THE BRITISH MUSEUM

A HISTORY

THE BRITISH MUSEUM

A HISTORY

DAVID M. WILSON

THE BRITISH MUSEUM PRESS

© 2002 David M. Wilson

First published in 2002 by The British Museum Press
A division of The British Museum Company Ltd
46 Bloomsbury Street, London WC1B 3QQ

David M. Wilson has asserted his right to be identified as the author of this work

A catalogue record for this book is available from the British Library

ISBN 0-7141-2764-7

Designed and typeset in Quadraat by Andrew Shoolbred

Printed in Spain by Grafos S.A.

CONTENTS

PREFACE

To write a history of an institution of which one was once the head is not an enterprise to be undertaken lightly. It has, however, been a rewarding experience and one that I enjoyed enormously. I am not an historian, so help was needed on a massive scale and it is a pleasure to acknowledge that help here.

A great deal of this book was written in libraries, but I am particularly grateful to Sarah Dodgson and her staff in the library of the Athenæum, with its remarkable collection of books of and on the nineteenth century, who looked after me with patience and kindness. The staff of the British Library, the University Library Cambridge, the London Library, the Niedersächsischen Staats- und Universitätsbibliothek, Göttingen, and the Library of University College London were unfailingly courteous. Helen Burton of Keele University Library and Gaye Blake-Roberts and Lynn Miller of the Wedgwood Museum helped me in matters to do with Townley and Wedgwood. Jørgen Jensen of the National Museum, Copenhagen, answered my questions about P.-O. Brøndsted and Arthur MacGregor of the Ashmolean Museum helped me with John Evans. Richard Edgcumbe of the Victoria and Albert Museum gave me useful information about the material brought back from the Abyssinian campaign; Signe Weill of the Aabenraa Museum discussed north German museums with me, John Hurst helped me with medieval pottery, Barbara Watterson helped with Egypt and Dick Shannon provided me with historical references.

My ex-colleagues in the Museum were incredibly considerate. Many of them read passages of this book in draft, others answered importunate queries and provided me with references and photocopies. I must, therefore, warmly acknowledge help received from Sheridan Bowman, Andrew Burnett, John Cherry, Brian Cook, John Curtis, Aileen Dawson, Antony Griffiths, Margaret Hall, Harry James, Bob Knox, Christopher Liddle, Terence Mitchell, Andrew Oddy, Jane Portal, Venetia Porter, the late Tim Potter, Tony Spence, Susan Walker and Leslie Webster. Ian Jenkins was a tower of strength in relation to the classical collections and their display, while John Mack read a number of chapters and strengthened my knowledge of the intellectual history of the nineteenth century. Joanna Bowring, of the Museum's central library, provided me with printed material, old and new, with immense courtesy and alacrity. Thomas Carlyle lamented, in compiling his edition of the letters and speeches of Oliver Cromwell, of the 'shoreless lakes' of unsorted documents. The Museum is another example of that genre – there is paper without limit – and without the constant help of the Museum's archivists this book could not have been attempted. Janet Wallace helped me initially, but I am deeply grateful to her successor, Christopher Date, and his assistant, Gary Thorn, who went to endless trouble when I was in semi-despair. Christopher also read the whole book in draft and sorted out many inconsistencies. Glennis Hoggarth and Christine Lawrence provided me with photocopies, files, keys and coffee and eased my path considerably. Elisabeth Ingles, my editor, and Teresa Francis of the British Museum Press were constantly helpful and courteous, saving me from much error and occasional hubris.

Else Roesdahl read the whole book in its roughest first-draft stage and saved me from many errors and inconsistencies. She also pointed to elements which would be unfamiliar to a foreign reader (this book is after all aimed at an international audience) and made me explain them (this is why I have tried not to use acronyms – although I have failed twice!). This is not the first time she has provided me with such help, and I would like to assure her that I am deeply appreciative. Philip Harris, historian of the British Library, read the whole text in draft and helped me in many other ways from his deep knowledge of both the Museum and the Library. My successor, Robert Anderson, and the Chairman of the Museum's Trustees, Graham C. Greene, read the manuscript in draft and provided me with much needed insight. It is almost a literary formula to thank one's wife, but my thanks are sincere. Only I can measure her support; not only did she read drafts, she put up with constant absences, irritable interludes and pleas for help; my gratitude is boundless.

It is, however, my erstwhile assistant, Marjorie Caygill, who deserves my deepest thanks. She should have written this book, as she has written so much about various aspects of the Museum's history; but she is at present far too busy in the Museum's service. No query was too small, no trouble too great. When I needed a reference she produced it immediately from her enigmatic filing system; she fed me with information, transcripts from manuscript sources, lists, obscure references and anecdotes by the score. She compiled the appendix which lists the staff and read the whole book in draft, commenting liberally. Much of this book was researched from a cubby-hole next to her office and I could shout questions at her, which she would answer with gay abandon. Thank you, Marjorie!

David M. Wilson
Castletown, Isle of Man
November 2001

INTRODUCTION

This is the story of the British Museum, the oldest and greatest publicly funded museum in the world. It is the story of the collections, the buildings that house them, and the people who have administered and curated them through two hundred and fifty years. It is above all the story of the curators who have shaped the collections and made them available to the public and to scholars; who have reflected or created the collecting taste of their own time; who at their best formed collections long before others saw the value of the material they were accumulating. It chronicles the developing and sometimes deteriorating relationships with government and an almost chronic lack of financial support from the Treasury. It is the story of trustees, directors and curators who fought battles, publicly or discreetly, to acquire, publish and display material to illustrate the whole history of mankind. Finally, it details the developing and generally supportive relationship with its public – scholarly and popular, national and international.

The purpose of this book is to celebrate the two hundred and fiftieth anniversary of the British Museum. This is of course not the first history of the Museum but, with the exception of an excellent small book by Marjorie Caygill,[1] all other formal histories have been written by librarians. Even the best of them, Edward Miller's brilliant *That noble cabinet*,[2] takes too bibliocentric a view of the institution. This book is intended to redress that balance by following the thread of what is now the Museum from its origin to the present day.

As the Museum faced its anniversary in 2003, there were discussions as to how the milestone should be celebrated. The commitment to publish this book makes clear that in the Museum's history lies its present and its future. What it did in the past has shaped what it must do today, and it is proper to examine its past in order to understand not only where it has come from, but where it is going. The Museum's *raison d'être* is to illuminate and explain the past of the whole world through material culture; it must, therefore, illuminate and explain its own past, for it has been a formidable element in the universal cultural history of the last two and a half centuries.

The Museum founded in 1753 is still discernible in the Museum of 2003. The library and natural history departments have been split from the main stem, but flourish as independent institutions, continuing the tradition, shaped in the European Enlightenment, of a universalist approach to knowledge that encouraged the foundation of the Museum. The history of the two separated institutions, the Natural History Museum and the British Library, has been told more than competently elsewhere,[3] and concerns this book only in so far as it impinges on the main story.

The Museum could well have developed in other ways. It could also have functioned as a national gallery of painting. In its early days it collected paintings and could have brought within its walls the national picture collection; indeed, one of the founding collections of the National Gallery – that of Sir George Beaumont – was given to the Museum in 1823. By a number of accidents the National Gallery was founded in the following year and for a number of years after was in some respects run by the British Museum Trustees, who occasionally met in Trafalgar Square and who, until well into the middle of the nineteenth century, still claimed ownership of more than fifty of the Gallery's paintings. In related fashion the Museum from its foundation haphazardly collected historical portraits. In 1856 the National Portrait Gallery was created and a few years later, recognizing an illogical position, the Museum transferred its collection of painted portraits to the new institution. Thus the location of the national collection of paintings was satisfactorily settled. The problem of the Department of Prints and Drawings remained. It seemed to many to have an anomalous position within the British Museum structure, and indeed in 1887 there was a half-hearted attempt to transfer its Old Master drawings to the National Gallery. But the Old Masters are only a small element in its diverse collections, which embrace everything from Michelangelo to cigarette cards; the Department's collections, consequently, fit better with the Museum's universal outlook.

The foundation of the South Kensington (now the Victoria and Albert) Museum in 1852 was a crucial element in shaping the British Museum. Established in the wake of the Great Exhibition of 1851, in its first rather muddled incarnation it reflected in its collections the material shown there – everything from food to machinery. Its philosophy was based on the education provided by the government's School of Design and carried through by the driving force of the Great Exhibition, Henry Cole. Cole and a number of colleagues bought what they considered the most important material from the Great Exhibition and displayed it in Marlborough House, from which it was to move in 1857 to South Kensington. Cole was omnivorous and built up a major collection in a very short time.

At that period, although a Royal Commission had urged the establishment of a section of the British Museum to deal with national antiquities, there was a strong feeling in the Museum that the future of its Department of Antiquities lay with artefacts from the classical world and with the newly emerging treasures of Egypt and the Levant. The proponents of this idea would happily have moved all other antiquities to South Kensington and were not slow to say so to official committees of enquiry. In 1854 the sale of the Bernal Collection of decorative art of the medieval period and the Renaissance allowed for co-operation between Cole's newly founded institution and the British Museum. A government grant was given to buy at the sale and a killing was made by both institutions; this was a signal that the British Museum had interests outside the ancient Mediterranean basin and that the South Kensington Museum had a brief to collect material from the past. Although Cole was often out of sympathy with the British Museum, he had a warm relationship with some members of staff and between them they managed to work out a series of *ad hoc* arrangements that established the unofficial briefs of both institutions. The British Museum was to collect on an historical and cultural basis and the South

Kensington Museum was to build a collection based on the history of design and applied art. In 1873 the government floated a lunatic proposal to amalgamate the two museums, but this very properly came to nothing. Although there were from time to time muddles, particularly on the South Kensington side, the distinction that was evolved in the middle of the nineteenth century survives to this day.

Each generation makes its own contribution to the Museum and it is often the actions of individuals that change its course or consolidate its strengths. In the decades at the turn of the eighteenth century it was a Trustee, the tyrannical Sir Joseph Banks, who strengthened the Museum's scientific work and fought for the institution in the corridors of power. In the first quarter of the nineteenth century the Swiss-born Principal Librarian (as the Director was then called), Joseph Planta, liberalized the regime and in practical ways encouraged the staff to publish the collections. To librarians Antonio Panizzi is simply the best Principal Librarian the Museum has ever seen, the man who tidied up the copyright laws, masterminded the building of the Reading Room, raised the book-purchasing grant to realistic levels and battled for his vision of the catalogue. Hawkins, Newton, Madden, Birch and Franks were the academic heroes of the nineteenth century to the antiquities departments; the greatest of these was Franks, who was as innovative in his scholarship as he was aggressive in his collecting and generous in his giving.

In the twentieth century, because of corporate memory, judgement is less sure. Sir George Hill vies with Sir Frederic Kenyon as scholar-director, while Campbell Dodgson, Keeper of Prints and Drawings and benefactor, arguably the most significant figure in the first half of the century, attains that position because he was backed by a remarkable group of colleagues. This is not to say that others did not contribute on a grand scale to the strength of the Museum as conciliators or innovative scholars, or that some few did not do positive harm through inertia or tunnel vision. At all times, however, the curators in the Museum were professionals, and for more than a hundred and fifty years – on the humanities side at least – they were among the very few professionals in the country. Until well into the twentieth century there were few professional archaeologists and even fewer art historians. Their specialities only gradually evolved as taught subjects in the universities; consequently, until the explosion of interest in them after the Second World War and the expansion of the number of universities, the 'experts at the British Museum' were the real professionals to whom many automatically turned for information.

For this reason I have paid a good deal of attention to the middle years of the nineteenth century, when the academic influence of the curators of the antiquities departments was in national and international terms at its strongest and most innovative. It was also a period when the collections increased almost exponentially, a period when government money was made available for the purchase of objects, although money for buildings was only grudgingly delivered. The first half of the twentieth century also saw much change as the staff became even more professional, and became more involved nationally in the development of their various subjects. It has been most difficult to write of my own period as Director, and even more difficult to write of the last ten years, which have seen many changes. Chapter 8 should therefore be considered as an essay, unavoidably biased, but communicating, I trust, enthusiasm for an institution which since its foundation has been much loved by those who have worked there, even if they have sometimes grumbled about personalities and conditions.

Chapter 1

BEGINNINGS

1753–9

You will scarce guess how I employ my time; chiefly at present in the guardianship of embryos and cockleshells. Sir Hans Sloane is dead, and has made me one of the trustees of his museum, which is to be offered for twenty thousand pounds to the King, the Parliament, the Royal Academies of Petersburg, Berlin, Paris and Madrid. He valued it at fourscore thousand and so would anybody who loves hippopotamuses, sharks with one ear, and spiders as big as geese! It is a rent charge to keep the foetuses in spirits! You may think that those, who think money the most valuable of all curiosities, will not be purchasers. The King has excused himself, saying that he did not believe that there are twenty thousand pounds in the treasury. We are a charming, wise set, all philosophers, botanists, antiquarians and mathematicians; and adjourned our first meeting because Lord Macclesfield, our chairman, was engaged to a party for finding out the longitude. One of our number is a Moravian, who signs himself Henry XXVIII, Count de Reus. The Moravians have settled a colony at Chelsea in Sir Hans's neighbourhood, and I believe he intended to beg Count Henry XXVIII's skeleton for his museum.

Thus Horace Walpole to Horace Mann on 14 February 1753, just over a month after Sloane's death.[1]

Sir Hans Sloane

The story of Sir Hans Sloane (pl. 1) has been often told and need only concern us in outline;[2] but concern us it must, as his will was the document that triggered the foundation of the British Museum. He was born in modest circumstances at Killyleagh, Co. Down, in 1660, the seventh son of the agent of Lord Clandeboye (later Earl of Clanbrassill), to whom he was probably related.[3] It was this connection which presumably gave a start to Hans and his brother William, both of whom, through influence and their own energies, became seriously wealthy. At the age of nineteen he moved to London and for four years studied to become a physician at the Apothecaries' Hall. He also pursued a growing interest in botany at the Chelsea Physic Garden and was taken up by the distinguished natural scientists John Ray and Robert Boyle. There was clearly enough money available for him to be able to extend his studies through travel. He spent three months in Paris; he took the degree of Doctor of Physic in France at the University of Orange in 1683 by disputation, and then went to the University of Montpellier (where Ray and Boyle had preceded him) and continued his study of botany, medicine and anatomy. His physical appearance at this time is described in the records of his university as, 'of medium height, hair very short, light chestnut, face rather long and grave, marked with small-pox'.[4] He returned to London in May 1684 and took up the practice of medicine. Clearly a personable and clever young man, he made friends easily and quickly became a Fellow of the Royal Society (1685) and of the College of Physicians (1687). He might easily have settled immediately into the life of a prosperous and fashionable doctor, but adventure came first in the form of an opportunity to travel to Jamaica as the personal physician to the Governor, the second Duke of Albemarle. Sloane was attracted to this opening for scientific reasons. Writing to John Ray he confessed that he wished to investigate the botanical resources of the island as a source of medicinal drugs, as well as in more general terms.

By the time the party reached Jamaica in December 1687, they had already called at Madeira, the Canaries, Barbados and many islands of the West Indies. Throughout the voyage Sloane made observations and collected specimens, both animal and botanical, as he did for the fifteen months of his residence in Jamaica before the death of the Governor. He returned to England with the embalmed body of his patient in May 1689. Clearly not blamed for the duke's death, Sloane became personal physician to his widow for four years before setting up practice on his own account in fashionable Bloomsbury. In 1695 he married money in the form of the widow of Fulk Rose of Jamaica, who was also co-heiress of her father John Langley, a London alderman. They set up house in what is now 3 Bloomsbury Place, two hundred metres from the building which became the British Museum.[5] His wife died in 1724.

Sloane was not simply a fashionable physician; in 1719 he became President of the College of Physicians and in 1727 succeeded Newton as President of the Royal Society. He was a physician to the royal household and attended Queen Anne on her deathbed, he was Physician General to the Army for five years from 1722 and a governor (and benefactor) of most of the London hospitals. He was created a baronet in 1716. He was an innovative doctor, promoting the introduction of inoculation and popularizing the use of quinine. He made a fortune from investment in the raw material from which this was distilled and also from the promotion of milk chocolate (his recipe was used by Cadbury until 1885).[6] Amidst all his other duties he continued his scientific work, publishing papers in the *Philosophical transactions of the Royal Society* and, in 1696, his great work on the botany of Jamaica, *Catalogus plantarum*. In 1707 he published the first volume of a major work entitled *Voyage to the Islands Madera, Barbados, Nieves, S. Christophers and Jamaica...*, which, with the second volume (published in 1725), was a definitive account of the natural history of this part of the world. His work was much admired, both in England and abroad, receiving praise from such diverse authorities as John Ray, John Locke and the *Journal des sçavans*. It must, however, be recognized that Sloane was writing about, and collecting, natural history in the period immediately preceding the establishment of the systematized taxonomy of Linnaeus. Consequently his methods seem to the modern scholar curiously old-fashioned and rooted in the past.

In 1712 Sloane bought the manor of Chelsea from the last Viscount Newhaven (the early sixteenth-century manor house was pulled down in 1760) and, while continuing to live in Bloomsbury, used it as a country retreat until the death of his wife, finally moving there in retirement after a serious illness in 1742. Here he was the landlord of the Apothecaries' Physic Garden, which he conveyed to the Society for an annual rent of £5. In the garden was erected a statue by Rysbrack of Sloane in his robes as President of the College of Physicians. It stood there until it was moved (much eroded) to the British Museum in 1985. Sir Hans died at Chelsea on 11 January 1753 and was buried a week later in the churchyard of Chelsea Old Church. A splendid monument by Joseph Wilton was erected in 1763 over his grave – it still survives.

Sloane was a friendly man, much esteemed by his associates, who included some of the greatest thinkers of his day. Patrick Blair wrote of him 'You will find him very affable and free'; while Birch described his person as 'tall and graceful, his behaviour free, open and engaging, and his conversation cheerful and communicative'.[7] He was the epitome of the rising middle classes of the eighteenth century and perfectly reflected the spirit of the Enlightenment rather than the dying fall of the Renaissance, to which he is sometimes ascribed.[8] He was a professional, trained professionally as a physician – a scientist who would merit the French description *savant*. He was not, as Voltaire described so many of his contemporary members of the Royal Society, an amateur.[9] As Secretary and then President of the Royal Society, he was what would nowadays be called an academic administrator; but he was more than that, he was a true – if not a great – scholar and a considerable polymath who assembled one of the greatest universal collections ever made by one man. In his professional life he not only himself practised medicine free of charge for the poor, but also encouraged others of his profession to do the same. Heartfelt tributes to him as a medical practitioner may be found; few are more illuminating than those of the poor scholar and great Saxonist Humfrey Wanley, who was for a short time employed as a cataloguer of Sloane's library.[10]

What is perhaps the most balanced tribute to him comes from the pen of one of his contemporaries and a trustee of his will, the antiquary William Stukeley, which chimes with more modern estimates:

> Sr Hans Sloane is an instance of the great power of industry which can advance a man to a considerable height in the worlds esteem with moderate parts & learning. industry may be said to have raised Sr. Hans... [He] has had this piece of luck too, that being a Vertuoso has made his fortune which generally ruins others. Indeed the whole business of his life has been a continued series of the greatest vigilance over his own interest, & all the friendships he ever makes are to himself. the same industry has made him perfect master of the knowledg of his immense collections... & may be said to be the greatest that was ever a private mans possession... he has no faculty of speaking, either fluently or eloquently, especially before any number of people, & and he do's it with great timidity. his most commendabl quality is his love for natural learning, & the pains he takes to promote it.[11]

The broad international spread of his interests and contacts is patent. This first emerges with his studies in France and his adventures in the West Indies. The contacts he made in these countries stood him in good stead, but as he became an established figure in the world of science (particularly through his offices in the Royal Society) he came into contact with many other international scholars. Many of them visited Sloane, among them Carl von Linné (the Swedish botanist Linnaeus) to whom he was introduced in 1736 by the Leiden botanist, chemist and physician Herman Boerhaave.[12] As he grew older and more famous, anybody who was anybody had to visit him – everybody from Voltaire to Handel to Franklin (who sold him an asbestos purse which is still in the collections of the Natural History Museum),[13] not to mention British and foreign royalty. He became a member of foreign academies – those of France, Prussia, St Petersburg, Madrid and Göttingen – and through such honours he made more contacts. Little is known of his linguistic ability, although von Uffenbach commented upon his facility in French and Nickson reckons that he necessarily read Latin (he published a book in this language, and probably disputed for his degree in it), had some Greek, probably read German, Dutch and Italian, and perhaps Spanish and Portuguese.[14] He collected books and manuscripts in languages far beyond his linguistic capabilities. His interests were as broad as those of any man of his period, as is demonstrated by the eclectic nature of both his collections and his publications. He was one of the makers of Enlightenment. Roy Porter puts him in the 'first team' of the English enlightenment.[15] The first volume of Diderot's great *Encyclopédie* was published in 1751, just before Sloane's death; he could only have approved of it. The universalist approach to knowledge exhibited by the *philosophes* was a reflection of Sloane's lifelong work with the animate and inanimate, sharpened by his sympathy and friendship with John Locke. He belonged to an age which, in the words of Isaiah Berlin, 'is perhaps the last period in the history of Western Europe when human omniscience was thought to be an achievable goal'.[16] It was this aspiration to universalism that informed Sloane's collecting and thereby shaped the British Museum. It is this idea that still differentiates the Museum from the great 'art' museums of the nineteenth century with which it is often in ignorance lumped together.

Sloane's Collections

Sloane's collections have recently been reviewed in some detail and with vast critical apparatus by a group of scholars led by Arthur MacGregor.[17] Importantly, Sloane collected not only for himself, but also for the whole scholarly world. The curious were made welcome in his collections and scholars were encouraged to use them in pursuit of their studies. To this end he not only catalogued the collections himself, but also employed cataloguers to assist him.[18] By the time of his death it was patent that the collections needed to be saved for the good of the scholarly community; perhaps it was for this reason that the trustees of his will had such an easy ride.

In their earliest form Sloane's collections concentrated on natural history and this remained at the centre of his interest:

> He buys for Topham, Drawings and Designs,
> For Pembroke, Statues, dirty Gods and Coins;
> Rare Monkish manuscripts for Hearne alone,
> And Books for Mead and butterflies for Sloane

quipped Pope of the architect Earl of Burlington.[19] John Evelyn (who consulted Sloane professionally and did business with him in the Royal Society) visited him on 16 April 1691 and provides one of the earliest descriptions of his collection:

I went to see Dr. Sloans Curiosities, being an universal Collection of the natural productions of Jamaica consisting of Plants, Coralls, Minerals, Earth, shells, animals, Insects &c: collected by him with greate Judgement, several folios of Dried plants & one which had about 80: severall sorts of Fernes & another of Grasses: &c: The Jamaica pepper in branch, leaves and flowers, fruits &c: with his Journal, & other Philosophical & naturall discourses & observations is indeede very extraordinary and Copious, sufficient to furnish an excellent History of that Iland, to which I encouraged him, & exceedingly approved his Industry.[20]

No purchased 'dirty gods and coins' here. Sloane was no magpie, but a selective collector, primarily of natural history, who planned his acquisitions with some care. Clearly not all his material was collected with his own hands; rather he set out to improve his collection in various ways. As he grew wealthier he would buy whole collections as well as individual items. Other collections were given to him. His first major acquisition (one of the most important he made) was a legacy, the collection of an old friend whom he had first met at Montpellier, William Courten, who died in 1702.[21] While this collection included natural history specimens, clearly of great interest to Sloane, it was more famous for its antiquities, coins and medals. Courten's collection was valued at some £50,000 (in 1686 Evelyn had estimated its value at £8,000, so it had obviously grown considerably in sixteen years) and it was left to Sloane with his residual estate on condition that he paid legacies to the amount of £2,500 and that he kept the collection 'intire'.[22]

Most of the collections Sloane acquired, chiefly through purchase, were of natural history; but some, like Courten's, included what were for a long time known in the Museum as 'artificial productions' (i.e. man-made objects). Few of the artificial productions were individually of supreme importance; in total, however, they made up a splendid and important collection and one that would not ultimately be overshadowed by the books, the manuscripts or the natural history collections as the British Museum developed. A remarkable number of the 'artificial' items still exist.

The collection of orientalia formed by Engelbert Kaempfer, the German physician who had been medical officer of the Dutch East India Company in Nagasaki in 1690–2, was perhaps the most outstanding of Sloane's collections not exclusively taken from the natural world. It included Japanese prints, paintings and lacquer, Turkish and Persian bazaar paintings and Chinese prints, paintings and various other objects.[23] Islamic items included a collection of seals and amulets and the famous and beautiful astrolabe, made in Persia for Shah Sultan Husayn, the Safavid ruler, in 1712/13.[24] From disparate sources Sloane amassed a collection of well over 20,000 coins and medals, which was already by 1721/2 important enough to be singled out by Stukeley as a major source in his attempt to make a 'Compleat description and history of all the Coyns relating to Great Britain from the Earliest times to our own'.[25] It is clear from the comments of his contemporaries that this part of his collection had a broader range than any in the country.

Sloane's ethnographic collection was perhaps his most remarkable 'artificial' assemblage. It was not only comparatively large (well into the hundreds), but it contained many unique items, some derived from first-time contact with indigenous peoples.[26] Sloane collected through a network of acquaintances who worked overseas or amassed material at home. Thus Mark Catesby, an artist and naturalist, who worked in Virginia as a sponsored observer and recorder, sent both botanical specimens and artefacts home to Sloane and other collectors – some of his material even fell into the hands of pirates on its way and was recaptured![27] Henry Elking, who sent him Inuit material from Greenland, was probably a trader in whale oil and other arctic products.[28] Often items came into the collection as incidental appendices to natural history collecting, such as the Chinese compass sent in 1701 to Sloane from Chusan by James Cunningham (a Scottish doctor working for the East India Company) – '200 botanical specimens and a compass'.[29] He bought from other collectors and from their heirs. In 1718 he paid £4,000 for James Petiver's collection, which included some hundred objects other than items of natural history, some of which may be identified by means of illustrated plates published during the collector's lifetime.[30] Many of the artefacts collected by Sloane from his correspondents abroad were made of materials in which he was, as a naturalist, interested – bark cloth, shoes, baskets, an Indian hat of cane, many semi-precious carved stones and so on. Some are of enormous interest historically. An Asante drum, for example, made of West African woods, said to have been collected in Virginia, may well, if this is true, have been taken there on a slave ship.[31]

Classical antiquities, much collected by gentlemen on the Grand Tour, apparently interested Sloane little. Ian Jenkins, who has examined the material, says of him, 'Sloane... appears to have had no more interest in antiquities, his own included, than he did in an account in his possession of maggots taken out of a man's ear on 27 August 1702 by J. Hare, Vicar of Cardington, Bedford'.[32] This is a little unfair, for Sloane was not unwilling to purchase classical antiquities – although on a small scale. Those he did acquire largely came incidentally with other collections. Most ultimately came from two Italian sources, Cardinal Gualtieri and the Abbé Sterbini; others came from the collections of John Kemp and the Soranzo family of Venice. Others came singly, as for example from the cabinet of the Neapolitan lawyer Giuseppe Valetta. If Sloane was simply a magpie in this field, he did at least collect within it, and it is fortunate that later in the century others built on the classical collections which he had (possibly accidentally) founded.

Sloane, like many collectors of the period, owned a few unremarkable Egyptian pieces, although some of them have some historical interest in that seventeenth-century English travellers had acquired them.[33] Similarly, his collection of prehistoric and provincial Roman antiquities is unremarkable but historically interesting. In the main he was interested in material of archaeological importance. Such, for example, was the Acheulian (Upper Palaeolithic) hand-axe found with some mammoth tusks and bones during gravel digging in Gray's Inn Lane, London, in 1696. This was thought to be a British weapon which had been used to kill an imported Roman elephant. While it was recognized as an artefact, the idea that this was really an extremely ancient implement would not fit with the then accepted date for the Creation of the year 4004 BC.[34] It was not until 1797 that John Frere boldly wrote of some similar implements from Hoxne, Suffolk, that 'the situation in which these weapons were found may tempt us to refer them to a very remote period indeed; even beyond that of this present world'.[35] Knowledge of prehistoric artefacts was nugatory at this period. Sloane recognized flint arrowheads for what they were, but was not so sure about stone axe-heads, which he says were 'called by some thunder stones'. Bronze Age implements were often identified as Roman, but the Roman material was rather better described and recognized. What is interesting, however, is that Sloane collected these objects and described them objectively and often with insight. The present-day archaeologist is happy to look at his collections and use them in his researches.

Sloane also collected objects of medieval and later date.[36] Certain groups of material clearly interested him – for instance, finger-rings, gems and mathematical instruments. Sloane was a contemporary of the great medievalists of the seventeenth century and was a friend of the Anglo-Saxon scholars Thomas Hearne and George Hickes. Sloane's coins and one or two Anglo-Saxon antiquities, for example a gold ring with a runic inscription from the Manchester region, reflect the revolutionary work of Hickes and his contemporaries (Hickes published the Lancashire ring), as by extension does his collection of seals, which even included a lead impression of the seal of Edward the Confessor. Other more mundane Anglo-Saxon objects were also to be found in his collection – cinerary urns, for example.

In general, however, his collection is a miscellany illustrating English history up to the Restoration – among the objects are a presumed death-mask of Oliver Cromwell and the Phoenix Jewel of Queen Elizabeth I (made about 1570–80). Other objects include the famous late thirteenth-century Sloane astrolabe (the earliest English astrolabe), a number of pieces of Italian majolica, the seal-die of Erik XIV of Sweden and what is probably the 'shew stone' of the magician John Dee. An interesting footnote to this group of later material is the fourteenth-century bronze lamp found on St Leonard's Hill, Windsor, which he presented to the Society of Antiquaries of London in 1738; this has since been used as the badge of the Society.[37]

Lastly among his collections, which now comprise the core of the British Museum, are the prints and drawings. A distinguished Keeper of the Department of Prints and Drawings has written concerning his collecting in this field:

> ... in so far as we can judge it, we can say that Sir Hans Sloane was a diligent, often well-informed, sometimes very fortunate, certainly influential, sharp and opportunistic accumulator, who, as far as North European art is concerned, had a good instinct for the interesting, and sometimes, for the very finest drawings.[38]

Apart from those drawings and prints relating to Sloane's interest in natural history, the corpus of drawings is remarkable, but clearly demonstrates that Sloane was not collecting them as a connoisseur of art; indeed, most of his non-scientific drawings were bequeathed to him by Courten. The collection is eclectic; he had major items from Holland and Germany, particularly of minor masters, but few French works and a rather disappointing array of Italian masters. Particularly important, however, are the copies of John White's drawings from his travels in the Roanoke colony in the late sixteenth century, a number of drawings of the first colonization of America, including two by Hans Burgkmair (1473–1531) of Tupinamba, a native South American, and the group of drawings and prints by the Bohemian artist Wenceslaus Hollar (1607–77). The most splendid works are the volumes of Dürer watercolours and drawings – among the greatest treasures of the Museum – which Sloane had acquired from Holland in 1724.[39] They include landscape watercolours, 'revolutionary both in imaginative power of observation and in execution, isolated in their excellence from all that had gone before, and unrivalled for many years by what was to follow',[40] but mostly they are concentrated on science and natural history, including some splendid and now famous images of animals – particularly those of a rhinoceros and a walrus.

It is difficult to reconstruct the contents of Sloane's collection of prints with any certainty, since they are now distributed between the Museum, the British Library and the Natural History Museum. Further, some of the albums which held many of his prints were broken up by order of the Trustees of the Museum in the early nineteenth century and many duplicates were sold.[41] His stature as a collector of prints is perhaps indicated by the fact that in 1735 the Society of Antiquaries of London presented Sloane with a complete collection of the prints they had published.[42] More importantly, in the previous year Louis XV gave him the *Cabinet du Roi* (the series of prints made for the kings of France since the 1660s, in twenty-three volumes), which remains in the British Library with many of his other bound sets of prints.[43]

Sloane also had a collection of paintings on canvas and panel. As the Trustees later took the decision not to collect such items, they have been distributed among other museums and galleries, although some few remain in the Museum.[44] The pictures varied in subject from paintings of animals to portraits of historical figures. Typical of the former is the painting of nine insects by Jan van Kessel (1626–79). The famous painting of a dodo 'drawn from the life' attributed to Roelandt Savery (1576–1639), now in the Natural History Museum, did not come from Sloane's own collection (as is often stated) but was presented in 1759 by George Edwards.[45] The portrait of John Ray, the naturalist, on which Roubiliac based his bust in Trinity College, Cambridge, was one of a series of historical portraits, which extended from medieval kings to Oliver Cromwell.[46] One such painting, which is still in the Museum, is a copied portrait of Franck van Borsalen, Count of Ooster-vant (d.1470).[47] Sloane's tastes in this field of collecting were eclectic, but included pictures that reflected his own interests, as for example the portrait of Thomas Briton, a 'small coal man who went about the streets of London with a bag of them on his back, but in his leisure hours he studied Chymistry, Antiquities, Books of which he had a consider-able collection …'.[48]

Sloane's library has until recently received less attention than it deserves. It started as the working collection of a man of science but grew into what in its time was probably the largest private library in England, and which had been systematically catalogued since 1694. By the time of his death Sloane had filled 3,944 pages of his catalogue of books and manuscripts, each page listing between twenty and forty books.[49] The existence of the library was to dominate the development of the British Museum immediately after his death and for half a century to come.

The Legacy

We do not know when Sloane started to consider the ultimate destination of his collection. Stukeley may be hinting at a solution in a sentence from the passage quoted above, 'his estate now being excessively great, does but double his diligence for getting more, tho he has no male heirs to leave it to, & his daughters are very richly marryd'. Further, it is inconceivable that he did not consult some of the great and the good who were the executors of his will. He must have talked of the problem to friends and visiting scholars and it has been suggested that comments of Frederic, Prince of Wales, during his visit to Sloane in 1748, may have encouraged him to leave the collection to the nation.[50] In fact Sloane had already in his first will of 9 October 1739 gone some way along this road. Nevertheless the thoughts expressed by the Prince of Wales must have been echoed by many of Sloane's circle:

> ... he [the Prince] express'd the great pleasure it gave him to see so magnificent a collection in *England*, esteeming it an ornament to the Nation; and expressed his sentiments, how much it must conduce to the benefit of Learning, and how great an honour will redound to *Britain*, to have it established for publick use to the latest posterity.[51]

Sloane apparently did not tell his royal visitor what he had in mind, but continued to revise his will.[52] He may well, however, have talked to one of the trustees named in his will about his intentions, for Dr Thomas Birch, one of the Secretaries of the Royal Society, in a manuscript memorandum which is one of the chief sources of our knowledge of Sloane, wrote:

> the Desire next his Heart was that his collection might be kept together for the Instruction and Benefit of others engaged in the same pursuits. And tho the intrinsic value of it was too much to be given away intirely from his own Children, he left it to the public on such easy terms, as he thought would readily be complied with.[53]

How many of these feelings were expressed with hindsight is not clear, but there is no reason to doubt the sentiment. As Sloane redrafted and added codicils to his will between 1739 and 1752, his plans took shape; he discussed the will with his family who put him under some pressure to exclude the manor and advowson of the living of Chelsea from his legacy to the nation. He also certainly discussed it with some of the people he named as trustees of his will, for, when he eventually died, they moved into action with great speed and efficiency.

When the will was published his intentions immediately became clear:

> Having had from my youth a strong inclination to the study of plants, and all other productions of nature; and having through the course of many years with great labour and expence, gathered together whatever could be procured either in our own or foreign countries that was rare and curious; and being fully convinced that nothing tends more to raise our ideas of the power, wisdom, goodness, providence, and other perfections of the Deity, or more to the comfort and well being of his creatures than the enlargement of our knowledge in the works of nature, I do Will and desire that for the promoting of these noble ends, the glory of God and the good of man, my collection in all its branches may be, if possible kept and preserved together whole and intire... that the same may be, from time to time, visited and seen by all persons desirous of seeing and viewing the same, under such statutes, directions, rules and orders, as shall be made, from time to time, by the said trustees... that the same may be rendered as useful as possible, as well as towards satisfying the desire of the curious, as for the improvement, knowledge and information of all persons....[54]

There was, however a sting in the tail, deliberately placed there by a wily old man, who knew his way around the corridors of power:

> ... and I do hereby request and desire that the said trustees, or any seven or more of them do make their humble application to his majesty or to parliament, at the next sessions after my decease, as shall be thought most proper, in order to pay the full and clear sum of twenty thousand pounds of lawful money of Great-Britain, unto my executors....[55]

This money was to go to his daughters (who were already rich and advantageously married and were in any case to benefit from the rest of his considerable estate). Further – a distinct piece of patriotic blackmail – if this clause were not to be approved, the collections were to be offered on the same terms to the academies of St Petersburg, Paris, Berlin and Madrid in turn. If all should refuse the collections should be sold.

All this must have presented real problems to the thirty-four trustees and executors of his will who gathered at Chelsea on 27 January 1753, a fortnight after his death. The trustees, however, seemed remarkably well prepared; they knew what they were doing, and first resolved to submit a memorial to the king.[56] Five days later they again met at the King's Arms Tavern in Westminster, and approved a draft petition. By this time the senior executor – Sloane's son-in-law, Lord Cadogan – had demitted the chairmanship of the trustees to the President of the Royal Society, the Earl of Macclesfield, who was deputed to present the petition to the king. Ten days later the trustees met again and heard that the king 'doubted that there was money sufficient in the Exchequer, but he had no direct answer'.[57] The well-briefed trustees then called a meeting of those of their number who were members of either House of Parliament. The upshot was that a rather weak MP, Edward Southwell, presented a petition to the Commons on 6 March asking them to accept Sloane's collections.[58] The petition asked for money to be provided in order to maintain the collections. The cause was nearly lost. The Chancellor of the Exchequer (who may well, as we shall see, have had a hidden agenda) tried to delay its consideration, which could have killed the project; fortunately, however, some quick footwork allowed the motion to be referred to a committee of the whole House. Negotiations then resumed and it became clear that the body of trustees nominated in Sloane's will was not acceptable to Parliament. The trustees agreed that the cause was too important for them to continue in office if the project would otherwise fail and agreed, if necessary, to resign, but they would not do so before they had on 15 March produced a remarkable document which has resonance and meaning to this day:

> Fundamental Principles from which the Trustees do not think they can in Honor or Conscience depart.
>   1st That the collection be preserved intire without the least diminution or separation.
>   2dy That the same be kept for the use and benefit of the publick, who may have free access to peruse and view the same, at all stated and convenient seasons agreeably to the Will and intentions of the Testator, and under such restrictions as Parliament shall think fit.
>   3dy That in case it should hereafter be judged the most… beneficial for the publick use, to remove the collection from the manor house at Chelsea where the same is now deposited, that it be placed properly in the Cities of London or Westminster or the suburbs thereof….[59]

The critical debate came on 19 March. The heroes of the hour seem to have been Charles Gray (one of Sloane's trustees) and the Speaker of the House, Arthur Onslow, who quit the chair to take part in the debate. Gray had James Empson (the curator of Sloane's collections and now in the employ of the trustees) called to the bar of the House; Empson gave evidence that the collections were worth well over the £20,000 which Sloane had wanted for his daughters – he valued them rather at as much as £100,000 – and presented some highly dubious figures which suggested that the running costs of the collection might be between £400 and £500 per annum.

Having agreed that the collection was worth more than £20,000, the House then debated the means of acquisition. The Chancellor of the Exchequer (Pelham), whose attitude to the project seems from the surviving documents to have been many-sided, now revealed his plan. He clearly wanted to get rid of Sloane's trustees in order that two major libraries which needed a home could be incorporated into the proposed institution. There is a distinct whiff of behind-the-scenes dealing in what follows, for the debate became almost glib. Gray immediately read out the trustees' resolution that they were willing to resign and Onslow then weighed in with a long disquisition on the two libraries and their history, salting it with a mention of Major Arthur Edwards's 1743 legacy (subject to a life interest) of £7,000 to house the Cotton Library (a major library of manuscripts, including a coin cabinet,[60] assembled by the Cotton family and left to the nation in 1700, which had been much neglected since it had been rescued from a fire in Ashburnham House in 1731 when many of the books had been damaged). Further, he airily suggested that another £3,000 would buy the Harleian Library (the manuscript collection of the Earls of Oxford, which was being offered for sale to the nation by the widow of the second Earl).[61] Onslow went on to propose the raising of £50,000 by means of a lottery to fund the project.

Finally, on 6 April the House approved the grant of £20,000 to the executors of Sir Hans Sloane, the provision of money to house the Cotton Library, and the transfer of the bequest of Major Edwards to the general use of that library. They approved the purchase of the Harleian Library in the sum of £10,000, and agreed that a lottery be initiated to fund these payments and to house and run the collections. This was enshrined in a bill which received Royal Assent on 7 June 1753, less than six months after Sloane's death.[62] What had started out as a museum had become embedded in a major library. By the Act of Parliament (pl. 2) it received a name – the British Museum. The origin of the name is not known; the word 'British' had some resonance nationally at this period, so soon after the Jacobite rebellion of 1745; it must be assumed that the Museum was christened in this light.[63]

A New Type of Museum

The Act established that the Museum should be governed by a body of Trustees (in many respects very different from the trustees named in Sloane's will), a body which would put the composition of all modern quangos totally in the shade. It was made up of the very great and the very good – forty-one in all.[64] At their first meeting at the Cockpit (part of the Lord Chancellor's offices in Whitehall) on 11 December 1753, not only was the Lord Chancellor present, but so were the Speaker of the House of Commons and the Archbishop of Canterbury (the holders of these three great offices of State were to be the Principal Trustees until the British Museum Act of 1963). Among the others were the Secretaries of State, the Master of the Rolls, the Lord Chief Justice, the Attorney General, the Solicitor General, the Presidents of the Royal Society and the College of Physicians, one duke, three earls, Lord Cadogan (Sloane's son-in-law) and Mr Thomas Hart. They proceeded to elect to the body another duke, another earl, a baron, two baronets, two peers' sons and a group of eight commoners.[65] Some of these had been trustees of Sloane's will and others (two each) were to be nominated by the Sloane, Cotton and Harley families. Eleven were fellows of the Royal Society.

To do it justice, this body worked hard. The full Board met six days later (17 December), first to authorize the payment of the £20,000 owing to Sloane's daughters and, among other business, to elect a committee, the embryo of the Standing Committee, which was established on a regular basis on 17 May 1755.[66] This committee was the real work-horse of the Board and was charged with the nuts and bolts of the new enterprise – initially with caring for the collections which now formed the British Museum, but also with finding, repairing, adapting and furnishing a 'repository' to house them.[67] By the time the Museum opened to the public in 1759 its main business was conducted by this committee, which from this time on met at fortnightly intervals. All Trustees were invited to come, but in practice an average of five or six conducted its day-to-day business.

The first concern of the Trustees was to establish their corporate identity and to take care of the money they had received from the lottery. A temporary seal was ordered and strict regulations for its control were laid down; there was much discussion about its design, before its final form and the inscriptions on it were approved (pl. 4).[68] In the early days the Trustees were much concerned with the safety and condition of the collections. The more valuable portable objects from Sir Hans Sloane's legacy had been placed in the Bank of England immediately after his death, and among the first duties of the embryo General Committee was the inspection of the rest of his collection.

The story of the lottery which funded the Museum has been the subject of amusing and lengthy discussion by every historian of the institution and need not be rehearsed again. Suffice it to say that it was as corrupt, dishonest and criminally mismanaged as any in the eighteenth century.[69] It did however produce for the Trustees, after deduction for expenses, the sum of £95,194 8s 2d.[70] This immediately had to provide the £20,000 due to the executors of Sloane's will, and £10,000 for the Harleian manuscripts. The Trustees, having paid these bills and purchased, refurbished and furnished a 'repository' for the collections, were left with a capital sum of about £30,000 which, invested, provided most of the running costs of the Museum for the next seventy years at an annual income of some £1,200.

The museum that had been cobbled together by Parliament was a very strange animal indeed, bearing little relationship to the make-up of Sloane's collection. The two libraries that had been added to it were soon joined by the King's gift of the old Royal Library, housed with the Cottonian Library and books from the Edwards bequest in the old dormitory of Westminster School.[71] While all these libraries together were only about the same size as the Sloane Library, their contents were much more important in that they comprised many of the major manuscript sources for the history of Britain and its literature, as well as a great variety of other manuscripts of wider importance.[72] This became in fact the national library of Great Britain, and overshadowed the collection of natural and artificial curiosities so carefully assembled by Sloane. The story of the British Museum is the story of how the three elements of the original collection grew and separated.

There was at this time no national library – much less a national museum – in Britain. What is more, there was no such institution abroad, where major collections of books and curiosities generally belonged to the sovereign. Although many of these royal collections came into the public domain in the nineteenth century, there was no experience of a national public museum when the Trustees of the British Museum started work. In England there were a few great libraries, particularly Bodley's Library at Oxford, the

University Library at Cambridge, the libraries of the Inns of Court and of the various learned societies. There was also the theological library at Sion College and Dr Williams's Library, which chiefly served nonconformist clergy. In Scotland there was the Advocates' Library and in Ireland the library of Trinity College, Dublin. Some aristocrats had their own libraries, which they occasionally allowed scholars to use, while interested prelates had founded a number of public and parish libraries. In the various European capitals and in many of the principalities of Italy the royal collections functioned in effect as public libraries – two of them at least (Berlin and Paris) were officially opened to the public before the foundation of the British Museum. Great university libraries also flourished on the Continent.

Museums were even thinner on the ground. The only substantial museum in England (the Tower of London cannot be counted as it was in effect a royal arsenal and secure place of deposit, some parts of which were open to the public) was the Ashmolean Museum at Oxford, founded some seventy years earlier, but now in a sorry state.[73] The smaller 'repository' at the Royal Society had been brought back into order during Sloane's presidency after years of neglect, but had a much narrower declared collecting policy, being largely confined to natural history.[74] Many of the great houses contained pictures and classical antiquities brought back from the Grand Tour or gathered together by discerning collectors – as for instance at Wilton. Such compilations were not always treated with respect. The great seventeenth-century collection of the Earl of Arundel, for example, was split up after his death; the Latin and Greek inscriptions were given to Oxford, but other objects were sold or given away (one or two ended up in the British Museum), and some were even broken up for use as rubble.[75] There had been little royal interest in collecting since Charles I, although George III, who came to the throne just after the British Museum opened its doors, was, like his father Frederic, Prince of Wales, a great collector. The present royal collection is mainly based on George III's wide and deep interest in art, clocks and furniture, while his important library came to the Museum as a gift from his son (see p.79).

In Europe many royal houses had curiosity cabinets (*Kabinett* or *Kammer*), the best-documented being that of the Danish king.[76] As early as 1587 an adviser was telling Christian I of Saxony how a *Kunstkammer* should be formed.[77] A single ruler could often create a considerable collection. In Schleswig-Holstein, for example, Duke Friedrich III with the help of one man, Adam Olearius, from 1648 onwards built up a cabinet of natural history, ethnography, Egyptian and oriental antiquities as well as a splendid collection of gems and *objets de vertu*.[78] In St Petersburg the *Kunstkammer* of Peter the Great was opened to the public for a few years in 1719, before being passed in 1724 to the Academy of Sciences. Other curiosity cabinets were used in university teaching; such was the museum assembled in the middle of the seventeenth century by the polymathic professor in Copenhagen University, Ole Worm (like Sloane a Doctor of Medicine), which, like Sloane's collection, was based on medical and natural historical materials.[79] While Worm was inspired by Italian examples, many of the curiosity cabinets being assembled by medical men in northern Europe may have been animated from the Low Countries, where early seventeenth-century anatomists had been engaged in the exploration of the human body. The most famous and bizarre of these cabinets was that of Frederik Ruysch of Leiden who in the second half of the century started to gather comparative anatomical material, partly as *memento mori* and partly for the interest of the curious.[80] By the end of the seventeenth century curiosity cabinets of all sorts had become such an accepted part of cultural life that general books were being published about them and their management. Such, for example, was J.D. Major's 1674 handbook showing how objects could be stored and systematized, while Michael Bernhard Valentini's description and illustration of objects from many existing cabinets, published in two thick folios between 1704 and 1714, was in reality a cabinet in book form.[81]

While the idea of a library and of a cabinet was familiar to the Trustees when they set about housing and servicing the new museum, they had to combine the two and make them accessible to the public. This was their unique challenge. Nowhere else in Europe did such a public institution exist.[82] This point is well made by a French visitor in 1784:

> The British Museum is a superb collection of... books, prints and antiquities voluntarily deposited for the instruction and gratification of the public... The house... in which a variety of specimens are brought together, is an admirable monument; but, considered individually the collections do not compare with what we have in France. If the *Bibliothèque du Roi*, the Cabinet and our medals and prints were brought together, the result would be something quite different from the British Museum. Here, as in everything else, the public spirit of the English is worthy of remark: a considerable portion of the exhibits has been voluntarily given and every day new legacies are recorded.[83]

The Trustees were certainly confident, and among their number were two or three people who had very strong ideas as to how they should proceed. After the excitement of the early days the Trustees' meetings were much less well attended (some were hardly quorate) and a small group of people seem to have done a lot of the hard work – Lord Charles Cavendish (father of the famous natural philosopher), Colonel William Sotheby (who was married to Sloane's niece), Dr Thomas Birch (Secretary of the Royal Society) and (Sir) William Watson (an apothecary and active Fellow of the Royal Society) were regular attenders. Other keen members were Lord Macclesfield (President of the Royal Society), Dr John Ward (professor of Rhetoric at Gresham College) and William Sloane (Sloane's nephew and a family Trustee). Apart from Cavendish, they had all, like Sloane, emerged from the professional middle classes, but all of them knew their way around Westminster and the Court and had recourse through the rest of the Trustees to anyone in the country. These were the people who inspected the collections, who arranged for their housing and the furnishing of the Museum, and debated problems of access. Their control was absolute and the staff, once appointed, was allowed little leeway. Their minutes and financial records are impeccable and easily legible. They were clearly keen managers – although inclined to fuss about minutiae. Their first objective was to identify a 'repository'.

Montagu House

Bloomsbury was at this time situated on the northern limits of London, a little to the north of the centre of the Anglo-Saxon town (between Aldwych and Covent Garden) and bounded by the City (the economic centre) in the east and Westminster (the royal centre) in the west. By the middle of the eighteenth century Bloomsbury was being developed with fashionable housing for the upper middle classes and the aristocracy. To the north was open countryside, leading to the heights of Hampstead and Highgate. There were two great mansions on the northern edge of the district. The first, on the site of the original manor of Bloomsbury, was known as Southampton House, after the Earl of Southampton, granted the manor in the reign of Henry VIII. The heiress of the last Lord Southampton married in 1669 William, Lord Russell, whose family inherited the estate and renamed the house. Bedford House, which stood on the north side of Bloomsbury Square, was demolished in 1800 as the Russell family further developed their Bloomsbury estates.

Next door, so to speak, was Montagu House, standing in grounds of some seven acres. This was destined to house the British Museum.[84] Unlike Bedford House it did not front on to a square, but on to Great Russell Street. The house purchased by the Trustees was possibly the second house on the site. The original house, partly destroyed by a fire in 1686, was a fine late seventeenth-century mansion in the style of a Parisian *hôtel*, designed by Robert Hooke and built for the francophile Duke of Montagu on land purchased from the Duke of Bedford. The new house (pl. 5) was rebuilt or reconstructed almost immediately under the direction of a 'Mons. Pouget'.[85] Behind a wall and entrance gate on Great Russell Street was a courtyard with a main building of seventeen bays, with two main floors, cellars and a mansard roof broken by the dormers of the attic floor. A fine pillared colonnade in the Corinthian style lined the wall on to the street, which in the French fashion presented a blank, unfriendly face to the public. The courtyard was entered through a large gate capped by an octagonal lantern with clock and cupola. The house was built of fine-quality red brick with stone quoins. Wings with a main floor and basement and attic rooms flanked the main edifice, both fronting a courtyard (that on the east side comprising the stables). The main building was entered up a flight of steps through an unporticoed doorway into a splendid painted hall with a grand, iron-balustraded stone staircase, reached through a screen to the left.[86] The walls and ceilings were decorated – again in the French style – with allegorical scenes representing Bacchic feasts, the triumphs of Caesar and the story of Phaeton painted by Charles de la Fosse. The saloon on the *piano nobile* had a painted ceiling which represented the fall of Phaeton.

Behind these two houses were great gardens; that of Montagu House, laid out originally in the French style with fountains and parterres,[87] was much cared for and altered by the Trustees over the years, and became a pleasant and safe resort for the *bon ton* of Bloomsbury. Beyond the gardens was open farm and common land, crossed by the conduits of the New River Company which were soon to be tapped by the Trustees. The land to the west was still open space when the Museum opened, but Bedford Square began to be developed in 1776. The houses beside Montagu House on Great Russell Street and for a little way to the south of it, as in Bloomsbury Square, housed the rich and famous of the newly created parish of St George's, Bloomsbury.

It had been clear to the Trustees from an early stage that Montagu House was the best choice as a 'repository' for the Museum. They had considered Buckingham House, but decided that it was too expensive (it was later sold to George III for £28,000 – £2,000 less than the sum for which it was offered to the Trustees).[88] They had also considered a putative new building within the Palace of Whitehall – in Old Palace Yard – and immediately dismissed it. On 3 April 1754 they decided to proceed with the purchase from Sir Edward Montagu and the Dowager Duchess of Manchester of Montagu House, for

£10,000.[89] It was advised that a private Act of Parliament would be necessary to confirm the purchase, but the Trustees were so anxious to get on that they sought to indemnify themselves for the alterations and repairs that would have to be undertaken before the Museum could be opened.[90] The building was insured, a fire-engine provided and a water main was laid on by the New River Company.[91] Plans (pl. 4) were made even at this early stage for the allocation of the rooms to the different parts of the collection, for the various elements had to be moved into the Museum with some expedition.

While basically sound, Montagu House was in a poor state of repair and some £17,000 had to be spent on repairs, alterations and fitting-out before it opened in 1759.[92] The roofs were repaired and covered with Westmorland slate; the cornice, which was in bad condition, was made safe, and many less urgent repairs were carried out, including the re-paving of the forecourt and the laying of larger paving slabs inside the house in order to minimize the risk of fire. All the rooms, other than those which had ornamental painting, were ordered to be whitewashed. The two rooms on the right of the entrance, which had painted ceilings, were hung with paper and appropriated by the Trustees – one functioned as a boardroom. The wall and ceiling paintings needed attention and £365 was laid out for their repair by Mr Pond.[93] Among all the serious business of the Trustees on 2 January 1756 five guineas was given for drink for workmen at the finish of re-roofing – clearly a memorable party!

Now that the house and its fabric were secure, the collections had to be moved in and the Museum had to be staffed and furnished.

The Staff

The Trustees had little money to play with – about £1,200 a year, as we have seen. First they had to create a staff structure. They took soundings abroad and considered the costs of the royal library of France. Among Dr Birch's papers is an undated note:[94]

Expences of the French King's Library

		Livres
2 Keepers of the Books and MSS each 3000 livres		6000
1 Keeper of the Medals and Antiques		3000
1 Keeper of the Prints and Plates		1200
4 Commis	each 1000	4000
2 Commis for extraordinary business	each 800	1600
3 garçons	each 800	2400
2 Froteurs or Sweepers	each 500	1000
2 (?)Sniss	each 500	1000
	Livres	20200

£

3000 Livres at 10½ amount to 131.5

20200.............................. 884.5

This was a little less than the sum that the Museum had available to pay its own staff, but the structure ultimately resembled the French model, although it was to have an identifiable chief officer, the Principal Librarian. After much discussion it was agreed that the Principal Librarian should have a salary of £200. Then there were three Under Librarians, each in charge of a department. One was to look after the Natural and Artificial Curiosities, one to look after Manuscripts (including coins and medals), while the third was in charge of Printed Books – each to be paid £100, with an assistant at £50. The wages of various other servants and the gardener were also decided.[95] The Principal Librarian's salary was immediately reduced by £40, to be restored to him if he were to take on the duties of financial officer. The Under Librarians' salaries were reduced to £80, but £20 a year was to be paid to each of them in turn if they acted as Secretary. They were given free coal and candles, service and a residence in the wings of the Museum, but had to provide their own furniture.[96] These were not enormous salaries (£100 in 1755 would be worth about £9,000 in 2000), but they were part-time posts; most of those ultimately appointed had other jobs as well. This was a period of inflation and those on fixed incomes, like the lesser clergy and civil servants, found it difficult to make ends meet,[97] so perhaps the salaries on offer were not unreasonable, although the level at which they were set was to cause trouble half a century later.

What did the Trustees expect of the officers? There exists a formidable job description for the Principal Librarian which appears to have been drawn up by Birch, one of the most active Trustees. It is quoted here in full as it gives a clear idea of their intentions regarding the Museum.

Qualification and Duty required of the Principal Librarian

The principal Librarian as to his qualifications, must not only be Studious and Learned, but One who has had the Education of a physician, and who has been abroad to compleat his Studies, by which means he may have learnt to Speak and write the living Languages, but the French in particular, as with that Tongue and Latin he will be able to Correspond with almost all persons of Learning or distinction in any foreign Country, as well as converse with them at home and he should also be a person Versed in Mathematical learning. A Gentleman thus qualified will at first be Chiefly employed in making himself the Master of the Books and MSS. and of that great and essential part of the Collection which relates much to the History of this Nation. It being Scarcely probable that if he was a person remarkable only in the knowledge of the latter, that he could be the Master of the first Qualification and with only such an Education as above, at least in any Degree Sufficient to Answer the design of the Legislature in that respect. As to the Duty of the principal Librarian it will be first to make the Several Divisions and parts of the Repository familiar to him which will take up a great deal of time and Constant Application. And as to the Sloanian Collection especially as well as to the MSS. to have the Books and the Subjects they treat of so much in his Memory and knowledge as to be able to call for any of them readily on all Occasions and to Converse with any persons of Learning & Curiosity on the matter of them. Also to make himself Master of the Physical and Anatomical Articles and Natural Rarities with their Virtues and properties and chiefly of the Herbs and plants, Fosils and Minerals and also the Jewells and to be also the Master of the several Artificial Curiosities and the knowledge of them and… of the Medals and likewise of their History and other the Grecian and Roman Antiquities. He must employ great part of his time and be Sollicitous in gaining the Conversation of the Learned and such who are remarkable for their knowledge in the liberal Arts and should sett apart certain times when they might meet at the Repository for their Studious Amusement which will tend to promote the great design of the Museum and lead the Librarian into a Correspondence with learned and Ingenious men. At such meetings might be Introduced any Curious Invention of

Art where the Inventors may be sure of a Candid and proper Examination and afterwards with the Assistance of the Trustees as the Patron of the Museum be encouraged according to their deserts and Inventions properly made known for the Use and benefit of the publick. This Officer thus qualified must as a Studious man be quite free from any other Engagements which may embarrass or intrude upon his Studies except the Daily duty of his Office as hereafter mentioned. This Officer should be constantly resident in the Museum and must not be absent from his duty for any length of time without the leave of the Trustees. He must have all Orders and Tickets of Admission Shewn to him before the Company enters the repository and if they are Foreigners or others who are persons of Quality or of great distinction or eminent in any Branch of Art or Science they should be led into his Study from whence he must attend them thro' the Repository, a respect which will certainly be expected by such persons and must be paid them, as the Under Librarians alone will not be so Capable to make the Visit agreeable to them, and therefore he must be in his Study or in the Repository, such Hours it is to be kept Open, and allowed to be Viewed, (which in the Winter Season are proposed to be between ten and three and in Summer between nine and four). The leisure hours besides every Saturday and Sunday will be sufficient Relief from the more constant attendance and leave him time to Employ himself in his Studies.

And lastly this Officer is to attend the meetings of the Trustees in all Affairs which relate to the Management and Conduct of the Repository and to execute their Orders relating thereto and to have the Direction and Management of all the Litterary Transactions & Correspondences both at home and abroad, the Under Librarian (who is proposed for Acting as Secretary for these purposes) to be herein particularly under his direction and Controul.[98]

This fascinating document clearly expresses the importance of the non-library parts of the collection to the Trustees. The idea that a medical doctor should fill this post clearly reflects the origin of the Museum, but also emphasizes the fact that medicine provided the chief training for the natural sciences at this period. The Trustees' choice as Principal Librarian fell upon Dr Gowin Knight, who (backed among others by Birch and Lord Royston) was appointed by the King's sign manual on 21 May 1756. His appointment was confirmed by the Trustees at their meeting a fortnight later, when he signed a bond in the sum of £1,000.[99] The other name submitted to the King and rejected was Dr John Mitchell, a distinguished botanist, Doctor of Medicine and Fellow of the Royal Society.[100]

Gowin Knight (pl. 7), who was forty-three years old and born in Lincolnshire, had been to Leeds Grammar School and to Magdalen College, Oxford. He became a physician in London and in 1745 was elected FRS. Interested in magnetism, he wrote a number of papers on the subject and developed a compass which had been adopted by the Navy (for which he had received in 1752 a reward of £300); he had also been awarded the Copley Medal of the Royal Society (this he later gave to the Museum).[101] Clearly a force to be reckoned with in the scientific world, he was a reasonably energetic head of the Museum, although later in life he got into financial hot water, from which he was rescued by a loan from John Fothergill.[102] He was a quarrelsome man, hated by the staff and sometimes acrimonious in his relationship with the Trustees.[103]

The men appointed on 19 June as Under Librarians were an interesting trio. Two (both of whom later became Principal Librarian) were MDs of Leiden University, the third had no apparent university training whatsoever; all three were Fellows of the Royal Society. The first MD, Matthew Maty (pl. 7), a Huguenot, was put in charge of the Sloane library; he later was to be Under Librarian of the Natural and Artificial collections. He was fairly well off and a bit of a gossip. Gibbon says of him:

By descent and Education Dr Maty, though born in Holland, might be considered as a Frenchman; but he was fixed in London by the practice of physic and an office in the British Museum. His reputation was justly founded on the eighteen volumes of the *Journal Britannique*, which he had supported, almost alone, by perseverance and success. This humble though useful labour, which had once been dignified by the genius of Bayle and the learning of Le Clerc, was not disgraced by the taste, the knowledge, and the judgement of Maty; he exhibits a candid and pleasing view of the state of literature in England during the period of six years [January 1750–December 1755]; and, far different from his angry son [also a member of staff of the Museum], he handles the rod of criticism with the tenderness and reluctance of a parent. The author of the *Journal Britannique* sometimes aspires to the character of a poet and philosopher; his style is pure and elegant; and in his virtues, or even in his defects, he may be ranked as one of the last disciples of the school of Fontenelle.[104]

Maty was trusted by the Trustees and was apparently much liked by his colleagues.[105] He became Principal Librarian on the death of Knight in 1772, but he was already ill and died four years later.

The other medical Under Librarian was Charles Morton who was put in charge of the manuscripts in the Royal, Cotton, Harley and Sloane collections. He succeeded Maty as Principal Librarian in 1776 and died in post in 1799 at the age of eighty-three. He was no ball of fire; of him the *Dictionary of national biography* states, 'His term of office was not marked by any striking improvements, but he is said to have always treated students and visitors with courtesy'. Like Maty he was comfortably off, if not rich – twice married into the aristocracy – which perhaps explains why he never completed his great project, the publication of Domesday Book.[106]

By contrast James Empson, the third Under Librarian, who had been Sloane's curator for fifteen years, is virtually unknown even to the historians of the Museum.[107] His mother (presumably a superior servant) had 'lived with' (in the most proper sense of the term) Sir Hans Sloane for twenty-nine years, and was warmly spoken of by Sloane's daughter Sarah Stanley.[108] Empson (d.1765) had been much consulted by the Trustees in the three years after his master's death and worked hard for them. He was appointed to look after the Natural and Artificial curiosities. He was not a formally trained academic and scientifically was perceived as a weak link in the scholarly hierarchy of the Museum. He was, however, clearly a hard worker who produced rather incoherent, but important, documents for the Trustees based on his knowledge of the Sloane collections and of the manner in which they were housed. In 1763 – seriously ill – he was sidelined by the appointment of a serious academic scientist, Daniel Solander of the University of Uppsala.

The academic staff was completed by the appointment of three Assistant Librarians.[109] The most competent was probably Andrew Gifford, appointed assistant to Morton in April 1757 as a result of the influence of the Trustee John Ward, whose pupil he had been at Gresham College.[110] He was a Baptist minister and a Doctor of Divinity of St Andrew's. A considerable numismatist, he wrote or edited two books on the English coinage. He married well and had sufficient money to collect a fine cabinet of coins, which was later purchased by George III. He also collected historical portraits and over the years gave at least twenty paintings to the Museum – the first in 1758 was a portrait on panel of Henry VIII. Most of these were transferred to the National Portrait Gallery in 1879 along with many other portraits of English subjects held by the Museum. Appointed as Assistant to

Maty was the Reverend Samuel Harper, a Cambridge graduate. He succeeded Maty in 1765 and served in the Library until his death in 1803; he appears to have been a dull, if hard-working, librarian, much praised as chaplain to the Foundling Hospital, where he was buried.[111] William Hudson was appointed to assist Empson. An apothecary, he resigned after only one year and went into business on his own account.[112] A Swiss parson, Andrew Planta, replaced him; he transferred, still as an assistant, to Printed Books in 1765 and on his death was succeeded by his son (later Principal Librarian).

In June 1758 it became apparent that an additional senior member of the staff was needed to supervise the Reading Room. Peter Templeman was appointed 'Keeper of the reading room or rooms' in December.[113] A man of some means, he had been educated at Trinity College, Cambridge, and was MD of Leiden.[114] He was a friend of Maty, being, like him, a member of the distinguished Medical Club; it may well have been Maty who influenced his decision to apply for the job.[115] He did not get on with the Trustees and resigned some two years later on being appointed secretary to the Society of Arts. He was succeeded by the Reverend Richard Penneck.

On the whole the staff were competent; but, with the exception of Empson, their knowledge of either libraries or museums was minimal – they had a lot to learn. They were not, in modern terms, specialist; they changed from one department to another, apparently without too much trouble, aided presumably by the fact that it was their job (once the Museum had opened) to conduct visitors through the whole collection and as a consequence became familiar with all its facets. At least some of these first appointees were reasonable linguists and all seem to have become competent curators. Many of them were active Fellows of the Royal Society and were, therefore, acquainted with the major scholars in their fields. Though well connected, their salaries were poor and, unless (like Gifford) they had private money, had to be supplemented by taking outside jobs. As with other employees of the Trustees they lived (rent free) in the wings of Montagu House with their wives and families, a circumstance which, although it relieved some of their poverty and was meant to encourage collegiality, led from time to time to awful quarrels and bickering over rooms. The poet Thomas Gray, for example, records that 'the Society itself, Trustees & all, are up in arms, like the Fellows of a College, the Keepers have broke off all intercourse with one another, & only lower a silent defiance when they pass by. Dr Knight has wall'd up the passage to the little-House [the privy], because some of the rest were obliged to pass by one of his windows on the way to it'.[116] Some wealthier officers had houses elsewhere – indeed, Morton later got into trouble for being absent at his summer residence in Twickenham when the Gordon Riots were threatening Bloomsbury in 1780[117] – but few staff had this kind of money.

The staff were augmented and serviced by a porter, a messenger and a number of housemaids. The Trustees appointed their first porter immediately after the purchase of Montagu House. He was Joseph Markland and had been an old servant of the Montagus. He was to be paid £20 p.a. and a chaldron of coal and candles. He 'absconded' in late 1756 and was replaced by Sloane's old porter, Raymond Payne, who soon needed an assistant.[118] The first messenger was Joseph Lockwood who was appointed on 19 February 1756. The female servants consisted of an upper housemaid (J. Wadell) and three housemaids, Dorothy Markland (presumably a relative, perhaps the wife, of the absconding porter), Elizabeth Chaplin and Judith Stanley.[119] The housemaids and other servants tended to stay long in post (they appear for many years in the general accounts of the Museum) and relatives and children of existing staff members were often employed by the Trustees, creating dynasties of servants in the institution. They served all the senior staff of the Museum and probably cleaned it as well. They lodged in the eastern turret[120] in rather cramped quarters which, by 1837, were described as 'barely wholesome'. The porter and his family lived in the gatehouse.

The officers of the Museum – already by 1759 known informally as 'keepers' – had a fairly light workload. Originally they were obliged to be on duty for six hours for five days a week, but this was reduced in 1761 to two hours for two days in one week and two hours for three days in the next week, after complaints that they could not look after their other positions otherwise. Only the superintendent of the Reading Room was required to be present for all five days.[121]

Arranging the Collections

Montagu House was completely empty when it was taken over by the Trustees; after their first meeting there it was agreed that the boardroom should be furnished with '2 doz chairs, a table with green cloth, grate with necessary furniture and three pairs of brass candlesticks', and a month later a bid was authorized for a bureau and glass case belonging to the late Martin Folkes.[122] So the Trustees were starting from scratch so far as both the administration and furnishing of the Museum were concerned.

Unusually, some records survive of the manufacture and costs of the storage and display furniture. It was agreed to re-use existing bookcases so far as possible; but many more had to be designed, approved by the Trustees, and built. Empson was consulted about cases for the objects.[123] Some of them were to be rehoused in Sloane's original cabinets, but others had to be built. Specifications appear to have been approved on 16 January 1755:

> A Cabinet of 11 feet high and 10 feet long and about 14 Inches deep in the Clear fitted up with shelves and seven drawers in hight in the lower part, with the Locks, Hinges and Glass Doors, all Compleat, without any carving will amount to £52 4s, which is about £2 19s p foot running.

The cabinets were all of deal faced with mahogany. A finished sample was inspected by the Trustees on 3 April 1756, and the estimate £3 7s 6d a foot was accepted.[124] Further details appear, in a later letter from Dr Ward, on the subject of the security of this part of the collections:

> That all the medals, coins, seals, cameos, intaglios, gemms, and other small curiosities of a like nature, in the Repository, be locked up in drawers, with glasses or wires over them, thro which they may be seen; but not taken out, and intrusted in the hands of any person, unless in the presence of the Keeper or his Assistant, who has the keys of the drawers.
> That no copy of any of the said curiosities be allowed to be taken, without the permission of the Superintendent.
> That other curiosities in the Repository, such as vessels, fossils, Instruments, drawings,

prints, etc., be locked up in cases, with glasses or wires before them; and shewn in the same manner, as those in the drawers.[125]

In March 1758, 'two cases for depositing medals, one of pear tree stained black, and another of mahogany', were submitted to the Trustees who chose mahogany.[126] None of these cabinets, as far as we know, survives, nor has any drawing or illustration been preserved of the rooms in Montagu House which contained antiquities.

By the time the staff had been appointed, preparations for the final housing and display of the collections were put in train. In June the Trustees ordered that all material not already in the Museum should be moved there. They had already decided the division of the collections. It was agreed:

> That the Repository be divided into Three parts:
> The First to contain the Books of the Sloanian Collections.
> The Second the Jewells Pictures Medals and the Natural and Artificial Curiosities... belonging to it.
> The Third the Cottonian Library with Mr Edward's Books and the Harleian Manuscripts.[127]

These were renamed in 1758 as the Department of Printed Books (under Maty), the Department of Natural and Artificial Productions (under Empson) and the Department of Manuscripts (under Morton, who also took charge of the coins and medals).[128]

Ever since its first days the Museum had received gifts. Donations of books and libraries need not concern us here, save in so far as they caused accommodation problems for the Museum and its staff. But some of the earlier acquisitions were of antiquities. The most important of these was undoubtedly the bequest of the collection of Egyptian antiquities formed by Colonel William Lethieullier, who had visited Egypt in 1721 and returned with a number of objects, many probably from Saqqara (to the south-west of Cairo) – among them the Museum's first mummy. The Trustees were excited by this acquisition and a group of them visited the colonel's son to express their thanks – a good move, as the family over the years continued to give to the Museum.[129] The Lethieullier family (his son, Pitt, and his cousin, Smart) added greatly to this collection up to 1770, giving among other items another mummy.[130] Even before the Museum opened to the public other gifts began to trickle in. Many of them were destined for the library or natural history departments, but a good number could be classed as antiquities. Thus in 1756 'Mr Watson' presented some 'specimens of tiles taken from Roman baths and sudatories lately discovered at Bath'.[131] In 1757 Thomas Hollis presented a group of Italian antiquities and inscriptions, including 'a considerable number of etruscan vases, sacrificing vessels and lamps'.[132] A couple of months later James Theobalds gave the Museum 'a wooden image, supposed by the donor to be an Indian idol from Jamaica'.[133] Pictures were also accepted as gifts.[134] Coins, medals, prints and drawings were also given, particularly in the early years by members of staff. All these were destined to remain in the library departments until the establishment of independent departments for these collections in the early nineteenth century. From the earliest days a 'Book of Presents' recorded all gifts and continued in use until the separation of the British Library in 1973.[135]

Purchases of objects or collections were apparently not even discussed in these early days. There was no grant from government towards the general acquisition of antiquities (although printed books were purchased regularly in the 1760s and onwards[136]), nor did the Trustees even consider applying for such monies. Whether they expected that the generosity of private donors would continue is not documented; it was not until the 1770s that purchases of antiquities were seriously considered, while a purchase grant was not initiated by Parliament until 1834. Even the purchase of a reference book for staff use was a matter for decision by the general committee of the Trustees.[137]

The collections were now tackled on a systematic basis. The books (where necessary) were dried out, rebound and set in order on the shelves. Empson started to arrange the collections in his department in some sort of order. Cataloguing also began of those parts of the library departments which had not yet been listed. A register of Natural and Artificial Productions existed but was apparently in a mess (as any modern user of the Sloane registers will witness); it was poorly ordered and Empson made various suggestions concerning it which were put to the Trustees early in 1757.[138] The problems presented by this register were never properly tackled, despite the fact that the Trustees returned to the subject from time to time (proper registers for the non-library departments were not standardized until the 1830s). Progress in physically setting the collections in order was, however, good and the Trustees began to allow limited access to the collections.

Privileged visitors had been allowed to see the collections since the passing of the Act. At first such permissions were mentioned individually in the minutes. Trustees were allowed to take visitors round; thus the Earl of Northumberland was allowed to escort the Princes Corsini around Sloane's collection in early 1754 and Lord Royston similarly escorted Count Poniatowski in May of the same year. More interestingly, on 17 January 1755 it was 'Resolved that leave be given to Mr Roubilliac, at the request of the Revd. Dr. Smith, Master of Trinity College in Cambridge, to make a Draught from the picture of Mr John Ray in the Mannor House in Chelsea, in Order for the making of a Bust of him to be placed in the said College'. A more casual visit in August 1756 is described by Catherine Talbot in a letter to a friend:

> One Evening we spent at Montague House, henceforth to be known by the name of the British Musæum, I was delighted to see Science in this Town so Magnificently & Elegantly lodged; perhaps You have seen that fine House & Pleasant Garden: I never did before, but thought I liked it much better now, inhabited by Valuable Mss, Silent Pictures, & Ancient Mummies, than I should have done when it was filled with Miserable Fine People, a Seat of Gayety on the inside, & a place of Duels without... Nothing is yet ranged but two or three rooms of Mss. Three & Thirty rooms in all are to be filled with Curiosities of every kind. A number of Learned and Deserving Persons are made happy by the places bestowed on them to preserve & show this fine Collection: These have Comfortable Apartments in the Wings, & a Philosophic Grove and Physick Garden open to the view of a delightful Country, where at leisure hours they may improve their health & their Studies together.[139]

Such visits became more common and the Trustees eventually decided to allow access to the books and manuscripts on a limited basis in 1757.[140] This got in the way of the preparatory work for the opening and the privilege had to be withdrawn about a year later, although people – particularly the smart Bloomsbury set of the period – were allowed to walk in the garden.

The garden must have been magnificent. Though it was much neglected at the time the Trustees had bought the house, a lot of care and attention had been lavished upon it (a gardener called Bramley had been appointed in 1756).[141] Presents of plants were received from many people, including some Trustees, so that by the end of the century there were more than six hundred species in the garden.[142] The first visitors were admitted in March 1757 and it soon became a popular refuge from the noise and smells of Bloomsbury. Admission to it was jealously controlled, tickets being introduced in 1762.[143] The extent to which it was appreciated by the privileged few with access to it is reflected in the words of a Victorian Principal Librarian:

> Let not such small records be accounted trivial. The vision of the porter and his handbell ringing out the loiterers under the glowing twilight of a summer evening is one to be cherished by dwellers in the crowded and fog-ridden Bloomsbury of the present day.[144]

Towards the end of 1758 it became clear that the Museum was ready for opening. On 2 December the Trustees agreed 'that the porter be allowed a Gown and Staff, and the Gown be of a plain drab colour with a yellow tuft, and the staff (pl. 2) be black tipt with silver on the top...'.[145] On 22 December, they approved the text of a ticket for admission and agreed that 'the Museum be opened on Monday the fifteenth of January 1759'. They then went away and did not meet again until 7 April.

Chapter 2

ACCESS AND ACCESSIONS

1759–99

The Museum was now theoretically open to the public. But it was a very circumscribed group of people who were admitted, under restrictive conditions – and for the senior staff the restrictions must have been almost unbearable. The Trustees had been as much exercised concerning access as any government at the end of the twentieth century, although the refinement of that access would justify the use of the pejorative 'elitist'. The pages of the various minute books and the private papers of the Trustees are shot through with proposals and draft regulations. Trustees sometimes seemed as much concerned with keeping people away as allowing them access. Sloane's declaration in his will, which has already been quoted, was always, however, in their minds:

> ... it is my desire and intention, that my said musæum or collection be preserved and kept... under such statutes... as shall be made, from time to time, by the said trustees... as well towards the satisfying the desire of the curious, as for the improvement, knowledge and information of all persons; and it is for this purpose I have reposed a sincere trust and confidence in my... trustees....[1]

Sloane had himself allowed scholars and the curious access to his collections as generously as a private gentleman might. It was now up to the Trustees to do the same.

Rules and Regulations

The Trustees were much exercised by the problem posed in Sloane's will but, in the draft statutes and rules drawn up in 1757, stated fairly and squarely in the true spirit of the Enlightenment:

> For altho it was chiefly designed for the use of learned and studious men, both natives and foreigners, in their researches into the several parts of knowledge; yet being founded at the expence of the public, it may be judged reasonable, that the advantages accruing from it should be rendered as general, as may be consistent with the several considerations above mentioned.[2]

The drafts of the statutes were batted back and forth among the more professional members of the Trustees, the President of the Royal Society (Lord Macclesfield), Dr Birch and Dr Ward, who produced draft printed regulations in 1758 and 1759.[3] Other Trustees joined in: Sloane's son-in-law, Lord Cadogan, for example, expressed the opinion of the whole board in answer to a specific proposal that people should be admitted whose names were entered on a register, '... many intolerable inconveniences must necessarily arise from very low and improper Persons, even menial Servants being entered into the said Register'.[4] Dr Ward, elderly and opinionated, went even further in discussing the admission of the lower orders:

> ... many irregularities will be comitted that cannot be prevented by a few Librarians who will be insulted by such people... If any such people should be in liquor misbehave, they are rarely without their accomplices... No persons of superiour degree will care to come on such days so that this low Class with the lowest of the Mobb, will make the Museum that day a place of diversion... If public days should be allowed [it will be necessary] for the trustees to have the presence of a Committee of themselves attending, with at least two Justices of the Peace and the constables of the division of Bloomsbury... supported by a guard such as one as usually attends at the Playhouse....[5]

The idea that the noisome lower classes should be allowed into the Museum with the middle and upper classes was to exercise the minds of the Trustees for the next seventy-five years.

Although this was a serious worry, it is clear that the physical security of the collections was uppermost. Ward, for example, was exercised that the lower classes would cause accidents. Nobody was to be trusted to wander through the rooms alone. The idea that warders should be appointed was adumbrated from time to time, but was never seriously considered by the Trustees, who could not be shifted from their opinion that the officers and nobody else should conduct visitors round the building, the better to control straying fingers.[6]

The conduct of the various reading rooms posed fewer problems of access, although some of the regulations were bizarre (particularly as to the number of books allowed on each visit) and were to cause great friction between the Trustees and the quarrelsome superintendent of the Reading Room, Peter Templeman.[7] Readers could be admitted only with the approval of the Trustees (later changed to that of the Principal Librarian). A record of the admissions to the reading rooms was kept, the first entry being for 12 January 1759.[8] Most of those who were admitted in the first few weeks were clerics, but the great lawyer William Blackstone was soon working there regularly, as was William Stukeley, the antiquary, and David Hume, the philosopher. Foreign readers in the first months included scholars from Kiel, Berlin, Uppsala and Stockholm, for the Trustees were always keen to encourage foreigners to use the collections. They were not always so keen to admit the natives, who had to know a Trustee to gain admission, and when a fifteen-year-old schoolboy, Samuel Wilton of Christ's Hospital, asked permission to use the Reading Room, it was decided that he was too young and an age limit was set.[9]

Once in, however, the readers seem to have developed a camaraderie which is still found in the present-day reading rooms of the British Library. Thomas Gray, the poet, a keen reader, expressed this well in a letter to the Reverend William Mason, only a few months after the Museum had opened:

> I this day passed thro' the jaws of a great leviathan, that lay in my way, into the belly of Dr
> Templeman, superintendent of the Reading Room, who congratulated himself on the sight
> of so much good company. We were – a man that writes for Lord Royston; a man that writes
> for Dr Burton of York; a third that writes for the Emperor of Germany or Dr Pocock, for he
> speaks the worst English I ever heard; Dr Stukeley, who writes for himself, the very worst
> person he could write for; and I, who only read to know, if there were any thing worth
> writing, and that not without some difficulty.[10]

The trials of the readers were gradually overcome, partly through the liberal attitude of the
otherwise difficult Templeman. The close examination of antiquities seems not, however,
to have been deemed worthy of a students' room, although natural history materials were
sometimes viewed in the reading rooms.[11] Thus Taylor White was allowed in for a month to
look at specimens of cassia and cinnamon. We must assume that the same courtesy was
extended to students of antiquities, although coins and medals – always a security
problem – could be examined only under very strict conditions.

It was represented to the Trustees that students might need more time studying the
material in the Department of Natural and Artificial Productions and it was even suggested
that officers might be paid to allow study outside normal visiting hours.[12] Decision on this
was continually postponed, but it is clear that, although no charge was allowed, medals
and Artificial and Natural Productions might be shown 'in a more private way' out of
visiting hours.[13] Prints and drawings were treated in the same way as books, although
there seems to have been a need to get special permission to look at them. Thus a Dr Nash
was granted permission to see prints and drawings, 'provided that no more than two
books of Prints and Drawings be carried into the Reading Room in one day'.[14] The Trustees
were somewhat exercised, however, by certain images: 'Dr Templeman is to observe that
the Miniature Paintings of Merian, Robert, and others are not included; Nor are they to be
carried into the Reading Room without particular leave; they being in continual use for the
Amusement of Persons coming to see the Museum'.[15]

Regulations for the admittance of the general public were brought into force at the
opening of the Museum and were made public in the pages of such periodicals as the
Annual Register.[16] The public found the very strict admission procedure burdensome, the
staff was unhappy and the restrictive ideas of the Trustees were allowed full rein. Despite
representations from the staff, who were clearly disgruntled at the amount of time they
had to spend showing people around the Museum, the Trustees were adamant '... that the
requiring the attendance of the Officers during the whole six hours that the Museum is
kept open, is not a wanton or useless piece of severity, as the two vacant hours (if it is not
thought too great a burden on the Officers) might very usefully be employed by them in
better ranging the several Collections'.[17] The Trustees sank their teeth into the problems of
public access, and regulations for entry were continually reviewed between June 1759 and
May 1760. The Principal Librarian fell out with the Trustees about the regulations and was
reprimanded for his rudeness to them,[18] but in the end a new draft set of regulations,
framed by Matthew Maty, was brought into force.[19]

Entry was by ticket, which had to be obtained from the porter. The Principal Librarian had to approve the name of the visitor and the applicant or his servant had to collect the
ticket before he could view the Museum. Ten tickets were allowed for each hour of opening

(normally six hours a day, save Saturdays, Sundays and festivals) and parties of no more than five were then conducted round the collections in a specified order by an under librarian or an assistant. Entry was free and gratuities were strictly forbidden. Although the system seemed simple (if tedious), it was a complicated and rickety procedure. It was to last for nearly half a century and was the subject of complaints and minor tinkering throughout that period. By the time more liberal access was achieved in 1805, fewer than 12,000 people annually had toured the Museum and only about 160 readers were admitted to the Reading Room.[20]

The tickets were often oversubscribed and, particularly in the summer months, delay was endemic. Edwards quotes an advertisement concerning tickets dated 9 August 1776, 'The Applicants of the middle of April are not yet satisfied. Persons applying are requested to send weekly to the porter to know how near they are upon the List.'[21] The system was also abused by ticket touts and even by the porter.[22] In 1784 William Hutton of Birmingham was desperate to see the Museum:

> I was unwilling to quit London without seeing what I had many years wished to see; but how to accomplish it was the question; I had not one relation in that vast metropolis to direct me and only one acquaintance; but assistance was not with him... As I did not know a right way, I was determined to pursue a wrong, which probably might lead me into a right... By good fortune I stumbled upon a person possessed of a ticket for the next day, which he valued less than two shillings, we struck a bargain in a moment, and were both pleased....[23]

Having achieved a ticket the visitor presented himself at the porter's lodge and was admitted to the Museum. In the southern colonnade of the courtyard were 'two pieces of greenish marble, which belonged to the mausoleum of Cleopatra... lately sent from Egypt by Mr Montague [Edward Wortley Montagu], to the Earl of Bute, together with four mummies and a large crocodile. His Lordship presented them to the King, who was pleased to bestow them on the Museum'.[24] Moving from the courtyard into the hall the visitors would be greeted by their guide and would see displayed there some of the heavier objects from the Department of Natural and Artificial Productions: fragments removed from the Giant's Causeway in Antrim (a great tourist attraction of the period), a stone from the Appian Way outside Rome, two granite columns, two terms, epitaphs and inscriptions in Latin, Greek and other languages and a number of other geological specimens, all overwhelmed by the painted walls and ceilings.[25] The Reading Room, the old Royal Library, the library of Major Edwards and the Sloane Library were on the ground floor, as was the boardroom. The grand staircase was adorned by a bust of Sloane and the first of many historical portraits which were hung around the building.

Through a great doorway at the top of the stairs the visitor passed into a small anteroom 'set for the immediate Reception of Presents', which was clearly intended as what would nowadays be called a 'recent acquisitions exhibition'. The objects shown here came from all departments. The main room on the *piano nobile*, described as the saloon, was used as a waiting room for visitors who arrived late; it contained a copy of the Belvedere Laocoon, and was later used for the display of antiquities. The visitors were then led into the five rooms of the Department of Manuscripts on the east side of the building, tucked into the corner of which was a room reserved to Sloane's collection of medals – upwards of 20,000 of them, although they were not initially on display (the Harley medals were kept with the Harley manuscripts). After leaving the room devoted to the Sloane manuscripts, the visitor passed through a room of antiquities, and then back into the anteroom and saloon. In these rooms was displayed a confusion of objects of all periods and from all areas of the world from Japan to Mexico (although there was little if anything from sub-Saharan Africa). Mixed in with the natural history specimens that occupied the rooms on this floor were other antiquities, gems, cameos and ivories (including one 'made by the late Queen of Denmark' – presumably Louise, the daughter of George II).

Returning to the ground floor, down a secondary staircase, visitors were able to view some scientific apparatus including some of the improved compasses developed by the Principal Librarian, Dr Knight. Finally, in one of the rooms on the ground floor the visitor was able to see some of the Sloane collection of drawings, 'perhaps the finest to be seen in the World'.

Most visitors were overwhelmed – after all it was unique as a public museum. The young Mozart at his visit in 1765 was presumably suitably affected and composed a motet, 'God is our refuge', dedicating it to the Museum.[26] Early visitors were most struck by the Egyptian antiquities and those described as Etruscan. Indeed, the Museum was itself rather impressed by the Egyptian material; one of the mummies even seems to have been displayed in a case that could be rotated by turning a handle.[27] Classical antiquities seemed at this time less than impressive, as the author of an anonymous series of letters wrote, 'I am sorry to acquaint you that the collection of these antiquities is far short of what I hoped to find. Among them, however, there is of brass, a noble bust of Homer. It is of the most exquisite Greek sculpture....'[28] Some were uncritically overwhelmed. Many (while being impressed) complained, particularly about the speed with which they were led around the Museum. Carl Moritz, a visitor from Germany in 1782, wrote:

> The company who saw it, when and as I did, was various and some of all sorts, and some, as I believe, of the lowest classes of the people of both sexes; for, as it is, the property of the Nation, every one has the same right (I use the term of the country) to see it that another has... The rapidly passing through this vast suite of rooms, in a space of time, little, if at all, exceeding an hour; with leisure just to cast one poor longing look of astonishment on all these stupendous treasures of natural curiosities, antiquities, and literature; in the contemplation of which you could with pleasure spend years, and a whole life might be employed in the study of them – quite confuses, stuns and overpowers one. In some branches this collection is said to be far surpassed by some others; but taken together, and for size, it certainly is equalled by none.[29]

There were also continuous complaints that the respectable classes had to mix with the lower classes, although many of these complaints came from the staff who had to show the visitors round. Sometimes the boot was on the other foot. When the Duke of Brunswick came to England in 1764 to marry Princess Augusta, he was generally mobbed by the populace as a hero of the recent wars. On a visit to the Museum he was apparently jostled by those who were being conducted round the collections and specific regulations had to be drawn up thereafter for the reception of royalty, so that when George III and Queen Charlotte came for the first time in January 1767 the visit passed off in staid fashion.[30]

Some characters, like Smollett's Mr Bramble, had their own agenda:

Yes, Doctor, I have seen the British Museum; which is a noble collection, and even stupendous, if we consider it was made by a private man, a physician, who was obliged to make his own fortune at the same time; but great as the collection is, it would appear more striking if it was arranged in one spacious saloon, instead of being divided into different apartments, which it does not entirely fill. I could wish the series of medals was connected, and the whole of the animal, vegetable and mineral kingdoms completed, by adding to each, at the public expence, those articles that are wanting... I could also wish, for the honour of the nation, that there was a complete apparatus for a course of mathematics, mechanics and experimental philosophy; and a good salary settled upon an able professor, who should give regular lectures on these subjects.

But all this is idle speculation, which will never be reduced to practice. – Considering the temper of the times, it is a wonder to see any institution whatever established for the benefit of the public....[31]

Others, like William Hutton (who had been taken for a ride by a ticket tout), while admiring the collections, were ultimately condemnatory of a parsimonious government:

We began to move pretty fast, when I asked with some surprize, whether there were none to inform us what the curiosities were as we went on? A tall genteel young man in *person*, who seemed to be our conductor, replied with some warmth, 'What! Would you have me tell you every thing in the Museum? How is it possible? Besides, are not the names written on many of them'... The company seemed influenced; they made haste and were silent. No voice was heard but in whispers. If a man spends two minutes in a room, in which are a thousand things to demand his attention, he cannot find time to bestow on them a glance a piece... It grieved me to think how much I lost for want of a little information. In about thirty minutes we finished our silent journey through this princely mansion, which would well have taken thirty days. I went out much about as wise as I went in, but with this severe reflection that, for fear of losing my chance, I had that morning abruptly torn myself from three gentlemen, with whom I was engaged in interesting conversation, had lost my breakfast, got wet to the skin, spent half-a-crown in coach hire, paid two shillings for a ticket, been hackneyed through the rooms with violence, had lost the share of good humour I brought in, and came away completely disappointed... I had laid more stress on the British Museum, than on any thing which I should see in London. It was the only sight that disgusted me... Government purchased this rare collection... at vast expense, and exhibits it as a national honour. How far it answers the end proposed this chapter of cross incidents will testify.[32]

Some gave a professional opinion. Barthélmy Faujas Saint-Fond, professor of geology at the natural history museum in Paris, was perhaps over-chauvinistic. He certainly made a point, however, when he wrote, 'The British Museum contains many valuable collections in natural history; but with the exception of some fishes in a small apartment, which are beginning to be classed, nothing is in order, every thing is out of its place; and this assemblage appears rather an immense magazine, in which things have been thrown at random, than a scientific collection, destined to instruct and honour a great nation'.[33]

The First Cash Crisis

At the root of the problem was, as so often in the Museum's history, a chronic shortage of money. In the euphoria of the opening the Trustees seemed to have ignored the fact that their outgoings already exceeded their income. At a Trustees' meeting in March 1760 it was observed somewhat laconically that 'It also appears by the state of the accounts of the Museum lying upon the Table, that the *annual Expences* of the Establishment *exceed* the annual Income by 516 £.0.0 per annum: which requires the serious Consideration of the Meeting'.[34] So anxious were the Trustees about their financial position that they called a series of emergency meetings. Less than a fortnight later they were told that their income was £900. As to the future, there were two sources of income in prospect, as the salary of the Royal Librarian would revert to them, as would the legacy of Major Edwards. The latter, however, was actually appropriated by his will 'to the Purchase of Manuscripts, Books of Antiquities and Coins and Medals'. Annual expenditure was shown to be £1,490 4s 1d, whilst additional expenditure on taxes, maintenance, and so on, brought this up to £1,608 19s 7d. In all the Trustees had a budget deficit of £708 19s 7d. A detailed account of the income and expenditure of the Museum since its foundation was drawn up and this was submitted to the Treasury with an application for help in late April.[35] The expensive war with France was at its height and the approach failed. Resources dwindled so that the Trustees' capital had by 1762 been reduced to £30,000. This time the Trustees sent a petition directly to the Commons and, on 26 June 1762, a grant-in-aid of £2,000 was reported to them. A similar sum was granted every two years thereafter until 1774, after which it rose to £3,000, paid every second or third year until the end of the century.[36] The reversion of the Royal Librarian's salary in 1774, and the receipt of the residue of Major Edwards's estate in 1769, slightly relieved the Trustees' finances and allowed them occasionally to purchase material – particularly books (sometimes helped by the sale of duplicates – somewhat loosely so designated if we are to believe Thomas Hollis).[37]

It was impossible on this limited budget to improve the resources of the Museum as regards either staff or amenities. As the century progressed the staff grew more cursory in their duties as guides and the public became more impatient with the service that was offered. Some of the younger staff, particularly Daniel Solander in Natural and Artificial Productions and Samuel Ayscough in Printed Books, were, however, more energetic and interested (in their own fashion) in the collections. On the death of Empson in 1765, Maty had transferred sideways to become Under Librarian of the Department of Natural and Artificial Productions and, with Solander, began to draw up a collections policy for the department. Maty was by far the most original and bright mind among the founding appointments; his successor as Keeper of Printed Books, Samuel Harper, however, was a plodder and for nearly forty years (until 1803) ran the department in a fashion that could best be described as dignified. (Less dignified was the one recorded colourful episode in his career, when he was hit on the head with a poker by Aaron Williams, the porter, who was clearly drunk – and not for the first time. Williams was subsequently dismissed.)[38] The egregious Dr Templeman, superintendent of the Reading Room, resigned – to the Trustees' delight – in 1761 and was replaced by the Reverend Richard Penneck, who held on to the job until he died, aged seventy-five, in 1803. Penneck was rector of Abinger and Horsley Down; gout-ridden throughout his career, he was absent for long periods with his foot up.[39] The gifted but sick Maty succeeded Knight as Principal Librarian in 1772, but only four years later was succeeded by the lazy and self-seeking Morton.

Coins and medals, then in the Department of Manuscripts, were looked after by extremely competent assistants. In 1784 Andrew Gifford was succeeded by another collector, the Reverend Richard Southgate, who died in 1795. Southgate, the son of a prosperous farmer, while still an undergraduate at St John's College, Cambridge, had started to collect coins and books and by the end of his life had amassed an impressive private collection of both. A curate at St Giles-in-the-Fields (where he is buried), he was presented to the living of Little Steeping in 1763 and, in 1790, to Warsop, Nottinghamshire, which had a stipend of £400. He was thus – at least towards the end of his life – comparatively well off. He worked on the Anglo-Saxon coinage but published nothing; after his death his collections were sold (the books and prints alone fetched £1,322).[40]

Daniel Solander was another officer of the Museum who published next to nothing, although a large number of his manuscripts survive in the Natural History Museum. [41] Widely known as the botanist who accompanied Captain James Cook on his first voyage, he is better known in the Museum today as the eponymous inventor of the hinged box which is used almost universally to store prints and drawings. Solander came to England in 1760, with good introductions from his teacher in Uppsala, Linnaeus, with whom he had collaborated in his native Sweden. In 1762, having turned down the invitation to a chair in St Petersburg, he started to catalogue the important natural history cabinet of the Duchess of Portland. He became an assistant in the Museum in 1763, recommended to some extent by Carteret Webb, an MP and a keen gardener and antiquary, who had consulted Solander on a number of occasions.[42] It was about this time that Solander met Joseph Banks, then an undergraduate at Oxford, but soon to be a great force in both British science and in the British Museum and Solander's chief patron. Solander was a smooth man of the world – Fanny Burney later described him as being 'very sociable, full of talk, information, and entertainment... a philosophical gossip'; Dr Johnson, however, reserved judgement.[43] His greatest claim to fame remains his presence, as an undoubtedly valuable member of Banks's party, in *Endeavour* on Captain Cook's first voyage to the South Seas. (The salary of £400 he received for participation in this voyage allowed the Museum to employ a deputy during his absence.) On his return, lionized and granted an honorary degree by the University of Oxford, he acted as a sorting house and distribution point for the collections brought back on this and subsequent voyages, which placed the Museum in the forefront of collecting in the newly explored parts of the world.[44] Solander became head of the Department of Natural and Artificial Productions in 1773 and died young of a stroke in 1782. He was succeeded by Maty's son Paul Henry Maty, who himself died five years later. From the minutes and other documents in the Museum archives it is clear that Solander, more than most other officers of the Museum, regarded the post as a gentle-manly sinecure. For example, when asked to act as deputy to Morton for three months in 1778, he at first declined.[45] Arrogant and snobbish though he undoubtedly was, Solander was a considerable scholar and his academic reputation has undergone a more positive re-assessment in recent years.[46] However, it must be said that, although a brilliant naturalist, he appears to have paid little attention to the antiquities for which he was responsible.

Joseph Banks – Dictator

Solander was a confidant, one might almost say a creature, of Sir Joseph Banks (pl. 8), the most influential manipulator of the academic community of the late eighteenth and early nineteenth century.[47] Banks became a Trustee of the British Museum, *ex officio* as President of the Royal Society, in 1778, and remained active in these capacities (as in many others) until his death in 1820, giving much material in his lifetime to the Museum and bequeathing it his vast collections of natural history material, together with many of his papers and his library. He was primarily interested in natural history, but had a small collection of antiquities, was a member of the Society of Antiquaries, and was not uninterested in field monuments. He was issued a Museum reading-room ticket in 1764 and, when he was elected a Fellow of the Royal Society in 1766 at the age of twenty-three, he numbered among his proposers the under librarian Charles Morton and William Watson, one of the original Trustees. When he became President in 1778 two officers of the Museum were Secretaries of the Royal Society – Paul Henry Maty and Joseph Planta, who had succeeded his father as assistant in 1773 and had been Keeper of Manuscripts since 1776. Banks, like many young men, tried to move quickly and lost a number of battles in the Society in which both Planta and Maty were on the opposite side.[48] Banks, however, did not lose the war. In a great row in the Society in 1784 Maty foolishly fought Banks and, although Planta tried to pour oil on troubled water, Maty had to resign his (paid) post.[49] He remained in the Museum but died three years later, unreconciled to one of his most powerful Trustees.

Banks, Solander and Maty were clearly involved in different capacities in the acquisition of much of the material from the Cook expeditions in the South Pacific and on the Northwest Coast of America. As scientists they were particularly interested in the natural history collections, but ethnographic material was also acquired, albeit in haphazard and grudging fashion, as though the Museum had little idea of what to do with it. No attempt was made to classify the acquisitions, which were not registered, so that over the years objects were subject to dispersal at the casual whim of the head of department or of the Trustees.[50] Banks and Solander spent much time systematizing and listing the botanical and zoological material that had been brought home. Neither, however, produced the publications they had planned, about which there was much talk (and for which many engravings were prepared). This failure may be chiefly due to the early death of Solander who, among other pupils of Linnaeus employed by Banks, was the most senior member of the team of scholars working on the reports and catalogues of the Banks collection, then housed in Soho Square.

Much work was, however, published by some of the other scholars, often heavily subvented by Banks. The offhand treatment by Banks and his team of the ethnographic material was reflected in the display in the much-visited Otaheite (South Sea) Room, cobbled together in 1775, in which objects were labelled only with the names of the donors, the items otherwise being unidentified.[51]

The main part of the South Sea collections from the first voyage was given by the Admiralty in 1775 to be displayed 'in a particular manner and in a distinguished place as a monument of these national exertions of British munificence and industry'.[52] Banks made a further contribution in 1780, which perhaps came from the collection he had inherited from Captain Clerke. Other collections and individual objects came at that time from a variety of sources, presumably stimulated by the display in the Otaheite Room.

A sidelight on the attitude of the Museum to such material (and perhaps to others) is recorded by one of Banks's assistants, the entomologist Johann Fabricius:

The British Museum is one of the public institutions where there are several superintendents but of whom none devotes himself with true zeal to that institution, with the result that many things remain neglected. A case in point are the objects which Banks had acquired from Cook's last voyage, dresses, weapons, instruments, and which according to his noble thinking he had sent to the Museum, in order that the museum could choose from them what they thought best. There they remained for about two years, without anybody taking any notice about them, until finally Sir Joseph – not uninfluenced by our arguments – gave permission for me and two other friends to bring everything back from the Museum to his house and divide it among ourselves. You may well imagine that I received no small quantity of different objects of different fabrication, mats, spears, bludgeons, nets, angle hooks and other things, with which I was very pleased. I shall certainly have some trouble in transporting everything of this precious freight back to the continent, however, quite a bit of what I take back shall serve for the pleasant entertainment of my friends.[53]

Jonathan King has estimated that there were in the eighteenth century some two to four times as many specimens from the Cook expeditions in the British Museum as exist today.[54]

While not entirely uninterested in the ethnographic material (the first authentic portrait of him (pl. 8), painted by Benjamin West in 1772, depicts him surrounded by ethnographic items and wearing a cloak from the South Seas),[55] Banks was certainly responsible for the Trustees' refusal to purchase some of the most important items from Cook's voyages, which made their way into the Lever collection. This was disposed of by lottery in 1786 and later dispersed by sale in 1806, whence most of the material ended up in Vienna.[56] Banks himself owned what has been described as the most valuable of the Hawaiian feather cloaks, which had belonged to the high chief Kalani'opo'u; he gave it to William Bullock and it is now in the National Museum in Wellington.[57] Compared with the tyrannical Banks, George III was much more perspicacious in dealing with the South Sea material, reserving material for the British Museum before offering it elsewhere in his dominions – to the University of Göttingen, where the term 'Ethnographie' was first used and where the most coherent ethnographic collection from Cook's voyages survives.[58] The King gave the Museum 113 objects from the Northwest Coast of America and the South Seas brought back in Discovery by Archibald Menzies.[59] Banks and his cronies were also clearly out of touch with the feelings of the general visitor to the Museum, for the South Sea room soon became the most popular attraction there; in the Synopsis of the contents of the British Museum (1808) it is described as 'one of the most conspicuous parts of the Museum'.[60]

Banks, despite his dictatorial tendencies, was an important influence. He was the ultimate fixer in a period when influence was all; he was used unmercifully by the Trustees on numerous sub-committees and consulted on many political and financial matters. Whether holding the ring in major purchases, as an arbiter of architectural practice when a new wing was planned, or in considering the design of new bookcases, Banks made his presence felt. He knew everybody and had contacts throughout Europe and in America, contacts that were frequently used by the Trustees. It is not surprising, therefore, that he took advantage of his influence. We have seen one example of this, but there were others; he was, for example, given permission by the Trustees (under fairly rigorous conditions which may not have been totally adhered to) to exchange material from his own collection for material from the Museum.[61]

It is difficult to overestimate Banks's services to the institution, both politically and academically. Amid his many other interests, he worked hard to better its standing in the eyes of the great and the good and to increase its natural historical collections. Even here he was exceedingly high-handed, turning down, for example, the opportunity to acquire the anatomical collections of John Hunter, which were consequently given to the Royal College of Surgeons.[62] His lofty attitude towards some of the artificial curiosities is less deserving of praise, although he gave and bequeathed to the Museum many antiquities and ethnographical specimens, and was influential in the acquisition of some major collections. His bust by Mrs Damer no longer stands alongside that of Sloane, as it once did in a place of honour on the staircase of Montagu House,[63] but his portrait broods over part of the Trustees' suite in the present building. After Sloane, his was the most important influence on the fledgling Museum in the first sixty years of its existence.

Not all stories of acquisition by the Department of Natural and Artificial Productions are so horrific as the tale of the ethnographic collections from the South Seas. The Museum had been receiving gifts since its inception. Some of them were very odd; but it was the kind of oddity found in any self-respecting eighteenth-century curiosity cabinet – a piece of lace made of the hair of Queen Elizabeth (1762); a Chinese bowl, disfigured in the fire occasioned by the earthquake at Lisbon (1763); a pair of glasses made of the beard of a shellfish found off the coast of Sicily (1764); a dried thumb dug up in the foundations of St James's coffee house (1766), and so on. Other gifts were more normal, such as the gift of Thomas Hollis, who in 1757 had 'presented that useful repository with a large collection of antique bronzes and etruscan ware, &c, which had cost him upwards of fifty pounds'.[64] The first pieces of European porcelain, the famous Cleopatra vases of the Chelsea gold-anchor period, made in 1762,[65] came to the Museum in 1763 through Empson; a faltering step on the long road in the creation of the Museum's internationally important collection of pottery and porcelain. One of the most famous pieces of sculpture in the Museum today, Roubiliac's statue of Shakespeare, came with the Garrick bequest in 1779.[66] This nicely supplemented the Roubiliac terracotta and plaster busts purchased by Maty at the sale of material on the sculptor's death in 1762 and almost immediately given to the Museum.[67] A portion of the collections made on Captain George Vancouver's voyages to the Pacific coast of North America came to the Museum in 1798.[68] The first major collection of antiquities to be purchased by the Museum was, however, the Hamilton collection of classical material – particularly Greek vases. The Museum was about to change.

Sir William Hamilton

Sir William Hamilton (1730–1803), known to popular history as the husband of Nelson's mistress, Emma, came from a cadet branch of an aristocratic Scottish family. His father held a number of appropriate senior offices and his mother was Mistress of the Robes in the royal household (and perhaps the actual mistress of George III's father, Frederic, Prince of Wales). He served in the army in Flanders (he was for some time equerry to George, Prince of Wales), but resigned his commission in 1758 and married an heiress (with £5,000 a year), Catherine Barlow. After a stint in Parliament, and partly due to his frail wife's need to live in a warm climate (she died in 1782, having lost her only daughter

45

in 1775), Hamilton went as Minister to Naples, where he was successful both socially and diplomatically – within the limits of a second-rate posting – until ill-health caused his retirement in 1800.

Hamilton had arrived in Italy at a period when the study of classical Roman antiquity was being revolutionized. The Capitoline Museum in Rome (founded in the mid-seventeenth century by Pope Innocent X) had been enlarged and reorganized under the patronage of Popes Clement XII and Benedict XIV and was made available to the public in 1734, at which time the great collection of Cardinal Albani was added to its holdings.[69] Rather earlier the collection of the Farnese family had been moved to Naples and that of the Medicis to Florence; the other kingdoms of Italy were thus able for the first time to see imperial Roman material. The avidity with which the royalty and aristocracy of Europe collected classical antiquities and sculpture had impoverished Italy, but it had on the other hand provided an opportunity for scholars north of the Alps to become acquainted with such material. Excavations at Herculaneum, which started in 1711 (some of the finds went straight to Dresden), and Pompeii were being carried out in great secrecy. These became the subject of an open letter of protest by a Brandenburg German of humble origins, Johann Joachim Winckelmann, whose great *Geschichte der Kunst des Alterthums* (1764) was to inform and lead European methodology in the study of classical – and particularly Greek – antiquity until well into the nineteenth century.[70] Winckelmann's letter was published in 1762, just two years before Hamilton arrived in Naples, and coloured the new diplomat's more discreet protests about the matter. It presumably also encouraged him to publish a report on the Pompeii excavations.[71]

Hamilton was a man of the Enlightenment. Like Banks, with whom he sustained a long correspondence on scientific and horticultural subjects, he was a member of the Society of Dilettanti, the Royal Society and the Society of Antiquaries, was keenly interested in music and was a many-faceted collector.[72] He was also interested in the eruptions of Vesuvius, which he observed with scientific detachment, and offered sober theories concerning them – an interest which earned him the title of 'the modern Pliny of Vesuvius' (*le Pline moderne du Vésuve*). This title he acknowledged but was somewhat scathing about it: 'As for my part', he wrote, 'if I live the rest of my life here, I shall content myself with collecting facts, and let those who will form them into a system afterwards'.[73] In 1767 he gave the Museum a 'complete collection of every sort of matter produced by Mount Vesuvius, which I have been collecting with some pains for these three years past'.[74] This was followed by a similar collection from Mount Etna. But he formed other collections, not only of lava but of splendid paintings, gems, classical antiquities, marine biology and various miscellaneous objects.[75] He was also the purchaser of one of the most famous objects of antiquity, the Barberini Vase (found in 1582 in the Monte del Grano, south of Rome, and dated to 30–20 BC). This he bought in 1782 through James Byres for the sum of £1,000 and sold it on two years later to the Duchess of Portland, from whom it received its present name – the Portland Vase. In 1810 the Portland family lent it to the Museum, which had to wait until 1945 to purchase it.[76]

The most important part of Hamilton's collection to come to the Museum was his first collection of antiquities, chiefly Greek vases found in South Italy. This was bought in 1772 for £8,410, a further £840 having been voted to house it – the first time the Trustees had been to Parliament for this purpose.[77] Hamilton (who later became a Trustee) advised the Museum on display of his collections. They were to be placed in the saloon and antechamber; the smaller objects were to be placed in cases 'of mahogany, but without any carving or useless ornament' – other objects had to be more closely packed and redistributed as a consequence.[78] The painter David Allan was so impressed by this acquisition that he painted a full-length portrait of Hamilton and presented it to the Museum. Writing from Rome on 6 October 1775, he stated:

> ... considering his great ingenuity and Merit in making such a Noble Colection of interesting & beautiful monuments of Antiquity which are at present rightly placed in the B. Museum has induced me to think that a portraite of the worthy colector might very properly find a place in that Colection, on this consideration I have ventured to offer the picture to the Directors....[79]

With the purchase of the Hamilton collection the Museum began to change its character, moving away from domination by books and natural history towards the institution it is today.

There was a bonus to this acquisition in that part of the Hamilton collection had been beautifully engraved and described (along with much additional material) by a French rogue, the self-styled Baron d'Hancarville (actually Pierre François Hugues),[80] in four volumes which Hamilton published in luxurious form between about 1766 and 1779 as *Antiquités étrusques grècques et romaines tirées du cabinet de M. Hamilton*.[81] Although Hamilton tried to sell the Museum other objects, including the Warwick Vase[82] and his second collection of vases, they were not accepted. Nevertheless, Hamilton remained a Trustee until his death and gave the Museum a number of important pieces, including some fine sculpture. It is particularly sad that the Museum did not purchase the remains of the second Hamilton collection (beautifully published with engravings by the German painter Wilhelm Tischbein), part of which was sunk in HMS *Colossus* off the Scilly Isles on its way back to England in 1798.[83]

The publication of d'Hancarville's work and the presence of the Hamilton vases in London helped to change and stimulate English taste, already influenced by such architects as Robert Adam – and not only English taste. Most commercial of those influenced by Hamilton was the entrepreneurial genius Josiah Wedgwood, who, with his partner Thomas Bentley (a Liverpool merchant with wide continental connections), had already begun to make a fortune from his refinement of creamware and tiles, which he was to sell to many prestigious clients. Queen Charlotte allowed him to call his creamware 'Queen's Ware' and the Empress Catherine the Great of Russia ordered two services from him – the 'husk' and the 'frog' – and a large group of Wedgwood plaques for her bedroom at Tsarskoe Selo.[84] Wedgwood was so impressed by the pottery of the type collected by Hamilton (then known as Etruscan) that he gave the name 'Etruria' to his new model factory, which opened on 16 June 1769. Here he started to produce vases of 'Etrurian' form and decoration – a move which led to an explosion of vase production in England in the 1770s.[85] This fashion led to the development of 'black basalt' stoneware, first sold in 1768, and 'jasper' ware, which Wedgwood launched in 1774 after much experimentation. The form and decoration of many of these wares were based on classical designs and motifs. One of the pieces which most exercised Wedgwood was a jasper-ware plaque modelled by Flaxman entitled 'The Apotheosis of Homer', which is first mentioned in correspondence in 1778.[86] The design was based on a published plate in d'Hancarville's publication of the Hamilton collection (from a *calyx* dating to the fifth century BC) and Wedgwood, for advertisement purposes, sent a copy to Hamilton in Naples. Plaques such as this were much used by the well-to-do as ornamental decoration in interior design, particularly on chimneypieces, and Wedgwood and Bentley saw a market for their product in Italy, as they had already successfully introduced it into other European countries. They had, for example, exported to Germany a vast collection of various classically inspired wares for Count Leopold III Friedrich-Franz von Anhalt-Dessau, who had visited Hamilton in Naples in 1766 and admired him greatly. Leopold used Wedgwood's pottery to embellish his new palace at Wörlitz, and continued to purchase Wedgwood's wares until the end of the century.[87] Beside this, the Prussian king Wilhelm II's purchase of sixty-five pieces of jasper and black basalt ware for the Marble Palace in Potsdam pales almost into insignificance.[88]

Wedgwood, so influenced by the Hamilton collection, gave the Museum copies of two of his masterworks – the Pegasus vase (a re-working of the 'Apotheosis of Homer' plaque) in 1786 and his version of the Portland Vase in 1802[89] – thus providing the foundation for the Museum's rich collection of Wedgwood, now one of the most substantial and best-documented in the country.[90] Wedgwood was constantly in correspondence with Hamilton on matters of mythology, design and even technology. It may have been due to Hamilton's trusteeship that these two important pieces were added to the collections, for there was at this time little interest in, or knowledge of, such material on the part of the staff. Indeed, it was more than half a century before the Museum was to record any further gifts of this nature.

Meanwhile, in 1769, the Museum received its first bequest of prints and drawings. These came from a collector of whom nothing is now known, William Fawkener.[91] The collection was bound up in thirty-nine volumes. Little trace remains of it, as many of the volumes were broken up in 1808 and the prints distributed in the collection. Some of the drawings, particularly those of the Northern schools, were remounted in albums containing drawings from the Sloane and Cracherode collections. Four of the original volumes contained 386 – mostly Italian – drawings. The Museum had no specialist staff to deal with this material and the works were housed with the manuscripts.

It has been pointed out that the Museum was collecting paintings, mainly concerned with English history; indeed, there was a slim chance that it might about this time have expanded to take on the function filled today by the National Gallery. On 16 May 1777 Mann wrote to Horace Walpole:

> Both my nephew and I were much surprised to see in the last public papers a speech of Wilkes recommending to Parliament the purchase of the collection at Houghton. Was it a thought of his own, or suggested to him by anybody? I approve the proposal, but fear the time is improper.[92]

Mann was referring to a debate in the House of Commons on the finances of the Museum on 28 April, in which Wilkes suggested that Sir Robert Walpole's great collection should be housed in 'a noble gallery... to be built in the spacious garden of the British Museum for the reception of that invaluable treasure'.[93] Mann was right; the idea proved impracticable and the collection was bought in 1779 by Catherine the Great for a sum variously estimated between £35,000 and £45,000.[94] The British were slow to believe in the collection of great paintings for public display; even the foundation of the Dulwich Picture Gallery by Sir Francis Bourgeois in 1811 did little to stimulate them.[95]

The Gordon Riots

Much of the energy of the staff at this time was expended on the library departments, where a great many important collections of books, manuscripts, music and maps continued to be acquired by gift or purchase. Cataloguing and sorting occupied most of the time left over after the completion of guiding duties, which were becoming more sketchy as the staff grew more and more bored with them. There was occasional relief from this tedium as when, at the time of the Gordon Riots in 1780, troops were stationed in the Museum gardens and in part of the building. These anti-Catholic disturbances, stirred up by Lord George Gordon, were occasioned by the passing (two years earlier) of an Act of Parliament in relief of a minor element of the civic disabilities of the Roman Catholic community, and caused mob violence on a hideous scale. Houses were burned, property was sacked and some 850 people lost their lives. Among the places attacked by the mob were the houses of the Lord Chancellor and the Archbishop of York in Bloomsbury Square, a few hundred metres from the Museum; the former's house was sacked and the archbishop fled from his. Colonel Stanhope Harvey's York Regiment of Militia was quartered in the Museum, chiefly to protect these grandees and their neighbours, but partly to guard the collections (the Trustees, who met in emergency session on a number of days in early June, even agreed to pay the regiment's expenses).[96] The gardener's tool-shed and its adjoining stable, fitted with a chimney and a skylight, served as an officers' kitchen, while some of the officers were quartered in the residences and cellars of the Museum. Once the trouble was over the encampment became a popular visitor attraction (pl. 6); even the King and two of the royal princes inspected the encampment. Solander was there to see the fun:

> The British Museum has ever since the Rioting time been a compleat Garrison. We have had there a whole Regiment... They muster with officers, women and children very near 900. They came by a forced march, without Tents or baggage, of course were for the first 11 days supplied by the Trustees and officers of the British Museum with necessaries of all kinds. It was a drole sight, to see about 700 people every night sleep under the portico of the museum & their women &c under a large cover by the great steps. The officers slept with the officers of the museum. I had 8 occasional beds in my Appartments. Now the Regiment is encamped in the garden and the Camp is by all esteemed the neatest of any seen. The King called it a fairy grove. The common men have their Tents in Lines on the Lawn and the officers in the Terrace the Captains on the west side & subalterns on the East side, opposite their respective Companies. The field officers have their state Tents in the Terrace fronting the House and their common Tents in the grove... Every Evening the camp is crowded with visitors. Tea & Coffee & other refreshments are given every night by the Field officer & officers of the museum in the Tents – to their friends and other gentlemen visitors... We can never speak too much in praise of the officers and men. It is hardly to be credited but not less true. That they have not pulled a single flower... I don't think they have done 10 shillings damage to the premises....[97]

Public access to the collections was naturally limited during this period and the soldiers stayed for nearly two months, formally thanking the Trustees on their departure in August, as well they might in view of the cost (£487 – which the Trustees hoped, vainly, would be reimbursed by the Treasury). Further, a considerable amount of damage caused by the troops – notwithstanding Solander's statement – had to be made good. The Principal Librarian, as we have seen, was told off by the Trustees for being absent during this period, his behaviour being 'highly improper and irregular'; he was ordered 'not to lie out of the Museum without leave of Absence from a General Meeting or from the Standing Committee'.[98]

It is noteworthy that during earlier riots, in May 1765, which culminated in the siege of the Museum's next-door neighbour, the Duke of Bedford's Bloomsbury Square house, the Museum itself was apparently not considered to be a target of the mob. It clearly only became a centre of attention during the Gordon Riots not because of any perceived threat to the institution itself, but because its garden provided a convenient camping ground for troops. Only after the disturbances of 1780 did the idea of the security of the building and its collections in the face of mob violence become an issue with the Trustees. Museum folklore has it that it was these disturbances that led to the mounting of a sergeant's guard at the Museum, as it was at the Bank of England. This is untrue. The guard was first mounted as a measure of general security in 1807, the guard marching each day with that of the Bank of England from their barracks, being strengthened at times of threatened public disturbance.[99] A guard-house was built in the south-west corner of the garden and the soldiers were a familiar sight in Bloomsbury until they were replaced in 1863 by the Metropolitan Police (who had been present in the Museum since 1837).[100] In 1798 the Trustees were again asked to allow volunteers to exercise in the gardens, but they refused to repeat the experience of 1780.[101]

Apart from such disturbances the even tenor of life continued, monitored in minutest detail by the Trustees, who in general meeting or standing committee regulated all details of the running of the Museum from the sweeping of the courtyard (at least once a week with a yard brush) to the repair of the roof after a storm. The staff quarrelled about their accommodation and were occasionally in hot water because they overspent on the refurbishment of their apartments.

The Trustees were sporadic in their attendance at full meetings, save when there was an emergency or a need to approach Parliament. Every so often after 1780 they were not quorate and six months would consequently elapse between full board meetings. The *ex officio* Secretaries of State rarely attended the meetings; rather one of the three Principal Trustees – the Archbishop of Canterbury, the Lord Chancellor or the Speaker of the House of Commons – chaired a meeting of between six and twelve of the elected members, who might include one or more of the representatives of the learned societies. The interested elected Trustees included collectors such as Hamilton (when he was in the country), virtuosi such as Banks, professionals such as Thomas Astle (Keeper of the Public Records from 1783),[102] together with the occasional family Trustee. It is noticeable that until well into the nineteenth century the Trustees who attended the meetings were not predominantly aristocratic or political grandees; they were either landowners like Banks (who was incidentally one of the two or three hundred wealthiest men in England), or semi-professionals.

At their meetings the board considered the general state of the finances (sometimes parlous),[103] reporting from time to time to Parliament and asking for further financial support.[104] They empowered their agent at the Bank of England to sell or purchase stock. They were keen to produce published catalogues of the core collections, particularly of the books and manuscripts, but also of the coins and medals; although such works were produced very slowly their progress was monitored with care and attention. They received reports on losses and damage.[105] They confirmed appointments made on the nomination of the Principal Trustees; they approved gifts and ordered that letters of thanks be written to donors. They spent an inordinate amount of time in considering who should hold keys, particularly recording the names of the Trustees who held the keys to the 'iron chest' and to the smaller chest that held the seal. They discussed and approved major purchases and clearly worked behind the scenes to raise money in Parliament for the acquisition of great collections. During the whole of the eighteenth century there seems to be no record of the Trustees agreeing to the purchase of minor antiquities (as distinct from books and natural history specimens). They also approved expenditure on the rapidly decaying buildings under various surveyors. The first to hold the post was Henry Keene (c.1767–76), then (1776–92) James Wyatt, who was followed by his nephew Jeffry Wyatt (later Wyattville). In 1799 Wyattville entered into partnership with the Pimlico builder John Armstrong; between them they continued to advise the Trustees for a number of years until the new galleries were designed by George Saunders in the early years of the nineteenth century. The surveyor had a tough job in that, as well as advising on new furnishing, he had to ensure that the building could stand the strain of a use for which it had not been erected. Floors were supported by disguising metal and wooden supports in bookcases, unnecessary external ornament was removed before (and sometimes after) it fell off, and chimneys and cellars were altered to reduce the risk of fire; dry rot was dealt with and books and people removed from damp corners. All this was reported to the Trustees through the Standing Committee which took the main business decisions of the Museum. Special meetings of the full board were convened from time to time in Westminster or Whitehall solely to elect new Trustees.

The Standing Committee, elastic as regards numbers, effectively had executive powers. Although matters were officially referred to the main board, the Standing Committee increasingly took decisions itself. Typical of its business was that of a poorly attended Standing Committee on 4 April 1783, at which Banks, Mr Duane and Dr Watson were present. The Trustees first heard general reports from the various senior officers, then:

> Dr Morton having desired to have some steps for the purpose of mounting his horse. Ordered That his request be referred to the next Committee.
>
> Mr Planta having applyed for some repairs to be made in his Apartments. Ordered That the Surveyor make an estimate of the charges and report thereupon.
>
> Mr Penneck having represented that his apartment, in Mr Goram's opinion, is render'd offensive by a Water closet constructed by Dr Gifford. Order'd That the Surveyor do apply to Dr Gifford, and having inspected the Water Closet in question report thereupon.
>
> Order'd that the Lamplighters bill amounting to twenty five pounds, sixteen shillings be payd by a draught on Mr Newland. A draught was accordingly made out, signed by three Trustees, and order'd to be sent to Dr Morton.[106]

The gardens caused problems and a complaint voiced at a meeting in 1784 was to be a recurring problem for half a century:

> The Inhabitants of the Houses in the Neighbourhood of the Museum with respectful Compliments to the Trustees or Gentlemen resident there, Beg Leave to Represent to them that the Burning of the Leaves in the Museum Garden is such a Nuisance And the Smoak and Smell arising from it are so disagreeable and offensive to the Inhabitants that they shall be exceedingly obliged to the Gentlemen if they will Take it into immediate Consideration And Give such orders to their Gardener as will effectually Prevent this great Annoyance in future.[107]

The 'Lower Orders'

Both the full board and the General Committee were much exercised by the domestic servants and the porters. Patronage was exercised in a manner normal for the period. The Archbishop of Canterbury, one of the three Principal Trustees, for example, wrote to the Principal Librarian on 10 March 1772 asking that Mary Kyffin be appointed head maidservant in the Museum.[108]

She got the job in the place of Sarah Jones (who had agreed to resign) and remained in post until her death in 1784. After her death Elizabeth Aulkin, widow of the porter, applied for her position.[109] The Principal Librarian, Morton, however, tried to appoint Martha Williams, wife of a porter dismissed for drunkenness, but this appointment was not confirmed by the Trustees. Morton persisted, but so did the Trustees who again refused to confirm the appointment and ordered him to look to give jobs to a long-established maid and to Elizabeth Aulkin.[110] The unfortunate Mrs Williams was paid off and Elizabeth Chaplin was appointed to the position.[111] There were no pensions for either officers or servants at this period. Elizabeth Chaplin must have considered herself lucky, as two years after her retirement she received a gratuity of 2s 6d a week, which, since she had started work for Sir Hans Sloane, was hardly over-generous (she died in 1804).[112] Twenty years earlier Dorothy Markland had been less fortunate:

> [being] now upwards of seventy three years of age, and is rendered incapable of doing her Work, having entirely lost her Sight, but [having worked for the Museum since its foundation] she is allowed to keep her place, during life, or as long as her daughter can officiate for her, her daughter doing her work for her... by the kindness of Dr Morton. That your humble Petitioner, being under the necessity of keeping her Daughter, and her allowance being but six shillings pr. week, humbly begs this Honble. Board to take the same into their consideration and grant her some small addition, that she may be enabled to Live, the remainder of her Life, in your Service....[113]

The Trustees turned down her request.[114] Her daughter was later employed as a maid, a bit of nepotism commonplace in the first two hundred years of the Museum's existence.

On the whole, according to the lights of the period, the Trustees looked after the servants well. A year before she retired, for example, it was ordered that Elizabeth Chaplin 'be provided with a stove & also a Curtain... those she had originally being entirely worn out and become useless'.[115] The junior maids, having petitioned the Trustees, got a rise of a shilling a week in 1792 (although wages in London had been stable for more than half a century) and the men got an increase in their board wages a year later.[116] The Trustees also looked after the moral welfare of the staff:

> Complaint having been made of great irregularities and inconveniences arising from Servants attending at the Museum being supplied with Drink, &c from Public Houses, ordered That the Porter prevent such Practices for the future.[117]

Tradesmen (of whom a number were employed by the Museum) were also discussed by the Trustees. At one meeting in 1788, for example:

> The Surveyor having reported that John Toothead Bricklayer to the Museum had been for a long Time very negligent in the Business, and that he thought him an improper Person to be employed any more, he had been discharged, and William Cromp, recommended by the Surveyor, had been appointed in his Room.
>
> Dr Morton having reported that Edith Gregory, Tallow Chandler to the House, is in a State of Lunacy, and incapable of conducting her Business, and he having, at the same Time recommended Martha Worthington as a proper Person to succeed her, the said Martha Worthington has been appointed accordingly.[118]

They were also tough on the officers, who were frequently reprimanded and occasionally dismissed. Maty's son-in-law John Obadiah Justamond's post as assistant keeper of Natural and Artificial Antiquities was declared vacant after persistent absences and much discussion at board meetings. He was clearly suffering from debt and woman trouble, which had driven him to live abroad.[119] Hard work on the part of the officers, however, occasionally brought reward. Both Planta and Harper were paid on the completion of their library catalogues of the Cotton manuscripts and of the printed books[120] – £500 and £525 respectively, equivalent to some £30,000 each at today's prices.

Free Entry

At all times the Trustees were exercised by what would nowadays be called 'access'. The perceived audience was the middle classes, but constant comments and complaints show that people of the 'lower sort' managed to visit the Museum. This factor, the boredom of the staff who had to guide visitors, and the wonted shortage of cash frequently raised the spectre of entrance charges. The earliest recorded serious consideration of this matter after its opening is found in the first illustrated handbook to the Museum, the van Rymsdyks' splendid folio, *Museum Britannicum*, published in 1778:

> Anno 1774. The Report from the Committee appointed to consider of proper Regulations to be observed for the Future, by Persons admitted to see the *British Museum*, was brought up, and a small Debate ensued on one of the Resolutions, which was for Money to be paid by every Person to see the Curiosities: the principal *Speakers* in which were General Conway, Capt. Phipps, and Mr Harris, but I am very glad for the Public, on a Division there were for Money being paid 56, against it 59.[121]

This argument has been continually rehearsed until the present day. At an extraordinary meeting of the Trustees in 1784, for example, at yet another time of acute money problems, it was agreed not to charge visitors for entry in order to raise revenue.[122] The leading voice among the Trustees calling for charges, if not at this time then a little later, was Banks, who for once did not carry his colleagues with him.

The van Rymsdyks' book (pl. 3), from which the above quotation is taken, was the result of private enterprise.[123] The van Rymsdyks ranged widely through the collections in the Department of Natural and Artificial Productions, illustrating some of the more extraordinary objects found there. The book was expensive, but it was a great success and was republished in 1791 with a dedication to the Prince of Wales. The Trustees, in the spirit of the time, had no intention of publishing popular accounts of the Museum and its contents. Instead they struggled constantly to publish the catalogues of the printed books and manuscripts, which they then proudly gave to libraries, academies and royalty throughout the world. The idea that objects should be labelled was rendered, in their view, unnecessary by the fact that the officers continued to conduct visitors around the collections.

It seems that the active Trustees were not, as the century drew to a close, against popular access to the collections. It would have been easy to stop the flow of visitors of the lower class, about which there were frequent complaints. They made an occasional regulation about dress (uniformed servants being admitted without question) – but at no stage did they erect barriers beyond the Byzantine methods which were still in force for obtaining tickets. It is conceivable that the fight against charging, so frequently won by the Trustees, resulted in part from the unuttered beginnings of a belief in the Museum as a tool for the improvement of the working classes which was to emerge in the following century. When in 1784 the Trustees were reluctantly considering charging, they made a statement almost delphic in its obliquity:

> That the number of persons admitted annually to see the Museum when all the Tickets that may be granted according to the subsisting regulations, are taken out, amounts to about 12,000. That the applications in the Spring and Summer Months are generally very numerous, but that in the Winter (as was the case when this enquiry was made) there are often too few applications to fill up the regular hours. On inspecting the list of those who had lately been admitted, they also found, that they consisted chiefly of Mechanics and persons of the lower classes, few of whom would probably have been at any expence to satisfy mere Curiosity.[124]

This surely means that the Trustees implicitly encouraged the free attendance at the museum of the 'lower orders'.

The Museum may not have been well displayed and the tours may have been cursory, but at the end of the century it remained a popular attraction for both native and foreign visitors. Other than the theatre and a handful of public buildings, there were few public spectacles in London. From time to time private attractions such as the Lever collection of natural history, displayed in the Holophusikon in Leicester Square, or Cox's museum of automata provided paid entertainment to the curious; but none of them lasted long. The Royal Academy (founded in 1768) and the Royal Society of Arts (founded in 1754) provided exhibitions of a type that continues to the present day, but the British Museum remained an unique element in the cultural life of the capital.

But there is another level of access – access to scholars and students; first, through the published work and accumulated knowledge of the staff and, secondly, through allowing scholars and students to handle and study material. The first took many forms. The Trustees paid for the rump of the work on the Hamilton catalogue, for example, and closely monitored the progress of the catalogues of the library collections (and, as has been shown, rewarded the staff handsomely when they completed a task). From time to time they even closed the Museum in order to expedite the completion of such work. They also encouraged the staff to classify and sort the collections under their care; thus, for example, Joseph Planta was given encouragement and resources, even extra money, to sort the coin collections. Second, the Trustees (perhaps sometimes with a hint of reluctance) were not averse to allowing established craftsmen and artists in to study. James Tassie, the Scottish plaque-maker and modeller, for example, was permitted to make casts of gems.[125] Third, Banks's group of followers and assistants were in and out of the Museum as though it were a second home. Access to the antiquities collections was allowed on the same basis as that to the natural history collections, although there was no official space for serious students to work, and no published catalogues (or even good inventories) to help them in their research.

The acquisition of the first Hamilton collection had started the Museum on its path to becoming one of the most important international centres for the study of classical antiquities; but it still had a long way to go. The staff beavered away at the coins and medals collections, and the Trustees had approved the first comprehensive display of material from the South Seas. Later, the Napoleonic wars were, as we shall see, to provide the Museum with some of its most popular antiquities – those from Egypt. But even before the end of the eighteenth century the continental war released vast quantities of art and antiquities into private hands as the result of looting. Many countries imitated stated French policy that works of art and antiquity should be in the hands of free men. There was thus a scale of redistribution unequalled since the Thirty Years War.

The Cotton, Royal and Harley libraries, with their vast array of English historical manuscripts, were made available to scholars through existing or newly written catalogues, and spawned a new generation of medievalists who provided background for the Museum's collection of medieval antiquities a century later. Joseph Strutt's influential books on the medieval antiquities and history of England, for example, drew almost all their illustrative material from the illuminated manuscripts that he had studied in the Museum. His books became important tools of the later antiquaries and served as a quarry of *realia* for European historical painters for over a hundred years.[126]

View at the End of a Century

As the century drew to a close personal memories of Sloane faded; the last of the original elected Trustees, the Earl of Hardwicke, died in 1796, and the last of the original under librarians (since 1776, Principal Librarian), the lazy, gout-ridden Charles Morton, in 1799. Samuel Harper, the last officer to be appointed before the opening of the Museum, died in 1803. A new era was to dawn as the Trustees appointed Joseph Planta to succeed him.[127]

The first forty-five years of the Museum's existence had not been unfruitful. In a rapidly shifting political scene it had retained its independence and consolidated its position both academically and financially through regular grants from the government. It had a powerful patron in the King, and many in the corridors of power held the institution in high esteem. It had become a place of pilgrimage for foreign visitors and (with some difficulty in view of the red tape surrounding admission) had even become popular with the general public. Intellectually the Museum had been close to the centre. It followed, in its emphasis on cataloguing and classification, the model of the Enlightenment. The presence of Solander (a pupil of Linnaeus) at a critical time in the formation of the collecting policy in natural history had put the institution in a pivotal position in the systemization of botany. Further, the Trustees' continuing interest in the rapid cataloguing of the library departments, as evidenced in the minutes of their meetings and the extra payments to staff on completion of major catalogues, set it firmly at the hub of European scholarship.

The staff of the Museum was international in outlook; quite a few of them were foreigners or second-generation Englishmen, and they were not overburdened with the complacency of the older English universities. Joseph Planta, for example, had studied at Göttingen and Utrecht; other senior members had studied at Leiden, St Andrews, Uppsala, Frankfurt an der Oder and Copenhagen.[128] The Cambridge graduates had been at the two most lively colleges, Trinity and St John's. The staff had considerable skill in language and, in the true tradition of eighteenth-century polymathy, were not unhappy when drafted into departments away from their specialisms. Thus the great specialist in the ancient languages of the Middle East, the Pole Carl Woide, was for some time an assistant in the Natural History section of the Museum, before moving to the Department of Manuscripts.[129] Strangely, the classics were not represented by specialists. Although the staff had a thorough knowledge of Latin and Greek, their knowledge of classical antiquity was rudimentary.

Planta, soon to be Principal Librarian, had in 1776, just after his appointment as an assistant in the Museum, published the standard work on the Romansh language (the native language of Grisons in Switzerland, where he had been born).[130] At this distance of time it is difficult to reconstruct his philosophical stance, but it could well be that he was following the intellectual trend of his student years in Germany. There, the influence of such romantics as Herder, with his interest in indigenous languages and his realization that man's behaviour could not be codified into the strict boxes of the taxonomist, was beginning to move against the mood of the Enlightenment, which had dominated, and was still to dominate, mainstream thinking in the British Museum. It would be interesting to know whether Planta knew his fellow countryman Fuseli, who had brought some of the ideas of the *Sturm und Drang* with him when he settled in England, and whose diploma piece for the Royal Academy was in the mainstream of the new interpretation of an emerging Germanic nationalism that was challenging the older classical tradition. So long as Banks remained a central figure on the board of Trustees, the move away from the ordered ideas of the Enlightenment must, however, have been slow; but the young Turks who had studied on the Continent were, we may be sure, conscious of the gradual change in the intellectual climate throughout Europe. Perhaps the popularity of the South Sea collections reflects the first stirring in the public mind towards this mood. Inevitably the Museum was to remain throughout its history a taxonomic-based institution, but in certain areas it now began to soar beyond the narrow limits of this product of the Enlightenment.

The work of the Museum was carried out against a political and economic background that seems scarcely to have impinged on the lives of the staff, although it had a clear effect on the collections. The end of the Seven Years War in 1763 had left Britain in a splendid position to expand and exploit a growing empire, which was over the years to contribute so much to the collections, as the loss of the American colonies forced the British to turn their attention to other areas from which they could derive profit. The French Revolution released confiscated and looted material – royal, aristocratic and ecclesiastical – on to the market. This material was avidly snapped up by English collectors and some ultimately made its way into the Museum (although the results of such collecting are most immediately seen at the Wallace Collection). The secularization of the Church in the Austrian Netherlands in 1783 released books, manuscripts and antiquities on to the European market – Sir Joshua Reynolds, for example, made a killing in the resulting sales – and foreshadowed similar actions elsewhere on the Continent in the early nineteenth century. It was at this time that London became a major centre of the art market, as the collections of paintings belonging to the Duke of Orleans and other grandees were sold there.[131]

Abroad the first national museums were emerging. Special pleading would assert that the National Museum in Stockholm was established by decision of the Cabinet on the death of Gustav III in 1792, but in fact the royal collections remained in the palace until 1866, until which time it was little different as regards access from that of most royal *Kunstkammer* of the period.[132] Of particular importance to the British Museum was the foundation in 1791 of the the Musées Nationaux de France, and its most important constituent the Louvre (initially known as the Musée de la République), constructed in 1793 out of the royal and aristocratic collections of France.[133] The old royal library (with its coins and medals cabinet) was converted into the Bibliothèque Nationale and became in effect a national museum of antiquities, quite unrelated to the Musée des Monuments Français in the monastery of the Petits-Augustins in 1795.[134] As yet there was, however, no universal museum of the stature or philosophy of the British Museum, although Catherine the Great's Hermitage – essentially a royal collection within a palace – was beginning to take on such a role so far as fine arts and antiquities were concerned – it was not, however, formally to open to the public until 1852.

Interest in the collections of the British Museum was growing as its British audience became more aware of its own surroundings. The appearance of *Chambers' Encyclopedia* and of the *Encyclopædia Britannica*, together with the publication of a number of periodical reviews and the burgeoning number of circulating libraries, provided the middle classes with easy access to learning and literature. The new literary and philosophical societies brought to the provinces an opportunity to discuss intellectual matters which were being aired in London. The audience of the Museum was becoming more sophisticated and more demanding; the next few years saw it attempting to live up to these expectations.

Chapter 3

LONG AWAKENING

1799–1836

Joseph Planta (pl. 7), the newly appointed Principal Librarian, was the son of the Reverend Andrew Planta.[1] He was born in 1744 at Castegna in Grisons, Switzerland, and studied philology at Utrecht and later at Göttingen. After a certain amount of travel he moved to England where his father was established as the pastor of the German Reformed Church in London (as well as being an assistant in the British Museum). The Church gave the elder Planta access to Court, for he taught Italian to the German Queen Charlotte.[2] Through this influence his daughter, Margaret, became some sort of teacher or governess to the royal children,[3] and Joseph secured a post as secretary to the British minister in Brussels, returning to England in 1773 at his father's death to be appointed to his father's post in the Museum.[4] Three years later he became Under Librarian of Manuscripts. In 1788 he was appointed to the sinecure of Paymaster of Exchequer Bills, a post he held until 1811. Fanny Burney, who knew his sister well, was discreetly taken with him, describing him as 'sensible, manly and agreeable'.[5]

A considerable linguist, Planta was an urbane, sociable man and a hard worker, writing, among other books, the majority of the great catalogue of the Cottonian manuscripts and much of the catalogue of printed books. He was not, however, narrow in his interests; he was, for example, much involved as Under Librarian in sorting and re-housing the coin collection, and had been, as has been seen, appointed one of the Secretaries to the Royal Society in 1776. His years as Principal Librarian (1799–1827) were some of the most significant in the history of the Museum and it was through his personality and careful use of influence that so much was achieved.

Charging for Admission

Planta's greatest virtue lay in his tact and his ability to move things in the right direction by stealth. In the aftermath of Morton's lax rule he was much needed – not that, initially, there was any extra money to help him reform the institution, but attitudes could be, and were, changed.

The first of the reforms to be tackled concerned the regulations for admission, the easing of which was to take much of Planta's time during his twenty-eight years as

Principal Librarian. Once again the question of charging for entry was raised. In 1801 the Trustees asked the officers to submit proposals concerning admission. Drafts were written on the one hand by Banks and on the other by Planta supported by the Under Librarians Gray, Harper and Nares. Banks argued for entry fees mainly on the grounds that 'persons of low education' visited the Museum out of 'mere motives of idle curiosity' and asked 'senseless questions' that distracted the officers and the normal visitors, 'who have prepared themselves by reading to receive usefull information'; they also posed a physical threat to the collections. The fact that the Museum had been founded and supported by public funds was, he argued, no reason to deny the possibility of charging, on the grounds that the Museum had initially not been funded out of taxes but by lottery.[6]

The officers did not risk a head-on encounter with Banks and contented themselves with a bland reply. While pointing out that 'very few, if any, of the other museums founded by public authority, either at home or abroad' charged for admission, they proposed that, if a charge should be made, the proceeds should be put towards the provision of staff to superintend the visitors.[7] The Trustees, uncomfortable, delayed decision, but returned to the problem in 1802, asking Planta to comment. He knew that he could not go too far, but won significant ground. Interested in easier access, he got the Trustees to agree not to sell tickets and to make them available on the day of admittance (the list of applicants had still, however, to be approved by the Principal Librarian or the senior officer present). The Museum was to be closed on Monday and on summer Friday afternoons, and the hours of opening were to be increased by two hours a day (9 a.m. to 4 p.m.).[8] New regulations were drawn up, with two additions – one of which increased the possibility of entry very considerably by allowing one person to apply for twelve tickets at one time. The second addition concerned the Trustees' continuing doubt about the behaviour and appearance of visitors, 'the Officers being instructed to refuse Admission to, or cause to withdraw, any one who shall disregard this Caution [as to appearance and behaviour] – Past Experience has shown the Necessity of this Injunction'.[9] (What this experience was has never been made clear[10] – perhaps it was more perceived than actual.) Further, the Trustees agreed to appoint three Attendants knowledgeable in languages at a salary of £75, to relieve the officers (among other duties) of the tedious business of showing the visitors round the collections – in effect the Museum's first education officers![11]

The Trustees continued to worry about admission, but the new regulations had doubled the potential number of visitors. By 1805 the Museum opened on Mondays, Wednesdays and Fridays and five groups of no more than fifteen people (including children over the age of ten) were admitted every hour on the hour between 10 a.m. and 2 p.m. Any overflow was accommodated on Tuesday and Thursday (although the Trustees clearly wanted these days to remain comparatively free for the benefit of the staff). Thus up to 360 visitors a week could be catered for. The Trustees were to return to a discussion of the admission system when the new Townley Gallery opened in 1808.

Planta next turned his attention to the structure of the Museum. In 1807 the Trustees resolved:

> 1st. That the Collections of Engravings be transferred from the Department of Printed Books to the Department of Manuscripts....
>
> 4th. That the Collections of Antiquities be separated from the Department of Natural History, & transferred to a new department comprising these, & the coins & medals, distinguishing

each collection by proper marks, & preserving the same together whole and entire.

5. That the present Keeper of the Coins and Medals be denominated Under Librarian of the Department of Antiquities and Coins and Medals; and that an Assistant Librarian in the same Department be appointed; and also an Attendant....

6. That the Offices and Salaries of Secretary and Accountant be united.

It was also agreed that each Under Librarian should be duty officer for one day a week, helped by an assistant librarian and an assistant. Further, the staff of the Department of Antiquities were enjoined to write a manual or inventory of their gallery, catalogue the Egyptian collection, complete and revise the Hamilton catalogue, and complete the catalogue of coins and medals; 'this, it is supposed, will be a work of very considerable length'.

This re-organization reflected in some measure the shake-up in staff in the period after the death of Morton. Salaries were increased in line with inflation.[12] Planta's replacement as Under Librarian of Manuscripts, the Reverend Robert Nares, was a philologist who had been appointed assistant librarian in 1795. An ecclesiastical pluralist,[13] he retired in 1807 to enjoy his various stipends and was replaced by that eccentric and learned antiquary Francis Douce.[14] In 1803 the Reverend William Beloe, characterized by Esdaile as 'a scholarly but extremely silly divine', became Under Librarian of Printed Books.[15] Dismissed in 1806, he was replaced by a future Principal Librarian, the amiable Henry Ellis, who had joined the Museum from the Bodleian Library, Oxford, in the previous year.[16] In 1801 Edward Gray, the Under Librarian of Natural and Artificial Productions, became the first permanent Secretary of the Museum – a post he held together with his keepership.

Gray's death in 1806 presumably triggered the creation of a new Department of Antiquities (although ethnography remained in the Department of Natural and Artificial Productions). A numismatist, Taylor Combe, became head of the newly created department, with an assistant, Horace Walpole Bedford, who died in 1808 and was replaced by William Alexander, destined to become the first dedicated curator of prints and drawings. Trained as an artist, Alexander had been attached as an artist to Lord Macartney's 1792 embassy to China; he had also illustrated the account of Vancouver's voyage. Even after his appointment to the Museum, he was employed to illustrate the first four volumes of the Museum's catalogue of classical marbles.[17] He had little expertise in the subject he curated, but was an amiable enough man.

Taylor Combe is important, as he was the first keeper of the department which was to grow into the present British Museum.[18] His appointment was originally urged by one of the Trustees, Charles Townley, because the Museum needed a man who knew about coins and antiquities.[19] In 1803 he had been put in charge of coins, which were then transferred from the Department of Manuscripts to the Department of Natural and Artificial Productions. He became Under Librarian of Antiquities in 1807 and held the post until his death in 1826. He belonged to the new generation of officers, most of whom had been educated not abroad but at Oxford or Cambridge (he had been to Oriel College, Oxford), and was well grounded in the classics.[20] At the time of his original appointment he had been charged with publishing the coins,[21] and, amid many distractions, succeeded in writing the Museum's first published catalogue of ancient coins in 1814 – his second catalogue appearing in the year of his death.[22] He also produced in 1810 a catalogue of classical terracottas and in 1812 started the great series of catalogues of classical sculpture.

Soon after Planta's appointment we gain some impression of the way in which the institution was displayed. In 1803 appeared a full, if rather eccentric, description of the British Museum buried in a multi-volume work by James Malcolm.[23] It is replete with a careful description not only of regulations for admittance, but also of the regulations, official and unofficial, for the use of the Reading Room, then in a north-facing room on the ground floor of the west wing. Malcolm was interested in painting and comments on the Museum's more important historical portraits, which ranged from the Duke of Monmouth to Louis XIV and from Cranmer to Sir William Hamilton by Reynolds. The pictures in the saloon, he writes, were hung above the bookcases, 'at least 15 feet from the floor; which circumstance injures every picture in the Museum'. He provides the first description of the display of medals, which were set in four wooden frames (up to nine medals in each) in the eastern window, and comments on their quality and appearance ('these two dukes wear armour; the latter very corpulent, wears an enormous wig'). He goes on to mention a few smaller frames which 'contain little reliefs, in brass, finely executed, by Valerius Bellus or Bello'.

Some things lead to patriotic reflection. In the hall is:

> A tin cap of liberty, suspended on the East wall, lately presented to the publick by Lord Elgin; who received it as part of the captured effects of the French army of Egypt, in the late memorable campaigns in that fervid climate, where the British gained so many laurels. Pompey's pillar is well known to the inhabitants of Europe, which exalts its lofty capital above the towers of Alexandria; nor is the dangerous and gallant exploit of the English sailors who scaled it, and drank punch on the summit, less known; whose example, it may be presumed fired the French to emulate the hazardous undertaking. When *they* ascended the pillar, this tin cap, elevated on a strong pole, was affixed to the capital, as a double memento of sovereignty and intrepidity; where it remained till our sons of Neptune, in the nautical phrase, struck it, in token of victory.

This leads naturally to a description of a Roman funerary monument from Great Chesterford in Essex, 'a large and curious wooden chest', and a canoe suspended from the ceiling, 'suited to the wants of the original owner, but utterly useless to the English fisherman'.

In discussing the first room on the first floor, which now housed part of the Hamilton collection (the rest was in the saloon), we get the first mention of a Museum label – a showcase inscribed with the words 'Imagines Deorum Egyptiacorum', which at least has the merit of being informative and short.[24] An interesting object is a 'model by De Bourg, of the temple of the Sibyl at Tivoli... the cork represents the decayed stone with great truth. It is coloured after the tints occasioned by damps and time'.[25] The saloon has in the centre 'a large handsome mahogany pedestal, supporting a glass case, in which is the finest vase in the collection', as well as four other cases holding altogether twenty-eight vases. Larger vases were in a case by the window which also contained small terracotta figures, finger-rings and other gems. A narrow case near the window held Cracherode's gem collection.[26] In the second room were two cased mummies, and a sloping table case containing miniatures, ivories and silhouettes.

There is a six-page description of the Otaheite (South Sea) Room, with its collections culled from the voyages of Captain Cook and his successors. Malcolm obviously ran out of steam or interest at this point; he dismisses the mineralogical and other natural collections and the medal room in four lines, and the basement in one line, 'The basement story contains the largest and most repelling specimens of Nature and Art'. He also mentions the newly acquired Egyptian sculpture ('the ponderous spoils of the Egyptian campaign'), housed in two sheds in the courtyard: 'Of those the huge baths and coffins covered with hieroglyphicks are the most interesting.'

The Cracherode Collection

The collections of the future antiquities departments were growing apace. In 1799 the Reverend Clayton Mordaunt Cracherode (pl. 11), a faithfully attending Trustee since 1784, died and bequeathed his entire collection to the Museum.[27] He lived in London, a shy eccentric, who called weekly on Thomas Mudge to have his watch regulated and daily met his 'literary friends'. He was rich, but his affairs were firmly placed in the hands of his agents and he hardly, if ever, visited his country estate at Great Wymondly in Hertfordshire. He never travelled further than Oxford (where he had studied at Christ Church) and never mounted a horse. He was, as might be expected, unmarried. A bit of a poet, he was a fellow of both the Royal Society and the Society of Antiquaries. He ordered all his personal papers to be destroyed, even his manuscript notations in interleaved copies of Walpole's catalogue of engravers and the Bible. The only personal manuscript to survive is his notebook of his dealings as a Trustee of the Museum, which is even less informative than the official minutes of the meetings he attended.[28] He did, however, write out catalogues of his collections, but unfortunately none relevant to the present collections of the British Museum survive. The Trustees were so impressed by the gift that they housed the books and prints and drawings in their committee room, where they provided new cabinets and wire-fronted bookcases.[29]

Cracherode collected in five distinct areas; in order of importance they were: books (valued at his death at £10,000), coins and medals (£6,000), prints and drawings (£5,000), cameos and intaglios (£2,000) and shells and minerals (£500). Unfortunately his coins and medals can no longer be identified as they have been distributed into their appropriate series and the catalogue was destroyed in the Second World War. He left the Museum 662 drawings, together with an album of drawings by Giovanni Francesco Grimaldi and between 5,000 and 10,000 prints.[30] The drawings are mainly by Northern artists – Dürer, Holbein, Rembrandt, Rubens and van Dyck. There are also some drawings by Claude. Of prints he had a few Dürers and Schongauers, and an excellent collection of Italian masters. His most important group was an almost complete collection of Rembrandt's etchings. He had engravings after the paintings of Rubens, van Dyck and Jordaens, a large collection of Hollars, and a scattering of other prints, including some of the eighteenth century, together with a remarkable collection of portraits, particularly of English sitters.

It was this collection that was pillaged by a crooked dealer, Robert Dighton, who had been systematically robbing the print collections since 1795. Between 1804 and 1806 he had wormed his way into the good graces of William Beloe, the Under Librarian of Printed Books, when his thieving seems to have increased. The theft was uncovered by another dealer, Samuel Woodburn, and the young Henry Ellis. In attempting to retrieve the situation the Trustees realized that they would have difficulty in recognizing the stolen items as they had not been properly and indelibly stamped. Accordingly they did a deal with Dighton, by which he would not be prosecuted if he co-operated in retrieving as many of the stolen prints as possible. Poor, weak Beloe was sacked for negligence. The detailed story, at once both sordid and interesting, is well documented and reveals the inner working of the Museum and the seriousness with which the Trustees took their duties, even though few members were present at the relevant committees.[31] On a magistrate's warrant Dighton's premises were searched and some £300-worth of stolen prints were found. Dighton made a full and detailed confession, describing how he had taken the stolen prints out of the Museum, 'in my pocket,... in the bosom of my coat, often in a roll in my hand... Having a particular desire to posses Rembrandts... I... kept them in my own collection. I sold the greater number of the rest to Mr Mortimer, to Davis in the Haymarket, and to Mr Woodburn...'. The report by a Justice of the Peace goes on, 'In consequence of this disclosure, a large portion of the most valuable prints have been recovered over and above those found in Dighton's house.'

Nobody knows how many of Cracherode's prints were lost in this episode, but a good number were recovered. It was this theft which two years later led to the establishment of a Department of Prints and Drawings within the Department of Antiquities, with William Alexander (who had trained at the Royal Academy as a painter) at its head in the rank of assistant.

At the time of the discovery of the Dighton robbery the Museum, almost incidentally, made its first purchase of prints. In February 1806 it paid £50 to James Monro for 'a collection of ancient prints';[32] although little is known of its contents, it was in effect the cream of the collection of John Monro, a doctor at the Bethlehem Hospital. The collection had been assembled in the late eighteenth century, and, although much of it had been sold at his death in 1791, the early prints had been saved, and possibly even added to, by his son. It is known to have contained at least ten early German engravings and a number of early Italian prints, including the famous church interior engraved by Prevedari after Bramante. Antony Griffiths, who has recently called the purchase 'one of the most brilliant and far-sighted in the history of the British Museum', has suggested that it is likely that the Monro collection contained as many as sixty-five early Italian, and two hundred German, engravings.[33] Who suggested this acquisition, in a period when there was no expertise in the subject in the Museum, is not known.

Egyptian and Roman Acquisitions

A major acquisition was the collection of Egyptian antiquities taken from the French in 1801. Carried home in the name of George III under the terms of the Treaty of Alexandria, they were immediately given by him to the British Museum. The material, mainly stone sculpture, had been collected by a group of French scholars whom Napoleon had sent out with his expeditionary force in 1798. The French had founded an Institute in Cairo and it was its head who had the bitter job of transferring the objects into British hands for shipment to England.[34] The most famous item in this group was the fragment of a stela from el-Rashid (Rosetta) in the Nile Delta, which is certainly the most important antiquity to have come out of Egypt. The Rosetta stone is 1.12 m high and is of dark grey granitoid, a quartz-rich rock which probably came from quarries more than 600 miles to the south in Aswan. The face of the stone bears parallel inscriptions in demotic and hieroglyphic characters and in Greek script, part of a decree issued in year 9 of Ptolemy V Epiphanes (196 BC). The three texts, which were quickly copied and published by the Society of Antiquaries,[35] provided the means by which the hieroglyphic script of Egypt was to be deciphered more than twenty years later by Jean-François Champollion, in a paper presented to the Académie des Inscriptions et Belles-Lettres in Paris.[36] The importance of the stone was, however, recognized long before this, and the words 'Captured in Egypt by the British Army in 1801' were painted on one side by some Museum triumphalist conscious of this fact (they can still be deciphered today). With the Rosetta Stone came a number of sculptures including a famous royal sarcophagus, some three metres long, which had been made for Nectanebo II of the thirtieth dynasty (360–343 BC), the last native pharaoh. Of breccia, it had been found in the Attarine mosque on the site of the church of St Anastasius in Alexandria, where it had been used as a public bath, twelve holes having been pierced in its bottom to allow the water to escape. Although the British brought home the material, it was left to the French to produce, between 1809 and 1825, the first major descriptions of Egyptian antiquity from the notes and drawings made during Napoleon's expedition, in a multi-volume work that was fundamental to all future Egyptology.[37]

The arrival of the Egyptian sculpture brought home to the Trustees the fact that Montagu House would not take their weight and that a shack in the garden was not a suitable place to exhibit such great treasures. A buildings committee was set up in 1802. The active members were Banks, Hamilton and Charles Townley, who, because his large collection of classical sculpture was set out for the benefit of his friends in his house in Park Street, was considered to be a specialist in the display of sculpture.[38] It was decided to build a new wing northwards from the north-west angle of Montagu House to which it could be joined by two passages cloaked by a colonnade. The building was also designed to obviate the normal *ad hoc* sins of museums throughout the ages – temporary buildings put up to house sudden accessions or to function for some new perceived need of accommodation:

> There will be, on the west side of the new building, a considerable space of ground, on which groups of Apartments, incapable of Architectural regularity, and always disgusting in appearance, such as detached Rooms proper to receive fine Statues and other valuable Works of Art, which require Skylights and recesses of particular Shapes, to shew them properly, may be placed, so as to be wholly hid from view, by the body of the new building.
>
> the building now proposed is part of a great Plan, which may be executed at such times as the Public has occasion for additions to the Museum... the opposite wing may easily be adapted, without any alteration in the outside appearance, to the arrangement of Books and natural curiosities of all descriptions.[39]

The chosen architect for the new building was George Saunders, who had made his London reputation in 1793 when he successfully extended Kenwood House for the second Earl of Mansfield. After examining and accepting a proposal that the building should follow the same style as Montagu House,[40] the Trustees decided (after work had started) that a plainer elevation in restrained palladian style was to be preferred to an 'approximation to the style of the worst period of French architecture'.[41] Parliament provided the money (£8,000) and work commenced on clearing the site in September 1804.[42] In January 1805, however, Charles Townley died and the problem of the future of his great collection faced the Trustees. Amid all the negotiations for its acquisition it was realized that space would have to be found for it, and work on the new building was suspended by order of the committee of the House of Commons considering the Townley purchase.[43]

Charles Townley, born in 1737, came from an old Roman Catholic landed family in Lancashire. His father had died in 1742 and he had been educated abroad.[44] He returned to England to claim his inheritance when he came of age. After spending some time at home he turned to Italy in 1767 where he immersed himself in classical art and started to collect sculpture. His Roman Catholicism and his Catholic education abroad presumably gave him entrée to houses not easily open to many on the Grand Tour, and it is not without interest that from 1776 one of his occasional companions (in effect a disciple of Townley) in Rome was another Roman Catholic from Lancashire, Henry Blundell, whose collection, formed between 1776 and 1810, is now in the National Museums and Galleries on Merseyside.[45] The collection of Roman sculpture formed by Townley, mainly between 1768 and 1774, was purchased from collectors and dealers in Rome at a period when such material was almost embarrassingly easily available to the wealthy.[46] His chief sources were Gavin Hamilton, Thomas Jenkins and James Byres, rich Englishmen who lived in Rome with rights to excavation at major sites like Hadrian's Villa at Tivoli. Townley did not visit Italy after 1777 but continued to make purchases at a distance; he also bought on the London art market until his death. He became a Trustee of the Museum in 1791. His collection was remarkable by any standards and contained some of the icons of the Museum's collections of Roman art. Such, for example, was Townley's favourite bust, 'Clytie', a first-century head and revealing shoulders of a wealthy Roman woman from southern Italy – represented as Ariadne – which was purchased by him from Prince Laurenzano in Naples.[47] Much of his collection of statuary, as was customary at the time, had been restored in Italy. Such, for example, was the charming relief of Nessos abducting Deianira.[48] Only the centre of this piece is ancient, the rest was restored by Bartolemeo Cavaceppi, who used the back of an ancient Latin inscribed stone which had been catalogued in the seventeenth century and was lost, until part of the text was re-discovered in 1982. Townley concentrated his collecting activities on the finest available sculpture, particularly Roman copies of Greek statues.[49] He laid his collection out with great taste and precision in his London house.[50] Here he was painted – surrounded by some of his favourite pieces – by Zoffany;[51] and it was here that the committee of Trustees looking into the construction of the new gallery at the Museum (of whom Townley was one) occasionally met to discuss the finer points of displaying sculpture.[52]

He had intended to leave his collection to the Museum, but, twelve days before his death, he changed his mind and, in a codicil to his will, left his collection to his family on the condition that they should build a gallery for it at his home near Burnley (as Blundell had done at his home). Such a building would have cost £4,500 and was allegedly beyond his heirs' means; they thus decided to sell the collection to the Museum, as stipulated in Townley's will. Throughout May and June of 1805 there were frantic meetings and a torrent of correspondence as the Trustees used the full weight of Banks's considerable influence. Banks and the Speaker of the House of Commons (Charles Abbot, one of the Principal Trustees) negotiated with Townley's heirs and then with the government.[53] Valuations were made, discussed, rejected and agreed, and deals were done. Finally, on 16 May, Banks was told by the Speaker that the Prime Minister had agreed in principle to the purchase and Banks was asked to devise a petition to a committee of the House of Commons. At meetings of the Trustees on 1 and 4 June the terms of the petition were agreed and were presented to the House on 5 June by the Master of the Rolls (another Trustee).[54] The speed with which the matter was dealt with was remarkable, for by 20 June all had been agreed, the House committee reporting favourably on the petition. A bill providing for the purchase was introduced on 25 June and passed through all its stages in two weeks, and the money was paid over in August.[55] Another committee of the House was formed (with six Trustee MPs among its members) to consider modifications to the new gallery which would now have to house both the Egyptian sculpture and the Townley collection. This committee also worked quickly; its members visited the Museum and took evidence and on 3 July reported that 'your Committee have therefore determined, that an enlargement is necessary in the connecting Galleries and the two Tribunes; and they have taken upon themselves to recommend that alteration; though they are sorry to find it will be attended by some additional expence'.[56] One can only marvel at the despatch with which the negotiations were carried out, all in the year of the battle of Trafalgar, when one would have thought that the government's mind would have been concentrated on other things.

The Townley Gallery

Work started again on the new gallery (pls 9, 18), which was now to have a greater floor space than originally conceived. Two short rooms (wider than the originally planned passages and without colonnades) connected the new building to the western end of Montagu House each led to rotundas, 24 feet (7.32 m) in diameter. From the southernmost of these a gallery or passage led to the new two-storey building. Where possible the sculpture was to be lit by roof-lights (Saunders started a fashion here), otherwise long windows in the main building provided sufficient daylight. Externally it was to be finished with ashlar, save for the west end which, to save money, remained as brick.[57] The alterations led to greater cost and a further £7,500 was granted by Parliament in June 1806. Despite some gratuitous interference by the parliamentary committee, the interior was decorated with plain distemper. The sculpture was laid out and installed on the advice of Nollekens (who was now too frail to be actively involved) and Saunders, under the paid supervision of Henry Tresham (a Royal Academician who had spent a long time in Rome in the company of artists such as Fuseli and Canova) and Richard Westmacott, the sculptor, with advice from Taylor Combe. The new building – the Townley Gallery – was formally opened on 3 June 1808 by Queen Charlotte, accompanied by the Prince of Wales, the Dukes of Cumberland and Cambridge, and four of the princesses.[58]

The contents of the gallery are recorded in the *Synopsis of the contents of the British Museum* (in effect the Museum's first official guide) compiled by Taylor Combe and revised at intervals between 1808 and 1856. Views of the room were widely circulated in prints and in the plates in Combe's catalogues of the terracottas and marbles.[59] In the short passages from the main building were displayed terracottas and Roman antiquities. The rotundas and the galleries leading to the main building contained sculpture, chiefly from the

Townley collection.[60] The first room in the main building held general Roman antiquities, including some found in Britain. In the main hall were Egyptian sculptures, and at the far end was more classical sculpture, centred on the Townley copy of Myron's discus-thrower (*Discobolus*). On the first floor were coins and medals, much of the Hamilton collection, and the first room to be dedicated exclusively to prints and drawings. All the marbles in the new building were numbered with black chalk in preparation for the compilation of a written catalogue.[61]

The opening of the gallery enabled Planta to increase public access to the collections. He persuaded the Trustees to employ a warder or gallery attendant and, after some havering, when the Trustees investigated the possibility of employing Chelsea pensioners, a man was appointed and provided with a light cloak of the same length and colour as the porter. The ticketing system, so long an irritation to the visitor and a cause of abuse, was abolished. The Museum was open to the public from Monday to Thursday, while Fridays were reserved for private visits and for the use of supervised students of the Royal Academy. Visitors were admitted at the main entrance, signed their name in a book and left their canes and umbrellas. They then went on a conducted tour of the house and the new gallery, to which they were admitted after ringing a bell.[62] The new *Synopsis* – in two forms, one more complete than the other – went on sale (at 2s and 1s) and provided the first written guide to the Museum.[63] The opening also triggered the publication of the first official catalogues of its classical sculptures.[64]

Two years later, in 1810, the rules were once more liberalized and the ludicrous waste of time on the part of the officers in showing visitors around was at last stopped. The Museum was now open on Mondays, Wednesdays and Fridays from 10 a.m. to 4 p.m., save for public holidays and the months of August and September. For the first time visitors were allowed to stay as long as they wished in the rooms of the upper floor (except the reading rooms) and in the gallery. Tuesdays and Thursdays were reserved for special visitors and students. Eight attendants were appointed,[65] and the duty officer now had to walk 'at least twice a day through the Rooms to see that Attendants are at their proper stations'.[66]

Planta continued to emphasize the long-held view that the English visitor was unruly. In an undated memorandum to the Trustees in 1814 he presses this point:

> It is to be observed in general that owing to the vigilance & strictness of the Police, the lower Classes in France are habituated to a far more orderly behaviour than ours, abundance of individuals being observed among our popular Visitors who, in the fervour of independence, pride themselves in shewing a disdain of order, & in doing essential mischief for which we have no means of obtaining immediate redress... Mr P. is informed by a gentleman of undoubted veracity, lately return'd from Paris, that the only instance hitherto observed of any trespass at their public exhibitions, was committed by two Englishmen. With us, three instances of mutilation, not very material indeed, have occurred within these few months.[67]

He continued, however, to press for greater access, and in November received the Trustees' permission to allow the public, by prior arrangement, to see the coins and medals on Tuesdays and the prints and drawings on Thursdays.[68] That he had some success in increasing public access is demonstrated by a remark of Sidney Smith in 1819:

> I passed four hours yesterday in the British Museum. It has now been put upon the best possible footing, and exhibited courteously and publickly to all. The visitors when I was there were principally maid-servants....[69]

The new galleries were well received, although a contributor to *The gentleman's magazine*, ironically in view of the fact that the gallery was conceived for just such a purpose, stated that 'the Egyptian Collection, consisting chiefly of large stone coffins, and massive uncouth figures, ought never to have been placed on an upper story and among the elegant Greek and Roman sculptures... it would be much more in character to see them in the solemn recess of a Catacomb....[70] But such perspicacious carping was unusual and a modern member of the Museum staff has said that the gallery 'probably provided the best setting the Museum ever had for the Graeco-Roman sculptures'.[71] This view reflects that of the German architect Karl Friedrich Schinkel, who visited it in 1826 while employed in building the first great museum in Berlin (the Museum am Lustgarten, now called the Altes Museum). He found the 'small rooms, lit from above, very restful and satisfying'.[72] The galleries were also some answer to the grand galleries at the Louvre (at that time the Musée Napoléon), which now housed the major collection of classical sculpture formed by Cardinal Borghese in the late seventeenth and early eighteenth centuries. This had been purchased in 1806 and (not being booty) stayed in Paris when much else taken by the French from Italy and elsewhere was returned to its original owners after the defeat of Napoleon.[73] Public and private collecting of classical sculpture was booming in patriotic guise.

Collecting Classical Sculpture

The next few years saw the Museum begin to be proactive in collecting material from the Mediterranean. This period started with a ludicrous failure. Because of poor intelligence the Museum lost the opportunity to purchase the marbles from a ruined temple of Zeus on the Greek island of Ægina, which had been discovered and acquired in April 1811 by two Englishmen and two Germans. After arranging an auction at Zakynthos, the centre of trade for the region, the marbles were shipped by way of Athens to Malta. In August Planta wrote to Charles Abbot, the Speaker, telling him of the find and repeating a rumour that the Prince Regent was interested in purchasing them and presenting them to the Museum.[74] In July of the following year, when the marbles had been landed in Malta, Abbot enters in his diary that Taylor Combe was to go to Malta and purchase them for up to £8,000.[75] Everybody was clearly at cross-purposes, Planta wrote to Abbot on 12 December 1812:

> Combe arrived last night somewhat emaciated. The tale of his miseries is a long one; and you will, I dare say, gladly dispense with it. As to the statues, he found them all packed and nailed up in cases, in a merchant's warehouse, and none of the proprietors on the spot. ...Cockerel [one of the excavators], however, was at Girgente, and was written to. He answered that he could not come over to Malta, but desired that Mr Combe might be allowed to open the cases one by one.... Nobody knew anything of a day of the sale. Cockerel only desired his correspondent to let him know what they sold for.

Combe's opinion is, that the statues are not so entire as he expected to find them… yet there are several so very superior that he cannot hesitate in recommending their purchase, even at the maximum allowed by the Government, which he found to be 8000l. This opinion he gave in writing to General Oakes, and, conceiving that this was the whole of his commission, he, with the General's approbation, took the first opportunity to embark for England.

The French have actually offered 160,000 livres for the collection, 10,000 to be paid down, and the remainder when it is safely landed at Marseilles or Havre. This offer has already been rejected; and as it appears that there are no other bidders, General Oakes will probably get it much below the maximum. Combe thinks we are pretty sure of it.[76]

The sorry story had, however, already ended in November, when Crown Prince Ludwig of Bavaria purchased them for a sum equivalent to £6,000 at the sale at Zakynthos, no English representative having been present. The British tried to buy the marbles from the Crown Prince for the price he had paid for them, but failed. They now adorn the Glyptothek in Munich. At least Combe was not blamed for the error and was even paid a gratuity by the Treasury.[77]

All was not lost, however, for the same group of Englishmen and Germans had continued their Greek travels in 1811 to Bassae, in south-east Arcadia, to view the well-known temple of Apollo Epikourios, which had been built between 420 and 400 BC. Having searched the ruins, the party found the remains of a fragment of sculpture and, with permission, proceeded to excavate twenty-three blocks of the frieze. This depicted a battle fought by Herakles and the Greeks against the Amazons, and another battle between the Lapiths (Greek inhabitants of Thessaly) and the Centaurs. They were then, not without some difficulty – both physical and political – moved to Zakynthos, where they were purchased by Sir John Campbell on 4 January 1814 on behalf of the English government for £15,000.[78] There was no mistake this time, and the sculptures were brought to England where they were unpacked – along with a 'torpid scorpion' – in October.[79] For many years they were known as the Phigalian Marbles after the name of a nearby town.

Unusually for the period, when they were mounted in the Museum under the direction of Westmacott (who used copper bolts to join them together), they were not restored. In the words of Taylor Combe:

> … we cannot refrain from expressing our strong disapprobation of the too frequent practice of repairing the mutilations of ancient marbles; these *reparations*, even when executed with consummate skill and ingenuity, are often any thing rather than *restorations*. In works of classical literature the scholar will never consent to admit conjectural interpolations into the text of an ancient author, and surely the same correct feeling ought to be extended to the remains of ancient sculpture, so as to preserve them from the injuries of conjectural restoration.[80]

Combe in this passage may in part have been less than tactfully criticizing the Bavarian Crown Prince who had the Ægina marbles restored by the Danish sculptor Bertil Thorvaldsen. Whatever the case, it was, for the period, a strong statement about the integrity of the original object.

The collections were well and tastefully laid out in a shed tacked on to the main building, as though in a grand house, and everybody was pleased with the acquisition of what are now known as the Bassae reliefs. Many were, however, still touchy on the subject of Ægina. In old age Nollekens visited the Elgin room and harried Combe, 'Why did you not bring the Ægina Marbles with you? They are more clever than the Phigalian Marbles. How could you be so stupid as to miss them?'[81] Another sculptor was more tactful, as Planta wrote to the Speaker in December 1815:

> Canova admired the Phygalian Marbles. He allows that the designs and composition are excellent, but he does not think the execution is of equal merit. He has said... that if these are worth 15,000l., the Elgin Marbles are worth 100,000l ... Canova was much pleased with several articles in our gallery, especially the colossal Venus [from the Townley collection] opposite the entrance, which he does not scruple to declare one of the first rate articles of sculpture.[82]

In the months following the defeat of Napoleon, as the allied leaders met in London, the Museum began its long history as a convenient place to which to send important visitors. Among those who visited were the Emperor of Russia and his sister the Grand Duchess of Oldenburg, Metternich, the King of Prussia, and many minor royalties. Some of them were characterized in small vignettes by Henry Ellis. 'At entering... [the Emperor] put his watch into his sister's hand, his time being limited'. His sister, the Duchess of Oldenburg, had also been earlier (her 'figure was genteel, but her nose pugged and her lips thick') and 'appeared to have none of the frivolity usually seen in a foreigner of French education; but was stade and affable'. Metternich was 'dressed in a green coat: of a spare figure, and rather frivolous appearance... He walked with a mincing pace';[83] the King of Prussia 'appeared tall and dignified, wearing a small quantity of hair on the upper part of his lips'.[84] Other lesser luminaries visited the Museum and at least one, the Norwegian patriot and the major player on the Norwegian side at the peace talks, W.F.K. Christie, was so taken by his visit that he seems to have modelled the museum in Bergen on the British Museum. In 1825 he outlined his plan for a museum of antiquities, art and native natural history. This, the earliest major museum in Norway, was founded soon afterwards and an imposing building constructed for it between 1831 and 1841.[85]

The Museum was much in favour at this period and seemed to have little difficulty in prising money out of the government for major collections. In 1811 the purchase for £4,200 of Barre Robert's collection of English coins nearly doubled its holdings in that field.[86] In 1814 a grant of £8,200 was paid for a supplementary Townley collection, mostly of coins, medals and small antiquities.[87] While small sums were not so easy to obtain, the Trustees did make a number of useful purchases, as for example the small collection of sculpture belonging to Edmund Burke.[88] Planta was, however, getting worried about the printed books and at the request of the Trustees wrote a long memorandum:

> The considerable additions made of late years to the ample stores originally deposited in the British Museum, and the various improvements lately adopted towards extending, by an easy access, the utility of the Establishment, have it is acknowledged at all hands, rendered it a rich & truly important repository, essentially conducive towards promoting most branches of Science and Erudition.
>
> Whilst however these Copious Additions have considerably extended the Collections of Antiquities, Coins, Manuscripts & Minerals, it is much to be lamented that the Library of printed Books should, since the... Establishment, have received very few accessions, and that it have, in its increase, by no means kept pace with the above mentioned Departments....[89]

This was part of a long-running campaign to persuade the government to pass a copyright act (an aim achieved in 1814)[90] to strengthen the existing requirement that publishers should deposit their publications with the Stationers' Company for transmission to the Museum. But it was also an appeal for more money to spend on books, and once again the Trustees were successful. In 1812, the annual parliamentary grant was increased by £1,000 for the purchase of printed books. A special grant of £8,000 was made for the purchase of the legal manuscripts and printed books belonging to Francis Hargrave in 1813. In 1815, however, the Munich library of Baron von Moll was bought for £4,700 by selling the bulk of the investments in the Edwards Fund. Purchases of collections of printed books became more frequent after this.[91]

The Elgin Marbles

But antiquities were still taking the lion's share of the extra money and the attendant publicity, for the Trustees now approached the problem of the Elgin Marbles. The story of the Marbles has been told many times, not only because they are among the greatest treasures of the Museum, but because they have from time to time – most stridently in recent years – been the subject of political and emotional controversy. The story has most recently been told in a lively fashion by William St Clair in a book which is more readily accessible than the magisterial study of A.H. Smith, Keeper of Greek and Roman Antiquities, published in 1916. On these two accounts, and on the report of the Committee of the House of Commons set up in 1816 to consider their purchase, much of what follows is based.[92] Such accounts are sometimes partisan, as few can avoid judgmental attitudes since Byron first triggered opposition to the removal of the sculptures from Athens: 'I opposed – and will ever oppose – the robbery of ruins from Athens, to instruct the English in sculpture (who are as capable of sculpture as the Egyptians are to skating)',[93] a swift change of view in a man who a few years earlier had excoriated the stones:

> Let ABERDEEN and ELGIN still pursue
> The shade of fame through regions of Virtù;
> Waste useless thousands on their Phidian freaks,
> Misshapen monuments and maimed antiques;
> And make their grand saloons a general mart
> For all the mutilated blocks of art....[94]

Lord Elgin was appointed Ambassador to the Sublime Porte at Constantinople in 1799. Although he had many diplomatic duties to fulfil in a period disturbed by the war with France in the Mediterranean, Elgin had a very real interest in classical antiquities and had been persuaded that it would be a good idea to disseminate knowledge of Greek art and architecture in Britain – at that time much steeped in Roman tradition – to provide inspiration for contemporary artists and architects. This was a genuine purpose, and one which activated all Elgin's actions with regard to the adventures of his agents in Greece. He failed to get government backing for this idea (although the government did eventually agree to send out a scholar with the embassy to attempt to recover lost classical and biblical manuscripts),[95] so he decided to spend his own money on the project.

On his way to Turkey, while visiting Sir William Hamilton in Palermo he met the Italian landscape artist Giovanni Battista Lusieri, whom he persuaded to enter his employment at a salary of £200 p.a. He also engaged through his secretary, W.R. Hamilton,[96] a number of artists, including a draughtsman for drawing figures, two architectural draughtsmen and two cast-makers. They were all sent, under Lusieri's charge, to Athens to record the monuments, and particularly those on the Acropolis. Athens, when they arrived in July 1800, was a small town of about 1,200 houses; a Turkish garrison was established on the Acropolis and the inhabitants were generally pleasant and co-operative, although the officials were steeped in the corruption usual in the Ottoman empire of that period. At first it was difficult for the artists to gain access to the Acropolis, so they contented themselves with making casts and drawings of buildings outside its walls while they waited for a *firmân* (official letter of permission) which Elgin was to obtain in Constantinople. At the same time they bought fragments of sculpture from the householders of Athens. In July 1801, the political climate in Constantinople being extremely favourable to Elgin, a *firmân* was obtained and sent to Lusieri; but, as Elgin said in an answer to the Committee of the House of Commons in 1816, the original was no longer extant, having been retained by the local authorities.[97] The *firmân*, if possibly somewhat vague in meaning, was of sufficient force to allow of the removal of stones from the Acropolis, for the party had gradually turned from recording and casting the sculptured and inscribed stones on the Acropolis to removing them from the site. At this distance of time it is difficult to interpret the exact tenor of the permission received by Elgin,[98] but he was clearly at the time seen to be within his rights and this was confirmed by the Commons Committee.

The removal of the sculptures from the decaying buildings and rubble of the Acropolis was mainly carried out under the supervision of the Reverend Philip Hunt (chaplain to the Embassy) and Elgin's artists. In defence of Elgin it must be said that sculpture had been removed from the Acropolis for many years – indeed, some had simply been burnt for lime. Thus, for example, eight of twelve figures from the west front of the Parthenon had disappeared between 1749 and 1800, while five slabs of the frieze, which had been drawn between 1750 and 1755, had disappeared and a whole Ionic temple had been completely destroyed. Elgin's party did not improve matters and did much damage to the monuments, although they were perhaps more responsible than many other collectors who visited Athens both before and after this period, in that they recorded their finds and did not distribute them through the trade. While nobody would today remove such antiquities from their original position, such a practice was normal then – and the subject of much pride on the part of the collectors of whatever nationality. Indeed, some ten years earlier the Frenchman L.-F.-Sébastien Fauvel had started on a grand scale to remove sculptures from the Parthenon and other monuments in Athens for the greater glory of France at the behest of the French ambassador, the Comte de Choiseul-Gouffier.[99]

The collection, as well as the sculptures removed and excavated from the Parthenon and the Erechtheion, included many other pieces of sculpture of both marble and terracotta, vases and other small objects, plus architectural fragments and a giant Egyptian scarab. The collection was removed to England in two parts. All had finally arrived by 1811 (although Elgin continued to receive comparatively small parcels of objects from Lusieri until 1819). Elgin's luck had long since failed; he left Constantinople in 1803, but was caught by the resumption of war with France. Contrary to the custom of the time with regard to the treatment of diplomats, he was made a prisoner of war as he passed through France on his way home. He was treated badly by Napoleon, imprisoned twice, and managed to return home on parole only in 1806. His marriage had broken, his political career was finished as a result of his parole, he had enemies in Parliament and he was practically bankrupt. In order to recoup his finances he decided in 1811 to sell his collection to the government. Expecting £70,000, he was offered £30,000 by the Prime Minister, Spencer Percival; this he could not accept.[100] He now suffered at the hands of one of the cruellest and most brilliant poets of the period, Byron, who totally destroyed Elgin's reputation for all time through the medium of two poems, *Childe Harold's Pilgrimage* and *The Curse of Minerva*:

> But who, of all the plunderers of yon fane
> On high – where Pallas linger'd, loth to flee
> The latest relic of her ancient reign –
> The last, the worst, dull spoiler, who was he?
> Blush Caledonia! Such thy son could be!
> England! I joy no child he was of thine:
> Thy free-born men should spare what once was free;
> Yet they should violate each saddening shrine,
> And bear these altars o'er the long-reluctant brine.[101]

'Nothing in his writing', says his latest biographer, 'approaches the malice and hysteria of his persecution of Elgin'.[102] Against condemnation in one of the most popular poems of the period there was no possible means of reply, and Elgin wisely kept silent. Few, save those who have studied the whole sad history, have since defended him, succumbing too easily to Byron's virulent rejection of the work of a man of honour who (by his own lights and those of many of his contemporaries) had only the general good at heart. P.-O. Brøndsted's description of him as early as 1818 as 'the plunderer of the Athens Parthenon' has been typical of much later comment.[103]

Elgin, under threat of being forced out of storage space at Burlington House in Piccadilly, and once again short of money, offered the Marbles to the government in early 1815. The matter was allowed to lie for nearly a year, when a Select Committee of the House of Commons was set up to examine his offer and decide a price. The sale was widely supported outside Parliament. Those who gave evidence were mainly artists, from the President of the Royal Academy (West) downwards – Nollekens, Canova, Flaxman (who as early as 1802 had proposed the erection of a temporary gallery at the Museum to house the Marbles),[104] Westmacott and Chantrey. Among others, most influentially, was a senior politician, the Earl of Aberdeen (a Trustee of the Museum and President of the Society of Antiquaries and one of the most respected classical antiquaries of his day), who had been in Athens in 1803.[105] Most spoke in favour of the purchase; only the collector Richard Payne Knight (a Trustee and future benefactor of the Museum), who believed the sculptures to be Hadrianic, and William Wilkins, the architect, in any way denigrated their quality. Even Payne Knight had the grace to say, 'I think my Lord Elgin, in bringing them away, is entitled to the gratitude of the Country; because, otherwise, they would have been all broken by the Turks.' The Committee vindicated Elgin's actions as totally legal and agreed on the merit of the sculptures, but – mean-minded – recommended that the

Marbles be purchased for a mere £35,000, which was considered to be their market value (the money spent by Elgin in obtaining and keeping them, which was double this sum, was ignored). They also recommended that the Elgin family be henceforth represented on the board of Trustees of the Museum. A sum of £800 was allowed for the removal of the Marbles to the Museum and £1,700 was granted to provide for their temporary accommodation. An Act of Parliament was passed which enabled the Marbles to be purchased and vested in the Museum in perpetuity.[106]

The officers of the Museum were clearly not considered important enough to give evidence to the Committee, despite the fact that Taylor Combe had just published his first catalogue of classical sculpture and had studied the collection at Burlington House in 1811.[107] Further, they must have been involved in negotiations concerning the Marbles early in 1815, when Elgin's secretary from his days in Constantinople, W.R. Hamilton, wrote asking if it would be possible to store the Marbles.[108]

Planta, and presumably Combe, were certainly privy to the negotiations, but the archives of the Museum are remarkably silent about them. After Elgin's offer in 1815 (discussed by the Trustees at their April meeting)[109] and the setting up of the Commons Committee in 1816, debate about the Marbles was very public. Apart, however, from a request from the Committee for an estimate of costs for moving and housing them, complete discretion seems to have reigned – at least on paper – in official Museum quarters. The acquisition is foreshadowed in May 1816, just before the Commons Committee's report was due, by the Trustees in terms of solemn and mysterious discretion:

> It having been reported from the Committee of March 9th, that they had directed a Letter to be written to Mr Harrison of the Treasury, informing him that as large sums would probably be wanted for more important objects the Trustees would beg leave to withdraw their request to the Lords of the Treasury respecting the purchase of Colonel Montague's Collection of Zoology.[110]

Once the Act had been passed the Museum proceeded with commendable speed to put the Marbles on display (pl. 12). The Trustees held a number of extraordinary meetings in late June and July to discuss the purchase and the way in which it was to be displayed. On 12 August it was recorded that everything had been arranged.[111] In just over six months a temporary gallery was built and the sculptures moved from Piccadilly and installed in Bloomsbury. They were then shown to the public and to the artists for whom, in a sense, the Marbles had been bought, and whose taste was, in some measure, to be formed by them.[112] Within a few months of the gallery being opened the painter Benjamin Haydon, long an enthusiastic protagonist of the Marbles, wrote in his diary:

> May 28. On Monday last there were one thousand and two people visited the Elgin marbles! A greater number than ever visited the British Museum since it was established. It is quite interesting to listen to the remarks of the people. They make them with the utmost simplicity, with no affectation of taste, but with a homely truth that shews that they are sound at the core. We overheard two common looking decent men say to each other, 'How broken they are, a'ant they?' 'Yes,' said the other, 'but how *like life*'.[113]

The temporary Elgin gallery (it was in use until 1831) was a simple brick-built shed (pl. 12). Designed by the Trustees' new architect Robert Smirke, it incorporated all the latest technologies of cast and wrought iron and was floored with pine.[114] It was tacked on to the west side of the Townley Gallery from which it was entered by way of a staircase from the second rotunda.[115] There was in addition a room to the west, in which the Bassae frieze was displayed (the Phigalian Room, retained until 1841). Also displayed in this gallery were a number of casts, mostly those made by Lusieri's party in Greece, including a cast of the west frieze which remained in Athens.[116] The marbles were minimally repaired by Westmacott and not restored. From time to time further fragments of the Parthenon were recovered from other collections and brought together in the Elgin room, although a metope from the Choiseul-Gouffier collection, sold in Paris in 1818, went to the Louvre despite the efforts of the Trustees to buy it.[117]

Despite the almost overwhelming interest in classical sculpture, the Trustees had time to negotiate for the much less popular Egyptian sculpture. In 1811, for example, they acquired a kneeling basalt statue which had stood on the premises of Messrs Fletcher Shaw and Co in Ironmonger Lane 'for the last twenty years'.[118] Henry Salt, recently appointed British Consul-General in Cairo, had been encouraged by Sir Joseph Banks to collect Egyptian antiquities on behalf of the Museum; in 1816 he received permission from Mohammed Ali Pasha, Viceroy of Egypt, to remove a colossal head, thought to be the younger Memnon, from Thebes and to send it to London. He instructed a colourful Paduan, Giovanni Battista Belzoni, who had spent some time as a professional strong man in England before becoming an unsuccessful hydraulic engineer in Egypt, to undertake the task.[119] The head was duly despatched to London, where it was an immediate success. It has erroneously been thought that it was the inspiration for Shelley's sonnet 'Ozymandias'. It was neither Ozymandias nor the younger Memnon. It is now thought to be Ramesses II. It is of granite, 2.47 m high, and dates from the thirteenth century BC.

This was only the first piece of Egyptian sculpture to be collected by Salt and Belzoni. Initially encouraged to collect by the aged Banks, they assembled a large and valuable collection which Salt, short of money, offered to the Museum. The Trustees, quite disgracefully, were growing cool towards Salt and his antiquities, feeling that in terms of art they were neither as good, nor as inspiring, as the classical sculpture that had taken London by storm. Further, the Trustees felt that Salt was trying to make too great a profit from his collection, but purchased the majority of the collection formed between 1817 and 1819 for £2,000.[120] They refused, however, to buy the great alabaster sarcophagus of Sethos I; it was eventually purchased by Sir John Soane, in whose museum in Lincoln's Inn Fields it remains today.[121] Their miserliness meant that Salt's second collection went to the Louvre (the collections of which were being rapidly increased through the activities of Salt's French equivalent in Cairo, Bernardino Drovetti, who also founded the collection of Egyptian antiquities in Turin). Much of Salt's third collection was purchased after his death by the British Museum at a sale at Sotheby's in 1835, for £4,800.[122]

A year later the Museum's greatest Egyptologist, Samuel Birch (see p.93), was appointed to the Department of Antiquities. The work of Salt and Belzoni established a base on which Birch could build the reputation of the Museum as one of the world's greatest centres of Egyptology. What is more, their work, together with a flood of new publications on ancient Egypt, encouraged private visitors to visit that country. Some of these visitors returned home with collections which often ended up in the British Museum, such as that purchased from Joseph Sams for £2,500 in 1834.[123]

The Passing of the Old Collectors

In 1824 the last of the old-fashioned virtuosi collectors in the eighteenth-century mould died. Richard Payne Knight (pl. 11) was seventy-five years old and had been an influential Trustee of the Museum since 1814 (he was a Townley family Trustee), despite the fact that he had made a fool of himself over the Elgin Marbles.[124] For fifty years he had collected coins, marbles, bronzes, gems, drawings and paintings in an idiosyncratic manner. He was a considerable theorist and critic of art, most famous perhaps for his supplement to Sir William Hamilton's *Discourse on the worship of Priapus*. This was published in 1786 through the Society of Dilettanti, a 'full and open discussion of ancient phallic rituals illustrated with engravings which would raise an eyebrow even today, and still more remarkable because it contended that it was from these cults that Christianity itself derived'.[125] But he wrote much more than this, including an *Analytical inquiry into the principles of taste* (1808), a work much discussed in the reviews.

Like his friends Banks and Townley, Payne Knight set up a museum in his London house, where he worked hard on a catalogue of his coins (he left more than 5,000 to the Museum), published by the Museum in 1830. He also left the Museum 111 gems, 1,144 drawings (of which 273 were by Claude) and about 800 bronzes, as well as marbles and other objects of *vertu*. He had bought widely in Rome, Paris and London, and exchanged objects with other collectors, including Taylor Combe at the Museum. It is assumed that his refusal to deal in art objects and his expressed intention to leave his collection to the Museum encouraged his friends to give him material. In appreciation of the bequest the Trustees agreed that his family should be represented on the board of Trustees, the last such recognition of a donor.[126]

Meanwhile, in 1820, the ancient Sir Joseph Banks had died. To the end this extraordinary man had served the Museum, with great influence. His unmarried sister, Sarah Sophia Banks, who died in 1818, had bequeathed her important collection of coins and medals to Lady Banks – this, after some muddle, Banks presented to the Museum.[127] The collection included coins of the newly independent United States of America, acquired as they were issued, which now provide a guide to this much-forged series. More important, the Museum also received her remarkable collection of printed and engraved ephemera, of which over 19,000 items – trade cards, visiting cards, admission tickets, invitations and so on – are now the core of the Museum's remarkable collection of such material.[128] Sir Joseph Banks himself now left (in a convoluted manner) his own vast collection of books and his herbarium to the Museum, a final addition to a long line of gifts of antiquities, ethnographic and natural history specimens as well as coins, medals and manuscripts. Much of his enormous international correspondence also came to the Museum (it is now in the Natural History Museum with the majority of his collection[129]). The herbarium and library were bequeathed in the first instance to Robert Brown, his curator and librarian, with reversion to the Museum. In 1827 Brown did a skilful deal whereby the collections came to the Museum in exchange for an extremely generous salary and leave package.[130] According to Stearn, 'Under Planta and König [Keeper of Natural History] the Museum was on its way to rival the Musée d'Histoire Naturelle in Paris, but it still had far to go'.[131] A few years later, in 1835, a sub-department of botany was created with Robert Brown at its head.

The staff at this period (1820) was still very small, although Planta had gradually strengthened its infrastructure (it would shortly grow with the addition of transfers from the Royal Library). The Principal Librarian was now paid £500 p.a. (unchanged since 1805) and the four Under Librarians (now more often known as Keepers) were paid £425 each. The four assistant librarians were each paid between £120 and £245 p.a. Extra assistants, of which there were two, were each paid a basic £200 p.a. There was an 'Accomptant', who was paid £30, plus £10 to assist the Secretary. The 'Attendant' in the Reading Room was paid £115 and the other five attendants £75. The nine warders ('extra attendants') were paid 5s a day for three days a week. To this must be added a messenger and porter at £52 4s p.a., an assistant messenger at £44, five housemaids and two night watchmen as well as a gardener and other manual staff. The total wages bill for the year ending 25 March 1821 was £5,397 19s 6d[132] (the total income of the Museum for that year was £11,789). There were no pensions, and officers and other members of staff tended to remain in post until they died.[133] Until the Select Committee of 1835 reported it was quite common for senior members of staff to have other part-time posts, mostly ecclesiastical appointments, while the maids and other museum servants were also known to do outside jobs – as waiters, for example.[134]

Eight of the officers lived in the Museum, in much-sought-after apartments which ranged in size from ten rooms (Planta) to four (Bean). The porter and the housemaids also lived in the Museum (see p.52). All members of staff were appointed through the patronage of the three Principal Trustees (although some of the manual workers and housemaids were appointed within the Museum by the Principal Librarian and reported to the Trustees). Candidates for posts of senior rank worked hard to be appointed. Typical is the story of the Reverend Francis Cary, minor poet, translator of Dante and curate at the Savoy Chapel.[135] In December 1825 he wrote to his father:

> My present fabric is in an office in the British Museum, which it is likely to be soon declared vacant. I have written to the Archbishop of Canterbury (in whose disposal it is), to offer myself a candidate and to the Bishops of London, Norwich and St David's... Beside this... I wrote to Mr Robinson (Chancellor of the Exchequer), Mr Croker, Mr Champagné and Digby; and intend doing so to many others... .
>
> The office at which I aim is that of keeper of the antiquities, about to be declared vacant consequence of the incurable illness of Mr Coombe who at present holds it... The value of it (including all advantages of residence, &c.,) is estimated at 500l a year.
>
> If I do not succeed in getting this, it is possible that I may obtain some other of less value in the British Museum, where it is supposed that several changes will soon take place.[136]

For six months he continued to write to sponsors, attempted to see some of them, particularly the Archbishop of Canterbury, and urged his father's help. He had a high opinion of himself and must have been disappointed when he eventually achieved an assistant keepership in the Department of Printed Books. He was lucky enough to get a residence in the Museum – where he was visited by such friends as Coleridge and Lamb – but was very cross when in 1837 he was passed over in favour of Panizzi as Keeper of the department (he appears to have been runner-up), writing a public letter of protest to *The Times*.[137] Having come into money, he resigned in a huff.[138]

Enter Smirke

The old building was gradually wearing out and new acquisitions were overwhelming the available space. For most of Planta's career as Principal Librarian he was engaged in plans for extension. By 1820 major works had become urgent. Not only were the Museum collections expanding at a vast rate, but Montagu House was beginning to collapse, the floors being continually reinforced by iron pillars and timber.[139]

The Trustees turned now to Robert Smirke, who had been associated with the Museum since 1814, and who was probably referred to them when the Board of Works took over the care of the Museum buildings in 1815.[140] It was Smirke who had designed the temporary Elgin Room and was consulted by them on both major and minor matters. At the age of nineteen he had, in 1799, won the gold medal of the Royal Academy School for his design for a national museum, and already by the time of his attachment to the Museum had had a glittering career as a classicizing and innovative structural architect. Trained under Dance and Soane, he was a rather heavy-handed exponent of the architecture of the Greek Revival, which he raised to new heights in the British Museum. In engineering terms, as at the Museum, he perfected the idea of a building dependent on a framework of cast iron and concrete with a stone shell.[141] He was also commissioned to produce some other very large buildings – the General Post Office, King's College London and the Custom House. The British Museum is, however, his master work and he was engaged on it until 1846, when he was succeeded by his hardly less gifted, much younger brother, Sydney, who had been associated with the Museum since 1823 and who designed the Round Reading Room and the Museum's splendid railings and gates.[142]

Smirke was asked to consult with the staff and the Trustees and to produce a plan for enlarging the Museum. He had already produced the beginning of a scheme, a single range to the north of Montagu House, which would ultimately form the northern side of a courtyard building.[143] The idea of the northern range was abandoned and a proposal was produced early in 1821 for 'an eastwards extension of the Townley Gallery for the Athenian and Phigalian Marbles' and a corresponding wing to the east for 'manuscripts and the more precious articles of natural history'. The idea was in general accepted by the Trustees, who decided to approach the government for money.[144] As so often, however, events overtook them. In the first place the Duke of Bedford took them to court on the grounds that the planned buildings would breach the agreement, made by the Trustees when they purchased Montagu House, not to build permanent structures in the garden.[145] Second, the new king, George IV (intent on re-designing Buckingham Palace – and particularly the rooms which held the Royal Library), offered them his father's great library as a gift.[146] Third, they were also offered much of the great collection of pictures formed by Sir George Beaumont.[147]

The first problem was successfully overcome by the lawyers, who argued that the Bedford Estate had already compromised the environment of the gardens.[148] The problem of Sir George's pictures (and the important collection of paintings belonging to Sir John Angerstein which was purchased by Parliamentary authority for £60,000) was ultimately settled by depositing them in the National Gallery, founded in 1824. The gift was to cause minor trouble for some years to come, as the 'Committee of six Gentlemen' appointed by the Treasury on 2 July 1824 to 'undertake the superintendance of the National Gallery of

Pictures' were basically Trustees of the British Museum and recorded some of their meetings in the Museum's minute books.[149]

Most immediately important to the Museum was George III's library.[150] The King had been a munificent donor in his lifetime; his first great gift was the Thomason tracts – some 30,000 printed ephemera concerning the English Civil War – which he had bought on the advice of Lord Bute for the ludicrous sum of £300. This purchase stimulated the King, who as Prince of Wales had already been buying books, to collect on a grand scale. (He was incidentally a great reader, not merely a collector.)[151] His next major purchase was the library of Joseph Smith, the British Consul in Venice, for which he paid £10,000. He bought widely, not only in England, but on the Continent, where monastic and Jesuit libraries were being secularized and their contents sold. Generally he spent at least £1,500 a year on books, both new and old, until at the time of his death he owned some 65,000 books, 19,000 unbound tracts and 450 manuscripts. The gift was debated in Parliament and it was agreed that the books, together with his maps, charts, topographical drawings and his collection of coins and medals, would come to the Museum – the books to be housed together. An initial grant of £40,000 was made towards a new building. Smirke's plans were hurriedly revised and it was decided that the King's Library would be housed on the ground floor, together with the Department of Manuscripts, and that the upper floor should be reserved for a picture gallery (ultimately it was to be allocated to natural history) on the eastern side of Montagu House.

By June 1827, when the King's Library building was handed over to the Museum, it had cost £157,000.[152] It was worth every penny. It was a splendid, state-of-the-art structure. The King's Library is a hundred yards (91.44 m) long (energetic assistant keepers within living memory used to race down its length after hours) and 31 feet (9.44 m) high; it is lined with oak cases, glazed only in the 1850s. It has an oak and mahogany floor (disastrously copied in the 1950s in poor-quality wood). In the wider central space of the room four polished brown granite columns (which cost £2,400) with capitals of Derbyshire alabaster are flanked by square grey granite wall-shafts; these in turn are flanked by marble pilasters framing scagliola panels; the pilasters at gallery level are of plaster. At either end of the room the moulded marble door-cases and the entablature are flanked by plain white pilasters of marble. Above the doors are inscriptions in brass on marble commemorating the royal gift. The coffered ceiling is broken by great panels, each containing a large roundel with a central rosette. There is a gallery with brass balustrade at window level, the windows being interspaced with bookcases. The room was heated, as was the upper floor of the building, by a hot-air system generated from stoves in the basement, which was at first difficult to control (the Print Room, however, was heated by hot-water pipes). It is, says Pevsner, 'one of the great rooms of London, restrained but festive'.[153] The room has now lost (not without a forlorn struggle on the part of the Trustees in the 1970s) its great library with the fine royal bindings (they now form a brilliant, shrine-like core to the new British Library at St Pancras). With it has gone much of the grandeur of the room, which can only be replaced gradually and with great taste.[154]

To the south of the King's Library was the manuscript room (later known as the Manuscript Saloon and today much altered) and two rooms south of this (the 'Middle' and 'South' rooms) which were used as reading rooms until 1838, when they were allocated to the Department of Manuscripts as the reading rooms in the north wing were completed.

The upper floor of the east wing was much plainer, it had no pillars and its plaster pilasters were undecorated. It was lit from the roof by great rectangular lanterns and the oak floor was supported on cast iron beams of elegance and strength (designed by the railway engineer John Rastrick)[155] which are still in place. These beams supported curved iron plates above the plaster ceiling of the library below.[156] Being originally intended for a picture gallery, it has no major windows. The main gallery was now given over to the natural history collections, the space above the wall-cases being taken up with the Museum's pictures from the pre-Beaumont era. To the south was the Print Room, which had been moved from its inconvenient and damp quarters in the Townley building.

Meanwhile a similar, if ornamentally less elaborate, building had been started on the west side of Montagu House, together with a shorter extension parallel to it which was to house the Elgin Marbles. The Elgin Room (it now houses the Nereid Monument) was completed in 1832; top-lit, it was described by Westmacott as 'one of the finest rooms in the world; and... as finely lighted as any room I know'.[157] A north wing, originally planned in 1823, was now contemplated.

The Old Order Changes

Taylor Combe died after a long illness on 7 July 1826 and Planta, aged 84, died on 3 December 1827. Their reigns, so far as the Antiquities Department was concerned, had been long and successful. The Museum now had one of the largest collections of classical and Egyptian antiquity in the world and the first Assyrian material was creeping in – notably in 1824 the collection of the remarkable linguist and antiquarian Claudius James Rich, the East India Company's Resident in Baghdad, who had died of cholera at Shiraz. This included (among an important collection of oriental manuscripts and coins) the first coherent assemblage of cuneiform inscriptions to reach the Museum.[158] In the following year Sir Gore Ouseley, following a gift by the fourth Earl of Aberdeen in 1817, gave a series of sculptures originating from the fourth- to sixth-century BC Achaemenid royal complex of Persepolis, in present-day Iran, which forms the basis of the large collection gathered by the Museum over the years.[159]

There was now a room devoted to British antiquities, although there was still a strange reluctance to collect such material. The numismatic and medallic collections were among the richest in the world and had been considerably enhanced in 1818 by the gift of the collections of the Banks ladies. In 1823 George IV had given the royal collection of coins and medals, and in 1824 came Payne Knight's classical collection. The ethnographic collections were increased almost by stealth as donations were received from travellers and merchants, particularly as a result of the trade with Central and South America. An important assemblage of Asante material, collected by T.E. Bowdich while on a mission for the Africa Company, was given in 1818, but not registered for ten years – the first major collection from Africa to enter the Museum.[160] The collections of prints and drawings grew gradually, although the opportunity to acquire some famous collections had been missed – John Thomas Smith, the assistant in charge, has been described by a later Keeper as 'indolent'.[161] The great series of catalogues of the non-library side of the British Museum had been successfully initiated (Combe's son presented the Trustees with the manuscript of his last unfinished catalogue)[162] and the torch was passed, rather slowly, to Combe's successors.[163]

The Museum as a whole has seldom had a more active and successful head than Planta. His achievements are often overshadowed in the literature by accounts of the extraordinary energy shown in the middle of the century by Panizzi – the librarians' librarian – as Keeper of Printed Books. The reason for this may be that all previous official histories of the Museum have been written by librarians, who, while acknowledging the ability of Planta, could not wait to start writing about the great reforming librarian, Panizzi, to them 'the great god Pan'. How much of the work was initiated by Planta and how much by the Trustees is unclear (he attended the Trustees' meetings only by invitation), but where his policy papers survive it is patent that it was he who formulated the policy – only Banks was more powerful.

Joseph Planta (and in this case it was certainly he) had opened up the Museum to a new, more popular, public (between 1807 and his death the number of annual visitors had risen from 13,046 to 79,131).[164] He had provided them with popular guides to the collections. Under his ægis student artists and others had been admitted to draw from the antique. He had liberalized the admission rules for library readers, and reader numbers had risen enormously. The annual Parliamentary grant had been increased from £3,000 to £12,877 in 1827.[165] He had split antiquities, coins and medals, and prints and drawings from the library departments. He had supervised the acquisition of a vast range of new collections that encompassed the whole area of the Museum's interests (£157,000 had been voted by Parliament for buildings and £125,852 for collections during his period in office).[166] He had nearly doubled the staff. Further, he saw the completion of two major new buildings and the planning of another and, with the aid of the Trustees, had persuaded the Treasury not to split the collection or move it elsewhere.[167] He had, as has been shown, energetically pursued the acquisition of printed books and manuscripts; but Panizzi's later criticism of the British Museum's collections as 'far inferior to the king's library in Paris', while true, was also unfair in that the Paris library had started from a greater base.

Planta's contribution must not, then, be underestimated.[168] Advised by him, the Trustees had squeezed money out of a reasonably acquiescent government and the Museum's general running costs were now set on a firm footing, backed by a regular government grant-in-aid. After the death of Banks he was more heeded, and the administration was tidied up. Established sub-committees of the Trustees were initiated, particularly a finance committee, which met intermittently before 1827.[169] In 1824 the Trustees had appointed a 'Sub-Committee of Three for each of the respective departments of the House, who may annually examine minutely into the same at the time of the Visitation, and report thereon to the General Meeting next subsequent' (the committee for the Department of Antiquities consisted initially of Payne Knight, the Earl of Aberdeen and the MP Henry Bankes).[170] Other committees were the precursor of what later became the building sub-committee. The sub-committee minutes are a mine of information concerning the domestic running of the Museum and its departments from that time to the present day. No longer were matters of moment normally referred to individual Trustees for consideration, as they had been in Banks's day, rather they were referred to the standing sub-committees.

Trivia continued to occupy the attention of the Trustees; the new Principal Librarian, like his predecessors, was much immersed in incidental managerial problems, from ordering and paying for coals to more delicate matters:

> Mr Ellis requests that the Committee will have the goodness to make an Entry upon their minutes for him to order Bed-linen for the Maid Servants of the Museum. They have had none since 1822, and Mr Ellis has ascertained by deputy that the same is really wanted.[171]

But more weighty matters concerning the collections and the building were much discussed.

While many major acquisitions had been achieved, many were missed. The supporters of the Museum continued to give generously, sometimes rather large collections, but often a few objects, which might range from natural history specimens to a Gainsborough, the Romano-British mosaic pavement from Withington in Gloucestershire, some souvenir of the Grand Tour or the Earl of Aberdeen's gift of sculpture from Persepolis. One of its most beautiful pieces of sculpture also came to the Museum at this period: the ninth- or tenth-century gilt-bronze Bodhisattva Tārā from north-east Sri Lanka was given by Sir Robert Brownrigg, Governor of Ceylon, in 1830.[172] Some objects (but not many) were borrowed, most notably the Portland Vase, lent by the Duke of Portland, at that time a Trustee.[173] Among collections not bought by the Trustees were, for example, the antiquities from the Bronze Age barrows of Wiltshire excavated by the pioneering English archaeologist William Cunnington, offered for £600 in 1815.[174] The Trustees also turned down the classical collection, offered for £890 in 1826,[175] of the Danish archaeologist and numismatist Peter Oluf Brøndsted, who had travelled widely in the eastern Mediterranean and been a diplomat in Rome. In the same year they turned down the much bigger collection of the Queen of Naples, which was offered at £14,000.[176] In 1827 a collection of Mexican antiquities was refused by the Trustees; it was offered for £8,000, but it was said that the French government was willing to pay £6,000 for it.[177] Individual items which would nowadays be snapped up were turned down, probably because they were not interesting to classically-biased Trustees – two (presumably Bronze-Age) gold collars from Ireland, for example.[178]

Some gifts were declined because the potential donors were too ambitious; thus a collection of Burmese antiquities was refused because the novelist Captain Marryat RN had offered them on condition that he be made a Trustee.[179] The most important loss came early in Ellis's reign; in 1830, despite a letter written in the most fulsome terms by the Trustees, the Treasury, in short order, refused to ask Parliament for £18,000 (an enormous sum, half the price of the Elgin Marbles) to purchase the old master drawings collected by Sir Thomas Lawrence, the purchase of which had first been refused by the King.[180] This collection, perhaps the finest ever formed, was distributed on the market; the Museum and many other collectors have been buying it up in small lots ever since.

A New Cast

Planta was succeeded by Henry Ellis (soon to be knighted),[181] who had been Keeper of Manuscripts and had acted as Secretary to the Trustees. He was fifty years old and looked so much like Mr Pickwick that one wonders whether Dickens, who knew him, used him as a physical model. He was bespectacled, round, benign and clubbable (pl. 10). He became Secretary of the Society of Antiquaries in 1814 and for forty years missed only two meetings.[182] Richard Garnett wrote of him, 'Panizzi was the real ruler of the Museum, and it says much for Ellis's placability that he should so cordially have accepted the direction of one who had assailed him with a contemptuous acerbity which would have been inconceivable if the condition of the museum at that time had not been absolutely anarchical'.[183] This has been very much the judgement of later historians (particularly Miller – the biographer of Panizzi – whose usual balance slipped when dealing with Ellis).[184] Perhaps the judgement of Edwards is more just than most:

> Those who had (like the writer) opportunity to watch, during most of the succeeding thirty years, the continuance of that service, know that the King's selection was justified. Sir Henry Ellis was not gifted with any of those salient abilities which dazzle the eyes of men; but he had great power of labour, the strictest integrity of purpose, and a very kind heart. He was ever, to the Trustees, a faithful servant, up to the full measure of his ability. To those who worked under him he was always courteous, considerate, and very often he was generous. He would sometimes expose himself to misconstruction, in order to appease discords. He would at times rather seem wanting in firmness of will than, by pressing his authority, wound the feelings of well-intentioned but irritable subordinates. No one could receive from him a merited reproof – I speak from personal experience – without perceiving that the duty of giving it was felt to be a painful duty....[185]

He was a serious scholar and worked hard throughout his career, being particularly involved in editing medieval sources, above all his *General introduction to Domesday Book*, which in its 1833 version has affected all subsequent scholarship.[186] He also published and edited many other books, including the first edition of Brand's *Observations on popular antiquities*, seminally important in the history of English folklore.[187] For 'The Library of Entertaining Knowledge' he wrote popular guides to the Elgin Marbles and to the Townley Gallery.[188]

Ellis did not start his Principal Librarianship trailing clouds of glory. Jobbery at the last moment nominated Henry Fynes Clinton for the post. Clinton, an ex-MP for a pocket borough of the Duke of Newcastle, a wealthy man and literary figure of some repute, was a protégé and indeed a relation of Manners-Sutton, the Archbishop of Canterbury, one of the Principal Trustees. The Archbishop's son, as Speaker, was another Principal Trustee and followed his father's recommendation, and for a short time it seemed that Clinton would get the job. Garnett was the first to publish the scurrilous story that Ellis obtained the post by influencing the King's physician, Sir William Knighton, by chasing after his coach and asking him to intercede with his master. The idea of the portly fifty-year-old indulging in such an exercise is Pickwickian in its absurdity; nonetheless the monarch chose Ellis rather than Clinton, probably due to the intercession of one of the most influential Trustees, the Earl of Aberdeen.[189] It was the better choice. Ellis has had a bad press; he was a good Principal Librarian, who had to struggle with some strong-minded colleagues, each of whom had their own agendas, and with a body of Trustees who were opinionated and accustomed to rule. As will be shown he presided over a period of enormous growth. In the twenty-eight years of his Principal Librarianship, Ellis – however reactionary – oversaw many revolutionary changes.

He could not have presided over a more selfish, partisan, devious and brilliant group of colleagues. Only one of the keepers with whom Ellis had worked as Secretary, Charles König of Natural History, survived long into the new reign (he finally went in 1851, five years before Ellis). The Reverend Henry Baber, the mild-mannered and occasionally daring Keeper of Printed Books, would be driven out as a pluralist to his country living in 1837. He was succeeded by one of the junior members of his department, an impoverished ex-revolutionary lawyer, an exile from Italy (where he had been condemned to death in his absence) and now professor of Italian at the newly founded University College London. This was Antonio Panizzi (pl. 7), later to be described as 'Prince of Librarians'.[190] Ellis's own successor, both as Keeper of Manuscripts and as Secretary to the Trustees, was the Reverend Josiah Forshall, Chaplain to the Foundling Hospital. Forshall was made full-time Secretary in 1837 as a result of the recommendations of the Select Committee of the House of Commons (he had held the post part-time since Ellis had become Principal Librarian). An unstable man (he was retired ten years later on grounds of insanity), he was, however, influential because of his friendship with the new Archbishop of Canterbury, William Howley.[191] He was also powerful because, as Secretary, he was present at the Trustees' meetings (the Principal Librarian was not); he has been seen by many as the *éminence noire* of the Museum at this period. He was succeeded as keeper by the brilliant, irascible Frederic Madden (pl. 10).[192] Madden came from a military background in Ireland, had been educated at Oxford and was a courtier, a gentleman of the chamber to both William IV and Victoria. Although relatively junior in the Museum hierarchy, his court connections led to him being knighted at roughly the same time as Ellis – and with the same orders. He despised Ellis and hated Panizzi, the latter ultimately with paranoid intensity.

Combe's successor as Keeper of Antiquities was Edward Hawkins. Like both Madden and Ellis he was a high Tory, immoderate in his unswerving Protestantism, which was to cause the Trustees much trouble towards the end of his career. Hawkins (pl. 14) was of a character very different from that of his predecessor. He had not been to university, but had been a volunteer in the militia, a banker and a landowner in Wales. He was not without means. A considerable numismatist, he had been a reputable botanist and was a Fellow of the Linnean Society, of the Royal Society and of the Society of Antiquaries (of the two latter he was Vice-President).[193] Born in 1780, he was older and more mature than either Panizzi or Madden, but had been employed only temporarily by the Museum during Combe's last illness in 1825. He was appointed Keeper early in 1827.[194]

Panizzi, Madden and Hawkins, with the formidable John Edward Gray, who became Keeper of the sub-branch of Zoology in 1840, formed the ingredients of a witch's brew of warring satraps, the like of which had never been seen before in the Museum – and has perhaps never been seen since. It is no wonder that Ellis did not wish to stir the pot!

But first the Museum had to face a public enquiry. Since the beginning of the 1820s, in an age of burgeoning reform, there had once again been considerable debate about access to the Museum, as readers of the reviews and the better-quality newspapers gradually became aware of the public nature of the institution and the fact that it was supported out of taxation. Criticism in press and Parliament concentrated on opening hours and closed months (particularly August and September), although there was some realization that limited access was largely due to lack of funding and only to some extent because of what would nowadays be called elitism.[195] In Parliament Henry Bankes and, later, Alexander Baring, both Trustees of the Museum, defended the institution with urbanity, while gradually giving ground. In 1833 William Cobbett, the newly elected MP for Oldham, typically turned the debate into a tirade against elitism, using language immoderate even for that great orator. The poor derived no benefit from the Museum, 'if the aristocracy wanted the Museum as a lounging place, let them pay for it... He wanted to know... the names of the maids who swept the rooms, to see whose daughters they were; whether they were the daughters of the heads of the establishment... this British Museum job was one of the most scandalous that disgraced the Government, and when he said that, he thought he could not make it more disgraceful'.[196]

Others, particularly in Parliament, questioned whether the Museum was doing enough to help art and manufacturing industry, but here they were on less sure ground, for many pointed to such relationships as that enjoyed by Wedgwood with Hamilton and the use of the Museum by students of the Royal Academy. A major irritant was caused by a dissatisfied member of staff – John Millard, a cataloguer of manuscripts – who had been sacked in 1833.[197] He was a friend of the radical MP Benjamin Hawes, who was one of the chief instigators of the Select Committee of the House of Commons set up to examine the 'condition, management and affairs of the British Museum' in 1835. Millard clearly provided Hawes, who was a member of the Committee and described by Madden as 'a dirty, pitiful blackguard – to quibble & lie & be insolent' and only qualified to be 'a country attorney',[198] with much ammunition. The Committee was chaired by T.G.B. Estcourt and included, alongside a number of hostile members, two Trustees of the Museum – the reactionary Tory Sir Robert Inglis and Lord Stanley (who later as Earl of Derby was Prime Minister and remained all his life an energetic Trustee). Although access had been a catalyst for dissatisfaction, 'the real purpose of this committee', in the words of Edward Miller, 'was to reveal the nepotism, corruption, inefficiency and maladministration said to be rife within the Museum. Also under attack was its alleged neglect of the physical sciences and the virtual absence of men of science and other specialists from the Board'.[199] In all these purposes it failed, as the Museum, its staff and the general public rallied to the Museum's flag. Critics had not yet learnt the lesson that the staff and their allies, while they may appear to be a flock of sheep, when threatened form a circle and face outwards. In fact in the final analysis it was clear that, in order to answer its critics, the Museum needed more support from government and particularly from the Treasury.

The Committee took evidence throughout the summer of 1835; it issued a report, but came to no conclusions.[200] Consequently another (rather less hostile) Committee was set up in the following year, which also issued a report, but this time it made recommendations.[201] The two Committees were thorough in their research, obtaining long memoirs from the Museum's European contemporaries, which were published as appendices and provide a unique and detailed account of the practices and constitutions of many of the major libraries (and a few museums) of Europe at that period. The breadth of their questions was limited and often hostile. The Museum's witnesses stood up well to the examination, in some cases (as in the evidence given by Ellis) with imperturbable equanimity, and in some cases (as with Panizzi) with passionate self-righteousness. The Secretary, Forshall, and the accountant, Mawer Cowtan, provided facts and figures, which were published in the appendices, and (in Forshall's case) made judgmental observations concerning them. All the keepers were examined, some more than once, and König, the Keeper of Natural History, made some telling points about collecting and accommodation. He even agreed that little had been done to explain the exhibits or make them attractive to the public. Madden (following a pusillanimous answer from Ellis) condemned the wretched Millard, whose dismissal was one of the elements that caused the Committee to be set up, as 'totally incompetent for the task to which he had been appointed'.[202] In his diary he was less moderate, apostrophizing him as a 'son of a bitch'.[203]

Initially, the Committee, having heard (probably to their disappointment) that Ellis had no patronage, save in the appointment of housemaids and watchmen,[204] was deeply concerned about the structure of the board. According to *Fraser's Literary Chronicle*, 'a crochet seems to have seized the head of the principal examiner' in this matter.[205] They were worried that Trustees 'were generally of high rank and wealth, and of great occupation'.[206] Imperturbably Ellis answered that while official Trustees were often too busy to attend, many of the others attended 'constantly', and that if a Trustee had not been to a meeting for a year he was not summoned until he again appeared. The Standing Committee, he admitted, basically consisted of those Trustees who wished to come. Yes, they were the great and the good (as well as the official Trustees, there were nine ex-ministers and three ex-ambassadors). As to the appointment of men of letters and scientists, he suggested, even when pressed, 'I would conceive that science and literature would be possessed by a well-educated gentleman in sufficient quantity to make him a Trustee of the Museum. Scientific men would not always be the best person for such an appointment'.[207] The Committee could get no further on this tack. Although the scientists in general pleaded for more of their kind on the board, Panizzi and others were quite happy with its structure. As Forshall put it:

> So far as my experience goes, the best trustees of the British Museum are those who have an earnest desire to promote literature, art and science conjointly, without a devoted partiality to one of the three. Men of good education and good taste, who love knowledge generally, are too wise to despise any branch of it whatsoever, and yet endeavour to give to each its due relative importance.[208]

Nor could the Committee get far in their accusations of nepotism – all the heads of departments had received their posts through promotion.[209]

The Committee, conscious perhaps of the fact that the population of London had nearly tripled since the beginning of the century, spent a good deal of time discussing opening hours and accessibility generally. They called for figures and harried Ellis on the admission of the working class to the Museum. But they got nowhere with him; he merely revealed his high Tory colours: 'People of a higher grade would hardly wish to come to the Museum at the same time with sailors from the dockyards and girls whom they might bring with them. I do not think such people would gain any improvement from the sight of our collection.' When asked whether he knew of any such sailors, he answered, 'I never traced them to the dock-yards, but the class of people who would come at such times [i.e. on public holidays] would be of a very low description.'[210] This, perhaps the most quoted statement of Ellis, has held him up to some ridicule by generations of historians of the Museum. It is worth pointing out, however, that five years later Ellis was quite willing to admit that he was mistaken. In evidence before another Select Committee, set up to examine the state of ancient monuments, particularly in St Paul's Cathedral and Westminster Abbey, Ellis was questioned about his expressed opinion and replied, 'My fears have not been realised...'.[211]

Much of the evidence taken (particularly in 1836) was concerned with the library departments, the number of books and the cataloguing of them; admission to the Reading Room was also much discussed. In terms of numbers, printed books compared unfavourably with those of the public royal collections of many of the European capitals (Panizzi had been to see them in the preparation for just such questions). Panizzi made a great impact with a series of impassioned answers to questions, which reflected his legal and radical background. Pleading for more money for books, he made some of the most resonant statements ever made by a member of staff: '... as to its most important and noble purpose, as an establishment for the furtherance of education, for study and research, the public seem to be almost indifferent'.[212] Apparently at odds with Ellis, he also stated that 'I want a poor student to have the same means of indulging his learned curiosity, of following his rational pursuits, of consulting the same authorities, of fathoming the most intricate inquiry as the richest man in the kingdom, as far as books go, and I contend that Government is bound to give him the most liberal and unlimited assistance in this respect.'[213]

In all this the Department of Antiquities was hardly mentioned. Hawkins was examined, but apart from some snide comments on his qualifications for the job, his examination compared with that of some of his peers was bland.[214] Some interesting facts did, however, emerge. He had not, for example, as head of department, been consulted in any way about the appointment of his assistant, the numismatist C.F. Barnwell.[215] Interestingly, he records a practice that obtains today, that of referring the valuations of objects to outside specialists rather than Museum officers. He also made it clear that the Print Room was in effect autonomous, and when asked whether, in his opinion, it should be made independent, he replied obliquely that if it were to be it would cost money. There was a great deal of discussion about catalogues and a long discussion involving Hawkins, Westmacott and the moulder Sarti, about moulds and copies of objects and coins.[216] Josi, the head of the Print Room, was also examined and seemed reasonably happy with his lot, saying incidentally that, although the Print Room was more accessible in England, students in Paris – which then had a much bigger print room – handled the objects more carefully.[217]

This wordy enquiry, which produced nearly 1,200 folio pages of evidence, in practice exonerated the Museum of any wrong-doing. Its first recommendation must have pleased staff and Trustees:

> *Resolved* 1. That the great accessions which have been made of late to the Collections of the British Museum, and the increasing interest taken in them by the public, render it expedient to revise the establishment of the Institution, with a view to place it upon a scale more commensurate with, and better adapted to, the present state and future prospects of the Museum.[218]

The Committee absolved the staff and Trustees from criticism and said that any imperfections were due to lack of money and space (they had incidentally interviewed Smirke at length about the building).

The other recommendations (numbered as in the report) were (2) to retain the 'Family Trustees' and (3) the official Trustees, although it 'might not be unadvisable' to reduce them in future. The Committee suggested (4) that some of the elected Trustees might resign if they were not sufficiently interested as to attend. Ellis and the others lost the argument about the composition of the elected Trustees; it was urged that the Museum should (5) look for Trustees with 'eminence in literature, science and art'. There should be more departments (6), and each department should have a keeper. It was suggested (7) that the keepers should meet once a quarter to discuss common matters and that (8) the Secretary's post should be separated from the keepership of a department. It was proposed (9) that the Museum should also open in the summer months on public days from 10 a.m. to 7 p.m., and that the reading rooms should open at 9 a.m. Further (10) the Museum should open during Easter, Whit and Christmas weeks, but should not open on Sundays or Christmas and Easter Day. Salaries (11) should be revised and no officer should hold another post in plurality. It was recommended that (12) keepers should combine to produce a better *Synopsis*, and (13) complete catalogues of all the collections of the Museum, 'with little regard' to making money out of them. Importantly (14), all objects should be registered, and (15) a facility should be provided to produce casts from statues, bronzes and coins. Finally (16) – pious hope – Parliament should fund all this.[219]

The Committee was a watershed in the history of the Museum. The Museum's value as a national institution was now officially acknowledged and the Trustees were encouraged to reform it. The Trustees immediately set up a sub-committee 'to report the best method of carrying into effect several of the recommendations made by the Select Committee', which submitted its answer (accepting most of the recommendations) in printed form to Parliament within two weeks.[220] A third Select Committee in 1837 examined Smirke about the building programme; it was chaired by Sir Robert Peel (always an active Trustee of the Museum), met for one day, and laid before Parliament a bid of £226,000 for the completion of the building.[221]

The staff of the Museum were well equipped to take it into the intellectual ferment of the mid-nineteenth century. They were, despite the Tory leanings of some, radical in their intellectual approach. There was still a good mix of senior staff who had not been pressed into the unreformed Oxford and Cambridge mould of classics and mathematics. Ellis, Forshall and Madden had been to Oxford, but Madden had never completed his degree and immediately on appointment successfully asked the Trustees if he might alter his leave arrangements in order to complete the residential qualifications to take his B.A. (Baber, the Keeper of Printed Books, a dyed-in-the-wool Oxford product, chose to retire to his country living after the Select Committee had reported). König had been educated in Germany; Panizzi in Italy, and he was still on appointment as professor at the newly founded anti-establishment institution, University College London. Hawkins had not been to university, nor had his nominal junior, John Thomas Smith (in charge of prints and drawings from 1816 until his death in 1833), who was a pupil of Nollekens and had been a print-maker.[222] Smith's successor, William Young Ottley, came from a slave-owning family and was trained as an artist at the Royal Academy schools. From 1791 to 1798 he had lived in Italy and collected many drawings, some of dubious origin. Returning to London he acted as a kind of amateur dealer and was one of the prime agents in the formation of the great drawings collection of Sir Thomas Lawrence. He was perhaps the greatest connoisseur of his day and wrote two important and original books, one on Italian drawings and the other on engraving. Appointed in 1833, he was in charge of prints and drawings until his death three years later.[223] Ottley was in turn succeeded in 1836 by the first independent Keeper of the Department of Prints and Drawings, Henry Josi,[224] a Dutchman who had worked with his father as a print dealer in London. George Robert Gray, appointed as assistant in the Department of Natural History in 1831, was another member of staff who had not been to university.[225] Most of these men were Fellows of the Royal Society, while Ellis and Hawkins were prominent in the Society of Antiquaries. When one considers the appointment of these men of such diverse background and nationality by patronage of the Trustees, the epitome of the high establishment of Britain (almost to a man educated at Oxford or Cambridge) in a period of reaction, one can only marvel at the Trustees' clear view of the needs of the institution.

At a time when there were few posts in science or antiquity in the universities, and none in archaeology or art history, the senior staff of the Museum were *faute de mieux* the leading professionals of their day. They had good contacts abroad and, in general, boundless energy. The physical proximity of the newly founded University College foreshadowed close collaboration with that radical institution (which had chairs in such subjects as Geography and Italian, not represented at the two ancient universities). Panizzi pursued his exceptional career as librarian, fighting for the enforcement of copyright deposit, for money to purchase foreign books, and for access to the books themselves; he burnt himself out in the process. Madden was a great medievalist and few manuscripts appeared on the market of which he did not have knowledge, although he could not buy them all. Gray and his colleagues in the Natural History sections were to fight their way towards the separation of the collections and the establishment of the Natural History Museum in South Kensington. Chairs were being established in their subjects at London and Cambridge, but formal education in natural history was only just beginning, although in Scotland it had existed for more than a century. A new dawn, however, was on the horizon as the undergraduate Charles Darwin was in the late 1820s being encouraged by John Henslow, Professor of Botany at Cambridge, to look beyond the Linnean system and see plants as living and observable organisms. The British Museum, steeped since Solander and Banks in Linnaeus, had still a central – if sometimes unfashionable – role to play in pure taxonomy. In other areas, however – as in mineralogy – its role was for the time being more innovative. It was also much concerned in the development of stratigraphical and historical geology and in discussions concerning the antiquity of man which were beginning to emerge, for example, in the work of William Buckland (later a Trustee of the Museum) and Georges Cuvier. Most important perhaps was Lyell's *Principles of Geology*, published 1830–3, which provided fodder for the young Darwin and for the archaeologists of the middle of the century.

Hawkins held what was to become the present British Museum in his hand. He tried hard. Within a few months of his appointment he wrote a remarkable memorandum to the Trustees proposing a collecting policy for British antiquities, drawing the attention of the Trustees:

> to the Propriety of appropriating a portion of the new building to the reception of National Antiquities; a letter lately addressed to the Earl of Aberdeen by Mr Markland,[226] the Director of the Soc. of Antiquaries is evidence for the general desire for the formation of such a collec-

tion, and the interest excited by the commencement of one at Edinburgh by the Soc. of Antiq. of Scotland, and by the extensive museum of such objects established at Copenhagen under the auspices of the Danish Government prove that a similar establishment here would be duly valued. Mr Markland proposes that it should be attached to the Soc. of Antiq. but even if the objection of their present want of accommodation were removed, their pecuniary means would scarcely be adequate to its collection, preservation and proper exhibition. The National Museum seems to be the proper receptacle of National antiquities; the appropriation of part of the new building would not be attended with any extra expence, nor would an increased number of officers, attendants or servants be required. It is desirable also that the objects in question should be under the same auspices and the same Roof with the unrivalled collections of MSS and Coins illustrative of our early History which are already deposited in the Brit. Mus.

Should the formation of such a collection be deemed advisable by the Trustees, and should Mr Hawkins be permitted to make known their wishes; he is induced to believe, from enquiries which he has been making for some time past, that several donations and bequests would be made which by the time the new Rooms are compleated would form a collection of considerable interest.[227]

Strong stuff, but much in keeping with antiquarian thought of the day which was beginning to perceive a pattern in the excavations carried out by William Cunnington and Richard Colt Hoare. These men, who have already been referred to, followed in, and developed, the tradition of the gentlemen excavators of the late eighteenth century; men like the Reverend Bryan Faussett, who had dug literally hundreds of Anglo-Saxon graves in Kent between 1757 and 1773,[228] or his slightly younger contemporary James Douglas, an officer in the Royal Engineers, who had excavated similar burials, published in 1793 in his influential book *Nenia Britannica*.

Hawkins's paper was discussed and decision 'postponed' by the Trustees at their next general committee meeting.[229] But Hawkins was not to be put off; he continued to accept gifts of British antiquities and even managed to purchase a number of single objects and small collections.[230] By 1837, however, the housing of British and miscellaneous antiquities was being adumbrated in Parliament and within the Museum a dedicated British display somehow became a *fait accompli*.[231] As Hawkins had pointed out in his memorandum, the Society of Antiquaries was taking a central role in this interest in the prehistoric and Roman past of the British Isles, emulating to some extent the work of their sister society in Edinburgh.[232] Much stimulus was given to this interest by the growth of the railways, which allowed of visits to sites and dealers. The annual meetings of the British Association for the Advancement of Science (founded in 1831 on the model of the Deutscher Naturforscher Versammlung as a meeting place for members of different scientific organizations) were made possible by easier transport, and this gathering of middle-class amateurs (with a sprinkling of aristocrats) and professionals (William Buckland, later a Trustee of the Museum, was the first president) allowed for cross-fertilization between many of the disciplines represented at the Museum and gave serious collectors access to newly found antiquities. Another element in the widening of interest in antiquity was the founding of county archaeological societies in the 1830s and 40s,[233] more or less on the model of the Yorkshire Philosophical Society, established in 1822 (and its museum two years later).[234] The next few years were also to see an increase in the respectability of medieval studies, long pilloried as dusty antiquarianism. The Tractarian movement and the equivalent Cambridge movement with its establishment in 1839 of the Cambridge Camden Society and its successor, the Ecclesiological Society, was to trigger an interest in medieval art at a time when the market for such material was at rock bottom.

Hawkins himself was fast becoming an expert on the English medieval silver coinage and he was to bring out his standard work on the subject in 1841,[235] having left his hard-working, slightly monomaniacal colleague Barnwell to plug away at the Museum's catalogue of Roman coins. The Numismatic Society was founded in 1836 and its journal (one of a number founded in Europe at this period[236]) provided a major outlet for specialist publication. Edward Hawkins, one of nine members of the Museum's staff to join, was its second President,[237] although it drew work away from the Society of Antiquaries in which he was also deeply involved.[238]

Burgeoning nationalism in the Napoleonic period had, particularly in Northern Europe, stimulated an interest in the past of individual countries. It is significant and understandable, therefore, that Hawkins had, in his memorandum to the Trustees, drawn attention to the situation in Denmark, a country crucial in the history of European archaeology and in the development of an understanding of prehistory in national and museum terms.

Northern Influences and Foreign Contemporaries

Denmark had declared itself bankrupt in 1813 and the following years were economically disastrous not only for itself, but also for Sweden and Norway. But the very troubles these countries faced brought about a renewed national vigour through an already well-established national romanticism. Central to the new cultural life of Denmark was an interest in the heroic past and its mythology, first expressed in the writings of Ewald, Grundtvig and Oehlenschläger, and in the paintings of Abilgård and his followers. This interest was soon to be reflected in Sweden and Norway and expressed itself partly in the study of antiquities both in the field and in the museum. In 1806 Rasmus Nyerup and Fr. Münter first advocated the creation of a national collection of antiquities for Denmark and in the following year an antiquities commission was set up by the king, which had as a sub-text the establishment of a universal museum.[239] Nyerup became Secretary and, with the Commission, worked through years that encompassed the bombardment of Copenhagen in 1807, the state bankruptcy of 1813 and the loss of Norway in 1814, to establish a museum in the tower and loft of Trinity Church. When Nyerup retired in 1816, a twenty-seven-year-old merchant, C.J. Thomsen, was appointed as his successor. He it was who arranged the exhibition, and opened the museum in 1819. Thomsen, faced with an inchoate mass of Danish antiquities collected by the commission and drawn from private collections, systematized the objects on the basis of the material from which they were made. He thus predicated a chronology for them which was to introduce the 'Three-Age' system – the division of prehistory into the Stone, Bronze and Iron Ages. While not altogether a new concept, Thomsen established it on a pragmatic basis, first experimentally in the galleries of the museum and then in his guide to the collections, published in 1836.[240] The new Copenhagen Museum – which gradually expanded beyond its original format with the accession of pictures, classical sculpture, a coin cabinet and, importantly, ethnography –

was soon internationally famous and was very much in the mind of the Scottish and London Societies of Antiquaries when Hawkins put his proposal to the Trustees in 1828.

Other museums were gradually springing up in Europe in the wave of nationalism kindled by the Napoleonic wars.[241] Within the Austro-Hungarian Empire the National Museum of Hungary was established in 1802, the National Museums in Prague and Brno in 1818, and those in Zagreb and Ljubljana in 1821. In Graz, the Johanneum, the first public museum in Austria, was founded by the Archduke Johann in 1811. The Hungarian National Museum was very similar in structure to the British Museum, in that it encompassed the embryo national library; but, growing out of national romanticism, it had a collection of Hungarian antiquities from its foundation. The National Museum in Stockholm, established in 1792,[242] was not, however, founded in the same spirit of nationalism. Like the Hermitage Museum in St Petersburg, it was based on the royal collections and (like its Russian contemporary) remained in the royal palace until 1866. In Berlin the Royal (Altes) Museum, also based on the royal collections, was founded in a rather stuttering fashion in the shadow of the instability of the Napoleonic wars. It finally opened its doors in 1830 and became the core of the great complex on the Museumsinsel constructed during the rest of the century.[243] Outside Europe museums were founded on a European model in Calcutta in 1814 and in Cape Town in 1825, inspired by British ideals of Empire as expounded by James Mill. The British Museum was still a distinctive institution, unlike any other; at the time of the first Select Committee report, however, it was struggling to cope with a major building programme, a burgeoning library problem, the beginnings of a collection of British antiquities and the temptations of further work in the countries of the Mediterranean basin.

Further, the British were, as always, looking over their shoulders at France. The comparative material garnered for the 1835 Select Committee included a considerable amount of information about institutions across the Channel. English visitors who flocked to Paris during the Peace of Orleans or after 1814 compared the Louvre, often to its advantage, to the British collections.[244] The Louvre, revolutionized by its minister/director Dominique-Vivant Denon during the Napoleonic period, was beginning to rival the British Museum in certain areas of antiquities. It was used as a propaganda tool by the French to demonstrate their dedication to the idea of a France as the protector of international culture.[245] During the years following the Select Committee report the Louvre was seen as a rival to the British Museum, and it seems highly likely that the energy and money spent by government in obtaining prestigious collections and single antiquities was to some extent a response to this perceived challenge. This may in part explain the vast strides made by the antiquities department of the British Museum during the middle decades of the nineteenth century, which soon filled the new buildings to overflowing.

Chapter 4

PROBLEMS AND SOLUTIONS

1836–60

The Department of Antiquities was clearly understaffed. In 1836 it consisted of a keeper (Hawkins), an assistant (Barnwell) and four attendants.[1] In the late 1830s and early 1840s the Trustees recognized this fact and recruited three new curatorial members of staff, who were to transform the collections and supplement the abilities of the energetic Edward Hawkins. Two of them, Samuel Birch (pl. 15) and Charles Newton (pl. 14), were quite remarkable men by any standard. The former, who was appointed in 1836, as well as being a good sinologist was perhaps the greatest Egyptian philologist the Museum has ever employed.[2] He was to succeed Hawkins as keeper of a much-reduced department in 1861, when the Department of Antiquities was divided. The second, who came to the Museum some four years later, was a towering (and arrogant) force in classical archaeology throughout the middle years of the century (he spent the years 1852–61 in the Consular Service, before being re-employed as Keeper of the new Department of Greek and Roman Antiquities).[3] The third assistant, William Vaux, was a numismatist of considerable distinction who also wrote a popular book, *Nineveh and Persepolis*, which went into many editions, and other books on Middle Eastern and classical antiquities.[4] He was initially much overshadowed by Hawkins, who already had a wide European reputation. Vaux, at the time of the reconstruction of 1861, became keeper of the newly formed Department of Coins and Medals. In 1848 they were joined by Edmund Oldfield, a Cambridge graduate who had become fellow and librarian of Worcester College, Oxford (posts which he retained throughout his Museum career).[5] He was chiefly responsible for the sculpture display, which he mounted with brilliance in a chronological rather than an aesthetic sequence.

This then was the new generation. Newton, Vaux and Oldfield were bright young men straight out of Oxford; Birch's career, however, was more unconventional. Samuel Birch was very much a Londoner; his grandfather had been Lord Mayor and his father was prebendary of St Paul's and professor of geometry at Gresham College. At school he started to study Chinese in the hope of entering the diplomatic service, but, not succeeding in this aim (and without going to university), was employed in the Public Record Office for seventeen months before being appointed to the Museum, where his first job was to register the Chinese coins. Soon, however, Birch turned to Egyptology and was, with the German scholar Richard Lepsius, the first to use hieroglyphic texts to reconstruct the chronology, and therefore the history, of ancient Egypt.

The New Building

Meanwhile Smirke's great design was slowly being completed – a courtyard building fronting on Great Russell Street, flanked by wings which held the officers' residences. The North Wing was opened in early 1838; the ground floor and basement housed the Department of Printed Books and had potential storage for 200,000 volumes.[6] At the east end of the ground floor were two high north-lit rooms with galleries that functioned as reading rooms. Access for readers was initially through a gated lane between two blocks of recently built houses in Montague Place. The geological and mineralogical collections were displayed in galleries on the upper floors.

In the centre of the north side was the so-called Large Room, a vast space, twice as broad as the Reading Room (it measured 24.4 × 27.4 m), which was divided into bays by means of bookcases and large square pillars. To the west of this were two further rooms of the same size as the reading rooms and, in the north-west corner of the building, the elegant Arched Room, added between 1839 and 1841. All these were used for library purposes. Apart from the Arched Room, which still survives (a rare and fine example of a 'three-decker' library, now the Students' Room of the Department of the Ancient Near East), the others have been altered beyond recognition. The Large Room was replaced early in the twentieth century by the North Library (now the Wellcome Gallery), and the other rooms of this range remain only as shells after alterations in the 1930s (they now contain the Mexican and North American collections). To the south of these grand rooms, and parallel to them, was a range of offices and specialist book-stores, with a public staircase in each corner. In 1840–1 the space behind the north-west staircase was developed as another gallery, the Insect Room, in line with the Elgin Room but not joined to it. On the first floor of this extension was the Print Room, 'a large well-lighted apartment'.[7] Josi, the keeper, enthused to the Trustees, writing that, as a result of the better accommodation, the department had in effect become 'a national school of design'.[8]

Only the southern and south-western ranges of the main building remained unfinished. The Trustees now met almost fortnightly to monitor the architect and his work. In March 1842 the Trustees agreed to the demolition of the northern portion of Montagu House.[9] The semi-derelict mansion, once one of the smartest buildings in London, died unloved, and by 1845 had completely disappeared.[10] Attempts to save the painted walls and ceilings failed, although Caygill and Date retail a Museum legend of dirty dealings by the porter, William Scivier (pl. 16), about their sale.[11] Work started on the south range of the new building in July 1842, and by 1846 the south front with its great colonnade of modified Ionic columns, but without its sculptures, was completed, to a great deal of aesthetic disapproval. Smirke, who had started work on the building nearly thirty years before at the height of the Regency, had designed it in a style now unfashionable. The Gothic-loving critic in *The Builder* castigated it appropriately:

> Sir Robert Smirke's conduct in this business leaves him with scarcely one to defend him... The public, if we are to judge by what is said by all its organs, by every authority on matters of art, have well-nigh lost all patience, and are abandoning themselves to the extreme of chagrin and disappointment... The thing is wanting in dignity, in character, in every thing except the most effete and out wrought mannerism; a portico and a pediment as the end of something stuck at the side of something, and the whole hemmed in as if two neighbour

proprietors had taken possession or broken a compact that had enjoined an undisturbed ground vacancy upon which Sir Robert had relied for setting off his building. Then there is the neat range of booking-office or counting-house windows, dignified by a screen façade of columns.

Oh, such botching and patching! We have no words for it.[12]

Thus the reaction to what is now accepted as one of the great buildings of London, an icon among the museums of the nineteenth century. It is recognized as perhaps the greatest Greek Revival building in the country, and it is pleasing that Smirke received the Gold Medal of the Royal Institute of British Architects in 1853, largely on the basis of this building.

The great colonnade of finely cut Portland stone was approached through the old Montagu House screen, across a courtyard with a gravel surface and up a great flight of steps. Entering the Museum through the tall central entrance, the visitor arrived in a main hall paved in Craigleith sandstone relieved by panels of green Italian marble. Its layout reflected the hall of Montagu House. To the left was a grand staircase, lined to the half landing with granite. Here it divided and the two staircases so produced, with their balustrades of Huddlestone stone, rose round a well of light to a top-lit central saloon on the first floor, from which the main display galleries could be reached, as could the medal room and the antiquities offices.[13]

The massive oak doors to the right of the ground floor were at first permanently closed, keeping the vulgar populace from the great rooms that contained the printed books and manuscripts – the Grenville Library, the Egerton room, the King's Library and so on. On the ground floor to the left, through another imposing door, a narrow, gloomy gallery containing Roman and British antiquities, poorly lit by windows from the colonnade, led after 1849 to the board room, the offices and the southern end of the sculpture galleries, containing Egyptian sculpture. Other galleries for classical sculpture were added in the south-west corner. From the middle of the Egyptian gallery a rectangular vestibule led to the Elgin room. Windows on the ground floor and the north staircases were set high in the walls, while light in the upper floors was provided through great wooden-framed skylights set in coffered ceilings. There was as yet no artificial light in the Museum, although there was, unofficially, some gas in the residences. In the 1850s the Assyrian sculpture was installed at the south end of the Egyptian galleries and in a series of newly built galleries along their western side.

In its original form the main entrance hall was not very deep (the original proportions have been restored as a result of the Great Court Scheme of 2000). The coffered ceiling was 'enriched with Greek frets, and other ornaments, painted in encaustic, in various colours most harmoniously blended' – the whole decorative scheme of the hall was designed by Leonard Collman.[14] In normal times it held only three pieces of sculpture – a bust of Banks by Chantrey, Roubiliac's *Shakespeare* and Anne Seymour Damer's *Genius of the Thames*; but, from time to time, it was used to display sculpture and other large objects before space could be found for them elsewhere.[15] A single door led from the hall into the central quadrangle, which was neither used nor seen. Sunless and untidy, this central space was architecturally mean, for Smirke had in 1833 been forced through financial pressure to reduce his plans for its internal porticoes.

The new building had many innovatory elements, not least its central-heating system which, while hit-and-miss by modern standards, generally kept readers and public warm. Ultimately the system chosen by Smirke proved unsatisfactory, but the Museum has never been a cold place.[16] The basements were all barrel-vaulted in brick, the better to carry weight on the floors above and also to act as fire-breaks. Cast iron, clad in plaster, supported all floors and ceilings; and the beams used to hold the floor above the King's Library (see p.80) were repeated throughout the building. The foundations, designed to take heavy sculpture, have generally stood the test of time. Squat cast-iron pillars supplemented the brick vaulting of the basement areas, while massive concrete foundations (between 90 cm and 2 m thick) were used after 1833 in the less stable subsoil of the site. Internally, slate flooring was used in panels along flues and pipe-runs as a precaution against fire – even on the ground floor where many of the floors of the sculpture galleries continued the use of the Craigleith sandstone of the Entrance Hall. The whole building was roofed in copper. The huge Portland stone facings (between five and nine tons in weight) were secured by iron clamps, and iron beams were used to support the entablature. The brick walls of the main galleries were up to six bricks thick, set with mortar of one part lime to three parts of Thames sand.[17]

Internally the upper galleries were lined with glazed mahogany wall-cases designed by Smirke (pl. 22).[18] The general design of these cases continued to be used in a more or less modified form from 1835 until well into the twentieth century (the last were installed in what is now the medieval room in the White Wing, which first became a public gallery after the First World War). Over the years most of these cases have been removed, as they do not conform to modern conservation and lighting requirements nor to the European Union's health and safety regulations; but original cases from the first phase of building have been deliberately retained in the northernmost Greek and Roman Gallery.[19] Smirke also provided the designs for the table-cases (pl. 22). These consisted of glass cabinets of table-like form (measuring approximately 2 × 1 m at the offset base), with a central ridge and gently sloping hinged lids on either side; the main surface elements were of mahogany. They stood on four legs, but could be adapted by replacing the legs with cupboards which gave a more stable base and could also be used for storage.[20] Some remained in use into the 1980s, but have gradually been removed on grounds of security and conservation (a few survive in store or have been given to other museums). The more elaborate table-cases in the King's Library, some of which we know to have been adapted by the addition of cupboards, are almost certainly original.[21] High-quality locks were provided for all the showcases, the method of bolting being changed from time to time. Generally each department had a single suite of locks made by Chubb, a firm that also designed the locking system for all the doors in the Museum. Only with the introduction of more sophisticated cases and the need for ever-increasing security in the course of the late 1970s and 80s were the original locks done away with. Oak benches for the public were also designed by Smirke (pl. 22). Over the years they gradually disappeared, but in the 1980s and 90s reproductions were made for some of the galleries, based on surviving fragments; these may be seen, for example, in the Front Hall.

The senior staff – still housed in the wings of Montagu House – lived in squalor as the buildings were more or less pulled down about their ears; some residences, indeed, were shored up in an effort to make them habitable. The new residences were grand and spaciously planned, but were all of different sizes and, in order to attain a new house to fit their own perceived needs, the Keepers indulged in appeals to the Trustees which gave new meaning to the term 'special pleading'. Hawkins was one of those who tried and failed to get one of the larger houses.[22] Madden, well versed in the art of impassioned letter-writing, attained new heights in July 1847, when he asked the Trustees to grant him, on the grounds of a seniority which only he perceived, the first choice of the residences then becoming available. He asked the Trustees to consider:

> the extreme annoyances, privations, and discomforts, which he and his family have suffered for four years, in being obliged to reside in a portion of the old Museum still standing, during which time the masons' work for hewing stones was carried on close beneath his windows, and not only the insufferable dirt and noise consequent thereon, but the indecencies of the work people and strangers in front of his residence, constantly to be endured...[23]

His complaints proceeded in like vein over a number of foolscap pages: he had received no civility from Smirke; his wife's health suffered, as did his; bugs crept out of the wall; rats ate his linen; the water supply was cut off; there was damp on the ground floor and the general structure of his house was unsound. Needless to say the Trustees refused to recognize his case.

The Museum has always seemed to resemble a building site, but until 1998, when the Great Court Scheme started, it was never as intrusive as in the 1830s and 40s (pl. 18). Railways, blacksmiths' hearths, horse-driven mortar mixers, masons' benches and piles of sand littered the forecourt, as well as the spaces between the residences and the Townley Gallery on the west side of the Museum. Materials from the old building were sold off by public auction.[24] A return of April 1848, when special constables were recruited at the time of the Chartist troubles, showed that 190 workmen were being employed by outside contractors.[25] Much of their activity was recorded in a series of watercolours by George Scharf the elder in the 1840s.[26] Because of the medium his pictures were painted in dry weather and give an almost idyllic picture of the proceedings, although they do illustrate one accident, when the ropes lifting a five-ton girder broke, with miraculously little damage to the workmen.[27] A truer picture of the mess and gloom of the site is perhaps provided by a photograph taken during the demolition of the screen towards Great Russell Street in 1847.[28] Madden's strictures were clearly justified.

The screen and gatehouse on Great Russell Street were replaced by smart new railings on a granite plinth. The great double gates were flanked by a pair of granite piers housing the porters' lodges.[29] Designed by Lovarti, John Evan Thomas and the firm of Collman and Davis, the gates and railings were made in York by John Walker and Sons. The iron gates with their carefully moulded detail each weigh five tons. The spears of the railings were of cast iron and the frieze was wrought. The main pillars of the railing carried gas pipes to a bowl-like torch. The railings, set in a granite base, were originally painted a bronze colour – later changed to Brunswick green, they are now (after a major refurbishment in the 1980s) painted in 'invisible' green with gilded spikes. To prevent people urinating against the wall a low rail was erected some five feet from the main railings, the major supports being crowned by cast-iron sitting lions which have become the symbol of the Museum (engraved, for example, on the inner glass doors of the main entrance).

Designed by Alfred Stevens after a drawing by Smirke, the twenty-five lions were removed when the railings came down. The Trustees allowed copies to be made and these appear outside a number of buildings in London – the Law Society in Chancery Lane, for example. Others appear in some very odd places – as a door-stop in the drawing-room of the Athenæum club in London and (bizarrely in oak) in the chancery of the British Embassy in Mexico City! [30]

The railings and the courtyard, with its two lawns surrounded by stone walls set with cast-iron gas lamps, were completed in 1852. The walls were bordered by pathways of York stone set in the red gravel of the court, while ribbed setts of granite formed diagonal pathways to the various residences. The basement areas in front of the officers' residences were protected by a stone screen, and attention was paid to details, such as the cast-iron foot-scrapers at the bottom of the residences' steps and heavy iron stops to prevent carts rubbing against the Portland stone of the walls.

The final embellishment was the sculptural panel of the pediment of the main colonnade. The commission was given to Sir Richard Westmacott, who had been employed for many years in mounting the sculpture in the Museum (see p.66). His scheme was approved in May 1848 after a great deal of discussion by a committee consisting of Lord Aberdeen, Sir Robert Peel and Dean Buckland. [31] In June Westmacott submitted an estimate for the work of £4,400 and insisted, despite Smirke's sense of urgency, that it would take three years to complete. [32] The tympanum, as it is now rather loosely described, is an elaborate and deep carving which has a meaning of considerable convolution. The description is, however, circumstantial:

> Commencing at the Western end or angle of the Pediment, Man is represented emerging from a rude savage stage through the influence of Religion. He is next personified as a Hunter and a Tiller of the Earth, and labouring for his subsistence. Patriarchal simplicity then becomes invaded, and the worship of the true God defiled. Paganism prevails and then becomes diffused by means of the Arts.
>
> The worship of the heavenly bodies and their supposed influence, led the Egyptians, Chaldaeans and other nations to study Astronomy, typified by the central statue: the key-stone to the composition.
>
> Civilization is now presumed to have made considerable progress. Descending towards the Eastern angle of the Pediment is Mathematics; in allusion to Science now being pursued on known sound principles. The Drama, Poetry, and Music balance the group of the Fine Arts on the Western side, the whole composition terminating with Natural History, in which such objects or specimens only are represented as could be made most effective in Sculpture. [33]

It was originally set against a painted light blue background and certain details were gilded. [34] Smirke had originally suggested other sculptural embellishments to the front of the building, but these had to be abandoned on the grounds of cost; only the pair of marble drinking-fountains on either side of the main entrance were added in 1859. [35]

The Public [36]

The Select Committee, which had so exercised the Trustees in the middle years of the 1830s, had urged greater public access. Opening hours were extended, but still only on three days a week (Mondays, Wednesdays and Fridays); it was not until 1856 that the Museum was opened during the summer months on Saturdays. It was open on most public holidays, but not yet on Sundays, an ambition constantly and agonizingly revisited by the Trustees. As it had become more publicly available, numbers had risen – from about 100,000 in 1831 to over half a million in 1842. During Easter week 1837, immediately after the new regulations were drawn up, 36,223 people visited the Museum and the 1841 Select Committee on National Monuments and Works of Art made approving noises about the progress, while Gray, the go-ahead Keeper of Zoology, stressed its importance to them.[37] Hawkins gave evidence to the same effect but, unlike Gray, did not believe in opening on Sundays.[38] Against this background of a more liberal attitude the annual figure rose – in 1850 it passed the million mark. The Great Exhibition of 1851 brought millions to London, and the British Museum became a popular additional attraction; the King's Library was opened to the public, as were a number of other library rooms, and the visitor figures rose to just over two and a half million.[39] In the following year numbers fell back to 507,000 and did not pass a million again until 1923.

That the Museum had been extremely popular in the years before the Great Exhibition is clearly demonstrated by both the press and the engravings produced for it. Ellis, one of many who continued to be frightened of popular enthusiasm, had written on Boxing Day 1838:

> Staid at home for fear of mischief from the Holiday people who visited us today to the number of more than 8800. We had eight of the Metropolitan Police scattered about our Rooms, to assist in protecting us.[40]

But soon even he had to accept the inevitability of popularity (pl. 20). Easter Monday 1845 was typical. Although more than 5,000 people attended the hanging of the Bethnal Green murderer and others went to Hyde Park and the Polytechnic Institute, *The Illustrated London News* recorded:

> Foremost among the more intellectual recreations of last Monday, must rank a visit to the British Museum; and, if any evidence were wanting to stimulate the liberality of Parliament in voting grants of money for the improvement and increase of this grand national treasury of Nature and Art, the living stream, which passed for hours continuously through the saloons in Great Russell-street, on Easter Monday, would surely have convinced the most obdurate economist; and even William Cobbett, who sneered at the Museum as 'a heap of dead insects', would have been moved by so many of the classes whose interests he claimed most especially to advocate.[41]

Fourteen years later Panizzi was still lamenting the popularity of the Museum in elitist fashion:

> ...many of them [the public] come to the Museum to pass their days comfortably and for no other purpose. They sit down musing, sleeping, reading a book or newspaper which they carry with them, or taking refreshment which they bring in their pocket. They throw what they don't eat on the floors, for instance orange peels in abundance, and the papers in which their victuals were wrapped up; the floors bear abundant marks of the butter and other greasy substances thrown on them.

> Not only are many children brought in who can just walk when led, as they pass before the porters and messengers at the gate and in the hall, and who must immediately after be taken in arms as they cannot move further; but a large number of children from four to ten years of age are brought to see the Museum, or sent to it unattended. These visitors occasionally cry, or run about, chase each other, shout and whistle (whistling is even indulged in by older persons). There is no bazaar in London no respectable shop no exhibition room in which this is allowed.[42]

But Panizzi was out of date, for public demand had become more focused as a result of the Great Exhibition, the importance of which in relation to both the country and the Museum cannot be underestimated. While emphasis was laid on the products – both raw and manufactured materials – of the industrialized nations, there were sections on countries of the Empire and beyond. The East India Company, for example, mounted one of the most successful sections, while the American section was rather thin. Other countries represented included most parts of the Ottoman Empire, China, Brazil and Mexico. Part of the exhibition was devoted to sculpture and the plastic arts, including a remarkable medieval section designed by A.W.N. Pugin. Visitors flocked from Britain and abroad, visitor numbers averaging 42,000 a day, with an entrance fee of a shilling. The railways laid on extra trains to bring people from all over the country, many of them visiting London for the first time in their life and eager to see as much as possible during their stay – hence the rise in attendance at the British Museum.

The results for the Museum were both negative and positive. They were positive in that the public became used to seeing exotic objects from a world outside the cultures of Western Europe, which was to lead to more sympathy for the collection of medieval and ethnographic material. They were negative in that numbers of visitors fell after the glory year. This was not merely due to the fact that there were fewer visitors to London, but because the public had warmed to the new, attractive design of the displays in the Great Exhibition and in any case had more with which to fill their time. Although transport to and within the capital itself was easier and cheaper and although the city's population had grown, the public, having experienced such an innovative show as the Great Exhibition, were becoming more sophisticated as more attractions became available. The National Gallery was now well established, the Museum of Practical Geology had opened in 1835, and the South Kensington Museum, founded in 1852, was soon to become more popular than the British Museum. The London Zoo, which had opened in 1828, although charging an entrance fee, was already by 1835 attracting 200,000 visitors a year. These were but some of many attractions for the general populace; while for the affluent, the annual summer exhibition at the Royal Academy was a social draw. Public parks and open spaces were being created and cared for, providing much needed lungs for leisure activity in London. Other entertainment was provided by the theatres and music-halls, which flourished after the deregulation of the Theatres Act of 1841 (in the second half of the century London theatre audiences totalled 100 million a year), and this, with the vast increase in the number of public houses with their grandiose decoration and comfort, provided well-lit space for much leisure activity. What a contrast to the Museum, which still had no artificial light! It was perhaps at this period that it began to gain its reputation for gloom, one that haunts it to this day. To those who remember it in a winter smog, there was until fifty years ago good reason for such miserable judgements. It might be that this was a contributory factor to the falling off in visitor numbers. Another element was the fact that it was still not open on Sundays – the day most easily available to the working man and his family. Frequent debates in Parliament from the 1840s onwards failed to move the Trustees (who included the Archbishop of Canterbury and the Bishop of London), until 1895 when opposition finally crumbled.[43]

Layard may give a clue to another reason for the fall in the Museum's popularity in a speech in Parliament in 1856: 'there was no place to compare with the British Museum in its resources, but there was no place worse managed. Everything was higgledy-piggledy... There was no system to guide [the visitor]; the people knew not for what purpose they were there; and thus they were without any motive for going again... .'[44] Labelling, for example, was haphazard – some of the geological specimens had printed labels, other labels were hand-lettered. A man called Kenneth Edward Mackenzie was employed as an attendant in the Department of Manuscripts in 1831 and undertook duties as copyist and label writer. Mackenzie was dismissed after a series of adverse reports in 1840, but it is clear that label-writing was in the hands of attendants until the appointment of the freelance Steele family to this task in the third quarter of the century.

The Museum continued to provide a printed guide, the *Synopsis* (which was frequently revised), although it was expensive at a shilling.[45] The last edition (the sixty-third) appeared in 1856 and was replaced in 1859 by the *Guide to the exhibition rooms of the Departments of Natural History and Antiquities*, which was priced at sixpence and was revised until the appearance of the last edition in 1878. Cheaper, unauthorized guides were produced commercially, pirating the *Synopsis* in abbreviated form and minuscule type-faces. Vaux wrote a rather grander and very well illustrated *Handbook*, which was published by John Murray.[46] The Museum provided neither lectures nor educational tours. A Select Committee of Parliament considered this in 1860 and concluded that '... though it would be of the greatest advantage that the meaning of the various collections should be rendered as intelligible as possible to the public, yet it is questionable whether the conversion of the Museum into an educational institution would not be a departure from the principle on which it rests. Your Committee look on the British Museum as primarily being a great consultative repertory'[47] – an elitist sentiment which was to persist and colour the journalistic view of the Museum for many years.

At this distance of time it is impossible to analyse the character and social status of visitors to the Museum in the mid-nineteenth century. We do, however, have some record of the more literate and serious students, not only in the library departments, but also in the rest of the Museum. Visitors to the Prints and Drawings students' room in the 1830s and 40s averaged about 4,000 a year, although in the 1850s and 60s numbers fell back to about 3,000. Visits to the Coins and Medals Room were first counted in 1854, when 1,310 were recorded; by 1860 they had stabilized at about 2,000 a year, these numbers included an increasing volume of interested visitors who wished to examine other small antiquities. It was perhaps more difficult for students to examine antiquities, for they had to work on corners of desks in the studies of the curatorial staff, and they were not enumerated, but there is plenty of testimony to the welcome they received.

Admission of artists to the sculpture galleries had from the beginning of the century been an important part of the Museum's function (pl. 21). The study of sculpture, and of the casts that now started to arrive in the Museum in increasing quantities, attracted students from the Royal Academy schools as well as professional and amateur artists. After 1855 special days were no longer set aside for their visits; artists had to work in the presence of the general public. Between 1830 and 1860 numbers varied between about 6,500 (in 1853) and 2,000 (in 1861, when they began to fall off seriously); in the 1870s they started to rise again, peaking at 15,626 in 1879. The reasons for such variation are difficult to interpret. Fashion among teachers of sculpture, the opening of the cast courts at the Crystal Palace, the development of the cast and sculpture collections at the South Kensington Museum, and the flight of arts students from the perceived tyranny of classical sculpture, the increased interest in the decorative arts, together with fickleness of taste, all presumably contributed to such fluctuation.[48]

The Department of Antiquities

The new building was already too small by the time Smirke's main design was completed in 1851. In the innocent days of 1836, before Panizzi (always voracious in his appetite for book space) got his feet under the table, Forshall, as Secretary of the Museum, could write to Hawkins in the simple belief that the new building would afford space for greatly extended displays and a collecting policy which would fill that space.

> The Trustees having a prospect of obtaining within a short time greatly extended space for the exhibition of the various objects contained in the Museum are desirous to secure the aid of H.M. Government in enlarging the Collections by every means in its power and more particularly through the Officers of the Navy and Army serving on foreign stations and other persons administering the affairs of our Colonial dependencies.
>
> In reference to an intended application to H.M. Government with this view I am instructed to request that you will favor me with any suggestions which in your opinion might be advantageously circulated among the Official persons, to whom I have referred, as to the particular objects connected with the Department under your care which are desirable for the Museum or the manner in which they can best be preserved and transmitted to England.[49]

In a period when all the major government ministers were *ex officio* Trustees of the Museum, a proposal to secure government aid could almost be honoured round its board table and it was not long before expeditions were being planned (with the enthusiastic help of the Royal Navy, whose enquiries had apparently triggered this move)[50] to bring home prestigious antiquities to London. Hawkins and others now cast round for projects.

The first major undertaking emerged through the energy of Charles Fellows, a rich amateur who had travelled in Asia Minor and discovered the ruined remains of Xanthos, the chief town of ancient Lycia. In 1839 he published the results of his first journey.[51] Hawkins clearly knew him (he lived close to the Museum) and early in that year urgently asked the Trustees to agree to the acquisition of sculptures from the site. So urgent did the opportunity appear to be that he pointed out that, if a letter were sent at once, it would catch the Admiralty despatches which would leave that same night for the British fleet in the eastern Mediterranean, where a Lieutenant Graves would be able to deal with their removal.[52] In a private letter to Forshall, Hawkins wrote that Sir John Barrow, Secretary to the Board of the Admiralty, felt that his Board would agree to a request from the Trustees. Hawkins also warned Forshall that the French had heard about the find and 'might antici-pate us'.[53] The Trustees, inspired by his enthusiasm, agreed to ask the Admiralty to instruct Graves 'to employ such measures as can with propriety be adopted for the removal of any of these Antiquities which seem to him to deserve the labour and expense'.[54]

Not for the first or last time did the Trustees (in this case particularly W.R. Hamilton and the Marquis of Northampton)[55] allow the enthusiasm of a member of staff to carry them away. Lord Minto, First Lord of the Admiralty, was, however, an experienced and cautious politician and first consulted the Prime Minister, Palmerston, who said that the matter should not proceed without a *firmân* from the Sultan. This he would try to obtain through the ambassador in Constantinople; Hawkins was reprimanded for talking directly to officials without formally going through the Trustees.[56]

In the weeks that followed Fellows set off on another trip to Lycia accompanied by George Scharf the younger, who was to act as draughtsman. The Sultan as usual procrasti-nated and the Trustees began to worry when Fellows reported that the French, Austrians and Prussians were all interested in the site and that the price for the removal was going up.[57] At last, on 25 September 1841, they were informed that a *firmân* had been granted and that the work of getting the sculptures to London quickly had been set in hand.[58] The first tranche finally arrived in December 1842, and Westmacott was employed to clean and mount them temporarily in the Phigalian Room.[59] The Trustees were so pleased with their acquisitions (among them the 'Lion Tomb', dated c.600–575 BC, and the 'Harpy Tomb', dated c.480 BC) that they immediately proceeded to set up another expedition, which was triumphantly completed with the arrival in late 1844 of more sculptures (including the Nereid Monument, dated c.390–380 BC, the most spectacular of the Xanthos monuments; and the Payava tomb, dated c.375–360).[60] Fellows was knighted for his part in the Xanthos acquisitions and a publication of the site was begun but never completed.[61] The Lycian room, which had been built for the display of this sculpture to the south of the Elgin room, was completed in 1845 and Hawkins, Westmacott and Fellows were asked to submit a proposal for the layout of the items.[62] The mounting of them was, however, handed over to Westmacott, despite protests from Fellows and Hawkins, whose more correctly archaeo-logical ideas for their display were overruled. The newly appointed assistant, Charles Newton, who was in the centre of this fight, thus had his first experience of dealing with the complications of major acquisitions of classical sculpture.[63]

Meanwhile the Trustees had been busy collecting in more normal fashion by purchase and gift. The main acquisitions in the 1830s and 40s were either classical or Egyptian. Month after month the Trustees considered the purchase, gift or transport of material to the Museum from the Mediterranean. Some ideas were bizarre: in 1839 a Mr G.G. Kelly offered, in no specific fashion, to bring home Cleopatra's Needle to the Museum, but the Trustees 'had no intention to take any steps at present with a view to the removal of this obelisk'.[64] One of the most important acquisitions was the purchase of a major part of the Durand collection of Greek vases.[65] The Danish antiquary P.O. Brøndsted was consulted by the Trustees and with Hamilton prepared a report on the collection. Brøndsted described it as 'the finest and most valuable treasure of ancient Greek painted Vases and terra cottas now in Europe, with the single exception perhaps of the Royal Museum at Naples... [judicious purchase at the Durand sale] might raise the Collection of

Vase and Terra Cottas in the Br. Mus. from a mere object of curiosity to a useful, instructive and classical collection'.[66] Brøndsted and Hawkins were sent to Paris to buy the collection at auction.[67] The Trustees applied for a Treasury grant of £4,000 for the purchase and spent 77,550 francs at the auction (just over £3,000).[68]

Brøndsted, one of the most distinguished classical antiquaries of his day, was the adviser to King Christian VIII of Denmark, who had amassed a considerable collection of antiquities, now forming the basis of the Danish National Museum's Greek and Roman collection. Brøndsted was clearly torn two ways. 'How often', he wrote from Paris, 'have I not thought, most gracious sir, of your collection. It made me deeply sad that I could not obtain these marvellous things for my Prince.'[69] This experienced courtier and traveller was not, incidentally, above a little genteel smuggling. He was roundly condemned by the Trustees for including a packet of '5 or 6 dozens of silk stockings for ladies' in the cases that brought the collection from Paris. The Treasury was not amused and in orotund terms regretted the incident and ordered the confiscation of the offending items.[70]

In 1839 an important decision was made about the Museum's collection of papyri. Although Madden had begun a catalogue of this material, which was at that time in the care of the Department of Manuscripts, it was clear that the speciality in Egyptian papyri lay with the Department of Antiquities and particularly with Samuel Birch. Despite a certain amount of growling on the part of Madden, the hieroglyphic, demotic and hieratic papyri were transferred to the Department of Antiquities on the somewhat specious grounds that there was more space for them there.[71]

With Hawkins in charge there was no lack of new acquisitions of coins and medals, mostly obtained by judicious purchase. Some of these purchases required special grants from the Treasury, and quite often such grants seem to have been forthcoming. In 1850/1, for example, a year in which the Department of Antiquities acquired 2,553 coins and medals of more normal sort, the Museum was granted £1,050 to buy a collection of nearly 1,000 gold coins, collected by an Egyptian, Ibrahim Pasha.[72] Sometimes the Trustees were not so fortunate, as with the Pembroke collection, when they had themselves to foot a bill of £1,271.[73]

Early in 1838 the Trustees tackled one of the most important problems of coin collecting – Treasure Trove. This was one of the regalities of the Crown administered in most of England by the Treasury, but where applicable by the chancellors of the duchies of Cornwall and Lancaster. Under this ancient law the Crown claimed all precious metal found in the ground having been deposited in the ground *animus revertendi* (with the intention of retrieval):

> ... respecting the Coins found at Lewisham, the Secretary was directed to draw up a letter to the Lords of the Treasury, to the Chancellor of the Duchy of Lancaster and the Lord Warden of the Duchy of Cornwall, expressing the anxious wish of the Trustees to be permitted, upon all occasions of Treasure trove, the selection of such Coins and other Antiquities as are desirable for the National Museum.[74]

The Duchy of Cornwall appears not to have replied to this appeal, while the Treasury cautiously acknowledged the Trustees' right to be consulted.[75] The Duchy of Lancaster enthusiastically stated that it would certainly pass all such material to the Museum.[76]

These approaches showed remarkable prescience, for within three years the Museum received much of one of the biggest finds of treasure trove as a gift from the Queen in her capacity as Duke of Lancaster. The vast Viking hoard from Cuerdale, on the banks of the River Ribble, was found on 15 May 1840 and was claimed as treasure trove by the Duchy of Lancaster.[77] The hoard, which was buried about 905, is the largest Viking silver hoard yet known from the Scandinavian homeland or from the Scandinavian settlements in the west. It consisted of some 7,500 coins and about 1,000 fragments of silver bullion, some in the form of ingots, some being 'hack-silver' (cut-up fragments of silver objects). Not all the coins and other objects from the hoard came to the Museum (although the vast majority did), but it remains a spectacular find and a fascinating attraction to visitors. Later finds of treasure trove did not always come to the Museum so easily, as the Treasury later demanded (and still demands) payment by the purchasing body of the full market value of the find; but the Museum has since the middle of the nineteenth century been deeply involved in the administration of this arcane medieval law, which was revised by Parliament in 1996.[78]

That the Scottish law of Treasure Trove (whereby all objects found in the soil can be claimed by the Crown) was not working at this period is demonstrated by the fact that the Trustees were able to acquire one of their most famous groups of antiquities in 1832 by purchase – the twelfth-century chessmen probably made in Scandinavia and found on the Isle of Lewis. Frederic Madden records most graphically the moment they appeared:

> Sir Walter Scott came at two o'clock and stayed about an hour with me. I had the pleasure of looking over with him a set of very curious and ancient chessmen brought to the Museum this morning for sale, by a dealer from Edinburgh named Forrest... They... are the most curious specimens of art I ever remember to have seen... There are 82 pieces of different descriptions, all made (apparently) of the teeth of the sea-horse, or morse, of which number 48 are the superior chess-men – forming parts of four or five sets, but none of them perfect *per se*, although two complete sets can be selected from them... an ivory buckle was also discovered with them... they will require some research and as the whole probably will be engraved in the Archaeologia, shall say nothing more of them here.[79]

The dealer was beaten down from a hundred to eighty guineas and, in making a case for their purchase, Hawkins wrote, 'There are not in the Museum any objects so interesting to a native Antiquary as the objects now offered to the Trustees'[80] – a serious comment to a board whose members were still attuned to the ancient Mediterranean. A further eleven pieces subsequently turned up and are now in the National Museums of Scotland. The Lewis chessmen have indeed become one of the most popular images of the Museum. Copies of them, marketed by the Museum's publication company, are sold throughout the world and pirated copies are found in airport shopping malls and souvenir shops everywhere (they have even appeared on the label of a brand of Norwegian spirits).

Then there was ethnography to be dealt with. The ethnographical collections had long been a cuckoo in the nest as they gradually took up more and more space in the Museum. They were transferred to the Department of Antiquities between 1836 and 1839.[81] A gallery dedicated to them was provided in the new building in 1844 and so urgent was the problem of accommodation that the Trustees, not always generous in such matters, agreed to Hawkins's request for extra showcases at a cost of £2,250.[82]

Hawkins, perhaps mindful of his defeat over national antiquities, made no attempt to form a department to look after the ethnographical material. He does, however, seem to have discussed the possibility in private. In 1842 a letter was received in the Department of Antiquities in which Henry Syer Cuming proposed himself as curator of the ethnographical collections, which implies that the idea was in the air:

> You must doubtlessly remember that I have frequently conversed with you upon the subject of *Ethnography*; and if I mistake not, you have expressed the same regret that I feel, that there is not a *National Collection* to illustrate the subject. I therefore now most anxiously appeal to you for your opinion and advice... in forwarding our views as to the formation of such a collection.
>
> I know you have spoken of the disinclination on the part of the Trustees of the Museum, to purchase modern works of art; you have also spoken of want of space, and of officers having sufficient and more than sufficient to do.[83]

There was clearly, in Hawkins's opinion, no point in pursuing the matter; but he continued to recommend ethnographical acquisitions to the Trustees (although hardly anything was purchased).

Assyria

The Museum in the early 1840s had begun to venture into the field of Assyrian antiquities.[84] We have seen that in 1824 it had acquired its first cuneiform tablets and inscriptions from Claudius Rich.[85] The interpretation of these inscriptions was, however, proving elusive, although a Dane, Carsten Niebuhr, who had copied inscriptions at Persepolis during his visit to the region in 1765, and a German, G.F. Grotefend, had made great strides towards interpretation – indeed Grotefend had cracked the problem in 1802, but his startling discoveries were not made public because he was not academically acceptable to Hanoverian academe. Other Danes, N.L. Westergaard, Christian Lassen and the polymathic philologist Rasmus Rask (who published a correct recognition of some elements of the Persepolis inscription in 1826), and the Frenchman E. Burnouf, brought the problem nearer to solution. It was, however, an English soldier in the service of the East India Company, Henry Creswicke Rawlinson, who was the real founder of Assyrian studies.[86] As military adviser to the Shah of Persia's brother, the governor of Kurdistan, 1835–7, he found himself stationed within thirty kilometres of the Rock of Bisitun, long known for its carvings and the enormous cuneiform inscription cut on a prominent cliff face in three languages, Old Persian, Elamite and Babylonian. Rawlinson set himself to copy the first two inscriptions and began to interpret them, publishing the first of a number of papers on them in 1838. (Later, in 1847, as British Resident in Baghdad, he was able to take squeezes – papier mâché impressions – of the Babylonian text, which survived in the British Museum until late in the century, and enabled the readings to be checked.) Rawlinson, because of the prominent position he later achieved and because of his subsequent publications, has rather overshadowed the reputation of Edward Hincks, an Irish parson, who worked for a short time in the Museum and who is now being seen as one of the most perspicacious of cuneiform scholars of this period. Hincks was not well regarded by Rawlinson, who considered him a poacher on private preserves, but his reputation is now undergoing re-assessment.[87]

Sir Stratford Canning (later Lord Stratford de Redcliffe) was, however, the most influential motor behind the development of the British interest in Assyriology. Canning, who had long experience as a diplomat in the Ottoman Empire during the Napoleonic wars and later, was appointed ambassador to the Sublime Porte in 1841, where he remained, with short breaks, for sixteen years. Much interested in the archaeology of the empire to which he was ambassador, he had in 1842 at his own cost employed as a kind of secretary/counsellor a young Englishman, Henry Layard,[88] who had travelled much in the Levant and had become interested in the Assyrian mounds. In 1845 Canning sent Layard to excavate Nimrud, the site of the ancient city of Calah, capital of Assyria after Ashur and before Khorsabad and Nineveh.

But the French were there first. Rich's collections had included two small fragments of carved stone from Nineveh and his study of the site itself convinced Jules Mohl, one of the secretaries of the French Société Asiatique, to encourage the French government to found a consulate in Mosul for the express purpose of excavating the Nineveh mounds. An Italian-born French consular agent, Paolo Emilio Botta, was appointed to this post and it was he who would introduce the world to the splendours of Assyrian sculpture.[89] In 1842 he started private excavations at Kuyunjik, the largest of the mounds of Nineveh but initially unproductive. Disappointed there, he had, in 1843, turned to another of the mounds, Khorsabad, and had uncovered numerous rooms and corridors in the palace of the Assyrian king Sargon II dated to c.710 BC, decorated with splendid scenes of gods, kings and battles, as well as winged bulls flanking the doorways. With great difficulty some of these sculptures were transported to Paris, where they caused a sensation when they arrived in December 1846. (In 1849 Rawlinson purchased from the French consul two of the largest sculptures – a human-headed winged bull and lion, each weighing 16 tons – for the British Museum and sent them to London.) A whole new civilization with fabulous images was emerging and the French government backed Botta's efforts with substantial money – apparently some £30,000.[90] Botta had discussed the finds at Kuyunjik with Layard and had generously allowed both Layard and Canning to read and copy his reports as they passed through Constantinople on their way to Paris.

Layard needed all his experience of wheeling and dealing in the Ottoman Empire to use to its best advantage his firmân to dig at Nimrud. Knowledgeable about the subject, he was also extremely lucky, almost immediately discovering, very close to the surface, rooms panelled with cuneiform inscriptions and then many sculptured rooms of the palace of Ashurnasirpal II (883–859 BC). He continued to excavate through the spring and summer of 1846, while Canning was obtaining permission to ship the new finds back to England and was trying to persuade the British government to take over responsibility for the excavations (and incidentally to reimburse the money advanced to Layard).

After considerable negotiation a grant of £2,000 (half the sum requested) was channelled through the Museum to enable Layard to continue his work at Nimrud. Having been offered and refused a fee of £500,[91] Layard complained at length about the amount of money available (as did his ally Rawlinson), but was generally treated by the Museum, in the person of the Secretary, Forshall, with extreme tact. Forshall advised him on how to write letters and often accompanied the Trustees' instructions with friendly, disarming covering notes.[92] The Trustees were conscious of the need to preserve the site, Forshall wrote to Canning:

> Mr Layard... shd be extremely careful not to do any injury whatever to those parts of the ancient monuments wh. he may not think fit to remove, but having taken Casts, Rubbings or Drawings, as the case may require of such parts, to cover them again with the soil & leave them as secure as he can for the investigation of future enquirers.[93]

Layard pointed out that this would add considerably to the cost,[94] but was perhaps not quite as shocked as his communications with the Museum would suggest; he wrote to his mother in March 1847:

> ... You need not be vexed about my affairs with people at home. I think I shall be able to do as much as I wish, and fully as much as, if not more than, the Trustees of the British Museum can reasonably expect. The last post has brought, in some respects, more satisfactory communications from England, and, on the whole, I think I ought to be content with what I have got ...[95]

Continuing his excavations in November 1846 with the aid of a local assistant, Hormuzd Rassam,[96] Layard revealed more and more sculpture. One of his most famous finds was the black obelisk of Shalamaneser III (858–824 BC), which depicts foreign princes bringing tribute to the king, and which played a major part in the decipherment of the cuneiform script. In 1851 Layard published an abridged account of his first results in Murray's *Reading for Rail* series, which became one of the great publishing successes of the middle years of the nineteenth century and told of his journeys in the Middle East and of his excavations up to 1847.[97] Meanwhile he had returned home, to find that the first fruits of his excavation had preceded him and were on show. His name was on everyone's lips; he was given an honorary degree by Oxford and was seen at fashionable dinner parties throughout London. Unusually, he was called into a Trustees' meeting, where the chairman, the Duke of Cambridge, 'conveyed to him the best thanks of the Trustees for his zealous, successful and in every respect satisfactory services'.[98] On the recommendation of the Trustees, Palmerston appointed him as attaché at Constantinople and seconded him to the Museum.[99]

He lobbied Palmerston and the Museum for more money, particularly for the publication of the finds. But 1848 was the year of revolutions and unrest throughout Europe and money was not easy to obtain. In despair, on 7 March 1848 he wrote to the English merchant Henry Ross, who was then at Mosul and in temporary charge of the excavations at Nimrud:

> Pray order the sculptures at Nimroud to be covered in. The Museum people are very desirous that what remains should be preserved. I think I mentioned in my last letter that they wished to continue the excavations, though not to spend more than £10 a month at present... The recommendation of the Trustees that £4,000 should be given by Government for the publication of my drawings, which would have been attended to at any other period, has been rejected, and I am inclined to think that nothing will be done. I am now trying to see what may be done in the way of subscriptions and personal sacrifices.... [100]

Gradually more money was screwed out of a reluctant Treasury and Layard returned to Nimrud and to Nineveh. By 1851, the year in which he withdrew from fieldwork to pursue what was to be a successful diplomatic and political career,[101] Layard calculated that more than 3,000 yards of the sculptured walls of Sennacherib's palace at Nineveh had been uncovered. The building also produced the tablet library of Sennacherib's grandson, Ashurbanipal (668–627 BC), the foundation of much modern knowledge concerning life and thought in ancient Assyria.

Rassam continued to work in Assyria under the Museum's auspices with the benevolent encouragement of Layard and, more importantly, Rawlinson (who later became a Trustee). In 1853 Rassam discovered at Kuyunjik the finest of all the sculpture-ornamented palaces, that of Ashurbanipal, retrieving from it, among other things, the splendid and justly famous scenes of a lion hunt. Rassam left Mosul (although he was to return later) in 1853, the year in which the Assyrian Exploration Fund was founded. Under their auspices W.K. Loftus started work at Warka in southern Iraq, and then, at the Museum's expense, tidied up at Nineveh.

Much of the material found was transported to London with difficulty by the Royal Navy, the East India Company and even through the diplomatic bag. Its arrival made a tremendous impact. The press was interested and the *Illustrated London News*, after a spat with the Museum and Layard,[102] published various drawings of the sculptures as they arrived.[103] The sculptures were installed (pl. 15) in what is known as the Assyrian transept at the south end of the Egyptian Sculpture Gallery and in two long narrow galleries specially prepared for them on the west side of this room, to the north and south of a central saloon also dedicated to Assyrian sculpture. After long battles with the Trustees, Edmund Oldfield, backed by Hawkins, gained general agreement to his plans to display the Assyrian sculptures in a reasonably logical sequence. The galleries were finally opened to the public in 1854. Later, other rooms were added, particularly the Assyrian basement to the west of these two galleries, now much remodelled.[104]

The public was fascinated and the learned world was intrigued and astonished by the skill of the Assyrian sculptors who worked long before the masters of fifth-century BC Greece produced what was then considered the greatest art of all time. Further, the Museum's publication of Layard's *Inscriptions in the cuneiform character*,[105] in 1851, and the subsequent five-volume work by Rawlinson, *Historical inscriptions*,[106] under various titles, began to build up the history of the hitherto mysterious Assyrians. These publications also fuelled discussion and controversy in biblical studies, as events and names as far back as 2500 BC were recognized, and legends – particularly that concerning the Flood – were drawn out of the texts.

Prints and Drawings [107]

Henry Josi was appointed Keeper of the newly created Department of Prints and Drawings in 1836 at the age of thirty-four. Between his appointment and his death in 1845 he revolutionized the department, which had coasted along under Smith and for a short time under an ageing Ottley. He had a background in the print trade and his many connections there were extremely useful to the Museum. His first project, in accordance with the wishes of the Select Committee, was the preparation of a new inventory. When it was completed in 1837, 9,302 drawings and 45,752 prints had been registered. At this point he adopted the new Museum cataloguing system, apparently invented by the natural historians, whereby the elements of an inventory number, say 1837,1–1,3, represent first the year (1837), second the month of the Trustees' meeting at which the item was reported (January), third the day or the number of the acquisition within that month, and last the number of the item within the group acquired. Two long papers which Josi wrote for the Trustees cover, in detailed fashion, the storage, arrangement and condition of the print collection, incidentally throwing light on the users of the Print Room. One group of visitors wish

> merely to hunt out a subject… These persons naturally care little about the beauty of impression, earliness of state or intrinsic value of the prints, beyond the subject it represents… The second class of visitors come to compare the work of the engraver. They include collectors, connoisseurs, and the numerous body of engravers.[108]

The Trustees were asked to allow the Keeper to 'enlarge the collection by increasing the works of our English school of engraving, in which branch of art the P[rint] R[oom] is deficient, and the first demand made by foreign and country visitors is to see the British school of engraving'. Throughout his short career Josi, however, was interested in acquisition far beyond this narrow range.

While still in the Department of Antiquities, acting as Assistant in the place of the dying Ottley, Josi started to build the collections up to the international status they were to attain by the time of his death. His first step in this direction was to recommend the purchase of the Sheepshanks collection. John Sheepshanks (1787–1863) is best remembered for his bequest of a large collection of English paintings – intended to form a National Gallery of British Art – to the South Kensington Museum. From a Yorkshire milling background, he had started to collect pictures in a modest fashion in his mid-thirties. His first serious foray into the prints and drawings market was at the 1824 sale of the collection of Count Moritz von Fries, and from then until 1828 he travelled widely on the Continent improving his print collection, particularly of Netherlandish prints and drawings. By the early 1830s he had become bored with works on paper and in 1836 he sold the collection – totalling 7,666 prints and 812 drawings – to the London dealer William Smith, who placed it on offer for £5,000. Josi, having called the attention of the Trustees to its availability, organized a series of letters to the Museum supporting its purchase, which, in the words of Antony Griffiths, demonstrated 'patriotic pride, and the potential usefulness of prints to modern English artists'.[109] As the result of this lobbying and on the basis of two reports by Josi,[110] supported by the signatures of thirty-seven artists ranging from Maclise to Cotman and Landseer,[111] the Trustees approached the Treasury for the full purchase price, a sum quickly voted by Parliament (the first sum to be voted for the purchase of works on paper). We shall never know whether the decision not to purchase the Lawrence collection of drawings for the National Gallery (which was being considered by the government at this time) was in any way influenced by this major purchase, particularly as the special grant for the Sheepshanks collection was being negotiated at the same time as the Trustees were trying to raise money for the Durand purchase.[112]

Using dealers, particularly William Smith and to a lesser extent Colnaghi and others, Josi now made a series of purchases at a period when the art market was in recession. He also bought at auction. In 1837, at the sale of the collection of his predecessor William Ottley, he bought, among other things, nineteen early Italian nielli.[113] He made numerous purchases for the Museum, culminating in February 1845 with the acquisition of 1,807 German prints through a special Treasury grant for £2,880.[114] Later in that year Josi died and his successor and close friend, William Hookham Carpenter, immediately initiated the purchase (again with a major Treasury grant) of the Coningham collection of 848 Italian prints for £4,200.[115] Josi had been successful in obtaining a departmental purchase grant from the Trustees, who were beginning to recognize the importance of the collection. Between 1835 (when the first grant was made to the department) and 1847 the annual grant rose from £100 to £1,200, a sum not exceeded until after the Second World War.[116]

Carpenter, who now became Keeper, built on the work of his predecessor and consolidated it.[117] His father had been a bookseller of some repute who specialized in books on art, and his son followed him into the business (he did not go to university). He could afford to give up bookselling and for a number of years haunted the Print Room at the Museum, during which time he wrote a substantial book on van Dyck.[118] Appointed Keeper of Prints and Drawings in 1845, he held the post until his death twenty-one years later. The collections grew dramatically. 1849 may be taken as a typical year: Felix Slade gave forty-one proofs of Turner's 'Views in England and Wales'; Ernst Harzen of Hamburg presented three rare early German prints and fifteen etchings by modern German and English artists; a Girtin watercolour was given by Chambers Hall. Most important was the outstanding collection of a hundred prints by Lucas van Leyden given by Henry James Brooke, many from the Denon collection.[119] Among other prints purchased in that year were works by Thomas Stothard, an impression of a niello ascribed to Peregrini, a number of prints by Cranach, Altdorfer, Claude, van Dyck and Murillo, and a collection of English portraits, broadsides and satirical prints from the collection of the Duke of Buckingham. It is noteworthy that contemporary or near-contemporary artists were being represented in the collections as a matter of policy, on a substantial scale; indeed, in 1865 Carpenter was to purchase four etchings by Edouard Manet.

Occasionally there was an opportunity to buy more substantially. Some major drawings from the Lawrence collection were, for example, purchased with the aid of a special Parliamentary grant of £2,273 in 1860 at the Woodburn sale. In 1854 Carpenter was even sent to Venice to report on an album of drawings by Bellini, which was purchased in the following year.[120] He did, however, fail to convince the Trustees that they should buy drawings (which included many from the Lawrence collection) at the King of Holland's sale in 1850.[121] Typical of the smaller, but important, purchases, was the acquisition in 1859 of works of Michelangelo from the Buonarroti collection (a purchase that included three wax models and a number of manuscripts). These were bought from the family, with the aid of Sir Charles Eastlake (a Museum Trustee as President of the Royal Academy) and his wife, in two tranches: the first for £110 and the second for £400, Carpenter valuing the drawings of the latter collection at £56 (the rest being made up of the manuscripts, valued by Madden at £350).[122]

From 1836 to 1866 over £50,000 was spent on acquiring prints and drawings. The work of the department was of such a standard and the collections so splendid that the Royal Commissioners of 1850 in an unusual burst of bonhomie stated, 'Of the condition and management of this department we are able to speak with very unreserved approbation'.[123]

Alarms and Excursions

On 7 February 1845, a bitterly cold day (it was the day Josi died), Madden and Hamilton were examining a manuscript when a messenger appeared and told them that 'an accident had happened to the Portland Vase! On proceeding up to the Room where it was exhibited, I found it strewed on the ground in a thousand pieces, and was informed that a short time before a young man who had watched his opportunity when the room was clear, had taken up one of the large Babylonian stones, and dashed the Vase, together with the glass cover over it, to atoms!'[124]

Hamilton and Ellis both wrote to the Duke of Portland and received two courteous letters in reply, displaying aristocratic *sangfroid* and indifference to punctuation:

> ... I beg you to assure the Trustees that I have no doubt that the breaking of the Barberini Vase is a misfortune against which no vigilance could have guarded it on the part of the Officers of the Museum.
>
> The indiscriminate admission of Visitors which they cannot control – which has been forced on the trustees makes perfect security impossible. I have no doubt that the man who broke the vase, whoever he is is mad... It is perhaps fortunate that his madness has shewed itself in the way it has done instead of some injury to human Life.[125]

The miscreant was taken to Bow Street police station. Here, under what turned out to be the false name of Edward Lloyd, he was sentenced to a fine of £3 or two months in jail for wilfully damaging the glass cover of the vase (a quirk of the law would not allow him to be charged for shattering the vase itself). His fine was paid for him by an unknown man and he disappeared from view. Later research revealed that his real name was William Mulcahy, a drop-out from Trinity College Dublin.[126]

In a further series of communications the Trustees, after a special meeting on 8 February, told the Duke 'that in the opinion of several persons who have seen the fragments of the vase it may not be impossible to put them together again so as to give a good idea of what the Vase was'.[127] A large number of people of many nationalities, many with patent adhesives of their own, offered to repair the vase, but the Trustees decided to use one of their own regular restorers, John Doubleday, and were able to write to the Duke on 1 November that the work was complete, 'more perfect than the Tr[ustee]s could have anticipated'. The Trustees paid Doubleday an extra £25 for his pains![128] Doubleday's work survived for nearly a hundred years, when, some small missing fragments having been discovered, the whole object was taken to pieces and restored once again by J.W.R. Axtell, a member of the Museum's conservation staff. The adhesive he used proved, however, to be unstable and a total reconstruction (this time properly recorded) was undertaken with great skill in 1988–9 by two other members of staff, Nigel Williams and Sandra Smith.[129]

Vandalism of a more ordinary sort was endemic. In 1857:

> A person called William Thomas was... convicted... at Bow Street of having defaced the banisters of the great stair-case of the Museum and fined £1 or fourteen days imprisonment. The man alleged that he saw so many names already written that he thought there was no harm in adding his own – a plea to which the Magistrate seemed to attach some weight. Mr Panizzi suggests that the parts of the banisters scribbled on be made good at once and put in such a state that any new writing may be at once visible and inexcusable.[130]

Thefts were surprisingly rare – or possibly rarely discovered. A serious loss was reported to a special meeting of the Trustees by Ellis on 4 April 1849:

> Sir Henry Ellis... was suddenly surprised at reading in a Newspaper that a Foreigner had been committed on the previous day to custody at Bow Street under remand for a Robbery of Coins, of great extent, at the British Museum... No notice, however, of such Robbery had been given to Sir Henry Ellis... previous to his seeing the Transaction in the Newspaper.[131]

People rushed here and there. Ellis saw the Archbishop of Canterbury. Sir David Dundas and W.R. Hamilton (two of the most active Trustees) turned up at the Museum, sent for the Dean of Westminster in order to discuss the matter, and constituted themselves a committee. Hawkins was asked to close the Medal Room until a special meeting of the Trustees could be convened. By one o'clock they had been joined by the Archbishop, Lord Breadalbane, Lord Mahon, Sir Robert Peel, Henry Goulbourn, Dr Paris and Macaulay.[132] Newton and Burgon (who had apparently reported the matter to the authorities without telling Ellis) were told to liaise with the police. The Museum's solicitor was instructed to take steps.

At the meeting it appeared that the man arraigned was a Mr Timoleon Vlasto, and Hawkins was called in and examined concerning him. It had emerged that Vlasto had also robbed a General Fox, who appeared before the Trustees with his solicitor. The Trustees set up a sub-committee, consisting of Hamilton, Goulbourn (a former Chancellor of the Exchequer) and (a real heavyweight) Peel, to look into the matter and to tighten up security – which they did with a vengeance. The coins (worth some £2,000) were all recovered; Vlasto pleaded guilty and was transported for seven years.

The Museum since the Gordon riots had been acutely conscious of the threat of mob violence and in the year of revolution it caught this fever again. The Chartist demonstration of 10 April 1848, so far as the Museum was concerned, contained more than an element of farce. Part of the Chartist procession was to assemble in Russell Square, and Ellis, like many in London, wished to be prepared. He consulted widely and sought outside aid. Troops and Chelsea pensioners were drafted in, and more than 250 members of staff and workmen engaged on the new building were sworn in as special constables, while an officer of the Royal Engineers advised on the erecting of barricades and produced a memorandum and a drawing showing lines of communication.[133] Forgetting his revolutionary past, Panizzi became the leader of the defenders and was in his element. Never one to discard a cliché, he encouraged his troops with the slogan 'England expects that every man this day will do his duty'! Touring the building like an experienced company commander, Panizzi examined weak entry points and fields of fire; stones from the builders' yard were raised to the roof to be dropped on the mob in case the outer defences were breached, and fire-engines, stretchers and medical supplies were on hand.[134] Scouts were despatched to report the actions of the enemy.

One of his most difficult members of staff, Edward Edwards – the great proponent of public libraries, later sacked on Panizzi's recommendation over a series of professional disagreements – refused to enrol in this makeshift army, and was bawled out by Panizzi because of it. Of working-class origin, Edwards was totally in sympathy with the Chartists' views and signed the Charter on 8 April on his way to work, 'as my humble and individual protest against the nefarious proceedings'.[135]

The danger, however, had seemed real enough; Madden (although unconvinced of the military capabilities of his colleagues) was sufficiently worried to evacuate his wife and children to Forshall's residence, which was considered more secure. He recorded an inconclusive meeting of the senior officers, but otherwise spent a muddled if somewhat disturbed day.[136] The 'riot', however, went off quietly. A more conventional member of staff, Robert Cowtan, wrote of the sense of anticlimax:

> Mid-day came and our eyes were gladdened by well-spread tables laden with cold beef and bread, to which were added a tankard of good beer for each man: some complained that the beef was rather tough, and that the beer was not so good as it might have been, but everyone gave practical proof of their appreciation of these creature-comforts by making a complete clearance of the tables, and the only thing needed to complete the banquet was a cigar, or a pipe of tobacco. This last indulgence was not to be obtained, as smoking is a thing strictly forbidden within the precincts of the Museum.[137]

The threat of mob rule receded and Panizzi's days of potential military glory were over.

On the other hand the Museum had its military side. Coventry Patmore, the poet and an assistant in the Department of Printed Books, was more militant than most and in 1852, against the background of a perceived threat from the French after Louis Napoleon's coup, wrote a letter to *The Times* saying that he had formed a rifle club at the Museum, which practised on ranges in and around London.[138] He even managed to beg a subscription of £5 each from Tennyson and his wife towards the club.[139] In 1859, with the formation of the national volunteer movement in view of yet another imagined threat of war with France, staff were allowed to join the rifle corps – they even tried to set up their own company in the Museum, but had some difficulty raising the money to support it. Instead they joined the 37th Middlesex Volunteers and were from time to time given leave to take part in exercises and reviews – indeed, the Museum was even closed for one afternoon in 1860 to allow members of staff to see their colleagues on parade in Hyde Park. Aaron Hayes, an attendant in the Department of Antiquities, was sergeant of the Museum company and was allowed four days' leave in 1860 to compete for the Queen's Prize in rifle-shooting.[140] In 1861 the British Museum Rifle Association was set up and prizes for marksmanship were given by some of the Museum's officers. At some stage the Association was allowed a shooting gallery in the basement; there was a succession of these, and the last functioned until it fell a victim to the Great Court scheme in the 1990s. Shooting was popular with the staff and by 1871 forty-four members of staff were in the volunteers, of whom the most senior – a captain – was Maskelyne, the Keeper of Mineralogy (the only senior member of staff ever to have been elected as a Member of Parliament). [141]

Royal Commission

During the years after the Select Committee the Trustees had been improving the library, under the energetic leadership of Panizzi. One of his greatest triumphs was the acceptance in 1846 by the Trustees, after eight years of sometimes acrimonious bickering, of his proposals for cataloguing the printed books in manuscript and not in print (although arguments of detail rumbled on). Meanwhile his pleading had increased the amount of money received by his department, including grants for special purchases, from an average of £1,296 in his predecessor's reign to an average of £4,197 between 1837 and 1845. The value of printed material received by the Museum under copyright in 1846 was £1,533.[142] After a considerable rise in grant in 1846 the number of books received by the Museum was 42,648 volumes or parts.[143] Space was becoming more and more of a problem, not least in the reading rooms, where an average of 784 volumes were issued to just over 200 readers every day.[144]

At the same time Madden, one of the most distinguished medievalists in the Museum's history,[145] had been reducing the chaos in the Department of Manuscripts and making splendid acquisitions, which also caused problems of space. Nearly £11,000 was spent on manuscripts between 1837 and 1845, a sum which increased to a total of £25,000 for the years 1847–56. In 1837 there were 23,900 manuscripts – both western and oriental – in the Museum. By 1848 a return to Parliament recorded that the department had 29,626 volumes, 23,000 charters and a few thousand miscellaneous items.[146] Accommodation for the library departments was stretched beyond reasonable limits. The expenditure on coins and antiquities, apart from special parliamentary grants, for the years 1837–45 was £12,481 and rose to about £35,000 for the years 1846–57.[147] As this was the period of the great Assyrian acquisitions, accommodation here was also at full stretch. The natural history collections were in even worse case.

The two major characters in the library were at daggers drawn. Madden had a hatred verging on paranoia for Panizzi, while Panizzi could not stand Madden. Madden's extensive private diaries record in unseemly language (quoted at length by historians of the library)[148] his feelings about him, particularly fastening on the fact that Panizzi was an Italian, and denigrating him as a result. This is not the place to detail this quarrel, which like so many in the Museum's history had two sides, but it must be said that neither of the protagonists hid their feelings and the staff inside the Museum followed one or the other star – Hawkins being close to the scholarly Madden. The two most senior natural historians, König (Keeper of Mineralogy and Geology) and Gray (Keeper of Zoology), were also sworn enemies. The unhappy state of staff relationships within the Museum was widely discussed in the world outside and spilled over into the press.[149] The Principal Librarian, Ellis, was ageing and could not reconcile the warring factions – even if he had had the power. The problem of staff relations was compounded by the chronic lack of accommodation for books, antiquities and natural history, and for the students who used the collections. Panizzi, increasingly frustrated by the power of the Secretary, Forshall (an ally of Madden) – the only member of staff with direct access to the Trustees – was adept at raising his problems in powerful political quarters.

An added issue – and one that would not go away – was the growing feeling among the increasingly vocal scientific community that the natural history departments were not receiving sufficient support. Its members were particularly incensed that there were no scientists among the Trustees (this matter had been aired earlier in front of the Select Committee, but nothing had been done about it). The scientists and their supporters were now better organized and, led by the then powerful British Association for the Advancement of Science and supported by other learned societies, they presented to Parliament a memorial addressing their grievances.[150] This was almost certainly the trigger that caused the previously reluctant Prime Minister, Lord John Russell, to set up a Royal Commission to enquire into the British Museum and recommend how it could be most effective 'for the advancement of literature, science and the arts'. It was formally constituted on 17 June 1847 under the chairmanship of the Earl of Ellesmere. Ellis and the senior officers of the Museum gave evidence, as did four Trustees and twenty-three members of the public. The quality of outside evidence varied. Particularly important was that of Richard Owen, professor at the Royal College of Surgeons, which was coherent and reflected the views of the majority of the country's natural scientists. Ellis's evidence was bland (everything in his opinion was going well), while that of some of the Keepers (Panizzi, Madden, König, Keeper of Mineralogy, and Gray, Keeper of Zoology) revealed some of the rifts and trivial quarrels of the institution. These the Commissioners attributed to a lack of communication between the various Museum hierarchies.[151]

As is the nature of such bodies, the Commission took a leisurely view of its duties and met rather spasmodically in 1848 and 1849, publishing its report early in 1850.[152] The Trustees immediately appointed a special committee to examine the report and make their own recommendations, which it did on 25 May 1850.[153]

The Commission's recommendations were of varying importance. Recognizing the ludicrous positions occupied in relation to the Trustees by the Principal Librarian and the Secretary, the Commission indulged in an extraordinary flight of bureaucratic fancy, proposing that these two posts should be abolished and that an Executive Council should be set up. This should consist of an independent chairman appointed for five years, four Trustees and two other (paid) members, one to be in charge of the natural history departments and the other in charge of everything else. This was seen as the nonsense it was and ignored, but one of the Commission's structural recommendations was implemented. It was clear from the evidence that Forshall, the Secretary, was not only inefficient, but also far too powerful. His salary of £700 was the highest in the Museum after that of Ellis (who was paid £800). He alone of the staff was present at the Trustees' meetings and could at will edit the officers' reports, which he read aloud at Board meetings. He it was who passed the Trustees' decisions to the staff (sometimes giving them a spin of his own), and informed the Principal Librarian and heads of departments of new staff appointments, concerning which there was no consultation. He also conducted all the official correspondence of the Museum. Forshall (who had not stood up to the strain) was retired on very generous terms – although he himself did not see it in that way.[154]

Although they did not accept the Commission's recommendations concerning an executive council (cleverly passing this back to Parliament), the Trustees, in the face of polite criticism from the Commission, tightened up the process of appointment to the Standing Committee. This was the real executive body and had worked hard over the years, as the main board only met quarterly. It was now to consist of the three principal Trustees, a Trustee appointed by the Sovereign (at that time the Duke of Cambridge) and fourteen others.[155] The Trustees for the first time invited the Principal Librarian to attend their meetings and, while not allowing the keepers to be present when departmental business was being discussed, granted them direct access to members of the board.

The Commission ignored the problems of the departments of natural history and of their accommodation, although the importance of their collections was recognized,[156] and came down against the physical separation of the natural history material into a separate building. The Department of Printed Books was considered at length in the report, although much of the discussion concerned the methods used in cataloguing the books. Panizzi's proposals for a hand-written catalogue were confirmed, and the rules of cataloguing were re-affirmed. The report rejected the opening of the reading rooms in the evening because of the risk of fire, and made various other minor suggestions about the accommodation of books. Madden's department came well out of the report, which also foreshadowed the creation of a department of oriental books and manuscripts.

Hawkins was examined three times by the Commission, who questioned him closely – as they did the other keepers – on communication with the Trustees and on such matters as establishment, recruitment and pay. The Commissioners were surprisingly interested in the qualifications of the officers. Hawkins made a point of saying that, as archaeology was not taught at university, 'we have been desirous of getting young men of considerable talents and attainments, and letting them derive their archaeological education from their employment and opportunities in the Museum'.[157] This attitude reflected Museum recruitment policy until well on into the twentieth century. Hawkins also expressed his dissatisfaction at the manner in which purchases were agreed by the Trustees. He agreed that delays in decision caused collections to be lost, although when pressed he could not remember any specific instance.[158] He also managed to raise the shortage of accommodation for display and for staff, a statement that led to an important question from the Chairman, 'Do you think... that, in an establishment of the description of the British Museum, a collection of antiquities should occupy a very prominent place?' to which he replied, 'Certainly'.[159] Prompted by Sir Roderick Murchison, he stated that he would like to form a collection 'somewhat similar to the Royal Collection of Scandinavian Antiquities in Copenhagen'.[160]

There had been a certain amount of lobbying concerning national antiquities (some of which, from Denmark, was presumably inspired by Hawkins), and this bore some fruit. In the proper language of a Royal Commission, the report stated, 'We can do no other than speak of such an object as one to which the liberality of Government might be directed with unquestionable advantage'.[161] The Commission, following evidence given by Sir Charles Fellows, agreed with Hawkins that the Museum's officers should arrange the display of sculpture (in chronological progression and archaeological context following the example of Ludwig I of Bavaria in the Glyptothek at Munich), thus ending the long history of Westmacott's involvement in this area of the Museum's work, which had come to an acrimonious head with the problems of mounting the Lycian marbles. Praising the work of the Prints and Drawings department, they approved the suggestion that a gallery be reserved for the display of its collections.[162] They also pointed out that there was, as always, insufficient space in the Museum as a whole for the adequate display of the collections.

Lack of space was also advanced as the reason for the lack of growth in the ethnographic collections. Hawkins was, as we have seen, keen on this area, and even suggested that the collections might be better cared for and displayed elsewhere.[163] He answered questions concerning his own speciality, coins and medals, with confidence, but equivocated somewhat about their display.[164]

The Commission listened to Owen, who wished to introduce handling sessions and lectures (he had cited the Hunterian Museum and the Jardin des Plantes as models), but dismissed his suggestions:

We consider the Museum as essentially a repository for the conservation and arrangement of a vast variety of material objects... We believe that the task of its superintendence and management, with a view to this main purpose alone, is sufficient to engross the time and the abilities of its own officers, and that the full attainment of that purpose might be... hazarded by the pursuit of every adventitious advantage which might appear of possible attainment through the instrumentality of its stores... we cannot... recommend the systematic adoption of the practice in question, nor to advise that any building in the nature of a theatre or lecture-room should form part of any future additions to the Museum.[165]

The most immediate problem of space concerned the library. Space was needed for more readers and a vast access of books, particularly as the Copyright Acts – which provided for the deposition of a copy of every British publication in the Museum – were tightened up and more rigorously enforced. The idea of a new building on Montague Place – enormously costly because it would imply the purchase and demolition of a large number of houses – was proposed and received in stony silence by the Treasury.[166] Longing eyes had for some time been cast on the inner courtyard of the Museum,[167] an unsatisfactory space, access to which had been denied to the public and, according to a correspondent in The Builder, was the home of all the neighbourhood cats.[168] Panizzi in April 1852 sketched out his (not altogether original) ideas for filling the space,[169] which were enthusiastically accepted by the Trustees, drawn out by Sydney Smirke (Robert Smirke's younger brother, the Trustees' new architect) and submitted in an official report to the Treasury on 7 June, with a request for a special vote of £52,000 towards its construction. This proposed a circular double-aisled space, surrounded by a rectangle of book-stacks, and was turned down by the Treasury in a terse letter ten days later.[170] Panizzi returned to the fray with a much modified design, consisting of a single domed room surrounded by iron book-stacks in the remaining quadrants of the courtyard.[171] In January 1854, having successfully lobbied the Prime Minister, Lord Aberdeen (a long-standing and active Trustee of the Museum), the Trustees were informed that £61,000 would be granted for the building and £25,000 for the fittings.[172] A contract was let to George Baker and Son of Lambeth and the first ironwork was erected on site in December.

In remarkably quick time, mainly due to the fact that much of it was constructed of cast iron, one of the most splendid rooms in the world was erected (pl. 19). The dome is 42.7 m in diameter (then exceeded only by the Pantheon in Rome) and 32.3 m high, and is lit by a central lantern and twenty round-headed windows – all double-glazed – set in a papier mâché ceiling. The roof was covered with copper. The Reading Room originally accommodated 300 readers at radially set tables which had longitudinal divisions to screen the readers from each other – divisions which also served to provide a conduit for warm air from a heating plant below the floor. In the centre of this spider's web, on a raised dais, sat the top-hatted superintendent and his acolytes, surrounded by two concentric circles of shelves which contained bound copies of the catalogue and larger works of reference. The drum which supported the dome was lined with three tiers of shelved reference books; the upper tiers were galleried and entered from the stacks by way of doors disguised with false spines of books; the shelves on the ground floor allowed open access to major works of reference. Outside the drum stacks for books filled most of the court, leaving a space of about nine metres between the stacks and the courtyard walls, which provided light for the galleries and a fire barrier. The construction work was photographed by William Lake Price and copies were sent to the Queen; this caused a certain amount of trouble, as Prince Albert disapproved of the shape of the windows, which had to be altered to his taste.[173]

As always, there were problems with interior decoration. Panizzi wanted the dome painted with scenes in either oil or tempera. Sir Charles Eastlake, President of the Royal Academy and therefore a Trustee, possibly mindful of the disastrous experience in the new Houses of Parliament,[174] agreed that these might be the best media and advised against fresco. The Trustees, however, turned down all idea of painted decoration.[175] This idea, like so many others in the history of the decoration of the Museum, did not go away and later schemes by Alfred Stevens and Sigismund Goetze (which included statuary) survive to show how grateful we must be to the Trustees.[176] The plain scheme of azure with gilded mouldings and ribs gave a light, airy feel to the room which remains one of its greatest pleasures. The surface of the floor was covered with a patent composition of cork and india-rubber to muffle sound.[177] A bust of Panizzi by Carlo Marochetti was placed over the doorway of the corridor leading from the Front Hall. The room was completed and opened to readers on 18 May 1857. The general public had been admitted to see the room from 9 until 18 May and, so popular was the demand, they were also admitted for two hours in the evening during the summer, when the room received more than 62,000 visitors.[178]

British Antiquities

The period between 1850 and 1860 was a period of development for the antiquities department, but also a period of great worry and overcrowding. The problems recognized by the Royal Commission were not to be resolved easily, despite the best efforts of Hawkins and his colleagues. A critical appointment was made to the department in 1851 in the person of Augustus Wollaston Franks (pl. 13), whose influence on the Museum over the next forty-five years was greater than that of any member of staff before or since.[179] His appointment was a direct result of the need felt by the Royal Commission for a more coherent attitude to be taken by the Museum towards the collection of national art and antiquities.

Franks, whose father had been an officer in the Royal Navy, came from landed and banking backgrounds and was comparatively rich.[180] Born in Geneva in 1826 and brought up in Rome, he had been educated at Eton and Trinity College, Cambridge. His career there had been enlivened by his membership of the Cambridge Antiquarian Society and (a rare privilege for an undergraduate) of the Ray Society. As a first-year undergraduate he had witnessed the destruction of the Cambridge Camden Society in a fury of ritual arguments concerning the restoration with a stone altar of the Round Church in Cambridge. The Camden Society had been founded in 1837 to advise restorers of churches of what its members conceived to be the true spirit of Gothic architecture; this was clearly of great interest to Franks (a budding medievalist), and he joined the Ecclesiological Society which rose from its ashes.[181] He was one of the founders of the Cambridge Architectural Society. Franks was already publishing on medieval subjects while an undergraduate – a paper on a palimpsest brass at Burwell, another on the Freville family and its monuments in Little Shelford church, and, in the year he graduated, a famous and well-illustrated book on medieval window glass.[182]

THE BRITISH MUSEUM: A HISTORY

Settling in London, he became actively involved in the work of the Archaeological Institute, which he joined in 1848. As a representative of the Institute he became a member and then honorary secretary of the committee which, in 1850, organized a ground-breaking exhibition of medieval art in the rooms of the Royal Society of Arts in the Adelphi (where incidentally he formed an important and lasting friendship with one of the committee members, Henry Cole, the effective founder of the South Kensington Museum). Through his work here he made lifelong friends among English collectors. He was thus well prepared for the British Museum when the Trustees at last heeded Hawkins's pleas for space for national antiquities and a post for somebody to work on them.[183]

Two factors now drove the push towards housing national antiquities which had exercised the Commission and Hawkins (p.117). First was the growing interest in medieval antiquities as a side-issue in the furious ecclesiological discussions of the period which Franks had witnessed – red in tooth and claw – at Cambridge, but which had their proper origins in the writings of the architect Thomas Rickman.[184] The second was the impact made on many influential people, including the chairman of the Commission, by the reorganization of the Museum of Antiquities in Copenhagen and the publications in English that grew out of it. More local issues also brought the matter to the fore, particularly an offer by Lord Prudhoe (later Duke of Northumberland) of the newly discovered Iron Age hoard from Stanwick, Yorkshire; this was made on condition that a room be found for its display, with other national antiquities, in the Museum.[185]

Renewed interest in artefacts of the medieval period was a direct result of activity within the Church of England. New churches were being built to provide for congregations in the fast-growing towns, and arguments about ritual were necessarily being addressed along the way. The Tractarians demanded more ritual in buildings that had mostly been turned into prayer-boxes by Protestant and puritan tradition. Taste had to be changed, colour and form introduced. The Cambridge Camden Society had started out by trying to inform opinion about details of medieval architecture and church furnishings and the appropriate stylistic use of ornament. Their influence was enormous. To use the words of a youthful Kenneth Clark, 'For fifty years almost every new Anglican church was built and furnished according to their instructions; that is to say, in a manner opposed to utility, economy or good sense.'[186] As churches were renovated and re-gothicized, cupboards were turned out to reveal all sorts of treasures overlooked for centuries. The new local archaeological societies began to publish (as had Franks) details of church furnishing; brass-rubbing became an acceptable hobby and, following Rickman, medieval architecture was systematized and studied by professional and amateur alike. In 1843 a new national archaeological society was founded, the British Archaeological Association, 'for the encouragement and prosecution of researches into the arts and monuments of the early and middle ages', in which aristocrats such as Lord Prudhoe, together with country gentry and parsons, took leading roles. By September 1844 it had a membership of 1,024 (including fourteen members of the Museum staff).[187] As a result the Society of Antiquaries, already at a low intellectual ebb, was seriously challenged, particularly in medieval studies. Within a couple of years, however, the Association was rent with feuds and the professionals – the architects and museum curators, with a few others – broke away and (led by a distinguished antiquary, Albert Way) in 1845 formed the Archaeological Institute, with a very similar remit, but allegedly more professional than the Association.[188] Two new annual journals appeared – *The archaeological journal* and *The journal of the British Archaeological Association*. Each society met annually, usually in a cathedral city, for lectures, excursions, discussions and dinners – meetings which incidentally served to stimulate the antiquaries who ran the local societies. The study of medieval remains was central to the two societies and to their journals. On the back of all this activity, medieval antiquities became collectable and were eagerly snapped up by connoisseurs. Rail travel on the continent became easier and the curiosity shops of Europe were ransacked, often by English travellers (of whom Franks was a notable example), for medieval objects turned out of churches and monasteries whose property had been secularized. The success of the Musée de Cluny in Paris, opened in 1844 and dedicated to medieval French antiquities, encouraged interest in the period in England.

While medieval objects were all the rage, a sense of Englishness was also growing; its academic base was fuelled by philologists such as Thorpe and Kemble, who edited many of the earliest English documents. They emphasized the pre-Norman roots of England for the first time since the early eighteenth century, an emphasis heightened by the publication of Kemble's synthetic book, *The Saxons in England*.[189] Kemble, who, with Thorpe, introduced into English history the rigorous methods of source criticism developed in Germany, was also interested in antiquities. He was the first scholar to point to a parallel between the material found in the homeland of the Anglo-Saxons in North Germany and that found in the cemeteries of Anglo-Saxon England.[190] Against a burgeoning interest in this period Anglo-Saxon antiquities were being excavated on a large scale, particularly in Kent, often discovered during railway construction. These became the special study of John Yonge Akerman, the new (paid) Secretary of the Society of Antiquaries, who in 1855, presumably stimulated by the graves found while he was Secretary to the Greenwich Railway Company, published his *Remains of pagan Saxondom*. Excavation had long been a gentlemanly pursuit, but it now became more popular as historians increasingly turned their attention to finds of all periods turned up by the plough or the amateur spade – Lord Prudhoe's hoard from Stanwick being a case in point. Already, in backing Prudhoe's request for a room for British antiquities in 1845, Hawkins had 'reported that the extensive excavations going on, and about to be undertaken in the construction of Railways, occurring at the same time that the enlargement of the Museum afforded additional facilities for exhibiting interesting objects, presented a peculiarly favourable opportunity of carrying out the intention of forming a Collection of National Antiquities...'.[191]

The interest in Anglo-Saxon antiquities was paralleled by English interest in contemporary finds on the Continent. Most important was possibly the publication in 1848 of the seventh-century graves from Selzen in Rheinhessen, which had been excavated by the Lindenschmit brothers.[192] In 1855 William Wylie, an amateur of Anglo-Saxon excavation, published a paper in *Archaeologia* about the Alemannic graves from Oberflacht in Swabia, which caused a great stir because of the quantity of wooden material recovered.[193] Of more immediate importance in relation to the Anglo-Saxon cemeteries was the work in Normandy of the Abbé Cochet (Curator of the Rouen Museum), whose excavations in the 1850s had much closer parallels to those of Akerman and his contemporaries in England.[194] Franks was well aware of his publications and in his numerous forays to France picked up a good number of Merovingian objects for the Museum.[195]

These two elements, the renewed interest in medieval antiquities and the burgeon-ing importance of excavation in the British Isles, so important to the future of the British Museum, were also catalysts in the foundation and growth of a number of other institu-tions in the British Isles. The period between 1845 and 1865 was one in which many of the great museums of the country were founded.

Undoubtedly the most interesting development, and one which was to cause considerable discussion in relation to the British Museum's collections in the 1850s and 60s, was the foundation of the South Kensington Museum. (This was renamed as the Victoria and Albert Museum in 1899. In this book it is referred to by the title current at the date.) It was established in the aftermath of the Great Exhibition of 1851, the brainchild of the Prince Consort and Henry Cole, to encourage British design education. First known as the Museum of Manufactures, it was opened to the public in 1852 and the following year was renamed as the Museum of Ornamental Art. It was moved to South Kensington in 1857.

Intended primarily as a museum of design and industry, it held collections initially consisting of models, casts and electrotypes of pieces of art of all periods and countries, as well as several hundred objects purchased from the Great Exhibition itself. Even before its opening, it began to acquire works of fine and applied art. Under the energetic leadership of Cole, head of the Department of Science and Art of the Board of Trade after 1853, it flourished. Central to its function was education in design and industry.[196] It was an *omnium gatherum* of higgledy-piggledy collections which included everything from geology to cotton-spinning equipment. It was the product of omnivorous, and sometimes uncriti-cal, empire-building by Cole, who saw it as a museum of popular education for all.

Always destined to be a museum of design and applied art, it had a fine-art com-ponent – the National Gallery of British Art – and for a short period under the influence of the brilliant J.C. Robinson, the first Superintendent of Art (equivalent to the post of director), it built a remarkable collection of medieval objects (particularly taking the lion's share of a government grant of £20,000 to purchase objects at the great Bernal sale of 1855),[197] as well as other major collections of both the fine and applied arts. But its brief was so broad that the South Kensington Museum's mission became rather muddled. Its component parts tended to break away and even return to their original home. The collec-tion of food and animal products, for example, was moved from pillar to post and much of it was destroyed in the 1920s. The Museum of Construction was frittered away in 1888. The Patent Museum ended up in the Science Museum. Fine and applied arts began to overtake design and industry in importance (modern manufacture was relegated to a branch museum at Bethnal Green in 1880). Policy was in effect made pragmatically and, because of the understanding between Cole, Robinson (until 1869, when he was eased out of his post) and Franks, the new museum concentrated on artistic content (its function in relation to current design and art gradually fading). The British Museum – as it had tacitly done from its foundation – continued to emphasize the historical context of the objects in its collection.[198] Apart from a blip in 1873 (see below, p.143) there seems throughout the rest of the century to have been a harmonious relationship between the two museums based on these two principles; the chief protagonists guided material each other's way – most notably perhaps Lady Charlotte Schreiber's collection of pottery and porcelain, given to the South Kensington Museum in 1884, largely steered thither by Franks.[199] The South

Kensington Museum meanwhile became perhaps the most influential applied-art museum in the world.

Stimulated by the growing importance of local collections made by antiquarian societies, by the growing interest in public art, as well as by civic pride on the part of the fast-growing cities, a Museums Act passed through Parliament in 1845 which allowed local authorities to found and support museums in the provinces.[200] And founded they were, in quick succession – Sunderland (1846), Warrington (1848), Leicester and Salford (1849). In the 1850s Ipswich and Winchester took over local society museums, and the Liverpool Museum was founded on the basis of a gift by the Earl of Derby. In 1858 Maidstone, soon to be the home of a major archaeological collection, was founded; Birmingham and the Royal Albert Memorial Museum at Exeter followed in the 1860s.

The National Museum of Ireland in Dublin was not founded until 1877. But in the 1840s the collections of the Royal Irish Academy were formally organized as the Museum of Irish Antiquities, in accordance with an Academy resolution of 1841 to press for the foundation of a national museum of antiquities in which it could house its remarkable – principally early Christian – treasures.[201] From the Royal Dublin Society the new museum received a considerable industrial collection. The National Museum of Ireland was administered in parallel with the South Kensington Museum (until recently many of its showcases were even of the same design as those of the Victoria and Albert Museum). In 1899, however, the control of the Museum passed from the English Board of Education to the Department of Agriculture and Technical Instruction for Ireland, where it remained until Irish independence.

The well-established museum of the Society of Antiquaries of Scotland was in process of being converted into the National Museum of Antiquities of Scotland under the influence of its remarkable secretary, Daniel Wilson, who was appointed in 1847. Backed by two Members of Parliament, Charles Cowan and the radical Joseph Hume, the Scottish collections were in 1851 transferred to the state, which undertook to house them, although the museum was still to be run by the Society, the members of which were to have a meeting room and housing for their library.[202] The Scottish archaeological establishment had always looked to Scandinavia for inspiration, and Wilson now started to order the major archaeological collections of the museum in line with contemporary thinking in Denmark. In 1854 the government also agreed to the establishment of a Scottish museum of art and industry to match that in South Kensington, for which the Department of Science and Industry was responsible. Originally known as the Industrial Museum for Scotland and later as the Edinburgh Museum of Science and Art, it was renamed the Royal Scottish Museum in 1904. In 1985 it was united with the National Museum of Antiquities.[203]

The Three Ages

In Denmark, as we have seen, a totally new method of arranging the antiquities of prehistory had been developed in the years following 1816 by C.J. Thomsen, the head of the Museum of Antiquities in Copenhagen. The division of prehistory by material, into Stone Age, Bronze Age and Iron Age (the Three-Age System), had in 1836 been published in theoretical form in a guide to that museum, translated into German in the following year.[204] An English edition was not published until 1848 (translated from the German by Lord Ellesmere, Chairman of the 1847–9 Royal Commission on the British Museum). This book and the system it put forward were widely discussed throughout Europe, but were most enthusiastically received in England.[205] Thomsen knew England well, spoke and wrote good English, and was well known to Hawkins, with whom he had discussed the Cuerdale hoard (p. 105) when Hawkins was struggling to publish it. In 1843 his young assistant J.J.A. Worsaae published a book entitled *Danmarks Oldtid oplyst ved Oldsager og Gravhøie* ('Ancient Denmark in the light of antiquities and grave-mounds'), which demonstrated by excavation the validity of Thomsen's museum-based system.[206]

In 1846 the Duke of Sutherland wrote to the Society of Northern Antiquaries in Denmark inviting a Scandinavian antiquary to visit Scotland. Thomsen and the King of Denmark recommended Worsaae, and the king paid for him to extend his journey to the rest of the British Isles (and incidentally Paris). Worsaae himself saw this visit in an almost missionary light; not only could he bring a better understanding of the Three-Age System to Britain, but he would also be able to examine and identify the Danish and Norwegian elements in the British archaeological record. There was also a political undertow to this visit, as Danish relations with Germany were not at all happy during the build-up of the Schleswig-Holstein problem. Worsaae was a political young man and his memoirs illuminate this side of his character.[207]

Worsaae, having been invited by the richest landowner in Scotland, had the best of all introductions and made many antiquarian and political friends in London. In archaeological terms the two most important people he met were Hawkins and Charles Roach Smith, an amateur antiquary with an enormous collection of London antiquities which was later purchased by the British Museum. Hawkins showed him coins and other material from the Cuerdale hoard as well as many other national antiquities. Worsaae was surprised to find that his book, *Danmarks Oldtid*, had been translated from its German version into English by William Thoms under the title *The Primeval Antiquities of Denmark* and that it was about to be published. He discussed it with the translator and later watched its success in the bookshops.[208]

In his letters home Worsaae was critical of much of what he saw in the Museum. But his patron, Thomsen, had been even more critical when he visited in 1837: 'One of the main reasons for my visit was to see England's ethnographical collections', he wrote. 'But everything was muddled, confused masses, where one jumped from antiquity to Greenland, from there to the South Seas and then back again to England... further within this chaotic collection are natural history items mixed in with everything, so that it is difficult to sort them out.'[209] In a letter to Thomsen, with the confident eye of youth, Worsaae condemns the Museum as a junk shop (*Ragelsekammer*): 'only the Egyptian and Roman antiquities have begun to progress under Dr Birch; but the national antiquities have a bleaker future. I preached to Hawkins and to a young man, Mr Newton, of how important it was that they took more notice of them than had been done. They agreed with this, but said that it was going to be hard.'[210] Worsaae met everybody in English society (Ellesmere, for example, invited him to dinner, where the young man was much impressed by the powdered footmen) and his visit may have helped to persuade Ellesmere and his Royal Commission to plead for a department of national antiquities within the Museum.

Worsaae, in his conversations with Hawkins, was preaching to the converted; but there can be little doubt that his presence in London and the close relationship he built up with his Museum colleagues (and particularly in later years with Franks) were ultimately to inform much of the future development of the Department of Antiquities.[211] When Franks came to re-display the British antiquities between 1856 and 1859 he was, after careful consideration, to use the Danish system as a base.[212]

Bodrum

The main collecting emphasis at this period was on Greece, Asia Minor and the Levant. For a few more years the Museum was able to collect classical sculpture on a grand scale. This time its main agent was Charles Newton, who in 1852 had resigned from the Museum to become vice-consul in Mytilene, on the island of Lesbos, then part of the Turkish Empire.[213] In 1845 the Museum had acquired a number of slabs from one of the Seven Wonders of the Ancient World, the fourth-century BC tomb of Maussollos at Halikarnassos; these had been built into the walls of the Crusader castle at what is now known as Bodrum, on the coast of western Turkey. Newton had already written an important paper concerning them and the topography of the area, the latter based on a chart of the town made by two English hydrographic surveyors, Graves and Brock. Arriving at Mytilene with instructions that, in addition to pursuing his normal consular duties, he was to acquire objects for the British Museum, he was, with financial help from the ambassador, Sir Stratford Canning, able to excavate on Kalymnos, a site which produced many inscriptions for the Museum.

In 1855 Newton visited Bodrum for the first time and in 1857 was granted £2,000 to remove some of the colossal lions that had guarded the base of the pyramidal roof of the Mausoleum and to excavate the monument itself. He asked for a naval vessel to help with the removal of the many spectacular sculptures he was unearthing, and was allowed a steam-corvette, the *Gorgon*, commanded by Robert Murdoch Smith. The original party included four sappers (some of whom had been trained as photographers at the South Kensington Museum) and various other craftsmen. Three young painters, Roderick Stanhope, Val Prinsep and George Frederick Watts, went along for the ride – officially to record the excavations. Much further evidence was recovered, and, a *firmân* having been granted, the rich finds, together with the marble figure of Demeter from Cnidus and figures from the sacred way at Branchidae near Miletus, were safely transported to London. There was as yet no space inside the Museum for the display of either the new finds or those from Carthage (excavated by the Reverend Nathan Davis) which arrived in the same summer, so the best of the Mausoleum sculpture was temporarily stored in sheds built under the portico.

Newton continued to work in the area, particularly at Cnidus, with the help of the navy and particularly of Lieutenant Smith and the architect Thomas Pullan. More important sculpture was found, including a colossal lion (pl. 17), estimated to weigh some ten tons, which was extracted from the site with great skill under Smith's direction and despatched to England by HMS *Supply*. Returning to England by way of Rhodes, where he negotiated the purchase of a large collection of vases and gold objects excavated from graves on the island, Newton left others to continue his work in Asia Minor.

Newton – an important man not only in the Museum's history but in the history of classical archaeology (see pp.147–51) – was a close friend of Panizzi, who had backed him through all his adventures abroad, and consulted him on political matters. He wrote a number of long letters to Panizzi between 1854 and 1861, describing in lively fashion his finds and his difficulties. They contain many of his thoughts about the Museum and how it should be run and controlled.[214] Newton had political aptitude and there is no doubt as to his intellectual ability, or indeed brilliance, as a classical archaeologist (as early as 1855 he had turned down the Regius Chair of Greek at Oxford, which was offered to him by Palmerston, because it had only a nominal salary – the post went to a scholarly lightweight, Benjamin Jowett). Newton's ambition sometimes led to ungenerous behaviour towards his juniors – Lieutenant Smith (later General Sir Robert Smith, Director of the Edinburgh Museum of Science and Arts) was but one of his associates not acknowledged in his published work. Not altogether a nice man, Newton made snide comments about his colleagues in the Museum, and Poole, perhaps the most brilliant of his numismatic colleagues, had reason to criticize this aspect of his character.[215] He was, however, a man of charm and wit; his letters are light-handed and his short marriage was clearly happy. He saw himself as a scholar, not as a museum man, and, before he became Keeper of the new Department of Greek and Roman Antiquities, insisted time and again to Panizzi that he wanted to pursue an academic career, free of all administrative and other curatorial duties.[216]

Casts[217]

The British Museum has an enormous collection of casts and moulds – Egyptian, Central American, northern European and Mediterranean. It remains a major, if now little used, resource for the study of sculpture from all these regions and is once again being appreciated by students. Louis XIV perhaps set the fashion for casts of antique sculpture through his presentation of them to the French Academy at Rome in the latter part of the seventeenth century; and the Polish and Scandinavian kings followed his lead in collecting them. There was, however, no serious patronage of casting in England until the early eighteenth century, when a few foreign and English craftsmen began to produce lead and plaster casts for the English aristocracy (who were also purchasing casts from Rome). The most important of these was John Cheere, who flourished in London in the middle years of the century.[218] The use of casts became even more popular as quality copying of classical sculpture in marble – as practised by such sculptors as Thorvaldsen and Canova – became prohibitively expensive. The mechanical copying of statuary in marble by nineteenth-century workshops in Italy was of such poor quality that casting in plaster became the accepted medium.[219] Casting was a highly skilled and expensive process and was particularly used after the installation of the Elgin gallery at the British Museum as a medium of exchange by the Prince Regent and others.

Casts made by Westmacott from the Phigalian Marbles in 1816, as part of the agreement with the original owners, were the first major set of moulds we know to have been commissioned by the Trustees. The six sets cost together £650.[220] At about the same time the purchase of the Elgin Marbles triggered a series of requests from as far away as

Württemberg for casts of the new acquisition, including an offer from the Royal Academy of two fragments of the Parthenon frieze in exchange for casts. Among the craftsmen who petitioned for the work the egregious Westmacott put in a proposal to make a complete set of moulds for £2,466, providing casts at £496 a set. The Trustees reduced this grandiose scheme to a total casting cost of £197 13s 6d and a number of sets were sold or given away on the government's instructions.[221]

In 1819 the Trustees were approached by the French for a set of casts of the Elgin Marbles in return for one of the Parthenon metopes. The Trustees were willing to pay £1,200 to achieve this end, but nothing came of the suggestion.[222] The Museum bumbled on, making occasional casts for anxious customers, but apparently having no firm policy or wish to indulge the undoubted demand.

In 1835 matters came to a head. First there was a request, again from the French, for a set of casts from the Elgin and other collections in exchange for casts from France. The Treasury having approved the plan, the Trustees asked Hawkins to produce the goods. The existing moulds were too damaged to be of further use and Pietro Angelo Sarti, a London-based specialist, and Westmacott were called in to fulfil the order. A contract was drawn up to provide the casts at a cost of £350. The second impetus was given by the report of the Select Committee of that year, which examined Sarti and others concerning the provision of casts, and more or less told the Trustees to start their own cast service at the public expense. The Trustees, in the face of greater demand, now became more assertive and, although still using outside specialists to provide the casts, started to keep master casts and moulds more carefully. They issued a catalogue and even started to make a little money from the process – as much as £1,755 was received from the sale of casts in 1838, although this was an unusually high figure. In the 1840s and 50s a considerable number of cement casts were sent to Athens, where they were originally exhibited in the Casts Museum in the Bath of Oula Bei.[223] It was not, however, until 1881 that a permanent member of staff, Saverio Biagiotti, was employed to make and provide casts, although an outside firm was often employed to provide new moulds or big orders. Although often threatened by closure, the service has survived in various guises (for some time in association with the Victoria and Albert Museum) to the present day, when it is under the control of the British Museum Company.

The Museum also acquired many casts, most famously the casts taken for Elgin from the west frieze of the Parthenon in 1802 by Bernardino Ledus and Vincenzo Rosati. Another set was acquired in 1872, and was used at one time in the Elgin Room to show the extent of the deterioration of the frieze in its original position. Casts of the Aegina pediment sculptures and of the Selinus metopes were early acquired by the Museum and were displayed to illustrate the sequence of Greek art, although generally the Museum policy in the middle of the century was 'that no cast of any sculpture that could be seen in a European museum should be exhibited in the galleries'.[224] Other collections were those taken in Egypt for Robert Hay in the late 1820s and early 30s and a collection of casts given by the Royal Academy in 1831.[225] Another interesting group was that taken at Persepolis by Colonel E.G. Stannus, who had the results shipped to Bombay, where they remained for a year before being presented to the Museum by the retiring Governor, Mountstuart Elphinstone. This group was added to at the end of the century by Herbert Weld, who took mould-makers with him on his excavations in Persepolis. Their products were given to the

Museum and to the Nottingham City Museum (who later passed their tranche to the British Museum).[226]

Probably the most famous collection of casts acquired by the Museum was that made for Alfred Maudslay in Central America at the end of the nineteenth century.[227] Maudslay's casts originally went to the Victoria and Albert Museum, where they were, to use his own words, 're-interred... whence they may possibly be unearthed in years to come by Macaulay's New Zealander if he happens to have a taste for excavation'.[228] They were rescued in 1923 by T.A. Joyce and installed in the British Museum in a room named after the man who had so adventurously taken them, together with original sculptures from Maudslay's collection, and furnished with a small popular guide. The Victoria and Albert Museum (like the British Museum) has always had an ambivalent attitude towards its casts; it gave its classical casts to the British Museum in 1907 and, between 1978 and 1993, having abolished its education department, while retaining its magnificent and recently refurbished Cast Court, it passed the majority of its reserve cast collection of moulds and master-casts to the Museum.[229] The later, and sometimes inglorious, history of the Museum's cast collection is discussed below (p.239).

Photography – A Missed Opportunity[230]

Newton – accidentally – was the first person to use photography on a Museum excavation (pl. 17). Since the foundation of the Museum the Trustees had been anxious to publish the collections and thus make them available to the public. When they initiated the great series of catalogues they had taken great trouble to engage draughtsmen and engravers of the highest quality. The advent of photography presented them with an opportunity to extend the knowledge of the collections which was never, unfortunately, followed through. The British Museum was, however, early in the field; indeed, as we have seen, a ghostly image of Montagu House was presumably made by Fox Talbot in calotype as early as 1843, just three years after he had presented his famous paper to the Royal Society. This was apparently made in an attempt to persuade the Museum to employ the process on Fellows's expedition to Lycia. The images taken at this time survive with a number of other views of the same date in an album collected by Gray, the Keeper of Zoology.[231] What is apparently the first use of photography in the Museum itself occurred in 1846 when Talbot and Birch collaborated to publish the text and translation of the hieroglyphic inscription on the stela of Sethos I. From the early 1850s gifts of photographs had been collected by the Museum and deposited in the Department of Prints and Drawings (see p.232). In 2000 the majority of the department's photographic collection was passed to the Victoria and Albert Museum.[232]

Serious photography at the Museum was instigated by Lord Rosse, a Trustee as President of the Royal Society, and Hawkins (presumably stimulated by Birch). As early as 1852 Roger Fenton (later to achieve fame as the photographer of the Crimean War) was allowed to photograph antiquities at the Museum. In the following year the Trustees agreed to build a 'slight and inexpensive' photographic studio with a darkroom on the roof and appointed Fenton as photographer. He did not last, leaving for the Crimea in 1854; he was re-appointed on his return, but, although he produced many fine photographs for the

Museum, he was seen merely as a technician. His services were terminated, with some ill-will on his part, by the Trustees in July 1859. His negatives passed to the Department of Science and Art, which was given permission by the Trustees to sell prints of them. The decision to dispense with a permanent staff photographer was partly caused by Panizzi's inability to understand either the process or its costs, and partly by a muddled decision on the part of the Department of Science and Art to concentrate all museum photography at the South Kensington Museum.[233] Fenton was not replaced and photography was put out to a number of private firms and individuals; it was not until 1927 that a full-time photographer, D.S. Lyon, was appointed.

Fenton's studio continued to be used by a number of individual photographers and companies, including the Autotype Company, who took official photographs for the Museum. In 1872 seven volumes containing nearly 1,000 pictures of objects in the Museum were published by Mansell and Company. The studio was, however, totally unsuitable for the much more sophisticated processes then being used and under pressure from the Autotype Company, which offered some of the funding, a new studio was constructed in 1884.[234] This consisted of a small daylight studio and darkroom and survived on the roof of the Greek and Roman Galleries as a draughtsman's studio until the 1960s.

The Apotheosis of Panizzi

Ellis was old, nearly eighty, and tired. In December 1855 one Trustee, the historian Macaulay, wrote of him:

> He is a faithful and laborious public servant. He has been very useful during many years. But he is now too old and infirm for his post. It is enough to say that, at the meetings of the Trustees, it is painful to see and hear him. We generally relieve him by reading the letters for him. He has most fairly earned a pension sufficient to make his last years comfortable.[235]

Tempted by the newly won possibility of a pension, Ellis resigned in early 1856 and machinations and special pleading flourished.[236] Madden and Gray both wanted the job, but were never serious contenders, while Hawkins was too old. Panizzi, uniquely successful as the Keeper of Printed Books, threw his hat in the ring and lobbied furiously, writing to many Trustees and well-placed friends.[237] He was worried that he would be seen as a foreigner and was indeed attacked as such in the xenophobic press; but he was more disturbed by the fact that one of the Trustees also wanted the job.[238] This was Sir David Dundas, a senior lawyer who had been in and out of government and seemed – as it turned out incorrectly – to be receiving the support of Lord Lansdowne and the Duke of Somerset. Panizzi turned to Ellis, who in his beautiful hand wrote a supportive note belying his years, describing his own feelings in a similar situation: 'I cannot help feeling your fears are groundless.'[239]

A not altogether unserious stalking-horse was produced (two people had to be recommended to the Queen) in the shape of the great Anglo-Saxonist John M. Kemble, who, apart from his work on editing Old English historical texts, had also for a time been employed as an archaeologist in the Royal Museum in Hanover (p.121). Macaulay, who did not want Panizzi (he judged him too narrow in his interests), would have preferred

Kemble, a pioneering historian, philologist and antiquarian. The objection, however, to 'his drunkenness was unanswerable'.[240] Lord Panmure wrote to tell Panizzi that he had heard that Kemble was his rival for the job, saying that he had been told by the Chancellor of the Exchequer 'that the *on dit* against you was that you were not on speaking terms with some of your confreres'.[241] It was clearly with relief that Panizzi heard on 4 March that he had been appointed Principal Librarian.[242] Although he received many congratulations, some merely sycophantic, joy was not totally unconfined within the Museum, where Madden particularly (but also Gray and Hawkins) had their doubts. Madden's private thoughts were indeed vituperative.[243] All the keepers, at Panizzi's request, wrote letters of support, although Madden, who thought Gray and Hawkins were pusillanimous in so doing, delayed until 3 April, when he wrote a formal note which gave few hostages to fortune.[244]

Panizzi now entered into his own and most of the librarians were overjoyed (to the historian of the library the years that followed his appointment are seen as a quiet period of consolidation[245]), but doubts as to his support of the non-library departments simmered. At almost the same time as they appointed Panizzi the Trustees, in an attempt to assuage criticism of the Museum by the scientific establishment, appointed the extremely distinguished zoologist Professor Richard Owen, Conservator of the Hunterian Museum at the Royal College of Surgeons, to the new post of Superintendent of the Natural History Departments.[246] Panizzi was deeply suspicious of this appointment, but was reassured by the Trustees that he was in supreme charge. In the end, however, Owen (whose appointment was resented by the keepers of the natural history departments) was to prove almost as distinguished a 'fixer' as Panizzi. Members of the non-library departments, on the other hand, had reason to be uneasy about a Principal Librarian who, in the words of Macaulay (a strong supporter of Owen), 'would at any time give three mammoths for an Aldus'.[247]

Panizzi (pl. 17) was a tough Principal Librarian and did not suffer fools gladly. He could be vicious if thwarted, as Oldfield and Edwards found to their cost. To one of the young assistants in the Department of Coins and Medals he was 'a steam roller'.[248] He had had a classic clash with the Royal Society in 1833 and, ever after, was deeply suspicious of the scientific establishment. He held no real brief, as will be shown, for either national antiquities or ethnography, and would ideally have wished to be head of a library with a museum of classical antiquities attached. As he said to the Trustees in 1857:

> All that space which is now occupied by Mediæval Antiquities, by what are called British or Irish Antiquities, and by the Ethnological Collection, might thus be turned to better account. It does not seem right that such valuable space should be taken up by Esquimaux dresses, canoes and hideous feather idols, broken flints, called rude knives, and so on...[249]

However, both he and the Museum had a problem – and he was attempting to resolve it.

At the root of the Museum's difficulties once again was the problem of space. The institution was bursting at the seams. Even as the new Reading Room and the stacks around it were completed, newly found sculpture languished unseen in the basements; the officers in the natural history departments had no room for their equipment; ethnographic specimens remained unpacked and natural history specimens were deteriorating. Something had to give, but few on either the antiquities or the science side wanted to move any of the collections out of Bloomsbury. The government wondered whether the fine art and archaeology should be combined on the new National Gallery site in Trafalgar Square, but decided against it.[250] Eyes turned to South Kensington, and, although the Trustees generally preferred to extend the Bloomsbury site to the north, they presented to Parliament a detailed proposal, drawn up by Hawkins and Oldfield, arguing this case.[251] The natural historians organized a letter to Parliament signed by everybody who was anybody in science, from Darwin to Lyell, from Wheatstone to Huxley (including – much to Panizzi's fury – a number of officers and Trustees of the Museum, one of whom was Owen), which stated, 'Her Majesty's Government, we trust, will never yield to the argument that, because in some other countries the products of Nature and Art are exhibited in distinct establishments, therefore the like separation should be copied here'.[252]

Letters were exchanged between the Trustees and Parliament, until finally in May 1860, in desperation, a Select Committee was set up, 'to inquire how far, and in what way, it may be desirable to find increased space for the extension of the various collections of the British Museum, and the best means of rendering them available for the promotion of science and art'. Having received limited evidence from Trustees and officers, as well as from one or two outsiders such as Albert Way (of the Society of Antiquaries) and Charles Newton, the Committee reported with commendable speed in August.[253] Panizzi's evidence was clearly pivotal – he was quite willing to separate out some of the collections and house them elsewhere. (Privately, as we have seen, he wanted to retain only the classical collections and the library departments. Publicly he set his face against some of the ideas of Hawkins and Franks as to the material collected in their departments.) Newton, who paid his own passage from Rome (where he was now consul) to appear before the Committee, argued for the separation of the medieval and ethnographic collections, and their combination in some way with the collections in South Kensington.[254]

Despite the powerful statements of Newton and Panizzi, the Committee inclined to the universal, historical view of the collections and tried to tackle the matter of space. It looked in detail at four options for expansion – Bloomsbury, Burlington House in Piccadilly, a plot of ground near Victoria Street in Westminster, and land in Kensington belonging to the Commissioners for the Exhibition of 1851. It compared costs and finally recommended a minimal solution: 'sufficient reason has not been assigned for the removal of any part of the valuable collections in the British Museum, except that of Ethnography, and the portraits and drawings...'. Extra space could be achieved by purchasing more land in Bloomsbury, which with a new building would have cost some £300,000 (compared with at least £620,000 in South Kensington). The Select Committee's recommendations were clear and acceptable at the time, but most of them – as is so often the case – were not to be carried out. Instead it became obvious that the sensible option was to move the natural history collections to South Kensington, although this was not officially agreed by Act of Parliament until 1878.[255]

Ten Years' Collecting

To understand the problems of the Department of Antiquities it is necessary to return to 1850 and the Royal Commission's recommendations concerning national antiquities. The advent of Franks had led, with the enthusiastic support of Hawkins whose hand had been strengthened by the Royal Commission, to a totally new collecting opportunity for the department. This was signalled in 1851 and 1852 when negotiations, mainly by Hawkins, resulted in the acquisition of a major collection of southern Baltic grave-goods of eighth- to tenth-century date from J.C. Bähr, professor at the Academy of Arts at Dresden – material which he had published in 1850.[256] This collection, which the vendor said was being sought by both Berlin and Copenhagen, was bought for £200 and was an entirely new departure for the Museum. It was soon on display in the British and Mediæval Room as a comparator to the Anglo-Saxon collections.[257] For the first time money was paid for a major northern European archaeological find; Hawkins, with Franks at his elbow, was testing the water.

But Franks had been appointed primarily to collect British antiquities and his first task was to arrange a British display in the room specially provided, sorting this material from other objects which had accumulated in distant basements. It must have soon become clear to him that there were enormous gaps in the collection and, almost symboli-cally, within a couple of months of his arrival he presented to the Museum a medieval brick from Guernsey and part of a stone axe from Lincolnshire (ironically, the latter is now agreed to be a natural object).[258] His first substantial gift, a couple of years later, was a collection of medieval lead-glazed tiles from, among other sites, Chertsey Abbey, Surrey, which had been discovered in 1852.[259] These gifts immediately encouraged other enthusi-asts (particularly Albert Way, with a series of tiles from Malvern Priory and elsewhere, and the Reverend John Ward, with tiles from Jervaulx Abbey) to give related material to the Museum, and thus lay the foundation of the Museum's incomparable collection of British medieval tiles.

Franks became active in the affairs of the Archaeological Institute and preached to the converted there about the value of national antiquities to the nation and to the Museum.[260] But the Trustees and the nation were slow to respond. In 1853 the collection of Anglo-Saxon grave-goods from Kent excavated at the end of the previous century by the Reverend Bryan Faussett came on the market. Hawkins and Franks desperately wanted to buy it. Its price was not high – £683 4s – but 'the Trustees declined to give so large a sum, as there were not sufficient funds'. In the middle of negotiations with the government about money for the new Reading Room, the Trustees had real financial problems. At the same meeting they had turned down requests for other purchases to the value of £380 and had also refused an appeal by Hawkins for a larger grant for his department. They were at the same time negotiating with Layard and Rawlinson for the transport and purchase of a colossal bull from Assyria.[261] Having turned down the purchase of the Faussett collection, they were then approached – twice – by the Archaeological Institute, presumably fuelled by information from Hawkins and Franks, asking them to reconsider their decision. They again rejected it, pleading lack of money; although, according to Vaux, one trustee, Dundas, had set his face against its acquisition.[262] This was a sad loss to the Museum and created something of a scandal, so much so that some years later Parliament called for papers.[263] When the Museum's option on the collection ran out it was bought by Joseph Mayer of Liverpool for £700 and ended up in the Liverpool Museum.[264] This had serious consequences for the British Museum: as a direct result of this decision it lost three major collections: the grave-goods from the Anglo-Saxon cemetery at Fairford, Gloucestershire, which went to the Ashmolean Museum; the collection of Anglo-Saxon grave-goods and the much larger general Anglo-Saxon and early medieval collection of W.H. Rolfe, both of which also went to Liverpool.[265] When, with commendable speed, Charles Roach Smith published the expanded notebooks of Faussett in 1856, he dedicated the book 'To Joseph Mayer... this volume, descriptive of a large and important collection of national antiquities, preserved by his liberality and patriotic feeling for public purposes, after being rejected by the government, is inscribed... by the editor.'[266]

Franks wrote to Mayer, '... you have surely conferred on English Archaeologists a great and valuable boon. The publication of the work is the only thing that reconciles me to the loss of the collection to the National Museum'.[267] The Trustees have been vilified by generations of archaeologists for not purchasing the Faussett collection.[268] It is worth emphasizing, however, that, as on so many similar occasions on which purchases have been refused, there was in fact no money available and the Museum was in the throes of bringing to fruition a major and expensive project about to be funded by the government. In similar circumstances a few years later Franks might, at the first hint of trouble, have purchased the collection himself and presented it to the Museum; but the atmosphere was not yet right for such grand gestures, nor was he yet well enough established in his post. He was, however, soon to make a gesture which was to benefit the country greatly.

It is clear that the general body of the Trustees – despite the recommendations of the Royal Commission – were not entirely happy with the direction the Department of Antiquities was taking in collecting archaeological material. This unhappiness was not the only reason why they initially turned down the important collection of antiquities assembled over a period of twenty years during building and sewage works in London by Charles Roach Smith – pharmacist, belligerent antiquary and polemicist – who had published it in 1854.[269] It consisted of more than 5,000 objects, mostly (but not exclusively) of Roman and medieval date, particularly medieval pottery (which made almost its first appearance in the Museum), but also Romano-British and Romano-Gallic pottery, stone axes, Bronze-Age weapons, pilgrims' badges, a considerable body of leather objects, the famous gold and enamel brooch of eleventh-century date from Dowgate Hill, many coins and much more. The collection, offered to the Trustees on 1 February 1855,[270] was accompanied by an enthusiastic report by Franks:

> The Collection would be a great and valuable addition to the British Room – the acquisition of it by the Museum would go far to remove from us the reproach under which we are labouring of neglecting the Antiquities of our own Country while we accumulate those of other lands. I have had many proofs that such a feeling exists and that it has prevented in several cases donations being made to us...[271]

Franks, however, considered the asking price (£3,000) excessive and the Trustees referred the matter back, but refused Hawkins's suggestion that they offer £2,000 for it. Smith was furious and, having rejected an offer by Lord Londesborough for his collection (because it would have meant that it would have been broken up), and, having in turn had the collection rejected by the City of London, he directed his considerable talent for polemic to persuade the Trustees to reconsider their position. National and local societies stirred the pot and petitions were presented to the Treasury and Parliament. A year later, after the collection was re-valued by Sotheby's, the Trustees – clearly affected by the mood of the antiquarian pressure group – agreed to approach the Treasury and were granted £2,000 to complete the purchase.

Once again the Trustees had been wrong-footed by circumstance. At the meeting at which they had rejected the purchase of the Roach Smith collection, they had also been asked by Hawkins for £6,000 to spend on objects at the sale of the Bernal collection, part of an approach to the Treasury with the South Kensington Museum for £20,000 (see below). Presumably the Trustees were conscious that there was little chance of getting two extra parliamentary grants for this department at the same time. But the Roach Smith purchase was – however grudgingly – made and the Museum's native archaeological collection now approached the critical mass necessary to build it up to a status worthy of a national museum. Franks was continually adding to it. In the year after the Roach Smith purchase, for example, Franks persuaded the Museum to buy for £40 one of its most spectacular British objects, the copper alloy, enamelled shield of Iron-Age date from the Thames at Battersea.[272]

Stimulated by the public statements of the Royal Commission (pl. 117) and of pamphleteers such as Franks and Albert Way, a flow of prehistoric objects now started to be offered by collectors who had been waiting for the Museum to take the problem of the nation's archaeological material seriously. In 1853 the Society of Antiquaries stirred its lethargic self and sponsored the excavations of its Secretary, John Yonge Akerman, at the Anglo-Saxon cemetery at Harnham Hill, Wiltshire; Akerman exceeded his brief and also charged them for his excavations at the similar sites of Wingham, Stodmarsh and Gilton, in Kent, and at a number of other sites including the deserted medieval town of Old Sarum. The finds from most of these sites were published in the Society's journal, *Archaeologia*, and ended up in the British Museum, as did the material from the important cemetery at Long Wittenham, Berkshire, which he excavated under the auspices of the Antiquaries in 1859.[273]

The Society of Antiquaries was to be increasingly important to Franks; not only did he meet all the collectors and excavators there, but he was able to steer to the Museum many of the objects exhibited and discussed at its meetings. Franks became Director of the Society in 1858 in succession to Ellis – not, however, without some opposition from the Trustees and Panizzi (the latter, who was what nowadays would be called a 'control freak', at one time gave the feeble excuse for his opposition that one of Hawkins's reports about the matter had reached him late).[274] Having after much trauma been elected, Franks now made the Society his main platform for communication concerning the Museum's collecting policy.

In 1855 Hawkins asked the Trustees to allow Franks £500 to spend on antiquities in Amiens. The Trustees, in agreeing this, cut the sum to £250 and asked that the South Kensington Museum be consulted in order to avoid competition. In the event Franks spent only £60 on the specific objects he had asked to buy, but asked permission – ultimately granted – to purchase two other objects, a copper-gilt figure and a Palissy dish.[275] This was an important moment. Previously such visits abroad had been allowed only for the purchase of books or classical antiquities. The Trustees now apparently recognized the importance of the medieval collections and began to trust the young Franks's judgement in a way that would have been unthinkable a few years earlier. The Trustees' concern that the South Kensington Museum should be consulted was also important; they were conscious that they were spending public money and that there were potential overlaps of interest here. They therefore initiated a practice of consultation and cooperation that continues to this day with other national and provincial museums.

Franks's immediate and specialist interest was the medieval collections. The Museum had failed to buy the ivory collection of Gabor Fejérváry in 1855, which, like the Faussett collection, had been snapped up by Joseph Mayer for Liverpool.[276] In the following year, however, Franks persuaded the Trustees to buy the much larger Maskell collection of ivories with a special Treasury grant of £2,400.[277] But it was the Bernal sale that showed Franks at his best and showed how far cooperation with South Kensington now went.

The collection had been amassed by an exceedingly rich MP, Ralph Bernal, who owned vast property in the West Indies. He was an early president of the British Archaeological Association and a ferocious collector. He died in 1854 and the dispersal of his collection in the following year triggered one of the great sales of the nineteenth century – it lasted thirty-two days and produced £62,690. An attempt, proposed by the Society of Arts and backed by the Prince Consort, was made to buy the whole collection for the nation for £50,000, as proposed by Bernal's heirs, and to spread the material round the country's museums.[278] This failed, and the South Kensington Museum and the British Museum took up negotiations with the government. Neither got as much as they had asked for, but the South Kensington Museum was granted £12,000, provided that it did not bid beyond the price marked in the catalogue, while the British Museum was granted £4,000 unconditionally. Franks worked closely with Cole and Robinson of the South Kensington Museum in planning the bids. A note by Franks bound in with one of two annotated copies of the sale catalogue in the Department of Medieval and Later Antiquities laconically notes 'many objects included in the estimate [£6,785] given up to Marlborough House'. On the other hand Franks was clearly skilled in handling the negotiations. Robinson told Coles that Franks and he had worked together 'in utmost harmony', while complaining about the constraints laid on him by the Treasury. There was considerable interest in the sale and prices were high. Many prize items went to wealthy collectors, including a number of members of the Rothschild family, and the two museums were outbid on a number of important items, so that the South Kensington Museum was only able to spend £8,583 and the British Museum £2,537. The Museum, however, was able to purchase 231 lots, out of a total of 4,267,[279] most of which were bought by private collectors.[280]

The most important of the Museum's purchases was the Lothar Crystal, which cost £267. Made about 865 for Lothar II, King of the Franks, it was given by him to the Abbey of Waulsort on the River Meuse; there, with a short interval, it remained until the French Revolution, when, according to tradition, it was looted and thrown in the river. Recovered, it was sold to a French collector for 12 francs, and it was from him that Bernal bought it. The crystal, 10.5 cm in diameter, is engraved with scenes from the tale of Susanna and the Elders, which refers directly to the stormy history of Lothar's own marriage.[281] This was but one of many important objects acquired in the sale, which included reliquaries, enamels, vessels of various materials, glass, finger-rings and all manner of objects – even a stall-plate of a Knight of the Garter.

Particularly notable was a group of seventy-two Italian maiolica pieces, mostly of sixteenth- and seventeenth-century date. Franks took special trouble with this acquisition.[282]

He had been interested in maiolica even before he had entered the Museum and, within a few months of his appointment, had persuaded the Trustees to buy twenty-one dishes of this ware from the collection of the Abbé Hamilton. Just before the Bernal sale he had himself given a group of splendid pieces of maiolica to the Museum, including a number of signed works.[283] Thus the Trustees were well attuned to the idea of collecting maiolica and did not cavil at the killing he had made at the sale. Franks focused his attention on documented objects – pottery bearing marks, signatures, heraldry or dates placing them in a firm historical context; his choice was a perfect foil to those bought by the South Kensington Museum, which were selected largely on the basis of design. By this one purchase Franks established the Museum's reputation as a serious collector of Renaissance and post-Renaissance pottery, a material which had hitherto only been collected incidentally.

The Department of Antiquities, although gradually acquiring more and more non-classical material, continued to purchase in its now traditional areas. Typical perhaps was a most prestigious object, a cauldron from the so-called Barone tomb, bought in 1854. Discovered in 1847 at Capua in Italy, the cauldron, dating from c.480 BC, has a tripodal foot and a lid embellished with three-dimensional figures of a man and woman dancing surrounded by mounted archers. On the shoulder is an engraved frieze of one of the exploits of Herakles, as well as scenes from a funeral procession.[284] It is a very grand piece. (Many years later the Museum bought a red-figured cup from the tomb, while the Bibliothèque Nationale in Paris acquired another pottery vessel.)

Reform

During the years following the appointment of Panizzi, Hawkins was a tower of strength to the Department of Antiquities. He was erratic, self-willed and growing old, but he was afraid of nobody and sustained his enthusiasm for the department's collections, particularly for the new national collections curated by Franks. He himself had been engaged in a massive book on English historical medals which was printed for the Trustees in 1852.[285] Only someone like Hawkins, having created a work so offensive to the susceptibilities of the time that it had to be suppressed and the edition pulped, could have continued to hold his post. The book was based on the Museum's collections, his own (much larger) collection, and medals from various other collections. It was a *tour de force*, but was at the same time so bigoted – not to say scurrilous – in its attitude to the Roman Catholic Church, to Oliver Cromwell and various historical figures that it could not be allowed to bear the imprimatur of the Trustees:

> The Trustees [growled their minutes] have observed with much dissatisfaction that the volume displays by far too many expressions of the Editor's private opinions, bearing with great severity, not only on persons conspicuous in English History, but on religious and political denominations. The Trustees are persuaded that such opinions cannot be declared in a work published under their authority, without derogating from the dignity and impartiality which it is their duty to preserve in all their proceedings. These objections are so powerful, that the Trustees do not think it necessary to specify several historical and literary errors in the book, which, though of minor importance, ought to have been avoided.[286]

The Trustees suppressed the catalogue, not even allowing Hawkins a copy. Questions were asked in Parliament, but it was to linger unpublished until Franks, Grueber and Vaux produced a new, enlarged – and expurgated – version in 1885, eighteen years after Hawkins' death.[287]

This was not, however, the end of the medal saga. During his long career, starting even before he was employed by the Museum, Hawkins had amassed a very distinguished collection of medals – he had 4,769 medals as compared to the Museum's 1,581 – which he offered to the Museum on a number of occasions. It was each time turned down. In 1855 Macaulay, who did not like Hawkins, had expressed a commonly held Trustees' view:

> As to Hawkins's medals, I am decidedly of the opinion that we ought not to buy them. It is the duty of the chief officers of the Museum to be constantly on the look out, each in his own line, for rare and valuable articles... It is to these gentlemen that we look for such information and advice as may enable us to expend judiciously the money entrusted to us by Parliament. But if our agents are to be our competitors at sales, if our agents are to forestall us, if they use that skill, which of right belongs to us who pay them, for the purpose of forming collections which they may afterwards sell to us at an advanced price, it is quite impossible that the public can be well served.[288]

Hawkins, aware of this criticism when he once again offered his collection to the Museum in 1859, countered, 'the collection was commenced many years ago and had become extensive before Mr Hawkins was connected with the Museum... As his object in collecting was historical, Mr Hawkins could not afford to allow any medal to pass away and consequently when obstacles opposed its acquisition for the Museum, he purchased it himself, but such purchases were compulsory not voluntary...'.[289] Which seems very fair since the Trustees were not particularly interested in this sort of thing, and certainly were not keen to pay for it. Perhaps looking to his retirement, the Trustees now assented to the purchase of what was a most important collection and one which raised the Museum's status in the field considerably.[290]

The painful discussion caused by this acquisition was presumably the reason why, three years later, Panizzi recommended to the Trustees that officers should not collect for themselves.[291] This was the first of many attempts to stop this practice, but in the nineteenth century it seems to have been honoured more in the breach than the observance. If Franks had followed this line the Museum would have lost one of its greatest collections. Other collectors (Franks's successor, Hercules Read, for example) were, however, less scrupulous. Meanwhile it became evident that Hawkins had also collected prints, specializing in personal and political satires – more than 10,000 of them. These were purchased without fuss from his widow in 1868 and formed the core of F.G. Stephens's catalogue of the Museum's holdings, which appeared between 1870 and 1883.[292]

Hawkins was feeling his age. On 22 June 1860 (in his eightieth year) he wrote to Panizzi:

> I am old and my activity is impaired and I feel that the time is arrived when I ought to make way for a more energetic succession. Will you then be good enough to let the Trustees know *privately* of my intention. There are a few things I wish to finish before I go, and when I see my way clear I will make a formal tender of my resignation. I wish now only to give a preparatory intimation of a future intention.[293]

He was not, however, as Miller has suggested, enfeebled;[294] he had stayed on for the first years of Panizzi's reign, fighting his corner against all odds (as early as 1856 Macaulay was rejoicing in his imminent departure).[295] He still, he said, had things to do. Chiefly there was his need to appear before the Select Committee, where his evidence and that of Edmund Oldfield, a trusted assistant, was crucial in begging for space. He saw the very real dangers Panizzi posed to parts of his vast empire (which was about to be split up), and wanted to make sure that Franks had his feet firmly under the table.[296] Hawkins presumably also wished to influence Panizzi's plans for the subdivision of the department, which were first aired before the Trustees in July (see p.140), and this he may well have done in view of the alterations made by the Trustees to the plans.[297] The time for reform had come.

Trustees

The Trustees were powerful and, as a result of the Royal Commission and the two Select Committees, well organized. The Principal Trustees (some more active than others) continued to do much of the official business; but real power lay with the Standing Committee (composed mostly of elected Trustees), which met about twice a month – no detail escaped them. As a body they worked well, seemed to be adept at getting money out of the government when they really wanted it and, through the presidents of the learned societies, had reasonable access to thinking in the academic world, as demonstrated in the frequent discussions on the natural history departments and on national antiquities. Ellis had, as has been shown, achieved direct access to Trustees' meetings only after the departure of Forshall, and always seemed to be somewhat in awe of them and unwilling to fight for his staff. The Trustees, as demonstrated in the evidence given to the Royal Commission, had a tendency to take things very much on themselves, ignoring the keepers – a case in point being their interference in the display of the Lycian marbles. They also tended – so far as the Department of Antiquities was concerned – to be oriented towards the classical and Mediterranean world, vociferously championed on the board by W.R. Hamilton and Sir Charles Fellows. It was only the presence of one or two powerful Trustees, such as Sir Robert Inglis and Lord Stanhope, the President of the Society of Antiquaries, that kept the Trustees' minds on a broader view of the Museum's duty. Panizzi, more worldly-wise than his predecessor, knew how to argue a case (as he had done so successfully as Keeper of Printed Books before the Royal Commission). Socially adept, legally trained and politically well-connected,[298] Panizzi played the Trustees skilfully and they backed most of his proposals, including some detrimental to individual members of the staff. But he did not win all his battles.

A measure of the Trustees' success can to a certain extent be measured by the increase in the size of the Parliamentary grant.[299] In the critical year of 1835/6 – the year before the Select Committee report was issued – the grant was £17,796, to which must be added the income from the Trustees' private funds, bringing the total at their disposal to £19,603. By 1860/1 the grant had risen to £100,850. The Trustees' own funds – together with income from the sale of publications – amounted to £1,360. Hardly a year passed without special parliamentary grants for purchases or buildings. From the years 1850/1 to 1860/1 Parliament provided special grants for purchase or excavation amounting to approximately £20,000. Although all the senior members of the government were on the board, the presence of the Chancellor of the Exchequer generally ensured that their more lavish demands did not succeed.

It is clear that the Standing Committee was all-powerful and an analysis of those who attended (and how often) is of absorbing interest and tempts the historian to speculate on their relative strength. Taking a year at random at a critical period in the history of the Department of Antiquities (May 1857 to May 1858), Dean Milman attended more than anyone else – seventeen times; Lord Stanhope attended thirteen times; Hamilton, Gladstone, Murchison, Dundas, the Duke of Somerset, Lord Lansdowne, Lord John Russell, Macaulay and Wrottesley eleven or twelve times. Of the Principal Trustees, the Speaker was the most constant in attendance, but the others occasionally attended meetings. Hamilton, who resigned in the course of the year, had long been one of the strongest supporters of the Department of Antiquities and of Panizzi – his knowledge of classical antiquity was deeply rooted. Stanhope, President of the Society of Antiquaries, represented the new generation and was to back Franks and his ideas in the next few years, while Gladstone (an elected Trustee since 1853, as well as being an Official Trustee when he was in government) eruditely – if parsimoniously – supported the classicists. Lansdowne collected books and antiquities and was a friend of Macaulay. There was here a vast hoard of experience and on the whole it was well used for the benefit of the Museum.

The full board meetings were still held quarterly on Saturdays and business could sometimes hardly be distinguished from that of the Standing Committee. Like all meetings, they could be tedious. As Macaulay put it in his diary, 'After breakfast to the Museum. Long, stupid and useless sitting.'[300] On the same occasion he gives a picture of the tedium in a letter to Margaret Trevelyan, who was holidaying at Brighton:

> But I am forced to sit here playing at doing business, – Goulbourn in the chair, – Inglis at my right hand, – the Bishop of London at my left, and further off Sir David Dundas. Here we shall stay dawdling till late in the afternoon, and shall do as little for arts or letters or science as if we had been, like you, lounging on the beach, gathering shells, and counting yachts and pleasure boats.[301]

Not everybody, however, took such a jaundiced view, and Macaulay died just before major decisions had to be taken about the Department of Antiquities.

Chapter 5

FISSION AND CONSOLIDATION

1860–97

The last forty years of the nineteenth century were the most important in the history of the Museum. In this period the natural history collections were moved to a grand new building designed by Alfred Waterhouse in South Kensington, and the space vacated by them put to good use by the library and the antiquities departments. A new wing was built on to the Smirke building and new galleries were built into vacant spaces. New departments were created and collecting in such new areas as ethnography and European prehistory grew almost exponentially. Many collections and objects were either given to the Museum at this period or, particularly in the 1860s and 1870s, were often acquired with the aid of government grants. More staff were recruited and better housed; they became more professional in their collecting, their scholarship and their recording. Those parts of the Museum that remained at Bloomsbury began to split into two disparate parts as the practices of the library departments grew apart from those of the antiquities departments, although the Department of Manuscripts served as a bridge between the two.

New Departments

Hawkins's long reign was over and his Department of Antiquities had grown ludicrously diverse. Panizzi acknowledged this and in July 1860, shortly after he had heard from Hawkins that he wished to retire, approached the Trustees suggesting that the department should be split into four – a Department of Greek and Roman Antiquities, a Department of Oriental (i.e. Egyptian and Assyrian) Antiquities, a Department of Coins and Medals and a Department of British and Mediaeval Antiquities and Ethnography. The two most senior keepers were to be paid £600 and the others £500 p.a. The Trustees havered for five months, at first suggesting that it be one department with three sub-departments. Eventually they agreed that there should be three self-standing departments, with Samuel Birch as Keeper of Oriental Antiquities, Charles Newton as Keeper of Greek and Roman Antiquities and William Vaux as Keeper of Coins and Medals.[1] The surviving papers about these appointments and divisions are exiguous, but it is clear that Panizzi was at odds with some of the Trustees. Even at the last minute he seems to have wanted Newton for Coins and

Medals and Vaux for Greek and Roman, but the Trustees disagreed.[2] At one stage he planned that ethnography and the non-classical antiquities should be attached to the latter department. Finally, in February 1861, it was agreed that this extraordinary conglomerate – British and Mediaeval Antiquities and Ethnography – should become a sub-department of Oriental Antiquities, headed by Franks, under the sympathetic Birch.[3]

It is difficult to reconstruct what had been going on, but there was clearly a hidden agenda and, in Newton's case, a hint of jobbery.[4] Nobody could deny Birch his post; he was the most brilliant scholar in the Museum and had a long-standing reputation as a specialist in hieroglyphic inscriptions. There seemed little opposition to the appointment of Vaux, whose interests straddled coins and sculpture, although he would have preferred to be in charge of the latter. Franks was probably too young to be a full-blown keeper; what is more, he was in charge of that part of the Museum with which Panizzi and the Trustees had the least sympathy. Newton, who was in Panizzi's confidence, had been busy lobbying since June, preferring the post of keeper of sculpture to that of keeper of coins.[5]

There was another possible candidate for one of the keeperships. Edmund Oldfield had taken on the arrangement of the sculpture when Newton left and, in the early 1850s, had presented papers to the Trustees on methods of displaying it in historical and cultural sequence in the limited space available. His proposals had been successfully carried through despite the constantly increasing size of the collection. He had backed Hawkins in providing many of the ideas when the old man was giving evidence to Parliament; indeed, unusually for a person in such a junior position, he had himself given evidence to the Select Committee.[6] Museum tradition has it that this fact was one of the reasons for Panizzi's undoubted dislike of him – another was that he had reported adversely on the collection of classical antiquities bequeathed to the Museum by an old friend of Panizzi, Sir William Temple, British Minister at Naples.[7] Hawkins wanted Oldfield to succeed him, and even the most active Principal Trustee, Speaker Denison, may well have favoured him.[8] When, therefore, Oldfield was appointed to the new Greek and Roman department under Newton, he felt hard done by and suggested that the department should be split in two and that he should be given the title of keeper, without any extra pay. The Trustees turned down his suggestion, and he had no alternative but to resign.[9] It was not a happy story and reflects badly on both Panizzi and the Trustees, for Oldfield, a good man, had served the Museum well and deserved recognition.[10]

Panizzi and Newton, together with many Trustees, still felt unhappy about the presence of medieval antiquities and ethnography in the Museum – although, strangely, they seemed to accept the presence of European prehistory. Panizzi and Cole (whose empire included the South Kensington Museum) were in some agreement that the medieval collections belonged in South Kensington. Cole, a predatory character, pursued the idea with diligence in evidence to the Select Committee on the South Kensington Museum, and Panizzi showed himself amenable to the proposition that the British Museum's medieval collections should be transferred there.[11] Panizzi and Cole were wrong; the British Museum was an historical museum, not an art museum. What is more, they both ignored the fact that there was already a major collection of medieval material in the Department of Manuscripts which was totally relevant to the antiquities.

The problem, however, also centred on the need to provide more space for the natural history departments in order to preserve the integrity of the idea of the universal museum, a concept still widely supported in the scientific community. Oldfield expressed the opinion of many in a letter to Layard in 1862, after he had left the Museum service, but while still well attuned to the grapevine. He argued for the purchase of one and half acres of land to the west of the Museum, which could be used to house the antiquities collection. This, he suggested, would cost £65,000, and the construction of the galleries would be a further £200,000. 'If this plan were adopted', he wrote, 'the present galleries of small antiquities on the upper floor could be surrendered to Nat. History: and then the Naturalists would be as completely severed from the archaeologists, and the sight, & smell, of stuffed animals, as effectively got rid of, as if they were 3 miles away'.[12] But it was gradually becoming clearer that Natural History would move. Owen, as Superintendent of Natural History, was on reasonably good terms with Panizzi and, despite the fact that he had in 1857 signed the memorial to Parliament against the separation of the two elements, had by the early 60s reversed his position and now agreed with the Principal Librarian that the two sections should be split. The Trustees were gradually brought round and agreed to a move in 1861,[13] but the South Kensington site was not finally agreed until the Act of Parliament of 1878.

This decision meant that enough space would be vacated to make way for prehistoric and medieval antiquities and ethnography, and the way was now open to create the fourth antiquities department – the Department of British and Mediaeval Antiquities and Ethnography. The proposal came from Franks in a seemingly audacious four-page foolscap letter to Panizzi on 6 March 1866 – seemingly audacious because such decisions were normally handed down from above, and also because Franks did not consult his keeper beforehand.[14] The tone of his letter does, however, suggest that Franks had been encouraged by Panizzi to take this step. Franks's hand had been immeasurably strengthened by his aggressive acquisition policy and particularly by his role in relation to Henry Christy's bequest of the vast collection of ethnography in late 1865 (see below, p.158). Franks – now aged forty – felt he needed the extra prestige of a keepership, having turned down a more senior post as head of the South Kensington Museum. Panizzi, now enthusiastic, put the proposal to the Trustees:

> ... the great increase in the mediaeval and ethnographical collections, and the great interest taken by the Public in the British antiquities most especially, render it highly desirable, or rather quite necessary that a separate department should be created for them. The necessity for adopting this course seems self-evident to Mr Panizzi, and he thinks therefore that he need not dwell upon it. Equally evident to Mr Panizzi are the advantages which the Museum would derive by securing the services of Mr Franks, as the head of the new department, on such terms as would be satisfactory to the feelings of so valuable an officer, who wishes no more than to secure for himself that higher position in the service of the trustees, which Mr Panizzi feels confident that he deserves.[15]

The Trustees agreed, and his appointment was signed on 24 May 1866.[16] The structure of the Museum's antiquities departments was now fixed for the next half-century. A few months later, in August 1866, George William Reid, an artist by education who had joined the Museum as an attendant (a post his father had held before him) in 1842, followed the highly successful Carpenter, who had recently died, as Keeper of Prints and Drawings.[17] It is noteworthy that all appointments to vacant keeperships seem now to have been made on the recommendation of the Principal Librarian (recommendations which were of course forwarded to the appropriate Principal Trustee).[18]

Panizzi had tendered his resignation to the Trustees in the previous year. This had been accepted, but he had stayed on while a successor was found.[19] The Trustees indulged in their now customary delay when presented with a problem. Panizzi wanted the Keeper of Printed Books, John Winter Jones, to succeed him. Jones (pl. 25) had acted as his deputy during a prolonged absence in 1863, and acquitted himself well. Some, however, felt that Newton would be a better Principal Librarian, but he was reluctant, although his name was one of the two submitted to the Queen.[20] Jones was finally appointed in July 1866 on the same day as the resignation of Madden, Panizzi's arch-enemy, was accepted by the Board – who allowed him an annual pension of £600 (the same sum as his salary).[21] Panizzi was made a Senator of Italy and in 1869 was persuaded by Gladstone to accept the KCB. He died in 1879.

Winter Jones – a pale shadow of Panizzi – had been an exceptionally competent Keeper of Printed Books and was a nice man. His twelve-year reign was pedestrian and, in the high period of the Victorian economy before the agricultural depression of the latter part of the century, he could have achieved more from the Treasury (in respect of extra staff for the antiquities departments, for example). He did, however, carry to its conclusion the battle of the move of the natural history collections to South Kensington. He came from a literary family (his grandfather wrote *Goody Two Shoes*), and went straight from St Paul's School in London to read for the bar, but gave this up and became travelling secretary to the Charity Commissioners. Joining the Department of Printed Books in 1837, he proceeded up the ladder of that department, pulled or pushed by Panizzi. His obituarists could find no ill in him, but were hard put to illuminate exceptional points save that he cared deeply for the staff.[22] The comment of one of his successors as Keeper of Printed Books, Richard Garnett, is typical: 'The institution, thoroughly reorganised during the last thirty years, required rest, and no impulse was felt towards the reforms and developments which proved practicable under his successor.'[23]

A Political Fugue [24]

One of the most delicate matters Jones had to deal with concerned the South Kensington Museum, and it must be said that his paperwork was impeccable. In June 1873 he was approached by the Chancellor of the Exchequer (Robert Lowe), enquiring whether the South Kensington Museum and the Bethnal Green Museum, at the time of the resignation of Henry Cole, should be transferred to the Museum. Jones consulted, at the Chancellor's request, the most active Trustees – Lord Derby, the Duke of Somerset, Lord Stanhope, Sir Philip Egerton, Spencer Walpole and Disraeli. The idea was that the education section should remain with the Board of Education and that the collections and exhibitions should be handed over to the British Museum. Somerset, like most on the British Museum side, was sceptical:

> It would be an advantage to get rid of a certain rivalry and competition in the acquisition of objects of art which is now inevitable.

> But the Kensington Museum I thought, is in the habit of lending articles for lectures &c in different parts of the country.
>
> The essence of that Museum was to popularize art amongst the manufacturing classes, and was so far educational. It seems to me difficult to divide that establishment into two parts.
>
> However I should be ready to assist in any *practical scheme*.

The Trustees discussed the matter on 4 July, and the Standing Committee met the Chancellor on the following day. The Chancellor dismissed most of the objections of the Trustees, for example as to the ownership of the building and the lending of material, as matters of detail and turned the matter over to Lord Ripon and W.E. Forster (Lord President and Vice-President of the Council respectively). Five days later there was a meeting and the Lord President answered all the Trustees' objections. Negotiations proceeded apace and everything seemed to be set fair, but parliamentary time was running out. By 30 July a deal seemed imminent and the Lord President drew up heads of agreement. Inevitably, there was then a leak (almost certainly from the South Kensington Museum, and probably from the retired Henry Cole) and on 4 August the matter was raised in the Commons. Gladstone, the Prime Minister, admitted that there had been conversations, but promised consultation. There was now a serious hiccup. Lowe was out of favour, deeply implicated in overspending at the Post Office and in the Department of Works, and within a few days was urbanely dismissed by Gladstone who added the Chancellorship to his own portfolio.

Meanwhile Jones, Franks and Newton, as members of a departmental committee under the chairmanship of Sir Francis Sandford of the Department of Education, tried to agree matters with representatives of the South Kensington Museum. A long printed report was produced in which the South Kensington members wrote dissenting appendices. They pointed to difficulties, particularly with regard to lending and the division of space, and insisted that the proposed scheme would not work. The government was getting cold feet and Henry Cole whipped up fury against the proposal in an intemperate speech in Hanley in October 1873, which attacked the Trustees and the British Museum in round terms. In November in London he also attacked Robert Lowe in similar vein.[25]

Somerset (at this time a supporter of Gladstone) comforted Jones (7 January 1874):

> ...I expected to hear that the Government had abandoned the scheme of transferring the S. K. Museum to the Trustees.
>
> I cannot... see how you, as our executive officer, could conduct the business with the continued opposition of the department at South Kensington. There will arise differences as to the purchases of objects, and remonstrances, and members of the h. of commons will be prompted to ask questions. It will be said that the education of the people is restricted, &c., &c. Few members take a real interest in the subject, but many will enjoy the opportunity of annoying government. I do not think it worth the trouble which the transfer would occasion.
>
> The organisation of the necessary arrangements would require a strong hand and the thankless task will bring no credit.
>
> I believe the management at South Kensington to be bad, and I should dislike to share the responsibility of conducting it on the existing system.
>
> But they consider their own system excellent, and the government seems helpless in controlling it....

Somerset was right. On 21 January the government kicked the project into touch and three days later the Trustees accepted the decision with some relief. In February the South Kensington Museum staggered into one of the less glorious periods of its history when Philip Cunliffe Owen was appointed as its head. If it had passed to the Trustees of the British Museum, Franks would have been put in charge of it and the story of both museums would have been very different.

Staffing

The staff of the Museum had grown considerably since 1836, the year of the first Select Committee, when the government grant, mostly spent on them, was £21,972. At this time the staff consisted of the Principal Librarian, Secretary and Accountant; in the Department of Manuscripts a keeper, assistant keeper, three assistants, a supernumerary and three attendants; in the Department of Printed Books a keeper, assistant keeper, an extra assistant librarian, three supernumeraries and thirteen assistants; while in the King's Library (still run separately) were a librarian, two assistants and two attendants. A superintendent and three attendants ran the Reading Room. The natural history departments had two keepers, an assistant keeper, four assistants and five attendants; while the Department of Antiquities had a keeper, an assistant keeper and three attendants. The Department of Prints and Drawings had a keeper and an attendant. There was a messenger and an assistant messenger, a hall porter, three housemaids and three labourers: a total establishment of sixty-four.

By 1861, the establishment had more than quadrupled to 284. The grant had kept pace with the growth in staff and now stood at about £100,000. Nearly half the staff were employed in the library – 109 in the Department of Printed Books – while the Department of Manuscripts numbered twenty-three. The natural history departments had thirty-four staff. The newly split antiquities departments had thirty-seven members of staff, comprising twenty-three shared attendants (as well as three attendants for the Department of Prints and Drawings) and eleven curators.[26] The ancillary staff, housemaids, labourers, heating and ventilation engineers, security staff, stokers and so on amounted to sixty-nine. Since 1863, when the military had been withdrawn from guard duties, the Museum was warded by three police sergeants and twelve constables on secondment (extra policing was bought in whenever necessary). The increase in library staff was largely the result of the rigorous pursuit of copyright material by Panizzi (as Keeper of Printed Books) in the early 1850s, and by his concerted effort to buy older books and foreign publications – the purchase grant for printed books, about £3,000 in 1837, was now about £10,000 and was to remain at this figure until the late 1870s. Acquisitions of volumes and parts of journals in 1839 (the first available figures) had been 6,500; by 1863 they had reached 76,000. In the 1860s the Department of Printed Books also began seriously to face up to the serious problem of the space taken up by newspapers (Harris, for example, quotes figures for 1865, when 798 volumes of newspapers were added to the library, occupying 142 feet (43.2 m) of shelving).[27]

By the time the Department of Antiquities had been divided, the library departments had reached a reasonably stable state. The collapse of Panizzi's health, however, which followed shortly, meant that the effort that should have been put into building up the staff of both the natural history and antiquities departments was not as effective as it might have been. Panizzi did, however, struggle with Civil Service reforms and with the problem of pensions for members of the staff. Pensions, as we have seen in the case of Ellis, were not granted by right; and junior members of staff, almost alone among public servants, often worked until they died or were incapacitated. Further, the Trustees had no right to offer any pension on their own authority; every case had to be referred to the Treasury. In 1837 the Trustees had approached the Chancellor of the Exchequer about pensions, but received a dusty answer: 'he did not apprehend that it would be expedient to introduce the principle of superannuation into the Museum, but that it is better to select carefully and to trust to the prudential habits of the persons employed'.[28]

But many members of staff were still poor, and could easily fall into debt. Even quite senior officers got into trouble. In 1840, for example, Ellis laconically informed the Trustees that 'Mr Cowtan [the accountant] is unfortunately absent from the Museum. He is at present detained in the prison in White Cross Street.' He had been imprisoned for debt. Released after two months, he returned to duty, without any disciplinary action being taken against him by the Trustees.[29] Some of the senior officers (Hawkins, Franks and Oldfield, for example) had money; but most (Madden and Newton, for example) were without significant private means and had to take outside work to supplement their income. Similarly, many of the housemaids and manual workers had no family and, if they left the Museum's service, were thrown on the parish. Many continued to moonlight as waiters in nearby hostelries or as scene-shifters at Covent Garden.[30] Panizzi, himself not wealthy, privately helped, it is said, some of the more poorly paid members of staff financially. In 1841 the attendants had set up the British Museum Attendants Mutual Life Assurance Society. Formally established under the regulations of the Acts of Parliament which controlled such institutions, it had three trustees and a committee of five. At the time of its foundation it had thirty-five members. Subscription was graduated between 4s a year at age twenty-five, and 15s 4d at age sixty-five, which was the upper age for joining; there was an entrance fee of 2s 6d. Next of kin received £10 on the death of a member. Meetings were held at the Museum Tavern opposite the Museum, where much unofficial business has always been conducted.[31] The Trustees were not entirely careless of the health of their staff, for in 1861 they appointed a medical officer at a fee of 10s 6d for each consultation.[32]

But such palliatives were not enough; the situation concerning pay and pensions was clearly inequitable and Panizzi and the Trustees addressed the matter seriously in 1857.[33] The Treasury were approached and appointed two senior civil servants, Sir Charles Trevelyan and George Arbuthnot, to examine pay and conditions. They proposed that henceforth members of the Museum staff should be treated as equivalent to civil servants, that posts should be pensionable, and that gratuities (special payments to staff) and the employment of supernumeraries should cease. The Trustees' Sub-Committee on Finance set a scale of salaries, which alleviated some of the inequities, particularly in the Assistant and Attendant grades. It did not, however, tackle the problem of the pay of the higher grades, particularly that of the keepers (£600) and assistant keepers (£400), which had remained at more or less the same level since 1837 – it was 1878 before anything was done to correct this anomaly.[34]

The most serious problem remained that of pensions. The Treasury and Gladstone, an influential Trustee, insisted that pensions would only be allowed if officers were recruited by examination under the system set up to reform the civil service after the Northcote-Trevelyan report of 1853. Gladstone, as Chancellor of the Exchequer, had invested much time in its implementation in order to remove patronage from the system of appointment within the service and insisted in carrying the reforms forward into the Museum.[35] The system of recruitment, which had changed little since the foundation of the Museum and still ultimately depended on the private decision of the three Principal Trustees, was precisely the sort of patronage that the reforms were meant to remove. The reforms were not, however, totally applicable to the Museum situation; the examinations were inflexible and had little relevance to the recruitment of the staff of the antiquities departments. As so often in relation to the Museum, adherence by the Treasury to bureaucratic principle (and a strict interpretation of the Superannuation Act of 1859) resulted in unsuitable people being appointed to posts on the basis of written examinations. These were set and marked by dons steeped in the unreformed traditions of Oxford and Cambridge, which were totally irrelevant to the specialisms needed. The Treasury was remarkably obdurate – even for that stone-faced institution – and a long public battle ultimately produced only marginal variations of the strict Treasury line until a major reform in 1921.[36] As a result of the straitjacket of civil service appointments, the keepers sometimes used devious methods to get round the civil servants. George Smith, for example, a brilliant linguist and specialist in cuneiform, was first recruited in 1867 as a temporary transcriber (what would in modern terms be a research assistant) to work with Rawlinson on the publication of the cuneiform inscriptions, but was quickly promoted as his abilities were revealed.[37] Franks was later to get into trouble by employing his ethnographic assistant at his own expense.

Attendants and messengers were also granted pension rights.[38] It is not clear whether other members of staff – at lowlier grades – were allowed pensions except *ex gratia*. In 1871, however, the Civil Service Commission insisted that labourers, window-cleaners and gatekeepers should pass a literacy test.[39]

Charles Newton

Curatorship was emerging as a profession and Newton, for one, saw its responsibilities clearly. Writing to Panizzi in 1856, he provides one of the earliest and best surviving views of the job of curator – one which strikes a chord today:

> … The duties of the officers of the Department of Antiquities are so varied and conflicting that it may be well doubted whether they can be efficiently combined in the manner adopted at present and whether the public service would not be more satisfactorily performed by another organisation and a more marked division of labour. To make this more clear I will state in what these duties consist. The Keepership of the Department… is pre-eminently an office of Custody. The safety of the precious objects confided to his charge ought to be the paramount consideration in his mind. Custody implies constant Residence at the Museum, and a considerable restriction of personal liberty.
>
> Next in importance to the duty of Custody, is the business of Acquisition, whether by purchase or thro' donations. This is a business perpetually going on & must necessarily occupy much of the time and thoughts of a Keeper of Antiquities. He alone is responsible for

the manner in which the public money invested in antiquities is expended; on his judgement every purchase is made, and his responsibility cannot be shifted to any subordinate officer. Anyone who examines the list of purchases yearly made by the Department of Antiquities and who is practically acquainted with the business of buying objects of this kind, knows how very much time and attention such business requires. Not only do the objects offered for purchase demand the most careful scrutiny, but they are in their nature more difficult matters for negotiation than those ordinary articles of commerce of which the market price is known & the quality can be easily tested.

The next function to be considered is that of Exhibition. It is not sufficient that Antiquities should be acquired, they must be arranged in an intelligent manner so as to convey the highest amount of instruction to the Archaeologist, the artist and the public generally.

In order that this function of Exhibition should be efficiently performed, a very active staff of officers is required in such extensive collection of Antiquities as those in the British Museum.

Where new acquisitions are constantly flowing in previous arrangements, however perfect, are constantly being disturbed and the ingenuity of the Exhibitor is continually put to the test in order to adapt the space at his command to new and unlooked for requirements. The future chances of Archaeological discovery being altogether Incalculable, no certain estimate of the amount of future Acquisitions of Antiquities can be made, and all arrangements for the purposes of Exhibition must be considered as liable to change. Hence the labour of arrangement is one that can never cease, nor is such an expenditure of the time of Museum officers to be grudged. Thousands of persons who walk through the Galleries of Antiquities in the course of the year desire instruction and pleasure from their visit exactly in proportion to the intelligent labour bestowed on the arrangement of the several collections. Scientific exhibition is obviously not complete unless explanatory titles, names and labels are attached to the several objects exhibited, and this work of labelling leads me to the consideration of the 4th function of the officers of the Department of Antiquities – this function is Interpretation with a view to Publication.

It is obvious that antiquities no more explain themselves to the ordinary eye without aid of catalogues and descriptions... No person can make a scientific catalogue of any important branch of Antiquities without having gone thro' a long course of previous training of the eye, the memory and the judgement. The explanation of a single object may involve the most intensive collations of similar objects, or the most tedious researches in branches of literature not generally known or accessible. The labour required for such catalogues is seldom to be appreciated by the public, to whom the apparent result is often only a single line of description.

The persons employed on the work of making Catalogues of Antiquities and in the general duty of Interpretation and Publication can hardly produce scientific works unless they are allowed to concentrate their attention on the severe labours imposed on them. They must not be distracted by the constant interruption of visitors; their work must be continuous from day to day, not merely in intervals of business.

Now by the present constitution of the British Museum the Keeper of the Department of Antiquities is not only responsible for the Custody and Acquisition, but also, for the due Exhibition, Interpretation and Publication of all the objects contained in the Department. All these functions centre in his one person, all these conflicting duties claim his attention simultaneously and must be discharged amid the constant interruptions of the visits from strangers. He has moreover to report constantly to the Trustees and reply daily to numerous correspondents. The officers under him are in like manner set to various duties according to the exigencies of the moment, as their journals and reports will show. A subordinate officer may be employed one day on a catalogue of coins, the next, he may have to attend a sale, the third day he may be in attendance on some distinguished visitor, & so forth. None of the officers are officially set apart for any one business, and the practical result is that the duty of

Interpretation and Publication which cannot be exercised at irregular intervals, but requires continuous application is very imperfectly performed. In making this observation I would in no way wish to impute blame to any of the present officers of the Department, the fault as I conceive, is in the system and not in them.

The three functions of Custody, Acquisition and Exhibition are, I would submit, the business of the officers of the Department. Interpretation & Publication are in my view, not business, but Literary labour, requiring individual attention and peculiar attainment, and not to be efficiently performed in combination with other severe duties....[40]

He then continues to sing a song chanted by keepers down the years, asking for a research post, separate from the Keepership with its duties of care, acquisition and exhibition. Despite Panizzi's sympathy for Newton, there was no hope of such a resolution.

Newton in this letter had identified with clarity the challenges and duties of curatorship; but he was wrong to separate out the scholarship attached to these duties. He himself, as he took up the keepership, was to publish a major academic report on his excavations (a model for its period), the lavishly illustrated book on Halikarnassos and his other discoveries in Turkey.[41] In future, publication of such reports, together with definitive catalogues of discrete parts of the collection, was to become a matter of pride for the Museum staff and for the Trustees. In another sense, however, Newton was right. Time taken in acquisition, at a period when there was so much material in private hands, was precious and, because of it, his younger contemporary, Franks, tended to write much more summary accounts of the collection which he himself was accumulating voraciously. Such accounts appeared in periodicals and journals – rarely in books. Franks was, nonetheless, of necessity in view of the wide range which he had to cover almost alone in a department with collections ranging from Japan to Peru and medieval Europe, a considerable scholar and polymath. He never in fact achieved the posthumous reputation of Newton.

Newton (pl. 14) was the most important and influential British classical archaeologist of his day. His work in Turkey had opened his eyes to the possibilities of excavation on a scientific basis and to the display and interpretation of the recovered material in context and in chronological order, a battle fought and won in the Museum by Hawkins and Oldfield when they took over the display of sculpture from Westmacott, to whom aesthetics was all. Newton returned to the Museum, after his period in the consular service, as Keeper of Greek and Roman Antiquities in 1861 as a mature scholar, hardened in the field, and with a knowledge of the wider political and social world more extensive than that of most of his colleagues. His publications after his return, apart from his report on the excavations at the Turkish sites, were generally short and specialist, although he was a co-author with Birch of two volumes of the catalogue of Greek and 'Etruscan' vases and edited the three-volume catalogue of Greek inscriptions in the Museum. He also wrote a volume entitled *Travels and discoveries in the Levant* and an influential volume of reprinted essays.[42] He was prompt and energetic in producing guides for visitors; although of high scholarly standard, they were narrow and arid in tone, making no concessions to a popular readership.[43] It has been shown that he was not an easy man to work with; indeed, his first assistant lasted only five years. The next one, Alexander Murray, appointed in 1867, was approved of – an appreciation which was mutual. Murray succeeded him as keeper.

Newton's main preoccupation was to obtain enough space to display the sculpture, expressing his ideas cogently in a series of memoranda to the Trustees.[44] This aspiration –

like that of the other keepers – was not in any measure achieved until the removal of the natural history collections in 1880. Even so, Newton's ambition to consolidate all the sculpture of his department into one chronological and contextual sequence was never fully realized.

The heroic days of collecting classical antiquities in the classical lands were drawing to a close – but Newton made the most of his opportunities. For a few years the Museum continued to fund excavations and receive material from them. Robert Murdoch Smith, for example, who had worked with Newton at Halikarnassos, moved in 1860 to Cyrene and, with E.A. Porcher, produced a wealth of North African classical material. This included the bronze head of what was probably a native Libyan of 300 BC and the famous second-century AD Roman copy of an Hellenistic statue of Apollo playing a lyre, all paid for by the Museum and brought home by the Royal Navy.[45] The Museum also funded J.T. Wood's excavations at Ephesus, which led to the acquisition of a substantial amount of material, including sculpture from the Temple of Artemis, one of the Seven Wonders of the Ancient World.[46] Other items came from the heirs of those who had been on the Grand Tour or whose fathers had been members of the Society of Dilettanti – the collection of the fourth Earl of Aberdeen, for example, presented by his son in 1861, and the sculpture from the Temple of Athena Polias at Priene, given by the Society itself in 1869.[47] Two years later the sixth Viscount Strangford gave three of the sculptures collected by his father, which included the famous Late Archaic figure of the fifth century BC known as the Strangford Apollo.[48]

Despite his jeremiad to Panizzi about the heavy burden of curatorial duties, Newton was exceedingly successful in acquiring objects for the Museum by purchase. He was, however, working in the well-established field of classical archaeology, understood by the educated and well displayed in the Museum, but in need of the type of close academic scrutiny which he was willing to supply. It was a subject particularly familiar to the Trustees and government, many of whose members had been trained in classics at Oxford or Cambridge. Such sympathy is undoubtedly the reason for the ease with which the Museum received permission to purchase, for example, the collection of the recently deceased Duc de Blacas, a former French ambassador to Rome. It was a formidable collection which, as well as the normal complement of distinguished sculpture and bronzes, paintings, glass and over 500 vases, included the remarkable late fourth-century silver treasure found on the Esquiline Hill in Rome. The treasure represents a Roman bride's toilet plate, including the famous casket which bears her name, Projecta.[49] One class of object opened up new possibilities for both collecting and display: eighteen oriental and Venetian silver-inlaid brass vessels (including the 'Blacas ewer' made by Shuja'ibn Nan'a in Mosul in 1232), which were immediately displayed in a specially ordered showcase.[50] Most important perhaps was a collection of 951 gems, of which the most noteworthy is the well-known oval sardonyx portraying the Emperor Augustus, who died in AD 14 (it is over 12 cm high).[51] The cost of the collection was enormous, £48,000 (the Blacas family wanted £60,000), but most remarkable was the speed with which it was purchased and the economy of the surviving paperwork. Newton reported its availability in early October 1866 and was authorized to go to Paris to view it. This he did on 14 November and was soon negotiating with the Blacas family. On 25 November he concluded a deal quickly in the light of a threatened purchase by the French government, and telegraphed the Chancellor of the Exchequer, Disraeli (who had instructed him to buy it), with the result of his negotiations. Napoleon III was furious; he struck the table on hearing the news and exclaimed, 'Ce n'est pas possible! J'avais donné l'ordre... de ne pas manquer de ça'.[52] No wonder that the Trustees were particularly effusive in their thanks to the Chancellor – clearly a sympathetic member of the Board.[53]

This purchase was made despite the fact that between 1862 and 1865 Newton had been engaged in buying other major collections of classical antiquities. First, eleven statues from the Farnese collection were purchased in Rome in July 1864 for a total of £3,873.[54] Then the collection of the Italian dealer Count Alessandro Castellani, which he had examined at Naples on an extended visit to the Mediterranean in April and May 1865, was picked over. He bought the best pieces, including a collection of gems and the famous Byzantine enamelled brooch which bears the dealer's name[55] – all for £5,000.[56] A little earlier in the same year, after a visit to Paris, he spent, through the dealers Rollin and Feuardent (much used by the Museum), £5,861 at the sale of Count Pourtalès's collection. In 1869 he 'took [his] portmanteau and went over to France' and within a few hours had purchased for £1,000 the Polykleitan Diadumenos from Vaison (Vaucluse), which had been on the market in fragments for a number of years.[57] But this was as nothing compared to the purchases made from Castellani in 1872 and 1873.[58] In 1872 he spent £20,000 on a group of objects that included more gems and jewellery and an important tomb group from Taranto, not to mention a famous 'Etruscan' sarcophagus, finally recognized as a fake in 1935.[59] In 1873, £27,000 was spent on another body of material assembled by Castellani, including the famous bronze head of Anahita in the guise of Aphrodite, which Newton described as the finest bronze he had ever seen. Newton's friendship and influence with Gladstone, both a Trustee and at this time Prime Minister, may well have been crucial in this last acquisition.

Newton and Gladstone were to come together again more publicly in relation to the Homeric claims of the German amateur excavator of 'Troy', Heinrich Schliemann. Gladstone himself wrote with 'lofty rhetoric' and sublime naivety about Homer and was serenely indifferent to the scholarly disapproval with which his books were received.[60] Newton (who knew which side his bread was buttered) was the person who introduced Gladstone to Schliemann. Gladstone, fascinated by Schliemann's story, was able to bend it in support of his own strange theories, and became the German's prophet in England.[61] Newton had first met Schliemann in 1871, when, according to the German, the plans to excavate Troy were greeted with heavy scepticism and a hearty laugh.[62] Soon, however, Schliemann and Newton were in close correspondence, as were Gladstone and Schliemann.[63] Newton supported Schliemann in many of his endeavours and lectured on his finds, particularly speaking for him when he was falsely accused of forgery in relation to finds in Mycenaean shaft-graves. For a scholar with only a vague perception of pre-classical Greece, Newton was remarkably open-minded about the new finds and was one of the first to take Schliemann seriously and help him support his case. Almost as a footnote, and it is difficult to know whether he was serious in intent, Schliemann offered the Museum the 'Treasure of Priam' for £50,000, but both Newton and Gladstone felt this was too much and, after being exhibited at the South Kensington Museum from 1877 to 1880, it was given to Berlin (it is now held as booty of the Second World War in Russia).[64]

The 1860s and early 70s were the glory years of Newton's purchasing power; never again was the department able to buy antiquities on this scale. The objects largely came from old collections or from dealers who garnered them, usually without provenance, throughout the Mediterranean. Britain was wealthy, politicians were willing and the Americans had not yet started to buy in quantity. The only real challenges came from Berlin and, to a certain extent, from St Petersburg. Further, limitations of space were beginning to prohibit the acquisition of large sculptures by the Museum. Excavations were now undertaken by the United States and European nations on classical sites in Greece and Italy, not to provide material for foreign museums but for retention by the country of origin. These were often carried on through the auspices of privately funded schools or societies, such as the British School at Athens which Newton helped to found in 1883.

It is true to say that there were few revolutions in the study of classical archaeology before the end of the century – merely shifts of emphasis and alterations in the angle of interpretation, or shocks caused by headline-makers like Schliemann.[65] The Museum was lucky to have a man as intellectually distinguished as Newton to lead his department at this period. Newton may have been brilliant, but he was no revolutionary. In hindsight the Museum was even luckier to have the polymathic Franks to guide it through the enormous changes in academic thought and attitude of the next twenty years – a man who was willing to lead it into areas of collecting and scholarship undreamt of by Newton.[66]

The Wider Picture

Intellectually the middle decades of the century formed a period both traumatic and stimulating for the Museum, as for the country. The federalization of University College and King's College into the new University of London in 1836, the governments' reforms of the universities of Oxford and Cambridge in the 1850s and 70s, together with the Public Records Act of 1838, led slowly to a new approach to history and science. The days of the gentleman historian – Macaulay and Carlyle – were largely at an end as the universities extended the base of English academe by broadening the base of examined disciplines. The founders of University College in 1828 had modelled their courses and examination systems on Scottish and even continental and American practice, which gradually broke the tyranny of both classics and mathematics. The words of the charter of the new federal university were quite startling to the English – if not the Scottish – educated public; the university was to ascertain, 'by means of examinations, the persons who have acquired proficiency in Literature, Science and the Arts'. It might be thought that the Museum would occasionally recruit historians to curatorial posts, but in truth they were rare birds, who made little impact on the Museum until the twentieth century – because of the poor quality of the historical education provided by the older universities.

This situation was beginning to change. In Oxford a group of historians grew up around the central figure of William Stubbs, whose *Constitutional history of England* was a landmark in the development of the study of history in this country, and whose *Select charters illustrative of English history* was still in use as a textbook nearly a century after its first publication in 1870. In 1866 he became Regius Professor of Modern History and fought for the full recognition of the subject, a status achieved in 1872. In Cambridge, where undergraduates had hitherto studied either mathematics or a slimmed-down version of the classics, a history tripos of sorts was founded by Seeley in the 1860s, but it was not until 1875 that it separated from jurisprudence, to be taught by towering scholars of the quality of Creighton, Acton and, more especially, Maitland (the latter Professor of the Laws of England). The provincial universities were less fettered by tradition and the University of Manchester soon became one of the leading schools of history in the country under T.F. Tout, who was appointed in 1890. The Royal Historical Society, founded in 1868, was a symptom of a new interest in the subject, as was the historical section of the Archaeological Institute, and – in 1886 – *The English historical review* (modelled on the *Historische Zeitschrift*, founded in 1859).[67]

Archaeology was also achieving respectability at British universities, although its real power-base until the end of the century and beyond rested in the societies and museums (and particularly the British Museum). Although there were ten chairs of archaeology in Germany (and one in France) in the middle of the century, they were all concerned with Greece and Rome. There was no such chair in England, but in 1851 John Disney endowed an archaeological professorship of a different sort at Cambridge. His agreement with the university clearly stated that the incumbent should each year give 'six lectures at least on the subject of Classical, Medieval and other Antiquities and the Fine Arts and all matters and things connected therewith'.[68] The first Disney Professor was John Howard Marsden, an old-fashioned antiquarian, who spent what little time he gave to Cambridge in the promotion of Greek and Roman culture. His successor, Churchill Babington, however, was (although a classical scholar) critical of his predecessor and wanted to broaden the field, saying in his inaugural lecture in 1865, '... I am glad that the Disney Professor is not obliged to confine himself to classical archaeology'.[69] Although the subject was not yet examined, a beginning had been made.[70]

At Oxford a chair of classical archaeology was founded in 1885 (see p.245), but there was to be no professorship of prehistoric archaeology until 1946. The Ashmolean Museum awoke from a long slumber in 1884 to provide a home to a series of distinguished archaeologists, beginning with Arthur Evans, the excavator of the Palace of Minos at Knossos, who collaborated with the new Professor of Classical Archaeology, Percy Gardner. The missing archaeological chair at Oxford was partly compensated by a readership in anthropology, held by the great pioneer of that subject (Sir) Edward Burnett Tylor (p.159), which was established in 1884. From the school founded by Tylor emerged many archaeologists, including a future Director of the British Museum, T.D. Kendrick. At University College London chairs of classical archaeology (held in plurality by Charles Newton of the British Museum) and, more importantly, Egyptology were established in 1879 and 1892. There was, however, no chair of archaeology in Scotland or Ireland.

Natural science, never entirely absent from the older English universities, had mainly been seated in London (in the Royal Institution and the university) and Scotland. A Natural Science tripos in Cambridge (Isaac Newton's *alma mater*) was introduced in 1851, but until 1861 it was available only to those with a first degree in another subject; the floodgates were opened with the foundation in 1868 of the Clarendon Laboratory for experimental physics. But now came Darwin, whose theories were only gradually accepted in the Museum. The great Owen, the Museum's head of natural history, was apostrophized by Huxley (who had his own agenda) as unacceptable to the new revolutionaries.[71]

Not only the natural historians, but the antiquarians, were central to the Darwinian controversies of the 1860s, as the antiquity of man was being investigated in the wake of the revelations of the geologists of the early part of the century. Franks was in the thick of it. His great friend John Evans, a rich paper-maker and a semi-professional archaeologist, was deeply involved in the recognition of Palaeolithic tools discovered in the gravels of the Somme and later the Thames. These finds at last allowed scholars to challenge the mind-set of those who believed the literal history of the origins of man as interpreted from biblical sources. In 1859 (the year of the publication of *The origin of species*), in papers read to the Royal Society and the Society of Antiquaries respectively, John Prestwich and Evans demonstrated that flint tools found in the Seine at Amiens and Abbeville by Boucher de Perthes, a local antiquary, and claimed by him to be 'haches antédiluviennes', were indeed contemporaneous with the laying down of the river gravels. One of the first people Evans saw on his return from France was Franks, with whom he clearly discussed his findings before his lecture.[72] John Evans's frequent references to Franks in his diary on his return from France, and the fact that Franks made a trip to Abbeville in August 1860 where he acquired some stone implements, suggests that he had early accepted the new ideas.[73] After Franks's visit Boucher de Perthes sent the Museum a complete set of his publications and, in 1862, some of the implements found in the gravels.[74]

Assyria provided another academic challenge. The Crimean War of 1855 had put a temporary stop to excavation in Mesopotamia, but in London the sculptures were gradually put on display. The staff now set to work on the rich finds from the area, and particularly on the inscriptions, which were overwhelming them. Here again the revolution in thought was felt. Against the background of German biblical criticism (and particularly that of Konstantin von Tischendorf), a group of English academics published one of the most scandal-provoking books of the century, *Essays and reviews*. The ideas expressed here even led to the prosecution of two of its contributors on the grounds of their alleged denial that the Scriptures were inspired. The authors demanded that their readers should not 'be afraid of any sane investigation of truth, whether by geologist or historian'.[75]

The new source-criticism of the Bible, fuelled by German scholarship and the work of the Tractarians, spilled over into hieroglyphic and cuneiform studies as the search was on for confirmation, or at least illumination, of episodes in the Old Testament. The British Museum provided much of the raw material, in that it had for many years been the repository of many texts relating to the Bible from Assyria and Egypt. As early as 1853 Layard had been able to list some fifty-five rulers, cities and countries which appeared in both the Bible and the newly discovered Assyrian texts.[76]

Biblical archaeology was soon put on to a more formal basis. In 1865 the first of a series of societies dedicated to the subject was founded, under the patronage of the Queen. This was the Palestine Exploration Fund. Three Trustees spoke at the foundation meeting but the only member of the Museum staff present was Owen, Superintendent of Natural History. More important was the Society for Biblical Archaeology, founded in 1870 by Birch and Joseph Bonomi, head of the Soane Museum. Birch (the first president) gave the inaugural address, which demonstrated the pragmatism of the English scholar:

> Its scope is Archaeology, not Theology; but to Theology it will prove an important aid. To all those it must be attractive who are interested in the primitive and early history of mankind;

that history which is not written on books nor on paper, but upon rocks and stones, deep in the soil, far away in the desert; that history which is not to be found in the library or the mart, but which must be dug up in the valley of the Nile, or exhumed from the plains of Mesopotamia.[77]

This, as Roger Moorey has pointed out, was very different from the American vision of biblical archaeology, which chimed well with those who tried to convict the Tractarians. In describing the work of the newly founded American Palestine Exploration Society in 1870, it was stated that:

the work proposed... appeals to the religious sentiment alike of the Christian and the Jew... Its supreme importance is for the illustration and defense of the Bible. Modern scepticism assails the Bible at the point of reality, the question of fact. Hence whatever goes to verify the Bible history as real, in time, in place and circumstances, is a refutation of unbelief.[78]

To the British scholar religious interpretation was, by contrast, a lucky accident, a by-product of the examination of texts.

One of the first papers given to the newly formed Society of Biblical Archaeology was by a brilliant young member of the British Museum staff, George Smith; it concerned a seventh-century BC tablet from Kuyunjik, which relates the Gilgamesh epic, a story reflecting the episode of the Flood as told in the Bible.[79] Published in 1873, it caused a great stir and the *Daily Telegraph* paid for Smith to go to Mesopotamia to seek more evidence, which he quite surprisingly did in two seasons' work. He died young from dysentery in 1876, perhaps the greatest loss to cuneiform studies in the nineteenth century.

The later prehistoric archaeology of Britain and Europe was at this time undergoing a gradual sea change. The Three-Age system was accepted only when it was demonstrated by careful attention to stratigraphy and to associated groups of material found in excavation on selected sites in Denmark – sites which had been deliberately targeted to demonstrate the validity of the model based on an empirical study of objects. While the British had always had an interest in field monuments, excavations, with one or two honourable exceptions in the early years of the century, were neither well conducted nor focused in the Danish manner. Many excavations were carried out almost as light entertainment by gentlemen at weekends, or to amuse the local archaeological societies on excursion. This was beginning to change in the 1860s. In the first place people such as Franks and Evans became interested in the contexts of the objects that they acquired; in forming their archaeological collections they carefully recorded provenances and associated finds.[80] Secondly, the French, who were fascinated by what Lubbock had christened the Palaeolithic, influenced by Louis Lartet and Gabriel de Mortillet, were confirming the finds of Boucher de Perthes by stratigraphy. Thirdly, one of the major figures of nineteenth-century field archaeology was beginning to excavate and survey monuments in a scientific fashion – this was Colonel Augustus Lane-Fox (better known as General Pitt Rivers, a name he adopted on succeeding to the rich Rivers estates in Cranborne Chase in 1880). Under the influence of a minor canon of Durham, William Greenwell, his excavations – at first tentative – were to grow in importance. The skill and organization attending them, together with the accurate observation and recording of what was found, set new standards for British field archaeologists.[81]

Franks knew Lane-Fox well, but had little hands-on experience of excavation, although he visited many archaeological sites in Britain and Europe. It is not clear in all cases where Franks spent his leave, but it is known that in the 1860s he frequently travelled with a group of archaeological friends, particularly Evans and Lubbock. A holiday visit by Franks to the Salzkammergut in Austria in 1863 almost certainly led to excavations undertaken on the already well-known site of Hallstatt in 1866, together with Evans, Lubbock, A. von Morlot (Professor of Geology at Lausanne and author of an influential work on the Three-Age system) and Lartet (a magistrate in the Gers, who had explored a number of French palaeolithic caves with Henry Christy). Hallstatt, first excavated in 1846, was soon to be recognized as an important Iron Age type-site, many grave-goods from which are in the British Museum.[82] This seems to have been a rare excursion by Franks into the field, but one he used tellingly in his discussion of Iron Age art.

This small group of friends – Lubbock, Evans and Franks (together to a certain extent with Lane-Fox) – was of great importance to British archaeology in that its members were in constant touch with their colleagues all over the Continent, from Madrid to St Petersburg and from Stockholm to Naples. They met not only in Britain, but at the annual meetings of the Congrès international d'Anthropologie et d'Archéologie préhistorique, founded in 1860, of which Franks was one of four vice-presidents at the 1867 Paris meeting and at a number of subsequent meetings. [83] These conferences provided the opportunity for exhibitions of recent finds, particularly finds from the country in which the Congress was meeting (in Paris it took the form of a section of the Exposition Universelle overseen by de Mortillet, the most influential French archaeologist of the period). Congress members were also actively encouraged to visit local museums and collectors. Congress proceedings were published and further disseminated knowledge of European archaeology. Franks went to many of the meetings of this congress in the next twenty years and was active as a vice-president in hosting the meeting in Norwich and London in 1868, of which Lane-Fox was secretary. Franks, alongside Evans, Huxley, Tylor and Lubbock, was also a contributor. These meetings and his less formal travels allowed Franks not only to keep up with the general direction of European archaeology, but also allowed him to purchase or otherwise acquire prehistoric material (sometimes sharing the spoils with Evans).[84]

Art history was seriously neglected in England. Part-time chairs of art history were established at Oxford, Cambridge and University College London as a result of the Slade bequest of 1868, in the administration of which Franks was involved (indeed he was himself Slade Professor at Cambridge in 1876), but there was in effect no formal discipline of art history in England in the nineteenth century. Curators, collectors, connoisseurs, dealers (and by long tradition) certain artists provided art-historical expertise. By extension, British historians in the middle of the century were not generally interested in material culture, as they were, for example, in Denmark. Here Fabricius's illustrated popular history of Denmark, first published in 1854, went into many editions, and was richly embellished with illustrations of material in the National Museum and with pictures of monuments, as well as reconstructed heroic incidents.[85] The first person who wanted to do anything like this in England was J.R. Green who, as Asa Briggs has pointed out, badly wanted to illustrate his great *History* with 'pictures which should tell us how men and things appeared to the lookers-on of their own day, and how contemporary observers aimed at representing them'. It was left to his widow to fulfil his dream in 1892.[86]

An important development in the middle years of the century was the staging of exhibitions following in the steps of that put on by the Society of Arts in 1850, of which Franks had been secretary. The model of that exhibition was followed on a massive scale in 1857 by the Art Treasures Exhibition, which was held at Manchester under the patronage of the Prince Consort and with the active encouragement of Henry Cole. Although dominated by paintings (the Old Master paintings were arranged by George Scharf, who for the first time in England juxtaposed the Northern Masters with the Italians), there was a major section on applied art, which included material lent from Marlborough House. Importantly, there emerged from attics, churches and private vitrines many hitherto unknown rarities. Their appearance allowed both the South Kensington and the British Museums the opportunity to purchase, or at least shadow, through its lush catalogue (to which Franks contributed the chapter on 'Vitreous art'), the more important objects in private hands in the following years.[87] Henry Cole even used the exhibition as a vehicle to manoeuvre the gradual purchase of the vastly important Soulages collection of applied art for the South Kensington Museum, which he in effect first leased after the exhibition closed.[88] In 1862 a further major exhibition – of medieval and Renaissance art – was staged at South Kensington. The exhibition consisted of nearly 10,000 objects belonging to more than 500 collectors and institutions and was visited by 900,000 people over a period of six months. For the rest of the century the South Kensington Museum, or its out-station at Bethnal Green, became the main centre in London for loan exhibitions of the applied arts.

The Fine Arts Club and its successor, the Burlington Fine Art Club (founded in 1866), which organized many of these exhibitions, were an important catalyst in prosecuting the understanding of the history of art in the nineteenth century. Initially they were very much social clubs at which connoisseurs, dealers and curators exhibited objects from their collections to each other. Gradually they broke away from the traditional comparative exhibitions mounted by the Royal Academy and the British Institution, and mounted small specialist exhibitions. Becoming highly critical, they refined judgement on matters of art history and provided reasoned opinions and a developing professionalism for nearly a century. Prominent among the early members were J.C. Robinson of the South Kensington Museum, the virtual founder of both societies, and his friend Franks; the staff of the Department of Prints and Drawings were also involved, particularly towards the end of the century. The specialist exhibitions sponsored by the Club, singling out the work of a single artist, school, or culture, became an annual feature of the London fine art scene and continued until the outbreak of the Second World War. At all times the Museum provided senior figures as members and sometimes as organizers of the exhibitions.[89]

Ethnography

The Trustees could no longer ignore the issue of the ethnographic collections. Time and again they had prevaricated, most recently as a result of the 1860 Select Committee's own equivocation. The Museum had since its foundation been passive in collecting ethnographic material. It has been shown how in the eighteenth century the reception and display of the Cook and Vancouver collections had formed popular attractions for visitors, and their popularity lasted until well on in the next century. In the first half of the nineteenth century the Museum acquired a fair amount of ethnographical material by gift, particularly from Central America, of which the most outstanding was the material brought back from Sir Robert Schomburgk's expedition to British Guiana between 1831 and 1835. It has been calculated that by the time Franks came to the Museum the ethnographic collection numbered 3,700 objects and that by the time he retired the collections had increased tenfold.[90]

The problem of the ethnographic collection started to come to a head in 1858, when the collection of Indonesian material formed by Sir Stamford Raffles some thirty years earlier was offered to the Museum for 1,000 guineas by the executors of his estate. The Trustees, who had never so far bought any ethnographical material, peremptorily turned down the offer. Raffles's nephew and heir, the Reverend William Flint, then offered it as a gift, which was grudgingly accepted. Some of it was put out in a disorganized fashion in a corner of the Ethnographical Room, presumably by Franks. The Trustees, nagged by the donor, continually questioned its display.[91] Franks at this time was already clearly involved with the ethnographic material, particularly with the Arctic collections. These had their origin in items brought back both by the Parry expedition in 1824 and Barrow's search for the ill-fated expedition of Sir John Franklin in the 1850s, which were the subject of the first catalogue – however slim – of ethnographical material.[92]

Early in November 1865, Panizzi received a letter in Franks's hand, signed by Joseph Hooker (who had just succeeded his father as Director of the Botanical Gardens at Kew), Daniel Hanbury (treasurer of the Linnean Society), John Lubbock and Franks himself:

> The late Henry Christy Esq. of 103 Victoria Street, who died in France in May last, has by his will dated February 5th 1863, bequeathed to us his Archaeological and Ethnographic Collections with their appurtenances, together with a sum of 5000£, all free of Legacy Duty, in trust for certain purposes, which will best be explained by the accompanying Extract from his Will....[93]

The letter explains how certain non-controversial archaeological objects had been split between the British and Ashmolean Museums, but states that the rest of the collection, which comprised both archaeological and ethnographical material, was to come to the British Museum. There was clearly no problem about the archaeological material, which was now acknowledged in the Museum's collecting policy. This largely comprised important groups of Palaeolithic art and artefacts excavated by Lartet and Christy from caves in south-west France, which had been visited by Franks and his friends in 1864.[94] What was not central to the Museum's interests at the time was the ethnographic material in the collection, probably over 1,000 items (mostly from Mexico). So marginal was it that Panizzi in his evidence to the Select Committee only five years earlier had actively opposed the collection of ethnographic material by the Museum.

Henry Christy was born in 1810, the son of the founder of the famous hat-makers and also of one of the earliest joint-stock banks. Although born to wealth, he served an apprenticeship as a hatter and became at the age of eighteen joint manager, with his cousin, of the family factory at Stockport in Cheshire. From 1850 he travelled widely as a representative of his firm and started to collect textiles; one of his earliest acquisitions was a piece of Turkish towelling, which (copied by his firm) was the model for the type of towel used in the West today. On a journey to Denmark in 1852 he met Carl Ludvig Steinhauer, who since the early 1840s had been working as Thomsen's assistant in charge of ethnography in the royal collections. This, Det Kongelige Etnografiske Museum (the Royal Ethnographic Museum), had opened in 1849, the first of its kind in the world, and soon filled twenty rooms in Prinsens Palæ, the building which now forms the core of the Danish National Museum.[95] Christy was impressed by Steinhauer, who clearly stimulated him to broaden his collection – indeed Christy later employed him to catalogue it.[96] Another great – perhaps mutual – influence was provided by the accidental encounter of Christy and E.B. Tylor on an omnibus in Havana. Tylor, considered to be one of the founders of anthropology, travelled for four months with Christy in Mexico. These travels resulted in a book, *Anahuac*, stamped on the cover of which is one of the famous stone masks of the Aztec god Xipe Totec, which came to the Museum with the Christy collection.[97] Among the objects collected on this journey were three splendid turquoise mosaics of the Aztecs, for which Christy paid £113. They are now among the chief treasures of the Museum's American collections.[98]

The letter written by Franks and his co-Trustees could hardly have been sent without some consultation with Panizzi, who even in old age was still a force to be reckoned with. Since the arrival of Franks, however, the Museum had accepted with no serious outburst from the Principal Librarian not only the Raffles and Barrow collections, but also Sir George Grey's Maori collection, the Fijian material from the voyages of HMS *Herald*, and the varied collection formed at the Haslar Naval Hospital.[99] Five years after his discouraging remarks to the 1860 Select Committee, Panizzi – presumably softened up by Franks – was willing to take the Christy cuckoo into the nest. The Trustees agreed its acceptance with 'cordial thanks'.[100]

Franks was soon recommending that the collection should be housed in Christy's flat in a newish mansion block in Victoria Street, and produced sketch plans and proposals for security and storage. The flat could be rented for £230 p.a., and, perhaps not without guile, the Christy trustees had in their original letter offered the Museum £100 p.a. in cash for five years from the Christy fund and the loan of enough glass cases to store and partially display the objects. Further, Franks offered to pay out of his own pocket the admittedly minute salary of Thomas Gay, who had been employed as a resident clerk/curator by Christy.[101] Negotiations over the next months with the Treasury and the Museum Trustees resulted in the setting up of an out-station in the flat, the employment of a resident porter and permission for Franks to sleep there while he was registering and arranging the collection.

It was nearly fifteen years before the Christy collection moved to Bloomsbury (until then it was opened in its temporary premises on Fridays). Only when the natural history collections were transferred to South Kensington was space made available for it in the main body of the Museum. Meanwhile, Franks tackled the registration of the collections with enthusiasm, devising a fiendishly complicated system of numbering. He drew heavily on the Christy fund to augment the ethnographic and prehistoric collections, and dipped deep into his own pocket to add more material, so that it has been estimated that by the time the collection arrived in its new home it comprised some 20,000 items.[102] He actively encouraged collection of ethnographical objects by travellers, missionaries and administrators and on his visits to the Continent arranged exchanges of 'duplicates' from the

Museum's collection or from his own with foreign colleagues and collectors. He also initiated the Museum habit of taking over unwanted collections from provincial museums which felt themselves saddled with such uncomfortable material.

Franks was clearly deeply committed to ethnography. He was a member (and officer) of the various ethnographical and anthropological societies and wrote many short notes on a variety of subjects for their journals. Nor was he exclusively interested in material culture. During the 1870s he was much concerned with the preparation of questionnaires concerning collecting for explorers and travellers (Franks never travelled outside Europe). Such questions concerned, for example, diet, marriage and funeral customs and even 'mental qualities'. He was, with Darwin, Lubbock, Tylor and others, a major contributor to a guide for serious travellers published by the British Association for the Advancement of Science, which advised collectors on how to record the primitive peoples with whom they came into contact.[103] He used carefully chosen colonial administrators to build up the collections. Perspicaciously, he realized that they might help with 'specimens which we most care for [which] are but seldom brought home by ordinary travellers, as they are but rarely of any beauty, and are in general the commonest things of the country'.[104]

This view of the purpose of collection was at odds with that of many of the other major collections of Europe. In Austria, for example, ethnographic collecting was, until the very end of the century and beyond, a matter of simple accumulation on the back of trade. This attitude was inveighed against in 1898 by the German Africanist Leo Frobenius:

> As far as I am concerned, to travel, collect and fill one cabinet after another does not even come close to preserving these records of the world's history. As such, the rags and rubbish to be found in some ethnographic collections are near to worthless. Rather, their real significance derives from the fact that they are evidence of a vigorous evolution. They are nothing more than tokens, dead hulks waiting to be imbued with living breath.[105]

Intellectually Franks was perhaps influenced in his approach to ethnography by his friend Lubbock (a fellow trustee of the fund set up under Christy's will), who in 1865 published his popular and wide-ranging book *Pre-historic times as illustrated by ancient remains, and the manners and customs of foreign savages*.[106] In this book, developing ideas put forward by Herbert Spencer in 1850,[107] Lubbock used the methods of the palaeontologists together with evidence provided by contemporary primitive societies to illuminate prehistory, demonstrating an optimistic emergence from dark savagery to Western European civilization. This theory was applied to the development of prehistoric societies in Europe, which was one of the reasons why so much of the early interest in anthropology and ethnology stemmed from archaeologists. (Christy, who collected both ethnographic and archaeological material, was a prime example of a person interested in the relationship between the two disciplines.) In proposing that the Trustees should acquire the Christy collection, Franks had expounded this idea: the collections, he wrote, 'have been brought together as materials for reconstructing the lost portions of European history; illustrating the manners, customs & religious faith of races using principally as weapons & implements those rude objects of stone which human research or the accidental operations of husbandry still bring to light in all parts of Europe'.[108] The ethnographic collections in the

Museum became central to the idea of social evolution, an uncomfortable theory never properly worked out in objective terms.[109] It was a theory, however, latent in the minds of most late nineteenth-century anthropologists. Indeed, it formed a backdrop against which the material culture of non-Western people was displayed by Franks in the British Museum, initially as an ideal type-series distributed geographically, but never displayed in strict evolutionary terms. The theory was tested not only in London, but also in Germany (particularly in the Museum für Völkerkunde in Berlin), in the United States and in the ethnographical museums of many other countries.[110] Indeed, it may well be that in such museum display was seen the most concrete expression of the idea of social evolution.

Lane-Fox (Pitt Rivers) was also collecting ethnography, but saw the development of artefacts in a straight Darwinian progression from the simple to the complex. He arranged his collection didactically to demonstrate his theory. The result was a system of display in which objects were arranged typologically, with little attention to cultural geographical distribution. The system which he insisted be used was probably one of the reasons why the government rejected his collection when it was offered to them (and consequently to the British Museum) in the 1880s. It is one which has ever since caused problems for the University of Oxford where it ultimately wound up.[111] 'With the collection inevitably', as John Mack has said, 'came Pitt Rivers.'

In the early stages of its collection of ethnography, the Museum appears to have had no imperial or missionary bias. Franks and his colleagues – coming to the subject from archaeology – were interested in ethnographic artefacts as reflectors of culture, as an extension perhaps of their typological view of prehistoric material. They were, as yet, not interested in the material as art – that came with the acquisition of the Benin bronzes at the end of the century – but more as representative of the life of the people who had made it. Franks himself was clearly fascinated by American material, and particularly by the archaeological remains of the native Americans. It was only with the appointment of his ethnographic assistants that a more professional anthropological approach began to take over.

Franks had employed Christy's assistant, Thomas Gay, to help him with the collection. In 1874 Gay was replaced by an eighteen-year-old boy, Charles Hercules Read, from the South Kensington Museum. Again Franks paid him out of his own pocket, but in 1880 Read was, amid much huffing and puffing from a starchy Treasury, formally appointed as an assistant in the department.[112] Although not university-educated (his father was a colour sergeant in the Royal Engineers), Read was formidably intelligent (if not very original in his ideas) and became in fact – if not by title – the first ethnographer in the Museum, although, like his mentor Franks, his interests and writing were polymathic. He was to be Franks's close friend and his successor as keeper, and ultimately his executor.[113]

Franks's Intellectual Position

The 1860s were crucial to the development of the antiquities departments, and particularly to that part of the Museum which formed the base of Franks's empire. It is difficult to underestimate the importance of Franks in the development of the institution. Intellectually, that development depended on a relatively short period of his life, his late thirties and early forties. At this period his mind roved restlessly over a broad range of subjects; he collected within that range, and was deeply involved with a number of young Turks who were altering the way in which the British looked at the past and at man's place in the world. It has been shown how Franks developed as a medievalist and as an authority on glass, but he has rarely been accorded the recognition he deserves as an influence in archaeological and ethnographical thought.[114] No history of archaeology has ever treated him to more than a passing mention, while to anthropologists he is seen as marginal to the intellectual mainstream. It is true that in the 1960s and 70s, when these two subjects were turned on their head, the sort of work that was done by Franks was much out of favour; but this does not excuse his neglect by earlier historians of archaeology and anthropology.[115] A book published by the British Museum at the centenary of his death (he died in 1897) out of proper *pietas* has carefully provided – from the point of view of many disciplines – the raw material from which we may judge his intellectual progress and stature.[116] Future scholars may now take his contribution more seriously.

Franks was a very private person. He left few private papers (unlike Evans), and had no biographer (unlike both Evans and Lubbock) and no students (unlike Tylor). His personality is, therefore, elusive.[117] His published work is fragmented; his bibliography embraces some 500 items; some were major works, but most were single pages recording the exhibition of an object or a group of objects.[118] In 1868, for example, he published his important *Guide to the Christy collection of antiquities and ethnography*, as well as papers and notes on objects from Kingston, on Gallo-Roman objects from the Seine at Paris, on 'Celtic' antiquities, on Roman pottery found at Bow, flint implements from Norfolk and Suffolk and a survey of additions to his department during the year. In his most active decade – the 1860s – he wrote on subjects ranging from Siberian antiquities to Bronze Age material from Denmark, a note on some of the Paston letters (part of an attempt to persuade the Museum to buy them), numerous publications on glass of all ages, material from Carthage and Bengazi and relics of the Order of the Garter. He wrote a paper on the manufacture of Chelsea porcelain and on palaeolithic material from the Dordogne; he also produced notes on Chinese and European enamels, scientific instruments, pilgrims' badges, and so on. Many of these were notes on objects exhibited to the Society of Antiquaries before or after they entered the Museum. In many cases he was breaking new ground, drawing attention to aspects of the ancient world little known to the world of archaeologists, antiquaries and collectors. His connoisseurship in many fields (oriental and western ceramics, Indian and Islamic antiquities, medals, scientific instruments and heraldry), which was unrivalled, is illustrated by many of these publications. This connoisseurship was based on true, broad and often innovative scholarship.

It is perhaps through his close archaeological associates of the 1850s and 60s that we may trace his true academic interests and influence. Franks, Evans and Lubbock travelled together and met often. They were all rich, all socially well connected, all ultimately knighted (Lubbock, a Member of Parliament, was later granted a peerage as Lord Avebury – a significant title); all were Fellows of the Royal Society and all became Presidents of the Society of Antiquaries and consequently Trustees of the British Museum. All were active members of the Athenæum, a meeting place of the great, the good and the intellectual. They knew severally, in different ways, the movers and shakers of the intellectual life of the country. Lubbock was a neighbour and friend of Darwin; Evans's son Arthur (the excavator of Knossos) married the daughter of a family friend, the historian E.A. Freeman; Franks, as

Director of the Society of Antiquaries, knew most of the active archaeologists and anti-quaries in the country. On the edge of this group – but frequently in contact – were Tylor and Lane-Fox (although in the 1860s the latter was still more of a soldier than an archaeol-ogist).

It was in their academic work that they were most closely allied. Lubbock's great work on prehistory has already been mentioned; in it he acknowledges the help of Franks and Evans. Earlier, in 1866, Lubbock had published a translation from the German of the Swede Sven Nilsson's *The primitive inhabitants of Scandinavia*, originally published in 1836, which was important in respect of the Stone Age, if rather eccentric in relation to the Bronze Age.[119] Evans at this time was preparing his first and most original book, *Ancient stone implements*, published in 1872, which depended very much on his dealings with his two friends.[120] As to Franks himself, he had already, in his edition of Kemble's *Horæ ferales* in 1863, seriously addressed the problem of Celtic art, a work 'of greater consequence than any which had yet appeared',[121] which prepared him for the observations he was to make as a result of the excavations with his friends three years later at the Iron Age type-site of Hall-statt – observations which still impress. Franks, as an Associate Commissioner of the Exposition Universelle in Paris in 1867, helped to arrange as part of this great show one of the most important exhibitions of prehistory ever mounted, a signal of 'the coming of age of archaeology'.[122] It celebrated in an international context the new extended chronology and social evolutionary structure of European archaeology, which Franks was now using in his treatment of the Christy collection, as demonstrated in the *Guide* he published in the following year.[123]

Franks was, particularly through his Museum work in the 1860s and 70s, a major innovator in the study of archaeology. At no stage after this was the Museum to have so great an influence in the study of archaeology, both in Britain and abroad. Franks's inter-national stature in archaeology at this period was enormous; he travelled more widely than his two friends, spoke several languages, and served on many important international committees of an academic nature.[124] Like his friends he was elected a member of a number of foreign academies, but it is noticeable that generally Franks was the first to be honoured.[125] Later his academic interests broadened and he had less time for archaeology, but the foundations he had laid in these early years were to form one of the main supports of the archaeological discipline in Britain. His influence on the development of ethnogra-phy has been demonstrated; he was no less innovative and scholarly in his approach to the applied arts. This is particularly true of his work on European and oriental ceramics, where the methods he introduced and his mode of collecting (particularly of pieces documented by inscription) established new standards. Franks, the polymath, was the archetype of those who helped to establish a reputation of omniscience for the Museum – 'an expert from the British Museum' became a literary stereotype.

Widening Horizons

The last forty years of the nineteenth century saw an unprecedented growth in the size and the geographical, cultural and chronological spread of the Museum's collections. In his area, Franks achieved this growth by purchase and gift, not by direct involvement in excavation. The Museum had already, before 1860 (when the evidence from the Somme gravels was beginning to be accepted), acquired material from the two most famous and controversial English Palaeolithic sites – Kent's Cavern, Torquay, and Brixham, both in Devon. The former, which had first been recognized in 1824, had not generally been accepted as biblically antediluvian – although a few bold spirits accepted the arguments of its great antiquity advanced by its excavator, a Roman Catholic priest, Father J. MacEnery.[126] Finds from the Brixham site, excavated in 1858, became, however, central to the whole problem of the antiquity of man. Franks, while recognizing that some of the flints found were of human manufacture, was cautious in giving any opinion as to their date.[127] Owen was a power in the land and in the Museum and Franks may well have had to move cautiously, for it was to Owen that the Trustees turned when first faced with a related problem. In 1864 a major assemblage of French Palaeolithic material was offered to the Museum for £1,000 by the Comte de Lastic St Jal, from the cave of Le Courbet at Bruniquel, near Toulouse.[128] It consisted of more than 2,000 objects, together with remains of contemporary fauna. The Louvre had turned it down and the Trustees, ignoring Franks, who by this time had accepted Prestwich and Evans's conclusions on the Somme material, had sent Owen (who had not initially recognized the implications of the early origin of man) to investigate the find, incidentally giving him the opportunity to accept publicly the new chronology. Fortunately he reported back favourably and 'made a meticulous record of the context of the finds and of the fauna', which was published shortly after the collection was received in the Museum.[129] This material, with that from the Christy collection, the Montastruc collection (purchased in 1887 from the Christy fund) and a small collection from the Somme gravels, provided the Museum with a collection of French Palaeolithic material unrivalled outside France. The Museum was rather less successful in acquiring English material; that from Creswell Crags in Derbyshire, for example, went to the Manchester Museum.[130]

The excitement of the recognition of early man overshadowed much of the later prehistoric material collected by the Museum and this is to a certain extent reflected in the quality of the collections, which nonetheless increased considerably in the second half of the nineteenth century. The most notable acquisition, the vast collection of chiefly Neolithic and early Bronze Age material excavated from burial mounds mostly from the north of England by Canon Greenwell, came to the Museum between 1879 and 1893.[131] The Greenwell collection also included material from the Neolithic flint mines at Grimes Graves, Norfolk, where further excavation was carried out by the Museum in the 1970s.[132] Foreign material of these two periods was not acquired in quantity. Worsaae sold for £150 a splendid and rich collection of Danish prehistoric artefacts to the Museum, while the general central European archaeological collection of Gustav Friedrich Klemm, a Dresden librarian, was acquired in 1868, but other Neolithic and Bronze Age material was acquired in dribs and drabs.[133] A major departure was the acquisition of a series of assemblages, including organic material from the waterlogged Swiss lake-dwellings of the Neolithic and Bronze Age, which had been investigated from 1832 onwards. These had been brought to the attention of the British public in a fascinating redaction of a series of articles by Ferdinand Keller of Zurich, published in English in 1866.[134] The influence of this book was immense and drew attention to the related Irish crannogs, first investigated by William Wilde and George Petrie in 1839, from which the Museum also acquired material.[135]

The Iron Age finds from Stanwick had been a catalyst in the foundation of the original British and Mediaeval sub-department in the Museum and Franks had written pioneering work on the art of the Iron Age, a type of material that has since been collected with great assiduity. Iron Age material from the Continent, particularly from the type-sites of Hallstatt and La Tène, a major preoccupation of the young Franks, was eagerly sought after.[136] The Museum's nineteenth-century interest in the continental Iron Age culminated in 1901 in the purchase for £2,100 of the large collection of La Tène objects from graves excavated in Champagne in the latter half of the nineteenth century by Léon Morel. Most importantly, these included the grave-goods from the famous chariot-burial from Somme-Bionne, Marne.[137]

The Romano-British collection of the British Museum is one of the best provincial Roman collections in existence. The Museum had been collecting such material since its foundation and a number of major pieces of Roman sculpture and some mosaics were acquired in the early years of the nineteenth century.[138] It had even been digging it up (a rare occurrence in the nineteenth century) – in 1845 Newton, together with Doubleday, a colleague from the Department of Zoology, had been sent to Colchester to search for antiquities; they were allowed six guineas in expenses.[139] The foundation of the Romano-British collection, however, lay in the great Roach Smith purchase of London antiquities (p.133). Objects acquired during the second half of the nineteenth century were drawn from the whole country, from Hadrian's Wall to the Iron Age and Romano-British hill-fort at Hod Hill in Dorset.[140] Franks was particularly interested in Romano-British bronzes, and in the course of his lifetime gave many examples to the Museum.

The mixed fortunes of the Museum in acquiring pagan Anglo-Saxon material have been recounted above, but it was during Franks's keepership that equivalent material was acquired from the Continent. The Morel collection acquired in 1901 contained much French material of the Merovingian period and was the culmination of Franks's consistent collecting in this area. In 1896 Franks arranged for the transfer of the rich collection of pagan Anglo-Saxon funerary material from Faversham, Kent, from the Victoria and Albert Museum, to which it had been bequeathed by William Gibbs as an educational collection. A new departure, however, was the gradual accumulation of antiquities that illustrated the culture and religion of Christian Anglo-Saxon and Celtic Britain. The most famous object, given by Franks and bearing his name, is the Anglo-Saxon whalebone casket, probably rediscovered at Auzon in the Auvergne.[141] The Franks Casket, which may be dated to the first half of the eighth century, has several inscriptions, mostly in runes in old English, accompanying scenes illustrating matter from the Old and New Testaments and from Germanic mythology. It was almost immediately, as a condition of gift, lent to the British section of the 1867 Exposition Universelle in Paris. Another runic-inscribed object acquired at this time was a ninth-century stone cross from Lancaster, given in 1868 by the Natural History Society of Manchester, the foundation of a small but distinguished collection of Anglo-Saxon sculpture.[142] Anglo-Saxon metalwork of the Christian period was also acquired by purchase or gift, including the earliest English chalice, which came from a rich silver hoard found at Trewhiddle in Cornwall (dated by coins to 873–5), given to the museum in honour of Franks by J.J. Rogers in 1888.[143] Another important piece was a nielloed gold finger-ring inscribed on the back of the bezel with the name of Queen Æthelswith of Mercia (853/4–873/4), the sister of Alfred the Great. This had been found between

Aberford and Sherburn in West Yorkshire and had been acquired in dubious circumstances by Canon Greenwell, who sold it to Franks.[144]

A group of ogham-inscribed stones from Ireland, the product of one of the first of Lane-Fox's archaeological expeditions, provided the Museum with its first major monuments of 'Celtic' Christianity.[145] The Museum acquired a representative piece of eighth-century Pictish sculpture from Burghead, Morayshire, in 1861.[146] Franks was generally remarkably tactful about collecting Scottish material, although it was not until after a row over the purchase by his successor of the massive Glenlyon brooch in 1897 that the British Museum formally accorded priority of acquisition to the National Museum of Antiquities of Scotland.[147] There was a brisk trade in antiquities in Ireland from the 1860s onwards, a source much tapped by John Evans and Canon Greenwell, although Franks also had his contacts there.[148] Through such sources the Museum acquired many fine pieces not only of the prehistoric periods, but of Early Christian metalwork, particularly ornamented penannular brooches. Two of the most impressive objects were shrines – the Kells Crozier, with its mounts of the ninth century and later, acquired in 1859, and the eleventh-century Shrine of St Cuilean's Bell (sometimes known as the Glankeen, Tipperary, bell-shrine).[149]

Strange, if important, donations were also received from time to time. Thus in November 1865 a letter was read to the Trustees:

> from George Witt Esqre proposing to present his Collection of 'Symbols of Early Worship of Mankind' to the British Museum, in the hope that a small room might be appropriated for its reception and arrangement with the specimens already in the Museum illustrating the same subject.[150]

These symbols were in fact erotica, more than 400 objects and a number of books collected in the early nineteenth-century tradition of Payne Knight and his contemporaries. The Trustees accepted them without apparent discussion.[151] A room was found for the collection in the north basement and Franks registered it in a separate volume. From time to time permission was asked of the Trustees to put some objects from the collection on display.[152] The Witt Collection, together with a similar number of pieces already in the Museum, became the basis of what was referred to in the nineteenth and early twentieth century as the *Musæum Secretum*, a collection paralleled by the 'Private Case' books in the Department of Printed Books.[153] Special permission had to be asked in order to see the collection; this was given readily, but Franks was dismissive of its value, writing to one such applicant, 'I should say that it will take you about ½ hour to make a careful examination of the whole'.[154]

The third quarter of the nineteenth century saw more money spent on the antiquities collections by the Trustees than at any other time in its history, but without the many donations – both large and small – the Museum would never have flourished. One of the greatest individual gifts was the bequest of a successful lawyer and landowner, Felix Slade.[155] He was a bachelor and a passionate collector, but intensely private, taking no part in public life. He had, however, a wide circle of friends, particularly among collectors. Perhaps foremost among them was Franks, thirty-six years his junior, whom he probably first met in 1850 when Franks was Secretary to the Mediaeval Exhibition at the Royal Society of Arts. Like Franks, Slade was a member of the Athenæum (he bequeathed money to it for the purchase of art books), the Fine Arts Club and (elected late in life) the Society of Antiquaries. He had no sympathy for the South Kensington Museum, specifically excluding it from his will. He collected antiquities, books (particularly those with fine bindings) and Japanese ivories, but specialized in glass (on which he spent some £8,000) and prints. During his lifetime, through his friendship with Franks, he had given a number of antiquities to the Museum, of which the most important is perhaps 'the Sword of Tiberius', dated to 15 BC, found in Mainz, which he purchased for the Museum in 1866.[156]

He died in 1868 and left estate valued at £160,000. The most famous part of his bequest comprised the sum of £45,000 to found professorships of fine art at Oxford and Cambridge, and a professorship and six studentships at University College London; the latter element was used as the foundation endowment of what was to become the Slade School of Art. In the first codicil of his will, however, he left his collection of glass to the Museum, together with:

> Such specimens of pottery and such other works of Art not specifically bequeathed by any other Codicil... as my friend Augustus Wollaston Franks one of my executors may select as desirable for the British Museum. And also my collection of Japanese carvings in Ivory and Metal... all my unbound collection of Engravings, Woodcuts and Etchings... and such of my... books in ancient bindings, which my friends Augustus Wollaston Franks and Richard Fisher... may think desirable for the British Museum... I particularly request that none of the bound volumes of Engravings and Etchings hereby bequeathed shall be broken up or otherwise mutilated... And it is my particular desire that no article... shall be at any time transferred to the South Kensington Museum.[157]

With this collection came £3,000, which Franks was allowed to spend within ten years at his absolute discretion on further pieces of glass. In a report to the Trustees Franks valued the collection at £28,000.[158] Slade also instructed that the catalogue of his glass collection should be completed and published, a wish quickly and faithfully fulfilled by Franks in a magnificent privately published volume.[159] A major contributor to the volume was Alexander Nesbitt, Franks's brother-in-law, who wrote about glass technology and built up a collection of glass sherds, mostly obtained in Rome. Franks, always keen to get hold of archaeological material to illuminate the Museum's holdings, acquired it and presented it to the Museum in 1886.[160]

While the glass collection is the most significant element of the Slade Bequest, in that it led the Museum in a new direction in its acquisitions policy, the enormous importance of the other elements in the collection must not be overlooked. The Japanese ivory netsuke were, for example, a new departure for the Museum, and one which was to assume greater relevance as Japan was opened up to the West and collectors could more freely lay their hands on both its fine and applied arts. Slade's collection of prints totalled 8,853 items of which 'up to 2,163 are individual images; the remainder are all sets of proofs of illustrations to nineteenth-century books, especially Shakespeare and the poets... In some cases there are several sets in duplicate...'.[161] The British school is very strongly represented among the individual items, as are the North European schools; there are 146 Italian prints – all fine impressions, collected with taste and selectivity. The remainder of the collection was intended for insertion in fine copies of already published works, although Slade apparently only did this once, to an edition of the *Decameron*.[162]

The glass collection, consisting of just under 1,000 pieces, is, however, unique and splendid. It was well known and often shown off; Gustav Waagen, for example, Director of the Berlin Museums, had visited and admired it in 1856.[163] Franks, who had written widely on glass,[164] had clearly been helping Slade with his catalogue and was aware of the impending bequest. So confident was he of its quality that, only a month before Slade's death, he recommended that the Trustees should not purchase the collection of glass offered by the marine artist E.W. Cooke, because of the potential bequest, producing a letter from Slade which confirmed his proposed action.[165] The Slade collection is eclectic and of the highest quality, spanning the period from classical times to his own lifetime; it is particularly strong in Venetian, Islamic and German glass. He also had some extremely fine pieces of English and Anglo-Dutch glass, although little was known at that period about English glass and Slade admitted that here he was swimming in uncharted waters.[166]

Before it received the Slade Bequest the British Museum had practically no glass of non-classical date; by one carefully engineered coup it now became a significant resource in European terms.[167] Franks clearly knew what he was doing, for he started to collect glass quickly and seriously with the money Slade had left him; between 1869 and 1873 he purchased some 700 items, including almost immediately the famous Anglo-Dutch Velzen covered goblet, made about 1690 and engraved in 1757.[168] When the Slade money had been spent Franks encouraged further bequests, gifts (many from Franks himself) and judicious purchases so that, almost without the Trustees knowing it, the Museum's glass collection became one of the most representative in the world.

As with glass, so with pottery. The Museum's post-medieval ceramic collection may not be very extensive by international standards (it numbers about 10,000 pieces), but the collection represents most of the European factories and fabrics. Its international importance lies in the number of dated and documented pieces of the kind that Franks was particularly keen to acquire. It was collected insidiously, in Franks's well-proven manner. We have seen how he had built up the Italian maiolica collections from scratch (p.135); he now proceeded by stealthy means to collect other ceramic material. In 1852 he purchased a Manises spouted vessel, the first of many pieces of Spanish lustreware to enter the collection.[169] So quickly had it grown that by 1867 Auguste Demmin, author of an early guide to pottery, was greatly impressed by the lustreware collection. It remains one of the best and least-known of such holdings and was in 1983 considerably enhanced by the acquisition of the collection of Franks's young friend Frederic Ducane Godman, which included many fine pieces.[170] Tinware followed, as did stoneware, of which Franks formed for the Museum a truly remarkable collection concentrating on its archaeological and documentary importance, recently catalogued together with the Victoria and Albert Museum's collection.[171]

Before the advent of Franks the European pottery and porcelain collection was insignificant, although the acquisition of the Chelsea gold-anchor vases and Wedgwood blue jasperware pieces soon after they had been made has been noted. The story of the porcelain collections is rather different from that of many of the other collections built up over this period, for this – with silver and finger-rings – was Franks's passion. He collected ceramics throughout his life for his own satisfaction and enjoyment (as early as 1860 John Evans tells of an evening spent with him looking at his porcelain, and by 1867 Demmin lists him as a collector of Chelsea porcelain). Only in his bequest did much of the most important part of his ceramic collection – the documentary continental porcelains, for example – come to the Museum.[172] Other portions came as gifts when he had assembled what he regarded as a significant or even reasonably complete collection; thus, for the first ten years of his keepership, hardly any porcelain was acquired by the Museum, though he himself was collecting energetically and privately. His first recorded interest in porcelain was in 1851, when he presented a paper to the Archaeological Institute based on a hand-written 1790 account by Thomas Craft of the method of decoration of one of the few pieces of English porcelain in the Museum, a Bow bowl. He had found the document in the card-board box in which the bowl was stored. He was to publish books and papers on the subject for the rest of his life, focusing largely on documentation. He was, for example, probably the first to use newspaper advertisements as a source for the history of the various potters' firms. It was presumably Franks's archaeological interests that in 1868 attracted the gift by G.H. Higgins of fragments of Bow porcelain and kiln furniture found on the site of the factory.[173]

Franks clearly intended from early on to pass his collections to the Museum either in his lifetime or at his death. Acquisition consequently was made cautiously, and mostly by gift. The Wedgwood collection is an example.[174] So far as we can tell, at the time Franks joined the staff there were only two pieces of Wedgwood in the Museum. In 1853 Joseph Mayer (as we have seen, a friend of Franks) gave twenty-four pieces, mostly portrait medallions. Small gifts of this nature, together with pieces given or bequeathed by Franks, brought the total to about 700 by the end of the century. Franks's friendship with his contemporaries seems to have ensured that the gift by Mr and Mrs Isaac Falcke in 1909 of a further 500 pieces of Wedgwood, which in no way duplicated the existing collections, was steered to the Museum. The Wedgwood collection thus became one of the most significant in the British Isles, and one which is added to year on year.

This is not the place to examine in detail the growth of the Museum's European ceramic collections during the last quarter of the nineteenth century. The tactics used in acquisition seem, however, to follow a well-tried course. First there was a period of caution during which hardly any material was acquired; then came a major gift by Franks (in two cases after he had first catalogued and displayed his collections at the Bethnal Green Museum).[175] He then prepared the way for his fellow collectors to give collections to the Museum. Figures are not without interest. His catalogue of continental porcelains (those displayed at Bethnal Green) amounted to more than 500 items. Soon after Franks's death R.L. Hobson, newly appointed to the Museum, catalogued the English pottery and porcelain; the porcelain items amounted at that time to more than 730 pieces, while the post-sixteenth-century pottery totalled more than 1,500 (of which some 800 were Wedgwood).[176] Some eighty per cent of this was given or bequeathed by Franks. He was not, however, entirely selfish for the Museum; it was his advice that steered to the South Kensington Museum the magnificent collection of English ceramics formed by Lady Charlotte Schreiber.[177]

Franks's interest in ceramics extended far beyond the European factories. He also laid the foundation of the Museum's unsurpassed comparative collection of oriental ceramics, Islamic, Chinese, Japanese, Thai and Korean – little understood or studied when he first arrived. Again he employed the tactics he had used in assembling the European collections – sparingly accepting gifts while he built up his own holdings and persuaded his friends to co-operate. Being interested in the interaction between Europe and Islam in the Middle Ages, he was deeply involved in early studies of Islamic pottery. In 1860, for example, he arranged an exhibition of this material at the Society of Antiquaries in which he attempted to identify three main groups (interestingly, some of the evidence he used was provided by Charles Newton, at that time consul in Rome).[178] Rachel Ward has noted that Franks acquired few pieces of this pottery for the Museum until 1878 because he was building up a representative collection of his own and discussing it with fellow collectors and friends – particularly John Henderson, on whose major collection Franks had designs.[179] He was not disappointed. In 1878 Henderson died and his varied material came to the Museum.[180] As well as ninety-six pieces of oriental and Venetian inlaid brass vessels and a vast array of oriental weapons, it included more than 130 pieces of Islamic pottery. Franks now started to add pieces that he had acquired himself and his plans for this area came to a triumphant conclusion in 1983 when the daughter of his friend Frederick duCane Godman steered her father's incomparable collection of Islamic pottery to the Museum.[181]

Far Eastern pottery had long been valued by wealthy European collectors who, since the fourteenth century, had used it to adorn their houses. The first pieces to enter the Museum came from the Sloane collection; but acquisitions of any sort of oriental pottery – or indeed oriental antiquity – until the arrival of Franks were haphazard and minimal.[182] Here again he formed his own collection, steering only a few items to the Museum, as for example two pieces from the Summer Palace in Beijing, bought for £35 in 1867.[183] His expertise in this field was widely recognized – it was almost unique in England – but, as he had no oriental language, he tended to depend on French literature for terminology and literary references. For immediate help with language and with inscriptions he turned to Birch or to Robert Douglas, a sinologist in the Department of Printed Books. Interestingly, in 1875 he edited a catalogue of Japanese pottery prepared by a Japanese scholar for the South Kensington Museum. By 1876 his collection of oriental pottery and porcelain was large enough to be placed on exhibition at the Bethnal Green Museum, for which he wrote a full catalogue.[184] Two years later he offered it to the Museum and, before it could be installed in 1885 (after the removal of the natural history material), he had weeded and increased it to a total of some 3,000 pieces. This included 180 ancient Japanese objects acquired at the 1878 Exposition Universelle in Paris.[185] Jessica Harrison-Hall has noted a letter from Franks to a dealer in 1888 after the completion of the display of this gift, which throws considerable light on his attitude. 'The British Museum', he wrote, 'does not purchase oriental porcelain and I am not now adding much to the collection I have given to the Museum.'[186] Having laid the groundwork, by what can only be described as frenetic collecting, he could afford to sit back, occasionally adding to the assembly, and wait for the important pieces and collections to appear, having encouraged various public servants and academics to collect for him. Thus, for example, when Lieutenant W.G.K. Barnes in 1896 offered twenty-three pieces of contemporary pottery from the Shiwan kilns in Guangdong or the French sinologist Charles Schefer sent him a case of ceramics from Korea, Vietnam and Cambodia in 1892, he was happy to accept them. The Museum's collection, he wrote in 1893, was 'less valuable perhaps from a commercial point of view than the famous collection at Dresden made about 1700 by the King of Poland, but more instructive'![187]

Asia and Beyond

Ceramics had introduced Franks to the high cultures of mainland Asia, while the opening up of Japan to the West as a result of the Treaty of Edo in 1858, and the subsequent flood of imported Japanese goods, clearly introduced him to the more general culture of that country.[188] Franks was to a minor extent involved in the London International Exhibition of 1862, where Japanese goods, chosen by the first British Minister in Tokyo, Rutherford Alcock, were exhibited in an international context for the first time and attracted wide interest. Some of the objects – bronzes, metalwork, ivories – shown at the exhibition came to the Museum, probably as a gift, the first Japanese objects to enter the Museum since its foundation. Franks was not the only one interested in these exotic arts; people of taste, particularly in Britain and France, became obsessed by them. Franks had more taste and experience and more contacts than most of the others. What is more, as Lawrence Smith has pointed out, he held himself generally aloof from fashionable, undiscriminating western *japonisme*. For example, he was apparently the first English collector to recognize the importance of the aesthetics of the Tea Ceremony. As a result he started a collection of the restrained (mostly stoneware) pots made for this important element of Japanese cultural life – a collection which is still continuously added to. That said, he also collected in fashionable areas – sword-guards and netsuke, for example – but almost without exception these are of the highest quality. An area in which he did not venture was Japanese painting, although it was through his influence that the Museum acquired the remarkable collection of some 3,000 paintings (mostly Japanese, but some Chinese) assembled by Dr William Anderson between 1872 and 1880, the foundation of collections which are now the best in Europe.[189]

While Franks was busily collecting oriental pottery and porcelain privately, he was being more open about the collecting of other Asian material for the Museum. The archaeology of this area was more or less a closed book to Europeans at this period, although Franks had himself published some stone prehistoric implements from Japan in a paper given to the London meeting of the International Congress of Prehistoric Archaeology in 1869.[190] He was, therefore, eager to accept judicious gifts of archaeological material from Asia. Early in Franks's Museum career A.F. Bellasis gave a collection of material excavated in Sind.[191] Other gifts followed, a Neolithic beaker probably from Annam in Vietnam, pottery and other artefacts from Japanese and Korean tombs, roof tiles and prehistoric weapons from China. The Gowland collection of Japanese archaeological material, principally from the Kofun period (third to sixth century AD), was purchased with its paper archive by Franks in 1889.[192] The Henderson bequest, which included many oriental weapons, and General Augustus Meyrick's gift of Japanese arms and ivories gave a whole new flavour to the Asian collections.[193] The first Korean pot was given to the Museum in 1888 by W.G. Aston. In the following year some early Three Kingdoms pottery was given to the Museum by Franks; it came from the collection of William Gowland, who was the first westerner to compare the tomb furniture of Japan and Korea.[194]

The most extraordinary lacuna in the Museum at the time Franks became keeper was India. 'It is something of a disgrace', Hawkins had written in 1836, 'to have so few memorials of our Indian empire.'[195] Although some effort was made to remedy this situation, Indian objects were very casually acquired and were thin on the ground.[196] In part this was due to the existence of the India Museum, which since its establishment in 1801 had been housed in the headquarters of the East India Company in Leadenhall Street.[197] Although often badly administered it continued to collect, particularly after it acquired much of the Indian material from the Great Exhibition of 1851. In 1861 it moved to Fife House in Whitehall, where it remained until it was closed down and its collections distributed in 1879. Franks may well have foreseen this closure, particularly as there had been frequent suggestions that the collections should be transferred in part or in whole to the British Museum. Meanwhile, in 1872, Franks had acquired by gift the Bridge collection of Indian sculpture.

This had mainly been formed by the purchase at Christie's 1830 sale of the collection of Major-General Charles Stuart, an Indian army officer who had been in the Company's service for more than fifty years. Stuart had collected Indian art, books and weapons widely and judiciously at a time when no other European was at all interested in this area. John Bridge, a London goldsmith, bought much of the sculpture from the collection and built it into his new mansion, West House in Shepherd's Bush, west London. Nobody knows why Bridge bought this material, although he had business contacts with India and may even have known Stuart. The sculpture collection remained in the family until the sale of West House in 1872, when it was given to the Museum.[198]

Soon afterwards a decision had to be taken about the India Museum, as the lease on Fife House had run out and the collections had been dispersed to various centres, including the South Kensington Museum. The India Museum had now passed to the India Office. After a certain amount of commotion, both in the Council of India and in Parliament, formal proposals were made to disperse the collections, dividing them between Kew, the British Museum and the South Kensington Museum.[199] Each of these three institutions was invited to nominate members to a committee to oversee the dispersal of the India Museum's collections – Bond, Franks and Günther (Keeper of Zoology) represented the British Museum. Although Franks bid for, and succeeded in acquiring, a substantial number of other items, he was anxious above all to acquire the Amaravati sculptures, and they were accordingly transferred to the Museum.[200] These now rank among the greatest treasures of the Museum and have since 1992 been displayed in the Asahi Shimbun Gallery in the King Edward VII Building. The Museum's collection consists of 133 fragments from a great domed *stūpa*, or Buddhist relic-house, from Amaravati, Andhra Pradesh, in south-east India; other pieces remain on the site and still others are in the Government Museum, Madras.[201] Most of the sculptures date from the first to third centuries AD and are the most important group of ancient Indian sculptures outside the subcontinent. By 1816 much of the monument had been quarried for building stone. At this time Colonel Colin Mackenzie, Surveyor General of India, started to record the site and removed eleven stones, sending two of them to the Madras Museum and nine of them to London. In 1845 Sir Walter Elliot of the Madras Civil Service removed another seventy-nine stones to Madras. Eventually 121 stones were shipped to London in 1859. In 1880 about half of the collection was mounted under glass on the main staircase of the Museum, where it remained until the Second World War.

With the Amaravati sculptures came other sculpture, including material from Gandhara, the north-west province of Pakistan, which became the core of the finest collection of this sculpture in existence.[202] The collection came largely from Buddhist enclosures abandoned in the seventh century AD, and comprises material mostly dating from the first to sixth centuries. The Mediterranean classical overtones of the ornament – clearly influenced from the west – astonished European students when the sculpture first appeared in the middle of the nineteenth century.

It is interesting that there had been little attempt to collect ethnographic material from the subcontinent and at this distance of time it is difficult to see why Indian sculpture was so sought after by the Museum. There must have been many reasons – the flight from classicism, the importance of India to Britain, the sheer quality of the carving, or a burgeoning interest in oriental religions and art. In many ways the interest must have been due to a fascination with the unknown, just as, forty years earlier, the Assyrian reliefs had fascinated the public. The Amaravati sculpture may have been placed on the main staircase because there was nowhere else to put it. This was, however, one of the most important sites in the building and it may be that the Museum was trying to challenge the public's taste. It seems as though a deliberate attempt was being made to get the public to accept cultures other than those of the classical world, which had hitherto so overshadowed the institution. Franks, as we have seen, was clearly fascinated by the Orient and had many contacts there; he was also by now (in the 1880s) a dominant figure in the structure of the Museum and influential with Bond, the Principal Librarian. He was, however, fighting for space. It is, therefore, quite likely that the strong statement made by the Indian sculpture was used by him not only to advertise the newly created oriental side of the Museum, but literally to drag the British public upstairs to galleries where the new and often more exotic material assembled during his keepership was now about to receive more visibility.

One of the less glorious episodes in the history of the Museum, in today's terms, was the Trustees' involvement in the punitive expedition to Abyssinia that resulted from the brutal idea of the Emperor Téwodros to twist the British lion's tail by taking diplomatic and missionary hostages. War became inevitable when the emperor refused the placatory British letter delivered by Hormuzd Rassam, a local British official (and incidentally, as we have seen, an agent of the British Museum in its Assyrian excavations). In October 1867 Newton approached the Trustees to pass on a suggestion from a Captain Sherwood, that the Museum should appoint a 'competent Archaeologist' to accompany the army to Abyssinia to investigate the cultures of the area.[203] He was supported by Franks, Vaux, Watts (Keeper of Printed Books) and Rieu (Keeper of Oriental Manuscripts).[204] The first choice, Emanuel Deutsch, withdrew on health grounds and was replaced by R.R. Holmes of the Manuscript Department.[205]

The emperor had been systematically collecting material from churches throughout the country and the British, who managed to gather most of them together during the last days of the campaign, put them up for auction. Holmes bid for the Museum and was particularly successful in purchasing manuscripts. The Trustees clearly applauded his collecting and, despite criticism of his actions by Gladstone, he was later given an *ex gratia* payment of £200 and was awarded the campaign medal.[206] The non-manuscript items, mostly minor ecclesiastical objects (but including a few gaudy secular ones), for which Holmes had paid £113 4s at the auction, were placed on temporary exhibition by Franks.[207] The Museum was then offered by the Abyssinian Prize Committee the most important items taken during the expedition, the gold mitre or crown and the chalice of the Abyssinian patriarch. Holmes had rescued them from a soldier, and had paid him £4 for them. Napier, the Commander-in-Chief, had apparently promised that he should retain them, but they were passed to the Prize Committee and were now on offer for £2,000.[208] This offer was strongly supported by Franks (who, as always, thought the price too high).[209] Approach was made to the Treasury, which waited some six months without replying and then turned the Museum down. There was a row about the delay and papers were called for by Parliament.[210] The Treasury retained the objects, which by 1878 had been deposited in the South Kensington Museum, where they remain.[211] Sixteen manuscripts taken during this expedition were presented to the Queen, who passed ten of them on to the Museum. On the request of the Emperor Yohannes IV of Ethiopia through the Foreign Office, however, one manuscript was handed back.[212] Holmes himself kept at least one particularly numinous item, the Kwer'ata Re'esu, an icon painted in either the Netherlands or Iberia, which he had taken from the bedroom of the dead emperor a few minutes after he was killed. The painting was sold by Holmes's widow in 1917 for £420 and, having again been through the saleroom in 1950, is now in a private Portuguese collection.[213] This was the only time that the Museum sent an official to collect with an army expedition.

Derring-do on the Frontier

One of the major donors of Indian material to the Museum was Sir Alexander Cunningham, a retired Major-General in the Indian army and the founder and first Director-General of the Indian Archaeological Survey, which between 1861 and 1885 published twenty-five volumes of reports. Cunningham travelled widely throughout India, particularly in the north, collecting coins, seals and inscriptions to illuminate the history of the subcontinent. As a young man in 1857 he had sold 118 coins to the Museum, but after his retirement in 1887 he presented it with three major collections: first, a collection of archaeological material, including a series of inscribed Buddhist reliquaries from Sanchi; secondly, in 1888, a group of Bactrian, Parthian and Mughal coins, and then in 1892 the residue of his archaeological collections. After his death, by gift and purchase the museum received a further 4,500 coins.[214]

Cunningham was one of a number of people involved in the acquisition – mysterious, opaque, even nefarious – of one of the Museum's most remarkable assemblages, the Treasure of the Oxus.[215] Excluding coins, the treasure consists of about 180 objects from the Achaemenid Persian Empire (6th–4th centuries BC). Many of them are of gold, sometimes ornamented with figures. Among them is a model two-wheeled chariot with four horses and a driver, with a representation of the Egyptian god Bes on the front. There are a number of gold figures and vessels and, the most impressive objects in the treasure, two massive gold arm-rings with terminals in the form of griffins. Many of the pieces were cut up, to be treated as bullion. There were probably some 1,500 coins in the treasure, of which some 200 are now in the Museum and a number of small parcels are scattered in collections round the world. The treasure is diverse in date and cultural influence. The earliest objects are of the sixth century BC and the latest suggest that the treasure must have been closed between 200 and 180 BC. It may have been a votive deposit, possibly a temple treasure, and includes objects of Achaemenid, Greek and Central Asian origin.

There is general agreement that the treasure was found in the sands on the northern bank of the River Oxus, probably at Takht-i Kuwad in present-day Tajikistan, between 1877 and 1879.[216] It was purchased in local villages by three merchants from Bokhara. In May 1880, between Kabul and Peshawar (somewhere on the border of present-day Afghanistan and Pakistan), the merchants were attacked, captured and carried off into the hills by a band of local tribesmen. Their servant, however, was able to escape in the night and summon help from Captain F.C. Burton, a British soldier who was Chief Political Officer in the border district. According to his account Burton, with a couple of orderlies, arrived on the scene while the robbers were dividing the spoil and quarrelling over the division; four of them were already lying wounded. Burton managed to abstract a major portion of the treasure from the robbers, who returned even more of it under the threat of force the following day. About three-quarters was restored to the merchants. There are various versions of the affair, but it is clear that Burton was able to purchase one piece, an armlet, which he later sold for £1,000 to the South Kensington Museum. The merchants continued on their way and ultimately sold the treasure in Rawalpindi, where many of the objects seem to have been bought over a period of time by Cunningham, who first published them. Between 1887 and 1893 Cunningham sold his portion of the treasure privately to Franks, who had already, through his contacts in India, started to collect other material from it – including, for example, the gold chariot, purchased separately for £120. It formed part of his bequest to the Museum.[217]

The Royal Gold Cup

Towards the end of the century the Americans – and particularly J. Pierpont Morgan – had started to collect medieval European items on a large scale. Franks was clearly conscious of this and towards the end of his life used this threat as a weapon in acquiring the Royal Gold Cup. In 1891 he wrote to Henry Tate: 'A very wonderful gold cup has appeared returned to this country after an absence of 287 years and I am anxious to see it placed in the National Museum and not removed to America.'[218] The Royal Gold Cup is 23.6 cm high and weighs 2,107 gm. It has a cover, the knop of which is missing, and stands on a foot of openwork cast gold and pearls. The lid and body are embellished with translucent enamels depicting scenes from the life of St Agnes. Applied to the neck of the foot are enamelled rosettes, above which is a collar recording its donation in 1610 by Juan de Velasco, Constable of Castile, to the nuns of St Clara at Medina de Pomar in Spain.

Its history is well known. It was made in Paris about 1380 for Jean, Duc de Berry, and was presented to his brother Charles V of France. It passed into the hands of Charles VI and then to John of Lancaster, Duke of Bedford, from whom it passed to his nephew, Henry VI. It remained in the English royal collection until in 1604 James I gave it to the Constable of Castile to mark the conclusion of an Anglo-Spanish treaty. From him it passed to the nuns of Medina de Pomar and remained there until it was sold in 1883 to Baron Jérôme Pichon, who paid £100 over the value of the metal and then offered it to Franks for £20,000. Franks did not bite and in 1891 Pichon sold it to Wertheimer, the Paris dealers, for £8,000. They offered it to Franks who purchased it privately at cost price.[219] Or that at least is the story. In fact Franks at first tried to raise the money privately, at first in

£500 tranches, but then in slightly lesser sums. In this he had some difficulty and the death of S. Wertheimer in the middle of the negotiations resulted in Franks himself putting up the sum of £5,500, although the Wertheimer heirs fulfilled their father's promise and gave £500 to the project. The Treasury granted £2,000, and ultimately made a supplementary grant of £830 to complete the purchase.[220] To Franks this was his greatest acquisition, and the one of which he was most proud.

HMS Topaze[221]

No account of the British Museum would be complete without mention of the two major pieces of Easter Island sculpture brought back by HMS *Topaze*, flagship on the South American station, in 1868. The more important is Hoa Hakananai'a, a magnificent example of Rapa Nui carving, 2.64 m high. The second, lesser figure was known as Moai Hava. Both cult figures had already been moved from their original site, the larger one to a stone house in Orongo. The larger figure probably dates from a late phase of a birdman cult which flourished between the eleventh and seventeenth centuries, with its ceremonial centre high up at the edge of the sea.

The main statue, which weighs four and a half tonnes, was transported for a mile overland and then brought on board the ship to the cheers of the islanders. Both statues were brought home to England and Hoa Hakananai'a was presented to Queen Victoria, who gave it to the Museum. Moai Hava was given to the Lords of the Admiralty, who – equally puzzled as what to do with it – likewise presented it to the Museum. With the sculptures came a number of other objects given by members of the crew, solicited by Franks. Queen Victoria's present became a much-loved object which now stands proudly in the Great Court of the Museum, and is still an inspiration to artists (p.226).

A Scientific Interest

There was in the nineteenth century no museum of science in existence anywhere in the world. The history of science was sorely neglected and its material remains languished in a few collectors' cabinets, in neglected drawers in various scientific societies and anatomical laboratories. Nobody was seriously collecting objects pertinent to the history of science. The exception was Franks who, together with a few of his friends, gradually amassed a collection of scientific instruments, mostly astronomical and mathematical. This was, until the gift of the Lewis Evans collection of scientific instruments to the University of Oxford in 1922, according to Robert Anderson, 'the largest and most impressive museum collection of early instruments'.[222]

Franks collected such objects himself and was supported as usual by his friends, particularly Max Rosenheim. Franks gave between a quarter and a third of the 267 scientific instruments added to the collection during his Museum career.[223] It is by no means an all-embracing collection, being largely confined to objects made before 1700 in Germany and England. It contains no serious optical instruments and no natural philosophical instruments. There was some ambiguity as to who should be collecting such material and a large loan exhibition of scientific instruments at the South Kensington Museum in 1876 has been seen as the first step towards the foundation of the Science Museum out of the Victoria and Albert Museum in 1909.[224] But in illustrating the history of scientific thought the collection formed by Franks and his successors is a formidable tool.

More important was the collection of clocks and watches, which now totals some 7,000 items and must be one of the largest in the world. Although Franks himself gave few clocks and watches to the Museum it is clear that he was interested in the subject – 'Old watches are rather a hobby of mine', he wrote to Mrs Swayne in 1892.[225] His friends Lady Fellows (widow of Sir Charles) and Octavius Morgan bequeathed fine collections to the Museum, perhaps the most visually outstanding being the carillon clock, 1.5 m high, by Isaac Habrecht of Strasbourg, dated 1589.[226] Modelled on the astronomical clock in Strasbourg Cathedral, it is paralleled by a similar clock in the Danish royal collections. More spectacular is the ship clock, probably made in Prague by Hans Schlottheim for the Emperor Rudolf II at the end of the sixteenth century. This extravagant object not only told the time, but rolled on wheels along the table, firing guns and playing a tune on a small organ concealed in the hull while soldierly figures moved and turned on deck.[227]

Not everything within the field of the Museum's interest was as noisily revolutionary as discussions concerning the antiquity of man or the historicity of the Bible. Smith's work on biblical archaeology had once again stimulated a more wide-ranging interest in Mesopotamia. Coincidentally, in 1877, Layard (who had so long worked for the Museum) was appointed British Ambassador to the Porte and was able to facilitate permission to excavate in the region. Through him, the Museum and its agent, Hormuzd Rassam, who had worked with Layard during his excavations some twenty years previously, obtained what was in effect blanket permission to excavate at almost any site in the region and retain all the finds with the exception of duplicates. Rassam, assisted by his nephew Nimrud Rassam and (in his frequent absences) by the British Resident at Baghdad, set to work with a will – and, it must be admitted, without great discipline, despite explicit instructions to the contrary – to travel widely and remit a great deal of material to the Museum.[228] First, with numerous other objects came the bronze plates from the ninth-century BC gates of Shalmaneser's palace at Balawat, some twenty kilometres from Mosul.[229] From Toprak Kale in eastern Turkey he sent back a rich collection of Urartian bronzes, some forming part of a throne, which now make up the core of the Museum's Anatolian collection. The discovery of the biblical Sippar (modern Abu Habbah) in 1881 produced, with other objects, some 60,000 to 70,000 unbaked clay tablets and was one of Rassam's last acquisitions for the Museum (and one which is still yielding information), before he finally quit the scene in 1882.[230] The Museum, although paying guardians to look after the sites they had been working on, did not return to the region until 1888, when a new assistant in the Department of Oriental Antiquities, Wallis Budge, with some difficulty obtained a firmân to dig at Kuyunjik for further tablets. Budge returned in the two following years to dig at Dêr; but generally he was more successful and more interested in purchasing tablets and other objects on the Baghdad market and, sometimes by devious means, sending them to the Museum.[231]

Birch himself dealt with the Egyptian collections and continued the series of works on the Museum's collection of hieratic papyri. More important, he put the collections in order and, by 1870, had registered them with a system of continuous accession numbers initiated by himself – a source of pride to the department, but of fury to every other department, which finds it difficult to relate to the standard system. Birch, having catalogued 10,000 objects, was not very active in acquisition in the field of Egyptology. His main acquisitions were papyri, most famously the Rhind Mathematical Papyrus, obtained in Thebes by the Scottish lawyer/antiquary Alexander Rhind, given to the Museum in 1863, and the Great Harris Papyrus of Ramesses III (which lists the donations of the king to Egyptian temples), presented in 1872. The activities of the Reverend Greville Chester, who visited Egypt for his health each year, produced a continuous stream of small objects eagerly purchased by Birch.[232] It was not until the foundation of the Egypt Exploration Fund (later Society) and the work of Wallis Budge in the 1880s that the Museum once again began to collect Egyptian antiquities in a planned fashion. Budge's earliest *coup* was the purchase in 1887 of the first tranche of the famous el Amarna letters. Although found in Egypt, these tablets are written in cuneiform and reflect the disturbed state of the region in the fourteenth century BC.[233]

Staff Changes

In 1878 Edward Bond, the Keeper of Manuscripts, succeeded a sickly Winter Jones as Principal Librarian.[234] He does not seem to have been the Trustees' first choice – they wanted the newly knighted Newton, who had acted ably in Jones's place when he was ill, but he turned them down, as did Franks.[235] Bond had in 1835 gone straight from Merchant Taylors' School to the Public Record Office; in 1838 he had joined the Department of Manuscripts and succeeded Madden as keeper in 1866. He was a major innovator in palaeography and was one of the founders of the Palaeographical Society. He was an odd choice as Principal Librarian, not least because he was sixty-three, and it is said that he was nearly as surprised as everyone else when he was appointed to the post. He was Panizzi's candidate and appears to have been persuaded by him to accept the post as 'a public duty'.[236] He seems to have been remarkably successful in a self-effacing manner, perhaps because he was willing effectively to delegate authority to his staff. He held the post for ten years, during which he initiated the printing of catalogues of printed books (long opposed by Panizzi and Jones) and supported Garnett, later Keeper of Printed Books, in the introduction of sliding bookshelves in the Department of Printed Books.[237] He reformed its book-purchasing policy and increased its senior staff. He also oversaw the move of the Natural History Museum to South Kensington, the subsequent carve-up of the newly vacant space and the building of the White Wing. He introduced electric light into the Museum. He arranged for the collection of British portraits to be transferred to the National Portrait Gallery and fought a Treasury suggestion that certain Old Master drawings should be transferred to the National Gallery.[238] More seriously, he saw off a threat by the Treasury, in one of its occasional periods of panic during a perceived financial crisis, to reduce the holdings.[239] He increased opening hours and started to develop an educational policy. He was a strong supporter of Franks and Newton. Retiring in 1888, he was replaced by his successor as Keeper of Manuscripts, the formidable Edward Maunde Thompson.[240] He was so revolutionary that Winter Jones felt moved to write of him, 'I fear there is too great a desire to court popularity and that the high objects for which the institution was founded may be lost sight of.'[241]

Thompson (pl. 25) became Principal Librarian in 1888 and governed (the word is used advisedly) for the next twenty-one years.[242] As was customary, two names were submitted to the Queen at the time of his appointment, the unsuccessful candidate being Sidney Colvin, the Keeper of Prints and Drawings. Thompson has, within the Museum, a reputation as a tyrant on much the same scale as Panizzi, although he has been much defended by some of his colleagues.[243] Outside the Museum he was known as a leading scholar in the field of palaeography and as a consummate academic politician. He came from an old Jamaican family; he was sent to school in England and then went to Oxford, but did not finish his degree because his father fell into financial trouble. He joined the Museum in 1861 in Panizzi's office, but soon moved to the Department of Manuscripts, where he was an energetic assistant and became a considerable scholar. When Bond was appointed as Principal Librarian he succeeded, with Panizzi's support, to the Keepership of Manuscripts.[244] His book on classical palaeography, which he revised after his retirement, is a landmark.[245] He was one of the founders of the British Academy, and preliminary discussions concerning its formation were held at the Museum; indeed, Thompson took the chair at its inaugural meeting in 1902. Although he hated making speeches, he moved in society with ease and entertained rather grandly. He was a successful administrator, but a bit of a courtier, being particularly close to Edward VII who, as Prince of Wales, had been a Trustee.

From the accession of Bond until the turn of the century, the staff and structure of the Museum changed fundamentally. In 1870 Vaux, the Keeper of Coins and Medals for ten years, having been put under considerable pressure as a result of trouble with one of his assistants, Madden's son (who was accused of peculation and had to resign), had a mental breakdown and himself resigned.[246] He was succeeded by Reginald Stuart Poole, son of an Anglican parson, who had between the ages of twelve and eighteen lived in Egypt; there he precociously assembled a book on the chronology of ancient Egypt, which was published under the patronage of the Duke of Northumberland. The Duke was a Trustee of the Museum and nominated Poole as a first-class assistant at the age of twenty in 1852.

Publication in the Department of Coins and Medals, which had produced great coin catalogues by Taylor Combe and Payne Knight, had ground to a halt. Only two catalogues were produced in Hawkins's reign – a privately published catalogue of French medals struck between 1793 and 1830, and the (suppressed) catalogue of British medals in 1852.[247] Nothing was published under Vaux. When, however, Poole succeeded as keeper in 1870 things changed; the department settled down to plan and execute the publication of the collections, and consequently produced a vast number of catalogues. The cataloguers did not attempt, as did those of so many foreign museums, to write a numismatic history of each ruler. Rather, they catalogued what existed in the collections according to mints and sequence of issues, and described the coins with an economy of style which enabled their work to appear regularly and quickly. Only thus could they produce, for example, the twenty-nine volumes of the *Catalogue of Greek coins* between 1873 and 1927. Naturally the volumes of the different series vary in content and accuracy, but in general they can still be used with benefit to this day and are frequently reprinted. The classical training of many of the staff led to a weighting towards classical and associated series. Medieval coins were largely neglected, although catalogues of the Anglo-Saxon and Norman series were produced in 1887 and 1916 respectively. Apart from the catalogue of Swiss coins published by Poole in 1878, no catalogue of continental coins appeared until R.H.M. Dolley and K.F. Morrison produced one on the Carolingian coins in 1966.[248]

The department had been active in acquisition. The collection of Bactrian and other coins of General Cunningham (acquired in 1888) has already been mentioned, as have the major collection of the Duc de Blacas (which added more than 4,000 coins to the Roman series, including many gold pieces) and the collection of 4,769 medals formed by Edward Hawkins. Indian coins were frequently acquired by gift; William Marsden presented his magnificent collection of oriental coins in 1834, and in 1886 came a well-documented South Indian series from Sir Walter Elliot. In 1861 Count J.W.F. de Salis, a great friend of the department and a considerable numismatist in his own right, gave a large collection of Roman and Byzantine coins on condition that he was allowed access to the Museum's collection in order to continue his study of the Roman series. In 1872 the department purchased the balance of Edward Wigan's collection of classical coins (he had given them his gold coins in 1864). The Bank of England passed its distinguished collection of coins and medals to the Museum in 1877 and Franks gave his large collection of Anglo-Saxon and medieval coins in 1893. Other coins came in small parcels through gift, purchase, or (increasingly) treasure trove.[249]

Poole was the keeper, more than any other, who brought coins before the general public: first by displays of electrotypes (a full-time technician was employed to make these), and then of original coins. In the rather jaundiced words of one of his successors, Sir George Hill, he 'had done something to stir up [activity in the department], though more by talking about it than by actual production'.[250] Poole always retained an interest in Egyptology and was one of Amelia Edwards's helpers in founding the Egyptian Exploration Fund (Birch, formally the Museum's Egyptologist, would have nothing to do with what he called 'emotional archaeology').[251] In 1889 Poole succeeded Newton in the Yates chair of Classical Archaeology at University College London, but did not retire from the Museum until 1893.[252] Barclay Head succeeded him as keeper, a scholar described by Hill as 'the best Greek numismatist this country has produced'. He had entered the Museum straight from Ipswich Grammar School in 1864 and had been deeply involved in the great catalogue series. A formidable scholar, he seems to have been a fairly typical monomaniacal inhabitant of the rarefied atmosphere of the Department of Coins and Medals at the end of the century.[253] He retired in 1906.

Birch, the senior antiquities keeper, continued to reign until 1885. A great scholar, he was a true eccentric; one of his successors, Budge, wrote of him:

> His dress was simple, the most characteristic of it being his long, black broadcloth coat, which was usually tightly buttoned and often awry. His trousers were made of some light material, with a black and white stripe, or check pattern. And he wore patent leather boots with spring sides, often the worse for wear. His broad-brimmed black silk chimney-pot hat was quite the worst in the Museum, which is saying a good deal, and no one remembered it when it was new... The dust on its brim was so well established that a friend once told him that, with the help of a little water, peas might be planted on it and they would grow... There was a good deal of truth in the remark of one of his American friends who told him that he looked like a 'cross between a jockey and a bishop'.[254]

He died in office in 1885, and was succeeded by a Guernsey man, Peter le Page Renouf, who was one of the rare keepers to be appointed from outside the Museum. (The Trustees for some reason ignored the claims of the brilliant Assyriologist Theophilus Pinches, who had been in the department since 1878.)[255] At the same time the Trustees, at Franks's suggestion, renamed the department as Egyptian and Assyrian Antiquities. Renouf was to hold the post for only nine years, being replaced by the brilliant and hyperactive Budge in 1894. Renouf had a chequered career before he came to the Museum. While at Oxford he had been involved with the Tractarians and had been received into the Roman Catholic Church. After a few years' desultory travel, Newman offered him a job at the new Catholic University of Ireland, where he became Professor of Eastern Languages. A pamphleteer, he subsequently quarrelled with the Church and left the university – but not the Church – to become a chief inspector of schools, a job he held until he succeeded Birch. Renouf was a philologist; he wrote a grammar of ancient Egyptian, and was hardly interested in archaeology, although it was not his fault that the Trustees formally abandoned excavation in Mesopotamia in 1888. He was, despite his later knighthood, a second-rate scholar – not a patch on Birch, Pinches or even his new assistant E.A. Wallis Budge, who had been appointed to the department in 1883. We may perhaps see Renouf's appointment as a mixture of unrecorded jobbery and as a holding exercise so that Budge could succeed him when he was more mature.[256]

Budge, who became keeper in 1894, was quarrelsome and uneasy in his relations with the British academic establishment, but brilliant and energetic; he wrote more than 150 books (which made him the most prolific author in *Who's Who*) and dealt with many languages – ancient Egyptian, Assyrian, Coptic, Syrian, Old Nubian and Ethiopic. Perhaps his greatest monument was the initiation in 1896 of the *Cuneiform texts* series, of which nearly sixty volumes have now appeared. He himself, probably because of some rivalry with Pinches, abandoned cuneiform and concentrated on Egyptian texts and antiquities. He visited Egypt in 1886, a few months after his appointment, and went to Baghdad in 1888, the first of many such visits. A text and objects man, not greatly interested in excavation, he purchased widely from dealers and fellow archaeologists in both Egypt and Mesopotamia, receiving also – rather grudgingly – material from Flinders Petrie's excavations for the Egyptian Exploration Society. One of his successors describes his activities there succinctly:

> On his first visit to Egypt in 1886 Budge was initiated into the technique of visiting and bargaining with antiquities dealers by Greville Chester; no better instructor in such a matter could he have had. But Budge soon outstripped his master in energy, knowledge and craftiness. His visits to Egypt on the business of the Trustees developed over the years into highly successful campaigns in which diplomacy, commercial acumen, a fine instinct for the exploitation of potentially advantageous circumstances, and irrepressible self-confidence all combined. Sometimes, in his desire to clinch a purchase, Budge was rather less than punctilious in his attention to the somewhat imprecise regulations concerning the acquisition and export of antiquities. But throughout his career he remained generally on good terms both with the civil authorities in Egypt and with the senior officials of the Antiquities Service....[257]

A great scholar, he was also an opinionated, quarrelsome man, who bore no grudge lightly. He was often in hot water, particularly in 1893 when he lost an ill-advised action for slander brought against him by the aged Rassam, supported by Layard, and had to pay £50 in damages.[258] It was a Pyrrhic victory for the two old men; henceforward Budge was to spend no little effort in denigrating the work of not only Rassam, but Layard. The Museum supported Budge and the case was clearly no obstacle to his career, as he was appointed Keeper of Egyptian and Assyrian Antiquities in the following year.

In the Department of Greek and Roman Antiquities, Newton, old and partly crippled, retired in 1886, to be succeeded by Alexander Stuart Murray (whose brother was to become Keeper of the Department of Botany in 1895). Murray was a Scotsman who had been educated at the universities of Edinburgh and Berlin. He joined the staff in 1867 and had probably lived too long under the shadow of his powerful keeper. He was an energetic scholar, a founder member of the British Academy, and rather conservative in his opinions, particularly in relation to Mycenaean chronology. His successor, A.H. Smith, wrote of him, '... his power of broad elementary exposition was limited, and although he was always interesting and suggestive, it was by no means easy to follow the general drift of his thought'.[259] The reallocation of space following the departure of the natural history departments in 1880 enabled him to rearrange the departmental galleries more spaciously and to re-label the objects. Acquisitions could no longer be planned with the abandon of the early years of Newton. Important purchases could, however, occasionally be made. Between 1889 and 1891 the Museum, for example, received special grants to purchase the gem collection of the fourth Earl of Carlisle (1694–1758) – some of which went to British and Mediaeval Antiquities.[260] Murray was from 1893 able, through a bequest of £2,000 by Miss Emma T. Turner, to initiate a series of excavations in Cyprus, one of the few areas of the classical world in which it was now possible to excavate and acquire material under licence from the government. Among the new Cypriot finds was material from the rich Enkomi tomb. The Museum had been acquiring material from Cyprus since a number of objects came with the Payne Knight collection in 1824, and now has one of the largest collections of Cypriot art in existence.[261] On the mainland work continued at Ephesus until 1905.

G.W. Reid, Keeper of Prints and Drawings, had kept his head down during the period of his tenure. He was the last of the old-style keepers. He had little formal education and had probably been appointed because of his long connection with the Museum (he had started his career as an attendant in 1842), his knowledge of the collection and because there was at that time no such thing as an art historian. His expertise lay in the field of prints; acquisitions of drawings were made almost accidentally, as, for example, with the Henderson bequest of 164 English watercolours. At a time when prints were cheap he bought enthusiastically and in vast quantity, building up particularly the department's magnificent series of nineteenth-century prints, including most notably the collection of proofs and prints of Turner's *Liber Studiorum*. He was also responsible for the purchase of the Hawkins collection of satirical prints. He spent £1,000 at the Durazzo sale in Stuttgart, £1,000 on the Hugh Howard collection, £600 on the Twopenny collection and sums between a few shillings and a hundred pounds on a multitude of small collections and individual prints. His most expensive acquisition was the Crace collection of London topography, which cost £3,000.[262] For the Galichon collection of prints and drawings, mainly Italian, which was sold in Paris in 1875, Reid requested the sum of £3,000. The Trustees agreed to approach the Treasury, which made a grant of £2,000, of which £1,704 was spent at the sale.[263] The Comptroller and Auditor General became agitated about this purchase but was roundly told off by the Trustees, who received an abject apology.[264]

Reid was a good housekeeper and his great achievement lay in the way he sorted and registered the collections. An indication of his application is that nearly all the records were written in his own hand. His assistants were of little importance in the history of the department; indeed, his appointment of his friends to write catalogues was ultimately his downfall, for although he himself worked manfully on building up and recording the collections, the work of his colleagues was based on little learning and no scholarship. He was eased, unwilling, out of his post in 1883 and was succeeded by an academic, Sidney Colvin, a star in the literary firmament, who was at the time of his appointment Keeper of the Fitzwilliam Museum at Cambridge and Slade Professor.[265]

In appointing Colvin the Trustees for the first time since 1803 had moved outside the Museum to fill a senior post, passing over the acting Assistant Keeper, Louis Fagan, a second-rate scholar who had enjoyed the protective patronage of Panizzi (of whom he wrote a biography).[266] Colvin came from a wealthy background. His father was an Indian merchant who lived in some style near Woodbridge, Suffolk. His mother was a friend of the Ruskin family and this friendship coloured Colvin's early professional career. Colvin did not suffer fools gladly and boldly restructured his department. His greatest achievement was the appointment of three young men – Campbell Dodgson, Laurence Binyon and A.M. Hind – who were to reshape the department and build up its scholarship over nearly fifty years.[267]

Colvin was keeper for twenty-nine years and, although he wrote little concerning the department's collections, he established its reputation for collecting Old Master drawings. He bought or was given many minor collections or individual drawings, as when he bought a major Raphael cartoon of the Virgin and Child for £900 in 1895.[268] Of particular importance was his acquisition of the collection formed by John Malcolm of Poltalloch, which included almost 1,000 drawings and more than 400 prints, for which the Museum received a parliamentary grant of £25,000 in 1895. The organization of the purchase was no easy task, but Colvin, who like all members of the department before and since was conscious of the loss suffered when the Museum failed to acquire the Lawrence collection, planned the operation skilfully. First, he persuaded Malcolm's heir to deposit the collection on loan in the Museum and to salt the purchase by offering a spectacular Michelangelo cartoon (now on permanent display in the Prints and Drawings Gallery) as a gift. On receiving the loan, Colvin put the collection on exhibition in order to emphasize its importance and announced both the loan and the gift in the newspapers.[269] Money for the purchase soon followed. But it was not only Old Master drawings that were acquired under Colvin's influence. One of the people who helped influence the purchase of the Malcolm collection was William Mitchell, who gave his splendid collection of early German woodcuts to the Museum to smooth the way.[270] The year 1895 was, for the Department of Prints and Drawings, in the words of the Museum's annual report to Parliament, 'probably, taking quality and quantity together, the richest in the annals of the department, at any rate during the present century'.[271] To add to these, Franks gave a large collection of nearly 1,500 title-pages and book illustrations and Lady Charlotte Schreiber gave her 'very comprehensive and valuable collection of playing cards', nearly 1,700 in number.[272]

The curatorial staff of the antiquities departments now stood at twenty (support staff consisted of forty-three attendants, seven masons and a mould-maker). In 1889 the library, with George Bullen, Keeper of Printed Books (to be replaced in 1890 by Richard Garnett), Charles Rieu, Keeper of Oriental Manuscripts, and the newly appointed head of the Department of Manuscripts, E.J.L. Scott, had together a staff of fifty-six librarians (the rest of the library establishment consisted of 116 attendants of various grades).

The Museum at Century's End

Acquisitions, particularly by Franks and Newton, had brought the antiquities departments near to crisis in relation to both storage and exhibition space. The staff was crowded into inconvenient and distant corners. A description of Birch's office in 1870 has a ring of truth:

> [It] was entered through a door in the south-west corner of the Nineveh Gallery, and was one of the additions made to the building when the architect realized that officials needed accommodation on the premises. It was built over a section of the basement containing apparatus connected with the heating of the Galleries, and the weird sounds which accompany the passage of hot water and steam through the pipes, and the hissing of the escaping steam, could be heard distinctly through the floor. Birch was firmly convinced that the engineer would one day lose control of his apparatus and blow the room and him in it up together... The room had two windows, one on the north side which gave a good light, and one on the west side, which faced and was close to a blank brick wall. Before the former stood a writing table at which students could sit and work, and before the latter a long low case, with a sloping top, which was much used by Birch when consulting the 'ponderous tomes' of Rosellini, Champollion and Lepsius... On each side of the fireplace stood an upright, narrow polished oak bookcase, and four other larger cases of similar pattern stood in other parts of the room. The floor was nearly covered by a very old and discoloured much-patched carpet, and in the centre of it stood another writing table at which Birch worked.
>
> In this room, which only measured 18 feet by 16 feet, the whole business of the Department had to be transacted. Here Birch had to draft reports, often of a confidential character, and to answer letters, and visitors could, and often did, read as he wrote what he was writing. Here his interviews with officials and colleagues had to take place; here he had to discuss purchases and fix prices with dealers, in the presence of students who were reading or copying at the table in the window, and who, for the most part, listened to what was being said, and whenever possible, joined in the conversation and gave their opinions on the business on hand.[273]

As has been shown, it had long been decided to move the natural history collections to South Kensington, where Alfred Waterhouse's magnificent new museum was built between 1873 and 1880. With the removal of this material the idea of the Museum as a universal museum was breached for the first time, although the British Museum (Natural History), as it was inelegantly christened, remained under the control of the Trustees, who met there from time to time. Although the zoological collections did not completely leave Bloomsbury until 1883, the new building was opened formally in 1881.

Some extra 5,713 square metres now became available to the antiquities departments, mostly on the upper floor of the building, increasing their space by two thirds.[274] Greek and Roman Antiquities now moved into the upper western galleries; Assyrian and Egyptian non-sculptural material was moved into the northern wing, ethnography into the long eastern gallery above the King's Library, and medieval material moved into the upper southern range. In 1875 the north wall of the Front Hall (including Smirke's internal south portico) was demolished and a two-storey extension was built, but space was still at a premium, particularly to house the ceramic and glass collections, but not least to provide the staff with decent working conditions.

Fortuitously, in 1879, the ninety-one-year-old widow of William White (pl. 11) died, releasing the interest in a bequest made to the Museum fifty-nine years earlier which had almost been forgotten. The will, made when White was a neighbour in the Montagu House days, specifically required that the money be spent 'in building or improving upon the said Institution'.[275] The Trustees were ready with a plan. In 1861 Sydney Smirke had produced a design for a building in the space occupied by the garden of the Principal Librarian's Residence (then the northernmost residence in the eastern wing). The Principal Librarian agreed to give up his very pleasant garden and looked forward to a great deal of disturbance during construction and to a subsequent lack of privacy.[276] The Smirke plan was handed over to Sir John Taylor, Surveyor to the Office of Works, who modified it to its present form. A grand entrance from Montague Street (which has been used only in emergencies) matched the eastern entrance to the residence and the Smirke-like exterior continued the architecture of the main building. The donor's bequest (£69,858 at the time of its liquidation by the Museum)[277] is commemorated in accordance with White's wishes by an inscription carved below the parapet, and the building was named, in his honour, 'The White Wing'. The Treasury, which had meanly insisted on the payment of £6,369 legacy duty, was dunned by the Trustees for £10,410 for furniture and fittings and rather unwillingly paid out.[278]

The White Wing, completed in 1885, was built round a small courtyard, which in 1956–7 was largely filled by an over-sailing, top-lit extension to the Department of Manuscripts' reading room at ground-floor level. Its basement was used for storage and workshops (one of which is now the horological students' room), serviced by a lift. The ground floor was given over to students' rooms and storage for newspapers and western manuscripts. On the mezzanine were the offices of these sections. The offices of the Department of British and Mediaeval Antiquities and Ethnography were in the south-east corner of the main building (where the offices of the Department of Ethnography remained until the late 1960s), but were transferred to the first floor of the White Wing in 1914.[279] On the top floor are top-lit galleries, the northernmost one being used until after the First World War as the Prints and Drawings Students' Room (after a brief sojourn in a small room on the first floor). The southern range was originally given over to ceramics and glass. The White Wing opened into the south-east corner of the Smirke building, which now became the Oriental Saloon.

White's bequest was spread quite widely; not only did it help to provide a new bindery and boilerhouse, but it also provided for the construction of a massive top-lit semi-basement gallery to house the sculptures from the Mausoleum at Halikarnassos. This was completed in 1881 by filling in a space to the east of the Nineveh gallery, while in 1887 another space, previously housing insects and the Print Room, was refurbished to house the Phigalian Marbles. The space left available by this move was used to house the Nereid monument. The final new build of the century was the construction of a new Medal Room above the Archaic Room in the south-west corner of the Museum.[280] In 1880 a new tea-room was opened in the north-east corner of the upper floor, a feature which had been absent for ten years. At the same time Birch moved into a more spacious office at the end of the north-western range of upper galleries.

A few years before the White Wing was finished, electricity was introduced into the Reading Room (until this time the Museum had closed when daylight failed). The Trustees were still chary of gas, although after much huffing and puffing they had permitted gas to be installed in the residences in 1866. In 1878 oil-lamps had been allowed into the offices of the keepers. But the situation in the winter was growing impossible and in 1878 Bond persuaded the Trustees and the Office of Works to agree to experiments by the Société Générale de l'Electricité into the lighting of the Reading Room. Although the experiments were successful, the firm could not meet the Museum's requirements, so the Trustees turned to the firm of William Siemens, which produced a system that, after two years' trial, proved satisfactory. Dynamos were purchased and early in 1881 an engineer was employed to run them. The system was gradually expanded. In 1889 electric light was installed in the galleries, which from 1 February 1890 were opened to the public from 8 to 10 p.m., to the great amazement of the public. Not for the first time the Museum, through caution or conservatism, had become a pioneer, for this was one of the first major public electric-light installations in London.[281]

Telephones were introduced in place of telegraphs for emergency communication with the fire-service and the police, in 1883 and 1888 respectively.[282] Internal communication in the newly built White Wing was by speaking tube, from the basement to the first floor (it still survives). In 1893 telephone links were introduced between the Principal Librarian's Office, the Front Hall and the main reading rooms, but the Treasury did not allow the museum to be linked up to the main London system until 1910,[283] when a telephonist was appointed at £70 p.a. Typewriters were introduced into the Museum at about the same time, although specialist typists did not appear until the 1920s. Esdaile, who became Museum Secretary in 1926, believed that he was the first man in the Museum to dictate a letter.[284]

It was the liberal-minded Bond who swept away the last traces of exclusivity in admission to the Museum. In his first statement as Principal Librarian he wrote:

> In order to prevent the disappointment of intending visitors occasioned by the closing of the Museum to the general public on two days of the week, as has been the custom, the Trustees have ordered that the Museum shall be open daily.[285]

Presumably because of lack of warding staff, some galleries were initially closed in turn in the middle of the week. Half-day Sunday opening was not to arrive (by resolution of Parliament) until 1895, but babes in arms were now admitted, despite crotchety complaints from Newton and Franks.[286] By 1882, when his opening reforms were complete, the Museum was open every weekday, save Good Friday and Christmas Day, from ten o'clock in the morning.[287] The short-lived attempt to open the Museum in the evenings was abandoned in 1898 as numbers quickly fell off.[288]

Numbers remained sluggish, particularly by comparison with the South Kensington Museum, which, for example, in 1896 had more than one and a half million visitors.[289] In 1870 visitors to the British Museum, including students, amounted to 543,791. By 1880 (the year of the opening of the Natural History Museum) numbers had risen to 839,374, its highest for some years. Between a third and a quarter of these visitors were using the various reading and students' rooms. Ten years later there were 789,216 visitors, of whom 66,339 came in the evenings. With Sunday opening beginning in 1895, the number of visitors had risen marginally to 943,858 in 1900, after which it started to rise more sharply.

There was the beginning of an attempt to make the Museum – still cluttered and under-explained – a little more user-friendly. Thompson, particularly, made efforts to improve the labels, although many of them were delphic in the obliquity of the information imparted, and many objects lacked any explanation at all. Nevertheless, the number produced was impressive and was recorded in the annual *Return* to Parliament; in 1897, for example, a total of 442 labels were written and painted for objects on display in the Department of Egyptian and Assyrian Antiquities.[290] The labels supplemented the gallery guide-books. These were rewritten and new ones introduced; in 1880 a general gallery guide had been published (copies were sold in the front hall).[291] Thompson, the martinet Principal Librarian, smartened up the attendants who sat in the gallery bearing their wands of office. The general appearance of the galleries was improved by waxing and polishing the hitherto rough wooden floors.[292]

In 1881 Bond had approached the Trustees in an attempt to provide teaching in the galleries, particularly in archaeology and natural history. The keepers gave a mixed response. Newton viewed the proposal favourably, writing 'that among the students of University College, King's College, and also among those who attend the archaeological lectures of the Slade and Disneian Professors at Cambridge, young men will be found who with a little training in the Museum would probably become efficient popular lecturers'. Franks, on the other hand, in the middle of reorganizing his galleries, put forward as many objections as possible. Poole went over the top and characterized the proposal as 'the largest and most public-spirited that has yet been proposed since the foundation of the Museum of Alexandria'. The Trustees kicked the idea into touch, as they did again in 1890.[293] In 1891 the Earl of Meath raised the subject in the House of Lords. The Trustees merely noted it and it was not until 1911 that lecturers were appointed by the Museum.[294] There was a certain amount of semi-professional lecturing in the galleries for which the Trustees granted (often rather grudging) permission. The influential, if rather batty, Jane Harrison (one of the Cambridge Ritualists and later a fellow of Newnham College, Cambridge) was, for example, employed informally as a lecturer in classics in the 1880s. She was a pupil of Newton, who apparently encouraged her work, not only as a scholar (where she had a profound influence with Sir John Myres in breaking down disciplinary barriers between classical studies and anthropology), but also as an extension lecturer of the University of London.[295] There was no dedicated lecture room and the Trustees refused to provide one, although from 1893 the Assyrian basement was used for this purpose from time to time.[296]

There was occasional trouble, with perceived threats. In 1883 a terrorist explosion in Westminster led to worries about security in public buildings and extra police were drafted to the Museum. In the following year bag searches were ordered; Samuel Butler wrote to his father on 8 March 1884:

> ... I have been within an ace of a better chance of distinguishing myself than I ever had, and missed it through want of a little ready wit. Last Friday... coming out of the Museum Reading Room I found the attendant in the Cloak Room in the act of refusing to accept from an

Irishman a most suspicious-looking box – and I blush to own that during the couple of minutes in which I was taking in the situation the man was gone... Perhaps there was nothing in the box, but this clearly is not the opinion of the authorities. I have been sent for and questioned but the whole affair did not take half a minute. The man never offered to open the box....[297]

Some trouble was caused by the merely dirty. In 1895 the sartorially conscious Maunde Thompson refused a man admission to the Museum when he appeared in the galleries wearing sandals.[298] One assumes that he did not question the habits of one of his Trustees, Lord Dillon, who was rarely seen not wearing plimsolls!

By the end of the 1880s the total establishment of the Museum at Bloomsbury was 344, together with a resident clerk of works, employed by the Office of Works, and twenty-four police under an Inspector, employed by the Commissioners of Police. The only women employed were six lady attendants (chiefly for the lavatories), four housemaids and a charwoman. The labourers included the indomitable figure of Henry Hook, who in 1879 had won a VC at Rorke's Drift during the Zulu War, and later became the Museum's 'Umbrella Man' (cloakroom attendant) at £67 16s 4d a year.[299] The departure of the police was foreshadowed by the presence of five members of the Corps of Commissionaires who were employed on specific supervisory duties.[300]

The removal of the natural history collections in 1880 provides a convenient date at which to note the cost of the Museum to the Exchequer. The grant to meet salaries at Bloomsbury in 1881/2 was £54,564, the purchase grant for both sites was £25,952 and the total government grant in that year was £132,939, a sum which rose to £152,333 in 1884/5. But in the following year, the economic depression was being felt strongly and, in a period of Treasury cuts, a Parliamentary committee was set up to consider the propriety of reducing the holdings.[301] Fortunately the Trustees were able to defend the collections, but the financial climate was turning and special grants from the Exchequer for purchase were never again so easily obtainable as they had been in the 1870s. (In the ten years before 1876/7 purchases – including books and the cost of excavations – amounted to £313,362, about double that in the previous ten years.) The Trustees must have felt very much at one with Lord Salisbury (never an active Trustee), who in 1885 wrote to a friend that the Treasury 'is a deity as inexorable as Pluto. They look upon the arts and sciences as so many excuses for extravagance'.[302] Franks was not alone in referring to the lack of public money for the support of the collections, and particularly for the lack of money in the purchase grant, which was gradually, if erratically, cut from 1877 onwards.

It has been shown that negotiation concerning salaries and pensions had been concluded reasonably amicably by Winter Jones in 1874. But it was more than twenty years before they were to be reconsidered. The remark of the notoriously tight-fisted Gladstone to Sidney Colvin has infuriated staff members ever since, 'I for one would never be party to increasing the salaries of you gentlemen at the British Museum, for a more delightful occupation I cannot conceive.'[303] In 1897, however, the officers received salary increases, but of a size which still did not bring them up to the levels of equivalent civil service grades. The Principal Librarian's salary rose from £1,200 to £1,500; keepers received £800 (previously £700); assistant keepers £620 (from £520); first-class assistants £500 (from £300) and second-class assistants £300 (from £150); leave allowances were tidied up.[304] At roughly the same time it was agreed that retirement should normally be at age sixty, although keepers and other senior staff could be recommended for extension to sixty-five, the age at which attendants retired.[305]

Junior members of the staff remained underpaid for years, the basic labourer's annual wage, for example, being £62 12s. Attendants, a sort of non-commissioned grade, were paid a maximum of £150 a year and many continued to supplement this income by taking on evening jobs.

A Victorian Community

For many of the officers the last years of the century formed a period of stability after the storms of the Panizzi period. The Museum seemed a calm and friendly place, although more perspicacious senior officers realized that the days of generous government finance were over. For the moment all was quiet and the Museum moved into a more professional and socially easy mode. Members of staff in the antiquities departments were busy filling the space vacated by the natural history material and the newly built White Wing, registering the new acquisitions and taking up work on the great catalogues which were to appear before the First World War.

The Museum was both a physical and an intellectual centre, in which members of this small academic, literary, journalistic and artistic circle met frequently. The library staff not only acquired and catalogued books, but were themselves involved in the literary world. Late Victorian writers of fiction and history worked in the Reading Room, and some visited the keepers in the residences around the courtyard or met each other and the more junior members of the staff in the tea room or in the cafés or bookshops of Bloomsbury. Sir Henry Newbolt, for example, tells how, as a young reader, he was introduced by Binyon (himself a poet) to a group of readers and staff who met daily for lunch at the Vienna Café in New Oxford Street – haunt of the more exotic element of 'Bloomsbury'. They 'talked faster and more irresponsibly than any group of equal numbers in my memory: by the noise we made, by the congestion of our table... and the recklessness with which we shared portions with one another... an onlooker might have taken us for a Bohemian society of students from some romantic foreign capital.'[306]

Many of the senior keepers, because they lived on site, attracted all sorts of visitors. Colvin, who had an ambiguous extra-marital relationship with a married woman, Frances Sitwell (whom he later married), was deeply involved in literary London and with her kept a 'salon'. Robert Louis Stevenson often stayed with them in their residence and is reputed to haunt it. Colvin was a friend of Edmund Gosse, who had for a short time worked at the Museum, and between them they knew everybody who was anybody in literary London and gossiped all the time. A close friend of both these literary figures was another denizen of the Museum's courtyard, Richard Garnett, Keeper of Printed Books, learned and open in his relationship with the readers, both academic and literary. The Museum, and particularly the Reading Room, began to feature more and more in light literature, as authors used it for warmth, companionship or research or as local colour in their writings.[307] Members of the various learned societies, in London for meetings and lectures, would visit friends there as they still do today. Foreign scholars came to work on the collections and would be entertained to tea by the staff, who would thus keep up with the work of their contemporaries on the Continent.

The social round was hectic for the lively children of the keepers, who had their friends among the craftsmen and other junior staff. The younger ones played cricket on the lawns after the Museum had closed for the night, lawns which Franks kept clear of daisies.[308] (Games were later forbidden by Maunde Thompson, who also objected to the older girls walking hatless in the courtyard.)[309] Thompson's son published feeble student poetry and Olive Garnett, daughter of Richard, pursued Russian anarchists and other disreputable characters and invited them to tea, chatting informally with the Principal Librarian about them and their beliefs.[310] The staff and the officers were in and out of each others' houses, for meals, gossip and (in the case of the older children) deep philosophical discussion. They were also able to use the Museum's facilities and went to private views; Olive Garnett, for example, in her lively diary records a party in the Print Room arranged by Colvin to publicize the Malcolm collection, which he was manoeuvring to acquire.[311] Some deeply privileged children were allowed to use the Reading Room as a place in which to do their homework, but how widespread this practice was is not recorded.[312]

The social life of the officers was conditioned by the presence of Maunde Thompson in his residence in the north-east corner of the courtyard. Olive Garnett, the lively feminist who lived next door but one and had a sneaking liking for him, records the noisy end to one of his parties, with the servants whistling for cabs for Thompson's guests at three o'clock in the morning.[313] Newton, who in his early years had been described as 'entirely jovial', had become more austere and serious.[314] He was never reconciled to the early loss of his wife and lived a quiet life close to the Museum in his house in Gower Street. In his later years he was much taken up by Sidney Colvin, who wrote warmly about him.[315] His political friends descended on him from time to time, as when Sir Charles Dilke visited Mrs Pattinson (wife of the Rector of Lincoln College, Oxford), who was staying with him as some sort of paying guest.[316] Very much of the world, he tended to take his few pleasures outside the Museum. Like Franks he travelled a lot (but mainly in the eastern Mediterranean) and was particularly involved in the Society of Dilettanti, of which he was an enthusiastic member.

Franks, the rich bachelor, took his entertaining seriously and gave rather grand dinner parties at his Museum residence for his antiquarian friends and fellow collectors. In May 1880, for example, having given an imposing dinner for his old friend the Danish State Antiquary, J.J.A. Worsaae, he gave a rather more intimate luncheon for Worsaae and another mutual friend, Sir John Lubbock. A day or two later Worsaae wrote to his wife, 'On Monday I shall again dine with many lords and scholars at Franks's'.[317] But there was a less formal side to Franks. Another old friend, John Evans, took his young daughter by his third wife to visit him (probably in the last year of Franks's life) and she was given a piece of turquoise, brought back from Leh by Younghusband.[318]

End of an Era

The British Museum as it is known today had largely been shaped by the end of the century. The natural history collections had been successfully removed to South Kensington and the antiquities now directly challenged the library for the limited available space. There was a particular problem with regard to the vast growth in the number of newspapers received, and the Trustees' Sub-Committee on Printed Books and Manuscripts reluctantly started to discuss this matter in 1897.[319]

In half a century the Museum had altered beyond all recognition; the raw, new, ill-staffed building had grown to be an internationally recognizable symbol of academic excellence. The scholarship represented within its walls was second to none in Britain in many areas of the humanities, although the universities were growing in number and diversity of subject, so that the Museum's own specialisms were gradually refined. The passing of the Ancient Monuments Act of 1882 (largely fought through Parliament by Lubbock, who was responsible for the appointment of Pitt Rivers as the first Chief Inspector of Ancient Monuments) was the first step in the official supervision of the built and buried heritage of the country.[320] It was to impinge greatly on the work of the Museum, the staff of which continued to excavate, but now concentrated more and more on the study of material. The universities still treated archaeology lightly, though the election in 1892 of Flinders Petrie to the chair of Egyptology at University College London provided an element of professional encouragement for practical archaeology as a university discipline. University College, as has been shown, was also the home of a professorship of classical archaeology, while Percy Gardner and Arthur Evans fought to introduce archaeology into the classical syllabus at Oxford. The Disney chair of archaeology at Cambridge was becoming a little more professional. Art history languished; the Slade professors gave less or more time to a discipline that was still basically amateur, and there were still no full-time posts in the history of art in the universities. Although some amateur practitioners who had cut their teeth in journalism, like the now-forgotten Emilia Dilke, wrote creditable and well-researched monographs on demanding subjects within art history, consistent scholarship could still only be achieved by learning on the job in a museum or gallery.[321] Anthropology as a taught subject was a mere twinkle in the eye of some doughty fighters at Oxford or Cambridge, notably Christy's friend E.B. Tylor, his followers R.R. Marett and H. Balfour, and the few members of an expedition to the Torres Straits (p.224).

In the wider world, museums had been founded throughout Europe and America. In England there were by 1900 probably some 300 museums and galleries, many founded under the various local government acts (most recently the Museums and Gymnasiums Act of 1891) – although Wales had remarkably few. In Germany the Berlin museums, under the active leadership of von Bode, were expanding at a phenomenal rate, building on the success of the Altes Museum, which had opened in 1830. In the German states public, 'national' museums were being founded almost by the year. The Germanisches National-museum at Nuremberg was founded in 1852 and the Bayerisches Nationalmuseum at Munich in 1855 (the Ethnographisches Museum was founded in 1868). After the conquest of Schleswig-Holstein in 1864, the archaeological collections of the Danish Kongelige Samling for Nordiske Oldsager in Flensburg were moved to Kiel to form the core of a new Museum für Vaterländische Alterthümer in 1873 (which incidentally was soon to appoint Johanna Mestorf as the first woman head of a major European museum).[322] In Austria the Imperial collections were gradually turned over to the state in lavishly grandiose buildings – the Kunsthistorisches Museum, with its many antiquities departments, was founded in 1891, the Naturhistorisches Museum (which also included the ethnographic and archaeo-

logical collections) in 1896 and the Heeresgeschichtliches Museum in 1906. In St Petersburg the imperial collections in the Hermitage were opened to the public in 1842 and the
Russian Historical Museum in Moscow was founded in 1897. National museums were
founded in Warsaw in 1862 and in Zurich in 1890 (Franks sat on the official planning
commission of the latter). In France the Musée des Antiquités Nationales at Saint-
Germain-en-Laye was founded by Napoleon III, encouraged by his Superintendent of Arts,
Emilien de Nieuwerkerke, in 1863 (its foundation stimulated in part by the gift of a collection of Danish prehistoric antiquities by Frederik VII).[323] In Germany the Kaiser's interest
in the imperial scramble led to huge patronage of the Museum für Völkerkunde in Berlin
(which had been founded as a separate entity in 1873). By the end of the century this, the
greatest ethnographical museum in the world, was established in its own building and
was organized into five departments with a staff of twelve specialists (one of these departments, European prehistory, became independent in its own building in the 1930s). O.M.
Dalton, a member of the British Museum staff, who wrote a report on the German ethnographic collections in 1898 (p.224), pointed out that 'On a moderate estimate the Berlin
collections are six to seven times as extensive as ours.'[324]

Major museums were now being founded in America. The Smithsonian Institution
in Washington was established, by the 1829 bequest of the English scientist John Macie
Smithson (an illegitimate son of the first Duke of Northumberland), as a national museum
by Act of Congress in 1846. The Metropolitan Museum in New York had its modest beginnings in 1870.[325] Within the Turkish Empire the foundation of two museums led to a closer
control on excavation and tomb-robbery. The Archaeological Museum in Istanbul was
founded in 1881, and an architectural competition was held in 1895 for a new Egyptian
Museum in Cairo, won by Marcel Durgnon; the building opened in 1902. The Indian
Museum in Calcutta was founded in 1866, based on the collections of the Asiatic Society of
Bengal. The National Museum of Japan in Tokyo was founded in 1877 and its first building
was opened ten years later. In Australia the National Museum of Zoology, Geology and
Ethnography was founded in Melbourne in 1854, while in Wellington the Dominion
Museum was founded in 1865. Public museums, which at the beginning of the century
were rare and confined mainly to the national capitals, were now becoming available to
almost every segment of the population.

The retirement of Franks at the age of seventy in 1896 was almost symbolic, for he
had seen most of this development in his lifetime and had done much to create the balance
of the institution which he had served for forty-five years. He continued to contribute to
the Museum, until his death the following year, as a member of the Standing Committee of
the Trustees (he had been a Trustee since 1892 in his capacity as President of the Society of
Antiquaries) and continued to shower it with gifts. In 1893 he wrote a short *Apology for my
life*, which, while used by Read in the *Dictionary of national biography*, has only recently been
rediscovered in the possession of a member of the family and published by Marjorie
Caygill.[326] It sets out Franks's own estimate of himself in relation to the Museum. His last
paragraph provides a summary of his achievement:

> I think I may fairly say that I have created the department of which I am now Keeper, and at a
> very moderate cost to the country. When I was appointed to the Museum in 1851 the scanty
> collections out of which the department has grown occupied a length of 154 feet of wall
> cases, and 3 or 4 table cases. The collections now occupy 2,250 feet in length of wall cases,

90 table cases, and 31 upright cases, to say nothing of the numerous objects placed over the cases or on walls.

All these items had been registered, and many had been published.

Franks made some attempt to value the collections he had given to the Museum. Contributions in gifts and expenses to the ethnographic section, particularly Asian and American material, amounted to not less than £5,000; a group of discrete Bronze and Iron Age material cost £1,000; the oriental ceramics were valued at £11,000; his collection of drinking vessels at roughly £8,000, and so on. He records some of the major gifts and bequests received through his capacity to charm collectors – Meyrick, Slade, Octavius Morgan, William Burges, Henderson, J.P. Nightingale, Henry Willett and, of course, Christy. He also mentions his own proposed bequest of a collection of 3,500 finger-rings, but omits to mention the other collections which he left to the Museum – his continental porcelain, the Treasure of the Oxus, his silver and gold plate and drinking vessels, jewellery, and Japanese netsuke and sword guards.[327] He also left an enormous collection of bookplates (which he estimated numbered some 30,000 items).[328] His total bequest was valued for probate at just under £50,000 (about £3.25 million at today's value – a sum that takes no account of the rise in the real value of antiquities over this period; Franks had always been ahead of the game).

Franks's bequest extended well beyond his private collection and even his lifetime. Years after his death his friends' collections came to the Museum. The Godman collection of Islamic pottery has been mentioned, but there were others. The Montague Guest collection of tickets and tokens is but one example, an extraordinary collection of great interest in the history of the theatre and of entertainment generally. This was given to the Museum in 1907 by the son of one of his closest friends, Lady Charlotte Schreiber (who had bequeathed it her collection of playing cards and fans).[329]

The most important collection to be acquired after Franks's death was that of his friend and fellow Trustee Baron Ferdinand de Rothschild, who died in 1898. As well as leaving a number of illuminated manuscripts to the Museum, he also bequeathed it nearly 300 objects, the contents of 'the new smoking-room' in the bachelor's wing of Waddesdon Manor, on condition that it be permanently displayed 'in a room separate and apart from the other contents of the Museum'. This was a remarkable collection, even for a family as experienced in connoisseurship as the Rothschilds. The Waddesdon Bequest, as it is known, is a veritable treasure-house of *objets d'art et de vertu* of the kind assembled by a sixteenth- or seventeenth-century prince. Much of the material is of Renaissance date and taste – jewels, sculpture, plate, pottery and glass – but it also includes other objects such as the early fifteenth-century Reliquary of the Holy Thorn, once in the Geistliche Schatzkammer in Vienna. A masterwork of French enamelling, it went missing from the collection in 1860 and was bought by Rothschild in 1887 after the Austrians had refused to buy it back. Most interesting historically is the Lyte Jewel, with its miniature of James I, but the strengths of the collection are too numerous to mention. The material in the collection is clearly very different from that accumulated by Franks and by the Museum, so much so that one wonders whether he and Rothschild had agreed in its ultimate disposal as a foil to the rest of the collections.[330]

Franks was a great man, the most important figure in the history of the Museum; but there is a negative side to him, which is clearly demonstrated in his *Apology*. In it there is no reference to the needs of the general public; labelling in his galleries was haphazard and uninformative, and unillustrated guidebooks of ineffable dullness were produced. He was basically concerned with acquisition and scholarship and it is for this that he is justly famed. He collected in all areas of the Museum's experience, but perhaps most importantly in the field of ethnography. It has been calculated, for example, that when he came to the Museum in 1851 there were only 3,700 ethnographic artefacts; when he retired there were 38,000, of which he had himself given 9,000. What is more, a large number of these items were on permanent display, placed hugger-mugger in vastly overcrowded cases (pl. 20). When a new acquisition was made objects tended to be moved up, and the new items introduced into grotesquely packed showcases. This was to change with the new century, but one might argue with reason that it is in the galleries that Franks worked out his academic salvation and displayed his genius. He used the collections displayed in his galleries as a living catalogue, placing objects in a cultural and typological sequence of highly flexible form, a form which challenged the rigid framework adopted by Pitt Rivers and used in his museum in Oxford. He fought for and left a Museum into which ethnography was fully integrated. Today, as the ethnographic material returns to a reintegrated Museum after the stimulating but misplaced adventure of the Museum of Mankind (p.282), the uniqueness of that vision shines out. Only in the Danish National Museum – and in a modified fashion the Smithsonian Institution in Washington – is there anything similar. He provided academic rigour to build a structure that forms the scholarly and physical core of the Museum as a universal institution.

Chapter 6

WAR AND SPACE

1897–1945

In approaching the history of any major institution which was already old at the beginning of the twentieth century, the tone and emphasis of that history inevitably change. The paper record is no longer the unique record; people and events of the first half of the century are held in a corporate memory – sometimes accurate, sometimes romanticized. There is a direct personal contact with the past. My own case is typical. When I joined the Museum as a young assistant keeper in January 1955, I would on most days arrive at the underground station at the same time as an elderly, slightly fragile gentleman, referred to in reverential terms as Dr Barnett.[1] He had joined the staff in 1899 and had been Keeper of Oriental Printed Books and Manuscripts between 1908 and 1935; having been re-employed as an assistant keeper, he was still working on his great catalogues when I knew him well enough to nod 'good morning'. We listened in awe to stories about him and knew him through his son, who later in 1955 became Keeper of Western Asiatic Antiquities. Another example: when in 1976 my appointment as Director was announced, not only were all my predecessors back to 1936 still alive, but I received a congratulatory letter from the first woman Trustee of the Museum. This was Dame Joan Evans, daughter of Franks's close friend Sir John Evans; she remembered visiting Franks in his residence in the Museum in the 1890s. Such memories begin to build up a folklore, which is the corporate memory of the Museum; it is still actively at work, piling legend on fact.

Trustees

Together with these memories, a sea of paper makes the task of the synthetic historian almost impossible. The Museum was becoming larger – more bureaucratic – and documentation and files became more urgently necessary. The Trustees were still all-powerful. They were still likely to interfere in the minutest detail, but the more complex needs of government thrust more power into the hands of the Director, who was the accounting officer to Parliament and could now control most of the Trustees' business. Although the three Principal Trustees remained the same, it was the Archbishop of Canterbury who normally functioned as Chairman. As the old generation of influential Trustees – for the antiquities department these were Lubbock and Evans – died out, new names came to the fore. Chief among them was the 27th Earl of Crawford, a politician who had published books on Italian sculpture and had become a Trustee in 1921. A man of taste (he was also a trustee of the National Gallery), he was greatly to influence the public face of the Museum. His diaries give an occasional, but unique, Trustees'-eye-view of the Museum, particularly in the inter-war period. He made his opinion plain after his first meeting in 1923:

> I rather fancy the B.M. wants tuning up – there are many aspects where the reforming eye would be serviceable. The Speaker [J. H. Whitley] feels this strongly, but vaguely also, because he is quite unversed in Museum problems, and does not know how to begin. Hitherto his efforts seem to have been very fumbling and ill-directed. The Archbishop [Davidson] is perfectly complacent, and believes that the great machine is rolling away to the perfect satisfaction of the public. Our agenda paper is really an object lesson: it is congested with every kind of trumpery report about messengers and window-cleaning, and no time is left for considering fundamental problems....[2]

His comment was shrewd; the agenda was indeed cluttered, and as much attention seems to have been given to the sale of an old coin-cabinet as to the acquisition of a drawing by Dürer. The Standing Committee did the detailed work and the Director presented the minutes of this committee to the General Meeting and led them through business, which was mostly a *fait accompli*. The Museum as a whole had sunk into a self-congratulatory mode, too conscious of its very real scholarship, and, save in a few areas, distinctly lacking in innovation. There were quite a few passengers among the staff and new blood tended to be cowed by the old men. The Museum was starved of money and there was little sympathy for it within government. Whether Crawford was really effective as a Trustee is difficult to say, but he was certainly powerful and knowledgeable and, reading between the lines of what little personal comment survives, he at least knew what the remedies should be.

It is reasonably clear from both the written record and Museum folklore that the Trustees – while grand – had become rather decorative, appearing outside the boardroom only on formal annual visitations to the departments. Archbishop Davidson was clearly bear-led by the powerful figure of Kenyon (Director and Principal Librarian after 1909), while his successor, the tough and opinionated Cosmo Gordon Lang, who became Archbishop of Canterbury in 1928, treated Kenyon's successors with rather distant courtesy and started to interfere in the actual running of the Museum. Unfortunately, as Crawford had observed, the other Principal Trustees (the Speaker and Lord Chancellor) no longer played a major role; it was now automatically assumed that the archbishop should act as chairman. Reading between the lines of a laudatory comment of a fellow Trustee, Lord Macmillan, it seems impossible to ignore the fact that Lang was difficult to deal with:

> He was an ideal Chairman, and dealt with the long and varied agenda not only with admirable tact and judgement, but with zest and interest. Apart from the actual meetings of the Committee, he concerned himself constantly and sympathetically with the solution of the Museum's problems, and especially with the elimination of the personal frictions inevitable in the working of an institution staffed by experts. When asked how he contrived to find time for all that he did for the Museum, he confessed that he found the work enjoyable and its atmosphere congenial by way of a change from his other duties. He liked to meet round the table colleagues from walks of life so different from his own, including personal friends such as the late Lord Crawford, Lord Ilchester and others. And perhaps, too, he rather enjoyed showing how efficient a man of business an Archbishop could be.[3]

Even after he retired he managed to stay on as a Trustee and – more startlingly – as chairman; his successor (Temple) 'was very willing, for the present, to be relieved of the duties of Chairman'.

The Trustees continued to elect non-family and non-official members of the board. The Prime Minister took a major role in this process, although there is a hint that his authority was sometimes questioned. In 1924, at a General Meeting held in the Speaker's Library, the devious Lord Esher 'called attention to the custom which first came into existence some fifty years previously, and which had been somewhat weakened previously by the practice of recent years, of assigning a special privilege to the Prime Minister in the proposal of candidates for election to the Trust; and emphasised the constitutional right of any Electing Trustee to put forward a candidate'. But the Prime Minister was too wily a fox to be taken in by such talk:

> Mr Baldwin agreed the Prime Minister had no right of nomination, but only of proposal, and that other Trustees shared that right. He thought, however, that the Prime Minister was often in a position to propose suitable candidates, and that his association with the interest of the Museum was beneficial. The Lord Chancellor and Lord Cecil concurred in this expression of opinion. It was, however, unanimously agreed that the Prime Minister had no exclusive overriding right of nomination, and that the concurrent rights of the other Electing Trustees are beyond doubt.[4]

The three Principal Trustees, throughout most of the period covered by this chapter, had few corporate functions in relation to the Museum, but continued formally to nominate and approve candidates for academic appointments. The Civil Service Commission, following a labyrinthine route to enable the form of the 1753 Act to be adhered to, carried out recruiting. In effect, each candidate as well as filling in an application form had to obtain a letter of recommendation (usually from their university) to one of the three Principal Trustees. The candidates, having sat a qualifying examination, were then reviewed by a selection board set up by the Commission which, in turn, recommended an appointment to the Principal Trustees, who approved it by letter. This burdensome method seems to have ceased during the Second World War, although letters of appointment were still signed by one of the Principal Trustees as late as 1950.[5]

Director and Principal Librarian

Thompson's title was changed – in line with the title of the head of the Natural History Museum – in 1898. He became Director and Principal Librarian – referred to as DPL or Director.[6] He retired on health grounds in 1909 at the age sixty-nine, but lived to be ninety. He was succeeded by Frederic Kenyon (pl. 25), Assistant Keeper in the Department of Manuscripts. Kenyon was young (he had been born in 1863), and had been employed by the Museum for twenty years; since 1898 he had been deputy to the Keeper of Manuscripts. The grandson of Edward Hawkins on one side and of the first Lord Kenyon on the other, Kenyon had a shining Oxford career (double first, Chancellor's Prize for an English essay, and Fellow of Magdalen). He was a considerable classical scholar and papyrologist, a specialist on Aristotle and deeply respected in biblical studies. He was perhaps the most distinguished scholar to hold the Director's post. Among many distinctions he was President of the British Academy, 1917–21.[7]

At least one of the keepers who had been passed over in favour of this young man was furious; this was Charles Hercules Read, Franks's successor as Keeper of British and Mediaeval Antiquities and Ethnography, who perhaps had too great a sense of his own importance.[8] Most people – outside the Museum at least – had expected Sidney Colvin, Keeper of Prints and Drawings, to get the post; but he was certainly too old for the job, as, possibly, were the other keepers. The inwardness of the appointment has never emerged, but one may guess that Maunde Thompson, who also came from the Department of Manuscripts, had some say in the matter.[9] It was certainly the right appointment.

Kenyon was an austere autocrat, a worthy successor to his mentor Maunde Thompson. It has been said of this cold and taciturn man that he would have made a good Chancery judge. He was a first-rate administrator and a good committee man. He also knew his way around the corridors of power, and was sociable enough to have been a member and joint treasurer of Dr Johnson's Literary Club ('The Club'), a monthly gathering of the great and the good to which a number of his Trustees belonged.[10] One such member was Lord Crawford, who was irritated by him (as he was by so many people):

> 13 July 1924. Board meeting at British Museum. What perfunctory affairs they are, with an agenda (not circulated in advance) sometimes containing sixty items, many of which are trivial or superfluous. Important topics are presented to us at a moment's notice, and our minutes, admirably printed on *papier de choix*, have to be returned to the Director after perusal by the Trustees. Nothing by way of reform will be feasible until Kenyon's departure; he is a stickler for etiquette and will defeat all our efforts to modernise the Museum and to revise our customs.[11]

Kenyon had a tough time as Director but was generally successful. He saw the King Edward VII Building through to completion and looked after the Museum during the war (although he had to be called back to his post from France). He stood up to a Royal Commission, began negotiations with Lord Duveen to build a gallery to house the Parthenon sculptures, formalized the guide-lecturer service and encouraged the production of a series of illustrated gallery guides. He initiated co-operation with the University of Pennsylvania Museum to excavate at Ur and generally encouraged the scholarly activity of the staff. He founded the Museum's Research Laboratory. He was successful in renegotiating the method of recruitment of the curatorial staff with the Treasury and the Civil Service Commission. He also reorganized the central administration of the Museum by appointing in 1926 a Secretary, A.J.K. Esdaile, from the Department of Printed Books, who was assisted by a graduate Assistant Secretary. Between 1922 and 1928 he renegotiated with Treasury and with the newly powerful unions the duties, pay and grading of the non-academic staff.[12]

Curatorial Staff before the First World War[13]

The Museum at the beginning of the century appears in retrospect a stuffy and formal institution. The staff were admonished to dress soberly and wear hats. Writing of the period in which he joined the Museum in 1902, a clerk remembered:

> The silk hat, morning or frock coat, with the usual accessories of white shirts and stiff collars, were the general order of the day; and if one could not affect these, nothing less than dark lounge suits and bowler hats was expected. Such a thing as a soft felt hat was not seen in the department [of Printed Books] until well on in the century.[14]

It was a period, famously, when Thompson told off an assistant keeper for riding a bicycle in the street. But it was a period of lively thought and learning, and not everybody was so formal beneath the sub-fusc exterior.

The early twentieth century was a period of modest expansion among the staff of the antiquities departments. The complement of the Department of Greek and Roman Antiquities and that of Coins and Medals remained the same in the ten years from 1894. The Department of Egyptian and Assyrian Antiquities, of which Budge became keeper in 1894, had then three assistant posts (one vacant, the others filled by Pinches and L.W. King). By 1905 this had increased by one (Pinches, a brilliant Assyriologist, had been eased out by Budge; the four assistants were now King, H.R.H. Hall, R.C. Thompson and P.D. Scott Moncrieff). Prints and Drawings, with Colvin as keeper, had only three assistants in 1894; by 1904 this had increased to include an assistant keeper (F.M. O'Donoghue) and three remarkable assistants (Campbell Dodgson, Binyon and Hind).

The Department of Greek and Roman Antiquities pursued the even tenor of its existence, although personalities changed. In 1904, the keeper, A.S. Murray, died and was replaced by Cecil Harcourt Smith, who five years later departed to become an extremely successful Director of the Victoria and Albert Museum.[15] The Museum was fortunate in his successor as Keeper, A.H. Smith, a well-connected Cambridge classicist, who had joined the staff in 1885.[16] His first publication had been a catalogue of the engraved classical gems, but his main interest was in sculpture, of which he wrote three extremely distinguished catalogues between 1892 and 1904, as well as an objective publication of the Parthenon marbles.[17] Towards the end of his career in the Museum (he retired in 1925) he published with F.N. Pryce the first two volumes of the Museum's *Corpus Vasorum antiquorum*. He is now remembered particularly for his remarkable article on the acquisition of the Elgin Marbles, which is used to this day by all who write on that subject.[18] J.F. Forsdyke (later to be Director) joined the staff in 1890 and F.N. Pryce in 1911. H.B. Walters, who had written catalogues of classical bronzes and Roman pottery, became Assistant Keeper of the Department in 1913.

The departure of Franks led to a complete shake-up in the Department of British and Mediaeval Antiquities and Ethnography. Read, as expected, was appointed his successor in March 1896. There appears to have been no other serious candidate.[19] A number of assistants had now to be appointed, particularly as F.L. Griffith, an Egyptologist *manqué*, who had joined the department in 1888, left in 1896 to take up an outstanding career in his preferred subject.[20] By this time there was a well-tried method of appointment for junior curatorial staff. The Principal Trustees, sticking to the original Act, still formally nominated to assistantships after having received applications for each vacant post. Three persons were sent forward by them for a written examination by the Civil Service Commission and the results were formally approved by the Principal Trustees who made the appointments.[21]

In June 1895 one of the most brilliant scholars to have served in the Department of British and Mediaeval Antiquities was recruited. Ormonde Maddock Dalton (pl. 14) took up his post in June 1895, having passed the written examination with exceptionally high marks in Latin, Greek, French and German and with 130 marks out of 150 for drawing – an essential accomplishment in the eyes of Franks.[22] Dalton had been to Harrow and was an exhibitioner at New College, Oxford (where he had taken a double first).[23] He was well connected (a cousin of the influential Canon Dalton of Windsor). Not only had he lived in Germany and France, he had, after leaving Oxford, travelled in the Far East for three and a half years, returning by way of North America. This massively shy man was to succeed Read as keeper, but his real claim to fame lies in his great catalogues. In these works he demonstrated his mastery of the post-classical world, and particularly of Early Christian and Byzantine antiquities, at a period when the Germans and French were his only challengers. Initially, however, he worked on the ethnographical collections, for which his travels had well suited him, and with Read published the seminal catalogue on the Benin antiquities.[24] Griffith's post was left vacant for nearly a year, and it was not until 1897 that he was replaced by R.L. Hobson, who produced in quick succession two massive and massively influential catalogues on English pottery and porcelain, based on Franks's collections.[25]

Another post having been allowed to the department, Reginald Allender Smith, an archaeologist, was appointed in 1898. Smith, another graduate in classics, had worked for a short time at the Royal Commission on Liquor and Licensing Laws – interestingly, since he was a teetotaller and a vegetarian. When in 1928 he followed Dalton as keeper, he developed by natural progression into a bureaucratic tyrant, typically, for example, persecuting the junior assistant keeper, Christopher Hawkes (a notorious night-owl), for turning up late at the office, eventually bullying him into a nervous breakdown.[26] Smith was an arid polymath who contributed large numbers of 'anonymous' notes on a variety of subjects to *The Proceedings of the Society of Antiquaries of London*, of which institution he was for many years secretary. He was deeply interested in the Palaeolithic and made many significant contributions to its study;[27] but some of his judgements were perverse and, finally, having attempted to re-date the Neolithic flint-mines at Grimes Graves, Norfolk, to the Palaeolithic, he retired hurt from this field. He was, however, a serious, if pedestrian, student of the Anglo-Saxon and Migration periods and kept warm the relationships with the museums of Scandinavia initiated by Hawkins and Franks.[28] His scholarship was oblique, but tough. As the Oxford Anglo-Saxonist E.T. Leeds, Keeper of the Ashmolean Museum, wrote, his work 'seems to march at ground-level. One misses that enlivening touch of imagination, that appreciation of human values, that inspiration, which would have helped to raise it to a higher plane'.[29]

Dalton, still comparatively young and trailing clouds of glory through his industry in cataloguing the Franks Bequest, was promoted to Assistant Keeper in 1901. In one of his roles he was replaced by the first person in the Museum to become a specialist ethnographer. T.A. Joyce – who like so many staff had read classics at Oxford, although with a special paper in Egyptology – became a pioneering Americanist. Read was clearly an adept empire-builder; the size of the department increased greatly during his tenure as keeper. He managed to squeeze another ethnographer, H.J. Braunholtz, out of the Trustees in 1913, and was able to appoint a rather reluctant medievalist, Alec Bain Tonnochy, to the department. Tonnochy was an Edinburgh graduate, who came six weeks before war broke out in 1914, and who was immediately sent down into the cellar to catalogue the Franks collection of plate. A dour Scot, he was not, however, without a sense of humour – to him is attributed the cross-reference in a departmental index, '"God", see "the Almighty"'.

The publication of the vast collection of tablets in the series *Cuneiform Texts* initiated by Budge in 1894 continued as one of the main exercises of the Department of Egyptian and Assyrian Antiquities for most of the twentieth century, and the staff consequently became leading figures in this industry. Chief of these was Leonard King,[30] who from the time he came to the Museum in 1892 to his death in 1919 had edited sixteen volumes in the series – a process that involved copying all the inscriptions by hand. But this was not all; he wrote a number of books based on these and other texts. He also reopened the Museum's excavations at Kuyunjik – in which he was later joined by his colleague C.R. Thompson, with whom he collated the inscription on the Rock of Bisitun. His health deteriorated as a result of his war-work, but he continued to write synthetically on his subject until his death. Of him Wallis Budge, not notoriously lavish with praise, wrote:

> ... it is an obvious truth that he published more Sumerian, Babylonian and Assyrian texts than all other Assyriologists in the world. And the quality of his work was as good as its quantity was great. He was easily the best and most accurate copyist of his generation... His work was eminently sound and sane.[31]

Not everybody stayed in the department for a long time. Pinches fell out with Budge and left in 1900, while P.S.P. Handcock left during the war and A.W.A. Leeper ended up in the diplomatic service. R. Campbell Thompson, however, had left the Museum in 1905 after just six years on the staff, but continued to work somewhat uneasily on its behalf. He knew the Middle East well and travelled there frequently from 1902 onwards. He continued the excavations at Nineveh, following on the work of Layard and the other heroic figures of the nineteenth century, and was part of the team sent out to excavate Carchemish. He was, in the words of his obituarist, 'the last representative in England of a phase of Assyriology that converted it from a discovery into a science'.[32]

In 1896 H.R.H. Hall came to the department as an assistant from Oxford, where he had studied ancient Egyptian languages. He was the first real excavator to join the department. Between 1903 and 1920 he dug in Egypt and the Middle East. He mended bridges with the Egyptian Exploration Society and forged the close relationship with it that persists to this day. He was a jovial character, wrote scurrilous verse, played the piano and smoked a foul pipe. His dress was to say the least unorthodox; Sir Max Mallowan describes his first meeting with him, rearranging sculpture in the gallery, 'dressed in a blue suit so old and shiny that one could see one's face in it'.[33] A good scholar, he was typical of many appointments made at this period, drawing expertise from a single course taken at university. His heart was always in his Egyptian studies, but he wrote a number of books on the classical world and when his colleague King died after the First World War he was sent out to start the excavations at Ur. 'Puzzling the military mind with the delightful legend "Captain H.R.

Hall, British Museum" on his kitbag, he rollicked out to Ur of the Chaldees, with seventy Turkish prisoners as his diggers, on 15 February 1919.'[34] Hall succeeded Budge, but died suddenly in 1930, having been keeper for only five and a half years, and was himself succeeded by Sidney Smith. [35] Smith was the first member of staff who after Cambridge studied Egyptology for a short time under Petrie at University College London, before moving on to Berlin to work on oriental languages. He joined the Museum in 1914; drafted into the army almost immediately, he did not return until the end of the war and was then put to work on the *Corpus of cuneiform inscriptions*.[36]

The recruitment of staff to the Department of Prints and Drawings has already been discussed (p.183). In 1893 Laurence Binyon, champion of Japanese art, was promoted to an assistant keepership with an allowance, a promotion urged on the Trustees by Colvin, who saw him struggling with an inadequate salary to keep a wife and three young daughters. As the old hands left, new assistants were recruited: A.M. Hind in 1903, A.E. Popham in 1912, Arthur Schloss (better known as Arthur Waley, his mother's name, adopted in the Germanophobia rampant in the first years of the war) and H.M. Hake, who was appointed in June 1914. Campbell Dodgson succeeded Sir Sidney Colvin as keeper in 1912, although Colvin wanted Binyon.

Dodgson (pl. 14) was one of the most influential keepers in the history of the department, not merely because of his vast knowledge of the early German School, but because of the important collection of 5,000 contemporary and near-contemporary works on paper which he built up throughout his career.[37] This collection he eventually bequeathed to the Museum, together with £3,000 to be administered for the benefit of his department by the National Art Collections Fund. Dodgson was rich, the son of a stockbroker, a scholar of Winchester and New College, Oxford (where he took a first-class degree in classics and married the daughter of its famous Warden Spooner). He was for a short time tutor to Lord Alfred Douglas and, through him, met Oscar Wilde, whom he treated with cautious awe. He was frugal in his habits (although he had a chauffeur[38] and was famed for his hospitality) and was a 'somewhat muscular' Christian, who swam regularly in the Serpentine. He was to take the department into the twentieth century with the reputation for accurate and innovative scholarship.

When Poole left the Department of Coins and Medals in 1893 he was replaced as keeper by the gentlest of scholars, Barclay Head, who retired in 1906.[39] Head was in turn succeeded by Herbert Appold Grueber, described by Hill as 'a painstaking plodder, with a certain facility for reading oriental coins – with how much accuracy was always doubtful'.[40] Hill was perhaps a little unjust, for the second volume of the catalogue of the Anglo-Saxon series, which Grueber wrote with G.F. Keary, remained a standard work for at least half a century. His great work was the three-volume catalogue of Roman Republican coins, based on notes left by de Salis. The assistant keeper was Warwick Wroth, who was expected to succeed as keeper, but died in 1911. He was responsible for six volumes of the Greek catalogues, two Byzantine volumes and a catalogue of the coins of the Vandals, Ostrogoths and Lombards. The orientalist at this time was Edward Rapson, who left in 1906 to become Professor of Sanskrit at Cambridge, having published a few papers and a small book on Indian coins.[41] He was to continue his association with the British Museum as he later helped to sort out the Stein collection (p.229).

George Hill (later to be Director) joined the department in 1893 on the retirement of

Poole.[42] Hill was the son of a missionary in India and his siblings were all distinguished in academe or the public service.[43] After a false start at University College London, he read classics at Merton College, Oxford, and, on arriving at the Museum, was set to work on the Greek catalogue (one of three people engaged on this series). He published six volumes on these coins and then turned his attention to medals, publishing in 1930 his great two-volume corpus of Italian medals before the time of Cellini. He was no narrow scholar; he collected Chinese enamels and contemporary art, published a book on Arabic numerals and what was for a long time the standard work on the law of Treasure Trove.[44] He also served on a committee that produced a memorial plaque to all those who had died in the Great War, and helped to draft new archaeological laws for Iraq, Palestine and Cyprus. In 1907 John Allan, a Sanskrit scholar, joined Hill in the department; in 1908 came the medievalist G.C. Brooke, while Harold Mattingly succeeded Grueber as the Roman specialist in 1910. In 1912 came E.S.G. Robinson, a meticulous scholar who nearly killed off the Greek catalogues, but, under the aegis of the British Academy, started the successful *Sylloge nummorum graecorum*. In the same year Hill became keeper of a department now filled with energetic young men.

New Building

The chronic shortage of space and the lack of will on the part of the Treasury to take the problem seriously were to hamper the development of the Museum throughout the first half of the last century and beyond. So seriously was the Treasury opposed to any increase in the Museum's space, or indeed collections, that in 1899, at a time of financial crisis during the South African War, a bill was introduced into Parliament demanding that the Museum should reduce its collections by disposing of 'valueless printed matter'.[45] The bill became entangled with plans for a new building on the north side of the Museum, which the Trustees did not want to be completely filled with newspapers. In the light of a suggestion of the Trustees' Sub-Committee on Printed Books and Manuscripts that local newspapers should be deposited with the boroughs and the newly created county councils, the Treasury insisted that the construction of the new building could be discussed only if the newspaper problem were solved by such deposits. Despite opposition from Maunde Thompson to the whole idea, it was a Trustee, Lord Peel, who introduced the bill into the House of Lords and, incredibly to modern eyes, it was an historian and Trustee, John Morley, who introduced it into the Commons. The First Lord of the Treasury, Arthur Balfour (a distinguished philosopher), was one of many who opposed it and a campaign, orchestrated by Maunde Thompson and the distinguished Shakespearean scholar Sir Sidney Lee, eventually led to the bill being withdrawn. Following a letter in *The Times* from Flinders Petrie, an alternative solution was proposed and accepted by the Treasury, that the nineteenth-century provincial newspapers be removed to a cheaper site on the outskirts of London.[46] An Act of Parliament was passed in 1902 allowing the Trustees to move newspapers and other printed matter into storage off-site.[47] Land was purchased at Colindale, Middlesex, which allowed for future enlargement, and a utilitarian store was erected and was operational by 1905 (although deposited material could be studied only in Bloomsbury until an extension was opened in 1932).[48]

Parsimonious Grandeur: the Edward VII Building

In 1895, after battle with a reluctant Treasury which eventually lent them £200,000, the Trustees had managed to buy from the Duke of Bedford (one of their body who gave them favourable terms) sixty-nine houses surrounding the Museum.[49] This created an island of property, which the Trustees envisioned would be developed throughout the twentieth century to form an outer shell to the existing buildings.[50] The first stage of this development – to the north – was eventually completed. The rest could not be built, initially because of lack of cash and the outbreak of the First World War, but later because of the need to conserve the threatened buildings purchased from the Bedford estate. This was particularly true of the Grade I listed buildings forming one side of the finest of all the surviving eighteenth-century London squares, Bedford Square.

But it was money, not issues of conservation, that initially delayed the scheme. The Treasury had forced the Trustees to borrow the money to purchase the Bedford estate properties (it was repaid over fifty years with an annual charge of 3 per cent). The Treasury also hedged the sale around with conditions, which were to haunt the Museum in the 1980s, when the Trustees wished to sell the leases of the Bedford Square houses to raise cash for the adaptation of the Montague Street houses for service purposes.[51] It was not, therefore, going to be easy to persuade the Treasury to finance any part of the new project. Fortunately the Trustees were once again rescued by an unforeseen legacy – this time from an eccentric, non-practising barrister, Vincent Stuckey Lean. On his death in 1899, he left the Trustees a number of manuscripts and £50,000, which should 'be appropriated at their discretion to the improvement and extension of the Library and the Reading Room'.[52] When the Trustees approached the Treasury with this money (together with £7,100, the residue of the estate of Franks's close friend C.D.E. Fortnum) and a plea for funding for the first stage of a building on the site of the Bedford estate houses, they got embroiled in the negotiations concerning provincial newspapers outlined above. After the trauma of the failed bill, with the South African War ended, and with Balfour now Prime Minister, the Treasury in 1903 offered £150,000 towards the project on condition that the Fortnum money would contribute to the cost of the fittings.[53] The Treasury did not let go of the money easily, for they and the Office of Works laid a heavy, discourteous and delaying hand on the project. Initial plans for the new building, which was to take up much of Montague Place, were sketched out in the style of the White Wing by the Office of Works architect, Henry Tanner, but his scheme was scrapped and, after a competition, John James Burnet was appointed as architect.

Burnet was a Glaswegian who had spent some time on the Continent and was much influenced by French architecture as a result of his training at the Ecole des Beaux-Arts in Paris. The Museum was his first major project outside Glasgow. His design for the Museum site and for its northern approaches was splendid in its strict classicism, which was later to become heavier as his partnership tackled buildings in Aldwych, Kingsway and Regent Street. Its scale ideally matches the Smirke buildings and, interestingly, if it had been completed, would even have impinged, rather tactfully, on the main Smirke frontage. The completed portion of his design – the King Edward VII Building and the North Library behind it – has received almost universal praise from authorities as diverse as Godfrey, Summerson and Pevsner. Of it Pevsner writes:

> The long range is a successfully eclectic mixture in the chastest Beaux Arts style: a dominat-
> ing parade of giant fluted Ionic engaged columns, which also echo Smirke, large plain
> openings which are clearly [twentieth century], the whole given dignity and repose by a high
> basement and a tall, plain attic. The weakest element is the central entrance at basement
> level, with its surround butting up awkwardly against the columns above.[54]

The façade is of Portland stone and the plinth and doorway are of granite (pl. 23). A domi-
nating inscription above the doorway was carved by Eric Gill.[55] The rather squat entrance
hall is relieved by an oculus (known universally throughout the Museum as 'the spittoon'),
which provides light from the immensely long, rather heavily detailed, marble and
mahogany gallery above. The staircase, of white marble with columns of black and white
marble, starts in a cramped space but then soars round a well almost to the full height of
the building, first to a mezzanine floor, which now provides access to the Korean Gallery.[56]
Above this were galleries for Prints and Drawings. To the east of these the mezzanine and
the main first floor were dedicated to offices and students' rooms for the Department of
Prints and Drawings. There is a lift behind the staircase which has a splendid gilt casing by
the Bromsgrove Guild. There was access to the North Library and the Reading Room off
the first half landing of the staircase and to the main Museum galleries from the half
landing above the mezzanine floors, although levels are awkward at this point. A mean
staircase then rose to storage and roof space, part of which was used as a photographic
studio after the appointment of a full-time photographer in 1927. The lower ground floor
and basements were used for library purposes and some storage; this area also provided
the Museum with its first purpose-built loading bay. In preparation for the fitting out of
the galleries, Burnet (at his own expense) and Read, Keeper of British and Mediaeval
Antiquities and Ethnography (much against the wish of the Office of Works), visited the
east coast of the United States to look at new museums there.

If the building process had been as successful as the ultimate product, the Museum
would have been a happier place. The Office of Works were clear that they were in control,
as a contemporary briefing note makes clear:

> It is to be noticed that, with a regrettable lack of official courtesy, HM Office of Works have
> never informed the Trustees of the commencement of building operations or completion of
> contracts. The mere fact of workmen being admitted to the premises, and the obtaining of
> information from independent sources, have been the only means by which the Trustees
> could guess that work was being undertaken on their own premises.[57]

There were endless troubles. First, the demolition of the houses in Montague Place led to a
considerable loss in rental revenue. Then, just before the King laid the foundation stone in
1907, the Office of Works announced that the estimate for the engineering service was
nearly double the original sum of £13,000. For two and a half years work came to a halt,
during which time the building was roofless. As a result some of the cement leached out of
the concrete floor of the gallery, which had to be re-laid, ancient parsimony which has
made it impossible to provide a worthy floor-covering ever since. Early in 1910 building
operations resumed and the new wing was finally handed over (late) to the Trustees for
fitting out in October 1913. King George V and Queen Mary formally opened the practically

empty building, with some pageantry, in May of the following year.[58] Unfortunately £11,000 could not be found to drive a major approach road from the entrance of the building to Torrington Square, so that once again the Museum had to be approached as though along a side street.

Although the architect had designed the gallery and North Library furniture, a good deal of cannibalization took place. The Prints and Drawings students' room, for example, was lined with presses taken from the old students' room in the White Wing (some of which had even come from Montagu House).[59] The ultimate meanness of both the Treasury and the Office of Works was demonstrated when they refused to pay for the two limestone lions that flank the entrance. Carved by Sir George Frampton, they had been commissioned for £2,000. The Office of Works, pressurized by the Treasury, thought this too expensive and agreed to pay only £1,200 of the cost. Despite protest, the Treasury proved adamant and the artist generously agreed to reduce his price. Two further sculptures, representing Art and Science, intended for the terminal pylons of the building were never executed – an interesting echo of the figural groups planned for the main façade of the building sixty years earlier by Smirke and Westmacott and never commissioned. As though to rub in Treasury control of finance, the entrance to the King Edward VII Building, from Montague Place, was not opened to the public until 1931 (and then only briefly), because of lack of financial provision for staff. The Director, Hill, was still complaining that the railings had not been finished in 1936 – they never were, which perhaps explains the odd appearance of the replicas placed there in 2000.[60] The architect, who had fought hard on behalf of the Museum, well deserved the knighthood awarded him after the opening of the building.

In August, three months after the King had formally opened the building, war broke out and the display in the Edward VII Gallery, already behind schedule, was put on hold. After the war, between 1920 and 1923, the main gallery was dressed, the Music and Map rooms were created on the mezzanine and the Department of Prints and Drawings moved into the top floor. At the western end the Waddesdon Bequest was displayed in ornate showcases, while at the eastern end much of the Franks Bequest was displayed; the main body of the gallery was taken up with an exhibition of ceramics – European at the west end and oriental, aptly, at the east. A bridge was constructed from the Franks Room to the north-east stairs of the Smirke building, a temporary structure that survives to this day. Until the beginning of the Second World War the dream of completing the Burnet scheme with galleries on the Montague Street and Bedford Square sides stayed alive.

The chief faults of the King Edward VII Building lie in the fact that the floor levels do not coincide with those of the main building and that the entrance hall and first stage of the staircase are rather mean.[61] Writing to his successor as Director in 1936, Sir George Hill puts the matter in context:

> As to the King Edward VII Building, the prospect is gloomy. It doubles (by the devilish ingenuity of which all the floors are put on different levels from those of the main building) the difficulty of all attempts at contact with new buildings on the West and East alike. The Northern Entrance gives a dismal welcome to the visitor. There is, however, Markham tells me, a plan for abolishing the 'spittoon' in the middle of the Ceramic Gallery, and making a good stair-case from the entrance up to that Gallery. It seems a sound idea.[62]

Display and Information

The mounting and labelling of objects in the collections was an ongoing task. Each year the departments reported to the Trustees and Parliament the number of objects mounted and the number of labels produced. In 1895, for example, the Department of British and Mediaeval Antiquities and Ethnography reported:

> Seventeen tablets and fifteen mounting boards have been covered with paper, and 1,752 objects have been mounted. Twenty-one boards and six tablets have been made. Sixty plinths have been made, and objects mounted on them for exhibition. Fifty-one labels have been painted; eighty card-labels with duplicates have been printed with the hand-press, and a large number written.... Fifty-eight numbers have been written upon exhibition cases.[63]

Gems and objects of precious metal were mounted on velvet-covered 'tablets'; other boards were either painted cream or covered with linen. The table-cases were in many instances curtained to protect the objects. In the Department of Prints and Drawings, after 1914 at least, upright cases were also covered with curtains. Some of the labels were of wood (for larger pieces the labels were often of triangular section), painted black, with white or gold lettering, while in the Department of Egyptian and Assyrian Antiquities we hear of oak plinths, although mahogany plinths were also used there and elsewhere. Caen stone, marble and granite were also used as plinths for sculpture and painted in gold or black with descriptive labels. Groups of antiquities were pinned to the 'tablets' or boards, descriptive text sometimes being painted directly on to those not covered with textiles. The tablets could easily be moved about the table-cases, and both they and the larger boards could be mounted on slopes or vertically in the wall-cases. Coins were exhibited in chronological sequence, often with electrotypes or casts to show obverse and reverse.

Labels were rarely very informative, it being assumed that visitors needing more information would refer to the gallery guides, which were, during the reigns of Thompson and Kenyon, produced in greater numbers and which referred the reader to numbered cases. Rooms also were numbered and labelled. The in-case labels normally gave the geographical provenance of an object, the date of the object and the material of which it was made. Registration number was always given (for the convenience of students and staff), as was any major reference in academic literature and, importantly, acknowledgment of all donors. Some labels were printed; most were hand-lettered on wood, painted strips of zinc, card or ivorine (a material replaced, after the Second World War, by Perspex), by three generations of the Steele family.[64] Typewritten labels appear to have been introduced about the turn of the century and may well have replaced labels written by hand by members of the staff.[65] There were as yet no information panels, although some showcases had general headings.

Showcases continued to be constructed to Smirke's design (pl. 22), although in the White Wing galleries some of the larger wall-cases were strengthened by the addition of a moulded, black-painted steel fillet within the frame. After the introduction of electricity the sealed panels at the top of the wall-cases were glazed.[66] Cases were lined with paper, which was painted. Only when the Edward VII Gallery was opened was there any serious departure from the original design for upright cases, which were now placed not on the walls, but were freestanding so as to form bays on either side of each window (pl. 23).

These were designed in Burnet's office on the basis of the Smirke design. They still survive, and are extremely inconvenient as each wall-case consists of three vertical sections, glazed back and front, of which only the central section opens. The long arm of a contortionist is needed to adjust objects in the outer portions of the case. It is likely, but by no means certain, that plate-glass shelves were first introduced into these cases.[67] The table-cases were built chiefly to the Smirke design, but a few much larger table-cases with rounded corners (known as 'tram' cases), the glazing framed with bronze, were modelled on cases introduced in the 1870s.[68] As in so many parts of the Museum, the table-cases were provided with cupboards for storage; some had glazed drawers for the exhibition of small objects or glazed doors in the base for the display of pots or other large objects. Mirrors were sometimes introduced to reflect details or lighten faces in shadow.[69] Free-standing showcases, some two metres high with glass sides and bronze frames – known as 'Director-type cases' – were introduced into the Edward VII Gallery in the inter-war period and were also used sparingly elsewhere in the Museum. They were not a success, as they were seriously unstable when opened at both ends.

The series of gallery and period guides enthusiastically commissioned from the curatorial staff by Maunde Thompson and Kenyon acted as a supplement to the labels. Paperbacked, with stiff boards, the guides sold, originally for a shilling, from a counter which also displayed postcards in the front hall; three salespersons were appointed in 1912 (previously an annual allowance of £10 had been made to the hall porter to oversee sales).[70] Warned by the example of the Victoria and Albert Museum, which had produced splendid – but unfocused and severely criticized – handbooks as 'companions to a visit to the museum', the British Museum guides placed the objects in the galleries in context.[71] They were well illustrated with photographs of a high quality and splendidly accurate drawings by the Museum's official draughtsman, C.O. Waterhouse, who in 1910 had been seconded from Waterlow's, the printers, and was given a permanent appointment in 1915 at a salary of £164 6s 6d.[72] While not unique, the guides were an important and original innovation. So important were they as synthetic sources that some, particularly those dealing with the European Iron Age and with Anglo-Saxon and 'Foreign Teutonic' antiquities (both written by Reginald Smith), were still used in university teaching in the 1950s.

Despite the success of the guides it took the Trustees a long time to face up to the problems of photography. Commercial photographers, particularly the firm of R.B. Fleming, were used exclusively until 1927. The photographer used for the guides was David Macbeth who worked on and off for the Museum for forty years until his retirement in 1940.[73] His standards were high and he was responsible not only for the innovative pictures in the guides but for many other photographs. His most prestigious work appears in the album commissioned for the opening of the King Edward VII Building in 1914.[74] Macbeth was not the only photographer used by the Trustees, but in 1927 they finally faced up to their responsibilities and appointed D.S. Lyon (who had been working for them since 1914 as an attendant in charge of photography) as Foreman of Photographers. He had one assistant and a new studio was built for him and the outside photographers on the roof of the King Edward VII Building. (Not at this stage worried by copyright problems, the Trustees allowed amateur photography with hand-held cameras from 1898.)[75]

Late in the day, official guide-lecturers – usually university graduates – were added to the Museum's establishment in 1911. In 1925, while struggling to obtain higher pay for

PLATE I Sir Hans Sloane, whose collections form the core of the British Museum. This terracotta bust by Michael Rysbrack, c.1737, is almost certainly a model for the statue of Sloane first erected in the Chelsea Physic Garden and now (in a much weathered condition) in the British Museum.

MUSEUM BRITANNICUM,

BEING AN

EXHIBITION

OF A GREAT VARIETY OF

ANTIQUITIES AND NATURAL CURIOSITIES,

BELONGING TO

THAT NOBLE AND MAGNIFICENT CABINET,

THE

BRITISH MUSEUM.

ILLUSTRATED WITH

CURIOUS PRINTS,

Engraved after the ORIGINAL DESIGNS, from NATURE, other OBJECTS;

AND WITH DISTINCT

EXPLANATIONS OF EACH FIGURE,

By JOHN and ANDREW VAN RYMSDYK, PICTORS.

When *Cicero* went to confult the *Oracle* about his future Conduct in Life, he received for Anfwer,

Follow Nature!

" No more you learned Fops, your Knowledge boaft,
" Pretending all to know, by reading moft,
" True Wit, by Infpiration, we obtain,
" Nature, not Art, Apollo's Wreath muft gain.   Mrs. A. BEHN,
                                     in Æfop's Life, 7th Plate.

LONDON:

Printed by I. MOORE, for the AUTHORS, CHARLES-STREET,
ST. JAMES'S-SQUARE. 1778.

PLATE 2 (*opposite*). The first page of the Act of Parliament of 1753 which established the British Museum. On it is laid the staff (popularly known as the mace) that was ordered for the porter at the opening of the Museum to the public in January 1759.

PLATE 3 Title page from John and Andrew van Rymsdyk, *Museum Britannicum*, 1778, the first major publication to illustrate and describe the collections of the Museum.

PLATE 4. (*Left*) The seal of the Trustees of the British Museum, 1754. (*Below*) Plan of Montagu House by W. Brasier, dated 1741, based on an original by Henry Flitcroft, 1725. Adapted by H. Keene, it was used to plan the housing of the collection and its staff. The housemaids lived in rooms at either end of the colonnade and the porter over the gatehouse. The wings were occupied by the officers; room G was the Principal Librarian's study.

PLATE 5 (*opposite*). The main façade, gatehouse and wings of Montagu House. Prints by John Buckler, 1828.

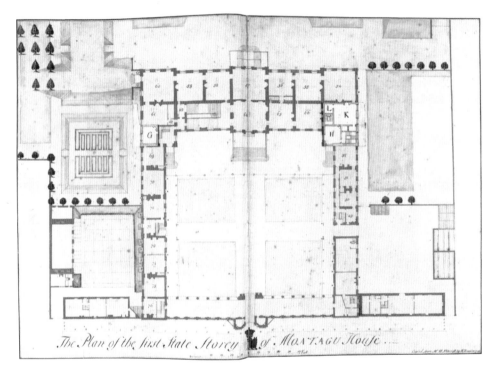

The Plan of the first State Storey of MONTAGU House.

PLATE 6 Encampment of the York Regiment of Militia in the garden of the Museum at the time of the Gordon Riots, 1780. This anonymous watercolour gives some idea of the pleasant nature of the Museum's gardens and the open country beyond Montagu House. It is taken from the north-east corner of Bedford Square and looks over the open fields towards Queen Square. The cart is roughly on the line of what is now the south side of Montague Place. The encampment was much visited by royalty and other generally curious people. One of the officers, Major Selwood Hewitt, so enjoyed his time here that he presented the Museum with a copy of an Irish translation of sermons on the principal points of religion, published in 1711.

PLATE 7   Four Principal Librarians. (*Above*) Gowin Knight by Benjamin Wilson; Matthew Maty. (*Below*) Andrew Planta; Antonio Panizzi.

PLATE 8 The young Sir Joseph Banks by Benjamin West, 1771–2. Banks is wearing a Maori cloak brought back from his voyage with Captain Cook. Usher Gallery, Lincoln.

PLATE 9 The Townley Gallery designed by George Saunders. 1808. (*Right*) Plan (after Cook (1977)). (*Below*) Interior looking north from the top-lit tribune (Room II) and east into Room I. (An external view is seen on plate 18.) The Townley Gallery was the first public museum building to use top-lighting consistently in rooms over which there was no upper storey. Schinckel saw it and was so impressed that he imitated it in the Altes Museum in Berlin. The use of top-lighting was continued by Smirke.

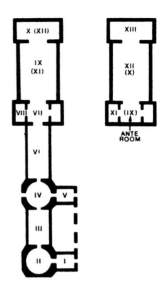

A POINT OF ANTIQUITY.

Payed to Karl ye Saron for his worship's hood off mail
with the blessed sign on the Forehead

PLATE 10 'A point of antiquity'. Left is Nicholas Carlisle, a librarian at the Royal Library from 1812 and (on transfer) at the British Museum, 1823–47. Resident Secretary of the Society of Antiquaries, he was 'one of the Society's most gifted exponents of the art of inactivity'. In the centre is Sir Frederic Madden, quarrelsome colleague, enemy of Panizzi and a great medievalist, Keeper of Manuscripts. The portly Sir Henry Ellis, much maligned Principal Librarian, is on the right. Published by Thomas Maclean 1833. Society of Antiquaries, London.

PLATE 11 (*opposite*). Four benefactors. (*Above*) William White; the Reverend Clayton Mordaunt Cracherode. (*Below*) Richard Payne Knight; Anne Hull Grundy (photograph by Eileen Tweedie).

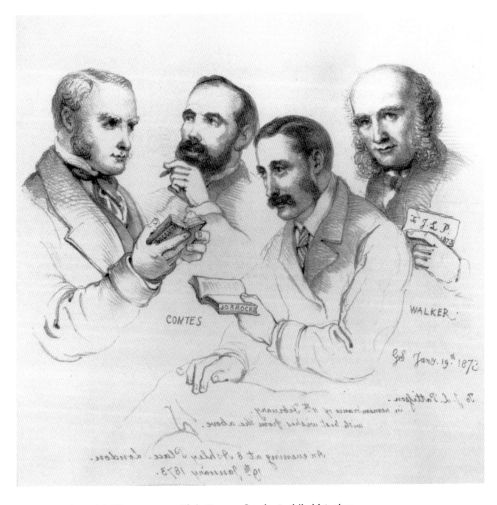

PLATE 12 (*opposite*). The temporary Elgin Room, 1819, by Archibald Archer.

Key: 1. Benjamin Robert Haydon, painter. 2. Charles Long (?), later Lord Farnborough, Paymaster-General. 3. Reverend James Bean, Assistant Librarian, Printed Books. 4. Reverend Thomas Maurice, Assistant Librarian, Manuscripts. 5. Sir Henry Ellis, later Principal Librarian. 6. John George Children, Assistant Librarian, Natural History (later Keeper of Zoology). 7. Benjamin West, President of the Royal Academy. 8. Joseph Planta, Principal Librarian. 9. Taylor Combe, Keeper of Antiquities. 10. Reverend Henry Baber, Keeper of Manuscripts. 11. John Thomas Smith, Assistant Librarian in charge of Prints and Drawings. 12. John Edward Gray, Assistant Librarian (later Keeper), Natural History. 13. The artist. 14. Charles König, Under Librarian, Natural History. 15. Thomas Conrath, Attendant.

PLATE 13 (*above*). A bachelor party, as depicted by Sir George Scharf, Director of the National Portrait Gallery and an artist who had been on Fellows's expedition to Lycia. Scharf entertains a cigar-smoking Augustus Wollaston Franks, William Frederick Beauford and Richard Worsley. A unique pictorial glimpse of the sociable Franks. National Portrait Gallery, London.

PLATE 14 (*opposite*). Four great keepers. (*Above*) Edward Hawkins, Department of Antiquities; Charles Newton, Department of Greek and Roman Antiquities. (*Below*) Campbell Dodgson, Department of Prints and Drawings; Ormonde Maddock Dalton, Department of British and Mediaeval Antiquities.

PLATE 15. (*Above*) Installing the Assyrian sculpture, *c*. 1852. (*Below*) Samuel Birch, Keeper of Oriental Antiquities, in his legendary high hat (see p. 180), placing material in cases in the upper galleries. He is assisted by the departmental Attendant, Thomas Vine Cooke. Drawings by George Scharf.

PLATE 16 Junior staff. (*Left*) William Scivier, porter, in the Windsor livery, the right to wear which was granted by William IV in 1837. (It is still worn by security staff on special occasions.) (*Below left*) Mary Bygrave, head house-maid, 1844. She was introduced in 1780 by her aunt, who had worked for Sloane. (*Below right*) A gallery attendant with his wand of office.

PLATE 17 (*opposite*). Two Museum excavations. (*Above*) Perhaps the earliest known excavation photograph. Newton supervises the removal of the Cnidus lion in 1856. (*Below*) The excavation of the Sutton Hoo ship-burial, 1939. Clockwise from left, Charles Phillips, T.D. Kendrick, Basil Brown, discoverer of the burial, Sir John Forsdyke, Stuart Piggott, and W. F. Grimes.

PLATE 18 (*opposite*). Smirke's building rises. Watercolours by George Scharf, 1845. (*Above*) The Townley Gallery stands in the middle distance between Montagu House and the rising south front of the new building. (*Below*) The foundations of the Lycian Gallery are laid. The west residences are being completed beyond the guard house (a building which survived into the second half of the twentieth century).

PLATE 19 The iron skeleton of the round Reading Room is here nearly complete. Photograph taken by William Lake Price in 1855 at the suggestion of Sydney Smirke.

PLATE 20 (*opposite*). (*Above*) Crowds in Great Russell Street in 1847 (from *Howitt's Journal*). The screen of Montagu House, the west corner turret and the gateway partially mask the nearly completed south front of Smirke's building. (*Below*) The south end of the Ethnographical Gallery in the late nineteenth century. The crowded nature of the display survived until after the Second World War. The showcase in the middle with legs was one of a group originally designed for the South Kensington Museum.

PLATE 21 Students' day c.1857–9. Photo by Roger Fenton, the Museum photographer. Easels had been banned from the galleries of the old Museum building some twenty years earlier, but were now once again allowed.

PLATE 22 Gallery furniture designed by Smirke: wall cases, bench and table cases (the latter produced in some variants).

PLATE 23 (*opposite*). The King Edward VII Building. Exterior (architect's model) and interior before the cases were dressed. Photographs 1914.

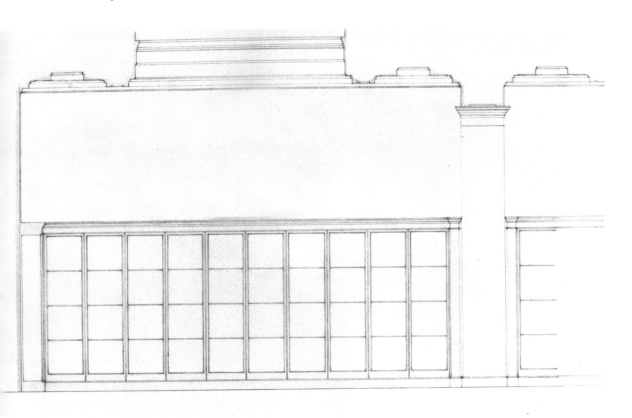

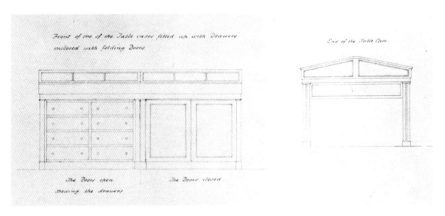

PLATE 24 (*opposite*). In 1905–6 the Danish artist Vilhelm Hammershøi painted two views of the Museum from the same spot. That in the Ny Carlsberg Glyptotek, Copenhagen, shows the corner of Montague Street with the White Wing. This one (in Storstrøms Kunstmuseum, Maribo) expresses the damp winter gloom of the main face of the Museum at the turn of the century.

PLATE 25 Three Principal Librarians. (*Right*) Winter Jones by William Salter Herrick; (*below*) Edward Maunde Thompson; Frederic Kenyon (both National Portrait Gallery, London; photographs by Bassano).

PLATES 26 & 27 The cause of much agitation: the Duveen Gallery. (*Below*) One of the original designs by the architect, J. Russell Pope, in which the Parthenon sculptures were to be treated as an ornamental motif set against grand architecture. Kenyon, Forsdyke and Crawford battled with the benefactor to produce the more clinical space which now houses the Marbles (*opposite*). Duveen's ignorance, wrote Crawford, was 'so dense as to make argument unserviceable'.

PLATE 28 (*opposite*). Contrasting styles. (*Above*) Two academic Directors: the highly respected numismatist George Hill; the frightening art-historian John Pope-Hennessy, through the eyes of Christopher Cornford. (*Below*) David Eccles, consummate politician of the arts and second Chairman of the Trustees after the 1963 Act; Burke Trend, powerful conciliator and fourth Chairman.

PLATE 29 (*right*). War damage, 1941. The bombed Central Saloon. (*Below*) Waiting for admittance to the Tutankhamun exhibition, 1972.

PLATE 30 The establishment of the Museum of Mankind enabled the introduction of innovative exhibition techniques. 'Nomad and City' in 1976, designed by Margaret Hall, set a trend towards the total recreation of the setting of the daily life of people outside the Western world.

PLATE 31 (*opposite*). (*Above*) The Japanese Galleries, opened in 1990, were created out of disused roof space in the King Edward VII Building. This was the first exhibition space to be constructed as the result of a targeted appeal. (*Below*) Part of the Sainsbury African Galleries constructed below the Great Court and opened in 2001.

PLATE 32 (*overleaf*). The Great Court, designed by Foster and Partners, was opened in 2000 to celebrate the Millennium.

these two officers (C.W.C. Hallett and W.W. Skeat, who were paid £315 p.a.), Kenyon described their function in a memorandum to Treasury:

> The Guides are not mere showmen, like the ciceroni who infest certain foreign galleries. They are educated, university-trained gentlemen, of the same class as the scientific staff of the Museum, who, without being experts in any of the special subjects represented in the Museum, yet know all of them sufficiently to be interested in them and to be capable of interesting others. They do not pretend to teach the specialist student, but to inform the seeker after knowledge and to give an intelligent response to the unintelligent curiosity of the casual visitor.

Programmes of lectures were circulated and relief lecturers were employed (with a special grant from the Treasury of £50!), as demand was great. The number attending the guide-lecturers' talks in 1924 was nearly 35,000, while nearly 4,000 attended the extra lectures.[76]

Serious students began to appear in some numbers in the various students' rooms of the antiquities departments. In the Department of Prints and Drawings and in the Department of Egyptian and Assyrian Antiquities they had to obtain a ticket of admission. These were issued on the back of regulations similar in many respects to those of the library departments, but with slightly different conditions: 'No Student shall pick with a pin, or knife, or any instrument, any character or characters, on a clay tablet, nor shall he scratch or scrape any part of the surface of the same...'.[77] In other departments tickets were not necessary. Here students, who were normally admitted by appointment, were closely supervised by staff sitting at neighbouring desks. Objects could generally be studied on every day on which the Museum was open (save Sunday).

Staff also provided a service of advice to the public, identifying objects brought to the Museum or sent by post. It is not clear when this practice started, but it is clear from the number of visitors recorded in the *Annual Returns* that it went back well into the nineteenth century. There was mutual benefit in such a service. The public learnt about the items they submitted, while the staff saw many important and varied objects, which were sometimes subsequently acquired for the collections. The practice continues to this day and still serves its dual role. Even today every newly recruited officer is expected to identify (or know how to identify) simple objects well outside his own immediate speciality. It has always been strictly forbidden to value submitted objects.

Visitor numbers remained low – between 650,000 and 800,000 annually – in the early years of the century, and did not hit the million mark until 1924, at which point the Museum overtook the Victoria and Albert Museum – which for many years had attracted more visitors. In this year the Victoria and Albert Museum had 1,112,617 to the British Museum's 1,181,242. Visitor figures for the Museum, save for the war years and the period of reconstruction after the war, never fell below the million mark, while the Victoria and Albert figures fell drastically until the war.[78]

The First World War[79]

One of the King's last official acts before the outbreak of war was the opening of the King Edward VII Building. On 4 August 1914 war was declared and a few days later a special meeting of the Trustees took place. It was reported that thirty members of staff had been called to the colours, including the Director. The bellicose Kenyon (a captain in the Inns of Court Regiment) was in Territorial Camp on Salisbury Plain on 4 August, but was immediately mobilized and had crossed to France on 9 August. Other members of staff wanted to go, and it was arranged that Lord Esher should sift applications. One attendant had been asked for by another government department; while the Trustees allowed the request, they were not at this time minded to let others go.[80] Kenyon, having spent a month with the advance troops in France, was recalled by the Trustees, but was allowed, for the duration of the war, to spend three weeks in every month training troops at Berkhamsted.[81] This was but the beginning. In the course of the war, out of a total staff of 384, 137 were recruited to the armed forces and forty-four were lent to other departments of government. Eleven men died in the war and twenty-three were wounded. The names of the dead are recorded on the war memorial carved by Eric Gill into the wall on the right-hand side of the entrance under the portico of the Museum. With the names is a verse from a poem by a member of staff, Laurence Binyon – 'For the fallen', which became one of the most quoted memorial verses after the war:

> They shall grow not old, as we that are left grow old,
> Age shall not weary them, nor the years condemn.
> At the going down of the sun and in the morning
> We will remember them.

The Museum was placed under great strain by the constant drain of men and was run on a skeleton staff, supplemented by a small number of volunteers. In the summer of 1915 Oscar E. Raphael (a collector of ceramics and glass and a generous donor, who in 1945 bequeathed his oriental collection to the Museum), Longworth Dames and the Romano-British archaeologist J.P. Bushe Fox (later Chief Inspector for Ancient Monuments) volunteered to work in the Department of British and Mediaeval Antiquities on a temporary basis (the two latter were paid £1 per day). Ex-members of staff were encouraged to return to work.[82]

There was perhaps a certain amount of overt anti-German sentiment, although it rarely appears in the documents. When one of the new members of staff, H.J. Braunholtz, was due to be confirmed in his appointment at the end of his second year in the Museum, his keeper, Sir Hercules Read, found it difficult to recommend him, 'owing to his want of zeal and efficiency and the departmental friction arising out of his family connection with Germany'. The Trustees, approving the payment of his increment, asked for a further report in six months' time, and then confirmed him.[83] When the Museum was asked to make a return of all staff of German parentage in 1917, Braunholtz was one of the three listed, by which time he was serving in the Royal Army Medical Corps.[84] Many of the staff fought in the armed services. A.E. Popham, for example, was a captain in the Royal Flying Corps and won the French Croix de Guerre. Others (particularly the linguistically gifted) were used in Intelligence and some were even used professionally, particularly a number of the members of the Department of Egyptian and Assyrian Antiquities. In 1918 Campbell Thompson, for example, was excavating at Ur and elsewhere on behalf of the Museum, and various officers were lent to the Mesopotamian administration for such purposes in the last year of the war.[85] In 1917 the Director, as if he had not enough to do, was, with the reluctant approval of the Trustees, allowed to accept an appointment to the War Graves Commission.[86]

The government's attitude towards museums in wartime was at first ambivalent; but as the war dragged on and the losses mounted, their patience grew less despite the fact that many outside government pointed to the need for the mental stimulus and refreshment which almost uniquely could be provided by museums. From the beginning of the war, the Trustees were aware of the threat of aerial attack and had to act to protect the collections. Generally, however, they kept their nerve and did not seriously denude the galleries until late in the war, when the demand for emergency office accommodation and the threat of more serious bombs led to the evacuation of many important treasures to the country. Initially, objects of special value were removed from the upper floors and hidden in basements, which were turned into strong-rooms. These and other well-protected areas within the Museum were reinforced and received the more important small items. Further precautions included a modified blackout, an improved high-pressure water supply and an addition to the night security staff of specialist firemen and electricians. In 1915 the sculpture was protected by sandbags and slag-wool. By the time air raids started in the summer of 1915, most of the collections were well protected. The nearest bomb fell some 150 metres away.

Until 1916 the Museum continued to fulfil many of its public service functions. But lack of staff and a reduced grant, combined with government pressure, forced the Trustees to close the galleries, although the reading rooms were kept open. All this merely led to a miserable saving of some £8,500 and the release of some staff for work elsewhere. Demands on the Museum now began to grow. First, the Trustees were asked to give a home to the statistical branch of the Medical Research Committee and space was found in the empty basement of the King Edward VII Building. Then they were asked to house the possessions of interned Germans from the Cameroons and other captured German dependencies; finally the Registry of Friendly Societies was housed in the upper Egyptian galleries and the Print Room. The Museum also provided shelter during air raids for as many as 250 people from the neighbourhood.

One of the more bizarre wartime ideas concerned the pigeons which infested the forecourt (as they still do). It was felt that they could be used as food, and they were gradually killed off until only about a dozen were left. Unfortunately flocks of starlings moved in to replace them, and these were eliminated only with great difficulty.

The most serious threat came, however, in December 1917. The Air Board applied through the Cabinet Committee on Accommodation to use the Museum to house their administration. Few seemed to understand the lunatic nature of a request which would house a legitimate target for air attack alongside some of the nation's greatest treasures. Without even bothering to consult the Museum the Cabinet agreed. Kenyon argued with the Air Board and stimulated a newspaper campaign in which all the learned great and good rallied to the cause.[87] The matter was due to be re-opened in the House of Lords when, on 9 January 1918, the Archbishop of Canterbury (Principal Trustee) and the Director were summoned to a meeting of the War Cabinet, where one of the Trustees, Lord Curzon, was fighting the Museum's corner. Let Lord Beaverbrook, who was present, take up the tale:

Even in the dark days of war Lloyd George was impatient and even intolerant of Lord Curzon's long and tedious harangues on public issues. There was at one time a proposal to take over the British Museum for the use of the Air Ministry. The plan found favour. Curzon then demanded a reconsideration and led off the discussion by reading a long statement setting forth his objections.

The Prime Minister checked him. Unhappily for his Lordship's pride, the Archbishop of Canterbury and Sir Frederic Kenyon, the Director of the Museum, were present to give evidence. When asked if he had any alternative suggestion, Kenyon replied, 'The Bethlehem Hospital – more commonly known as the Bedlam Lunatic Asylum.' The Ministers felt that this would hardly be suitable accommodation.

No doubt Kenyon's good-humoured comment helped the Ministers to the revocation of the decision.[88]

This major threat overcome, the Trustees then addressed the perceived threat of damage from heavier bombs. The evacuation of material to more secure accommodation was now started, with the aid of women volunteers as packers. The best prints, drawings and manuscripts were sent to the National Library of Wales in Aberystwyth and, after careful consideration of the implications for conservation, important antiquities and coins were removed to the underground tunnels below the Holborn sorting office, where the relative humidity was carefully monitored, with less than successful effect. Eight hundred of the library's most valuable printed books were housed in the private strong-room of C.W. Dyson Perrins at Davenham, Worcestershire. All this was accomplished between February and May 1918, and a special wartime exhibition was opened to the public on 1 August, which was seen by some 100,000 visitors by Armistice Day, 11 November. The exhibition provided the public with a taste of the collections through casts and electrotypes of some of the Museum's greatest treasures, but also displayed items of more immediate interest, including German propaganda medals obtained in Holland, together with documents, manuscripts and maps relating to such places as Mons and Ypres, names only too familiar during the war.[89]

The Museum continued to collect books from Germany and occupied Europe and various other objects, such as the medals quoted above, came out through Holland or Scandinavia.[90] There is in Museum folklore (unfortunately poorly documented) a certain amount of anecdotal evidence of a rather detailed knowledge of academic activity in enemy countries during the war. Non-combatant countries sometimes kept a watching brief on the Museum's local interests, and reported back to London. Perhaps most noteworthy was the occasion in September 1917, when the Swedish legation in Constantinople reported that Otto Walter of the Austrian Archaeological Institute had found that the Museum's Ephesus stores had been disturbed. He had moved the contents into Austrian protection – a gesture for which the Trustees returned thanks.[91]

General collecting continued, albeit on a minor scale, during the war. It is interesting to note that objects and documents concerning the war itself were collected with some enthusiasm. The German propaganda medals and their rather pathetic British counterparts were a notable acquisition, but the library departments were greatly enriched by maps, books and manuscripts directly connected with the hostilities. Drawings by official war artists – particularly Muirhead Bone, Pennel and McBey – were added to the collections. The Greek government after the war presented a number of antiquities recovered by the British on the Salonika front. Some antiquities from von Oppenheim's Syrian excavations at Tell Halaf were captured at sea and brought to a Prize Court in Alexandria. In order to avoid their dispersal, the Museum intervened and acquired the material. After the war the objects were studied and published by the excavator and the collection was restored to him (the Museum – by mutual agreement – retaining a type series).

In many respects the Museum recovered easily from the war; members of staff who had been temporary soldiers or civil servants – including the Director (now a lieutenant-colonel) – returned on the whole quickly. A few had done so well in the war that they went on to higher things elsewhere in the public service or academe. There had been no bomb damage; evacuated objects were returned with despatch and the sandbags removed from the sculptures – the Assyrian transept, relieved of its protection, was reopened on 2 December, within three weeks of the end of the war. By the end of April 1919 all the evacuated objects had been returned or uncovered and much was redisplayed. There remained one cuckoo in the nest, the Registry of Friendly Societies, which proved difficult to remove, but went somewhat reluctantly after questions in both Houses of Parliament had stirred up a harassed Board of Works to find them alternative accommodation in the spring of 1920. Later in the year the new galleries in the King Edward VII Building began to fill up, starting with the Prints and Drawings Gallery on the top floor. By March 1922, with the opening of the Coins and Medals Gallery in the old Waddesdon Bequest Room, the Museum was now – so far as the exhibits were concerned – fully operational.

The Museum was singularly successful in the post-war period in raising its annual grant-in-aid from the government: this increased from £216,863 in 1902–3 to £430,125 in 1927–8 (these figures included the grant for the Natural History Museum, as well as capital works at both sites). By the late 1930s the grant for Bloomsbury alone had reached around £200,000 (not including capital projects).

Conservation[92]

An unfortunate side-effect of the wartime evacuation of objects into the Holborn tunnel was that, despite conscious monitoring of environmental conditions, certain objects had suffered physically – despite Kenyon's carefully worded public statements which suggested the contrary.[93] The problems, basically caused by damp, included mildew on inorganic objects, efflorescent crystals on pottery and stone, and staining. The treatment of such conditions was far beyond the capabilities of the departmental technicians who were responsible for much of the remedial work carried out on the collections. In these circumstances Kenyon applied to the Department of Scientific and Industrial Research (DSIR) for help, and a consultant, Dr Alexander Scott, who had been Director of the Davy-Faraday Laboratory at the Royal Institution from 1896 to 1911, submitted a report recommending the establishment of a laboratory at the Museum. The Treasury approved the proposal and funded it for a period of three years from the DSIR vote. Scott was given an honorarium of £250 p.a. together with the services of an assistant, a restorer and a lab boy. He was also given a grant of £100 p.a., to cover equipment, chemicals and everything else.[94]

The DSIR was still the funding body and the smallness of the departmental grant nearly killed the project at birth. Scott was, however, resourceful; equipment was bought at sales and Scott himself lent instruments from his own laboratory and borrowed from friends. Responsibility for the laboratory eventually passed to the Museum as a result of a recommendation of the Royal Commission on National Museums and Galleries of 1928–30.[95]

Harold Plenderleith, who was to succeed Scott as head of the Research Laboratory in 1938, was appointed in 1924 and describes in fascinating detail the primitive housing of the laboratory at 29 Russell Square (a building which backs on to the north-east corner of the Museum). Particularly impressive was:

> ... the gas meter – the largest of its kind I have ever seen! It stood six feet high and could easily have accommodated six grown men within its ample girth; from the top radiated heavy black tentacles in the form of gas pipes made of cast iron, actually three inches in diameter, serving an assorted mixture of ancient Bunsen burners as well as some furnace equipment of doubtful utility. This meter could well have supplied most of Bloomsbury with gas.
>
> The Museum... engineers had done their best for us, but unfortunately with inadequate guidance as to scientific requirements or any idea of the work that lay ahead, a stricture that applied pretty generally all round.[96]

This was hardly surprising as there had been little experience of the work of such a department at home or abroad. The Berlin Museums had had a laboratory since 1888 and its first director, Friedrich Rathgen, had produced in 1898 the first text-book on conservation, *Die Konservierung von Alterthumsfunden*, which, translated into English in 1905, was to be much consulted for many years.[97] Gustav Rosenberg had also pioneered conservation in the National Museum of Denmark. Only the first of these provided any sort of model for the British Museum, as it had published some of its methods. Scott and Plenderleith were in reality working from first principles, providing simple chemical analyses and technical descriptions of objects.

Having advised on the conservation of the material affected in the Holborn tunnel when it was returned after the war, the Laboratory continued to deal with some pretty problems, many of which were purely advisory, as when Arthur Lucas, Howard Carter's scientist, consulted them about the contents of Tutankhamun's tomb. Others were more directly related to the Museum's collections, as for example when it consolidated some of the material that had been imaginatively and cleverly conserved in the field by Leonard Woolley, at that time excavating in the royal cemetery at Ur (p.220). As they were short of staff they employed volunteers of some distinction to help in the work, among them W.F. Grimes (later head of the University of London's Institute of Archaeology), Margaret Binyon, one of the twin daughters of Laurence Binyon of the Department of Prints and Drawings, and Agatha Christie, novelist wife of Max Mallowan who was excavating for the Museum in Mesopotamia.

The head of the department had a difficult furrow to plough, as he had to depend on the goodwill of the individual keepers, satraps jealous of their control over their collections. Many thought that they and their technicians knew best and consulted the Laboratory only when it was absolutely necessary. The Elgin Marbles story (see p.242) might have been very different if Plenderleith had had supervisory control of their cleaning. Beyond the Museum the Laboratory had a good reputation – it was, it must be remembered, the only one in the country – and was soon undertaking work for outside bodies, being involved, for example, in the conservation of the relics of St Cuthbert for Durham Cathedral.[98] In the late 1930s the department came into its own as it became deeply involved in planning the packing and evacuation of the Museum's collections at the beginning of the Second World War.

Establishment and Pay

Throughout Kenyon's period as Director he was involved in ceaseless negotiations about pay and staff structure. In 1914 the Royal Commission on the Civil Service recommended that the pay of certain members of staff should be re-examined. This examination was interrupted by the war, but negotiations concerning the status of the staff were reopened with the Treasury in 1920. Agreement was reached in the following year.[99] The Treasury – almost uniquely – agreed that there were anomalies and proposed restructuring. They did, however, try to reduce staff; but in view of the imminent reorganization of the Department of British and Mediaeval Antiquities and Ethnography agreed to drop their proposals for a few years. Although the structure agreed in 1921 for the curatorial grades was reasonably satisfactory, that for the clerical grades was not and Kenyon set to work to renegotiate terms. He argued for a different structure for the support grades (whose structure had been tinkered with at the end of the war) and for a more formal central administration. Leave entitlement and working hours were also reviewed.[100] By 1928, when his negotiations with the Treasury and with the Museum's own staff were finally completed, the establishment consisted of the Director at £1,500 p.a., a Secretary at £850–1000 p.a. and an Assistant Secretary at £500–600 p.a., nine keepers at £1000 p.a., nine deputy keepers (formerly assistant keepers) at £900 p.a., thirty-four assistant keepers (Class 1) (formerly first-class assistants) at £475–800 p.a., nineteen assistant keepers (Class 2) (formerly second-class assistants) at £250–440 p.a., an accountant at £550–700 p.a., a staff officer at £400–500 p.a., seven clerks at £60–250 p.a., 166 assistants and attendants of various grades at various salaries between £70 and £400 p.a., sixty-one commissionaires at a weekly rate of 30s and sixty-seven labourers, window cleaners, etc., at 29s–34s. In 1932 the Civil Service Commission agreed that written examinations for the curatorial staff should cease and that they should be chosen by interview.

One of the by-products of the 1920/1 negotiations was that keepers now paid an annual rent of £100 for their official residence. For the time being the Director lived rent-free. The keepers were not enamoured of this proposal; servants were difficult to obtain and expensive, and the houses were poorly maintained and costly to run. What had been a pleasant perk became a burden; further, the Museum was greedy of office space and the residences could easily be converted for such purposes. Gradually, as the number of resident keepers diminished, keepers and deputy keepers were required to live on a weekly rota in a flat in one of the residences during the closed hours in order to help the night security staff to deal with emergencies.[101] Thus was the original collegial atmosphere of the Museum broken. There is still a duty officer in residence on a rota basis, now living in one of the perimeter properties.

Towards the end of the war unions began to appear in the Museum and were recognized by the government. As a consequence a consultative committee – the Whitley Council – was set up in the Museum, as in other government departments, where unions and officials discussed and often settled matters of mutual interest. From time to time industrial action was taken, but it was rarely serious. During the General Strike of 1926 no corporate action was taken by the unions – indeed forty members of staff volunteered for emergency work.[102]

In the period from 1914 to 1933 the Director and Trustees were much exercised with the organization of the members of staff responsible for the day-to-day security of the building and its collections. In 1914 this staff consisted of fifty-two commissionaires (drawn from the Corps of Commissionaires), thirty-six policemen and six firemen. After the war the Treasury was anxious to make savings and, after a few skirmishes, was able to reduce the police presence by appointing a number of police pensioners in their place. In 1934, however, a scheme was worked out which was satisfactory to both sides, and which in general terms (under different labels) survives today. Fifty-three warders, under a chief and his deputy, were responsible for general gallery security; a further twenty-seven men (there were no women uniformed staff at this time) worked on a shift basis as security staff round the clock. All were now recruited by the Museum and paid for out of the Museum's grant.[103]

Women had made their presence felt during the war, when the Trustees agreed to the temporary appointment of female reading-room attendants.[104] In 1921 it became theoretically possible for women to reach the curatorial grades, but the Trustees did not agree this until 1925.[105] The first woman to be appointed was Marjorie Hoyle, who in 1931 became an assistant keeper in the Department of Manuscripts; she retired in 1965. The first woman assistant keeper in an antiquities department was Elizabeth Senior, in the Department of Prints and Drawings, who had trained at the Courtauld Institute. She came to the Museum in 1934, appointed in the face of such strong male candidates as Alec Clifton Taylor and Neil MacLaren, who both went on to establish major reputations in the history of art.[106] Women had to resign on marriage until after the Second World War, and many potentially valuable members of staff were lost through this rule, including one of Kenyon's daughters, N.G.M. Kenyon, who was an assistant cataloguer in Printed Books, 1934–8.

Purchasing

Apart from the war years, the Museum had an annual ring-fenced grant for the purchase of objects which gradually rose from £22,000 at the beginning of the century to £25,000. With the occasional blip it stayed at this level, but rose as high as £32,500 immediately after the Royal Commission had reported (see below, p.218). The grant hovered at this level until the 1950s, but varied from time to time and in periods of economic crisis. It fell as low as £15,000 in 1932 and 1933 and disappeared entirely during the Second World War.[107] The library departments had the lion's share of the grant, and the Department of Printed Books retained its enhanced grant of £9,000-plus even when the financial crisis was at its worst. Although the Museum was still allowed to apply to the Treasury for large sums for important purchases, the need for outside funding to buy antiquities became paramount. Private benefactors, such as J. Pierpont Morgan and Sir Percival David, were cherished by the Director and the individual departments, but institutional donors (not so numerous then as now) picked up most of the shortfall. Chief among them were the National Art Collections Fund and the Pilgrim Trust.

The National Art Collections Fund was founded in 1903 by a group of men and women who wished to devote private money to the saving of art treasures – particularly pictures – for the nation.[108] The causes for its foundation were twofold: the growing challenge of purchases by American museums and the reduced purchase grants for the national museums. The founders persuaded Lord Balcarres (later Lord Crawford) to become chairman and were soon joined by a small semi-private society known as 'The Friends of the British Museum', founded on Franks's death by a group of his friends, led by Fortnum and Max Rosenheim. This society was devoted to carrying on Franks's work in giving material to the Museum. The two bodies joined together and formed two sub-committees, the first to consider purchases of paintings, the second all other objects. The few hundred members in 1903 have grown to many thousands today, with an annual income of about £4 million, heroically used on behalf of collections throughout the country. Although the acquisition of paintings, because of their high cost, seems to have dominated the Fund's agenda, this is not in fact the case; its generosity has been immeasurable – some 40,000 objects have come to the Museum with help from the Fund. Generally it has contributed part of the cost of an object, often as a pump-primer for raising other money – even from the government. It has also, particularly in its early years, acted as a conduit through which objects are given to institutions. Thus in 1904, of the seven objects or groups given in whole or in part by grants to the national museums, four were given by individuals to the Museum and £400 was given towards the purchase of a Greek bronze relief from Paramythia. An imaginative extension of the parameters of grants was the occasional donation towards excavations in the acquisition of new material. An early and striking example of this was the bronze head of Augustus, found in the excavations at Meroë in the Sudan, which the Sudan Excavation Committee obtained permission to sell to the Museum.[109]

The Pilgrim Trust was founded in 1930 with the gift of £2 million from Edward Harkness as a thank-offering to Britain for its part in the Great War. From time to time it gave money to assist major purchases, but it had many other calls on its purse and now rarely gives for such purposes, although it supports museums in other ways. These funds and others (City companies, for example), together with generous private donors, enabled the Museum to venture into the market despite its exiguous government purchase grant.

Royal Commission[110]

In July 1927, after a direct approach from the Trustees to the Prime Minister about the lack of money for building,[111] a Royal Commission, chaired by Lord D'Abernon, was appointed to examine the national museums and galleries. There was wide dissatisfaction on a number of fronts about the funding and conditions of the national museums and the Commission was given a very general brief. The commissioners were set a massive task –

they were charged to look into problems of space and costs and asked to consider whether admission charges would be of advantage in raising money towards running expenses. A major question concerned the governance of museums and whether they would be better placed under the control of a central authority. The perennial problem of space was again raised.

Most of the national museums and many public and private bodies gave either written or oral evidence. Kenyon was an impressive and well-prepared witness before the Commission, quoting chapter and verse of practically all parliamentary acts and procedures concerning the Museum.[112] The arcane Trustee structure was examined at length and the Commission stated that they did 'not think the reconstitution of the government of the British Museum would effect any useful purpose'. It did, however, recommend that a special standing committee and a separate and independent director should be appointed for the Natural History Museum (against slight resistance from Kenyon).[113] The question of charges was ignored after Kenyon had made an impassioned plea:

> In 1923 the Geddes Committee recommended the imposition of fees, and a clause authorising it was introduced, in spite of the strong reluctance of the Trustees, into a Bill of that year. This elicited vehement protests outside the Museum which took voice in Parliament and in the Press; and after the clause had passed (with amendments) through the Steering Committee by the smallest possible majority, it was withdrawn by the Government on Report. It was quite clear that public feeling was against the proposal.
>
> The question at issue is a very simple one. Is it desired to encourage the use of the museum, or is it not? There is not the smallest doubt that the imposition of fees discourages attendances... The question, therefore, simply is whether it is worth while to exclude the public (and especially, of course, the poorer members of the public) for the sake of the pecuniary return to be expected from fees....
>
> The Trustees would, therefore, regard the imposition of fees as a retrograde step, inconsistent with and harmful to the policy of the development of museums which they desire to encourage.

The Commission praised the Museum's pre-eminent position with regard to excavation abroad, but, on the advice of Sir Charles Peers, Chief Inspector of Ancient Monuments, encouraged it, together with the Society of Antiquaries, to take a major role in archaeological excavation in England.

They were worried about labelling and signage, and encouraged a re-examination of the method of lighting exhibits. They pointed to the value of liaison with the press and encouraged more attractive bookstalls and more energetic marketing of publications and souvenirs. They wanted evening opening, but this they did not get. Inspired by Kenyon, they concluded 'that to initiate a more general system of admission fees would be unjustifiable from any point of view'. They further recommended 'that as soon as possible steps should be taken to abolish fees in the case of those Institutions where they are at present charged'.

They recommended that the entrance to the King Edward VII Building should be opened to the public. Shy of recommending any building work, save in so far as fire risk was concerned, they did propose increased accommodation for the Department of Printed Books and for the Newspaper Library. They encouraged loans, including the possibility of loans overseas, against which the Trustees had firmly set their faces.[114] They fostered collaboration between the various national museums, particularly between the British Museum and the Victoria and Albert Museum in relation to ceramics and watercolours. Most importantly, they encouraged the national museums to co-operate and collaborate more closely with their regional counterparts. In order to facilitate this they proposed the establishment of a standing commission without executive power (a body which was duly formed and is now dimly discerned in its descendant, Resource, the strangely named government council for museums, libraries and archives).

One of the main representations of the Commission was that a museum of ethnography should be erected in Bloomsbury (Kenyon had suggested that it be on the Montague Street side of the Museum's site) on the basis of the country's 'unrivalled' collections. The Commission proposed folk museums for the constituent countries of the United Kingdom and for London (and if the latter was not forthcoming they suggested the creation of a department in the British Museum for this material). The eternal problem of a cast museum was merely noted, temporary housing being provided for casts from the Museum and the Victoria and Albert Museum at Bloomsbury. They also commended the generosity of Sir Joseph Duveen in giving galleries to the British Museum and the Tate Gallery.

Carchemish and Ur

The Museum's most lively and original work immediately before and after the war was in the Near East. Here, through its agents and with the help of some of its young members of staff, it was breaking entirely new ground. The ancient site of Jerablus (or Djerabis), on the right bank of the Euphrates some sixty-three miles north-east of Aleppo, had been known to the English since Henry Maundrell had visited it in 1699. But it was George Smith of the British Museum who first identified it as Carchemish, an important Hittite citadel, when he visited the ruins twice shortly before his death in 1876. Layard, by then British Minister at Constantinople, obtained a *firmân* to excavate there. Some preliminary work was undertaken on behalf of the Museum by the British Consul in Aleppo, Patrick Henderson, who sent stones and inscriptions to London which showed the site to be Hittite, but his work there lapsed in 1881.

In 1908 Budge proposed that the Museum should resume work at the site and, Maunde Thompson and the Trustees having been persuaded, David Hogarth of the Ashmolean Museum was sent out to investigate it and other neighbouring sites. Hogarth reported favourably and later in the year the Museum applied for permission to excavate. When it was granted Hogarth was able to excavate there in 1908 and 1910. As a result of local political troubles work was interrupted until 1911, when he returned with R. Campbell Thompson of the Museum as his assistant. At the last moment Hogarth included in the party a young man, T.E. Lawrence, as a supernumerary member of the team, financed by means of a junior post at Magdalen College, Oxford.[115] At the end of the season Thompson was nominated by Hogarth as director of the excavations, but in 1912, on his marriage, he turned the offer down and Leonard Woolley, a member of the Ashmolean's staff, was appointed to replace him.

Excavation continued up to the outbreak of war in 1914, often against a lurid political and military background, the detail of which is recounted largely in Woolley's hyperbole, but occasionally more factually (though no less excitingly) in his and Lawrence's unpublished letters home.[116] Indeed, only in these is it possible to retrieve some of the sense of the academic excitement of the dig and of the associated adventures.[117] The excavations were funded by a substantial gift of £15,000 from a businessman, Walter Morrison, who for many years remained anonymous; the income from this fund provided much of the cost of excavation at Carchemish and later at Ur and other sites in the region.[118] In 1920, Lawrence being engaged elsewhere, Woolley returned to the site, which was now astride the newly created and very sensitive Syrian/Turkish border. Woolley found it almost impossible to continue the work there, particularly after some newly found sculpture was smashed by a predatory Turkish army officer.[119]

In 1969, when the first two volumes of the excavation report were reprinted, the then Keeper of Western Asiatic Antiquities said, 'The publication of the important excavations at Carchemish has proved to be, as was expected, one of the chief landmarks in the history and archaeology of North Syria and Anatolia alike.'[120] The identification of the Hittites was the most important result of the excavations, which most significantly revealed Neo-Hittite monuments (1000–717 BC), particularly fortifications and a great staircase and gatehouse. Within the fortifications of the outer town were a number of private houses, which were carefully excavated and recorded.

The fact that excavations could not be resumed at Carchemish after the war caused the Museum to look elsewhere in its continuing work in the ancient Near East.[121] Excavations in 1919 and 1923–4 at Tell al Ubaid were directed first by H.R.H. Hall and then by Woolley. Here, a small Sumerian temple platform was excavated and copper furnishings of the temple – including life-sized lions and the lion-headed eagle Imdugud – were recovered. The finds were divided, in a system known as *partage*, between the local authorities of the British Protectorate (this *partage* controlled at that time by Gertrude Bell) and the Museum. The Museum turned to two sites, the ancient town of Eridu where, according to ancient tradition, Babylonian civilization began, and the much more famous site of Ur, the original home of the prophet Abraham. Thompson was initially put in charge of the excavations at both sites. On his return the project was handed over to another departmental assistant, the overworked L.W. King, who died following complications caused by his preparatory inoculations. In his place H.R.H. Hall went out to Ur, but was ultimately succeeded by Leonard Woolley, who was to be employed on a freelance basis by the Museum at Ur and elsewhere for many years, with joint sponsorship from the University of Pennsylvania Museum.

Through his excavation from 1922 to 1934 Woolley established a continuous sequence from waterlogged levels of the fifth millennium to the fourth century BC. For the first time large areas of a major Sumerian town were excavated, shedding new light on the civilization it represented.[122] Important in this context was his discovery of texts and sculpture, but the most spectacular results came from the royal cemetery. It produced unique, incomparable treasures of the period around 2500 BC, which enriched the Iraq Museum, the British Museum, the University of Pennsylvania Museum and Iraq itself. The Museum received as a result of these excavations some of its most important objects, the Standard of Ur, the 'Royal Game of Ur', the 'Ram caught in a thicket', two remarkable lyres and some splendid jewellery. Woolley was a great archaeologist of flair and imagination. Although he was less well versed in the textual, art-historical and historical disciplines than many of his colleagues, his energy was enormous. He popularized the site through clever journalism and in popular books and, from 1927 onwards, he published (through the Museum) the work at Ur with commendable speed.[123] Among his junior colleagues there was Max Mallowan, who was to dig on a number of sites in the region. He continued his digging career as assistant to Campbell Thompson at Nineveh, then struck out on his own at the prehistoric site of Arpachiyah. In the early 1930s there was a change in the Iraqi attitude to foreign expeditions, so Mallowan moved to Syria and excavated at Chagar Bazar (assisted by Richard Barnett of the Museum) and at Tell Brak in the upper Khabur basin. Many finds from these sites came to the Museum, of which he later became a Trustee.

Co-operation

Much of the Museum's work in the Middle East was now carried on in co-operation with the various schools and societies of archaeology which would cover the whole region. Typical of such co-operation was that with the British School of Archaeology in Iraq, founded in 1932 as a memorial to Gertrude Bell, which, from 1934, published an annual journal, *Iraq*. The Museum's commitment to this venture is demonstrated by the fact that two of the first three editors of the journal, Sidney Smith[124] and J.C. Gadd, were staff members, while the third, R. Campbell Thompson, had also once been on the strength. Mallowan's Arpachiyah site was one of the first to be excavated under the auspices of the Iraq school.[125] The days of the decaying and corrupt Ottoman Empire's *firmân* were now over. The Museum, both here and elsewhere in the region, now benefited in the *partage* of the finds from many excavated sites by agreement with the local archaeological services, like those pioneered by Gertrude Bell in the British Mandates of the region. The scale of the excavations which produced this material was enormous. Mallowan's Arpachiyah site, for example, was dug in six weeks, but involved 180 local workmen. Excavation may have produced vast quantities of material, but the recording process was often rudimentary.

By this time the illegal trade in antiquities had been much reduced. The period between 1880 and the end of the First World War had seen a vast growth in the buying and selling of antiquities in the Near East. Stimulated by the wholesale acquisition of material by Rassam (p.177) and by the vast sums Ernest de Sarzec (the French vice-consul in Baghdad) paid for the tablets from Telloh in 1877–8, the trade grew and enabled Budge and many others to purchase material on the Baghdad market. Lawrence and Woolley, for example, were thus following a customary pattern when they collected for both the British Museum and the Ashmolean Museum until 1914. The situation in Egypt was analogous. As a result associated finds were distributed, provenances lost, and sites ruined by illegal digging. The new generation of specialists in the region now co-operated with the local authorities and trained local archaeologists and inspectors of ancient monuments, to try to control the trade. They were not entirely successful, but ethics began to enter into the process of collecting and soon no self-respecting museum officer of any nation would encourage such pillage; an end which, to give him his due, even Budge had long recognized as desirable.[126] The schools and institutes of Britain and other western countries – particularly Germany and the United States – were influential in achieving this change. They were also influential in training local archaeologists. J. Garstang, for example, at once Director of the British School in Jerusalem (founded in 1919) and head of the Department of Antiquities in Palestine (from 1920), was particularly successful in this respect and in encouraging other foreign schools to do the same.

Budge's collecting proclivities in Egypt have been mentioned above. Not very keen on excavation, considering provenance of secondary importance and concentrating as much as possible on textual studies, he was happy that the excavated Egyptian material acquired by the Museum during his keepership was largely derived from the work of the Egypt Exploration Society (initially Fund).[127] Budge was a near-contemporary of the towering Egyptological figure Flinders Petrie, who was every bit as arrogant and hardworking.[128] Petrie was, however, a more original scholar than Budge and, between 1882 and 1903, changed the whole understanding of ancient Egypt and its outside influences through excavations sponsored by the Society. In this pioneering period Petrie emphasized the importance of careful observation and record-keeping during excavation, which he achieved by building up a close supervisory role over his workmen and rewarding them properly. He was, however, a man of his time and, usually assisted by a very small team, never achieved the detailed control of his workforce or of his sites that Pitt Rivers did in Britain. Nor, it must be said, did many of his successors in Egypt until well after the Second World War.

Petrie's ideas could not be avoided, both inside and outside the Museum. In retrospect some of them were wild and over-complicated. He introduced a new method for establishing a chronology in the uncharted Predynastic and Early Dynastic Periods (sequence dating – a floating chronological sequence without actual dates). While much celebrated by Egyptologists, the method is no more than a restatement of the principles of typology and was of little help in establishing or confirming problems of absolute chronology. One of his wilder ideas (and one that was not his alone) insisted that the accumulation of debris could be gauged against a specific time-scale. Some of his ideas, however, were of enormous value to the subject and could not be ignored. He stressed the value of cross-dating with other cultures outside Egypt, particularly with those of Palestine and Greece. He was a pioneer in scientific study of the materials used in antiquity.[129] He insisted on full and prompt publication of excavations. In 1903 he fell out with the Egypt Exploration Society and founded his own 'British School of Archaeology in Egypt', which was based not in Cairo but at University College London. So far as Egyptology was concerned Petrie was the most original and influential thinker of the first half of the twentieth century; it is a pity that he and Budge could not stand each other – for they were complementary in method and knowledge.

The initial chilly relations between the Museum and the Egypt Exploration Fund gradually grew more cordial and the Museum became the chief recipient of the official distribution of finds from its excavations. Thus material from many of Petrie's early excavations came to the Museum. After Petrie founded his own institution, however, he steered little its way, although the Museum occasionally bought important pieces from him.[130] It must be said, however, that he was generous in giving papyri to the Museum; particularly important were the Ramesseum papyri, although Sir Alan Gardiner deserves much of the credit as he persuaded Petrie to give them and paid for their conservation.[131] Much of the material excavated by Petrie, both in Egypt and – after 1926 – in Palestine, went to the museum he had founded at University College London.[132] Other material – often turned down by the Museum because of Budge's long-term feud with Petrie – went to regional museums throughout Britain as well as to foreign museums as far away as Tokyo which had given him financial support.[133]

The Museum, however, continued to benefit from the work of the Egypt Exploration Society (as it does today), particularly after 1903 when H.R.H. Hall became co-director of the Deir el-Bahari excavation with Edouard Naville (one of Petrie's many *bêtes noires*). Much fine material came from this site and continued to flow in from other sites over the years. After the war the German permit for excavations at Tell el-Amarna lapsed and the concession passed to the Society, where Woolley was one of the excavators. The division of excavated material from sites by the Egyptian authorities became more rigorous; although the division was still relatively generous, many fine pieces properly went to the Cairo Museum. As a result much more ordinary day-to-day material – type series of pottery for example – which had been neglected by the text-bound Budge now happily appeared in the Museum's collections for the first time, not as casual collectors' items, but properly documented and provenanced.

The Museum itself continued to build up its reputation for scholarship in Egyptian texts, and continued to acquire them. From time to time, as collectors and landowners turned out their attics, it would also purchase or be given finer material of the kind that it had been collecting since the days of Belzoni. Until very recently (see below, p.320), however, the Museum has generally excavated in Egypt only in co-operation with the Society. Two important exceptions were the digs at sites in Middle Egypt – at Deir Tasa, near Mostagedda, and at Matmar – financed by the excavator, Guy Brunton, which were carried out in the name of the Museum between 1928 and 1931. This produced important material from the early Predynastic period which added a completely fresh dimension to the collections, illustrating the newly labelled Badarian (late fifth millennium BC) and more shadowy Tasian cultures, which were at that time being identified by Brunton and Gertrude Caton-Thompson.[134] Members of the staff were, however, frequently lent to the Egypt Exploration Society for a season's work in Egypt, thus increasing their hands-on archaeological experience.[135]

After the death of Hall the Department of Egyptian and Assyrian Antiquities fell into the hands of Sidney Smith, who was appointed keeper in 1931. Deeply learned, but a rather uncomfortable colleague, he had spent 1929–31 in Iraq on secondment as Director of Antiquities and Director of the Iraq Museum; he wrote two major synthetic works and produced four of the volumes of Cappadocian tablets in the Museum's *Cuneiform texts* series. C.J. Gadd, a Sumerologist who had succeeded L.W. King in 1919, was now joined by two lively young men, Richard Barnett (son of the erstwhile Keeper of Oriental Printed Books and Manuscripts) and I.E.S. Edwards (son of a Persian specialist in the same department). Barnett was a classicist by training whose interests were archaeological; he tended to work on the geographical margins of the department's academic territory.[136] Edwards – 'a better talker than listener', in the words of Archbishop Coggan[137] – had studied oriental languages at Cambridge and worked on Arabic as a postgraduate student.[138] He replaced Stephen Glanville, who went to the Edwards Professorship of Egyptology at University College London and later to the chair at Cambridge.[139] Edwards's interests were more textual than archaeological; although he edited two volumes of hieratic texts for the Museum, he was better known for his popular books on the pyramids.

Splitting a Department – Ethnographical Problems[140]

When Hercules Read retired in 1921 the problem of his vast empire was tackled. His natural successor was O.M. Dalton, now renowned as a Byzantinist, who was duly appointed. But everybody recognized that the Department of British and Mediaeval Antiquities and Ethnography was too big and amorphous to continue as it was. Read had wanted it to be split into three, but economic considerations ruled this out. Unfortunately the next most senior member of staff was R.L. Hobson, the immensely distinguished specialist in European pottery and oriental ceramics. It would have been possible and logical to have passed him over and split the department into two by separating out the ethnographic section and creating a sub-department, or even a self-standing department. The senior ethnographer, T.A. Joyce, who had had a 'good war' in the Intelligence Department of the War Office where he had been awarded the OBE, could then have taken over, either as deputy keeper in charge, or as keeper. He was a respectable – even innovative – Americanist, and in his early days in the Museum had written two synthetic works on South and Central American archaeology, which were, in the words of one American archaeologist:

> The first of [their] kind to give an archaeologic-ethnohistoric story of the whole continent. Based wholly upon library and museum research, it is a remarkable and admirable summary of the state of archaeological knowledge for South America at the close of the Classificatory-Descriptive Period [i.e. 1840–1914].[141]

Despite the self-evident claims for a separate department of ethnography, two sections of the old department were now brigaded together under Hobson in an entirely irrational, if correctly named, new Department of Ceramics and Ethnography. Joyce now became his deputy and took charge of ethnography. To do him justice, Hobson hardly interfered in this side of the department, the offices of which were almost deliberately located at some distance from those of the ceramics section. But a monster had been created which was soon recognized as illogical and was to survive only until 1933.

Ethnography was still a new subject, gradually becoming academically embedded in the fast-developing discipline of social anthropology; it now achieved respectability under the influence of A.C. Haddon, part of whose seminal collections from the Torres Straits (which separate Australia and New Guinea) came to the Museum in the 1890s.[142] In 1900 Haddon was appointed lecturer in ethnology at Cambridge and became involved in the work of the university's ethnographical collections, of which he took charge in 1920. Both Cambridge and Oxford now had formal teaching in the subject. The British Museum, however, still took a leading role and, despite its subsidiary position in a large department, ethnography was now well established in the main structure.[143] Members of staff were deeply involved in the national development of professional anthropology. Read, for example, was closely involved in the affairs of the [Royal] Anthropological Institute, being twice elected President, and was for some time – like Franks before him and Joyce and Fagg after him – editor of the Institute's monthly journal, *Man*. A tremendous propagandist for the subject and highly knowledgeable about it, he had done no fieldwork, nor had his colleagues, and the Museum largely depended on purchase and gift to increase its collections. Dalton, who had travelled widely, was a reluctant ethnographer, but an energetic scholar. During his work on his seminal catalogue of recently acquired material from the Nigerian kingdom of Benin, he had, through the medium of a report published by the government in 1898, pointed to the vast amount of money being spent by the Germans, particularly in Africa and the Pacific, on building up the Berlin ethnographic collections, which were many times larger than those of the British Museum.[144] In those days of imperial rivalry this report was to be influential in attracting money and aid for ethnographical expeditions.

Such expeditions included those carried out by an impoverished Hungarian, Emil Torday, who had worked in an official and commercial capacity in the Belgian Congo and had amassed a considerable, but poorly documented, collection of material from Katanga.[145] In 1904, increasingly unhappy at the actions of the Belgian king against the indigenous population, he did not seek re-employment with government and (after a short period with the Compagnie du Kasai) became in effect a full-time ethnographer. In this he was encouraged and guided by Read and more particularly Joyce. From February 1905 Torday became an agent of the Museum, which gave him some financial support. Joyce and Read now guided his steps towards a full recording of the ethnographic material in the context of the social background from which it was acquired. With the help of others they produced for him a document based on that which Franks had helped draw up for the British Association for the Advancement of Science in 1874 (p.160). This *Questionnaire ethnographique*, published by the Institut de Sociologie in Brussels, was distributed to officials throughout the Congo, requesting them to respond to Torday in the Congo or to Read at the British Museum. The booklet, together with the responses, were used by both Torday and Joyce, alongside Torday's field notes, to produce a series of reports under their joint names on the work in the Congo. Torday also used, rather inexpertly, a camera and a phonograph to record people, material and music in the course of his travels (although on his last expedition he passed the responsibility for photography to W. Hilton-Simpson).

Torday's work, which extended until 1909, brought to the Museum one of the best-documented collections of Central African material in Europe and formed the basis of a series of publications up to the time of his death in 1931. His collections were to have far-reaching influence among ethnographers and artists. Interestingly, the Congo material was displayed together and not mingled typologically with material from the rest of sub-Saharan Africa. Many anthropologists since – not least the famed Bronislaw Malinowski, who had been working in the Trobriand Islands – were to assemble collections that would document the culture of a society or region for the British Museum. The Museum's role here, as elsewhere, was to be an 'archive' of comparative material from all over the world. But it was becoming more than that. Since the eighteenth century the ethnographic collections had been one of its most popular attractions. Through the period of Empire, people of all classes became familiar with exotic parts of the world, through family connections, illustrated newspapers, travellers' and missionaries' tales and such fiction as Rider Haggard's *King Solomon's Mines* and its many imitators, so there was a demand to see more of the material culture of the world. The Museum provided this, displayed alongside other material from antiquity. Thus Torday's material told not of noble savages, but of a sophisticated African nation, with a strong and identifiable culture of its own. Further, the quality of indigenous art, which was so accessible, began to be appreciated by western artists and connoisseurs.

The display of Torday's African material was a revelation to people like the art critic Roger Fry. One of those most affected by it was the sculptor Jacob Epstein, who, having lived in Paris for a few years, was conversant with the influence of native art on Gauguin and, later, Picasso. Epstein himself studied African, Indian and Polynesian art in the Museum and was to be strongly influenced by it, an influence which is to be seen in his major work *Maternity* (1910); later he began to collect ethnographic art himself, including Central African objects thought to have come from Torday.[146] One of Epstein's contemporaries and friends, Henri Gaudier-Brzeska, then living in London, was much influenced, for example, by the Easter Island figure Hoa Hakananai'a, from which he drew inspiration for his famous *Hieratic head of Ezra Pound*.[147] He was a leading member of the Vorticist group of artists who drew great inspiration from the Museum collections.[148] After the war Henry Moore was also to be much influenced by the African and Oceanic art in the Museum and later expanded his interest to Cycladic and Egyptian art. In his old age Moore was to write a book on the Museum's influence on his sculpture, which makes it clear that he spent many hours there in his early twenties and – like Epstein – did not neglect classical sculpture.[149] The Museum's long-nurtured tradition of encouraging artists to work in the galleries thus changed direction and paid off in a spectacular fashion and, in a real sense, justified the gradual accumulation of ethnographic art, which is now appreciated for its own sake, and not simply as 'primitive' art. Torday and Joyce contributed influentially to this new understanding.

The Museum, meanwhile, was acquiring other African collections, particularly from Kenya and Uganda. These had been formed by colonial officers such as (Sir) Claude Hollis and (Sir) Harry Johnson. Others were formed by private collectors, such as W.S. Routledge, whose Kikuyu material was collected specifically for the Museum. From Nigeria came major collections formed by P.A. Talbot and Mr and Mrs Temple. The Museum's African collections, which had been rather slim, were now growing to a respectable size. One of its great strengths had always been its Pacific material; this was greatly enhanced in 1911 by the acquisition, for a nominal sum, of the collections of the London Missionary Society which had previously been deposited on loan. This included much 'first contact' material collected by missionaries, for example, in Polynesia; its collections from Papua New Guinea were of enormous importance. Material was acquired from all over the world, from Paraguay, the Upper Amazon, British Guiana, the Nicobar Islands, Borneo, Sarawak, Ceylon and Malaya. After the war the trend continued. Accessions poured in until the lack of storage space initiated the possibility (never fulfilled) of building a wing for this material on the west side of Montague Street. Many of the Museum's great ethnographical collections were displayed in increasingly chaotic galleries and described in the frequently revised guidebooks.[150]

Although Joyce had wished to join Torday in Africa, official and family commitments made it impossible; it was not until after the war that he was able to mount his own expeditions – but this time to America, where his real interests lay. These expeditions, which took place between 1926 and 1931, were financed by the Museum's Roebling Fund and by private benefactions, particularly those of Harry G. Beasley. Joyce went to British Honduras to work on the Maya, a subject in which he was a specialist. At home his colleague, Hermann Braunholtz, an Africanist and the only other ethnographer in the department, kept his head down, having collaborated with Joyce in 1925 to write a greatly expanded *Handbook to the ethnographical collections of the British Museum*. In 1929, tacked on to his attendance at the British Association's South African meeting, Braunholtz was able to spend some five months collecting documented Stone Age material in that country.

The idea of marrying two such incompatible disciplines as ethnography and ceramics was bizarre. In the first quarter of the twentieth century anthropology and its attendant, ethnography, were caught up in an exciting and revolutionary dance, in which scholars as diverse as Sir James Frazer, J.L. Myres, A.C. Haddon, Malinowski, W.H.R. Rivers and E. Evans-Pritchard were participants. All these, save Frazer, had long-term experience in the field, which was the catalyst for the revolution. The Museum encouraged the work of the new university-educated anthropologists and much anthropological field-work was geared to produce documented collections for it. To combine this vibrant discipline with the stately connoisseurship of the study of ceramics in a new department was perverse, and it is little wonder that Joyce, who had worked well with Dalton from whom he was now separated, left for America as soon as he could.

Joyce was an agreeable man. His colleague Braunholtz wrote:

> By disposition he was sociable and cheerful. Indeed the spirited sounds of whistling and song, which might sometimes be heard emanating from his corner of the room, exasperated the austerer temper of at least one of his older colleagues [R.A. Smith], who regarded such unbridled manifestations of gaiety in the study as improper, if not positively demoralising... One of the writer's earliest impressions of him was as he lay stretched full length on the floor poring over the unwieldy volumes of Kingsborough's *Mexican Antiquities*, which were far too large to be opened on any of the desks or tables in the study.[151]

A man of many friends, he was also a productive scholar – a bibliography of his work suggests that he published at least 131 items.[152] He was also energetic in acquisition. His friendships brought to the Museum such splendid collections as that of H.G. Beasley, who had formed the privately owned Cranmore Museum. Beasley's widow gave this highly significant collection to the Museum in 1944. Consisting of material from Africa, Oceania and America, it was particularly rich in Polynesian material and Benin bronzes and considerably enhanced the existing collections.[153] In the same year the Museum purchased W.O. Oldman's important general collection of American and African material, which was strong in wooden and ivory carving of the native Americans and Inuit.[154]

It took twelve years to undo the mess caused by the creation of the Department of Ceramics and Ethnography. One maverick element, which did not improve the prospects for the department, was the appointment of William Winkworth. A classicist from Balliol College, Oxford, he had won an MC in the war and joined the new department as a specialist in Chinese ceramics in 1922. One of the new generation of aesthetes, he was a friend of Arthur Waley of the Department of Prints and Drawings, who was fast becoming a major figure in the understanding of oriental painting. He did not last long. 'The post', in the words of an obituarist, 'was seemingly ideal for one with such broad interests in the arts of the East and West, but Winkworth's irregular attendance at his desk must have made his resignation in 1926 not wholly unwelcome to his Keeper, R.L. Hobson'.[155] He kept in touch with the Museum through Waley, Soame Jenyns (one of his successors), William King and Roger Hinks of the Department of Greek and Roman Antiquities.

The idea of a 'department of ceramics' was foreign to the whole ethos of the Museum, which had for years eagerly embraced the universality of its approach to world cultures, even in the Department of Prints and Drawings. It was an idea based perhaps on the Department of Ceramics at the Victoria and Albert Museum, whence it now drew a new member of staff, the eccentric W.A.H. King, specialist in European porcelain and one of the brighter young things of the 1920s, who knew everybody from Augustus John to the Duke of Wellington, and joined in 1926.[156] In the short period during which this bastard department existed the most remarkable events on the ceramic side were the gift of a collection of German and other continental porcelain by one of the Trustees, Viscount Dillon, in memory of his son,[157] and the publication of Mr and Mrs Frank Lloyd's bequest of Worcester porcelain, which was acquired in 1922.[158]

In 1933 in another shuffle the Department of Ceramics and Ethnography was abolished and a Department of Oriental Antiquities and Ethnography was created, of which Hobson was to remain keeper for five years. Joyce was made Deputy Keeper of a self-standing Sub-department of Ethnography, to which had recently been recruited Adrian Digby, the first professionally trained anthropologist appointed to the Museum. Joyce was clearly already in poor health and retired early at the age of sixty in 1938, to be replaced by J.H. Braunholtz. The oriental section now consisted of Basil Gray (formerly of the Department of Prints and Drawings) and Soame Jenyns. Western ceramics were to remain in the department until the retirement of Hobson, when they would be returned to their original home in British and Mediaeval Antiquities, along with King, the other western pottery specialist. Lord Crawford, who was in the chair at the meeting when the new department was created, clearly saw this appalling mismatch as a stitch-up and pressed in vain for a separate ethnographic department.[159]

The Museum was clearly restrained by the Treasury at this period. This was the time when, infamously, twenty assistant cataloguers, of which the Department of Printed Books particularly had great need, were, at Treasury insistence, appointed on an unestablished basis without pension rights to do the work normally done by assistant keepers.[160] It would have been extremely difficult in the climate of the depression of the early 1930s to create a new department; but Joyce was certainly treated badly and there seems to have been some sort of active resistance to his appointment as keeper. In a letter from the Director, George Hill, to his successor Forsdyke appears a mysterious sentence which shows that, while Hill was in favour of a Department of Ethnography, he was not in favour of Joyce as keeper, a sentiment which presumably reflected the latter's ill health.[161] In the event the Department of Ethnography did not come into being until 1946, when Braunholtz was appointed keeper. At the same time a new Department of Oriental Antiquities was formed under the keepership of Gray.[162]

Collecting the Orient

The twentieth-century curators of the various oriental collections (other than those in the Department of Coins and Medals) until recently had a standpoint based chiefly in aesthetic connoisseurship. And the collections reflect this approach. Few of them had been trained in oriental language or culture; most came to the speciality after they had come to the

Museum. Basil Gray, later the first and most important Keeper of Oriental Antiquities, is typical.[163] He began his career by reading history and classics at Oxford, took part in the British-led excavation of the palace of the Byzantine emperors in Istanbul and joined the staff as a member of the Department of Printed Books in 1928. Two years later he found himself in the Sub-department of Oriental Prints and Drawings, learning his trade as an Islamicist under the eye of Laurence Binyon, one of whose daughters he was to marry. With Binyon, Gray worked on the major international exhibition of Persian art mounted at the Royal Academy in 1931. A puritanical autocrat, Gray was competent in many areas from China to Persia, but wrote only one major work, *Persian miniature painting* (1933; together with J.V.S. Wilkinson), although his other writings made a great impact. A first-rate administrator, he was Keeper of Oriental Antiquities from 1946 to 1969 and served the department well through his friendship with important collectors who gave generously to the Museum. The new specialist in oriental pottery was Soame Jenyns, who was appointed in 1931 and served two years in the Department of Ceramics and Ethnography before the new sub-department was created.

The orientalists were first and foremost collectors and they did very well for the Museum, although they may well have been rather less than happy in an institution where connoisseurship was not properly understood. There was indeed continuous pressure outside the Museum, reflected in the report of the Royal Commission, to combine the collections with those of the Victoria and Albert Museum and form a separate museum of Asiatic art.[164] Fortunately this never came to fruition, Lord Crawford putting the Museum's case forcibly in speaking against the project and against the feelings of some members of the departments concerned:

> Here we are deliberately going to separate the art of the continent from the ethnography of the continent, the fictile work of their beautiful hands from the whole history and evidence of their civilization. If you do that you must abandon all hope of attaining any unity in expressing the mind and the genius of the Asiatic peoples. If we now at this stage separate the art from the culture and religion and so on, we are going in the teeth of the whole tendence of modern scientific research, which is based on the unity of civilization.[165]

The Trustees (perhaps rather unwillingly) followed Crawford and Hill and not the aesthetes, led by Hobson, in the embryo department. Discussion of the project rumbled on as part of the Museum's perpetual bid for space, but foundered through lack of funds.

Perhaps the most important oriental collection to reach the British Museum was that retrieved from Central Asia by Sir Aurel Stein. Stein was a Hungarian who, having studied in Budapest, Tübingen, Vienna and Leipzig, came to England in 1884 to study in Oxford and London. In 1886 he worked on his own in the Museum and was much influenced by Sir Henry Rawlinson, through whom he obtained employment in India as Principal of the Oriental College at Lahore. In 1900, with the encouragement of the Viceroy, Lord Curzon, he started on the first of his expeditions to Central Asia; there he discovered an immense amount of material of Chinese, Indian and Hellenistic origin, which he brought home and despatched to the British Museum. The Museum first officially heard of his work in 1902, when it was agreed that E.J. Rapson should help him in sorting material 'from Chinese Turkestan, which has been deposited in the British Museum and portions of which would finally be presented to the Trustees'.[166] From then on the Museum supported his work financially, as did a number of other bodies, such as the Government of India and Harvard University.[167]

In 1904, having become a British citizen, Stein became Archaeological Surveyor of the North West Frontier Province and Baluchistan. In 1906 he rediscovered the 'Caves of the Thousand Buddhas' at Qianfodong, near Dunhuang. Here he found manuscripts in various languages, temple banners and paintings on silk which had been walled up in the eleventh century.[168] His third and longest journey was in 1913–16, when he ranged widely over the roof of Asia from Turfan to Persian Baluchistan. He spent years writing up his finds and then, in 1927–8, worked in north-west Iran, Waziristan, Baluchistan and Maran. Attempting to return to China in the early 1930s he was more or less expelled by the Nanking government; but, backed by the Museum and the Fogg Museum at Harvard, he returned to Persia and continued to work throughout the Middle East and the west of the sub-continent until his death in Kabul in 1943.[169] Much of the rich material he found in his travels was first examined in the British Museum and was then divided between a number of museums in England, France, the United States, India and Iran.

Such fieldwork was not followed up by the orientalists on the staff – indeed, before the Great War none of them had been to the Far East.[170] They collected in the market and through other collectors. The most important single item ever bought for the oriental collection was the 'Admonitions scroll', or as the text is properly titled, *Admonitions of the instructress to court ladies*. Purchased by Colvin and Binyon in 1903, the scroll is attributed to one of China's most famous early masters, Gu Kaizhi (c.344–406 AD), and is probably the oldest extant Chinese painting.[171] It was at one time in the imperial collection. Paintings and prints were much sought after by Binyon and prints particularly tumbled into the department: the Ernest Hart collection of Japanese prints in 1902, the major collection of Arthur Morrison in 1906, the Tuke collection in 1907, Sir Ernest Satow's collection and that of Sir Hickman Bateman. W.C. Alexander completed the departmental set of Hokusai's views of Fuji. By 1916 the collection was large enough to enable Binyon to publish a major catalogue of Chinese and Japanese woodcuts.[172] This encouraged other gifts of works on paper. In 1926, for example, one of the Trustees, Dr William Bateson, bequeathed a major collection of Chinese and Japanese paintings.[173]

R.L. Hobson, the ceramic specialist, led the field in collecting the applied arts of the orient. Through his connections with the collectors of the Oriental Ceramics Society, he accumulated many gifts to supplement the Franks collection. There were many consistent donors. In 1924 Oscar Raphael, for example, gave seventy-eight pieces of Kiang-su pottery.[174] More was to follow as major purchases, gifts and bequests. First came the vast collection formed by George Eumorfopoulos, for which Hill had to raise £100,000 in 1935. Soon after Hobson's retirement the Museum received the small, if choice, bequest of Ming pottery formed in Jingdezhen in south China by a young assistant keeper in the department, A.D. Brankston, who died in Hong Kong in 1941.[175] In 1941 Oscar Raphael, long a generous friend of and donor to the Museum, bequeathed his collection, which was particularly rich in Chinese funerary jades and Japanese woodcuts, to be shared with the Fitzwilliam Museum at Cambridge. Included within his collection were thirty-three Egyptian and Western Asiatic antiquities, including two important Luristan bronzes.[176]

The purchase of the Eumorfopoulos collection of oriental art was more complicated (in fund-raising terms) than almost anything else the Museum had acquired because of the looming purchase of the Codex Sinaiticus. George Eumorfopoulos, who had already given material to the Museum, including fifteen Chinese frescoes of fourteenth-century date, was a Liverpool merchant whose family had fled the Massacre of Chios at the beginning of the Greek War of Independence. He had been collecting for nearly forty years, spending between £5,000 and £10,000 a year on oriental antiquities.[177] The collection was (through the generosity of the vendor) offered to the Museum in 1934 at a price less than half its valuation – £100,000.[178] This was too much to find, so it co-operated with the Victoria and Albert Museum to purchase the collection on a three to two basis. Money from a fairly recent bequest to the two Museums by J.R. Vallentin started the fund rolling. The National Art Collections Fund and Sir Percival David each contributed £5,000, and the money slowly rolled in to complete the purchase of one of the Museum's greatest oriental acquisitions.[179] The collection comprised three sections – paintings, ceramics and objects of metal, glass, ivory, lacquer and jade. Between 1935 and 1938 it was moved into the Museum and transformed the collections of the new department.

Prints and Drawings

The non-oriental side of the Department of Prints and Drawings showed a remarkable continuity of taste and scholarship throughout the first half of the century. Its staff, until the appointment of Elizabeth Senior in 1934, were not trained as art historians – indeed, until the 1930s there was no formal art-historical training in England; they came from an Oxbridge background and, having read history or classics, slotted easily into a mould of scholarly connoisseurship. But it was a rigorous scholarship that was pursued, and, with few exceptions, the staff dedicated their lives to the Museum. Occasionally a member of staff would move on to another post, as did Karl Parker, who after five years left for Oxford and after the war became head of the Ashmolean Museum. He was replaced in 1933 by the florid figure of Edward Croft Murray, who made the Museum his career, but did it few good turns.

Throughout the first half of the twentieth century the department pursued a consistent and aggressive collecting policy. It was particularly fortunate in its keepers. Colvin, keeper until 1912, was, as has been shown, gregarious and on good terms with collectors, factors that brought to the Museum by bequest, purchase and gift major collections and individual items. Physically the largest collection he received was the bequest by the second Lord Cheylesmore of nearly 11,000 portrait mezzotints and portraits of Queen Victoria, which came in 1902 and was exhibited in 1905, accompanied by a sixty-three-page guide. Most important, however, was one of the last collections received during his keepership – the Salting Bequest. George Salting, born of Danish parents in Australia in 1835, was described by *The Times*, in its announcement of his death in 1909, as 'the greatest English art collector of his age, perhaps of any age'.[180] From the age of thirty he had an annual income of £30,000, which enabled him to become a full-time collector of art.[181] An exceedingly mean bachelor, he lived in a two-roomed flat above the Thatched House Club in St James's Street, and characteristically drove very hard bargains with dealers. His collection was extensive and broad-based. Ninety-three paintings were bequeathed to the National Gallery, while his oriental porcelain and Renaissance bronzes (more than 2,500 objects) went to the Victoria and Albert Museum on condition that they be displayed together. His prints and drawings were left to the Museum – any that were not needed were to go to the Victoria and Albert. The collection comprised 291 drawings, most importantly seventeen Rembrandts, eighteen Turners and thirty-three portraits by the Clouets and their school. Among the 141 prints were forty-nine Rembrandts and twenty-one Marcantonios. Shortly afterwards Colvin mounted an exhibition of the bequest and accompanied it with a catalogue.[182]

One of the failures of this period was the 'National Photographic Record and Survey'. Devised by an MP, Sir John Stone, it was intended to produce a complete photographic survey of the British Isles at the turn of the century. He himself gave the first 200 photographs, taken by himself, of the architecture and monuments of Westminster and of Members of Parliament. Other photographers' work was added until 1904, but the scheme was never a success; the Museum, however, retained until 2001 some 3,000 prints of high quality made for the project. (These, together with other photographs of artistic merit, have now been transferred to the Victoria and Albert Museum.) There was certainly a lack of expertise concerning photographic images in the Museum, but this was a missed opportunity, particularly as it holds vast photographic archives, mostly in the individual antiquities departments.[183]

Colvin was succeeded in 1912 by an even more remarkable keeper, Campbell Dodgson (pl. 14), who almost incidentally supervised the move of the Print Room from the White Wing to the King Edward VII Building, where for the first time the department had a dedicated exhibition gallery. Dodgson's 1948 bequest of his collection of contemporary and near-contemporary works on paper has already been mentioned (p.202). Remarkably, it was assembled not by a specialist on the modern period, but by an expert on the prints of the early German masters. It was the most important gift of prints received by the Museum in the twentieth century.[184] Frances Carey, emphasizing that the Museum's policy at the time precluded the purchase of contemporary artists' work, estimates its importance:

> [It] amounted to more than 5,000 items, almost all of them prints of the late nineteenth century onwards, with approximately 2,500 by British artists, another 1,500 by French artists and 1,000 by those of other nationalities including concentrations of work by German, Scandinavian and American artists. It has provided the point of departure for most aspects of the late twentieth-century acquisitions policy, yet in its totality represents a mode of collecting which has all but vanished from the post-Second World War art world.[185]

The images he collected for the Museum are stunning. As early as 1926 he gave Edward Hopper's iconic piece, *Night on the El Train*, but he also bequeathed works by artists as diverse as Muirhead Bone, Pissarro, Gauguin and Käthe Kollwitz.

The Trustees' decision not to buy contemporary art inspired Dodgson to give many modern prints during his lifetime, but in 1919 he also hijacked (or perhaps founded) the prints and drawings fund of the Contemporary Arts Society, money which was until 1945 administered by the Keeper of Prints and Drawings. The fund was a means by which the Museum could acquire a considerable amount of contemporary material from both Britain and abroad, although, in the words of a present member of staff, 'there was individually, institutionally and nationally a real failure of nerve when it came to embracing Cubism'.[186] Generally, however, the department's main interests lay elsewhere. Thus in 1925, for example, the Trustees (having turned down Dodgson's request to purchase the whole series) bought for £3,000 forty-one proofs of one of the most important groups of French eighteenth-century engravings from *Monument de costume* after Freudeberg and Moreau le Jeune. This was part of a deliberate policy by Dodgson to improve the much-neglected French eighteenth-century collections at a time when such items were both fashionable and expensive. In the same year they bought a self-portrait by Gustave Courbet, with the help of contributions from the National Art Collections Fund, Samuel Courtauld and others; they also acquired a large collection of Napoleonic material, some purchased from, and some given by, Lord Crawford. In the following year they purchased a study of Adam by Michelangelo for the Sistine Chapel.[187] As in other departments, gifts and purchases, large and small, accumulated.[188]

Dodgson was a hard act to follow and it must be acknowledged that his successor, A.M. Hind, who was appointed in 1933 (after a one-year interregnum, when the orientalist Laurence Binyon was keeper), did not live up to his predecessor. Hind – 'a kindly man with a prominent white moustache, and a slightly grand manner'[189] – loved to exert control; by means of a series of buttons and lights he summoned staff to his room with a minimum of trouble to himself and a deal of pain to his colleagues. He had a bad memory and worked basically from thousands of index-slips on his window-sill; nevertheless, this tool enabled him to complete his great seven-volume catalogue of early Italian engravings.[190] He managed to fall out quite seriously with the Trustees just before the Second World War, but despite this succeeded in continuing an eclectic acquisitions policy. To take but one example at random, he purchased 120 sporting prints and seventeen drawings from the Schwerdt collection.[191] It was during his keepership that the Museum started to subscribe to Walter Gernsheim's 'Corpus photographicum'. This extraordinary project, which continues to this day, set out to photograph Old Master drawings in public and private collections throughout the world. In Britain only two institutions subscribed and the other – the Victoria and Albert Museum – ceased its subscription in 1985. The Museum now has over 165,000 photographs, which are much consulted by students.

Until 1933 the Department of Prints and Drawings sheltered Binyon and Waley, the specialists in oriental prints and paintings. Waley retired in 1928, but Binyon stayed on for a further four years. Binyon was a totally nice man and it was universally felt within the Museum that he needed especial consideration.[192] Almost the same age as Dodgson, he was rewarded by being promoted to succeed him in 1932, although his tenure only lasted one year, after which the Department of Oriental Antiquities and Ethnography was created and the oriental works on paper were removed from the Department of Prints and Drawings.[193] After his retirement Waley, who wrote widely for commercial publishers, at last published for the Museum his great catalogue of the Central Asian paintings from Dunhuang collected by Sir Aurel Stein (see p.230).[194]

Coins and Medals

If one department kept its old traditions of scholarship untarnished, it was the Department of Coins and Medals. Staff came and went, catalogues were written and, through close attention to the trade and cultivation of collectors, acquisitions were made on a considerable scale. Nothing seemed to change. The curatorial staff, all considerable scholars, had few challengers (although there were active coin rooms at the Ashmolean Museum, staffed for the first time in the 1930s, at the Fitzwilliam Museum and at the Hunterian Museum in Glasgow). They ruled the roost in Britain and were widely respected abroad. Almost without exception they became Fellows of the British Academy. They were also active as officers (particularly as editors) or members of the Royal Numismatic Society, and sometimes, but rarely, of the rival British Numismatic Society, established in 1903 – largely by amateurs – to face up to 'the historical importance of the great coinage of Britain'.[195]

The first half of the twentieth century saw remarkable progress in the study of numismatics. The days of gentle antiquarianism passed peacefully away and a new critical professionalism, largely stimulated from the Museum, came to the fore. Barclay Head's *Historia Nummorum*, published in 1887 and subjected to a major revision in 1911, was a turning point in the study of classical numismatics and is still consulted today. Senior and innovative historians, such as the Anglo-Saxonist Sir Frank Stenton (himself a collector), began to apply the numismatic evidence to their studies. Stenton, in writing his volume of the Oxford History of England, had, together with other historians, the advantage of a synthetic work by the Museum's medievalist – Brooke's *English Coins*, which appeared in 1932 and supplemented the medieval catalogues.

When George Hill became Director in 1931, he was succeeded as keeper by John Allan. John Walker, who had studied Semitic languages at Glasgow and then worked in the Ministry of Education in Egypt, joined the staff. Walker was to revise and update the ten-volume catalogue of oriental coins and write catalogues on the Muhammadan coins.[196] Derek Allen, who became a specialist in Celtic coins, joined the department in 1935, Stanley Robinson becoming deputy keeper in 1935. Robinson, a Greek specialist, was rich – his family had made its money from developing the paper bag in England. He was a consistent donor to the Museum, as he was to the Ashmolean Museum (generosity recognized by a knighthood long after his retirement from the British Museum).[197] Although he helped Nubar Gulbenkian build up his collection of Greek coins, now housed in Lisbon, he carefully kept many of the most important coins in Britain by purchasing them himself and passing them on to London or Oxford. Of him C.M. Kraay, Keeper of the Heberden Coin Room in the Ashmolean Museum, wrote: 'This was not collecting in the normal sense nor from the normal motives. The object was to have readily available in this country, whether in London or Oxford, adequate material for teaching and research – and the more complete the material the better.'[198]

Robinson was a broader scholar than most of his immediate colleagues. He revolutionized the dating of the earliest coinages and worked fruitfully, for example, with Ashmole, shortly to become Keeper of Greek and Roman Antiquities, on stylistic problems in Greek art. In this he followed Hill, who had similar interests.

Robinson and his colleagues, as is revealed through their own purchases and gifts, were intent on increasing the holdings in a scholarly manner, by the acquisition of either individual coins or specialist collections. In the period covered by this chapter one of the most important acquisitions was the Lloyd Collection of coins of Western Greece, 1,687 pieces of splendid quality.[199] But there were many more – too numerous to mention. The

Mavrogordato Bequest of coins of Chios and Athens, the Cox gift of Scottish communion tokens, and the 950 medals related to the French Revolution presented by the family of Dr S. Fairbairn are but three acquisitions which significantly increased both the holdings and the understanding of a series. They were, however, but three of many collections of all countries and dates which made their way into the Museum at this period.

British and Mediaeval Antiquities

In the reorganization after the departure of Read the core of the old department remained under Dalton's keepership. It was still an anomalous and uncomfortable amalgamation of European prehistory, Romano-British and Anglo-Saxon antiquities, a wide sweep of medieval material and a major body of material of post-Renaissance date – but until 1933 deprived of European ceramics. In charge of the archaeology was Reginald Smith, who in 1928 humourlessly succeeded Dalton. In 1922 Thomas Downing Kendrick (a future Director) joined the Department.[200] Wounded in 1916 at the battle of Delville Wood so that he thereafter walked with a pronounced limp, he came from a relatively wealthy background and had studied natural science and anthropology at Oxford, beginning a BSc thesis on the megaliths of the Channel Islands. After a brief foray into the Neolithic[201] he turned his attention to the early medieval period, writing successful books on the Vikings and Anglo-Saxons, but never a Museum catalogue. He was a perfect foil to the gloomy Smith, who enlivened his more dismal moments by sorting offprints, a task that he also forced on his younger colleagues.[202] The medievalist Tonnochy, encouraged by the gentle Dalton, went his own very slow way, writing an occasional paper for *The antiquaries journal* and preparing his catalogue of seal-dies.

The medieval side of the department flourished in acquisitions of all periods. One important purchase, among many, was the collection of some 400 objects and 100 coins, largely of the Vendel and Viking period, collected from the Swedish island of Gotland by James Curle of Melrose between 1888 and 1902. It was bought in 1921 for £1,200 with the aid of a grant from the National Art Collections Fund.[203] Probably the largest collection of Swedish antiquities outside its country of origin, it was assembled with the active help of the Swedish State Antiquary, Oscar Montelius, with whom Curle was in constant correspondence. This collection, together with the Worsaae collection from Denmark, the Bähr collection from Lithuania and the Cocks collection of Norwegian antiquities, mostly from Gudbrandsdalen, acquired in 1891, and some eighty pieces from the collection of Sir John Evans, allows the British Museum to display a representative collection of Scandinavian prehistoric and Viking Age material.

In 1918 an enormous collection arrived which delighted Smith, but few others in the department, when W. Allen Sturge, a doctor from Icklingham in Suffolk, bequeathed to the Museum his vast collection of flint implements. He and his wife had spent much of their life field-walking in search of prehistoric antiquities. They had also bought flints from dealers, including a major collection of continental material. From England alone they had assembled more than 86,000 flint implements which, with the glass cases in which they were displayed, came to the Museum and were installed in a basement in the White Wing. Select catalogues of the two elements of the collection – British and continental – were written by Smith, assisted by a newly appointed assistant keeper, Christopher Hawkes, and an erstwhile Edinburgh solicitor, E.M.M. Alexander.[204]

Hawkes, an extrovert prehistorian, was appointed to curate the later prehistoric and Romano-British collections when Dalton retired in 1928 to seek a quieter life in a flat in Bath and later (one of his neighbours having purchased a gramophone) to an even quieter cottage in the Quantocks.[205] From his time at Winchester and Oxford Hawkes had been deeply engaged in archaeology with his contemporary Nowell Myres (later Bodley's Librarian at Oxford), excavating sites of various dates in Hampshire and elsewhere. He was opinionated, wilful and brilliant, verbose, charming and careless of timekeeping. He formed a close friendship with Kendrick, but fell out disastrously (see above, p.200) with Smith, who bullied him to a nervous breakdown. Alexander, delighting in the Sturge collection, dealt with the Stone Age and for a short time, during the Irish Troubles, E.C.R. Armstrong was seconded from the National Museum of Ireland, where he had been Keeper of Irish Antiquities.[206] Hawkes was involved with a group of young archaeologists whose revolutionary approach had its apotheosis in the conversion of the semi-moribund Prehistoric Society of East Anglia into a national body, the Prehistoric Society, which was to provide a forum for the publication of a new scientific non-antiquarian archaeology. Kendrick and Hawkes had earlier produced a book summarizing British archaeology for the reconstituted International Congress of Pre- and Protohistoric Sciences, held in London (with Hawkes as one of the joint secretaries and Smith as one of the vice-presidents) in 1932.[207] The congress provided an opportunity for the two younger men to meet their contemporaries from Europe and America, scholars who seldom failed to visit when they were in London, giving the department a firm footing in the international archaeological landscape.

Members of the department excavated either privately or for the Museum. Hawkes, taking his full leave, had three seasons at Colchester between 1930 and 1933, where, under the general direction of J.P. Bushe-Fox, Inspector of Ancient Monuments for England, he supervised the excavation of the Romano-British site at Sheppen Hill. He also excavated at a number of other sites both in France and Britain. Kendrick dug in a much more gentlemanly fashion in both England and Ireland (at Gallen Priory), but, more importantly, started a major photographic index of Anglo-Saxon sculpture, recruiting helpers from different parts of the country to gather material, among them the painter John Piper and his wife Myfanwy.

The department retained a major role in British archaeology. Smith, for example, was the Secretary of the Society of Antiquaries (he was succeeded by Kendrick), and Hawkes was Secretary of the Royal Archaeological Institute. But this pre-eminence was fast being eroded by the introduction of a full archaeological degree in prehistoric archaeology at Cambridge, which produced a new generation of young scholars, most importantly J.G.D. Clark (later a Trustee). Properly trained prehistorians were now available for appointment to the British Museum and elsewhere. Medieval archaeology was not, however, catered for in any meaningful way, so that when Reginald Smith retired, to be replaced by Kendrick in 1938, the vacancy as curator of the Anglo-Saxon and Migration Period collections was filled by an Oxford historian, Rupert Bruce-Mitford. The first trained prehistorian to be appointed was John Brailsford, in the reconstruction after the Second World War. The medieval side of the department was meanwhile strengthened by the temporary appointment of a German refugee, the art historian Ernst Kitzinger, who was to produce an influential book for the Museum, *Early medieval art*; this – revised – was still in print more than fifty years later.[208]

Sutton Hoo and Mildenhall

The Department of British and Mediaeval Antiquities was in a more fortunate position than most departments whose collections were based on archaeological material and whose activities were curtailed by new antiquities legislation and the growing ability of local archaeologists. Because of the national character of the department's collections, it and its successor departments have received, by acquisition and gift, some of the major English finds of the twentieth century. Regional claims, however, began to be appreciated by the Trustees and much material was steered to local museums.

The most important and exciting acquisition in the twentieth century was undoubtedly the material from the seventh-century royal Anglo-Saxon ship burial at Sutton Hoo, Suffolk, which was given to the Museum in 1939 by the landowner, Edith Pretty. The story of its discovery has often been told and Rupert Bruce-Mitford, who spent the major part of his Museum career working on it, has, with the help of many collaborators, published the find in a monumental catalogue.[209] The finds at present displayed in the Museum come from a major group of burials, in both flat graves and mounds. They were initially investigated in 1938 at Mrs Pretty's request by a freelance amateur archaeologist, Basil Brown, for the Ipswich Museum, who excavated three mounds containing cremation graves; these produced rich finds of Anglo-Saxon date (now in the Ipswich Museum), of which the most exotic was the portion of carved limestone plaque of Byzantine character. Returning to the site in 1939, Brown started to excavate a fourth mound, in the process revealing the first traces of a major ship (some 29 m in length), preserved as a sand-stain, with many of its rivets clearly visible. At this stage, after discussion with officials of the British Museum and the Inspectorate of Ancient Monuments, a Cambridge archaeologist, C.W. Phillips, was called in to direct the excavation. Together with a number of young professionals, he proceeded to uncover the most important treasure ever found in English soil (pl. 17).[210]

The ship had been used to provide a worthy burial place for a royal figure. It is dated by French coins to a period before 625 and may be the grave of either Raedwald or Sigeberht, kings of East Anglia. All traces of a body had disappeared, but the contents of the grave in the centre of the ship included material of gold, silver, iron, wood and even a single pot. The most imposing object is a gold buckle weighing nearly 420 gm, decorated with interlaced animals inlaid with niello. There were a number of weapons, including a mail shirt and a helmet, shield and sword. The gold hilt and belt mounts of the sword and two great gold shoulder-clasps were inlaid with beautifully cut garnets. Other finds included a large amount of eastern Mediterranean silver plate, two vast drinking-horns and six maplewood cups, all with gilt mounts, which would have furnished the royal table. Cooking gear, lamps, buckets, bronze bowls, a lyre, together with a monstrous whetstone topped with the figure of a stag, and an iron 'standard', completed the main equipment found in the grave.

A coroner's court determined that it was not Treasure Trove and its ownership, therefore, reverted to Mrs Pretty, who gave it to the Museum. By this time war had broken out; there was just time to photograph the objects before they were placed in safe storage for the duration. The Museum has returned to the site from time to time and, in a major archaeological campaign in the late 1980s and early 1990s, placed the burial in its context in the middle of a major cemetery in an Anglo-Saxon landscape. The conservation of the finds from this site provided some of the most interesting work carried out by the Museum and has particularly shown the value of reversible work, as some of the items – particularly the helmet and the lyre – were initially wrongly reconstructed and have had to be remounted. In tackling these problems the Laboratory and scientific conservation came of age.

The other great acquisition of the period – the precursor of a number of such treasures – came from Mildenhall, Suffolk. Found by two farm workers, it was originally retained by their employer and only revealed when a local doctor brought a number of objects to the Museum for identification in 1946.[211] It was seized by the police and declared Treasure Trove and the Museum acquired it, paying the finders a reduced award (£2,000 – a tenth of its value) following advice that it had been illegally concealed for some four years.[212]

The Mildenhall treasure consists of thirty-four pieces of silver tableware of the late Roman Empire, deposited at some time in the late fourth century.[213] Some of the pieces are highly decorated, particularly the largest dish (60.5 cm in diameter), which bears scenes in low relief. In the centre the sea-god Oceanus is depicted full-face, his beard of seaweed, dolphins in his hair, surrounded by mythical sea creatures. In the field that surrounds this figure are Bacchic scenes – Bacchus himself, Pan, Hercules, satyrs and maenads. Interestingly, three of the spoons are decorated with the Christian *chi-rho* symbol.

Parthenon Problems

The period after the retirement of Kenyon in 1931 was not a happy one.[214] Hill (pl. 28), the new Director, was sixty-two years old and, although Kenyon's first preference,[215] could only be considered a stop-gap appointment; indeed, he retired four years later, to be replaced by Forsdyke, who had been Keeper of Greek and Roman Antiquities for the same period.[216] Hill (p.202) was much respected, even loved, by the staff. He had been the voice of the keepers in all negotiations with Kenyon and the Trustees and had a wide range of contacts outside the Museum. He was, privately, a sad man, much affected by the death of his wife in 1924, but he rose above it and put on a brave face. He was genuinely reluctant to take on the Directorship, writing:

> I think I was regarded both by [Kenyon] and the Trustees as a *pisaller*. In fact Kenyon told me that I was not expected to hold the position for more than a few years until someone in the Department of Printed Books or Manuscripts might be ripe for it; and from a remark made by Archbishop Lang it was clear that he had been advised to the same effect. Kenyon was a librarian above all things, and although he made gallant attempts to cope with the archaeological side of the Museum's activities, he never had his heart in it, and could not reconcile himself to anyone but a Librarian being head of the Museum.[217]

Hill was an archaeologist at heart and the first keeper of an antiquities department since the eighteenth century to be appointed as head of the Museum.[218] It was ironical, therefore, that his greatest acquisition was the purchase from the Soviet government of the Codex Sinaiticus, an early manuscript of much of the Bible, for £100,000, of which some £40,000 was provided by the government, the rest being raised with great energy by Hill and Archbishop Lang by public subscription.[219] The purchase was completed in 1933 and almost immediately Hill had to face up to the purchase with the Victoria and Albert Museum of the gigantic Eumorfopoulos collection of oriental material (p. 230). Again Hill had to go begging for another £100,000 and strained every resource to raise it in a period of economic depression – including a (surely unique) loan from the Bank of England of £10,000 at 1 per cent.[220]

Given more time he could have been an exceptional director, as is shown by the manner in which he tidied up the administration of the law of Treasure Trove. But age was beginning to be a barrier and the rather unlikely figure of John Forsdyke was appointed to the post. Kenyon's suggestion to Hill that the next director should be a librarian was not implemented, partly perhaps because W.A. Marsden, Keeper of Printed Books, was too lightweight and Idris Bell, Keeper of Manuscripts, was too devoted to his very considerable scholarship. The main reason for the appointment seems, however, to have been Forsdyke's perceived ability to deal with a demanding benefactor, Lord Duveen.

Forsdyke was not an easy man, nor in general was he popular with the staff.[221] Modelling himself as Director perhaps on Kenyon, he lacked Kenyon's aggressive personality and thus appeared to be full of his own importance, a fact emphasized by his official portrait, painted by his friend Sir Gerald Kelly, which shows him in full civil service uniform, wearing the star of the Order of the Bath. He was, however, to prove his worth in the Second World War, when the Museum depended on his forward planning and, later, on his steadiness under bombardment. Unlike his predecessor he came from a lower-middle-class background, but had won a scholarship to Keble College, Oxford, where he studied classics. On the outbreak of the First World War he was commissioned into the Royal Field Artillery and served in France, Macedonia, Egypt and Palestine. He was not an innovative scholar, but his catalogue of the Museum's Aegean pottery is lucid and important. With his predecessor as keeper, H.B. Walters, he compiled three fascicles of *Corpus vasorum antiquorum.* In 1926–7 he was asked by Sir Arthur Evans to complete the excavation and publication of the Middle and Late Minoan cemetery at Mavrospelio, Crete, a task he fulfilled with despatch. He was seen as a safe pair of hands and was appointed with a purpose, to complete the negotiations for re-housing the Parthenon sculptures.

In 1909 a display of casts of classical sculpture (including the majority of what was once the Victoria and Albert Museum's collection of classical casts) had been opened in a temporary shed built to the west of the south range of galleries in the space now occupied by the New Wing. Arranged chronologically to demonstrate the development of sculpture from the pre-Hellenistic period to the late Roman Empire, a vast quantity of casts were squeezed into the available space and proved to be a little-used teaching resource, even for nearby University College London, which housed not only a department of classical archaeology, but also the Slade School of Art. In 1913 F.N. Pryce (who succeeded Forsdyke as keeper) published a guide to the casts. Although the magnificent collection was of great academic importance, it took up a great deal of space and purists felt that it was of little use to the general visitor to the Museum. In 1930, at the suggestion of H.B. Walters, the then keeper, who urgently needed to display the Cypriot sculpture, most of the classical casts were passed on long-term loan to University College London.[222] The moulds and many casts were, however, retained by the Museum and in 1934 two moulders, J. and A.G. Prescott, were transferred from the Victoria and Albert Museum to the British Museum and continued to produce casts on demand.[223]

The Parthenon sculptures were still in the room in which they had been installed in 1832.[224] Throughout most of the nineteenth century they had been subjected to re-arrangement as each generation of curators studied them and attempted to make their display fit their theories and the building. By 1910, the year in which the newly appointed keeper of the department, A.H. Smith, had published his magisterial series of studies of Greek sculpture, they were displayed together with casts of those which had never reached Bloomsbury.[225] This didactic display was not to last. Backed by a Royal Commission, a group of aesthetically inclined university-based classical heavyweights – John Beazley, Donald Robertson and Bernard Ashmole – intoned:

> The Parthenon Marbles, being the greatest body of original Greek sculpture in existence, and unique monuments of its first maturity, are primarily works of art. Their former decorative function as architectural ornaments, and their present educational use as illustrations of mythical and historical events in ancient Greece, are by comparison accidental and trivial interests, which can indeed be better served by casts.[226]

Although Smith, whose life's work had been devoted to reassembling all the wide-scattered fragments of the Parthenon in one splendid pictorial record, disagreed – and many may argue that he was right – he could not carry the day and the Museum had to accept the judgement of those who conceived themselves to be his betters.[227] There were cogent arguments on the other side. There is no doubt that the myriad additions and in-fillings of the display gave an untidy and even ugly impression. The sculptor Jacob Epstein had (in a slightly different context) well described the revolt of the aesthetes in a letter to *The Times* in 1921:

> All those who care for antique sculpture will view with astonishment and dismay the present policy followed by the British Museum authorities in restoring the marbles – that is working them up with new plaster noses etc. I have remarked with growing alarm marble after marble so treated during the last year. I felt the futility of protesting, and so held my peace but now the dreadful crime of 'restoring' the head of the Demeter of Cnidus has at last been committed, the atrocity calls for immediate protest. No doubt the museum authorities do not like the Greek marbles in their possession, but why they should translate the master-pieces into something more nearly approaching the Albert Moore ideal of a Greek passes my understanding....[228]

Epstein was in some measure right about the figure of Demeter – although he continued to build fantasies about its cleaning which are demonstrably false. The case of the Parthenon sculptures was, however, different in that many of the attached casts were taken from original fragments, now scattered in many places. Some casts had been taken before the sculptures had been further damaged by the elements. Thus casts did indeed complete the story, and by using them in this way misplaced pieces of sculpture had been restored to their rightful position, and misunderstood subjects had been reinterpreted. There was a perfectly logical argument in favour of leaving the plaster and the marble together. But the idea of 'art for art's sake' triumphed and those without a classical education were to lose out as all explanatory and contextual material was moved away from the sculptures. What followed was not perhaps consistent with the true ethos of the Museum, which had long prided itself on not making exclamatory judgements. As for the repairs and additions to other sculptures, these were generally removed when Ashmole himself became Keeper of Greek and Roman Antiquities at the end of the 1930s, an action in keeping with the sentiments expressed by Taylor Combe more than a hundred years earlier in condemning Thorvaldsen's restoration of the Ægina marbles (p.69).

The Trustees now addressed the task of housing the Parthenon sculptures in a fitting fashion. The display had by this time become cluttered with models, casts, photographs and odd bits of sculpture from other buildings and periods. Responding to the climate created by the Royal Commission, Sir Joseph (later Lord) Duveen, prince of picture dealers and a totally tricky customer, offered to finance a new gallery for the marbles, and put up £200,000. It was the first time that the Trustees had experienced a living benefactor, and they could not have had a more difficult one. From the beginning things went ill. The Trustees, who had very clear ideas of what they wanted, and who consulted widely on the subject,[229] at first assumed that Duveen would just give them the money and go away. In their normal manner they set up a special sub-committee and discussed a number of architectural schemes proposed by Sir Richard Allison. But Duveen was completely hands-on and determined to have an architect of his own choice. He produced the distinguished American architect J. Russell Pope, whose most enduring monument is the old wing of the National Gallery of Art in Washington. The problems now emerged (pl. 26). In the succinct words of Ian Jenkins:

> ... Pope seems to have begun by using the sculpture as an ornament to his own architectural design and not, as was required, subordinating the gallery to the needs of the sculpture. In particular he had placed the sculptures at inaccessible heights away from the immediate gaze of the spectator. Further, he proposed to treat the sculptures from the east pediment as though they comprised the entire composition without allowance for the great quantity of material lost from the centre.[230]

This had to be sorted out. Lord Crawford – who also suffered Duveen at the National Gallery (where they were co-trustees) – tried to do this, with little initial success:

> After a long talk about the new Elgin room he [Duveen] said in effect that if the wonderful scheme prepared by Russell Pope were modified, he would chuck the whole thing. I said I regretted that menaces should enter into the problem and left the room. He then telephoned Kenyon in a fright and annoyed as well, and K. pacified him, or at least hopes he did so. Duveen's ignorance is tiresome, but his obstinacy and his impotence to understand an argument, are really galling.[231]

In May 1931 there was another showdown with both Pope and Duveen, whose ignorance Crawford considered 'so dense as to make argument unserviceable'. Eventually the message started to get through. On the day after the meeting, Crawford records that Duveen was 'in a much chastened mood. I think D'Abernon has given him a talking to; Pope also less inclined to pontificate. Anyhow the main principles of the Trustees' contentions were accepted and Pope is to try again...'.[232] The main burden of the continuous design and redesign was carried by Kenyon and later Hill and Forsdyke, as Keeper of Greek and Roman Antiquities. So central to the Trustees' thinking had the problems with this benefactor become that Forsdyke, on Hill's departure, was perceived as the only person who could manage the maverick Duveen; he was consequently promoted to the Directorship and seems to have established a reasonable working relationship with the obsessive donor. As late as 1937, however, he was still writing in tough terms to Pope on behalf of the Trustees:

> You may be inclined to think that the trustees are preoccupied with the free and unembarrassed presentation of the sculpture, but this charge is laid upon them by their Trust... In case of an elaborate setting they not only foresee but would have to agree with the universal objection that the sculpture of the Parthenon is being used to decorate the British Museum, and this is a position in which they cannot allow themselves to be placed.[233]

Pope passed the letter to Duveen and the matter was settled by a telephone conversation with the donor, who was in New York.[234] By now Duveen was dying of cancer, although he bravely hid it for as long as he could.[235] After some problems with a tenant in the Bedford Square property which was to be impinged upon by the building, work started in 1936 on the great new gallery, with its *gris d'Alésie* marble walls and floor of black marble from Trieste. It was finished in 1939 (pl. 27). Although the first panels of sculpture were put in place, the outbreak of war, the evacuation of the marbles and a direct hit by a bomb ensured that the gallery was not to be occupied for another quarter of a century.

Associated with the building of the new gallery came the problem of the cleaning of the Marbles, which developed into a scandal. This was a period when the cleaning of paintings and antiquities was highly fashionable – and highly controversial. Kenneth Clark at the National Gallery in London, for example, was continually in trouble as he cleaned the pictures there.[236] Duveen, a dealer, was an enthusiastic 'cleaner'. Lord Crawford, one of those who disapproved of the practice, had in 1931 noted Duveen's predilection, even with regard to the marbles:

> Duveen lectured and harangued us, and talked the most hopeless nonsense about cleaning old works of art. I suppose he has destroyed more old masters by overcleaning than anybody else in the world, and now he told us that all old marbles should be thoroughly cleaned – so thoroughly that he would dip them into acid. Fancy – we listened patiently to these boastful follies....[237]

The facts of the case are easily stated.[238] In 1932 the Laboratory had recommended that the Marbles be cleaned with a neutral solution of soft medicinal soap and water, a process which proceeded through 1932 and 1933. In 1937, however, some of the masons, led by A.S. Holcombe, foreman mason in the Department of Greek and Roman Antiquities, apparently (but not certainly) encouraged by Duveen, started to remove some of the secondary encrustation of the surface of the Parthenon sculptures with copper chisels and carborundum. The surface of those sculptures treated in this fashion was considered to have been damaged. When this was drawn to the attention of the Trustees an internal enquiry was held, as a result of which Holcombe, the keeper (F.N. Pryce, who was on sick leave for a long period in early 1938), and Roger Hinks, the assistant keeper officially in charge, were in effect sacked. Pryce was allowed to resign on medical grounds and Hinks was allowed to remain in post with a severe reprimand and the loss of ten years' seniority and consequent loss of pay. His position had clearly become intolerable and he resigned early in 1939.[239] Forsdyke and Lord Macmillan (chairman of the board of enquiry), against the advice of many, attempted to play down the affair and merely issued a statement to *The Times*,[240] which left them open to charges of conniving in a cover-up. People were gunning for Forsdyke, but he survived, partly due to adroit answers to questions in Parliament.

Nobody had behaved well. The press was handled particularly badly by Forsdyke, who deliberately understated the seriousness with which the Museum viewed the affair. One wonders why the Laboratory was not involved in supervising the cleaning, until one remembers how jealous the departments were of their independence; it was many years before this element of curatorial satrapy was tackled by Sir John Pope-Hennessy. Minor damage was done to the Marbles, but, if the matter had been handled with more openness at the time, and the damage (which has since been judged by experts to be not all that serious) demonstrated to press and public, the matter would have died down permanently. It would not have kept resurfacing – amid claim and counter-claim – for sixty years after the events. These ill-managed events are still used in polemic against the Museum. John Goldsmith, in editing the diaries of the unfortunate Roger Hinks, however, puts the matter in perspective:

> The final irony of the 'Elgin Marbles scandal' is that the whole thing was, in any case, a monumental fuss about nothing. Majority opinion is that the cleaning of the dirt of ages from the sculptures vastly improved them, and has indeed preserved them. Miss Melina Mercouri, the zealous Greek Minister of Culture, who has demanded the return of the sculptures to Greece, and who would have every motive for criticizing British stewardship, has publicly acknowledged 'the excellent care given to the Marbles by the British Museum'.[241]

The Department of Greek and Roman Antiquities had lost two curatorial staff in the course of the 1930s and, with the departure of Pryce and Hinks, was now reduced to one, Martin Robertson, a specialist in Greek vases who had joined the Museum late in 1936. The Trustees quickly found a new keeper. They turned to a popular figure, a friend of Forsdyke and acceptable to all, Bernard Ashmole, a specialist in sculpture, who had been Director of the British School at Rome and was now Yates Professor of Classical Archaeology at University College London.[242] Appointed in an honorary capacity in January 1939, he was immediately able to appoint, by transfer from the Victoria and Albert Museum, Denys Haynes, a specialist in bronzes.[243] Ashmole, a rich man, was apparently surprised to find that the Museum post was to be paid and was thus, by agreement, able to continue as professor at University College for two and a half days a week during term-time.[244]

Ashmole was specifically appointed to deal with the redisplay of the Parthenon Marbles in the now completed Duveen Gallery, but, although he started on the task, gathering war clouds turned his – and everyone else's – attention to harsher realities. His secondary task of dealing with the press concerning the cleaning scandal faded into insignificance.

Scholarship

The first half of the twentieth century seems in retrospect a halcyon period for scholarship in the Museum. Although the academic staff had little technical back-up, catalogues – long the building bricks of the study of material culture and texts – were produced at a substantial rate. Further, in 1926 Kenyon initiated *The British Museum quarterly*, a publication at once scholarly in content and gossipy enough to be a form of house journal. Here acquisitions were recorded and new information about old material was published; it also listed the names and qualifications of all new academic recruits. It even chronicled briefly exceptional periods of special leave and excavation. BMQ, as it was referred to, was widely distributed by exchange and sale and added greatly to the profile of the Museum and of its younger staff members, who through its pages were afforded an opportunity to experiment in publication.

The Museum's scholarly reputation up to this point was firmly grounded in its great series of catalogues, many of which have been mentioned in this chapter. Each assistant keeper in the antiquities departments was assigned a catalogue. The volume of production was enormous. In the Department of Egyptian and Assyrian Antiquities, for example, the main publications were texts. The series of cuneiform texts (initiated by Rawlinson in 1851) was continued and twelve volumes were produced between 1900 and the Second World War. These were supplemented by excavation reports on such sites as Carchemish and Ur, and by studies of particular monuments and texts – the legends of the Deluge and Creation were revisited. The series of coin catalogues ground on, rarely a year passing without the appearance of a new volume, and Hill produced two medal catalogues.

The Department of Prints and Drawings was breaking new ground. In general the mainline catalogues produced in this department in the nineteenth century were not well researched, while catalogues on bookplates, fans or trade-cards were little more than useful hand-lists. The reign of Colvin changed all that. The first serious catalogue published by the Department of Prints and Drawings was Dodgson's catalogue of the early German woodcuts, which appeared as two volumes in 1903 and 1911.[245] These have been described by the present keeper of the department as 'among the first works of British art-historical scholarship that matched up to German standards, and were immediately recognised as standard works in Germany itself'. Dodgson's first volume was followed by Hind's catalogue of early Italian engravings, which was published in 1910.[246] This was the foundation stone of his life's work, *Early Italian engraving*, published in seven volumes between 1938 and 1948. Hind also wrote a major synthetic work, *A short history of engraving and etching*, which, published in 1908, became an indispensable handbook for all interested in the subject – it is still in print. He also wrote four volumes of the catalogue of the Dutch School of drawings.

Throughout the first half of the century the department continued to publish its series of catalogues. But perhaps most important was Popham's *A handbook of drawings and watercolours in the British Museum*. Published in 1939, it is a fundamental and critical evaluation of strengths and weaknesses of the department's collection. It has been outdated only by later accessions. Further, the exhibitions mounted by the department fulfilled an important scholarly and public role through a most varied diet, from Girtin to Blake, from

Tiepolo to Rembrandt, as well as exhibitions of woodcuts, etchings, drawings and water-colours of all periods.[247] Summary catalogues sometimes accompanied the exhibitions. New acquisitions were put on display as quickly as possible, and there was usually a display of Turner's watercolours and of the techniques of print production.

In the Department of Greek and Roman Antiquities and the various offspring of the Department of British and Mediaeval Antiquities and Ethnography, the production of cata-logues slowed down in the 1930s and ground to a complete, if temporary, halt in the 1940s. This was partly due to the gradual realization that archaeology was not completely bounded by the material in the British Museum and a few other major collections. Kendrick, Hawkes, Hinks and their contemporaries now published commercially syn-thetic books of some importance. Their more detailed work was published in the profes-sional journals. Only the less adventurous members of the departments, such as Tonnochy or Jenyns, plugged away at the traditional catalogues – and even the apparently laid-back Jenyns wrote works of critical synthesis after the war.

Academic Specialisms

Catalogues certainly lost momentum in parts of the Museum, in some measure because the academic world was changing and demanded more from the institution. In the early years of the century the civic universities – and particularly, from the Museum's point of view, Liverpool – were growing stronger, challenging the traditionalists of Oxford and Cambridge and even the more maverick University of London. As a result, new or neglected subjects gained respectability. Prehistoric archaeology, anthropology and art history, for example, began to be taught as undergraduate disciplines, while Near Eastern and classical archaeology were achieving a much higher profile. At Liverpool a department of archaeology was founded in 1904 with funds provided by Sir John Brummer and John Rankine. Among its early teachers were the Professor of Classics, J.L. Myres, and the Egyp-tologist John Garstang. Cambridge was the first university to teach prehistoric archaeol-ogy at undergraduate level, with Miles Burkitt, a Palaeolithic archaeologist who had learnt his trade in Paris under the Abbé Breuil, as lecturer. Introduced in 1921, it was usually taught alongside anthropology or Germanic and Celtic languages. The part-time Disney chair of archaeology had gradually been transmogrified into a full-time post and was held after 1927 by Sir Ellis Minns, author of a standard work on Russian archaeology.[248]

At Oxford anthropology, but not prehistoric archaeology, had been taught as a post-graduate diploma since 1907, under R.R. Marett.[249] As, however, it was based at the Pitt Rivers Museum it naturally had a strong ethnographical and prehistoric element (members of the Museum staff, including, for example, Christopher Hawkes, were exam-iners in the subject in the 1930s).[250] This is not to say that archaeology was totally neglected there.[251] Classical archaeology was taught as a matter of course and became one of the great ornaments of the University.[252] The second professor of the subject, Percy Gardner, who was appointed in 1886, had been an assistant in the Department of Coins and Medals since 1871 and later (in plurality) Disney Professor at Cambridge.[253] Gardner was tough and knew his way round the power bases of the university; he struggled hard alongside Arthur Evans to get classical archaeology accepted as an examination subject and also curated the university's collection of classical sculpture and casts.[254] In 1907, the year in which a diploma in classical archaeology was introduced, the teaching of archaeology was much strengthened by the appointment of Francis Haverfield, the leading Romano-British specialist of his generation, to the Camden Chair of Ancient History, thus opening the doors to northern European archaeology in the university. In 1910 John Myres, much interested in both archaeology and anthropology, further strengthened the Oxford school when he came from Liverpool to the Wykeham Chair of Greek History, where he taught a course entitled 'Homeric Archaeology'. Classical archaeology received a further boost in 1925 when John Beazley suceeded Gardner and for thirty years made Oxford the world centre for the study of Greek art based on minute study of Greek vases – a discipline which was greatly to influence the Museum.

In Scotland a chair in prehistoric European archaeology was founded in Edinburgh in 1927 through the bequest of the fifth Lord Abercromby, himself a distinguished amateur prehistorian.[255] One of the most influential prehistorians of his day, Gordon Childe, was the first to hold the post and taught an undergraduate course to a handful of students.[256] Elsewhere the PhD had begun to appear and archaeologists started to look for postgraduate qualifications.

It was for postgraduate teaching at both diploma and higher degree level that R.E.M. and Tessa Wheeler had founded the Institute of Archaeology in London University in 1932, with the enthusiastic support of the British Museum.[257] Here a new generation of archaeologists was to learn clean and precise excavation techniques refined down from the Pitt Rivers model, but not yet embracing the ideas of area excavation being developed in Holland and North Germany. Oxford had no undergraduate teaching in prehistoric archaeology or anthropology (although a small amount was taught for the mainstream classical degree) – a proposal that it should be taught at undergraduate level was shot down because it was seen as a dangerous competitor to classics.[258] Postgraduate degrees were available at Oxford, as at a number of other universities, in classical archaeology and anthropology.

After the First World War art history – which had its true home in Germany and Austria – became academically respectable in Britain, as professorships were established at Edinburgh and Birmingham. A full degree in the history of art was instituted in the University of London with the foundation in 1932 by Samuel Courtauld of the Courtauld Institute of Art – the first such degree to be taught in England – which combined English and continental traditions of scholarship. Knowledge of continental scholarship in the field was also influenced by a number of German and Austrian art historians who, refugees from Hitler, came to England in the 1930s and ultimately gained teaching posts. Most influential in this context was the Warburg Institute, a research institute of the University of Hamburg founded by Aby Warburg, which took refuge in London in 1933 with its staff and fabulous library of continental literature built around a central theme of the survival of the classical tradition into the Renaissance. It became an institute of the university in 1944. In general, however, the staff of the Department of Prints and Drawings held themselves aloof from the new institutes (although one of their number, Elizabeth Senior, had been a student at the Courtauld). More interest in the new art-historical institutes in pre-war days came rather from people like Kendrick, who in compiling his index of Anglo-Saxon sculpture (p.236) worked with both institutes.

The young scholars in the Museum were carried along on the wave which had affected the universities. As always the vast scope of the Museum's interests and collections saved it from becoming too narrow in its academic approach. There was much inter-departmental co-operation; it is alleged, for example, that one of Kendrick's books on Anglo-Saxon art was vastly improved by his daily discussions with the great manuscript scholar Francis Wormald, as they passed each other on the way to the lavatory used by the two departments. Roger Hinks of the Department of Greek and Roman Antiquities wrote the first book in English on Carolingian art, a subject that was really the preserve of the Department of British and Mediaeval Antiquities. Members of this latter department and of the Department of Prints and Drawings also wrote synthetic works. Publication of its excavations both in Britain and abroad kept the Museum in the mainstream of international archaeology, a position based on experience steeped in first-hand knowledge of texts and material.

While the connoisseurship of the Department of Prints and Drawings was founded on deep scholarship, that of its oriental sub-department, separated from its earthy roots in ethnography, while still scholarly was more biased towards the collector, less to scholarly publication. In no other department did the ethos so closely resemble that of the Victoria and Albert Museum, with its inward-looking sensibility and its cultivation of the collector of art.[259] The same was true of the orientalists, too many of whom were collectors.[260]

The Museum was, in the small world of early twentieth-century scholarship, an important academic influence. Its scholars provided expertise in little-practised – but growing – areas of knowledge which now began to appear in the universities. The Museum controlled much academic raw material and was proud to make it available to all, eschewing attempts to establish a *Prioritätsrecht*. Its scholarly status is measured to some extent in the *Proceedings of the British Academy*, where year-on-year the obituaries of fellows contained the name of at least one ex-member of staff. Its reputation abroad was high, and in the print rooms and museums of Europe particularly its staff were welcomed and their opinion eagerly sought. With the expansion of higher education in the late twentieth century, its influence has been somewhat diluted. Perhaps never again will it achieve the pre-eminent position it held in the 1920s and 1930s; but its reputation for research still rides high.

The Museum, because it made its collections so easily available, became a magnet for foreign scholars as travel became more comfortable and easier. Although the universities received their fair share of foreign visitors, the position of the Museum in the capital, together with its long history of co-operation with foreign colleagues, enabled it for a short time to retain its leading role. Foreign scholars were welcomed and given hospitality, which was returned when members of staff travelled abroad. Many long-term academic friendships were cemented over lunch in the Holborn Restaurant. Staff working in the Mediterranean and Near Eastern countries had ample opportunity, through the medium of British schools of archaeology for example, to keep contact with their foreign contemporaries. Contacts with scholars in Europe had long provided an edge to the Museum's academic achievement; now the Americans began to appear in the Museum in order to study its holdings. At the same time staff began to travel in the United States to study in its rapidly expanding museums and libraries and to lecture at conferences and meetings; but sea-crossings took time and few members of staff could expect to make intercontinental official journeys in the pre-war period.[261] International conferences were rare, so that, when they were held, the contacts were more immediate and important than they are today when hardly a weekend passes without an international academic seminar. Contacts made at such gatherings first alerted the outside world to the political problems of Jewish scholars in Germany and led to offers of employment for refugees from Nazi tyranny.[262] The influx of art historians has been specifically mentioned, but similar stories could be told in many academic fields as the Museum staff helped the refugees to find employment in Britain or America. The presence of such people leavened the Museum's scholarship considerably.

Tinkering with Mezzanines

Much of the energy of the Trustees in the inter-war years was taken up with problems of space, the Duveen Gallery being the main product of their deliberations. The chronic shortage of space, however, particularly in the library departments, continued to be more than an irritant. Whatever the problems encountered in the construction of the Duveen Gallery, they were as nothing compared to a radical (and almost certainly impracticable) scheme proposed by Sir Richard Allison, Chief Architect of the Office of Works, which would have involved the reconstruction of most of the west side of the Museum.[263] The Trustees realized that this was a fantasy and proceeded more cautiously. With the help of the Royal Commission, a plea to move all the newspaper service to Colindale succeeded and the money was voted in 1928/9; the building was completed in 1932 and space was freed up in Bloomsbury.[264] Attempts to add a storey to each of the iron bookstacks surrounding the Reading Room in quadrants failed when (after one had been built) it was discovered that they could not carry the weight. In the light of the Royal Commission's recommendations it was decided to replace the quadrants, and indeed two of them were replaced before a bomb in 1941 demolished a third one. Again, following the recommendations of the Royal Commission, there was a rash of construction of mezzanine floors in the old North Wing for library purposes, with a heavily glazed wall to give light. The east and west staircases were rebuilt and provided with metal-framed windows. An extra floor was added in 1936–8 above the North Library.[265] This provided desperately needed storage and office space for the Department of Egyptian and Assyrian Antiquities. The roof of the Manuscripts Saloon was strengthened with heavy – and ugly – beams to take the weight of oriental sculpture in the room above. A temporary building was provided to the west of the boardroom for the display of casts.

But, as the Royal Commission had recognized, these were palliative measures. The government was tinkering with a major problem. The Museum really needed something much more radical; pivotal was the completion of the Burnet scheme, particularly on the Montague Street side, where it was planned to house the Department of Ethnography.[266] It was in the light of the shortage of space that the Commission had proposed the establishment of an oriental museum in conjunction with the Victoria and Albert Museum, a proposal that was considered and carefully kicked into touch by the Trustees (see above, p.229). The ground was being prepared for a solution to these problems when war broke out.

War[267]

The Museum was strangely well prepared for war. In large measure this preparedness was due to Forsdyke. Since 1933, only a few months after the Nazis came to power in Germany, he had been involved in planning for the eventuality of war, following a meeting of directors of national museums and galleries called by the First Commissioner of Works. The directors, in the face of the threat of aerial bombardment, were fatalistic: '... the crisis, should it arise, would be decided so quickly that all arrangements for [evacuation] would be futile, and that nothing less than the provision of bomb-proof repositories in immediate contiguity with the museums would be of any service.'[268]

Hill, the Director, did not accept this and put Forsdyke in charge of planning for the eventuality of war. This Forsdyke did with painstaking brilliance. Two depositories were identified in country houses in Nottinghamshire (Boughton and Drayton) and a little-used underground railway tunnel at Aldwych was by 1938 earmarked for the Museum – although the humidity of the latter was a serious disadvantage. Spare space in the National Library of Wales (which had been used by the Museum in the Great War) was set aside for the library departments and a supplementary rock shelter was constructed nearby. This was completed, with full temperature and humidity control, by 1940 (the Museum and the Library sharing the costs of construction). Packing material was laid in. Three thousand flat-pack, 'no-nail' plywood cases were bought (although delivery was stopped in 1938 in the face of an Admiralty requisition) and stored in the basements of the newly constructed Duveen Gallery. Thousands of millboard boxes, some of which were designed to take coin-cabinets, were also acquired. Wood wool and tissue paper were provided for packing, but in the event supplies ran out and were replaced by newspaper, including a vast consignment of copies of the News of the World![269]

Within the Museum the collections were listed in order of priority for evacuation, and a sixty-page handbook edited by Forsdyke was published, entitled Air-raid precautions in museums, picture galleries and libraries (1939). This relied largely on Home Office advice and on that of the staff of the various laboratories in the national museums and galleries – it was much praised. Sandbags were ordered and anti-gas precautions put in place. A range of basements on the east side of the Museum was reinforced with steel and timber. Details of transport were worked out with the railway companies and loading points for containers were identified.

The first containers were in place when, on the evening of 23 August 1939, the Museum was warned that war was inevitable. Members of staff were summoned by telephone and telegram and packing began at 7 a.m. the next morning. The whole staff and a number of experienced volunteers packed and moved the material with a sense of urgency, but also with a sense of order and calm. Lists were made in triplicate and the packing cases were all individually labelled. On the first day ten tons of library material had been despatched to Aberystwyth, twelve tons of antiquities to Boughton and Drayton and a first tranche of heavy sculpture to the Aldwych tube.

By the time war was declared a hundred tons of library material, three-quarters of the Prints and Drawings and the whole of the Coins and Medals collection had been sent on their way; the most valuable antiquities had been put in store. The rest of the evacuation went more slowly. Some objects were moved unpacked: the vast collection of textiles, for example, was transported on its existing hangers on bars erected in the containers. The best of the sculpture was put in the underground tunnel, the rest protected by sandbags. The large totem pole from Queen Charlotte Island languished under the colonnade. Gradually the stores filled up and by the time the bombing started most of the antiquities collections and some 135,000 books had been evacuated.

As members of staff were called up for military service (130 served in the armed forces during the war), or for service in various intelligence departments (including the highly secret code-breaking operation at Bletchley Park), a skeleton staff ran the Bloomsbury building and controlled the various depositories. Members of the senior curatorial staff were assigned to Boughton and Drayton, reporting to the Deputy Keeper of Coins and Medals, Stanley Robinson, a figure perhaps less than sympathetic to the conservation problems of the ethnographers, who were worried by the presence of damp, moth and too much light. The work at the depositories was rather dull, being chiefly concerned with security, conservation and the maintenance of equipment.[270] Things were more exciting in London when the bombing started.

At the beginning of the war most of the Museum was closed down. A reduced library service was introduced, first in the Reading Room and then from October 1940 in the North Library; other students' rooms were serviced with the little material available. As the period known as the 'phoney war' intervened, the Museum started to mount a few exhibitions. The galleries in the south-west corner housed exhibitions of prints, drawings, printed books and manuscripts. A photographic exhibition of the recently discovered Sutton Hoo material was mounted in the Front Hall and a 'sacrificial' exhibition of duplicates and folk-life material from the Department of British and Mediaeval Antiquities was put on in the Central Saloon at the top of the main staircase. When the first bombs fell on London, all the remaining manuscripts were evacuated and the exhibition on the ground floor was closed down. From now on the Museum had to function from various bases. It did not, however, cease to collect; indeed, it made some outstanding acquisitions, as is testified in the volume of the British Museum quarterly which deals with the wartime years.[271]

The Museum had trained its staff in fire-fighting, and auxiliary firemen were recruited for night work alongside the night security staff. The Director had taken a very personal interest in this training; when the bombs came, he was everywhere in a steel helmet marked D (for Director). His encouragement of the staff and his gratitude to them for their help, not to mention his own personal courage, contributed greatly to the rapidity with which problems were tackled. When, for example, an oil-bomb went through the roof of the Reading Room on 16 October 1940, leaving its burning oil on the copper skin of the roof, the fire was extinguished in seventeen minutes. Apart from small incendiary bombs, the Museum was hit by seven high-explosive bombs. Two fell in the courtyard and caused only minor damage, three others caused some damage, and two did not explode. The two latter fell on the Prints and Drawings Gallery, the second falling through the hole caused by the first. A further bomb all but destroyed the Russell Square building housing the Research Laboratory. On 23 October a high-explosive bomb destroyed part of the newspaper repository at Colindale, destroying some 6,000 volumes.[272]

It was the incendiary bombs, normally extinguished by the firemen, that caused the worst trouble. On the night of 10/11 May 1941 the Museum was hit by dozens of incendiary bombs and for the first time the fires got out of hand to the extent that the Fire Brigade had to be summoned. On this occasion the worst damage was caused by bombs lodged between the copper roofs and the ceilings of a number of the galleries. Those burned out were the Roman Britain Room, the Central Saloon (pl. 29), the Prehistoric Room, the roof above the main staircase, the Greek and Roman Life Room and its annexes, the Medal Room, the Greek Bronze Room and the First Vase Room. The temporary exhibition was completely destroyed. Where hose-pipes could be introduced the floors survived. The worst loss was to the Department of Printed Books. On the same night some 150,000 books were destroyed when the stacks in the South-West Quadrant were severely damaged by fire as the hoses ran dry.[273] No more bombs struck the Museum.[274]

The shock caused by the raids of May 1941 caused the Trustees to think about the safety of their evacuated material. It was thought that the collections at Boughton and Drayton might be at risk, as an airfield had been built in the neighbourhood. A search was mounted for safer storage and a quarry was found at Westwood, near Corsham, in Wiltshire. When the Air Ministry tried to hijack it a direct appeal was made to the Prime Minister (an ex-officio Trustee) and the Museum got its quarry. Thirty metres below ground, it comprised 2,500 square metres of storage space, had horizontal access and a roof height of four metres. In six months, after the expenditure of £20,000, it was converted into a perfect air-conditioned store and the material from Boughton and Drayton started to be moved there in February 1942. The quarry also hosted material from many other collections and museums, including the Free French Government Museum of National Antiquities, of which little is known. Meanwhile Skipton Castle had been equipped to take a major portion of the collections of the Department of Manuscripts and this, with a number of very isolated country houses, completed the storage space for the collections of the library departments. The collection of Coins and Medals and some of the ethnographic collections were, for example, sent to Compton Wynyates in Warwickshire, under the supervision of Stanley Robinson.

The stores were not emptied until some time after the end of the war, but at the time of departure Cyril Gadd, of the Department of Egyptian and Assyrian Antiquities, wrote a fitting inscription in cuneiform script on the wall of the Westwood quarry:

> In the year of our lord 1942, the sixth year of George, king of all lands. In that year everything precious, the works of all the craftsmen, which from palaces and temples, were sent out, in order that by fire, or attack by an evil enemy they might not be lost, into this cave under the earth, a place of security, an abode of peace, we brought [them] and set [them].[275]

Chapter 7

RECONSTRUCTION AND SEPARATION

1945–73

The war was over and the Museum now had the horrendous task of recovering itself, a process that took far longer than it had done in 1918. Those who had remained there throughout the war were tired, and – after the initial euphoria – an austere greyness settled on the institution, as it did on a country faced with enormous bomb damage, high debts and an exhausted industry, not to mention a severe shortage of material and even food. Members of staff who had served in the armed forces or in other branches of government were slow to return.[1] Money was short; successive governments, their minds engaged on greater problems of reconstruction and recovery, were unhelpful, and the physical rebuilding of those parts of the Museum that had been gutted by bombs took many years. Indeed, one 'temporary' roof remains to this day, while the scars caused by shrapnel on the colonnade will never be removed.

The Trustees had fair warning of future difficulties. In September 1944, with other representatives of the national museums and galleries, Forsdyke attended a meeting at the Ministry of Works:

> ... at which the prospects of restoring the various public institutions to working conditions were discussed. The Ministry explained that little or no labour would be available for Museums until demands for housing had been met, and Museums must therefore be prepared to confine their activities to parts of their premises which would need no serious reconditioning...[2]

But the Museum had more bomb damage than any other national museum and, despite a certain amount of initial optimism, it was to be a long haul.[3]

It is a brutal fact that for nearly twenty years successive governments neglected the national museums; and the British Museum, more bomb-scarred than most, suffered most seriously. Local authority museums were in like case; it was many years before civic pride re-asserted itself and grand municipal buildings were restored to their former glory. Post-war austerity did not help. Shortage of fuel meant that public buildings were neither heated nor lit adequately. The drabness of people's war-worn clothes was reflected in the make-do and mend spirit which became endemic in all public buildings. Materials – everything from paper to timber – were in short supply and quality was poor, repairs were

neglected or bodged, and craftsmen lost pride in their work. The maintenance of infrastructure was neglected, at great cost to later building projects, a trait which almost
became a national disease. Further, an over-stretched public service was unable to think
laterally about the problems ahead, and the museum service itself was suspended in a
1930s time warp. In hindsight it seems that this was the period when museums began to
gain their reputation for gloom, a judgement which has become a haunting journalistic
cliché.

The Museum began to recover physically in the late 1960s and 70s as the public
demanded more sophisticated and accessible displays. There were in the intervening
period few new museum buildings in the country, while display only gradually broke away
from an inward-looking elitist attitude aimed at a small percentage of the educated population. The medieval treasury and some of the ground-floor displays of the Victoria and
Albert Museum were innovative, while at the British Museum only the temporary
Parthenon display looked good – and even that provided merely minimal information.
Only science museums seemed to attract a broader public, and what was true of the
Science Museum in London was paralleled in such foreign contemporaries as the
Deutsches Museum in Munich. The great European national museums in Paris and Berlin,
for example, were in like condition, as anyone who visited the Louvre in the 1940s or 50s
will attest. In America and Scandinavia there was some movement; the Statens Historiska
Museum in Stockholm had been redesigned in the 1930s and 40s, and the displays of the
Germanic Iron Age and the Viking Age set new European standards. But the great National
Museum in Copenhagen, which had been so influential in the understanding of material
culture in the nineteenth century, retained displays which in some cases were nearly a
hundred years old. The museums of Spain and Italy, almost without exception, were in a
similar state. The majority of the museums in the British Isles gradually pulled themselves
out of this mire in the last thirty years of the century, led by such provincial museums as the
Castle Museum at Norwich. The British Museum started to move only in the late 1960s,
with the appointment of a professional in-house designer who could make some headway
against the dead hand of the civil service departments hitherto responsible for design and
layout. The Museum was to have a turbulent half-century and this chapter covers a period
of trauma, leading to the beginning of a recovery which saw the self-esteem and accessibility of the Museum rise from the depths and begin to soar.

Reconstruction

The repair of the comparatively minor damage caused by the high-explosive bombs in the
King Edward VII Building was put in hand almost immediately, largely dealt with by
Museum staff. The Post Office, which had used the old Elgin Gallery as a sorting office,
was evicted; the evacuated material was gradually moved back to Bloomsbury. The Department of Printed Books, having made a general appeal for the replacement of books lost in
the blitz, received generous help from institutions and private individuals throughout the
world, but these acquisitions had to be stored and sorted. This held up the opening of the
Reading Room, where the sorting was taking place, until June 1946.[4] In late April 1946 an
inter-departmental exhibition was opened in the main Edward VII Gallery, to muted press

interest.[5] The gallery remained shabby and the labels were largely re-used from the pre-war displays, but the exhibition made a stunning impact in that some of the Museum's greatest treasures were exhibited in a small compass for aesthetic effect. This arrangement in some cases played a scholarly role as, for example, when the Sutton Hoo jewellery and the Lindisfarne Gospels (closely related in their ornament) were juxtaposed. Another related treasure of the Anglo-Saxon period – the Kingston Brooch, on loan from the comprehensively bombed-out Liverpool Museum – was also displayed nearby (although it had to survive a train crash to reach London).[6] The upper galleries in the King Edward VII Building re-opened in September 1947 and the undamaged sculpture galleries on the ground floor were progressively re-opened between 1946 and 1954. The first of the upper Egyptian galleries was opened in June 1947.[7] Ethnography moved itself back into the upper east galleries and Islamic antiquities were displayed in the room to the south of this. The western range of upper galleries remained largely deserted and it was often necessary until the mid-1950s to use umbrellas and cross on duckboards the roofless space where the upper Greek and Roman Galleries had been. Between 1958 and 1961 four of the upper Greek and Roman Galleries were re-opened and a newly designed Greek and Roman Life Room was built in undistinguished Ministry of Works style in place of that destroyed in the blitz, but the two other bombed galleries were not rebuilt until the 1980s. The war-damaged galleries at the top of the main staircase were rebuilt in the mid-1960s and offices, a students' room and storage space for the new Department of Prehistoric and Romano-British Antiquities were added to the north.

The Duveen Gallery had been seriously damaged and the Parthenon frieze and pediment sculptures were brought back to their old rooms (the metopes being consigned to an adjacent room). Ashmole, the keeper and a specialist in sculpture, removed all the old photographs, the clutter of models and comparative material, and retrieved the sculptures from the Underground, where they had spent the war. Ashmole appreciated the original top-lighting of these galleries and removed the Victorian colour scheme ruthlessly, commenting:

> The old Elgin Gallery was painted a deep terracotta red, which, though in some ways satisfactory, diminished its apparent size, and was apt to produce a depressing effect on the visitor. It was decided to experiment with lighter colours, and the walls of the large room were painted with what was, at its first application, a pure cold white, but which after a year's exposure had unfortunately already yellowed. The small Elgin Room was painted with pure white tinted with prussian blue, and the Room of the Metopes was painted with pure white tinted with cobalt blue and black: it was necessary, for practical reasons, to colour all the dadoes a darker colour.[8]

The result was widely acclaimed when the room opened in July 1950 and the colour scheme remains an ideal to many to this day. Labelling and explanation, however, were practically non-existent.

The worst-affected department was Coins and Medals, which had lost not only its gallery, but also its offices (with, sadly, most of its archive). The staff were temporarily housed in the old Greek and Roman Gold Room while they waited agonizingly long years to move first into temporary quarters in the south-east Residence, a move delayed for years by a supine Ministry of Works, which seemed incapable of finishing a comparatively simple job. As late as June 1951, after years of procrastination, the Trustees resignedly noted that the south-east Residence was still not ready for the department.[9] At last, in 1959, they were able to move back to their reconstructed quarters next to the Greek and Roman Life Room. The opportunity was taken to increase space by adding a mezzanine floor.

Although the repair of bomb damage was important, the reconstituting of the staff was perhaps even more urgent. In this the Trustees, by stealth and political string-pulling, had some success. The formation in 1945 of the two departments of Ethnography and Oriental Antiquities has already been noted. But they were bereft of staff. The Department of Oriental Antiquities in 1945 was reduced to the keeper, Basil Gray (Soame Jenyns, the only other surviving member of staff, was likely to be sent to China on government service). The Department of Ethnography consisted of Braunholtz, Digby and Fagg (both seconded on war service) and a German refugee, Dr Samson. Even before the Japanese surrender the Trustees accepted that additional staff were needed; they approved an unspecified number of temporary appointments in the case of Oriental Antiquities and, with ambitions to increase the staff of Ethnography to six, approved the immediate appointment of an additional assistant keeper.[10]

The Treasury had ruled that all appointments should, until reconstruction was complete, be temporary, and the first appointment under this resolution was a German refugee, W. Cohn, a specialist in China and Japan, previously employed in the Museum für Völkerkunde in Berlin.[11]

At the same time the Trustees agreed that a Sub-department of Prehistoric and Romano-British Antiquities should be created in the Department of British and Medieval (by now altered from Mediaeval) Antiquities and that extra staff should be found. Hawkes was to be offered a special allowance to take charge of this when he returned from his employment as a temporary civil servant in the Ministry of Aircraft Production.[12]

Gradually the staff trickled back. Hawkes and Fagg returned to duty at the end of October and others followed. The Museum, however, was drastically understaffed as a result of the slow demobilization process. The Trustees had to appeal directly to the Prime Minister for alleviation of the problem, and received a sympathetic hearing.[13] New members of staff were gradually recruited. The first to be appointed was Philip Pouncey, who came from the National Gallery to the Department of Prints and Drawings, soon followed in the same department by John Gere (a refugee from a voluntary post in the Tate Gallery). Soon after, John Brailsford and William Watson were appointed to what was now the Department of British and Medieval Antiquities, and Thomas French to Greek and Roman Antiquities. The trickle became a flood, and in July 1947 (Scrutton and French having resigned),[14] Brailsford, Watson, Douglas Barrett, Kenneth Jenkins, Robert Carson and Reynold Higgins were certified as established civil servants in the various antiquities departments alongside Bryan Cranstone and D.H. Boalch.[15] Meanwhile the administration had been bolstered by the appointment of Frank Francis, a future Director, from the Department of Printed Books, as Secretary (in the rank of deputy keeper) in the place of the unattractive J.H. Witney.

Gradually pay and conditions throughout the Museum were sorted out. The maximum salary of keepers was set at £1,400, of deputy keepers at £1,200, of assistant keepers at £1,000, with the initial pay of the cadet grade (assistant keeper, class II) at £250 at the entry age of twenty-three.[16] The Trustees – not to mention the unions – thought the last rate too low by comparison with the salaries of equivalent grades in the civil service, and initiated a long series of discussions with Treasury. Other negotiations allowed for the establishment of five scientific assistants of various grades in the Research Laboratory and eleven craftsmen (the equivalent of today's conservation officers) in the departments, all on consolidated incremental salary scales between £290 and £370.[17] Attendants and technical assistants were now to be graded as clerical officers. Warders and housemen were to be paid between 95s and £5 per week. And so the reconstruction went on, the Treasury calling a halt to expansion of the basic establishment in March 1947 at a figure of 457.[18] By 1950 the staff had been restructured and consolidated, and the pay scales of the assistant keepers were finally settled, Class I being placed on a scale of £780–£1,250 (women £575–£985), and Class II on £400–£600 (women £400–£500). In the latter case increments were allowed for postgraduate experience and wartime service. The rates were still below the equivalent salaries in the Principal grade of the civil service and this caused much ill-feeling, particularly as they were also below equivalent rates in the universities. This was especially true of the pay of the Class II recruits.

Occupation of the officers' residences dwindled in face of the demand for departmental space, particularly by the departments of Manuscripts, Ethnography and Coins and Medals.[19] By 1948 only two residences were in use, that of the Director and of the most senior keeper. A small portion of one residence was still reserved for the duty officer.

Towards Normalcy

The war may have left its scars and the staff may have been dispersed, but the business of the Museum during the hostilities continued, on a lower key. Most of the work was routine – correspondence, registration and cataloguing, as well as the occasional purchase of objects. As circumstances permitted officers were allowed special leave for academic purposes, as when Kendrick was given a few days to photograph Anglo-Saxon sculpture.[20] In the public area the Museum had been involved in the foundation of the important archaeological pressure group, the Council for British Archaeology, and had advised government in many areas. As the prospect of victory in Europe became clearer some quite remarkable proposals reached the Trustees. In January 1945, for example, the Colonial Office approached the Museum asking 'at some later date' to advise the colonial governments of West Africa on archaeological excavations and the establishment of museums: a request the Trustees agreed to, and which brought fruit in the immediate post-war years, after visits by Braunholtz and others to these countries.[21]

Sir Leonard Woolley, a wartime lieutenant-colonel and adviser to the military on archaeological sites and monuments, with the strong support of Churchill recruited specialists from all over the country, including members of the Museum staff such as Denys Haynes of the Department of Greek and Roman Antiquities, first to identify, and then to help protect and preserve such sites during allied advances.[22] In early April 1945 when the end of the war in Europe was imminent, as though to signal a return to normalcy, Woolley wrote proposing the resumption of the excavations at Atchana. The site had been protected during the war and the Turkish authorities were willing for him to continue his work there; the Trustees backed his plan and Gadd, Deputy Keeper of Egyptian and Assyrian Antiquities, was given permission to go with him.[23] International travel to re-establish academic contacts, through both study trips and conferences, became the norm, and excavations in both Britain and abroad were resumed. Soon after his appointment to the Sub-department of Prehistoric and Romano-British Antiquities, John Brailsford went to Little Woodbury in Wiltshire to help complete important Iron Age excavations and J.P.T. Burchell, a part-time assistant in the same department, excavated sites of various periods in Kent and Essex. Perhaps more interestingly, William Watson joined a team which went to Cyrenaica to study Pleistocene sites. I.E.S. Edwards was given permission to accept a prize from Liverpool University which allowed him sixteen weeks' travel in Egypt.

There was a hectic quality about the late 1940s. Demobilization had been slow and cumbersome, and people wished to get on with their lives in the face of pervading auster-ity. Those who had been confined to England during the war needed to get out of the country, while those who had been abroad in the services needed to settle into a more even tenor. Many of the new recruits – graduates from university immediately before the war – had held relatively senior wartime posts and found some of the petty bureaucracy irksome. Having been flung about the world in haphazard fashion for most of their mature life, these new members of staff felt more or less disorientated and some were impatient of lost years and of their future. [24]

They were handled on a loose rein. Set to work on catalogues, handbooks and guidebooks, they wrote articles for the revived *British Museum quarterly*, and, while unpack-ing material returned from evacuation, learnt to know the collections and handle the public's questions. The first faltering steps towards a special exhibition programme were taken. Members of staff were also keen to plan the redisplay of the galleries, but were constantly frustrated by lack of money and technical support. In 1949, for example, the Director had to tell the Trustees 'of notices recently received from the Ministry of Works to the effect that the Treasury had made a 20 per cent. reduction in all Works services costing less than £10,000, that no supplementary estimates will be accepted in the current year, that works of alteration cannot be done without delaying maintenance and decoration, and that future requirements will have to be very closely scrutinised.'[25] Frustration turned into something approaching resignation.

But there were chinks of light. For some reason the Ministry of Works had been persuaded to provide accommodation for the bomb-damaged Research Laboratory quickly. By 1947 it was temporarily housed in 1 Montague Place and work on the Sutton Hoo finds continued to a stage where it was ready for display.[26] Rupert Bruce-Mitford produced an excellent handbook on the find, which – in days of great austerity – was visually highly attractive and set a new standard for future publications. But this was not the only work done by the Research Laboratory. Even before wartime damage to objects had been assessed, the Trustees agreed to outside conservation work such as the comple-tion of the restoration of St Cuthbert's relics for Durham Cathedral, which had been started before the war.[27] Plenderleith was involved in the committee which looked into the van Meegeren forgeries, and the Laboratory advised on the conservation of the prehistoric boats from North Ferriby, Yorkshire, for the National Maritime Museum.

Scientific archaeology was now beginning to play a major role in the discipline and the Museum was at the centre of this development. New initiatives included approval to take part in a project of the Bristol Museum for the invasive petrological identification of Neolithic stone axes to establish their place of manufacture. Surprisingly early, the Trustees also agreed to the establishment of a laboratory for radiocarbon dating, almost immediately after the discovery and development of the method by Willard Libby. The proposal came from I.E.S. Edwards of the Department of Egyptian and Assyrian Antiquities, backed by the Atomic Research Station at Harwell and by a number of colleagues in the Museum and the British Museum (Natural History). The first positive steps were taken by the Trustees in 1949.[28] Initially Harwell was to have undertaken the measurement of samples by gas counting, but this did not happen and in 1953 Harold Barker started to build the equipment in the Museum, publishing his first results in 1959.[29]

Such archaeological initiatives within the field of the natural sciences were in keeping with the spirit of the time. Before the war archaeologists at Cambridge – which had a close relationship with the British Museum (Natural History) – had been combining with botanists and others to investigate the vegetation, climate and land usage of prehistoric people: work soon to be paralleled at the University of London under F.E. Zeuner. At Oxford there was the beginning of a process which led to the foundation in 1955 of a Research Laboratory of Archaeology and History of Art, based on the physical sciences. Among its main supporters were Lord Cherwell and Christopher Hawkes (who had left the Museum for a newly created chair of European Archaeology at Oxford in 1946). This laboratory, under the leadership of Edward Hall (later a Trustee of the Museum), was to have a major influence on the Museum in later years. If Hawkes had possessed either the will or the interest to establish an undergraduate school of archaeology, Oxford, through this combination of science and the humanities, could have challenged Cambridge and London much earlier as a centre of archaeological innovation.

In the Museum the temporary accommodation of the Research Laboratory was replaced in January 1962 by state-of-the-art offices and laboratories in 39 and 40 Russell Square, built behind the façade of the bombed-out buildings. It included a modern single-storey extension in the gardens behind, which housed conservation research. The Laboratory building had air filtration to exclude dust and humidity was maintained below 50 per cent. Water, gas, and other services were provided with maximum flexibility on all floors and a vibration-free room was provided for delicate weighing operations. In the basement was the purpose-built radiocarbon-dating laboratory. The Museum could now boast that the Research Laboratory was 'one of the finest of its kind in any museum'.[30]

Faltering Steps, Itchy Feet

By 1950 the reconstruction and enhancement of the staff were complete and a new Director was in post. Geoffrey Fisher, the Archbishop of Canterbury, was an active chairman of the board of Trustees, of whom the most energetic members were perhaps the new Lord Crawford (who had succeeded his father on the board in 1940) and Lord Ilchester. Forsdyke retired as Director in 1950 and was succeeded by T.D. Kendrick. This appointment seemed inevitable to all save the runner-up, Frank Francis, Keeper of Printed Books, who badly wanted the post and had to wait until 1959 to fulfil his ambition. Kendrick was a friendly person with a sometimes outrageous sense of humour. Much liked by the staff, he was a competent administrator, but was perhaps too easy-going for the challenges faced by the Museum in the aftermath of the war.

The Festival of Britain of 1951 proved, for a short time, to be an energizer. The Trustees were encouraged to provide for the thousands who flocked to London to see the spectacle.[31] Despite a 20 per cent cut in all works accounts, money was found to repair the damage in the King's Library and much of the damage in and about the main staircase. Some of the upper galleries were re-opened, although the burnt-out Prehistoric Saloon and Greek and Roman galleries remained boarded up, while most of the galleries in the White Wing were reserved for storage. Ethnographic, Egyptian and Assyrian and some oriental antiquities were redisplayed, often re-using the same labels and showcases as before the war. In the case of Ethnography the re-shelving of the wall-cases was completed by means of a gift of Swedish timber – much appreciated at a time when the supply of building materials was severely controlled.[32] But money was still hard to come by.

Despite the general austerity and a chronic shortage of funds, the Trustees had by the early 1950s managed to add considerably to the staff. They also reviewed and reorganized the departmental structure. The departments of Coins and Medals, Prints and Drawings, and Greek and Roman Antiquities retained their names, with slightly enhanced staffs. John Allan, Keeper of Coins and Medals since 1931, was succeeded by Stanley Robinson, the Greek specialist, who held the post for only three years before passing it on in 1952 to John Walker, the orientalist. The two classical numismatists appointed in 1947, Kenneth Jenkins and Robert Carson, were joined in 1951 by Michael Dolley, a medievalist.[33] A graduate of King's College London, Dolley had transferred from the National Maritime Museum. He wrote widely on Anglo-Saxon coins; a masterly (and quarrelsome) historical theoretician, he liked to put forward theories that sometimes descended into the polemical.[34] John Kent joined the department in 1953. A Roman numismatist, he had considerable practical interest in British archaeology, and thus added a new dimension to a department steeped in the tradition of literary history of which he later became keeper. He was to write two catalogues in the Roman Imperial Coinage series and completed two catalogues, started by Derek Allen, of the continental Celtic coinage. D.W. MacDowall, who joined the department in 1956, understudied the keeper as orientalist, but left after a few years for a career in university administration.[35]

The Department of Prints and Drawings was full of comings and goings. A.E. Popham succeeded Hind as keeper in 1945 and remained for nine years. Writing first on the Dutch School, and then on the Italians, he was a towering scholar of the Renaissance in the traditional mould; one of his successors has said that he 'reinvented the subject'.[36] Popham was responsible for establishing in the post-war period the department's international distinction in the study of Italian drawings. He persuaded Johannes Wilde, for example, to catalogue the Museum's Michelangelo drawings – in the opinion of many the finest drawings catalogue ever published. He also initiated the great series of Italian drawings catalogues, which have enormous prestige and respect. In 1954 Popham was succeeded by Edward Croft Murray, who played the drums in an eighteenth-century band with skill and panache.[37] He was a specialist in English watercolours, in which subject he was joined by Paul Hulton, who found an agreeable home in the department, having irrevocably – but not unusually – fallen out with Sir John Rothenstein while an assistant keeper at the Tate Gallery.[38] Croft Murray's deputy was Philip Pouncey, a major Italian scholar, whom Popham had enticed from the National Gallery in 1945 (he later left the Museum to become a director of Sotheby's). His great friend and co-worker in the field of Italian drawings, John Gere, joined the department in 1946 and later became its keeper.[39] Hugh Scrutton was appointed at the same time but soon left for a distinguished museum career elsewhere. Christopher White, a Dutch specialist, joined the department in 1954, but left eleven years later for Colnaghi's, the dealers. He later joined the Mellon Foundation in London and ultimately became Director of the Ashmolean Museum.

The Department of Greek and Roman Antiquities had by the 1950s built up its staff and recovered some of its resilience. In 1956, however, Ashmole went to Oxford and, Robertson having already left for University College London, was succeeded as keeper by Denys Haynes. R.A. Higgins,[40] who wrote the great catalogues of terracottas, and Peter Corbett (specialist on Greek pottery, who was to succeed Robertson at University College) came to the department in 1947 and 1949 respectively. Donald Strong, light-hearted and urbane, replaced Ashmole in charge of sculpture in 1956. The most promising and original scholar in the department, he left to become Professor of the Archaeology of the Roman Provinces at the London University Institute of Archaeology and died prematurely in 1973.

Elsewhere in the Museum there was an attempt at departmental rationalization. It has been shown that Oriental Antiquities had split from Ethnography in 1946, with Basil Gray as keeper and Soame Jenyns as deputy keeper. Douglas Barrett, an Oxford-trained classicist who was to become an Indian specialist, was appointed to the department in 1947, as was Donald Boalch, an 'original' who resigned on grounds of ill-health in 1948. William Watson, later Professor of Chinese Art and Archaeology at the University of London School of Oriental and African Studies, transferred from his post as a Palaeolithic specialist in the Department of British and Medieval Antiquities in 1948, replacing Boalch. Ralph Pinder-Wilson, an Islamicist, joined in 1949. Braunholtz remained as Keeper of Ethnography until he retired in 1953, to be replaced by Adrian Digby. In 1955 William Fagg, a pre-war appointment as Africanist, became deputy keeper. Bryan Cranstone (later Curator of the Pitt Rivers Museum at Oxford) joined in 1947, and Margret Bennett-Clark (later Carey) in 1953.

The Department of British and Medieval Antiquities was now too diverse to be covered by a single keeper. Before Kendrick became Director in 1950, to be replaced by the stopgap appointment of Alex Tonnochy, it was already clear that prehistoric and Romano-British antiquities would have to be split off. This decision was delayed when Hawkes left for Oxford. A sub-department was, however, re-created of which John Brailsford, an experienced Cambridge-trained archaeologist and specialist in the Iron Age, became head.[41] His part-time assistant, E.M.M. Alexander, having resigned, Gale Sieveking – a specialist in the Palaeolithic – joined the department from the Raffles Museum in Singapore in 1956. The rump of the department now consisted of the ageing and tipsy figure of William King, Rupert Bruce-Mitford, and a new recruit, Peter Lasko, a medievalist. Lasko, who had come to England with his parents as a German refugee in the mid-1930s, trained as a painter at the St Martin's School of Art and went on to read art history at the Courtauld Institute (of which in 1974 he became Director, having first served as the founding Professor of the Visual Arts at the University of East Anglia). In 1948 Elizabeth Eames, who had been working on a voluntary basis in the department, was allowed £1 a day to prepare the catalogue of the medieval tile collection – nobody realized that it would take her thirty years to complete this formidable task![42]

Bruce-Mitford became keeper of the department in 1955 in succession to Tonnochy. King retired at the same time and two replacements were found, Hugh Tait and myself. The first was an honorary curator at the Fitzwilliam Museum, Cambridge, and an art historian; he was to specialize in ceramics and metalwork of the Renaissance and later. Having been an Assistant in Research at Cambridge, I was employed as an Anglo-Saxon and Viking archaeologist. I later became Professor of Medieval Archaeology at University College London and in 1977 returned to the Museum as Director.

The personalities in the Department of Egyptian and Assyrian Antiquities did not mix. Sidney Smith, an uneasy character, retired to a chair in 1948 and was succeeded by Cyril Gadd, who had been deputy keeper of the department since 1938. Donald Wiseman, an Assyriologist, was appointed in 1948, but did not stay long; in 1961 he became Professor of Assyriology in London University. In 1950 Edwards, the Egyptologist, on rather dubious grounds was appointed deputy keeper over the head of Barnett who had two years' seniority and took some umbrage.[43] Another Egyptologist, T.G.H. James, who had studied Oriental Languages at Oxford, was appointed in 1951. In 1955 Gadd resigned and, to everyone's relief, Edwards and Barnett became keepers of two newly created departments – Egyptian Antiquities and Western Asiatic Antiquities respectively. Edwards and James were joined in 1957 by a Coptic scholar, A.F. Shore, a Fellow of King's College, Cambridge, who in 1974 left for the Brunner Chair of Egyptology at Liverpool University. Terence Mitchell from Cambridge joined Barnett and Wiseman in the new Department of Western Asiatic Antiquities in 1959.

Plenderleith, Keeper of the Laboratory, resigned to pursue a career in international conservation in 1959. He was succeeded by A.E.A. Werner, an engaging Irishman who had taken his doctorate at Freiburg im Breisgau in 1937. He had returned to his native Dublin first as a lecturer and then as a reader, becoming a research chemist at the National Gallery in London in 1948. In 1954 he had migrated to the Museum as Principal Scientific Officer. He was to remain as keeper until 1975. On his elevation he appointed A.D. Baynes-Cope to be Principal Scientific Officer, in effect his deputy. They were supported by Harold Barker and Mavis Bimson and a number of more junior staff. Most conservation was carried out by technicians in workshops in the antiquities departments, loosely controlled by the Laboratory. The research side of conservation – which included the more delicate work in this area – was centralized under Werner. Among the conservation staff were three appointed in the late 1920s and 30s – B.A.F. Nimmo, Leonard Bell and Arthur Prescott, who was in charge of casts.

In 1959 a new director was appointed: Kendrick was succeeded by Frank Francis, a genial Liverpudlian classicist, who had joined the Museum in 1926.[44] Having served as Secretary for little over a year, he was appointed Keeper of the Department of Printed Books in 1947. Genial he may have been, but he was a tough and reforming director, whose great monument was the completion of the publication of the catalogue of printed books. He took over from Kendrick the drafting of the new British Museum Bill (see p.269) and struggled for more money for the redisplay of the collections. He was also responsible for negotiating the incorporation of the Patent Office Library in the Museum as a step towards the creation of a National Reference Library of Science and Invention.

This, given legal standing in a new Act, resulted in the move of the lending element of the scientific section of the library to Boston Spa in Yorkshire. He was totally dedicated to the prospect of building a new library to the south of Great Russell Street and was deeply disappointed when the government reneged on its promises to build it. One of his interests was greater public access to the Museum, and it was during his term of office that a design department was inaugurated and the education and publication service strengthened. Though a librarian to the core, he was sympathetic to many of the antiquities departments' aspirations and fought hard, for example, for some of their greater acquisitions. He was particularly involved in the purchase of the Ilbert Collection of Clocks and Watches, which haunted his early days as Director (see p.292).

The general administration of the Museum was controlled by the Secretary, who from 1948 to 1973 was Bentley Bridgewater; he was supported by an Assistant Secretary, seconded from one of the library departments after 1959 for a spell of three years. This latter was seen to be a good career posting by members of these departments; although there were attempts to persuade members of the antiquities departments to take the post, they were reluctant to accept such blandishments.[45] In 1973 Bridgewater retired and was replaced by George Morris (Assistant Secretary 1965–8). In 1960 the Director's office, apart from typists and messengers, was supported by a Senior Executive Officer, a Higher Executive Officer and seven Executive Officers. This, as pointed out by Philip Harris, who served a term as Assistant Secretary at this period, was not enough to 'cope with preparing papers for Trustees' meetings and writing the minutes, establishment and financial matters (including negotiations with the Treasury), public relations, works and accommodation matters, security, publications, the photographic service, the guide lecturers, and staff welfare'.[46] An extra Higher Executive Officer was, therefore, appointed in 1960 to deal with works and accommodation (there was already a clerk of works) and a publications officer and a welfare officer were appointed in the following year. In 1964 the Accountant's post was upgraded to Senior Executive Officer. Negotiations were opened with the Treasury for extra help in the shape of two deputy directors, and finally in 1966 a post of Assistant Director was approved. Unfortunately, T.A. Hume, later Director of the Museum of London, who was appointed to the post, failed his medical examination and the post was put on ice.[47]

There was clearly a need for more junior curatorial staff. The Treasury was reluctant to allow this, so the Trustees occasionally promoted clerical officers to the executive grade because of the specialist knowledge achieved by years of service. Such a case was Dudley Snelgrove, who knew better than anyone how the Department of Prints and Drawings worked, and was promoted in 1956.[48] A major breakthrough was, however, made in 1959 when the Treasury approved the appointment of a new curatorial class of research assistants (which already existed in other institutions). Initially these posts were envisioned to be held by people whose academic attainments was not as high as those of the assistant keepers. Research assistants were to work to the keeper grade and (so far as the antiquities departments were concerned) the posts were mainly seen as stepping-stones to senior curatorial posts outside the Museum. From the beginning, however, the quality of candidates was high and, although many of the initial intake did indeed go on to universities and museums elsewhere, many stayed and some began to resent their lowlier position in the Museum hierarchy. The Museum authorities and the Association of First Division Civil

Servants in their turn fought to prevent this class becoming the cadet grade for curatorial entry to the Museum, a position vehemently argued by some civil servants. Although at least three of the present keepers (including John Mack, the Senior Keeper) were recruited as research assistants, the matter is still not entirely settled. The two curatorial grades (keeper and research assistant) are now integrated and promotion between them is frequent, but keepers are still faced with the problem of appointing curators to head major sections of their departments from outside over the heads of older members of staff at research assistant level.

Although the curatorial and administrative complement increased in the post-war years, pay was low and job prospects poor, much poorer indeed than in the Principal grades of the civil service, and the increase in staff was insufficient to cover the work. Further, many of the keepers had ten or more years to run before their retirement would provide opportunities for promotion of the junior staff. More frustrating, however, was the lack of money and drive to push the Museum's displays and buildings into the post-war era. As a consequence junior members of staff tended to move to what they perceived as greener pastures. Although one or two went into the art trade, many more found a haven in universities in the aftermath of the Robbins report of 1963. This report had not only encouraged the foundation of more universities, it had also suggested a broadening of the curriculum. New departments of, and new posts in, archaeology and art history were consequently established. The Museum could provide universities with mid-career academics for such new posts, where research was still encouraged. For poorly paid assistant keepers with young children, the opportunity was too good to miss.[49] The loss of some of the brighter members of the staff caused the Trustees some concern. Various irresolute enquiries were initiated into the problem and came to no conclusions – perhaps because they did not inquire of those who had left. In the 1970s the salaries within the Museum were to increase substantially, while they sank in the university sector, and there was consequently less movement.

This was the era of the first television programmes of mass appeal, and members of staff increasingly had opportunity to appear either officially or privately in their own time in items concerned with archaeology and, occasionally, art history. Television also demanded synthetic studies of periods and places, as did radio, and again many took advantage of such opportunities. Although no member of the Museum staff ever became famous as a 'tele-don', opportunities for popular synthetic work were there for the taking and some took them with eager hands. Other hard-up members of staff taught extra-mural university classes in the evenings, thus gaining experience in teaching along with a modest extra income. The Museum tried to encourage synthetic work by paying members of staff to produce short booklets on special subjects. They also somewhat grudgingly welcomed television cameras into the building.[50] The Trustees were reasonably generous with special leave, although they did not always provide expenses, so it became possible to travel on the back of lecture invitations canvassed from university colleagues abroad. Nobody begrudged the taking of a full allocation of the rather generous annual leave allowance (all the keeper grades were allowed six weeks), and this time could also be used in some measure for academic purposes.

The Museum did not employ its own designers before 1964, nor was there a coherent policy concerning display. Major new galleries were designed by Ministry of

Works architects in reluctant consultation with Museum staff. When opportunities occurred for minor improvements, as for example when material was moved out of some of the bays in the Edward VII Gallery into the re-opened galleries on the upper levels, the assistant keepers did all the planning, arranging and mounting of the objects in the newly available space. Mounts for objects were made in departmental workshops and the Museum painter would be persuaded to wash the mounts and the inside of the show-cases with cream emulsion paint – then all the rage. The assistant keeper would himself type labels on card scrounged from stationery stores. Museum carpenters produced bases for larger objects and built new walls of plasterboard to enhance the display of larger objects – these had to be removed to reveal the architecture of the building in the 1970s and 80s. Temporary exhibitions, other than those mounted in the Prints and Drawings Gallery, were normally confined to a case in the Front Hall (often used to display new acquisitions) or to a number of cleared cases in the Edward VII Gallery. Such, for example, was a ground-breaking exhibition of early Bow porcelain mounted by Hugh Tait in 1959, which was accompanied by a short catalogue.[51] The Assyrian Basement was from time to time used for special exhibitions. Max Mallowan, for example, was given permission to celebrate the twenty-fifth anniversary of the British School of Archaeology in Iraq with an exhibition there in 1956.[52]

One bold spirit, Gale Sieveking, went outside the Museum and got free advice from designers and students in art schools about display and display technology. Thus in the early 1960s a back-lit screen was provided for the first time, on which a projector threw images of sites and objects to supplement the exhibition of prehistoric material in a small gallery in the White Wing. The projector frequently jammed and it was many years before more reliable visual aids could be introduced – and then only into temporary exhibitions.

The day-to-day work of the Museum was at no time boring, although the painstaking registration of new acquisitions fascinated few. Enquiries from members of the public, from dealers and collectors provided great stimulus, challenging expertise, and sometimes produced spectacular acquisitions by way of purchase or gift. Further, the re-sorting of material hastily packed at the outbreak of hostilities allowed new members of staff to learn the collections in a more detailed fashion than before the war, when the objects firmly remained year-on-year in the showcases. There was time to trawl the antique shops, and good relationships were established with the major dealers and with the learned staff of Sotheby's and Christie's, the two major auction houses. The minuscule purchase grant was used to good effect. Members of staff took office in various learned societies and helped to found and run others, thus building relations with professionals and curators in many fields, although the Trustees from time to time looked sideways at such activities. New journals provided space for publication and the curatorial staff contributed eagerly to them. Excavations were undertaken in both the Middle East and Britain, the latter including in the early 1960s one of the first scientific investigations of an industrial site, the eighteenth-century Longton Hall porcelain factory in Staffordshire.[53] The guide-lecturers were able to return to work and were soon in great demand in the newly opened galleries. The Museum was gradually regaining its self-confidence and its reputation for expertise in universal material culture. If one event symbolized the beginning of a new confidence it was the major reception given by the Trustees in 1957 to celebrate the centenary of the

Reading Room, at which the Queen handed over the Royal Collection of music. It was a glittering evening occasion; white tie, tails, decorations and tiaras added lustre to the drab galleries. Everybody's spirits were lifted.

A Personal Interlude

I joined the staff of the Department of British and Medieval Antiquities on 2 January 1955 as a very young assistant keeper, class II. The Museum at that time was a dark and unremittingly gloomy place. The portico was black with the soot of a hundred years. Those galleries that were open were dimly lighted, but many were still in their bombed-out state or closed and used for storage. In winter the London smog filtered through the imperfectly fitting windows and spread a greasy dampness on cold surfaces. Due to lack of warding staff and perennial fuel crises, the upper galleries were divided into two groups and closed on alternate days. There was no public restaurant, no information desk; only a few publications and black-and-white postcards were sold at a counter in the Front Hall. On the left of the entrance were a key pound and a glazed box for the hall superintendent, where the post was delivered and sorted. At the back of the Front Hall there had been a bold attempt to lighten the gloom by placing the Amaravati sculpture and the colossal Chinese Buddha against the wall. The Museum craftsmen had just discovered plasterboard and cream paint, and were busy covering up scars and casing in the rough edges of sculpture at the whim of the keepers. Behind the scenes, dirt and dust were augmented by the smell of the feral cats that lived – and died – in the under-floor conduits of the semi-defunct central heating system. The cellars were, with a few shining exceptions, indescribably filthy, as they had largely been left untouched since the beginning of the war.

My lot as a young curator was fairly typical. Issued with a house-key, I was given a desk in a large well-lit room, one of four junior curators who conducted their business in an open-plan office of a form developed in the Victorian period. The core of the departmental library was housed around the room and in the rooms at either end, which were occupied by the keeper, Rupert Bruce-Mitford, and the deputy keeper, John Brailsford. These rooms had iron doors, for they had open fires, which were covered by locked fireguards. The doors were kept open to allow access to the book-cases and the key safe which for some ancient reason of control and security was placed under the keeper's eye. Thus staff wandered in and out of these rooms at will, although the doors were closed when the officer needed privacy. The main room served as a corridor for the curatorial staff; it also gave table space to any special assistants and to scholars who needed to study material. The room was a centre for gossip and discussion and private visitors – scholars or collectors with whom it was necessary to have long discussions – sat by the assistant keeper's desk. With uncontrollably ringing telephones it sometimes approached bedlam. While the curators called each other by their Christian names, formality was still observed. Members of staff junior to oneself were addressed by their surnames (as were senior members of the curatorial staff in other departments). The junior grades addressed us as 'Mister X'. The men, including the clerical and executive officers, wore suits (except on Saturdays, when sports coats were permitted); the warders and technical staff were issued with long brown cotton coats.

All letters were drafted in longhand and were typed by the one secretary, who also acted as secretary to the keeper. If you were very lucky you might be allowed a few minutes of dictation. The rest of the staff consisted of a Higher Executive Officer, Ernest Barnard, who had started as a boy-clerk and was reasonably efficient in identifying ceramics. He had charge of a clerical officer named Bowles, who, living up to his nickname, Biffer, dealt in a rather slapdash fashion with photographic orders, and two messengers, who were allowed to handle objects. There were two technicians, who lived in a basement and made mounts on which objects were to be displayed, but were largely concerned with simple conservation.[54] The illustrator, a post shared with the Department of Greek and Roman Antiquities, was C.O. Waterhouse, who had joined the Museum before the First World War (see p.208), but he was soon replaced by Carey Miller.

Initially we worked a five-and-a-half-day week – this was soon changed to a five-day week, but we had to cover the whole day on Saturdays, as well as every public holiday, save Christmas Day and Good Friday. For these we were allowed days off in lieu. The curatorial duties were well defined. We had to identify and access objects in our own speciality and the junior members of staff had to enter all acquisitions in the register. We provided scholars and interested members of the public with physical access to the collections, whether the items were on display or in store. We answered queries, both within our own discipline and outside it – we all had to have a measure of expertise in such things as silver marks and heraldry, and we were expected to make simple judgements about the commoner antiquities. The public came to the department with or without appointment within the Museum's opening hours, and were, as a matter of pride, seen with expedition and without fuss. Their queries were mostly cogent and interesting, but sometimes on the wild side: one New Year's Day, for example, I was asked by a Canadian couple whether they could see Joseph and Mary's wedding-ring! While we were allowed to give opinions on objects, we were not allowed to give valuations, even when an object was produced which we might like to purchase – all such requests were referred to the auction houses. We had to mount our own exhibitions and type our own labels, pinning objects to boards and planning our own layout. I was given the task of unpacking the early medieval material which had been evacuated at the beginning of the war and was still in now crumbling boxes in the unheated Iron Age Gallery, the majority of which was taken up with the ceramic reserve. I was also given the job of creating an index of Anglo-Saxon grave goods, for which I took all the photographs myself.

Research was encouraged and I was set to work on a catalogue which was published as I left the Museum in 1964. Photographs for this book were produced by the central studio, but the drawings were largely made (without charge) by my wife, a profes-sional book illustrator. I was encouraged to write papers and, at home in the evenings, wrote a synthetic book on the Anglo-Saxons, which was to go into three editions. There was not much money for study leave, so I accepted every invitation to lecture, whether from women's institutes or foreign academies, and thus travelled to museums all over Britain and Scandinavia. There was a strange reluctance to allow staff to apply for outside funding, so that, when I received a three-month travelling studentship from the Lever-hulme Foundation to visit museums in Scandinavia, Germany and Austria, I was not allowed to take it at one time; I had to split it into two. I was never a great excavator, but I was encouraged to go out in the field and at least my few excavations are published!

It was the academic stimulus provided by the Museum which made it all worth while. It was a splendid place in which to meet colleagues. Foreign scholars turned up in droves and I got to know most of the European specialists in my field as they passed through London. Curators and archaeologists from all over Britain also visited the Museum, which acted as a clearing-house for opinions on newly found material. Lectures at the learned societies (all London-based) – which took place almost weekly – allowed of more contact with colleagues and kept one up to date with the subject. We were allowed much latitude, and perhaps stretched it to the limit. I helped to found, and became secretary of, one national archaeological society and chaired another. These were heady days. There was no university teaching in my subject, so I started an informal seminar for the few who were interested, which drew colleagues from Oxford, Cambridge and London to monthly gatherings, followed by supper at one of our homes. Through contacts in University College London, I learnt to use sources in neighbouring disciplines – onomastics and philology, for example. In our day-to-day work we had the inestimable advantage of the Department of Printed Books. Books were brought to our desk – often, to our shame, remaining on them for months.

Most important were interdepartmental contacts. A small group of us daily had coffee at 9 a.m. in the staff canteen and discussed matters which, in the days before the information explosion, ranged over most of Europe and Asia. Here we brought potential acquisitions for discussion with our peers in other departments – a practice unthinkable in these conservation-minded days. A coffee-bar in Soho served as another informal meeting place where, gossip exchanged, we were also able to hone our knowledge of material on the borders of our special disciplines. For me the presence of the Department of Manuscripts staff was of great importance, as I was developing theories about style history which drew on the illuminated books in that department.

I count these days as most productive – as did almost all my colleagues. We soaked up knowledge like blotting paper and made contacts that lasted us all our lives. We were, however, arrogant and impatient and conscious of the strict hierarchical structure of the Museum, which blocked promotion prospects. My keeper was wayward and interested mainly in his own research on Sutton Hoo; he disappeared for long periods into the bowels of the building or on continental tours, where even his secretary could not reach him. He was not particularly supportive of our academic ambitions, nor did he really trust our judgement. Like many of my colleagues I felt that a change of scenery would be timely – so in 1964 I went.

The New Act of Parliament

By the late 1950s it was becoming increasingly clear that the Trustee system was creaking. Attendance was at a low ebb; sometimes as few as eight members attended the board meeting and the business had become monotonous and formulaic. In 1952 an MP, W.R.D. Perkins, raised the matter in an attempt to reform the Museum. He had four proposals:

> The first is that we should start at the top and reform the whole system by which the trustees are appointed... There are 51 trustees of the British Museum, the vast majority of whom are far too busy to take an active part in the running of the Museum. Some of them are back-

woodsmen who long ago might have been transferred into the Museum itself... I suggest to the House... that we should appoint seven trustees only, that they should be appointed for five years by the Government of the day, and that they should not be eligible for re-appointment. My second proposal is that these new trustees should have power to lend any objects vested in them for public exhibition anywhere in the world. There are many objects which are in fact rubbish... My third proposal, therefore, is to allow the new trustees to sell off anything they like... My fourth proposal is that... the new trustees should have permission to destroy [infected objects]... after they have obtained permission from this house.[55]

This was good knockabout stuff and permission was given to bring in a bill for this purpose; it was duly introduced, but not passed.[56]

Perkins's arguments were not without merit. The criticisms of Lord Crawford in the 1920s (see p.198) are reflected in a slightly over-egged account of the proceedings given by Edward Heath (a Trustee by virtue of his position as Lord Privy Seal from 1960) of his attendance at a meeting in 1961:

> ... Sitting at an enormous table laden with exhibits of every kind were a dozen trustees. In the chair was the Marquess of Cambridge... The Marquess called on the Secretary to read the agenda. 'The minutes of the last meeting –' he began. 'They've been confirmed,' interrupted the Marquess. 'Go on.' 'The election of the Standing Committeee for next year –' announced the Secretary. 'They've already been re-elected. Go on.' 'The estimates for 1951–2 –' 'They've been settled,' interjected the Marquess. 'Now we can get down to business.' The whole procedure had taken just three minutes. The Marquess then turned to me and said, 'If you would like to stay for the rest of the Standing Committee meeting... we will have a spot of lunch. Now item 176.' I was astonished.[57]

There was an element of truth in this caricature; there were indeed many done deals.[58] It should be said, however, that Heath showed little interest in the Museum's collections when he was shown round by the Assistant Secretary on this, his only visit as a Trustee.[59] If he had been more assiduous he might not have made the great error of forcing through the introduction of admission charges for national museums when he was Prime Minister (see p. 296). The most interesting part of the Trustees' business concerned gifts and purchases and the reports of the departmental keepers. These latter first went to three sub-committees; the library departments and the Department of Prints and Drawings reported to one, the antiquities departments to a second, and a third (separated out in 1956) dealt with the Research Laboratory and technical services. A Planning Sub-committee, concerned with the building, was set up in 1958. The attention given to the keepers by the Trustees at the Standing Committee meeting could only be cursory. In the case of antiquities, the reports on the year's work of as many as seven departments were dealt with at a meeting that began at 11 a.m. and finished in time for a quite appalling lunch of sandwiches and coffee in the staff canteen. Visitations to the departments, which preceded the Sub-committee meetings, had become equally cursory. Discussion of gifts and purchases took up a major portion of the meeting and was much enjoyed by the Trustees, who sometimes made idiosyncratic decisions. In order to make judgements on acquisition, objects for approval were brought to the boardroom and displayed on sideboards before the meeting. This afforded junior staff their only contact with the Trustees.

The board's mill ground exceeding small. The minutiae of appointments were still recorded, down to that of the most junior cleaner; sick absences were noted and promotions, establishments, and retention of services of staff beyond retirement age were also dealt with. Curatorial staff applied for and reported on special leave. Payment of fees and expenses for assistance by outside specialists in sums as small as £30 were approved.[60] Damage reports were received; loans were sanctioned and accepted.

There was a hard core of active Trustees of whom the most influential was Lord Crawford, closely followed by Lord Radcliffe, a Lord of Appeal in Ordinary, who had been elected in 1957, and Lord Boyd (Alan Lennox-Boyd, previously a Trustee as Colonial Secretary), who was elected in 1962. The only active Family Trustees were the representatives of the Harley family, Sir Victor Goodman, and of the Cotton family, Richard Thompson.[61] These were the Trustees who led the reform movement. In 1958 discussions began to bring before Parliament a new Bill, triggered by the possible transfer of part of the collections to a new library site.[62] The Marquess of Cambridge, Lord Radcliffe and a few other Trustees took the lead in all discussions concerning the bill, which was passed as the British Museum Act in 1963.[63] Although it avoided the worst excesses of the Perkins Bill, the new Act radically altered the governance of the Museum and particularly the structure of the Board of Trustees.

A board consisting of fifty-one members was replaced by one of twenty-five. The Family Trustees were abolished and the Officers of State no longer had a place on the board. Importantly, the Trustees were allowed to nominate their own chairman and also five members of the board. The Sovereign would nominate one member. The learned societies retained their representation – but on the basis that their representatives should not necessarily be their presidents, as in the past. Fifteen members were to be appointed by the Prime Minister and all members would serve initially for five years. A more liberal approach was taken to out-stations, which enabled the temporary separation of the Department of Ethnography. A long-awaited reform – permission to lend objects abroad – was introduced. The appointment of the Director was now to be confirmed by the Prime Minister, not the Sovereign. Service in the Museum was put on a par with that of the civil service. Finally, the Trustees were required to report to Parliament on a triennial basis. As a pendant the Trustees sorted out their private funds in Chancery.[64] A new board was set up to govern the Natural History Museum. Quickly following on the Act, the sponsoring Department of State became the Department of Education and Science in place of the much-criticized Treasury – a case of 'out of the frying pan into the fire'.

In undramatic fashion the Trustees concluded their last meeting under the 1753 Act on 13 July 1963 with a record of thanks to Lady Epstein for the gift of a Baule mask from the Ivory Coast. The minutes were signed at the first meeting of the reconstituted board on 12 October by Michael Ramsey, Archbishop of Canterbury (now an appointed Trustee), as 'acting chairman'.[65]

Things now started to change. Lord Radcliffe was elected Chairman and the board continued to meet on Saturday mornings; but there was an attempt, not realized until the reforms of 1999, to reduce the number of meetings to six a year. Members now tended to take their attendance at meetings more seriously, and soon between eighteen and twenty attended regularly. Business was streamlined; a fixed format for the agenda was agreed, whereby formal business – accounts, appointments, reports on special leave, non-controversial loans and so on – was despatched separately and without discussion. The new committee structure was approved in December 1964. The first committee looked after Printed Books, Manuscripts, Oriental Printed Books and Manuscripts, and Prints and Drawings; the second, Coins and Medals, Egyptian Antiquities, Western Asiatic Antiquities, Greek and Roman Antiquities (later known as Antiquities I); the third, British and Medieval Antiquities, Oriental Antiquities and Ethnography (Antiquities II); and the fourth, the Research Laboratory and Technical Services. Three other committees were set up – Buildings, Publications and Finance.[66]

At this distance of time it is difficult to untangle the relationship between the Trustees and the Director. In the 1920s the Director, Kenyon, had been tough and influential and it was not until Archbishop Lang had become Chairman and Kenyon had retired that the Trustees became more influential in the business of the Museum. Forsdyke lived out most of his directorship in a period of continuous and changing crises with an appropriate management style. Kendrick, an economical and tidy administrator, appears to have dealt with the Trustees on a need-to-know basis in an unadventurous manner. His chairman was Archbishop Fisher – a prelate of headmasterly mien who had a tendency to be autocratic in his dealings with his fellow board members. Francis on the other hand was much more active as Director, but ultimately fell out with Lord Eccles, the most hands-on of the new-style Trustees, who followed Radcliffe as Chairman.

The Sculpture Galleries

In the late 1950s money began to be made available for some restoration work and in 1959 the Coins and Medals office suite, completely destroyed during the war, was rebuilt and re-opened. Attention turned towards the gallery work, beginning with the sculpture galleries on the ground floor.

Ashmole, the Keeper of Greek and Roman Antiquities – an architectural minimalist – had never liked the Duveen Gallery:

> It is, I suppose, not positively bad, but it could have been infinitely better. It is pretentious, in that it uses the ancient Marbles to decorate itself. This is a long outmoded idea, and the exact opposite of what a sculpture gallery should do. And, although it incorporates them, it is out of scale, and tends to dwarf them with its bogus Doric features, including those columns, supporting almost nothing which would have made an ancient Greek artist architect wince. The source of daylight is too high above the sculptures, a fault that is only concealed by the amount of reflection from the pinkish marble walls. These are too similar in colour to the marbles... These half-dozen elementary errors were pointed out by everyone in the Museum, and by many scholars outside, when the building was projected. Gifts can be a great danger to museums, the larger the more dangerous, especially when they have such strings attached as that the donor must nominate the architect.[67]

He would much have preferred not to put the Parthenon sculptures there and delayed the process as long as he could; indeed, he tried to persuade the Museum to use the gallery for other purposes. In 1962, however, six years after he left, the Duveen Gallery was finally restored and the Parthenon sculptures were moved into it to general acclaim, once again at the heart of the Museum (pl. 27). It was not, however, until the 1980s that the installation of an award-winning lighting scheme removed his greatest criticism of the building.

The transfer of the Parthenon sculptures from their old galleries allowed new possibilities for the display of the rest of the major Greek pieces. It also, to the disgust of the aesthetes, included within the galleries a chronological display of early Greek archaeological material, beginning with Cycladic material of the third millennium BC. The galleries were no longer to be totally devoted to sculpture, although the Nereid monument, the Bassae frieze (in a newly constructed mezzanine) and the Mausoleum sculptures were kept entirely separate from smaller objects and displayed (in the case of the first-named most imaginatively) in their own rooms. The Payava monument was surrounded by a mezzanine gallery, to save space and allow it to be viewed from above. The caryatid from the Erechtheion, however, was squashed into a rather ungainly space between the Nereid and Payava monuments. A floor was built over the basement lecture-theatre (originally the Mausoleum room) which, reached by steps, showed some of the most important Hellenistic material.

The designers, commissioned by the Ministry of Works to refurbish the galleries, were the Russell and Goodden partnership, two important members of whose team were Mary Shand and Robin Wade (who was to redesign the Egyptian Sculpture Gallery between 1976 and 1979). The taste of the time suited a minimalist approach of the type favoured by Ashmole, which is now largely out of fashion. In some cases Smirke's ceilings were masked or blocked out. The walls were painted in light colours and the floors (save in the main south range and the Hellenistic gallery) were tiled in a stone-coloured ceramic material, which replaced everything from York stone to blue rubber. Some labels were inlaid in ceramic lettering in the floor. The cases were visibly secure, and consequently too heavy to move, so that certain elements of the design became fossilized. The design partnership believed that Smirke's architecture challenged the objects:

> ... its main shortcomings were threefold: first, the strong competition between the reproduced classical detail in the architecture of the building and the authentic but weathered, and often damaged, forms and details of the exhibits; then, a pervading drabness of colour and similarity of tone which resulted in a total lack of dramatic impact; and finally the quality of lighting, both natural and artificial, which generally speaking was very different from that for which the exhibits were intended and which made no attempt to show particular things to their best advantage.[68]

These galleries, opened by the Duke of Edinburgh in 1969, 'were the first in the Museum to depart radically from the nineteenth-century tradition of even-handed symmetrical presentation in tune with Smirke's architecture. They adopt a selective, chronological presentation and make use of dramatic lighting, emphatic display cases, and ingenious viewing points at different heights'.[69] But the Townley collection was removed from display and the chronological sequence of sculpture, so long striven for by generations of keepers and never quite achieved, was broken.

The Assyrian sculpture galleries were treated in the same way by the same designers, and were re-opened with much better lighting in 1970. In the opinion of the Keeper of Western Asiatic Antiquities the exhibition reflected the feel of the original site and lighting.[70] At last the famous Lion Hunt frieze from the seventh-century BC palace of Ashurbanipal at Nineveh – perhaps the finest animal sculpture surviving from the ancient world – was worthily displayed.

Nor were storage areas neglected. In 1965, for example, the vast collections of Palaeolithic and Mesolithic flints were finally reorganized and re-boxed in a basement that doubled as a students' room in the White Wing.

In-house Design at Last

In October 1964, almost unnoticed among a large number of new appointments, a new phenomenon appeared in the Museum, a professional designer in the form of Margaret Hall.[71] Appointed as Exhibitions Officer, she arrived from the commercial world with no brief other than to advise the keepers on display. There was no culture of museum designers; indeed, only two other museums in the country at that time had an in-house designer – the Natural History Museum and the Leicester City Museums. On her first day, ushered into an office with a desk and chair and no equipment, Hall was interviewed by Francis, the Director, who clearly had no idea how she should proceed. She was taken on a tour of the Museum, introduced to the keepers, and told to get on with it.

Hall was faced with a great deal of hostility and resentment on the part of the senior academics, who were used to mounting their own displays with the help of the Museum carpenters and painters, using their own (sometimes questionable) taste. Gray, who had just mounted a Chinese exhibition, welcomed her appointment and – amid mutual incomprehension – told her that it was a pity that she had not come earlier as she would have been useful in arranging flowers! She was to have no responsibility for the design of the permanent galleries, a right wrested away from the Ministry in the late 1970s. Indeed, as has been shown, the lower sculpture galleries were being refurbished and redesigned at the time of her appointment.

It says a great deal for Hall's tact and energy that she was able to build up over the rest of the century a department which was to deal with practically all the design of permanent galleries and special exhibitions. In the course of her career she was ultimately responsible for more than 700 design projects and provided training for many of today's leading museum designers. She started modestly, arranging a case of comparative silver for Croft-Murray, who was mounting an exhibition on Hogarth. This was such a success that other keepers began to consult her and ask for her help. She was herself a designer in the round – in 3D – and soon had to recruit a graphic artist to deal with texts and labelling. She had no budget for external technical help and relied initially on the Museum's carpenters and painters, who, under her tutelage, began to produce more original and better-finished work.

In 1965 she mounted, at one end of the Edward VII Gallery, her first special exhibition. Curated by Bryan Cranstone, it was based on material he had brought back from an expedition to the Central Highlands of New Guinea. Despite difficulties with the keeper (Fagg), her partnership with this department was most fruitful, for she became responsible for all exhibitions in the Museum of Mankind when it came on stream in 1970 (see p.282). Because of the organic nature of most of the material in the collections of the Department of Ethnography, practically all its exhibitions were, on conservation grounds, planned to be temporary. These exhibitions were, therefore, controlled by the Museum and not by the Property Services Agency, the supply arm of the Department of the Environment, which had charge of all the major changes in the galleries at Bloomsbury. After the New Guinea exhibition Hall was able to mount in the new Upper Assyrian Gallery a large exhibition of glass based on the Slade collection.

The Museum was now beginning to challenge the traditional exhibition venues – particularly the Royal Academy and the Victoria and Albert Museum. The Museum's first 'blockbuster' came in 1972 with the mounting of the Tutankhamun exhibition (see p.284). Initially it was intended that a distinguished and senior outsider, Alan Irvine, should design it. Hall, however, appealed to the Director, who reversed the decision and passed the project over to the Museum's design team. Hall's leadership in this enterprise led to her being awarded an OBE and she later received the even more distinguished award of RDI (Royal Designer for Industry of the Society of Arts) – the only time it has been awarded to any museum employee. To many her most innovative exhibition was 'Nomad and City', mounted in 1976 in the Museum of Mankind as part of an Islamic festival (pl. 30), which introduced the smell of eastern spices and a taste of Arab sophistication into the centre of London. Soon after this she became swamped with administration as head of a large and growing department, and the last exhibition for which she was personally responsible was 'Captain Cook in the South Seas' in 1979.

Building Plans

The appointment of an exhibitions officer was a straw in the wind. The new Board of Trustees set about planning the future of the Museum in relation to its own needs and to the perceived needs of the public. In fulfilment of the obligations laid on them by the 1963 Act, the new Trustees published their first triennial report in 1969.[72] This was ground-breaking in that it not only laid out the achievements of the post-war years, but also began to present a plan for the future. It was a hard-hitting document aimed specifically at the Government. The first post-war report, it had, therefore, to cover:

> ... a period of more than twenty-five years, during which the normal progress of the Museum has been interrupted by a succession of distracting experiences – the evacuation and dispersal caused by the War of 1939–45, shattering bomb damage suffered by the fabric of the great Bloomsbury building, and a long and still uncompleted struggle to restore the ruined galleries. In the post-war years, moreover, it has had to try to take the strain of those vastly enlarged demands for facilities and services which museums are now called upon to provide for a general public that is at once more educated and more critical. ... the general situation of the Museum, one of this country's great institutions, appears to us to be so little satisfactory that we think it necessary to... [point out] the three or four outstanding problems that are urgently calling for solution.[73]

The Trustees outlined their needs – more space, more staff and more money for acquisitions and the repair of the bomb damage. They pointed to the fact that they had received two major financial benefactions since the war. The first was from a merchant banker, T.P. Brooke Sewell, who died in 1958, and who had created two funds by gift and bequest for the purchase of art objects from India and the Far Eastern mainland (the bequest, but not the gift, could also be used for the purchase of Japanese objects). The two funds at the time of the report amounted to about £1 million, and, unlike other Museum trust-funds, were invested in equities and not gilt-edged stock, so that capital appreciation became an actuality.[74] The second benefaction was the bequest of George Bernard Shaw which, after what proved to be a maverick attempt to produce a new alphabet, was to be shared between three institutions, the British Museum, the National Gallery of Ireland and the Royal Academy of Dramatic Art. At the time of the report the Museum share stood at £600,000 – enhanced as it was by royalties from the musical *My Fair Lady*. The Trustees pointed out that these funds were beginning to benefit the Museum's ability to acquire objects in a few specialized areas. Such private funds, however well invested, could, they stated, make only a minute difference. The report detailed the Grant-in-Aid, which for 1966–7 was £2,070,000, a sum which included an earmarked purchase-grant of £262,000 (of which £182,000 was used for the library departments). A further £1,666,000 was borne on the vote of the Ministry of Public Buildings and Works for building, maintenance and utilities, and £359,000 on the Stationery Office vote for publications. More than £1.5 million was spent on staff, publications and photographic services (of which £135,000 was returned to the Exchequer as 'appropriations in aid'). As a consequence only £142,000 was available for all general running costs.

The Trustees stressed that the money available for maintenance and other costs, including rebuilding the bomb-damaged galleries and providing a proper display of ethnography and a public restaurant, was quite insufficient. The ten-year programme of refurbishment put forward by the Ministry of Public Building and Works was already two or three years behind schedule.[75]

The Trustees were, however, principally concerned at this time about a new building to house the British Library. It had now been accepted that development on the Montague Street and Russell Square frontages to the east of the main building was unacceptable on conservation grounds. In 1952, after a public enquiry into the post-war County of London Development Plan, space was designated for a new national library on the site between Great Russell Street and New Oxford Street/Bloomsbury Way. This designation had been approved by the Minister of Housing in 1955, and in 1962 architects – Colin St John Wilson in association with Sir Leslie Martin – were appointed to draw up a scheme. Their imaginative plan of a two-winged library to the south and an open piazza between the Museum portico and St George's Church was approved in outline by the government in 1964.[76] The Ministry of Public Buildings and Works gradually purchased buildings in the area to be developed – some £2 million was spent on this exercise – and the scheme seemed set fair. In 1966, however, problems began to appear. Lena Jeger, the local Member of Parliament, started to agitate against the new plan on the grounds that historic buildings and much private housing would be demolished if it were to go ahead. In this she was backed by the Borough of Camden, the local planning authority. She raised the matter in Parliament in July 1967, but had obviously lobbied ministers strongly before this. On 26 October the project was killed stone dead by an announcement in Parliament by Patrick Gordon Walker, Secretary of State for Science and Education. The manner in which this decision was reached and the way in which it was conveyed – without any consultation or prior warning to the Trustees – affronted many on both sides of Parliament and outside Westminster. Protests were loud, but ineffective.[77]

Lord Radcliffe, Chairman of the Trustees, was incandescent, and, in a debate in the

House of Lords, made a memorable speech – later published – of such passion and length that it probably did the cause no good, but which was nonetheless a splendid parliamentary performance. As John Carter put it, 'a great public servant who is also a great jurist delivered, in a style compounded of fire and ice, a withering attack on the arbitrary and discourteous nature of the... administration'.[78] Radcliffe probably realized he had gone over the top, but was unrepentant, writing to Warden Sparrow of All Souls:

> It had impact... and that was what was intended. Indeed no one can say that he failed in his publicity who has received in one morning (a) an affectionate Christmas card with photograph from Godfrey Winn, (b) a request from David Frost for a television interview, (c) an invitation from Curtis Brown to write my memoirs for me. I think the British Museum affair a sheer scandal so I tag along though I am sick at heart over the whole thing.[79]

What lay behind the decision to cancel the library project will probably never be known.[80] Camden Council and Lena Jeger were the public face of the protest, but there may also have been a hidden agenda in that the Office for Scientific and Technical Information – which at that time carried a lot of clout – was involved in the affair. This body seems to have objected to the Museum's role as the national library, particularly in view of the transfer of the Patent Office Library to the Museum in 1966 and the establishment, under the Museum's ægis, of a National Reference Library of Science and Invention.[81] It may well have acted, with Camden, as spoilers of the scheme.

Credence may be lent to this hypothesis by the fact that at the end of the House of Lords debate, Lord Longford, for the government, announced the establishment of a committee to investigate the national libraries under the chairmanship of a scientist, Frederick Dainton, at that time Vice-Chancellor of Nottingham University and a skilled operator in the public arena. The structure of the committee – on which no librarian sat – indicated the interests of ministers and signalled the beginning of the end of the presence of the library departments in Bloomsbury. Only one member of the committee was drawn from the humanities. This was the Professor of the History of Fine Art at Edinburgh University, David Talbot Rice, who was a specialist in Byzantine art, not notably a user of libraries, nor even a significant figure in the corridors of power.[82]

Dainton

The new Chairman went to work quickly. He was charged with examining all aspects of the various government-funded science libraries, including that of the Science Museum, 'to consider whether in the interests of efficiency and economy such facilities should be brought into a unified framework'.[83] The Trustees set up a committee to give evidence. They produced a major document (edited by Lord Annan), printed in an appendix volume to the *Dainton report*,[84] and also gave oral evidence to the committee.

Dainton's report was published in 1969 and its main proposals are simply summarized. A new statutory body should be set up which would take over all the bibliographical and library responsibilities of the British Museum, together with the National Central Library, the National Reference Library of Science and Invention and the British National

Bibliography. It would also encompass certain information functions of the Office for Scientific and Technical Information. The Science Museum library was excluded from this body, it being suggested that it should be brigaded with the Lyon Playfair Library to form the central library for Imperial College, London. The National Central Library should be moved to join the National Lending Library for Science and Technology at Boston Spa in Yorkshire. The committee called for an investigation into automatic data processing in the library. They recommended that a board – the British Library Authority – be set up to administer the new body, and that a number of advisory councils should report to the board on major library units. Members of the board should be paid. On balance the committee backed the Bloomsbury site for a new building. The Museum's Trustees were in general agreement with Dainton, although they clawed back the Department of Prints and Drawings, which had in some way slipped into the library maw.[85]

There was at this critical moment a change of government. Harold Wilson was replaced by Edward Heath, and Lord Eccles (who had in 1968 succeeded Lord Radcliffe as Chairman of the Trustees) was suddenly catapulted into the post of Paymaster General, which gave him responsibility for the arts. He now held ministerial responsibility for the implementation of the Dainton report. His first act was to re-christen the putative authority as the 'British Library'. Eccles and the government accepted the main tenor of Dainton's recommendations in a White Paper in January 1971.[86] After a series of consultations, a bill was drawn up which, enacted in July 1972, established the British Library as a separate entity, finally divorced from the Museum.[87] The only formal remaining link was the Trustees' right to nominate one of their own members to the board of the new institution. The first such nominee was Sir Denis Hamilton. Although the British Library was not physically to leave the Museum until the late 1990s (the bindery remains at Bloomsbury at the time of writing), the two institutions had to live together – but separately governed – under one roof after the vesting day of 20 June 1973.[88] A civil servant, Harry Hookway, was appointed as Chief Executive of the British Library Board, whose Chairman was Lord Eccles, no longer a minister. A new building was to be provided for the Library and the government approved expenditure on it up to £36 million, although its site next to St Pancras Station was not decided until 1976. No consequential financial provision was allowed to the Museum, which would have to deal with an enormous problem when the library departed. On this matter successive governments remained obdurate.

A number of awkward matters still remained to be settled, but over the years they were agreed with surprisingly little rancour. There was an attempt by the keepers of the antiquities departments to retain the illuminated manuscripts, particularly those in the Department of Oriental Printed Books and Manuscripts, but this fell at the first hurdle. The Trustees, more tenacious, were worried about the appearance of the King's Library and entered into futile negotiations to try to retain the books in Bloomsbury, a matter which dragged on for nearly four years. The destination of the Shaw Bequest caused some in-fighting. It was decided that this should stay with the Museum, but that the Museum would continue to listen sympathetically to requests from the British Library for funding from it. Other purely library funds were passed to the new institution.[89]

From the point of view of the staff of the antiquities departments the one major matter on which no agreement could be negotiated, and one which still causes a certain amount of ill-feeling, was the withdrawal in the late 1990s of the right of the Museum staff to borrow printed books from the Library for use in their own offices. Although the departmental libraries had been built up separately from that of the Department of Printed Books, it had always been recognized that there should not be too much overlap and thus certain books were purchased by the central library to save money, or were received under copyright legislation. Such books could be borrowed at will by staff of other departments. These included expensive nineteenth-century luxury publications, but also, and more importantly, run-of-the-mill publications, such as standard historical texts and editions of poetry, as well as periodicals of local and national archaeological and historical societies. The obduracy of the Library had to be accepted, but the gaps will take years to fill.

New Faces at the Top

The Museum was not helped at this period by the fact that there was constant change at the top. Because of the necessary political manoeuvring of the 1970s, the Chairman of the Trustees became more deeply involved in the governance of the Museum. The Director was, to a certain extent, relegated to a back seat. Only under Lord Trevelyan and Sir John Pope-Hennessy after 1976 was the position reversed and power handed back. Radcliffe, the skilled negotiator, resigned the chairmanship in 1968 and was replaced by Eccles (pl. 28), a bibliophile politician of great charm and skill, who saw it as his duty to reform the way in which the Museum was run internally. In his two years he oversaw many changes. First, in 1969 he insisted that an Assistant Director be appointed, and brought into the post the formidable Maysie Webb, who had come to the Museum with the Patent Office Library to take charge of the National Reference Library of Science and Invention. A year later she also took over the Museum Secretary's responsibility for the establishment and in 1971 her job was re-designated as Deputy Director. She was to be a pivot at the top until her retirement in 1983. Eccles was deeply involved in staging the departure of the Director, Frank Francis, and the appointment of his successor. Francis's tenure had been extended by two years beyond the normal retirement age of sixty-five, and in 1968 he was probably, in view of the political problems inherent in the library situation, expecting a further extension. Eccles, however, realized that he was tired and that a new appointment would have to be made. Rather hurriedly he began to look round, but could find no obvious candidate. The senior keeper, Basil Gray of the Department of Oriental Antiquities, was drafted into the post as Acting Director. Many thought he should have been appointed on a permanent basis, but he was considered, at sixty-four, too old. So Sir John Wolfenden, a man of sixty-three, was appointed in his place in 1969 – the first outside appointment to the post since the foundation of the Museum. He was to be head of the institution until 1973, and the last to hold the title 'Director and Principal Librarian'. In 1970 Lord Trevelyan succeeded Eccles as Chairman.

Wolfenden was astonished to be offered the job, which, if his memoirs are to be believed, was proposed out of the blue in an informal manner by either the Permanent Secretary or the Secretary of State for Education.[90] He was enormously distinguished. He had in turn been an Oxford don, headmaster of two public schools, vice-chancellor of Reading University and Chairman of the University Grants Committee. He had also produced for the government a highly sensitive and sensible report on homosexuality which led to the liberalization of the law. He was seen as a safe pair of hands – the epitome of 'the great and the good' – and it seems certain that Eccles suggested his name and forced the appointment through. There was a row in the press when it was announced. Although polite, the academic staff generally resented him because he had no knowledge or experience of museums, but there was nobody among them of sufficient stature to take the post. Douglas Barrett, just appointed as Gray's successor as Keeper of Oriental Antiquities at the age of fifty-four, would perhaps have made a good director and would have been respected by his colleagues, but seemed to lack the necessary experience. The Museum never learnt to love Wolfenden and it is easy to believe that he was never really comfortable in the post, which he was to occupy for only four and a half years.

Despite this Wolfenden had attributes desperately needed by the Museum. Chief among them was a knowledge of both the theory and practice of administration. Ably abetted by Maysie Webb, he now set about reorganizing the central administration, restructuring it from top to bottom and charming money out of the government. Until Webb was established as Assistant Director, the common services of the Museum had been run by the Secretary and a handful of middle managers. These services covered accounts, security and the warding and security staff, publishing, maintenance, establishments and so on. Bridgewater, the Secretary, although urbane, amusing and full of knowledge about the way the Museum was run, was by now fairly indolent. He was due for retirement in 1973 and was in effect sidelined during the reorganization which now started.

The Museum, at the time of its separation from the Library, took a long look at its establishment and bid for 191 additional posts in the financial year 1972–3, mostly in administration and support staff in the departments. This was steep by any standards and, faced by the bid, the Department of Education and Science called in an outside firm of management consultants to examine the central administration.[91] Its report, which appeared in 1972, accepted much of the Museum's case and must have influenced the department's extraordinary agreement in that year to the appointment of ninety-seven extra staff – another seventy-six were funded in the following year and fifty-five in 1974–5.[92]

At last the Museum could be run properly. Three service departments were created. First, the Secretariat was reorganized. The Secretary's grading was reduced to Deputy Keeper level – George Morris, a Slavonic specialist from the Library, was appointed.[93] He was largely responsible for Trustee matters, aided by an Assistant Secretary, Edward Schofield, at Assistant Keeper grade. To this department was attached the registry, and a librarian/archivist post was established to bring order to the long series of central records. The archives so created were now designated an official depository under the Public Records legislation, although the extensive departmental records did not come under the control of the central archivist. (The post split in 1979 and a qualified archivist and a qualified librarian were appointed.)

In 1970 Wolfenden set up a properly constituted education service. For the first time the Museum got to grips with the need to make contact with teachers, not least so that education in all aspects of its collections could be provided for parties of schoolchildren between the ages of six and twelve. This department did little formal teaching; rather it provided education packs and inducted teachers into the usefulness of the collections in

their work. Research assistants were gradually appointed in each of the antiquities departments to provide educational services. The education section also embraced the information desk in the Front Hall. In the wake of the consultants' report the service was brigaded,
under a keeper, S.P. Cooper, with the Exhibition Office (now renamed the Design Office,
with a staff of fourteen), a newly reorganized photographic service (with twenty-eight
photographers) and an information and press office, to form the second major service
department.

A third department, Administrative Services, was created under a senior principal
brought in from the mainstream civil service. His empire embraced the establishment,
personnel, training, welfare, works, stationery, security and an accountant's office.
(Payroll functions were transferred to the Civil Service Department's Computer Centre.)
Many of the new elements had been there in embryo, but they were now reorganized and
properly staffed. Most of the service departments were headed by civil servants of the executive grade, but the specialist departments, such as education, were placed under graduates whose ranks were equivalent to the curatorial grades. In effect all these staff, other
than the Secretary, reported through their heads of department to the Deputy Director.

The Director's role was now more formally defined. It was recognized that he was
the Museum's chief executive and that he should take a wider managerial role than previously, particularly through the keepers in relation to the departments. The Director thus
became responsible for all curatorial and academic policy and, through the Deputy
Director, for the administration. In practice the Deputy Director took over responsibility
for finance and personnel matters (although the Director still remained responsible to
Parliament as Accounting Officer), while the Director gradually took the lead position with
regard to building and design matters. This distinction of roles between the Director and
Deputy Director, while not without occasional difficulty, was to last with minimum
problems of demarcation for the next twenty years, when in the light of changed circumstances the roles had once more to be redefined.

Such major reorganization could not, however, be achieved without initial stress.
Lord Eccles was a very hands-on Chairman. Wolfenden, who had a great public persona,
extensive administrative experience and a broad base in the outside world, was, however,
at sea in the intimate organization of the Museum. He was stuck between Eccles and
Webb, who had – in his words – 'pretty clear and forceful ideas of what there was to be
done', and could, if meticulous, occasionally be wilful.[94] Even when Lord Trevelyan was
appointed Chairman in 1970, Eccles, as Chairman of the British Library Board, was still a
slightly uncomfortable neighbour.

Outside, in the main body of the Museum, the keepers for the moment circled and
growled, imagining that their independence and power were being eroded, and criticizing
what they saw as creeping bureaucracy. They had, for example, for the first time to provide
an acquisition policy to the Trustees – one of Wolfenden's initial demands – and this
annoyed some, who trusted largely in serendipity to increase the collections.[95] Such a
policy document was, however, necessary to control the wilder flights of fancy not only of
the staff, but of the Trustees, whose judgement about purchases were not always soundly
based ('but it's the sort of thing we've got at home,' exclaimed one of the older-established
Trustees when asked to approve the purchase of a rare – if rather ugly – pair of Chelsea
vases of the 'gold anchor' period). It took some Trustees a long time to learn that the

Museum is not an art museum, but one with an historical base – taste is only peripherally a reason for the acquisition of objects for the British Museum.

There was a sub-text to all this reorganization. It was perceived by the far-sighted that when the Library left Bloomsbury, the Museum, under-serviced administratively, would have to stand on its own feet and would need a radically different core of services. Further, the rapid growth in visitor numbers (they had reached two and a half million by 1971) and a new exhibition policy were beginning to strain the Museum's human resources to breaking point. The curatorial departments were also reorganized, gaining in the process more staff, but this process was largely completed under Wolfenden's successor, Sir John Pope-Hennessy.

Another innovation, the groundwork of which had been laid under Francis, was the foundation of a friends' organization, 'The British Museum Society'. Founded in 1968 on the model of the successful Tate Gallery body, it had two functions, to make the general public more aware of the Museum and its problems, and to provide a base for fund-raising. Through its lectures, tours, and particularly its magazine it has now gained a solid core of informed and popular support for the institution. The first chairman was Sir Richard Thompson, a Trustee, but he soon made way for the dynamic and colourful Lady Hartwell, who was to take it from strength to strength.

British Museum Publications

Museum publications had long been a drain on resources. In the ten years from 1962 to 1972, the financial loss was £87,531, a sum that did not include the overheads of accommodation, services and so on, although the publications officer was a useful professional. The great catalogue series was run down almost to extinction and there were no souvenirs or merchandise other than books, postcards and slides. The Trustees were anxious that there should be more scholarly and popular publications. In January 1971 an outside consultant submitted a report to the Publications Committee of the Trustees recommending:

> That the Publications Department... be separated from the general administration of the Museum, and be administered by a separate body with capital raised from outside which would enter into contractual relationships with the Trustees of the British Museum to act as their publishers.

This was the first shot in a campaign, immediately approved by the Trustees, to found the company known as British Museum Publications. The Trustees emphasized that it should have charitable status and could be funded from Trust funds.[96]

Energetically led by Sir Denis Hamilton, whose drive was really responsible for the foundation of the future company, the Trustees now pursued the project through the Whitehall thicket. It took a long time, for this was new ground; no national museum (indeed no other government department) had erected a company totally free from departmental control. Against all odds the company was incorporated as 'British Museum Publications' on 2 November 1972, with a board of directors mainly composed of Trustees, but including a member of staff;[97] Hamilton was elected chairman.[98] It had been proposed that photographic services should be part of the company's remit, but in the end only the casts came under its control. Its main purpose was to provide a vehicle for the scholarly output of the Museum; more popular publications and souvenirs were to subsidize this. It was also intended that it should contribute to the Museum's income. The company started business in November 1973; the managing director was Michael Hoare, recruited from the old-established publishing house of Longman's.

The company was beset by financial difficulties from the beginning, particularly because it was immediately saddled with a debt of £182,362 – the independent valuation placed on the stock held by the Museum, which the Treasury insisted should be paid over by the new business. This was a ridiculously high assessment, but one against which there was no appeal, and the Trustees had to make provision to cover it from Trust funds. There was a great deal of scepticism outside the Museum as to whether the company could ever become profitable, not least in the Parliamentary Committee of Public Accounts. In his evidence to this body, the head of the government's Department of Education and Science gave a succinct account of the rationale behind his Department's agreement to the establishment of the company, saying that it would have 'a jolly difficult task' to turn the deficit round:

> [The Museum's] trading was always at a loss. What we thought we were doing was to protect the taxpayer from this function and we deduced that it was always likely to be a loss because the British Museum was not properly staffed to discharge that function. It was quite alien to their normal one, and therefore it seemed a reasonable proposition for the safeguarding of public money that we should take the loss off the taxpayer and create a separate company that would have to live or die on its own with no public money going to rescue it... At the moment the company is committed to the idea that if it has the right professional people (which it has never had before and for which you will have to pay something) and that if the business is organised on a suitably dynamic basis, there is money to be made here... Given that they have cut themselves off from the Museum, that they are not getting public money, that they have recruited first-rate staff, that they have good things to sell and that they develop the right policies, and allowing them two or three years to get over the initial inheritance of having to acquire the stocks that were going, there seems to be no reason why they should not make a profit... and, above all, not make a loss at the taxpayers' expense.[99]

At every stage of the negotiations it had been determined that there should be no public subsidy of the company and that the Museum should charge for all services. Such matters were largely agreed before the company was set up. But one problem was seized upon by the Parliamentary Committee of Public Accounts and would not go away. The committee made a great fuss about the rental charged by the Museum for its offices, then in Bedford Square (one of the perimeter buildings owned by the Trustees), which had been fixed at £2 per square foot for the initial three years of the company's existence in a letter from the Paymaster General, Lord Eccles, in June 1973.[100] Two years later the newly appointed Director, Pope-Hennessy, suffered greatly at the hands of the committee, which said that this level of rent amounted to a subsidy from the public purse. Pope-Hennessy fluffed his answer and was roundly – and unjustly – condemned in its report:

> Your Committee were disturbed and displeased at what we may regard as a departure from the normal standard of accuracy and frankness in the information given to that Committee and which a Select Committee of the House is entitled to expect from witnesses.[101]

There were strained apologies all round, but the Museum felt sore and its arm's-length relationship with the company was stretched almost to breaking point.

British Museum Publications, although primarily founded as a medium for the production of scholarly works, from the beginning built up a general publishing list and initiated the manufacture and licensing of souvenirs. After careful negotiation it was allowed to pay royalties not only to outside authors but also to staff who wrote more general books in their own time. It has been a financial success and under its three managing directors, Michael Hoare, Hugh Campbell and, until 2001, Patrick Wright, built up such a reserve fund that it was able to contribute almost £4.9 million to the appeal for the construction of the Great Court which opened in 2000 – a long way from the company's initial £182,000 deficit. Now known as the British Museum Company, it has a staff of about seventy and is still wholly owned by the Trustees. It now comprises various sections – the publishing arm (The British Museum Press), a merchandising division, a retail division and a division that organizes tours (British Museum Traveller). It runs book and souvenir shops both within the Museum and outside it, including one at Heathrow Airport.

The Museum of Mankind and Off-site Storage

Proposals to provide adequate accommodation for the vast and important collections of the Department of Ethnography had foundered consistently over a hundred years.[102] The new British Museum Act finally allowed the Trustees to abandon all pretence that they were going to construct a new wing on the Montague Street frontage. With the approval of the department they now cast around for space to help solve this problem and eventually leased a building in Burlington Gardens, behind the Royal Academy in Piccadilly. Originally built as the Senate House of the University of London, it had for many years been the headquarters of the Civil Service Commission (many senior members of staff had been interviewed for their posts in a room at the head of the main staircase). Importantly, it provided some 2,700 square metres of exhibition space. Between 1969 and 1972 the building was prepared to receive the display of the department's collections, the library (soon to incorporate the library of the Royal Anthropological Institute which had been given to the Museum), offices, workshops and some storage of material. For a short time the building had housed the British Academy and there was consequently an existing small lecture theatre. The stated intention of the exhibitions in Burlington Gardens was succinctly put in the *Report of the Trustees, 1966–9*:

> The new exhibition will not attempt to display, as has been the practice in the past, a small sample of every culture, but will concentrate instead on more intensive changing displays of a much smaller number of cultures. The public will thus be able to see much more of the collections over a period of time.[103]

To this end new and flexible modular showcases were designed which, while lightweight, lasted for nearly twenty-five years and housed many splendid exhibitions. In 1970 the department opened its first ten exhibitions in the new out-station, which in 1972 was, unhappily, named the Museum of Mankind.[104]

While the Museum of Mankind was well displayed and had a programme of splendid exhibitions, it had many physical drawbacks. In the first place it was leasehold – most undesirable for a museum, as such institutions are, by definition, intended to last for ever, and cannot depend on the whim of a ground landlord. Secondly, not having been built as a museum, it had many inconveniences. The ground floor was easily adaptable as a fine and elastic space for temporary exhibitions. The first floor was a muddle. At the head of the staircase was the senate room, flanked by other grand rooms of the old Senate House. These had to be dealt with tactfully, particularly since their panelled walls could not be touched. Galleries on this floor had to be approached through narrow passageways which were difficult to signpost. The Museum was also inconveniently situated between Bond Street and Regent Street, in a street little used save as a taxi rat-run. The building could not take the department's reserve collections, which were in 1972 out-housed in an old warehouse (also leased) in Shoreditch, in East London – later named Franks House. Curators were literally miles from their basic study materials; they and students had to visit them by means of a specially provided bus service – and, when they finally got to the store, there was no library. But perhaps the greatest disadvantage was the separation of the Department of Ethnography from its natural intellectual base. Overlap with other departments is important throughout the Museum; cross-disciplinary access to the collections was and remains a unique quality of its academic base – and one of its greatest strengths on the world scene.

Little thought seems to have been given to the future of the Department of Ethnography. There is some evidence of a hidden agenda to create a separate museum; indeed, the department occasionally needed a nudge from the centre to remind it that it was still part of the main Museum. For many reasons, not least the universal nature of the Museum's collections, it soon became clear that the creation of the Museum of Mankind could only be a temporary solution, and, thirty years later, with the departure of the Library, its future is assured as a main plank in the Bloomsbury structure with new galleries on the north side of the Great Court.

The space vacated by the Department of Ethnography in the Bloomsbury building allowed the expansion of other departments. Oriental Antiquities got a basement; Coins and Medals, Oriental Printed Books and Manuscripts and Western Asiatic Antiquities were to share the main Ethnographic gallery (although in the event only Western Asiatic Antiquities moved in – the rest of the space was used as a temporary exhibition gallery). Medieval and Later Antiquities received the old departmental offices and the Maudslay Room, which were later to become galleries.[105]

The Public Face

The Museum became much more conscious of its role in relation to the public, particularly as more and more television programmes increased the public's awareness of archaeology and art. A professional publications officer had been appointed in 1961, who was able, with the aid of the Gulbenkian Foundation, to initiate small and cheerful guides on specific subjects; the Museum's publications began to be seen in book fairs and exhibitions abroad, as far away as Japan. An information desk was opened in the Front Hall in the mid-1960s and educational services were becoming more proactive. The Friends organization (p.280) produced a popular magazine for members. Labels and displays were improving and the galleries were repainted and furbished in the contemporary image, which depended on plain-coloured walls, clean lines and minimal ornament. The Trustees began to investigate the possibility of cleaning the now deeply grimy façade of the building. The physical changes that took place in the years preceding the opening of the Museum of Mankind did a lot for the institution's public image. In 1960 the number of visitors was 805,846; by 1970 this had risen to 2,260,784, which includes the visitors at the Museum of Mankind.

A lecture theatre was created in the space below the Hellenic room in the early 1960s. It was much used. Gallery lectures were still given twice daily, except on Sundays, and short illustrated lunch-hour lectures, introduced in 1965, were very popular. In 1974 the lecture programme was substantially overhauled; only one daily guided tour was provided, but illustrated lectures were introduced on a daily basis. An education officer was, as we have seen, appointed in 1972, and schools and colleges were increasingly encouraged to visit the Museum. An *ad hoc* advisory committee of lecturers and teachers in the early 1970s drew up pilot schemes for making the Museum's resources available to teachers. The Education Office was located in 1 Bedford Square, a spacious building which provided rooms for classes and for meetings with teachers.

An enormous boost to the Museum's image and to its *amour propre* was the Tutankhamun exhibition in 1972. The achievement of this exhibition was a great diplomatic triumph for the Museum and for I.E.S. Edwards, Keeper of Egyptian Antiquities, in particular. A key figure in the negotiations was Sir Denis Hamilton, a Trustee who not only had political contacts in Egypt but, more importantly, as Editor-in-Chief of Times Newspapers was able to provide sponsorship for the exhibition by *The Times* and the *Sunday Times*. The catalogue was written by Edwards, who was allowed access to unpublished manuscript material deposited by Howard Carter, the tomb's discoverer, in the Metropolitan Museum, New York, and in the Griffith Institute at Oxford.[106] 1,694,117 visitors queued, sometimes for hours (pl. 29), to see this splendid show, which was extended to nine months from its original six. Visitors were charged entry and all profits (£654,474) were given to the UNESCO fund for the preservation of the temples of Philae.

Exhibitions mounted by the Department of Prints and Drawings (and the Department of Printed Books) had often been successful, but with the emergence of an exhibitions office, professionalism and taste came to the fore. The number of special exhibitions was impressive – ten in 1965, fifteen in 1966, eighteen in 1967 and 1968, and so on. Many of these (particularly those in the Library departments and in Prints and Drawings) were easy enough to mount (especially after the introduction of modern cases in a light-controlled gallery); but now they had professionally produced graphics. Some were more complicated, particularly as there was no dedicated exhibition gallery until 1979 (although for many years the southern end of the great first-floor gallery on the eastern side functioned in this role). Thus, for example, the loan exhibition 'Swedish Gold' in 1966 demanded extra security, specially built mounts and intelligent graphics in a section of the Edward VII Gallery. Others demanded more space, 'Glass' for example. Space had to be found where there was a temporarily empty gallery. Loan exhibitions were still rare and most exhibitions drew on the Museum's collections; some recorded gifts, as the Sedgwick collection of Chinese art, or recent finds made by the Egypt Exploration Society; others celebrated donors, Campbell Dodgson or Sloane for example; still others were thematic, or celebrated artists. The opening of the Museum of Mankind provided much space and many splendid exhibitions for the public, who flocked to see them – 300,000 by 1974. Some were enormously popular; none quite matched Tutankhamun, but in the years after this most popular of exhibitions they grew in importance and sophistication and were almost always accompanied by catalogues or professionally produced booklets.

Curatorial Changes

Basil Gray and the enigmatic Denis Haynes, Keeper of Greek and Roman Antiquities from 1956 until 1976, were the last of the pre-war appointments to retire as keepers. Staff appointed after the war now started to fill the senior posts. Barrett's appointment as Gray's successor has already been mentioned. Kenneth Jenkins had been appointed as Keeper of Coins and Medals in 1965, after nine years as deputy keeper specializing in Greek coins. R.A.G. Carson was now his deputy. Edmond Sollberger, a specialist in Sumerian who had been recruited in 1961 from the Musée d'art et d'histoire in Geneva, became Keeper of Western Asiatic Antiquities on the retirement of Barnett in 1974. He himself left in 1983 and was succeeded by Terence Mitchell. In 1974 T.G.H. James followed Edwards as Keeper of Egyptology and was to remain in that post until 1988. John Gere succeeded Croft-Murray as Keeper of Prints and Drawings in 1973 and, although sometimes appearing difficult, through his own work and that of his new appointments returned academic respectability to the department, which had suffered greatly under his predecessor.[107] His Italian speciality was balanced by the Northern interests of John Rowlands, who was appointed his deputy in 1974. Rowlands had come to the Museum in 1965, having first worked in the Birmingham Museum and Art Gallery and for five years as an editor at Clarendon Press, Oxford. Ian Longworth, a specialist in the Bronze Age and Neolithic, succeeded John Brailsford as Keeper of Prehistoric and Romano-British Antiquities in 1973. Longworth – a laconic and reliable Lancastrian – was only thirty-eight years old; he was, like his predecessor, a Cambridge graduate in archaeology. He had started his professional life in the National Museum of Antiquities of Scotland, before coming to the Museum in 1963.

While these senior members of staff were promoted, the complement of the antiquities departments gradually grew. There were by now so many staff that it is no longer possible to detail their careers as so far in this book. The reader is referred to Appendix I.

Scholarship

The basis of much academic endeavour both inside and outside the institution was changing, but the Museum's base remained the collections. As they increased, so the curatorial staff had to keep up with specialist knowledge and opinion on the periods which the objects represented. In some areas, where collections increased only marginally or along traditional lines, the catalogue remained central to the Museum process. Thus catalogues of coins, medals, prints and drawings, of discrete collections such as classical terracottas and of major gifts could still be produced, providing, as they had always done, primary but often innovative sources for scholars working in the various associated disciplines. Even in quickly developing fields like European archaeology, the catalogue could still play a major role. As late as 1960 it was still possible to catalogue late Anglo-Saxon metalwork because there had as yet been no major development in electronic metal-detecting, which was to flood museums throughout the country with this material in the 1970s and 80s. Such catalogues were conceived as necessary in that the material they recorded provided basic tools in interpreting and dating the sites and monuments of the period.

Archaeology in Britain was particularly fast-moving at this period, both as regards work in the field but also in the application of natural scientific methods to archaeological material and in the examination of the basis of archaeological theory. Television and synthetic books, such as the *Ancient Peoples and Places* series published by Thames and Hudson (of which two of the first ten were written by members of the Museum staff), stimulated a wider interest in archaeology, at both popular and academic level. Specialist journals were founded and made their impact alongside the publications of the period societies. Excavation in Britain increased almost exponentially from the late 1960s with a growing awareness of the threat to archaeological sites caused by uncontrolled development in town and countryside. The foundation of the pressure group 'Rescue' was a symptom of this interest, which helped to stimulate a rise in government expenditure on rescue excavation. Professionalism in field archaeology was underlined by the foundation of regional archaeological trusts to undertake rescue excavation, and in 1982 a professional body of field archaeologists was founded to set and preserve standards.

Excavation had moved away from the trenching and grid methods pioneered by Pitt Rivers and Sir Mortimer Wheeler. Excavators in Britain now began to follow techniques developed in the 1930s on the lighter soils of the Soviet Union, Denmark, Holland and Germany. These techniques, which were introduced into England by the German archaeologist Gerhard Bersu at Little Woodbury immediately before the war, were driven by an interest in settlement archaeology and its relevance in the interpretation of the development of society. The new techniques involved the opening up of large areas to reveal a site period by period, by shaving off the layers. More material, not just artefacts, could now be recovered and studied. British archaeologists from Cambridge, particularly Eric Higgs and Claudio Vita-Finzi, pioneered new processes of extraction by flotation of seeds and other organic remains from large-scale excavations in Northern Greece and their work was paralleled on the Continent, particularly in Czechoslovakia. Waterlogged sites were eagerly sought so that organic artefacts, long missing from the archaeological record, could be found and wooden structures investigated. The horrendous development of town centres throughout Europe demanded the excavation of urban areas of Roman or medieval origin on a scale undreamed of before the war. All these developments affected the Museum departments most involved in European archaeology – Prehistoric and Romano-British Antiquities, Medieval and Later Antiquities, the Research Laboratory and, to a lesser extent, Coins and Medals. The new developments not only brought in more material, but they demanded the use of the Museum's expertise on a greater scale than before, particularly as the new excavators had little detailed experience of material culture.

The Museum itself was now, with the universities, a major provider of research, rather than rescue, excavation.

Nor was it unaware of the theoretical developments, particularly in archaeology, that were taking place in the universities. On the one side Grahame Clark at Cambridge had written influentially about the economic basis of societies revealed by archaeology, and particularly through the application of the natural sciences. On the other hand there was a move away from the cultural-historical methods of the first half of the century developed in Germany by Carl Schuchardt and Gustaf Kossina, who by analogy with the methods used in studying the continental semi-historical Migration Period had identified and interpreted people ethnically through their material culture. While the right-wing Kossina (who died in 1931, before Hitler came to power) developed strongly nationalistic theories of race which were much to influence Nazi thinking, other scholars, like the Marxist Gordon Childe and his followers, used similar methods, rejecting, however, all racial theories. They identified individual cultures by their archaeological assemblages as seen in museums, postulating a continuous wandering of peoples and ideas out of the East. Strict cultural-historical methods were widely used elsewhere. In the years before and after the war one of Kossina's students, Józef Kostrzewski, turned his methods against his master to develop theories about the ethnic migration of the Slavs, an element which dominated Eastern European archaeological thinking under the Communist regime in the post-war years. Such writing was based on the study of material culture, and therefore, by definition, on material in museums. It was of only limited success as it denied the possibility of the evolution of culture, refusing to accept outside influences. Discussion of ethnic issues of this sort is still important today as we consider, for example, the Anglians, the Thracians and, more controversially, the Celts.

Under American influence anthropology and archaeology moved closer together and cultures of widely different date and geographical area were now compared. From this grew the 'New' or 'processual archaeology' of the 1960s. Its aim was to use rigorous scientific methodologies to test hypotheses about cultures and assemblages. Theoretical systems, like those developed in the biological sciences, were postulated in order to describe ancient situations in general terms, without making assumptions based on historical analogy of the type developed by Kossina and Childe. Hypothetical patterns of material culture were erected which could be reconstructed without reference to ethnicity, on the basis of hierarchical judgements concerning the types of sites uncovered by archaeology. Theoretical archaeologists ventured into structuralism, systems theory and other such abstractions against a more open political background as Fascism and Communism collapsed. They tested their hypotheses with much-vaunted rigour, wrapped their results round with some private jargon, and moved to compare different cultures in different parts of the world, as though to erect natural laws of human behaviour.

These were stirring times, but the new theories left Museum scholars floundering and unfashionable, although some, like the African ethnographer John Mack, fought back.[108] Museum archaeology was firmly based in historical mode and it was not until there was a reaction against many of the new models which had placed human societies in a strait-jacket, alterable only through environmental variation, that the work of the museum-based scholar became more relevant to the archaeological profession. There was, however, a return to an interest in historical method which, combined with archaeology and ethnology, produced a more linear perception of human development and cultural influence. Further, greater attention was now paid to laboratory analysis, to wider interpretative use of objects and ecological factors produced by the expanding excavation archive. In the early 1970s Colin Renfrew, breaking away from some of the models of the New Archaeology and from Childe's diffusionist theories of *ex oriente lux*, built a series of historical postulates for prehistory. His arguments were based on the dating methods introduced by the natural and physical sciences (radiocarbon dating, dendrochronology, potassium-argon dating and so on). Such postulates, however much they were argued, rested more happily with the work of the Museum in that they illuminated its work on the actual material and allowed its archaeologists to communicate with the theoreticians on a similar level. Indeed, by this time the Museum was deeply involved in laboratory dating techniques.

The arguments of the theoreticians chiefly affected the prehistorians and ethnographers in the Museum and, at a later stage, its classical and oriental archaeologists. Historical archaeologists in the Museum, as in the universities, managed to avoid too deep an involvement in either processual or post-processual archaeology. They were, however, like their 'prehistoric' colleagues, able to use the new scientific methodologies to build up a much more refined chronological framework for the Museum's ever-expanding excavation archive, some of which came from their own research excavations (see p.293). Curators of all periods were able to use the new methodologies alongside their own expertise to explain both new material and that from older collections in safer contexts. Their position was not unlike that of archaeologists in China or in Communist Eastern Europe, who bowed to theory but spent much time studying the expanding archaeological archive to document technological, economic and ecological change against a background that was becoming clearer through the application of scientific methods of conservation, dating and analysis. The pages of *the British Museum quarterly* from the mid-1960s onwards demonstrate increasing collaboration between the Research Laboratory and the antiquities departments.

At its simplest level new conservation techniques were developed in the Department of Western Asiatic Antiquities to increase the rate of production of the publication of cuneiform texts by means of baking and desalinating tablets so that they could be more easily handled by staff and students, a process started in the 1950s.[109] On a more sophisticated scale the development outside the Museum of good dendrochronological series allowed of narrower dating of objects as well as structures. Thermoluminescent dating of pottery was now routinely used and research was being carried on into extension of the technique. In the early 1970s computers began to appear in the Research Laboratory and were used for a number of purposes, including analysis of X-ray diffraction patterns.

To a lesser extent other fields of the Museum's interest – particularly the fine arts – were affected by fashionable (although now often outmoded) theory. In the applied arts, however, contact with collectors and connoisseurs was still of great importance, and as the connoisseur became more rigorous in his methods – as for example in Bernard Watney's study of English pottery – such contacts became increasingly valuable. Similarly, the more rigorous amateur coin collectors, such as Christopher Blunt in his study of Anglo-Saxon coins, worked with the professionals in the Museum to build a modern approach to numismatics. Analytical technologies based in the Research Laboratory were increasingly used. From the mid-1970s these were used on archaeological material, as for example in the analysis of the composition of copper alloys from the fourth millennium BC to the fifth century AD, which produced significant information concerning the development of metallurgy. Later, similar analyses were applied to coins and other historical material. The Laboratory began to have an increasingly important role in deciding on the authenticity of objects offered for purchase to the Museum, or indeed of material already in their collections. In the Trustees' *Report* for 1972–5, for example, it is stated that (other than ceramics, for which thermoluminescent dating techniques were available) of 148 objects examined, forty-two proved doubtful.[110]

The value of the traditional Museum catalogues was still recognized and in some areas produced ground-breaking work; but the information explosion, to a certain extent based on the computer, made the publication of such catalogue series as those of Dodgson and Hind nearly impossible to achieve. The work of curators was now more often fined down in comprehensive exhibition catalogues and in such later synthetic works as Antony Griffiths's *Landmarks in print collecting*, which stands alongside Hind's *A short history of engraving and etching* as an indispensable tool for the student of prints. In a different mode, material could now be made available more economically, as with the British Academy's *Sylloge of coins of the British Isles*, where the Museum has conformed to a publication format created externally. The publications company now enabled the Museum to deliver research more efficiently.

Some scholarly works were more difficult to bring to fruition than others and the publication of the Sutton Hoo catalogue presents a precautionary, if unique, tale of procrastination and obfuscation. Rupert Bruce-Mitford was a stubborn and devious man, a scholar of international repute but limited vision, who irritated practically everyone he worked with. He had since the war been engaged on the production of a great definitive work on this greatest of all Anglo-Saxon graves. But he could never bring it to conclusion and was generally secretive about the results of his research and the progress of the project. In 1964 the Trustees, having allowed him a great deal of rope, lost patience and took serious action, demanding that he deliver the report by 1969. Backed by Werner, Keeper of the Research Laboratory, he asked for an extension to allow further scientific research and analysis and, when this was granted, resumed his former procrastination. The Trustees, exasperated, took drastic action and in 1968 appointed a full sub-committee to oversee the project. This consisted of three of the archaeological heavyweights on the board – Stuart Piggott, professor of archaeology at Edinburgh, who had taken part in the 1939 excavations, Dr Kathleen Kenyon, excavator of Jericho, and Lord Fletcher, a distinguished amateur of Anglo-Saxon archaeology. Piggott was soon replaced by Sir Mortimer Wheeler, the most famous archaeologist of his day. They stopped Bruce-Mitford's plans for further excavation on the site (he had dug there briefly in 1967), seconded him from his keepership, provided him with a number of research assistants – particularly Angela Evans, who bore much of the day-to-day burden – and monitored his progress on a monthly basis. In 1971 Bruce-Mitford reported that the work was finished, but it was not; and the first volume did not appear until 1975. The third volume appeared in two parts in 1983. The whole is a triumph of detail, perhaps over-elaborate and, in some respects, blinkered. The Trustees, however, had fulfilled an obligation to a uniquely important excavation which had taken place forty years previously.

Collecting

The Department of Ethnography had already become more adventurous. Bryan Cranstone, in 1963–4, investigated the mountain people at the headwaters of the Sepik and Fly rivers in the Central Highlands of New Guinea. He produced 437 well-documented specimens for the collection, which were first exhibited in 1966, accompanied by a small catalogue.[111] Central America still continued to attract attention and Adrian Digby, the keeper, was granted special leave in 1956 to excavate in British Honduras, with the aid of a grant from the Pilgrim Trust.[112] Later, in 1970, a British Museum excavation in Honduras, jointly sponsored with Harvard University, worked on Joyce's old Maya site at Lubaantún (see p.226), confirming his dating and many of his observations, and adding interesting supplementary material to the collections.[113] Staff in the Department of Ethnography were now expected to undertake field-work and in 1967 and 1968, for example, Shelagh Weir worked in Palestine and Elizabeth Carmichael in the British West Indies. From such expeditions the ethnographers were able to bring back contemporary material typical of fast-disappearing cultures, which now became an important target of the Museum's collecting policy.

The period immediately following the war was one of great collecting opportunity, partly because increasing tax burdens forced collectors and heirs to realize assets that would not otherwise have come on the market. Further, as the period of Empire drew to a close, collections formed by missionaries and colonial administrators were found too burdensome to retain privately. The Museum, within its limited resources, was in some respects able to take advantage of the circumstances. In some areas it was, for almost the first time, stating its priorities and taking action. In others serendipity continued to hold sway. Accessions stood almost at a record level. In 1966, for example, the Department of Ethnography was able to state that since 1939 nearly 50,000 items had been added to the collection, of which the largest single element was 15,000 items given by the Wellcome Trust.[114] Other collections included, for example, the mostly African material held in the museum at Kew Gardens,[115] and the important collection of African art built up by two London-based Americans, Mr and Mrs Webster Plass, given in 1956.[116] In 1971 first steps were taken to draw up a formal acquisitions policy for the department, but this was not finalized until the appointment of Malcolm MacLeod as keeper in 1974.

Even in more traditional areas of collection there was progress. Only a few of the many major acquisitions can be mentioned. Some 131 items from the Southesk collection of cylinder seals were purchased for the Museum by the National Art Collections Fund.[117] In 1960 the Department of Greek and Roman Antiquities was enabled by a grant from the Fund to acquire the collection of classical jewellery formed by the seventh Lord Elgin, which had long been on loan to the Museum.[118] The National Art Collections Fund appears frequently in the list of donors at this period, as it does to this day. Not only, however, did the Fund give money towards purchases, but it was used more and more as a conduit for the channelling of gifts and bequests. Other individuals and bodies which helped the Museum purchase objects included Chester Beatty, I.D. Margary, the Isaac Wolfson Fund, the Pilgrim Trust and the Worshipful Company of Goldsmiths.

In 1945 the Duke of Portland realized one of his assets and the Portland Vase, for so long an ornament of the collections (see p.46), was finally purchased by the Museum.

Bequests continued to flow. In 1947, for example, a Chinese collection, chiefly of pottery vessels and jades of all periods, was received from Harry Oppenheim,[119] and in 1963 Dr Louise Samson bequeathed twenty-four sculptures from Thailand.[120] In 1958 A.D. Passmore presented nearly a hundred items, mostly of English pottery.[121] Treasure trove increasingly provided a method of acquisition by purchase. Perhaps the most important such find of this period was the first group of the Snettisham gold collars, which came in 1948 and 1950. This was the prelude to the Museum's excavations at this Norfolk site in 1990, which produced further hoards, with a combined weight of 20 kg of silver and 15 kg of gold – the richest such find from Iron Age Europe.[122]

One major item got away. This was the 'Bury St Edmunds Cross', a major English Romanesque ivory, which appeared in mysterious circumstances in the possession of an expatriate Yugoslav, Ante Topic Mimara.[123] A full-scale photograph of this hitherto unknown and totally unprovenanced object (then in a Swiss bank vault) was brought into the Museum one Saturday in 1981, when I happened to be on duty. I had only a short time with the photograph, but I was convinced of its authenticity and asked Mr Topic Mimara to return on Monday and show it to Peter Lasko, the Romanesque specialist, who with Rupert Bruce-Mitford spent the next year and a half trying to acquire the object. Eventually the money – £200,000 – was raised with the aid of a Treasury grant; but, because Topic Mimara could neither prove his title to the cross nor give it a provenance, the Museum had to turn it down, to its great regret. These ethical considerations did not disturb the Metropolitan Museum in New York, which purchased the piece in 1983. It is now the chief ornament of the Cloisters Museum.

The most traditional of the departments as regards collecting was Coins and Medals. They purchased widely in the salerooms and received some splendid gifts and bequests of which one of the most important was the bequest of Sir Allen George Clark; although generalist, it included some fine gold specimens, Greek, Roman, English and American.[124]

An emerging source was the acquisition of objects in lieu of estate duty. Although this method had been theoretically possible since 1930, the Museum had never benefited from such unusual benevolence on the part of the Exchequer.[125] An early acquisition under this heading was the Chatsworth Apollo – a fifth-century BC bronze head found in the early nineteenth century at Tamassos in Cyprus, which came from the collection of the Dukes of Devonshire.[126] The Treasury still occasionally made special grants for the purchase of objects; almost the last such was £60,000 granted for the purchase for £240,000 of the medieval Savernake Horn in 1975. The National Art Collections Fund and the Goldsmiths' Company helped the Museum buy this splendid object, and the Treasury also advanced £130,000 which was reimbursed over two years.[127]

The loss of major national treasures to the nation had been discussed by the Museum since the end of the century and was one of the spurs to the foundation of the National Art Collections Fund in 1903. Despite various attempts to set up a system for the control of the export of works of art and antiquities, the only pre-war success was the establishment in 1922 of the 'paramount list' of a very few outstanding pictures, for the purchase of which the Treasury was willing to grant money, if they were sold to purchasers outside the country. Between 1922 and 1952 only two pictures – the Wilton Diptych and Titian's *Vendramin Family* – were saved in this way. By clever use of wartime emergency legislation some works of art were stopped for export, but, as the art trade revived after the war, this legislation proved inadequate and a Reviewing Committee on the Export of Works of Art, consisting of civil servants and a number of directors or keepers of national institutions, was set up in 1949. In the following year Sir Stafford Cripps, as Chancellor of the Exchequer, set up a departmental Committee on the Export of Works of Art under the chairmanship of Lord Waverley. The Waverley Committee reported in 1952 and confirmed the importance of the Reviewing Committee's powers to stay the export of objects of art, antiquities and manuscripts considered to be of outstanding national importance.[128] They also set out the 'Waverley criteria', which have been used by the revamped Reviewing Committee ever since. Unfortunately the Reviewing Committee was given no funds and its only available sanction was to delay export. (Purchase was sometimes funded by the Treasury using the National Land Fund – a memorial fund set up to commemorate those who died in the two wars.) The procedure allowed the committee to put an indefinite stop on the export of objects which had been stopped and for which a public institution had made an offer at the full market price. The system was very occasionally abused by crooked dealers, but on the whole worked well. Generally, foreign museums respected the British law and, if the money could be found, allowed British museums to purchase the objects withheld by the committee. But not always: in one notable case an album of drawings by Claude Lorrain was purchased by the National Museum of Stockholm, which (after it had been stopped by the Reviewing Committee) refused to sell it to the Museum and deposited it in the Swedish Embassy in London for a number of years. It is now (quite legally) in Stockholm. Most museums acted in a more colleaguely fashion.

Perhaps the most important acquisition by the Museum in the middle of the century was the collection of clocks and watches formed by C.A. Ilbert. It consisted of 277 clocks (of which seventy were Japanese), thirty-eight chronometers, more than 1,000 watches, 741 watch movements and miscellaneous associated material. The negotiations in 1957 and 1958 were long and arduous; Bruce-Mitford as keeper wrote memorandum after memorandum to the Trustees, until they became heartily sick of them. They criticized him, for example, for bringing the collection to the Museum without authorization at a cost of £87 10s – but he persisted. Frantic fund-raising began, particularly when a sale of the collection at Christie's was threatened – a catalogue of the watches was even published. The Treasury refused a special grant. At the eleventh hour a benefactor appeared. Gilbert Edgar of the Worshipful Company of Clockmakers purchased all the clocks for the Museum and made a substantial donation towards the purchase of the watches and other objects, the balance being raised by a public appeal organized by the Master of the Worshipful Company, M.L. Bateman. The Company also agreed to pay the salary of Philip Coole, an experienced watchmaker and horologist, who had looked after the collection for Ilbert. The British Museum, which already had a substantial collection, thus became the owner of perhaps the finest historical collection of timepieces in the world, suitably housed in a students' room and workshop in the White Wing as the result of a further benefaction from Mr Edgar. Michael Inchbald gave an horological library and a gallery was set aside in the early 1970s to display the collection.[129]

Between 1941 and 1950 the Department of Prints and Drawings boasted that it had acquired nearly 30,000 'prints, drawings, books of prints and books of reference', despite the fact that no purchase grant was available between 1941 and 1946.[130] The greatest acquisition was the collection of (chiefly Italian) drawings that had belonged to one of the most famous and eccentric collectors of the nineteenth century, Sir Thomas Phillips, many of which had come from Sir Thomas Lawrence's collection (mostly bought in 1860 at the Woodburn sale). The drawings had been inherited by his grandson, T. Fitzroy Fenwick, who in 1935 had commissioned Popham to catalogue them.[131] The Museum received 1,277 drawings from this collection in 1946, presented anonymously by Count Seilern, who had bought them for the Museum. This was a great coup by Popham, who was aided and abetted by Johannes Wilde, Seilern's expert adviser. Seilern kept a few outstanding drawings for himself and bequeathed them to the Courtauld Institute, where Wilde worked. Single acquisitions included the great sixteenth-century botanical album by Jacques le Moyne de Morgues, which was purchased with the help of many funds in 1962, later to be triumphantly published in facsimile by Paul Hulton.[132] Among other acquisitions were 8,000 bookplates, collected by Eric Viner specifically to supplement Franks's bequest, 9,000 paper items concerned with the London retail trade bequeathed by Sir Ambrose Heal, which brought up to date Miss Banks's trade-card collection, and eighteen volumes of Christmas cards collected by Queen Mary between 1872 and 1947. This last must have caused the scholarly and aesthetically-minded Popham some trauma, particularly as Queen Mary continued to add to the collection until her death – a total of 2,621 cards.[133]

Although linked to the Bloomsbury Group through family connections (his daughter was married to Quentin Bell), Popham was unable to appreciate much contemporary art, and was particularly antagonistic to German Expressionism. Thus he rejected the offer by Dr Rosa Schapire, a German refugee, as a gift or bequest of a virtually complete set of prints by Schmidt-Rottluff. Although he resiled from the modern, Popham importantly reached an agreement with the Trustees that the purchase grant could be used for the acquisition of modern material, but it must be said that the fund was rarely used for this purpose.[134] In 1967, however, at the insistence of Lord Radcliffe, the Trustees established a fund for the purchase of modern graphic art which was for the time being used in a haphazard, and sometimes offhand, basis – Bomberg, Frink, Grosz, Munch, for example, and, strangely, some Kokoschka stage designs.[135]

Just discernible was the beginning of a more considered collecting policy. It has been shown that the Department of Ethnography was now seriously committed to systematic fieldwork in order to provide well-documented collections. The Department of British and Medieval Antiquities also began to consider the balance of its collections. To take an example, in a lecture to the Museums Association in 1956, Bruce-Mitford stated: 'The British Museum does not possess material from a single inhumation cemetery of the Anglo-Saxon period that has been scientifically excavated and properly recorded by modern methods...'.[136] He proceeded to rectify this omission in 1963 by acquiring the material from the cemetery at Buckland, Dover, excavated by Vera Evison.[137] A little later, in 1970–1, the department itself excavated a cemetery at Broadstairs, Kent, directed by Leslie Webster, a newly appointed assistant keeper.[138] Material from other cemeteries and settlement sites (which were also under-represented in the collections) followed.

Excavation had in fact been a tool for contextual acquisition for some time. John Brailsford and Ian Richmond carried out excavations between 1951 and 1958 on an Iron Age and Romano-British hill-fort at Hod Hill, Dorset, which put the material acquired with the Durden collection in 1892–3 in context and allowed the publication of the older acquisition.[139] In the late 1960s Gale Sieveking excavated a well-known Palaeolithic site at High Lodge in Suffolk, which produced Acheulian implements in context on a well-known gravel site.[140] Excavation by Grahame Clark of Cambridge University brought to the Museum a part of the major find of organic material from the first properly excavated Mesolithic site in the country, at Star Carr, Seamer, Yorkshire.[141] An important acquisition came through the Museum's excavation of a fourth-century Romano-British mosaic pavement at Hinton St Mary, Dorset, which provided the earliest known British portrait of Christ.[142] Other excavated material was acquired through the Ancient Monuments section of the Ministry of Works and its successors. An important documented collection was the Testot-Ferry material from the original Palaeolithic excavations at the type-site of Solutré in France.[143] A new method of acquisition of English material was initiated by Bruce-Mitford in 1961, when he received permission from the Trustees to use the departmental purchase grant to acquire representative material from the excavations of the Anglo-Saxon cemetery at Loveden Hill, Lincolnshire. The sum was modest (£200) – it helped finance the excavation – but the method used, which benefited both the Museum and the excavation, gradually became a major method of acquiring new and properly excavated material.[144]

But excavation was not the only way in which archaeological scholarship was served. A little later Bruce-Mitford was responsible for the initiation of a national reference collection of national and international medieval pottery, which became an invaluable tool in the burgeoning study of medieval archaeology.

In the Department of Western Asiatic Antiquities, excavations by Max Mallowan at Nimrud on behalf of the British School in Iraq continued work which had been started in 1845 by Layard and continued by Smith in 1873–6 – putting their finds into a more up-to-date context. Division of objects between the country of origin and the excavator was still possible in some areas and the most remarkable material acquired by the Museum as a result of such excavations was a group of eighth-century BC ivories, including a now-famous plaque of a lioness mauling an African.[145] Barnett, the keeper after 1955, was basically an archaeologist and not bound, as had been so many of his predecessors in the department, by texts. He sought to make the collections more representative of the region. A typical new departure was the acquisition of material from the excavations by Kathleen Kenyon at Jericho of the contents of a Middle Bronze Age tomb group and a plastered human skull of the Neolithic period. Material was also acquired from the Gulf, particularly the Higham collection of Bronze Age and Parthian grave-goods from Bahrain deposited on loan in 1971 and finally purchased in 1999.[146] In general there had always been a tendency in this department to carry on the excavation work of its predecessors; Barnett had thus brought a more pragmatic approach to acquisition, an approach that continues to be successful. The Department of Egyptian Antiquities for much of this period, on the other hand, relied mainly on two sources in its acquisition policy – objects in private hands and excavated material made available through the Egypt Exploration Society, to which the Museum contributed financially.

The Department of Oriental Antiquities, particularly in the early 1970s, was the fortunate recipient of many gifts, especially the Seligman collection of Chinese bronzes and pottery – 408 pieces – and another collection of Chinese material, including eighty-seven superlative pieces of lacquer of the thirteenth to eighteenth centuries, given by Sir

Harry and Lady Garner.[147] A further gift of twenty-two outstanding pieces of Jingdezhen porcelain of the fourteenth and fifteenth centuries came from Sir John Addis (later a Trustee), who also published them.[148] While pursuing its traditional collecting policy through gift and purchase, the department had also embarked on a systematic improvement of the Indian sculpture collections. Encouraged by good relations with the Indian Archaeological Service, Douglas Barrett, on a number of visits to India, filled in many gaps, helped by the Brooke Sewell Fund. He himself was a generous donor to the Museum and, with his wife, later gave the Ashmolean Museum at Oxford a major collection of similar material. Excavation was also undertaken by the department in Thailand.

Alone at Last

Wolfenden's departure in 1973 coincided with the separation of the British Library from the Museum. As the Trustees began their search for a successor they could be well satisfied with the preparations that had been made for independence. The Trustee body itself had been totally reconstructed; the political element was now much smaller, Lord Boyd being the most senior of the ex-ministerial Trustees to survive (he was also perhaps the most influential of all his colleagues). Academic Trustees were very much to the fore. They included three archaeologists (Kathleen Kenyon, Max Mallowan and Mortimer Wheeler), an art historian (Lord Clark) and various vice-chancellors and heads of Oxbridge colleges (one of whom was Edmond Leach, the anthropologist); the scientists included Edward Hall, head of the Research Laboratory for Archaeology at Oxford. Lord Trevelyan, who it is said distrusted Wolfenden,[149] was for a short period very much hands-on, appropriating an office in the Director's Corridor which he used regularly.

The administration had been reconstructed and the Museum, under the effective leadership of Wolfenden and Maysie Webb, had been put on a firm financial footing. For the moment, the government grant (which stood at £2.968 million) appeared to be index-linked against inflation. The academic staff, having suffered the changes in silence, were buoyed up by the thought of a new Director, the search for whom now got under way.

Chapter 8

FREEDOM OR CONTROL?

1973–2002

The appointment of Sir John Pope-Hennessy (pl. 28), Director of the Victoria and Albert Museum, to Wolfenden's post was as surprising as it was necessary. By his own account he was a reluctant candidate, being approached on three occasions in early 1972: 'The idea of exchanging a museum I understood for one covering areas in which I had no special competence was disconcerting, and I [said]... that in no circumstances would I accept the appointment.' However,

> ... at the annual dinner of the British Academy, I found myself seated next to Lord Boyd, a long-standing trustee of the museum. Halfway through the meal he gave me a list of the candidates being considered for the post. It was so weak that I agreed to reconsider my decision. Next morning at ten o'clock the chairman of the trustees, Humphrey Trevelyan, and Alan Boyd came down to my office and offered me the post, promising their support in modernising the museum and its procedures. [1]

The upshot was that Pope-Hennessy agreed to accept the post, on the one condition that he would not have to live in the 'director's rather forbidding residence'. One of the main reasons he accepted was his admiration of Trevelyan and his commitment to making fundamental changes at a time when the British Library was finally split off administratively from the Museum.

Wolfenden retired with a peerage, and on 2 January 1974 Pope-Hennessy took up the post. It was hardly an auspicious beginning. The Heath government was failing, a miners' strike had forced the introduction of a three-day working week and a ham-fisted ministry had, without consultation, introduced admission charges for all national museums. The charges were strongly opposed by most of the arts community, but Heath remained intransigent despite pleas from many close to him. The introduction of charges coincided with Pope-Hennessy's first day at the Museum. On the advice of the Department of the Environment the ticket machines had been placed under the portico in the open air; the machinery had seized up since their installation and the new director's first executive decision had to be to waive the charges until the problem was solved. (Charges were withdrawn as one of the first acts of the Labour government after the general election in March.)

Union Trouble and Staff Development

The climate of the times and the political state of the country had its effect on staff relations within the Museum. Trade unionism was in the ascendancy and the Museum reflected the national picture. The museum unions included their fair share of militants, including one or two who had won their spurs in the London docks. Loyalty to management was almost non-existent and leaks to the press were consequently endemic. Administrators had to tread delicately and Maysie Webb, who dealt with staff matters, with her small group of advisers steered a discreet course through the tangled demands of union officers. They were not helped by the fact that their own union, the Association of First Division Civil Servants, vacillated, partly because they resented much of what Wolfenden and even Pope-Hennessy stood for. This union felt particularly slighted by the appointment of outsiders not only to the post of Director, but also, under Pope-Hennessy, by the appointment of keepers from outside the Museum, and the consequent effect on career prospects. The new Labour government also had its fair share of trouble with the unions and had to bow to them, to the extent that it was even thought that there might have to be a union representative on the board of Trustees.[2] The unions expressed their power from time to time; there was an occasional 'day of action' and, more seriously, a full-blown, twenty-four-hour strike by members of the security staff. Most ludicrously, the place reserved for a staff member on the board of the publications company – intended for a curatorial representative who could advise on the academic side – was hijacked, due to supine neglect by the First Division Association, and a militant clerical officer was forced upon it.

Generally, however, the unions were more of an irritant than a threat, and over the next fifteen years relations returned to normal. This process, although conditioned by the political climate of the Thatcher years, was helped by more informal contact of management and staff and by the introduction by Webb of a number of emollient measures, including a staff suggestion scheme (with financial sweeteners) and awards for all staff who had served more than twenty-five years. Further, the greatly increased government expenditure on the public services in the 1970s supported the more logical and efficient staff structure trailed under Wolfenden; and the staff became happier as, for almost the first time in the Museum's history, an adequate purchase grant was provided.

Pope-Hennessy took more interest than his predecessor in the appointment and grading of the curatorial staff. There was now more money available and he was able to persuade the Treasury to allow the appointment of six deputy keepers on the basis of scholarly merit. He also recognized gaps in the coverage of the collections. As a Renaissance scholar he was instrumental in appointing the first specialist in medals since Sir George Hill, and thus launched Mark Jones (now Director of the Victoria and Albert Museum) on a successful career. Two important appointments were those of Antony Griffiths to look after prints, an area of the collection neglected since Hind, and of Frances Carey to collect twentieth-century drawings. Other similar far-seeing appointments were made in the antiquities departments.

When it came to the appointment of keepers he was more doctrinaire. He believed, with some reason, that promotion to keeperships had become too automatic and rightly insisted that appointments should be made through public advertisement and competi-

tion. He appointed all but two of the new keepers from outside the Museum. Neil Stratford, a lecturer in art history at London University, became Keeper of Medieval and Later
Antiquities. This was at the time a controversial choice in that he was a specialist in
Romanesque sculpture, a subject unrepresented in the Museum. Stratford wrote success-
fully on enamels during his long tenure, but his heart was in France; he continued to work
on Cluny and other major French sites throughout his keepership and retired to a professorship at the Ecole des Chartes. Malcolm McLeod, who (after some discussion by the
Trustees) was appointed to succeed Fagg as Keeper of Ethnography, was a substantial
West African specialist and – although young – was a successful leader of the department.
It is arguable that he was appointed a little too early as Bryan Cranstone, who was passed
over for the keepership, was a leading figure in the ethnography of the Pacific and immediately left to be a most successful head of the Pitt Rivers Museum at Oxford. McLeod
resigned in 1990 to become head of the Hunterian Museum in Glasgow University; later he
became a Vice-Principal of the university. Much more messy was the attempt to appoint a
Keeper of Greek and Roman Antiquities. An outside scholar was chosen, but Pope-
Hennessy seems to have lost his nerve and refused to let the Trustees confirm the appointment he himself had originally recommended. Passing over Reynold Higgins, who
promptly resigned, he appointed Brian Cook at the end of 1976. Cook, an Englishman and
a Roman specialist, had come to the Museum after nine years at the Metropolitan Museum
in New York in 1969.[3] The only straightforward promotion to keeper was that of T.G.H.
James (one of only two candidates at open competition) as Keeper of Egyptian Antiquities
at the beginning of Pope-Hennessy's directorship.

Pope-Hennessy's appointments to keeperships caused internal resentment. To
many they seemed to show a lack of confidence in the ability of existing senior members of
staff.[4] The problem had to be resolved and, after Pope-Hennessy had resigned, although
posts were still publicly advertised and the appointments were made not merely on
grounds of seniority, it was fairly easy to appoint new keepers from existing staff on
grounds of pure ability. It was not until 2000 that another external appointment was made,
although in 1998 an external candidate withdrew after being offered a post.

Pope-Hennessy soon tired of a Museum which he did not entirely understand; he
stayed for only three years. He took up an attractive offer of 'a consultative chairmanship
of the Department of European Painting [at the Metropolitan Museum in New York] and a
professorship at the Institute of Fine Arts'.[5] Although the Trustees had advertised the
Director's post when Pope-Hennessy was appointed, they had not, as has been shown,
followed the process to a normal conclusion. In 1976 they not only advertised, but also
interviewed ten candidates. I was appointed (I was on the River Neva when I heard that I
was successful) and Michael Jaffé, Director of the Fitzwilliam Museum at Cambridge, was
the runner-up. When in turn my retirement was announced in 1991, the post was again
advertised and Robert Anderson, Director of the National Museums of Scotland and a
specialist in the material remains of the history of science, was appointed. He took up the
post in January 1992. In the last quarter of a century since there have been too many
changes of personalities in the senior posts to be related here, but some need to be
recorded. Maysie Webb retired as Deputy Director in 1983 and was replaced by Jean
Rankine, head of Public Services, who herself retired in 1997. After much discussion and
internal wringing of hands, at the insistence of the Department of Culture, Media and

Sport a new post of Managing Director was created in 1997 and Suzanna Taverne, formerly of the Financial Times Group and with no museum experience, was appointed to take over the administrative side of the institution. On her appointment she was designated Accounting Officer, previously a function of the Director.[6] Soon after, John Mack, the Keeper of Ethnography, who had held the unofficial title of Senior Keeper, was confirmed officially in that post and left his department on secondment to become a full-time administrator on the academic side. Following the arrival of Taverne the public service departments were reorganized and considerably augmented, and a certain amount of 'downsizing' took place to free up cash for the new appointments.

The new structure of dual control was based on two separate branches of administration reporting to the Trustees. One, under the Director, comprised the curatorial departments, Education, a new Department of Libraries and Archives (under Alison Sproston, the Eccles Librarian),[7] the British Museum Company and the British Museum Development Trust. Under the Managing Director came a Director of Marketing and Public Affairs, Carol Homden, controlling commercial and corporate services, exhibitions and design, marketing, media relations, the British Museum Society, photography and imaging, and visitor services. Also under the Managing Director was a Directorate of Operations, under Christopher Jones (basically dealing with the building, security and IT), a Director of Finance and a Director of Human Resources (i.e. personnel).

This structure of dual control, which has been tried with varying success elsewhere in the world, did not work in the British Museum. When Anderson's retirement was announced in 2001, the Trustees decided to revert to the original formula, with a single scholarly Director, and dispense with the post of Managing Director. Neil MacGregor, Director of the National Gallery, was appointed in his place (with effect from June 2002) and Taverne resigned amid a flurry of ill-considered press interviews.

There were changes within the curatorial structure of the Museum. The Department of Oriental Antiquities was too big, covering all the countries and periods of Asia save the ancient Near East. In 1987 a split became inevitable when the Museum started to raise money to create a series of galleries to house the Japanese collections. Jessica Rawson became keeper of the rump department, which retained its name when Lawrence Smith moved sideways to become Keeper of Japanese Antiquities in 1987. All posts within the Museum are now advertised, but internal candidates then filled all keeper posts, which do not, however, always go to the most senior members of the department: an example of the minor resentment this caused was when Andrew Burnett was appointed Keeper of Coins and Medals in 1991 in succession to Mark Jones. The first women were appointed keepers at this period – Jessica Rawson in 1987 and Sheridan Bowman, in the Department of Scientific Research, in 1989. In 1998 there was a slight hiccup when an outside appointee to the Keepership of Medieval and Later Antiquities withdrew his name and John Cherry was given the post. On Ian Longworth's retirement as Keeper of Prehistoric and Romano-British Antiquities in 1995, Timothy Potter (a Roman specialist) succeeded him, only to die prematurely five years later. Caroline Malone, the editor of Antiquity, was appointed to the post in 2001.

In 2000–1, the names of four departments changed. Western Asiatic Antiquities became the Department of the Ancient Near East; Prehistoric and Romano-British Antiquities became the Department of Prehistory and Early Europe; Medieval and Later

Antiquities became the Department of Medieval and Modern Europe; and Egyptian Antiquities became the Department of Ancient Egypt and Sudan.

Committees

Pope-Hennessy overhauled the Trustees' committee structure. Since the new Act the Trustees had become more energetic and more professional. Attendance at board meetings had almost doubled and new Trustees' committees were formed to make the best use of the more specialist knowledge of the members. To the existing Finance, Building, and Laboratory and Technical Services Committees, and the newly formed Education Committee, were now added committees on Scholarship, Excavation and Fieldwork, Staff, and Conservation. For a short time there was a Committee on Design, but this was soon subsumed into the Committee on Buildings. The Trustees who chaired these committees were often professionals in nearly related disciplines who could speak with authority to both the administrators and to the senior staff who attended the meetings. Their contribution was much appreciated by the staff of the Museum and helped to relieve a number of tensions. The Museum functioned more efficiently as a result.[8]

A wise and successful Pope-Hennessy innovation was the establishment of annual visitations to departments, in a more informal mode. A Trustee was provided as chairman of visitation for each department and other Trustees could attend at will – often as many as ten being present.[9] Trustees toured the department picking out problem areas, examining, for example, potential purchase policy and proposed development. They then joined all the departmental staff for drinks and informal conversation. Such visitations took place in the week before the presentation of the annual departmental report to the Trustees, and allowed the staff much-needed informal contact with them. At each board meeting an annual report was presented by a keeper, and the half-hour discussion allowed on such occasions was useful on all sides. (This latter practice ceased in 1997 and the keepers' reports to the Trustees were reduced in size.) The chairman of visitation – normally not a specialist in the department's disciplines – kept in touch with his designated department throughout the year and acted as its spokesman at board meetings. The quality of the Trustees' lunch after board meetings was gradually upgraded under Wolfenden and his two successors. It became the practice to invite more curatorial members of staff to meet the Trustees on these occasions on a less formal basis than had been possible in the rather stilted atmosphere, accompanied by gastronomically dire collations, of the old regime.

The last quarter of the century saw great changes in the manner of government funding of the Museum.[10] Until 1975 it received a direct parliamentary vote to pay for salaries and general administrative expenses. It also had a purchase grant which included a sum for books. The buildings were looked after by the Board of Works and its successor Departments of State, while Her Majesty's Stationery Office provided all paper materials and published the Museum's books. Such services as superannuation, catering and legal advice were provided by central government. The first of these services to be withdrawn was that of the Stationery Office, the main function of which had already been taken over by British Museum Publications. Gradually the Museum's grant was consolidated to provide more and more services: the most important and beneficial was the devolution to each of the national museums and galleries of responsibility for its own buildings in 1988. In each case the Museum's grants were adjusted. In 1986 all national museums were changed from vote-funded to grant-aided bodies, which enabled them to generate and retain additional revenue to supplement government funding. All the grants – for running costs, buildings and the purchase of objects – were consolidated into a single grant in 1993. Such changes were accompanied by high-sounding ministerial phrases, such as 'new freedoms', 'additional allocations' and 'greater flexibility'. A much desired funding plan (by which a given level of funding was promised over a three-year period), allowing better planning opportunities, was lobbied for hard and was implemented by the government in 1983. Unfortunately, they reneged on it ten years later. Responsibility for pay and conditions was devolved to the national museums at this time and a certain amount of latitude was now allowed in setting the level of salaries, as pay based on performance was encouraged by the government. Extra money was not provided to fund it; museums were simply encouraged to earn more money. At the same time the government demanded the appointment of extra staff to cover new legislation (as for example that to do with health and safety and disability), but again did not provide the extra finance. Many of these changes, if they had been properly funded, were for the good; but the consolidation of the purchase grant in the main grant was not (p.311).

Conservation Comes of Age

The retirement of A.E.A. Werner, Keeper of the Laboratory, in 1975 enabled the Trustees and Director to take a long look at the anomalous structure of conservation in the Museum. It has been seen that, although research into conservation methods was carried on under the aegis of the Laboratory, practical conservation was separated from it and carried on in the individual departments, mostly unsupervised from the centre. This nonsense had to stop, and Pope-Hennessy created a new unit, the Department of Conservation and Technical Services. As far as possible all members of staff who were conserving objects were now placed under the control of the new department, leaving only a few technicians (museum assistants who were employed to specialize in exhibition work) in the antiquities departments. The masons and mounters of works on paper were also ultimately transferred to Conservation. The new department was originally divided into five sections, but these are now grouped together as three – organic materials (including paper, wood, textiles, skins and fibres), inorganic materials (including metal, stone, wall-paintings, mosaics, ceramics and glass) and a research group consisting of five scientists. Harold Barker, who had worked on the Museum's radiocarbon dating programme since the 1940s, was appointed keeper and was succeeded by Michael Pascoe in 1979, by which time there were fifty-seven conservation officers in the department. Pascoe resigned in 1981 to become head of science at Camberwell School of Arts and Crafts, and was ultimately succeeded by Andrew Oddy, a specialist in metalworking techniques, who had been at the Museum since 1966. When the department was set up conservators were consigned to one speciality (stone or metal, for example), on which they worked exclusively. More recently they have been given a broader training and have thus been able to move between sections to develop their careers. Initially the photographic service of the Museum was brigaded with the Department of Conservation, but this was soon recognized as inappropriate and it was transferred to the Public Services Department.[11]

The establishment of the new Department of Conservation was not carried through without opposition from some keepers, who felt that responsibility for the objects under their care was being compromised. Their complaints rumbled on for a number of years but, as personalities changed and as the validity of the new structure became more evident, tempers cooled and the new order was accepted.

In its early days there was a national shortage of trained conservators and little training was provided by universities. Staff who had worked in conservation capacities within the Museum had been recruited straight from school or art school. Selected mainly on the basis of their manual dexterity, some 40 per cent of the conservators in the new department were relatively untrained juniors. Formal training was, therefore, set up in-house to enable them to reach the standards set by the Museums Association's Certificate in Conservation, for which they studied. Teaching was mainly carried out by senior members of staff, supplemented by a series of videotaped lectures by an ex-member of staff, Robert Organ, head of the Conservation Analytical Laboratory at the Smithsonian Institution, Washington. This proved extremely successful, but pressure eased as conservation began to be taught on a more formal basis in more universities and art colleges. In the late 1970s it was agreed that junior staff should study for the Conservation Certificate at the Institute of Archaeology at University College London.[12] Reduced fees for their courses were negotiated with the university in return for lectures by members of staff.

The discipline of conservation had now gone far beyond the cleaning and repair of objects, although this remained the chief activity of the department. As the number of objects lent by the Museum increased, so the work-load of the conservation officers grew, as all potential loans had to be examined for fitness to travel and advice given on packing. In the Museum itself humidity and light levels in the galleries and stores were now monitored regularly, and all materials used within showcases had to be tested to eliminate anything that might damage the objects. The cautious approach of conservation officers often made life difficult for curators and designers, and sometimes tried patience to the limit, but in the end conservation had to win if the objects were to survive. There is still an element of tension (which is a good thing), but the intervention of the Conservation Department is accepted generally as both sides have become more pragmatic.

The development of new techniques and materials for conservation has long been one of the prime objectives of the Museum's conservation scientists. In the 1930s they developed and licensed one of their most famous products, a liquid to treat leather bookbindings. There has since been no similar commercial venture, as new techniques have been made freely available for the general good, although advice is sometimes given on a commercial basis to manufacturers of showcases and storage materials. Conservation had tended to be interventionist, the products of corrosion were often removed without reason, and make-up was applied to surfaces to produce an aesthetically pleasing effect. Emphasis was now placed on minimum and reversible intervention. There were occasional failures, as for example an attempt in the 1970s to conserve crumbling limestone by impregnating it with polyethylene glycol wax which, while initially successful, changed the colour of the stone and began to display other problems.[13] Careful monitoring of the process enabled the Museum to call a halt with only a few pieces minimally affected. This particular problem was tackled in another fashion by strict control of the humidity of the environment in which the objects were kept. This is most notably demonstrated in the air-conditioned Asahi Shimbun Gallery, specially built in 1992 to house the Amaravati sculpture, which, on conservation grounds, had been withdrawn from exhibition for a number of years.[14] A new data system was introduced which recorded all interventions on individual objects; this has saved enormous time and energy when, as sometimes happens, an object is years later returned for treatment. This system was later computerized. In a rather different area, a successful programme was initiated to remount the Museum's collection of classical mosaics on lighter backing, so that they could be more easily moved and displayed on walls.

By 1996 the Department of Conservation (as it was now called) had a staff of about eighty-four, of whom sixty-four were conservators; there were also six conservation scientists, seven technicians and seven administrators. Although it had been possible to bring many of the staff together, the department is still spread among twelve locations (in 1981 it was distributed over twenty-three different sites). Of these the most significant are the workshops for textiles and wood, located at Franks House in Shoreditch, together with the ethnography stores, which hold the largest concentration of organic material. In 1985, after much hassle from the Treasury, which insisted on the letter of the 1894 Act, the Trustees were able to apply the money from the sale of leases of the Bedford Square property to the refurbishment of a number of basements and rooms in Montague Street as up-to-date and properly equipped conservation studios. This brought together most of the rest of the department, other than the masons; they in 1986 were provided with a new building, which also housed the locksmiths. In 1994 a conservation studio for Eastern Art was opened in the 'drill hall' behind 1a Montague Street. This provided state-of-the-art facilities for the most important Eastern paper conservation centre in Europe; it was largely paid for by Professor Ikuo Hirayama, whose name it bears.[15]

The size of the department enabled it to work on a wider stage. The Museum's conservation expertise had always been much sought after by outside bodies. In the 1960s, for example, two of the greatest treasures of the National Museum of Ireland – the Ardagh Chalice and the Tara Brooch – were conserved and recorded in great detail. Such specialist work continued to be done, as for example when the mace of the House of Commons was damaged by an irate MP. More conventionally, the Museum conserved some of the Crown Jewels. The department, however, now works on a broader base. With such institutions as the British Council it provides advice to museums in developing countries. In 1983, for example, a member of staff was invited to advise the Republic of the Maldives on the establishment of its National Museum. The Museum also collaborates with outside institutions by providing internships on a significant scale for trainee conservation officers from all over the world.[16] Conservation officers are also sent out with the Museum's archaeological expeditions in order to provide first-aid work to objects in the field.

The Department of Scientific Research and Computers

As a consequence of the establishment of a Department of Conservation the Department of Scientific Research, as it was now named, became more focused. Its work was concentrated in two main areas – dating and materials science. Radiocarbon dating continued to produce results, although there was a hiccup in the 1980s when it emerged that there was a possible systematic error in results; the system had to be reworked and procedures modified. The introduction of accelerator mass spectrometry (AMS) at Oxford in the late 1970s produced better, more refined (although more expensive) results from smaller samples. This did not for many years affect the work of the Museum's conventional radio-carbon work (which used liquid scintillation counting), as the samples came from archae-ological sites which were rarely too small to produce results. At first AMS was not entirely accurate, but, with improved precision, the need for the Museum radiocarbon laboratory became less obvious and it was closed down in 2001. An interesting departure in the mid-1980s was when the department acted as a co-ordinator (under the chairmanship of one of the Trustees, Professor Hall) in the radiocarbon dating of the Turin Shroud, believed by many to be the burial shroud of Christ. The resultant calibrated date was 1260–1390 AD (at 95 per cent confidence level), a result which did not resolve the controversy concerning its origins, but at least gave one scientific parameter to this extraordinary object.[17] Thermolu-minescent dating was introduced from Oxford in the early 1970s, initially for the authenti-cation of ceramics. Later it was applied to other areas, such as burnt flint from Palaeolithic caves.[18] Other dating techniques, for example dendrochronology, were not tackled by the Museum, which relies on results produced by other laboratories.

Even before the war, in both Britain and Germany, attempts were being made to locate the sources of metals used in antiquity by means of characteristic trace elements in artefacts – the ultimate intention being to recognize workshops and trade patterns. After the war the Research Laboratory focused much attention on such matters, leaving the use in archaeology of environmental and life sciences to scholars working in the field. Much of the Museum's work was initially targeted at authentication of objects submitted for purchase or by curators doubtful of the genuineness of material in the collections. The Portland Vase, for example, although generally accepted as a Roman object, was some-times postulated as of Renaissance date. Examination of fragments in the scanning electron microscope by means of X-ray spectrometry showed that the vase, like compara-tive Roman material, has a low potash and magnesia content. Renaissance glass does not exhibit this feature, and the vase's Roman origin was thus proved.

Such analytical methods have been much developed in the Department of Scientific Research. The preparation of the report on the Sutton Hoo find concentrated a great deal of energy into the scientific examination of the metals used in this seventh-century burial. This was taken further into wider chronological and geographical contexts and into other materials. Examination of trace elements and the microscopic sampling of methods of manufacture and techniques of ornament demonstrate the progress of technological change in all materials down the ages.

Until the sixth century BC, for example, gold artefacts usually contained a signifi-cant silver impurity, but the first gold coinage, introduced at this time in Lydia (in modern Turkey), was usually silver-free; it may thus be inferred that the introduction of coinage stimulated major advances in the refining of gold. Co-operation between the natural scientists and the antiquities departments has helped to develop an understanding of many manufacturing processes throughout the pre-industrial world, and has led to many fascinating discoveries. For example, an interest in the Museum's Roman brass figures engendered research into possible sources of the zinc (one of the metals used as an alloy in the production of brass). This led to a joint project with Hindustan Zinc Ltd in a remote mining area in the Aravalli Hills of Rajasthan, India, where some of the world's oldest zinc-smelting remains were excavated. The fourteenth-century furnaces, retorts and condensers found there allowed the reconstruction, by a team of metallurgists, chemists, geologists and physicists, of the early history of zinc smelting, until then practically undocumented in Europe.[19] This work has now been extended as far afield as remote areas of China. The Museum has developed expertise in the technology of many early materials, as diverse as Korean porcelain and Egyptian pigments. Its strengths in the physical sciences have been supplemented, more recently and on a lesser scale, by work in the biological sciences. The collections themselves can be better interpreted by understanding how natural resources are exploited (the basis for all environmental archaeology), as, for example, with the discovery that foreign woods were often imported into Egypt in the Roman period for high-status mummy portraits.

A great deal of the work of this department was illustrated in 1990 in a remarkable exhibition *Fake? The art of deception*. Here the Museum bared its soul and, with the help of generous lenders, was able to examine the physical and psychological side of the authenticity of objects. While to a great extent the identification of the fakes in this exhibition depended on the subliminal judgement of the human eye, the proof of such judgement often lay in the hands of the analytical scientist. Radiocarbon and thermoluminescent dating were particularly used to reinforce the eye of the specialist, or to persuade the specialist that his first judgement of an object was flawed. Thus, for example, an 'Etruscan' figure of a banqueteer, wholly convincing to the educated eye, was proved to be a forgery because it was made of brass, an alloy not available in the sixth century BC.[20] (What could not of course be explained – one of a curator's most interesting problems and one which will remain a matter of metaphysical speculation – is why, when an object is revealed as a fake, it loses its mana.)

Much of the equipment used in the physical examination of most of this material could not have been processed without the use of computers. The first computers were introduced into the Museum in the early 1970s as a necessary tool for such processes as thermoluminescence. It was soon realized that the computer had wider applications and had great potential for the Museum inventory, which was now so vast as to be almost unmanageable, and certainly incapable of being audited.

The total number of objects in the possession of the Museum had never been realistically computed, but educated guesses placed it in the region of five to six million. Repeated requests since the early years of the twentieth century by the Parliamentary Committee of Public Accounts for an audit of the collection had run into the ground. Much of my own examination by the committee in 1981 was taken up with this matter and, although by this time certain pilot schemes had been undertaken (particularly in the Department of Egyptian Antiquities), it was not until we had the committee's backing that money was made available which enabled the Museum to investigate the possibility of a full computerization of the collection. Using a super-minicomputer and software developed partly by ourselves and partly by the Museum Documentation Association, the Museum began in 1978 to computerize the whole collection. A section of the Department of Scientific Research was set up under the ponderous title of Collections Data Management Section to provide an on-line database for the whole collection. This was serviced by a specially recruited staff. The computerization of the collections in the Department of Ethnography had been completed by 1991 and the departmental staff had taken over its management and updating. By March 2000 1.2 million records, containing information on 1.9 million objects, had been completed,[21] including, triumphantly, 42,000 records of all the drawings in the Department of Prints and Drawings, 'the first drawings collection in the UK and possibly the world to be documented to such a high standard'. By this time the Egyptian, Ethnography, Medieval and Modern Europe, Oriental and Japanese departments had completed their computerized database. There are many years of work in prospect before the whole Museum is covered; the total number of records still to be entered in the system is about 1.5 million. The Department of Prints and Drawings presents particular problems for it contains an estimated two million prints – some of a most complicated nature – which, if present staff is not enhanced, will take 480 years to be added to the database! The original basic system of recording was specialist and not user-friendly; a new Windows-based system – Merlin – was consequently developed, which began to come on-stream in 2000.

A further application of the computer began with the inauguration of the COMPASS project – which may be found on the Museum's website, and which is also available in the Walter and Leonore Annenberg Centre. COMPASS is an educational resource which uses both text and three-dimensional imaging to explain the collections to the general public, through (in 2001) some 5,000 images. Educational multimedia programmes were introduced in 2001 with initial sponsorship from the Japanese television company NTT.

Planning

The British Museum for a long time seemed to run on serendipity. Things happened, and nobody seemed to know how they came about. That this was not completely true is demonstrated by a number of scholarly projects which continued through the years. Moreover, there is plenty of anecdotal evidence of planned acquisition by continuous social contact with collectors. New buildings were planned long ahead, but were often not delivered. It has been shown that some far-seeing keepers, Rupert Bruce-Mitford for example (see p.293), initiated novel and formal collecting policies in individual departments. Such moves were, however, exceptional and most innovations were introduced casually from the top down. The 1970s was a time of planning and examination of entrails. Wolfenden restructured the administration, Pope-Hennessy tackled the Trustees and curatorial staff, and I tackled the buildings and the collecting policies. The Museum, however, remained locked in the civil service cycle of annual grants, a cycle that inhibited longer views, save in regard to staffing (alterations to which were subject to Treasury approval).

In early 1977 I set up and chaired a long-term planning committee to consider the future development of the Museum. Although the committee included a Trustee and senior members of the administration, it otherwise consisted of a broad spectrum of curators of all grades who gave an entirely new perspective to the normal Museum process. Many minor proposals were acted upon as they arose in the course of deliberations. The committee reported early in the following year, and most of its recommendations were accepted by the Trustees. Much emphasis was placed on problems of space. The Trustees accepted the key recommendation that the Department of Ethnography should ultimately return to the main building. It was also felt desirable to return the storage of the ethnographic material to Bloomsbury, and a number of locations (some of which were then under negotiation) were suggested which, while they came to nothing in themselves, stimulated much future thinking and action. The departure of the Library was still too far away to demand serious planning, but a marker was laid down that it should soon be brought under more detailed consideration. It was, however, realized that there was an urgent need to form a central, general library to ameliorate the loss of the British Library's collections.

The committee took a hard look at its relations with the Victoria and Albert Museum. It roundly rejected the idea, then in the air, that the Department of Oriental Antiquities should be amalgamated with the equivalent department at South Kensington. Its stated terms for such an amalgamation made it quite clear that if it did happen the British Museum should be in control of the whole. In looking at other clashes of interest between the two museums greater co-operation and inter-museum loans were urged to avoid duplication in the national collections. In many ways recommendations concerning co-operation were cosmetic, partly because the collecting and loan policies of the two institutions were already very different, while collaboration in the saleroom was already automatic. The Victoria and Albert Museum, under its energetic new director, Roy Strong, was at this time concentrating on its position as a museum of art and design of the post-1920 period, while the British Museum continued to stress the historical basis of its collecting.[22] There was thus little clash of collecting policy.[23]

Co-operation within the Museum itself was examined. The committee argued for a deeper intellectual co-operation between all the departments, and particularly between the Departments of Ethnography and Oriental Antiquities, and made concrete proposals to achieve this end. An early result was a collaborative publication by Brian Durrans and Robert Knox in 1982 entitled *India: past and present*. Other aspects of departmental co-operation included the integration of coins and medals in the display in the period galleries, the transfer of objects more freely between departments, and a more rigorous control of duplication of equipment and staff in the Department of Scientific Research and the Department of Conservation. The committee considered the position of the Roman element of the Department of Prehistoric and Romano-British Antiquities in relation to classical antiquities and recommended the *status quo*.

Some matters were overtaken by events. The committee proposed establishing a collection of photographs of personalities and historical events since the beginning of photography. The Trustees were interested in following up this suggestion, but tended to think that it was a matter for consideration by the British Library. The foundation, however, of the National Museum of Film, Photography and Television immediately following the delivery of the report took the wind out of the Museum's sails and the idea was never followed up. Further, the Victoria and Albert Museum at this time started to develop its previously moribund photographic collections, to which most of the photographs in the Department of Prints and Drawings have now been transferred. The committee proposed that the Department of Ethnography's important photographic collection should be curated by a specialist. Unfortunately this recommendation has not been entirely fulfilled, although the value of the collection has been recognized and it is now looked after by an appropriately trained librarian.

There was much discussion about the ethnographic collections. The keeper – a member of the committee – was full of gloom, saying that in most countries collection would only be possible for another five to ten years. The Museum consequently initiated an aggressive collecting policy in areas where the collections were weak by filling obvious gaps, for example, in parts of Malaysia, tribal India and savannah Africa. Where the collections were strong, as on the west coast of Canada or Mexico, more adequate documentation should be sought. European folk-life material should also be collected where possible. The committee encouraged the collection of what has been termed 'airport art', tourist souvenirs created by indigenous populations, which reveal an interesting syncretism between the artist and his client. Alongside this material the department collected at little expense some of the multifarious 'fake' objects manufactured specifically for the tourist industry. At the same time the committee encouraged the collection of such items as Australian Aborigine acrylic paintings which take forward an older tradition of sand painting on bark, the graphic arts of the Northwest Coast of America and the sophisticated art of the North African littoral. Generally these ambitions were achieved partly through direct collecting by curators collaborating with local colleagues, and partly through financing research trips by trained outside anthropologists. A recommendation that more excavation should take place in the Pacific, South-East Asia and Africa was not taken up, although Robert Knox, later to be Keeper of Oriental Antiquities, has excavated over a number of years in Pakistan.[24]

A major change of policy concerned the Department of Coins and Medals. The importance of the social and economic use of money was now emphasized. As a first step the department was urged to collect paper money. A new curator, Virginia Hewitt, was appointed, who was successful first in acquiring a major historic collection and then in collecting contemporary bank notes. A major exhibition was mounted in association with the Bank of England in 1987. Entitled *As good as gold, 300 years of British bank note design*, it tackled a subject not previously even thought of by the Museum.[25] Credit, debit and charge cards were also collected, as were cheques and bankers' drafts, and a special exhibition on the subject of money was mounted. This paved the way for a new gallery sponsored by HSBC (the Hong Kong and Shanghai Banking Corporation), which opened in 1997 and dealt not only with coins, but with money and barter in all its aspects. Displayed in this gallery is such related material as minting machinery, cash-tills, money-boxes and safes. At last the department broke away from the study of myriads of little round things – and did so willingly – although the taxonomic work continued. The committee also encouraged the collection of modern coins and medals on a more systematic basis. This was pursued energetically and the Royal Mint was persuaded to deposit its own collections in the Museum, only to withdraw the offer at the last minute when space had been prepared to receive them.

The display of machinery in the HSBC Money Gallery reflected one of the more innovative suggestions of the Long-Term Planning Committee. It argued that more emphasis should be placed on technological aspects of the material displayed in the Museum and that the Department of Scientific Research should acquire material illustrating early technology without treading on the toes of the Science Museum. This ambition has been only partially achieved, although such projects as the investigation of zinc extraction (see p.304) are a result of this suggestion. A specialist curator of scientific instruments, Silke Ackermann, was appointed to the horological section by Robert Anderson to fill a long-perceived gap.

The committee placed great emphasis on the collection of twentieth-century material in areas outside the Department of Ethnography. Whereas in the early years of the Museum's history members of staff collected contemporary or near-contemporary material, curators of the twentieth century, with certain notable exceptions such as Campbell Dodgson and Hill, had avoided the modern. Such material was collected in the most desultory fashion. Pope-Hennessy recognized this and, in appointing Frances Carey to collect twentieth-century prints and drawings, breathed a little more life into the Modern Graphic Fund. She was never really supported by him and was often thwarted by Lord Clark, at that time a Trustee. In appointing her and two other assistant keepers to look after long-neglected areas of the collection – Mark Jones to curate medals, and Antony Griffiths to curate prints – Pope-Hennessy probably did not realize that he was admitting to the Museum energetic members of staff who, while specialist in earlier periods, took the widest possible view of their responsibilities and were almost predatory in their ambition to add to the collections of the modern period. The committee built on this potential and expanded it, demanding a collecting policy which embraced all areas of the twentieth century, without duplicating the policy of the other national museums, and particularly of the Victoria and Albert Museum. An increasing amount of money was set aside to build in these areas. Agreement was easily reached with the other museums and the staff was further augmented in 1979 by a modern curator in the Department of British and Medieval Antiquities, who was given an annual grant of £15,000 for general purchasing. The grant soon rose to £20,000 and was supplemented from time to time out of central funds.

The result of these recommendations in the Department of Prints and Drawings was startling. Two separate annual funds of £25,000 were established, one for prints and one for drawings (the latter was subsequently doubled), and the curators went out and bought quickly and while it was still possible to acquire material in certain unfashionable, or only partly fashionable, areas. The department was also extremely successful in encouraging donors (one of whom, Dr Birgit Rausing, gave £100,000 to build on the Museum's existing Scandinavian print collection). Three exhibitions in the Department of Prints and Drawings, with their accompanying catalogues, demonstrate the success of the new policy and the Museum's commitment to bring its collections up to date.[26] These exhibitions displayed American prints of the period 1879–1979, German Expressionist prints, and Scandinavian prints.[27] A further exhibition in 1990 showed British avant-garde prints. Nothing succeeds like success, and other ways were found of increasing the collections. The British Museum Society, for example, was very supportive. From 1983 it granted an annual sum of money, now between £7,500 and £10,000, for the purchase of contemporary works of art on paper (a risky procedure which calls for mature judgement). This was the first of a number of similar 'Running Funds' established by the Society to collect in specific, cross-disciplinary areas, as, for example, board games and eastern European and Central Asian ethnography. The Society, imaginatively, also became a conduit through which the duplicate British material could be collected together and exchanged in 1986 with the National Gallery in Prague for a comprehensive collection of modern Czecho-slovak prints.[28]

Other departments followed suit. A small twentieth-century gallery was opened by the Department of British and Medieval Antiquities in 1982 and a major catalogue of the decorative arts holdings from 1850 to 1950 was published.[29] An exhibition in 1991, *Collecting the twentieth century*, was arranged to coincide with the publication of this catalogue and included a large amount of material from other departments, most of which had been acquired since the Long-term Planning Committee had reported.[30] The Department of Coins and Medals was particularly active. Mark Jones purchased medals on a broad scale and founded and ran the British Art Medal Society from the department, a society which revitalized a moribund art form in this country. Alongside this a large collection of twenti-eth-century lapel badges was assembled and acquisition lists of them were published in the Museum's *Occasional Papers* series. The Keeper of Japanese Antiquities, Lawrence Smith, developed a taste for modern Japanese prints and decorative arts and made some stunning purchases, which in turn stimulated gifts of a value far beyond the Museum's purchasing power and resulted in a number of splendid exhibitions.[31] The Department of Oriental Antiquities also collected twentieth-century material, particularly prints and paintings. Anne Farrar over a number of years collected a large number of contemporary prints from schools of art in various regions of China, from Beijing, Hangzhou and Chonqing for example; while Gordon Barrass, an ex-diplomat, assembled a major collec-tion of Chinese calligraphy which was given to the Museum in 2002. The department esp-ecially extended the Korean collection, some of which is now housed in the new Korean Gallery in the King Edward VII Building. The Department of Ethnography built on the collecting policy it had initiated after the war, collecting for itself and sponsoring collect-ing by others to build the holdings as rapidly as possible before a sea of international plastic wiped out visual traces of local culture.[32] In the fifteen years to 1990, the objects in this department increased by 25,000. The keeper's original doom-laden prophecies were shown to be only half true and the departmental collecting policy continues to this day; a fascinating temporary exhibition in 2001, for example, displayed and explained the contemporary Japanese souvenir industry.

In 1984 a new long-term planning committee reported to the Trustees in much tighter financial circumstances. The aspirations of the original committee with regard to space were now realized to be over-ambitious and, apart from putting down a few markers for when the British Library should go, the new committee concentrated on detailed discussion of how best to use the space available. It argued for a new conservation block, rationalization of the basement area, and the sharing of students' rooms and storage space between departments. It argued (with a few dissidents) for the complete redesign of the galleries and began a battle to take over the total responsibility for their design from the Crown Suppliers and the Property Services Agency (the agency of the Department of the Environment which then dealt with public buildings). Only interior case design and the labelling were then controlled by the Museum. The battle was ultimately won, as it matched government plans for devolution from the centre. The break-up of the Property Services Agency was some time away, but the committee obviously had some inkling of what might happen and considered ways of breaking free of its stultifying embrace.

Noting the success of the collecting policy initiated by the previous committee, the second body examined in some detail problems raised by its implementation. It pointed to lacunae – the haphazard collecting of graphic material produced in developing countries, for example – and discussed such *faits accomplis* as the growing collection of modern lapel badges. It stressed, in a way that the previous committee had not, the importance of excavation for acquisition. It set up a mechanism to encourage exchange of objects with other collections, although this often proved difficult for legal reasons.

In some ways the discussions of the second committee were more wide-ranging and detailed than those of the first – but perhaps less imaginative. The recommendations were often more easily fulfilled, but even here some kites were flown. There was long discussion on departmental structure and particularly of the possible creation of a modern department. This was dismissed, but the division of the Department of Oriental Antiquities was foreshadowed. The work of the two committees stirred up the Museum and allowed some of the younger and livelier members of staff to try out ideas on each other and on the central administration. There were many practical results, perhaps most important being the sense of community engendered by the discussions. The staff, seeing the Museum as a whole, felt less isolated, their opinion more valued.

Acquisition

The late 1970s and the 1980s were, in terms of acquisition, some of the most productive in the Museum's history. Until the mid-1980s the purchase grant-in-aid increased year on year, from £424,000 in 1975/6 to £1.617 million in 1983/4, and even after it had been frozen in 1984 by Lord Gowrie, then Minister for the Arts, this was still a substantial sum. Further, the release by the Treasury of what remained of the National Land Fund, set up after the war in memory of those who died and subsequently much milked by the government, provided for the establishment of the National Heritage Memorial Fund, which was to benefit the Museum by many grants for major purchases. There was, however, a sting in the tail in that direct Treasury grants for special purposes now apparently disappeared. In 1986 the purchase grant was consolidated within the main vote. The Museum fought this innovation, since it was foreseen that it would gradually be eroded as the money was used to plug funding gaps elsewhere. This happened in 1996/7, when, despite the major inflation of the late 1980s and early 1990s, the Trustees (who had kept the amount of money available for purchase at rather less than its 1984 level) cut it to £925,000.[33] By 2001/2 it was budgeted at £500,000. The responsibility for this decrease lies firmly at the door of successive governments, which have persistently cut the grant-in-aid in real terms (an estimated 23 per cent between 1994 and 2004).

Many of the staff are depressed by these constant cuts, as relatively cheap, but important, acquisitions are lost almost daily. In real terms the amount allowed for purchase from the grant-in-aid is now less than it was in 1930, and all the good work of the 1970s and 80s in increasing the grant has been eroded. On the other hand the various friends' organizations, together with the National Heritage Memorial Fund, the Heritage Lottery Fund and the National Art Collections Fund, have raised the total spend to a rough annual amount of about £2/3 million, but even in the late 1980s the Museum was in real terms receiving roughly the same amount from these sources. The problem with such generosity is that the two big national funds rarely give the full amount for a purchase, and the balance tends to bleed the small amount available for general purchases. Further, the National Heritage Memorial Fund cannot buy foreign material not in British collections. At some point the government must face the fact that this is no way to treat a major national institution; but at the moment the Department of Culture, Media and Sport does not seem to be interested in acquisition.

The support of the British Museum Society (since 2001 known as the British Museum Friends) has increased exponentially since its foundation in 1968; it now funds major purchases and contributed to the Great Court scheme. Further, a number of departments have managed to form their own groups to provide private funding for more day-to-day purchases. In February 2001, for example, the Keeper of Prints and Drawings could report to his departmental friends that the seventeen Patrons of Old Master Drawings, organized by one of the assistant keepers, Martin Royalton-Kisch, had contributed £60,000 for purchases in that field. One of these was a real find in a bundle of drawings bought for £950, a work by Amico Aspertini (c.1540). The Arcana Trust gave the department $295,000 between 1996 and 2001. Further, an anonymous donor had given £128,000 to fund the purchase of modern works, with an emphasis on Israel and Italy; while the Rootstein-Hopkins Trust has given £500,000 to endow a fund to purchase works on paper by living artists or artists who have died within the previous ten years.[34] The Department of Greek and Roman Antiquities is supported by a body of international friends known as the Caryatids, who each annually contribute $2,500 or $5,000 for departmental purposes. The departments of the Ancient Near East and of Japanese Antiquities have similar bodies.

The size of the purchase grant in the 1980s enabled the Museum to allocate various sums to the departments for specific purposes. The purchase of twentieth-century collections has already been mentioned. Other sums were granted for specific projects. Nicholas Turner, for example, was sent to France to buy nineteenth-century French academic drawings. With a few thousand pounds and the blessing of the export authorities he was able to strengthen considerably the Museum's rather weak holdings of this material. Collections were identified which chimed with our purchasing policy, and acquired. Two random examples will suffice. A major collection of Victorian decorative tiles was bought, which nicely supplemented the Museum's holdings of tiles of earlier periods; and the Museum bought, on extremely favourable terms, the Vergez collection of Japanese prints. This latter, with the existing holdings and subsequent purchases, made the Museum's collection the largest of such material in the world. The staff was more proactive with dealers, and, because the Museum was seen to be working the market aggressively, dealers began to bring more and more items to its attention, often offering special terms. In general the Museum bought material in unfashionable areas before the market rose; thus, for remarkably small sums, it was able to build up the best international collection of twentieth-century prints and drawings. With the aid of the National Art Collections Fund, the National Heritage Memorial Fund and, later, the Heritage Lottery Fund many magnificent and interesting objects and collections were acquired by purchase. From its own purchase grant the Museum bought many less grand objects.

Donors were unusually generous in the last twenty-five years of the twentieth century. The character of the gifts varied as much as did the character of the donors. Contemporary artists, Henry Moore, Ronald Searle, Jim Dine and others, chose from their own art and gave generously, as did a number of Japanese artists. Not all metal-detector enthusiasts were interested simply in the monetary value of their finds and some made gifts of important objects. Some donors gave special collections built up over many years. A.G. Poulsen-Hansen, for example, who had worked in Korea in the 1950s, gave a large amount of socially interesting material assembled in that difficult period. Other specific gifts included, for example, Patrick Donnelly's bequest of his lifetime collection of Blanc de Chine porcelain and Mrs Stella Greenall's gift of her husband's collection of Venetian coins. Gad and Birgit Rausing gave a coffee-service by the mid-twentieth-century Swedish silversmith Wiven Nilsson, while others gave money to purchase objects. Most recently Dr Hahn Kwang-ho gave £1 million to purchase Korean antiquities and also loaned material from his own collection. A village in Romania, Cimpeni, gave many items towards a systematic collection of textiles, a gift that encouraged the British Museum Society to purchase more. Others used the Society as medium for gifts; Hans Schmitt and Mareta Meade gave their collection of Himalayan material and Japanese tea-ceremony pottery in this way. There were many bequests: Major J.P.S. Pearson, for example, bequeathed an album of wonderful botanical drawings by two unknown nineteenth-century Indian artists. The list is endless.

Two donors stand out, Anne Hull Grundy (pl. 11) and Edward Wharton-Tigar. The Museum has had many eccentric donors, none more so than Mrs Hull Grundy, who, with her husband John (a lecturer at the Royal Military College), gave a priceless collection of jewellery, and a collection of Japanese netsuke, ojime and other small carvings.[35] She also gave a major collection of Martinware pottery to supplement that bequeathed in 1945 by Ernest Marsh, as well as a number of other individual and sometimes odd pieces.[36] But nothing was as odd as the donor.[37]

Anne Hull Grundy was born in Nuremberg, the daughter of one of the Ullmann banking families. At an early age she took a strong dislike to gem-set modern jewellery: 'I hate diamonds; they're just for call girls and rich dumb wives. I hate merchants' shop jewellery, and anything to do with social climbing.' She bought decorative jewellery with a hard-nosed abandon which reflected both her taste and her knowledge. Her interest in the subject was wide and she showered museums all over the country with gifts, despatched almost weekly by taxi or post from her house in Chilbolton in Hampshire. Although she had started to collect by visiting the dealers' shops, she soon retired to bed and for years summoned dealers from all over the country to attend her in her bedroom, where she sat wrapped in the most extraordinary furs (latterly pink fun fur), often wearing a balaclava and mittens. Pigeons flew in and out of her open windows, for she was a passionate conservationist. Like a French monarch she dispensed her patronage or dismissed hopeful dealers in a language which was as earthy as it was succinct. 'For God's sake shut up and let me see the bloody things – I hate oily salesmen', was one of her kinder and less obscene greetings. Her gifts to museums throughout the country were glorious and a mixed blessing; often they were deposited on loan and she would telephone museum directors in vituperative terms enquiring after the fate of 'her babies'. The average director was nonplussed and presumably rarely matched her invective; 'you can only get a grunt out of a pig', she said of museum curators.

She targeted the British Museum late in her life, and the capable Maysie Webb dealt with her with flair and imagination. First, Mrs Hull Grundy withdrew a major loan from the Victoria and Albert Museum in excoriating terms and deposited it with us. We then had to try and convert the loan into a gift, for we could not put so much energy into negotiation with such a capricious eccentric without real hope of a positive outcome. The ultimately successful negotiations were conducted like those of two warring Renaissance princes attempting to make peace. Insult was followed by a gift, which would be followed by nego-tiations, which might involve the gift by the Museum of seven pounds of pigs' brains despatched by the Museum car to Chilbolton. This would result in her donation of a number of Dundee cakes, or on one occasion of three pigskin attaché cases. Then war would break out again, and Miss Webb started to record her telephone calls. Then more jewellery would arrive. Finally, in October 1978, to the great credit of Maysie Webb, the gift was finalized and the donor said that she would haunt us if the jewellery was ever not on public display. Mrs Hull Grundy continued to shower us with gifts until her death in 1984. There have been no hauntings and her jewellery is permanently shown as an integral and important part of the Museum's eighteenth- and nineteenth-century display.

It was an extraordinary gift, nearly 1,200 pieces of decorative jewellery illustrating and documenting the skills and techniques of the jeweller's craft from the seventeenth to the mid-twentieth century. Not only did it bring the Museum's collections in this field up to date, it also allowed an academic appraisal of the marks on the jewels and the associated documentation, which put the decorative jewellery of the period into an entirely new light. The collection was published, as the donor wished, in a two-volume catalogue in 1984, a collaborative work of innovative scholarship which has stimulated the Museum to continue to buy in the same and related fields.[38]

Edward Wharton-Tigar had from his schooldays collected cigarette cards, a passion continued and expanded throughout a long career as a mining engineer with a break in the Special Operations Executive during the Second World War.[39] By the time he approached the Museum in 1984 he owned about one million trade cards stored in two houses in Kensington. The Museum was initially worried by the size of the problem, espe-cially since it had been turned down by the Victoria and Albert Museum which could not see how it could be incorporated in their collections. It clearly marched well with the Museum's collection of trade cards and ephemera given by Sophia Banks in 1818 and by Sir Ambrose Heal in the immediate post-war years. Antony Griffiths, the Museum's print specialist, was enthusiastic and Sir David Attenborough (a Trustee) and I went to see his collection and were bowled over by it. Mr Wharton-Tigar belied both his name and his fearsome reputation and proved to be a most co-operative prospective donor. He agreed to our chief condition that he should himself arrange the collection in conservation-standard melinex sleeves and would provide us with a complete index. He did this all at his own expense, but the task was incomplete at his death in 1995. The first 300 boxes were, however, transferred to the Museum in 1996 and the sorting is being completed by the Cartophilic Society. The collection is of value in many ways – in the history of printing, advertising, trade, popular culture, and so on. But it is also of enormous monetary value. One example, albeit exceptional, illustrates this: a cigarette card showing the American baseball player Honus Wagner, which had been withdrawn after its fanatically anti-smoking subject sued, was bought by Wharton-Tigar immediately after the war for $100 – another example was sold in 1996 for $644,500!

Collecting is central to the life of a museum. It is also fun. There are many other attractive sides to a curator's life – scholarship, education, communication and discovery – but without the collector's eye a museum becomes dull and boring. The last quarter of the twentieth century saw a vast increase in collecting activity. Most material is acquired for study – not 'hidden away in the basements' in a self-indulgent fashion, as populist politicians and journalists assert. It is constantly studied, used, displayed, shown to students and made freely available to specialists and all who wish to see it. The immense amount of time spent by the curatorial staff in showing reserve collections to the interested public and the value they receive through discussion with visitors is the stuff of which knowledge of material culture is made. From it history can be constructed. Not everything can be placed on display to the public – even distributed throughout the country. A museum gathers together objects, and with them expertise. The fact that the British Museum has twenty-six boxes of Rembrandt prints means that students can study and compare them in one place, advised by specialists, without searching them out all over Europe. The prints reveal not only Rembrandt's art, skills and technique; they also add to the sum of knowledge of the man and his period. They give clues to his religious beliefs and those of his period; they illustrate the life of the countryside, the appearance of the towns, sport, topography and a multitudinous series of life's facets. They can be used by historians, topographers, botanists, architectural historians and art historians and applied to many kinds of educational and other purposes. They are used in exhibitions to illustrate aspects of Rembrandt's art and his period. Much of the stuff collected by the Museum – pottery sherds or belt buckles, for example – is often intrinsically boring, but when studied, interpreted and set in context it can tell fascinating stories about the past. This is what museums are for. Collecting lies at the heart of their function, not through simple acquisitiveness, but as a means of adding to knowledge and of communicating that knowledge visually to others. The British Museum is – through its vast collections – an international resource of knowledge which variously affects the perception of the whole world.

A long line of generous benefactors has supported the British Museum, and continues to do so. The Museum has a well-thought-out collecting policy, which is sometimes thrown out of kilter by the necessity of purchasing nationally important objects in haphazard fashion because an owner needs to raise money. Although the Museum should collect 'heritage items' threatened by export, it is perhaps more important that it collects to create a new heritage. Wharton-Tigar's collection of trade cards was a more important acquisition for the British Museum than the lost Old Master drawings from Chatsworth discussed below, simply because there is no other comparable collection in the world – the cards give limitless opportunities for pleasure and research. The Museum, together with the Royal Collection and such museums as the Ashmolean, ensures that this country has its fair share of Old Masters, perhaps one of the biggest and most diverse collections in the world. This Chatsworth loss in global terms was relatively insignificant. The acquisition of Old Master drawings will continue – indeed, the Museum received an important and generous bequest (through the National Art Collections Fund) of German Old Master drawings from Rosi Schilling in 1993. But the Museum has other functions, other ambitions, which extend far beyond the art of sixteenth- and seventeenth-century Italy and the Low Countries. Let our successors, not our contemporaries, pass judgement on such policies.

The problem of archaeological antiquities looted from heritage sites, with the consequent loss of their cultural context, is ever-present and the source of much trouble to museums all over the world. In 1988 the Trustees adopted a policy statement codifying their long-accepted practices, stating that they would not acquire objects illegally excavated or exported from their country of origin. The statement was refined in 1998, condemning the illicit trade in antiquities and stating that the Museum will acquire significant antiquities only if there is documentation to show that they were exported from their country of origin before 1970. The Trustees recognize, however, that in the case of minor antiquities such documentation often does not exist and in such cases, 'the Museum's curators... use their best judgement as to whether such antiquities should be recommended for acquisition'. To emphasize this commitment Robert Anderson sat on the Ministerial advisory panel on illicit trade, which reported in December 2000.[40] The panel made firm and realistic recommendations by which the government could, through legislative and non-legislative means, play a proper part in preventing and prohibiting the illicit trade in antiquities. For British antiquities the Museum acts as a repository of last resort for objects without documentation.[41]

The Museum has long co-operated with foreign governments in assisting the return of illegally exported property. In similar vein it – along with most other museums in the west – has been examining the collection to trace material looted by the Germans during the Second World War from Jewish owners or institutions and is collaborating with the official Spoliation Advisory Panel set up to deal with this problem. So far only a handful of objects have been identified and the whereabouts of the heirs of the original owners are being sought.[42]

Some Failures

Ever since the Museum failed to acquire the Lawrence collection of drawings in 1838, there have been a number of spectacular failures of acquisition. The post-war period also had its failures. The most notorious and most publicized was the 'Chatsworth affair'.[43] The Duke of Devonshire's collection includes some 2,000 Old Master drawings. In 1982 the Museum was offered seventy-four of these by the trustees of the Chatsworth Estate; they were valued at £7 million by the auctioneers Christie's. This with the 'douceur' under Capital Gains Tax regulations suggested that the Museum would have to raise some £6.275 million in order to purchase them. In its negotiations with the Duke the Museum made it clear that a sum of £5.5 million would be the most that could be considered. This sum was agreed with the National Heritage Memorial Fund, which had the drawings valued independently. The Duke played it long, and in June 1983 stated that the list of drawings was not negotiable. By September the Museum, after a meeting with the Duke's solicitor, thought that, by a slight variation in the contents of the package, it had a deal to buy at about £5.5 million, a sum which was some quarter of a million pounds beyond the resources available to the Museum. This was later raised to £5.669 million. The package was turned down abruptly in November 1983. Despite an offer to purchase by a private consortium, the Duke was set on selling at auction, and was well justified in doing so. Christie's sold the drawings for £21 million in July 1984, which, even without the 'douceur' on Capital Gains Tax, represented to him a most successful gamble.

The prices reached by the drawings at the sale were unprecedented (the Museum bid for six and did not get them). This represented one of those inexplicable hikes in auction prices with which all collectors are familiar; the sale set a new index for the price of Old Master drawings. The Museum was, however, pilloried by the chattering classes; even the *Burlington Magazine*, which might have been thought to be more sympathetic, criticized it severely; the Committee on the Export of Works of Art was, however, more gentle and understanding when it had to pick up the pieces.[44] The Keeper of Prints and Drawings, John Rowlands, received some unpleasant criticism in the broadsheets, and a number of major figures in the art world are still aggressive about the matter more than fifteen years later. It seemed that nobody would listen to the Museum's reasons, or understand the restrictions under which it was working. These can be simply stated. First, the Museum had not got the money; it was in fact bidding beyond the limit of its purse and the National Heritage Memorial Fund was not willing to go higher. If it had succeeded in the bid the Museum would have had to raise well over a quarter of a million pounds from other sources, including the National Art Collections Fund and the city companies, none of which had previously given us that sort of money. Secondly, even if the money had been available from public sources, the Museum and the Memorial Fund, as publicly funded bodies, would have been hamstrung by the valuations which the Fund by its constitution had to accept. It would have been impossible to justify to Parliament payment so far in excess of such official and independent valuations. The grant offered by the Fund would have made a large hole in its resources and might even have prevented the purchase for the nation of the major country house, Belton, a few months later. Thirdly, the Museum had a carefully worked out acquisitions policy. Only six of the drawings on offer fell within the terms of that policy, and the Museum attempted to buy them all only because it seemed in the national interest to keep a major and distinguished collection in the country. It was certainly not in the Museum's interest. Fourthly, by the time the Museum thought – with good reason – that it was on the edge of a deal, the Duke of Devonshire was determined to go to auction. The drawings are not lost; many of them are now in museums in the United States (one, a Rembrandt, is even in the British Museum) and can be studied by all who need to see them. This was not a repeat of the Lawrence affair, it was simply an inroad of a little less than 4 per cent into one of the last private collections of importance in the country. Perhaps the interests of the country have been best served by the better preservation of one of the greatest houses in England as a consequence of the money fed into the Chatsworth Trust by means of a successful ducal gamble. That the Duke bore no ill-will is demonstrated by the fact that, in 1993, he lent the Museum 220 drawings from his collection for a most successful exhibition.[45]

The loss of two other major collections was more painful, but less public. One of the main collecting areas identified for development by the Long-Term Planning Committee was icons. The Museum had a small, but fine collection of Greek and Russian icons, some of which had been transferred from the National Gallery. It had long been neglected. With the presence on the staff of a new curator of Byzantine material – David Buckton – the Museum now proceeded to expand from this core. Two early acquisitions under the new policy in the early 1980s were the 'Black George', a late fourteenth-century icon from Pskov in northern Russia, and a splendid Constantinople icon of St Peter (dated c.1320) which was discovered in a London restorer's studio on the back of a seventeenth-century icon.[46] In 1983 the Museum attempted to buy for close on £2.5 million a collection of fifty-eight icons belonging to Mr Eric Bradley. Here it fell between the Treasury and the National Heritage Memorial Fund. In no way could the icons be considered as part of the national heritage (although the Fund battled hard to be sympathetic) and the Trustees could not get permission from the Office of Arts and Libraries to approach the Treasury for a special grant.[47] The Museum thus lost its chance and the icons were sent for auction. It will take many years to build such a collection, although the Museum is gradually acquiring a rich holding of icons through the generosity of individual donors, particularly from Mrs Dyne Steele.

Much sadder was the attempt to purchase a remarkable collection of 242 ethnographical musical instruments, together with recordings and transcriptions, from Jean Jenkins in 1978.[48] In this case there was no worry about the purchase price, which could have easily been met from the Museum's resources. There was, however, a complicating factor in that it was a condition of the purchase that Mrs Jenkins should be employed to curate and catalogue them. This was so academically attractive that the Museum agreed to the proposition, only to withdraw because the union and the staff of the department felt threatened by precedent and by the volatile personality of the vendor. There was a failure of nerve all round and Mrs Jenkins sold her collection elsewhere. This was personally the saddest loss to the collections while I was Director.

The other great failure of the last twenty-five years had a happier ending. In 1978 the Salisbury and South Wiltshire Museum was in trouble. Its collections had outgrown its building and a major acquisition – the Pitt Rivers collection of local prehistory – could not be properly housed. After long, complicated and careful negotiation with the Salisbury Museum and the Office of Arts and Libraries it was agreed that the British Museum should take over most of the local collections and run the museum as an out-station in a newly purchased building in Salisbury. The rationale behind this was that the Salisbury Museum's rich archaeological collections were complementary to those of the British Museum. They included much of the material excavated in the nineteenth century in the Salisbury region by General Pitt Rivers (see p.155), which was critical to an understanding of the archaeology of Wessex, an area richly represented in the British Museum.[49] The Trustees were clear that they were not in the business of rescuing failing museums, but that this case was unique. They, therefore, welcomed the idea. In the period during which discussions were taking place, there was a change of government and the Deputy Director and the Office of Arts and Libraries grew cooler towards the idea. The governing body of the Salisbury Museum, now more motivated, started to raise money towards a completely new museum. The British Museum withdrew gracefully from the project and was delighted when the Salisbury Museum opened its doors in the cathedral close in November 1983.[50]

The Museum and Excavation

By the 1970s it had been tentatively established that the purchase grant could be used to support archaeological excavation and ethnographical fieldwork, so long as it resulted in the acquisition of material for the Museum's collections. For years it had, for example, given money to the Egypt Exploration Society and received material important for both study and exhibition. It had ranged over the world to support excavations. The Museum's excavating interest was not confined to the Mediterranean; in 1973, to give but one example, it granted £5,000 to the Cambridge University expedition to Corozal in Belize, which produced artefacts of all periods, and support for this series of excavations was continued for a number of years.[51] Even when the use of the purchase fund for excavation was eventually formalized and the Museum was allowed from its general funds to contribute to excavations without expectation of return, funding was decided on such a haphazard basis that a committee was much needed.

In October 1974 the Trustees' Committee on Excavation and Fieldwork, set up by Pope-Hennessy, met for the first time and began to set parameters for the Museum's involvement in future archaeological excavation.[52] The Committee decided that only the Departments of Prehistoric and Romano-British Antiquities and Medieval and Later Antiquities had sufficient expertise to undertake their own excavations.[53] This, though generally true, was disappointing as the Museum wished to widen its role as a hands-on excavating institution. It had two reasons for expanding this role: first, to set the existing collections in a more modern perspective by targeting key sites that could be directly related to material already held; secondly, to acquire material which placed such collections in context and which could also provide a more modern scientific approach to the interpretation and study of the collections themselves. The committee recognized the limitations of staff experience, but encouraged the departments to participate in excavations in certain specific areas, particularly in the Near and Middle East. The committee, while insisting that staff should take part in excavations, did not envisage that, with increased experience, they would be able to run their own excavations in these areas. Rather, they felt that they should be seconded to the excavations of the various regional British archaeological institutions abroad, such as the British School of Archaeology in Iraq or the Egypt Exploration Society. The Trustees also encouraged the Museum to collaborate with universities and institutions excavating in foreign countries, in India, Africa and the Far East. Against the wishes of Haynes, Keeper of Greek and Roman Antiquities, who felt it inappropriate for members of his staff to indulge in such an ungentlemanly activity, Anne Birchall was allowed to take part in a dig at Torone. Other members of the department later followed suit to dig in the Mediterranean countries. The committee was happy with the archaeological competence of the two European-oriented departments and commended Ian Stead's work at Menil Annelles, in France, and Ian Longworth's excavations at Grimes Graves, Norfolk. They also approved the continuing use of money from the purchase grant for excavations in Britain and elsewhere to acquire material found in context. Later, permission was given to support financially excavations abroad from which there was no expectation of return in the form of objects for the collection 'subject to the participation of a member of the Museum staff'.[54] The Museum thus became, after the British Academy, perhaps the chief British source of funds for research excavation.

British archaeology at this period was beset by the need for rescue excavation in advance of development, initially funded by the Department of the Environment but later by the developer. The volume of material recovered was so great that it became an embarrassment to the excavators and to the museums that had to store it. The acquisition in 1980 of a major portion of the old Post Office Savings Bank near Olympia, in West London, allowed the Museum to accept a certain number of complete archaeological archives which could not be housed elsewhere. Excavation was becoming more professional and consequently more expensive, and universities found it easier to train their students on rescue excavations and with few exceptions were unable to afford to undertake research excavations in Britain. The Museum was, however, one of the few institutions able to run a consistent research excavation programme from the 1970s onwards.

In Britain the Museum undertook many excavations, of which only a few can be recorded here. Area excavation at Stonea Grange in Cambridgeshire between 1980 and 1985, supervised by T.W. Potter and R.P. Jackson, focused on a major second-century Romano-British settlement around an extravagantly planned stone tower-like building (the stone having been brought 40 km to the site). The settlement must have been an important element in the Imperial estates in the English fens. Further excavation demonstrated settlement and ritual on this site from the Lower Palaeolithic to the post-medieval period. While such usage may not have been continuous, Stonea Grange was for long intervals clearly a high-status site and is of great importance in the understanding of the history of the Fenlands.[55] Many other excavations were carried out in Britain and in Europe by members of the staff of the Department of Prehistoric and Romano-British Antiquities. Stewart Needham, for example, excavated the Late Bronze Age waterfront site at Runnymede Bridge and Ian Stead, a serendipitous excavator, dug at a number of Iron Age sites in France and England, always producing rich finds, most notably the great gold torcs from Snettisham, Norfolk. The Department of Medieval and Later Antiquities preferred to fund excavations by outsiders in return for material, but collaborated with the Society of Antiquaries to excavate the Sutton Hoo site under the direction of Martin Carver. Here they tidied up problems left by the excavations of 1938 and 1939 and put the great ship-burial into its local and national context in more modern terms.

The idea that members of the departments of Egyptian and Western Asiatic Antiquities were not qualified to run excavations was harsh, but was soon reversed. In the early 1980s John Curtis, of the Department of Western Asiatic Antiquities, excavated at five sites threatened by building of the Eski Mosul dam in Iraq; the site of Khirbet Qasrij, dated to 612–539 BC, cast new light on an obscure period of Assyrian history;[56] and at Khataniyeh a provincial Assyrian palace destroyed by fire in 612 BC was uncovered.[57] A long-term project was started in 1985 with the excavation by Jonathan Tubb of a multi-period Jordanian site in the Jordan Valley at Tell es-Sa'idiyeh, a site continuously inhabited from the Chalcolithic period of the mid-fourth millennium BC to early Islamic times. By 2700 BC it was already a prosperous city. Most surprisingly, twelfth-century BC levels revealed a major Egyptian presence. Museum specialists in palaeobotany and conservation formed part of the team and worked with the Museum's archaeologists on site. Jordan is one of the few countries in the Middle East which still allows the division of excavated material and the Museum has benefited very considerably from the items it has been able to retain from this excavation. The Jordanians in return have received a great deal of help from the Museum in the conservation of their retained material.

From such small beginnings has grown a Museum involvement in excavations on its own account or in support of other institutions in, for example, China, Pakistan, Sri Lanka, Sudan, Egypt (where the Museum for the first time conducted its own excavation – at El-Ashmunein on the Middle Nile), Italy, Libya and Syria. This work, alongside that carried out by the Department of Ethnography in collecting and recording the culture of many countries, enables the Museum to fulfil its boast that it is 'illuminating world cultures'. The Trustees have recently codified their policy on excavation:

> Four main reasons for undertaking or supporting excavations or other types of fieldwork have been identified: to acquire material for the collections; to put the existing collections into better context; to enable staff to work in their areas of specialism and make important contributions to scholarship; and to develop contacts and good relations with institutions and colleagues overseas... Many of these enterprises are joint projects, undertaken in conjunction with other bodies, highlighting the fact that collaborative efforts are the pattern for the future.[58]

International Relations

The rapid growth of easier and cheaper travel enabled the Museum to build on its unique long-standing relations with scholars abroad. As the railways had opened up Europe in the nineteenth century, so air travel now opened up the rest of the world. The Museum had long been much involved in fieldwork abroad, but now the horizons widened as ethnographers worked *inter alia* in Aden, Cameroon, Papua New Guinea and on the Northwest Coast of America. Sometimes, as in Madagascar and North Korea, the Museum was one of the first western institutions to be allowed back into a country after the re-opening of its frontiers. In nearly all these cases the Museum staff worked with local colleagues to their great mutual benefit. In another instance, Richard Blurton adventured into politically unpopular Burma and managed to compile a splendid collection of lacquer, keeping in touch with academics and dealers and stimulating a major gift from Ralph Isaacs. Academic contacts were strengthened by frequent short visits; these replaced the long, tedious, over-planned surface trips which had made the Trustees sometimes reluctant to allow staff members to go far. American contacts became more reciprocal, and visits, particularly to the Far East, became regular occurrences. Relations are complex and varied and only a few examples can be mentioned. Computer staff advised colleagues in India, a curator sat on a national art jury in Japan, the Design Office was consulted by museums as far away as Hawaii; while conservators (often with the backing of the British Council) helped train their opposite numbers in countries throughout the Third World – sometimes by giving them bench space in London, sometimes by working abroad. In other cases, as when a paper conservator from the Shanghai Museum was received, the Museum has learnt more than it has taught. Similarly, foreign curatorial colleagues, often on exchange, have spent time in the departments to the mutual benefit of both sides – and this traffic has been two-way.

The growth of international exhibitions has not only raised the Museum's profile abroad, but has also made the collections accessible to a wider public. In 1988, for example, the Museum lent 646 objects, worth £30 million, to fifteen countries, some of them on long-term loan. These figures had more than doubled by 1998 and the number of dedicated travelling exhibitions originating in the Museum has greatly increased. Such activities cost staff time on a considerable scale and are often unthinkingly criticized by bean-counters, but the returns have been more than worth while. Curators, travelling with objects to exhibitions, have not only improved their knowledge of foreign collections, they have been able to network with their contemporaries on an active and personal basis for the good of the academic status of the Museum. The appearance of the Museum's material in published catalogues of exhibitions has made it more accessible to scholars, particularly as individual objects are often technically and academically re-assessed before travelling. The Museum has also, to its own great advantage, borrowed material never before seen in this country. In some cases it was uniquely assembled from a number of sources and countries – as with the Viking exhibition of 1980, which borrowed items from all over Scandinavia, as well as from Germany and the British Isles.

The growing confidence of the staff in their areas of expertise abroad has also affected the Museum's capacity for fund-raising. In their travels curators meet the influential and the rich and have consequently been able to fund-raise through such contacts, often helped by British diplomats in those countries which see the gain in good international relations as an uncontroversial bonus. In 1989 it was true to say that 'save for a number of significant contributions from the Wolfson Foundation, most of the privately funded galleries... have largely been paid for out of non-British generosity'.[59] Today, thanks largely to the energy of Sir Claus Moser and the British Museum Development Trust, this is no longer true; but the foreign relations so carefully nurtured over the years have been of enormous financial value to the Museum and to the country generally.

Return of Cultural Property

The Museum's foreign relations are not always entirely comfortable. In the mid-1970s various countries began to ask for the return of objects in the Museum which they perceived to have been taken by force – even stolen. One ex-colony sent a list of every item originating from it in the Museum and asked for the return of all. This was a perplexing request as, in the main, the material was well duplicated in its country of origin and indeed that country was in process of sending the Museum, through official channels, a group of newly excavated material to enhance our collections. After amicable discussion, the demand was dropped. A Benin ivory mask, adopted as a logo by a pan-African arts festival in Lagos in 1976, became the centre of a year-long battle for its return to Nigeria before the demands died down.[60] The chief problem of this period concerned the Parthenon sculptures.

In 1981 Melina Mercouri, high-profile actress and patriot, became Minister of Culture for Greece and took up the cause of a few philhellenes in both Britain and Greece in demanding that the British government return the Elgin Marbles. Interestingly, although there had been an occasional suggestion that the Marbles should be returned, this was the first official request. The battle was long, but neither side wavered and the British government insisted on the legal and moral right of the Museum to keep one of its greatest treasures. After Mercouri left office the demands became less vociferous and ultimately died down, now occasionally bursting into life for a few days as one side or the other thinks up a new argument or puts a foot wrong. The present policy is to be open about the whole matter and not repeat the communication errors of Forsdyke and his successors. To this end the Museum hosted a conference in 2000 which allowed a full airing of views on all sides.

The Museum's arguments against the return of property were first formally expressed in a statement made by the Trustees in 1984:

> Demands by Greece and others for the return of parts of the collections of the British Museum have consumed considerable time and energy in recent years. The Museum – with the support of government – has continued to withstand these demands and has sought to correct the lack of understanding of its proper function as a universal museum which plays a unique role in international culture. The Museum's collections are vested in its Trustees in accordance with legislation enacted by Parliament, which since 1753 has prohibited them from permanently disposing of any object (other than duplicates) and has required them to ensure that the collections are preserved for the benefit of international scholarship and the enjoyment of the general public. In fulfilment of this responsibility the Museum is open seven days a week, free of charge, throughout the year. The Trustees would regard it as a betrayal of their trust to establish a precedent for the piecemeal dismemberment of the collections which recognise no arbitrary boundaries of time or place in their enduring witness to the achievements of the human spirit.[61]

The Museum's arguments, which have since been restated on a number of occasions in different contexts, do not rest purely on a legalistic view; rather they encapsulate a moral position which has been forcibly repeated.

Treasure

The lure of buried treasure is a potent force, and the final thirty years of the last century saw a vast increase in the number of treasure hunters who went into the field armed with portable metal detectors. Unscrupulous dealers encouraged illegal searchers and, initially, treasure hunters were secretive about provenance and in some cases trespassed on private land or even ancient monuments in flagrant disregard of property rights or antiquities legislation. While much material was recovered, the context in which the object was buried was often lost; sometimes, however, careful enquiry could recover it. Thus, for example, of the eighteen Anglo-Saxon cemeteries excavated since 1972, sixteen were discovered by the use of metal detectors. Over the years museums at all levels have spent much energy in encouraging the co-operation of those who use metal detectors – and with a measure of success. Of particular concern to the Museum was the vast increase in the number of hoards discovered. The British Museum, because of the role it played in the administration of the law of Treasure Trove, had to steer carefully in these muddy waters, dealing with players on all sides of the process, detector users, dealers, museums and collectors.

One of the first major hoards discovered with the aid of a metal detector and acquired by the Museum was that found in a ploughed field at Water Newton, Cambridgeshire (the site of the Roman town of Durobrivae), in 1975. It was correctly reported and officially declared Treasure Trove. It comprises a group of thirty silver objects, a number of which bear the Christian *chi-rho* symbol. It is considered to be the earliest group of Christian liturgical silver yet found in the Roman Empire.[62] Yet another hoard from the same period found at Hoxne, Suffolk, contained 15,000 coins (the largest coin hoard found in Britain), as well as pieces of plate and jewellery.[63] One Roman hoard of the late fourth century, from Thetford, Norfolk, found in 1979, was not immediately reported and its context was lost as the site was built upon. Ultimately it was declared Treasure Trove, and the Museum managed to acquire it two years later. It includes thirty-three silver spoons, twenty-two finger-rings set with semi-precious stones and glass and a splendid gold buckle decorated with the figure of a satyr, as well as much other jewellery.[64]

Other hoards have proved even more elusive. Such was the Salisbury hoard, the story of which reads like a thriller and has been told in racy terms by Ian Stead, who acted as detective.[65] The first intimation of the existence of the hoard was when Stead was shown a group of objects by Lord McAlpine, a dealer who had a large number of unprovenanced objects from Britain and the Continent. The items that started the ball rolling consisted of twenty-two miniature bronze shields of Iron Age type (c. 200 BC), of which four were delicately decorated and unique. The group was so important academically that the Museum felt duty-bound to buy them so that they would not disappear piecemeal into the trade or be sold abroad, with a consequent loss to knowledge of a major find of the English Iron Age. All attempts to find a provenance through the vendor failed and the Trustees, rightly worried by the dubious provenance, agreed to indemnify the National Heritage Memorial Fund, who in 1989 gave £55,000 towards the purchase of the group, in case the title were to prove faulty. They also issued a statement clarifying their position about the purchase of such finds.[66] The Museum enthusiastically supported the purchase and agreed to make an effort to discover the origin of the find.

Stead, through a series of contacts – some of dubious respectability – with police co-operation ultimately discovered and investigated the exact find-place of the hoard. He was able to recover from the finders, through the trade and from other museums about half the original find, which had consisted of 50 kg of bronze – the second largest hoard of prehistoric bronze objects found in Britain. It had been assembled by the inhabitants of an Iron Age settlement at Netherhampton, near Salisbury, and consisted of objects of the third, second and first millennium BC clearly collected in the Iron Age from cultivated land in the neighbourhood, an area which has always produced vast amounts of Bronze Age material. The hoard has cast new and unsuspected light on the Iron Age as well as providing much original material of hitherto unknown type and form. Stead's investigations, and those of his colleagues both inside and outside the Museum, led to the trial and conviction of two metal-detector users and the return of many of the objects to the landowner. The Museum returned to the owner those bought from Lord McAlpine (who did not repay the purchase price). In 1998 the story came to a happy ending when the shields and another nineteen objects came to the Museum in lieu of inheritance tax, and the same year it acquired from the owner much of the other material in the hoard.

This was but one of a number of cases of concealment. The law of Treasure Trove did not apply in this case and was indeed becoming unworkable. Lord Perth (backed by the Museum and the Surrey Archaeological Society) introduced a reforming bill into the House of Lords. It was not, however, until 1996 that a government-backed Treasure Act, applicable to England, Wales and Northern Ireland, passed through Parliament.[67] This refined the simple terms of the law, which laid down that treasure subject to this law consisted of objects of precious metal placed in the ground *animus revertendi* (i.e. with the intention of retrieval). Treasure was now defined as any object other than coin which contains at least 10 per cent of gold or silver and is at least 300 years old; and all coins from the same find provided they are at least 300 years old. If the coins contain less than 10 per cent of gold or silver, the find must consist of at least ten coins. Importantly, objects found in association with treasure (for example the find's container) are subject to the same law. All such finds must be reported to the coroner for the district within fourteen days. The Museum was much involved in the formulation of this law, and the adviser seconded to the Secretary of State to deal with it was a member of the Department of Coins and Medals, Roger Bland. Associated with the new Treasure Act was a 'Portable Antiquities Scheme' which encouraged the voluntary recording of archaeological finds that fall outside the definition of treasure in the Act. A pilot scheme, paid for by government, covered half the country; some 20,698 items were recorded in 1998–9. The Museum is deeply involved both in this scheme (which has engendered a large amount of paperwork) and in the adminis-tration of the Treasure Act, and provides a great deal of the specialized knowledge that helps archaeologists to interpret the material in context. To a certain extent these two measures have curbed the worst excesses of the metal detector users, although some material clearly slips through the net.[68]

Building and Refurbishing

The Museum was still strapped for space, particularly to house the greatly increased administrative staff. In 1975, after much havering, the government finally approved the construction of a new building in the south-west corner, behind the screen connecting the main building to the residences. Designed by Colin St John Wilson (the architect of the new British Library), it had been reduced in size from that originally planned, partly due to planning problems and partly because the government did not provide all the necessary funds. The building provided a new gallery for special exhibitions (but on a smaller scale than originally planned), with associated basement workshops, storage and loading bay, new public and staff restaurants, a new boardroom suite – the old boardroom had been demolished as part of the scheme – and two floors of offices. It was completed in 1980 and apart from trouble with solar gain, which had to be corrected by the provision of openable windows, has lived up to most expectations. A bonus was the creation of a new room above a void in the corner of the Smirke building, which was converted into a hospitality suite, used by staff and Trustees alike. This was furnished and embellished by Lord Hartwell in memory of his wife Pamela, a Museum Trustee and Chairman of the British Museum Society, and has proved of immeasurable benefit as a setting for hospitality in recent funding activities.

A bonus for the Director and his wife was the complete refurbishment of the Director's Residence, which had temporarily been used as offices for those displaced by the new building. The Residence, which had become rather tatty, was transformed and once again became a social centre for the Museum, its Trustees and its staff. Although there was little consistent domestic help my wife managed to create both a home and a centre for entertainment in this grand house.

The Museum was only one of a number of national museums searching for govern-mental funding for new buildings. There was only a certain amount of money available and in some respects the Victoria and Albert Museum and the Science Museum, which became trustee bodies in 1983 (previously they had been an integral part of the Department of Education and Science), were suffering from greater neglect and needed money more urgently. It was becoming clear that the Museum could not depend to any great extent on the Exchequer for the improvement and expansion of the buildings. Fortunately the cleaning of the main front, which had been planned for so long, was put in hand in 1978 and the Front Hall was redecorated, cleared of clutter and provided with a new information desk and a new shop. The Museum was beginning to have a more welcoming aspect and visitor numbers began to improve; they had reached 3.1 million in 1975. It was decided to encourage the Department of the Environment to concentrate on the maintenance of the neglected infrastructure. It was a constant battle. Buckets and heaps of sawdust gradually disappeared from the galleries as eleven and a half acres of roof were repaired and ceased to leak. The last of the bombed Greek and Roman galleries was made watertight, although the walls were still bare brickwork. A new electrical ring main with its associated sub-stations was installed, and problems of heating in at least some of the upper galleries were solved. Drains and telephones were dealt with. The floor of the gallery above the King's Library was strengthened and made more fireproof, but lack of vigilance on the Museum's part led to the lazy laying of cables and the installation of a temporary floor here, which was to take some years to correct. The roof of the Duveen Gallery was repaired and new lighting and air filtration introduced. A mezzanine floor was slung below the Department of Coins and Medals to give it more space and greatly improve security; a gallery for the reserve collection of Greek pottery (unfortunately rarely open to the public) was carved out of a cellar below the Archaic Greek gallery and a small room for the temporary display of coins and medals was constructed off the Greek and Roman Life Room. The railings at the front of the courtyard were stripped back to the metal and repainted; their tips were gilded. A new lecture theatre and education room were constructed in the Museum of Mankind, and so on. A more systematic approach was taken to the state of the building as plans and surveys were gradually filed and indexed. Finally, in 2000 a group of members of staff produced a full conservation plan, recording the history and detail of the complicated Bloomsbury building.

During my period as Director I had a personal blitz on the basements, which had been neglected for years. One of my first acts was to insist on visiting every room in the Museum, chief among which were the cellars. It was a revelation. In one basement I found an ancient fish-fryer, which we despatched to the Science Museum; in another was a free-lance cycle repair workshop; yet another was filled with out-of-print and largely useless books published by the Museum. The emergency equipment for use in disasters was housed in a cellar, which was also used to store empty fire extinguishers and two ancient bicycles to enable the staff in time of emergency to move around site. In one basement under the boilerhouse we found a man doing yoga. There were workshops for picture-framers and packers, a room for the housemaids to store linen and make tea, photo-graphic studios and rooms used as stores by the day contractors. There was far too much smoking taking place and a number of unofficial canteens. Many of the basements were filthy with the dust of ages and the passages outside were lined with covered antiquities and builders' junk. A major lacquer figure of the Buddha, for example, was in pieces in a barrow in a passage open to the elements, where it had lain for years (it now takes a proud place in the middle of the Joseph Hotung Gallery). Some basements were in apple-pie order, with modern storage or top-of-the-range conservation equipment. Over the years the corridors were cleared, the dust being laid by painting the walls and floors; new shelving and simple air extraction systems to minimize dust and damp were installed and basements were reallocated to the needy. Every door was labelled with the name of the department responsible for it, and huge quantities of junk were removed – some of which was even sold. Harassing the departments with succinct notes telling them to clear messes, I was able to bring into proper use vast swathes of neglected space.

A number of galleries were also refurbished, particularly on the south side of the Smirke building, where new displays for the Departments of Prehistoric and Romano-British Antiquities and Medieval and Later Antiquities were refurbished with standard cases provided by the Property Services Agency. One of the first galleries to be dealt with was the Medieval Room, where the Museum won a famous battle with the Agency, which allowed the Design Office to place, dress and provide texts for the cases. But it was clear that there was not enough money available to carry out the improvement and refurbishment that were so clearly necessary. The Museum consequently started to raise money for such work. In 1976 Robin Wade had drawn up a design for the Egyptian Sculpture Gallery, providing it with side rooms which together would make a more logical and understandable display. Direct negotiations with the Minister secured a promise of matching funding for the project if the Museum could provide the balance. A number of private donors (chief among them Henry Moore) were successfully approached and the gallery was triumphantly opened by the Prime Minister in 1981. This was the first gallery to use the house style of labelling and information panels developed by the Design Office. (Unfortunately, for they were very attractive, the side rooms were removed during the construction of the Great Court.) The next project was to provide galleries for the Townley and much of the reserve collections of classical sculpture and inscriptions. A suite of cellars beneath the Duveen Gallery was identified and converted into galleries with the aid of a major grant from the Wolfson Foundation.

Much more, however, was needed. Recognizing that a considerable time would lapse before the British Library was re-housed, the Trustees laid out in their triennial report in 1984 a scheme for the development of the non-Library portions of the building.[69] Much of it proved to be unrealizable, but much was done and the statement triggered planning which was to lead up to the successful take-over of the Library portion of the building. The Museum now went all-out to raise cash. First came the Japanese Gallery appeal. The Japanese collections were growing, and interest in them was also on the increase. A space was identified in the roof of the King Edward VII Building which would provide more than 1,000 square metres of exhibition space; the Trustees agreed to dedicate this to a display area for Japanese art and antiquities. No public money was available and the Museum settled down to ambitious fund-raising. This would have been impossible without the commitment of Teruko Iwanaga, a Japanese businesswoman living in England, who gave her time to the project in a totally unselfish manner. Together with Lawrence Smith, Keeper of Japanese Art, and a strong English committee, she raised more than £5 million (£4 million of it in Japan) towards these galleries, which were opened in 1990 (pl. 31). A happy legacy from a former Trustee, Sir John Addis, provided an Islamic gallery in the lower ground floor of the King Edward VII Building, opened in 1989.

It had become quite clear that money had to be sought from the private sector. We felt that we needed to make a splash. A dinner for nearly 1,000 influential people was given in 1988, funded privately by a number of individual Trustees. All the planning for this was done in-house; a committee chaired by the Hon. Mrs Marten, one of the Trustees, ran what was one of the most successful events ever put on by the Museum, the practical side being dealt with by my assistant, Marjorie Caygill, aided by Harriot Tennant. The dinner was held in the Duveen Gallery and in the adjoining Nereid Room; the Queen and the Duke of Edinburgh were the chief guests and the profile of the Museum was raised vastly. In the words of Sir Stephen Runciman, an erstwhile Trustee, 'it was social death not to have been there'. Patrons at £1,000 p.a. were recruited afterwards and a large number of Associates contributed £100 annually. The team that organized this event now became specialists in running fund-raising and other major events in the Museum; they gave them style and understated glitter.

The enormous generosity of Sir Joseph Hotung was one of the first fruits of the new approach to fund-raising. He gave £2 million to refurbish much of the main floor of the King Edward VII Building for Chinese, South-East Asian and Indian material. The Japanese newspaper *Asahi Shimbun* gave £500,000 to fund one end of this gallery for the Amaravati sculpture, while the Museums and Galleries Improvement Fund paid the balance.[70] It was completed in 1992.

Others followed. Two very generous donors appeared in the shape of an American couple, Raymond and Beverly Sackler, who have since become staunch friends of the Museum. They paid for a series of major refurbishments on the north side for the departments of Egyptian and Western Asiatic Antiquities, which have completely transformed the appearance of these galleries. To this was added the refurbishment of galleries funded by Roxie Walker and the Bioanthropology Foundation to house the ever-popular collection of Egyptian mummy-cases and wooden sarcophagi. The refurbishment of the upper Greek and Roman galleries was stimulated by the gift of money by the A.G. Leventis Foundation to fund the display of Cypriot antiquities. The Wolfson Family Charitable Trust completed the run of the five western galleries by paying for one of the two Roman galleries opened in 1991. The last wartime bomb-damage visible in this area was thus rectified. On the ground floor, the Bassae Gallery was refurbished and provided with a new staircase by Mr and Mrs Lawrence Fleischman, who with other American friends have funded other gallery projects on the same floor. The Korea Foundation provided money for a Korean Gallery, while the Museum collaborated with the Mexican National Council of Culture and the Arts to fund the Mexican Gallery – two of the first galleries carved out of British Library space. The Chase Manhattan Bank paid for the second, a gallery of North America. Mr and Mrs T.Y. Chao funded the nineteenth-century gallery and HSBC paid for the new Money gallery. The Garfield Weston Foundation contributed to the new galleries covering Europe in the Bronze and Iron Ages, together with Roman Britain. The Sainsbury family funded the African Gallery as part of the Great Court Scheme.

Great private generosity has transformed the galleries in the last twenty years. The drab interiors and displays been brought up to date and glow with newly exposed brilliance. While this is chiefly due to the donors, the hard work has fallen on the antiquities departments and the Design Office, as well as those in the works department.

Storage space remained a problem. In the 1980s additional storage space was added to Franks House in Shoreditch and in 1992 the last remaining freehold of this group of properties was acquired. A ceramics centre was opened for the study of European pottery and porcelain in two of the Montague Street houses; the removal of this material from the main building at last allowed the full restoration of the old Iron Age Gallery to display the sixteenth-, seventeenth- and eighteenth-century European collections. These developments, together with the Olympia property, held storage problems at bay while a search for a solution proceeded. Soon after he became Director, Robert Anderson set up a working party to look for storage to serve the Museum for another half-century. By good fortune the enormous Royal Mail sorting office on High Holborn became available and was bought by the Trustees in 1995, using up most of the free capital in their private funds for the purpose, a project since aborted through lack of funding support.

The Great Court[71]

The greatest challenge and greatest success, however, was the Great Court (pl. 32), which opened in December 2000 – the biggest single museum scheme to be completed in the country since the war. The heroes of the project were Graham Greene, Chairman of the Trustees, Robert Anderson, the Director, and above all Sir Claus Moser, Chairman of the British Museum Development Trust. They had the vision, raised the money, and suffered the press.

When building work began on the British Library in 1982 the Office of Arts and Libraries ignored all pleas from the Museum to discuss the future of the space to be vacated in Bloomsbury. Despite the fact that the Trustees owned the building, the Office even suggested that the Museum had no presumed right to move into the library space. As work on the new British Library building proceeded, the Ministry became more and more disturbed by the escalating costs in a period of high inflation and started to interfere more in the project management of what was one of the most expensive public building projects of the post-war period. They thus had little time for the Museum's requests for dialogue. By 1988 it became clear that as the British Library was indeed going to move out of Blooms-bury the Museum would have to do something about planning with or without support from the Ministry. On a domestic basis a joint working party between Library and Museum was set up to discuss the logistics of the move. More importantly, a committee of Trustees and staff, chaired by Sir Peter Harrop (a former Permanent Secretary at the Department of the Environment), was set up to examine all the implications.

The committee had a broad brief.[72] Uppermost in its mind was the Trustees' resolve to relinquish the Museum of Mankind and move the Department of Ethnography back to Bloomsbury into the vacated space, bringing the reserve collection back from Franks House in Shoreditch. The committee consulted widely and produced a bold plan. Its main objectives were to improve circulation in the Museum, to placate sentimentalists among readers who wished to retain the Reading Room as a reading room of the British Library, and to provide a positive and useful space for storage, display and education. The commit-tee proposed the demolition of the book-stacks in the quadrants to ground level. The existing basement space below the courtyard would be used for storage. Many of the larger vacated rooms and galleries, of which the most important were the North Library, the remains of the north wing of the Smirke building, the Manuscript Room, the South Room, the Grenville Library, together with the old Official Publication Library on the lower ground floor of the King Edward VII Building, were to be used for major new displays. The Reading Room would be returned to its original decorative scheme and retained to house part of the vast library of the Department of Ethnography.[73] The public was also to be allowed access to view one of the great rooms of London. The shelves of the King's Library would be furnished with appropriate books, interspersed with a display of pottery and porcelain, and the original table-cases would house a display of material appropriate to a gentleman's cabinet of the eighteenth century. A lecture room, shops and a room for the British Museum Society would be fitted into the space left by the demolition of the southern quadrants. The space taken up by the northern quadrants would be adapted for offices and storage. The estimated cost of this outline plan for the whole of the vacated library space (including what later became the Great Court), allowing for inflation, was £138 million. The committee was working in the period before the National Lottery was set up, and the sum seemed almost unobtainable. The Trustees, however, wanted a firm commitment from the government over a number of years to fund the major part of the project, but the Department of National Heritage (as the Office of Arts and Libraries had become in 1992) was less than helpful. Courageously, the Trustees decided to go ahead on the lines proposed by the committee and produced a lush brochure outlining their plans – the first of a number of such public relations exercises;[74] the elements of a business plan were constructed. As I was about to retire, further planning was left to my successor.

Fresh from the initiation of a major building project in the National Museums of Scotland, Robert Anderson had a broader vision. Unhappy with the existing plan and particularly with its piecemeal approach, in December 1992 he reconstituted the Harrop committee. He was particularly critical of the proposed use of the Reading Room and convinced the Trustees that it should be converted to provide a library of general reference. The Trustees were persuaded by one of their number, Sir William Whitfield, to look at Smirke's courtyard as a whole, and the Great Court scheme was born.[75] An international architectural competition was held, not to produce a finished design but to identify an architect with 'a broad, imaginative view of how the space could be used'.[76] Some 132 firms submitted schemes and in July 1994 Sir Norman Foster and Partners were declared winners. Foster, one of the most distinguished of contemporary architects, had designed many prestigious buildings both in Britain and abroad, from the Sainsbury Centre of the University of East Anglia to the reconstruction of the Reichstag in Berlin. His concept was basically simple. Smirke's internal courtyard was to be restored, paved and entered from the old Entrance Hall. The Reading Room, faced in stone, would become a freestanding entity with an elliptical extension. New basements were to be constructed for storage and educational purposes. Access to the galleries would be provided in the middle of each of Smirke's internal façades. The most striking feature was a cushion-like roof of plastic panels (glass was later substituted) supported on a steel grid, which would cover the space between the Reading Room and the internal walls of the courtyard. The cost of the scheme, as revised in the light of Foster's proposals, was estimated at £100 million.

The new Director was helped by the fact that his appointment more or less co-incided with the announcement of the establishment of a National Lottery, which placed the proposed development within the bounds of financial possibility. In 1994 it was announced that the product of the National Lottery should be divided into five; one part – designated the Heritage Lottery Fund – was to be run by the National Heritage Memorial

Fund, and another part should form a fund – administered by a newly established Millennium Commission – to celebrate the coming millennium. The Museum was eligible under the terms of both these funds; what is more it had by this time worked up a scheme for the Great Court which enabled it to apply for money in the period when there was least restriction on the spending of either fund. The first application was to the Millennium Commission, which in March 1996 granted a sum of £30 million.[77] The main condition attached to this grant was that entry to the courtyard should be free and that it should be considered as a general public square, open for a period significantly longer than the normal opening hours of the Museum. An application was then made to the Heritage Lottery Fund for work directed at the restoration and conservation of Smirke's forecourt; the restoration of the polychromatic decorative scheme for the front hall devised by L.W. Collman; and the replacement of railings outside the King Edward VII Building, which had been removed during the Second World War. For this the Museum was granted £15.75 million. A further £52 million had to be raised if the scheme was to go ahead and a highly skilled and influential Trustee, Sir Claus Moser, agreed to undertake the task and ratcheted up the fund-raising activities.

A British Museum Trust had been set up in the 1980s to raise money; renamed the Development Trust, it was now revitalized by Moser. With Princess Margaret as Patron and Dr Gerard Vaughan as director, the Development Trust built up a staff and started to raise money, particularly from big donors. Aided by the British Museum Society and the American Friends of the British Museum, the balance – and more – was raised. The most important private donation – the biggest in the Museum's history – was £20 million from Garry Weston's Garfield Weston Foundation. Other major benefactors included the Japanese newspaper group *Asahi Shimbun*, British Petroleum, The British Museum Company, Donald and Jeanne Kahn, and Peter Moores. Gifts from Sir Joseph Hotung and members of the Sainsbury family provided for two galleries and the Clore Foundation and the Vivien Duffield Foundation paid for the Education Centre. The Paul Hamlyn Foundation established a reference library in the Reading Room. A large number of other major donors and supporters contributed to the scheme.[78] Altogether this was the most successful fund-raising exercise ever undertaken for a museum in Britain.

The holdings of the British Library had first to be moved to its new building and enabling work costing £8.5 million had to be undertaken. This completed, demolition and construction work finally started in March 1998.[79] The Museum heroically remained open throughout the building work, despite closed galleries, some noise, much dust and frequent false fire alarms. It caused most serious disruption for the staff of the Department of Prehistoric and Romano-British Antiquities, whose offices and library had had to be demolished to allow the scheme to go ahead. Access to the enclosed building site was difficult and practically all material had to be lifted over the portico by two giant cranes to and from a temporary builders' yard in the forecourt. The huddle of buildings around the Reading Room was demolished and earth to a depth of ten metres around the drum was removed to create basement space.

As finally opened by the Queen in December 2000, the Great Court provided a series of new facilities for the Museum. At basement level on the south side, and linked to the vaulted basements of Smirke's building, is the Museum's first purpose-built education centre. This includes the Ford Centre for Young Visitors, the Clore Education Centre with two lecture theatres – one of 320 seats, given by BP, and one of 150 seats, given by Hugh and Catherine Stevenson – as well as a series of seminar rooms (one named in honour of Sir Claus Moser, another for Mr and Mrs Sackler). The Court above the basement area is dominated by the drum of the Reading Room, clad in Spanish limestone (*Galicia capri*). It stands in the middle of a newly refurbished courtyard, with a totally reconstructed south portico giving access to the Front Hall. The interior of the Reading Room was redecorated and restored to its original appearance, while the reading desks and other fixed furniture were retained. A surprising discovery was the amount of gilding in the original decorative scheme – the restoration of which added significantly to the contingency costs of the project. The post-war chairs were refurbished and a display of a collection of books by readers who had used the library in the past – from Karl Marx to Louis MacNeice – was mounted in the area immediately inside the door. The shelves in the ground floor of the room have been filled with a general reference library for the public, while those in the two upper galleries hold books from the library of the Department of Ethnography.[80] The windows, their form originally suggested by the Prince Consort, admit daylight and provide the visitors in various parts of the Museum with a glimpse of the glory of the Reading Room's decorative scheme.

The stone wall of the Reading Room is continued to the north as an ellipse. This contains, at ground-floor level, shops (including a magnificent bookshop) and other services. In either northern corner of the Court is a self-service cafeteria. The floor of the courtyard also displays symbolic sculpture, an Anglo-Saxon cross, the lion from Cnidus, two Egyptian heads and so on. Perhaps the least successful element is the display on a vast plinth of the Easter Island statue, Hoa Hakananai'a, which is demeaned by the towering space. By means of grand stone staircases on either side of the drum one may reach the Joseph Hotung Great Court Gallery for special exhibitions. Above this is a restaurant and access by a bridge to the upper level of the northern range of galleries. The great glory of the Court is the undulating glass roof, which edges up to the bottom of the dome. Through its amazing computer-planned lattice can be seen the scudding clouds and sky.

The Front Hall was restored to the Collman scheme and the forecourt gently remodelled, being partly re-paved in York stone. The grass plots were preserved, but seating facing on to the grass was incorporated in the renewed stone wall. As part of the Great Court scheme the Sainsbury African Galleries were installed at basement level (pl. 31), entered from the old North Library. A grant from the Wellcome Trust will enable the construction of another ethnographical gallery in the old North Library shell, which will open in 2003; meanwhile it serves to give access to the North Entrance.

While critics who had seen the completed project were almost universal in their praise, *The Evening Standard* and Sir Jocelyn Stevens, the ex-Chairman of English Heritage, led a sustained attack on the Museum about the stone used in the reconstructed south portico.[81] There was trouble here. The specification provided that the portico should be built of 'oolitic limestone, Portland-base bed or similar'. The stone was chosen from a number of samples but it was in fact a similar oolite, Anstrude Roche Claire, from a French source. The stone is certainly whiter than the weathered stone of the rest of the courtyard – hardly surprising since beds from which the original stone was taken have long since disappeared. What is more, much of the rest of the façade was patched and stained after exposure to the elements and building schemes over a period of a hundred years. The fuss caused the Museum to commission a report from Pricewaterhouse Coopers on the matter. The report states that 'The Museum was deceived... [and] let down by its professional advisers' procedures.... The ultimate decision of 30 July 1999 to continue with the use of Anstrude stone was probably correct...'. They found no evidence of a cover-up, but pointed to some minor management deficiencies in communication and record, which the Museum has promised to correct. It was a tornado in a teacup, but threats of litigation proceeded for a time as the London Borough of Camden made tough-sounding noises. Eventually they backed down and dropped their complaints.[82]

The creation of this magnificent space has, however, produced difficulties for the logical viewing of the Museum. The main staircase, restored to its original decorative scheme, is now so gloomy and poorly signed that the public tends to ignore it and go straight into the Great Court. It is now clear why Franks placed objects on the half-landing to tempt people up the stairs. If members of the public ignore the stairs they tend to enter the Museum in a back-to-front way, either halfway through the sequence of Egyptian sculpture, into the middle of the King's Library or into the King Edward VII Building. They tend to miss the early classical sculpture as they head directly for the Duveen Gallery through the Assyrian transept and the Nereid Room. All these problems will be solved in time, but other urgent matters have priority.

The remaining portions of the British Library space are still to be developed. The King's Library is already partly funded by the Wolfson Foundation and Simon Sainsbury, but a great deal of money needs to be raised before all the plans can be brought to fruition.

Education

The completion of the Great Court scheme and the provision of a specialist education centre has led to a significant growth in the provision of educational opportunity in the Museum. It has been shown how, under Wolfenden and Pope-Hennessy, a properly organized and funded educational policy was developed, and staff and infrastructure provided. In the 1970s and 80s the smallish education staff concentrated largely on teaching teachers, particularly those of children up to the age of eleven, especially by providing teachers' packs throughout the country. Although other audiences were reached through gallery talks, text-books and specially focused programmes, resources were inadequate. By 2001 the educational staff of the Museum (which included its various central libraries) had increased to forty with a budget of £1.3 million, of which in 2001/2 nearly £200,000 was sponsored. Ethnic groups were particularly targeted. Museum websites were created in a number of subjects and languages, which supplement the Museum's main website.[83] A relationship was built up with the Department of Education and Employment to develop the Museum's resources for use in the public examination of schoolchildren.

Another section of the Museum's Education Department concentrates on lifelong learning, and some resources have been slanted towards various postgraduate university courses. For example, a diploma in Asian art is taught in the Museum, while various MA courses are taught in collaboration with outside bodies, as, for example, University College London, Birkbeck College, London, and the Open University; there are as well outreach programmes with local education authorities. A more specialist approach is the Michael Bomberg Fellowship, endowed in 2000 in perpetuity, to bring in young students of prints for periods of three months. Fellowships funded by British Petroleum allow staff from foreign museums to spend periods of six weeks at the Museum as interns.

Members of the Education Department still deliver talks in the galleries, but their work is now supplemented by others. Outside gallery lecturers appeared on a planned basis in the 1980s; first through the London Tourist Board and the 'Blue Guide' lecturer scheme, and then in 1992 by means of trained volunteer guides, within a scheme entitled 'eyeOpeners'. By 2000 nearly a hundred volunteers are providing eight short introductory tours daily in various parts of the Museum. This scheme, based on the American 'docent' system of volunteer gallery lecturers, has proved extremely popular, particularly for office workers at lunchtime. Since the 1980s the Museum has been open for an evening each month on which members of the public and the British Museum Friends are able to go behind the scenes and listen to the curators talking about the collections. Since the opening of the Great Court these have continued, but in addition much of the Museum is open to the public on a number of weekday evenings.

A major new element in the success of the Education Department has been the increased space in the basements of the Great Court. The two state-of-the-art lecture theatres, together with seminar rooms, children's cloakrooms, classrooms, lunch-rooms and a large foyer, have improved facilities out of recognition for both staff and public. Even before the opening of the new Education Centre the Museum was offering a full programme of courses and events to more than a quarter of a million schoolchildren; this is set to rise dramatically. Adrian Mole's fictional diary comments on a form visit to the Museum in the early 1980s will, we trust, no longer ring true:

> Enter British Museum. Adrian Mole and Pandora Braithwaite awestruck by evidence of heritage World Culture. Rest of class Four-D run berserk, laughing at nude statues and dodging curators.[84]

Exhibitions – A Vicious Circle?

There is nowadays a craving for exhibitions by a public fed on such successes as 'Tutankhamun' – the Museum's biggest blockbuster – and the many major shows at the Royal Academy. A great deal of time and energy is expended on such exhibitions by the Museum staff – although such visitor figures have never been realized again. The return is worthwhile in that not only do members of the public enjoy major, well-displayed expositions of artists or cultures, but also there is a permanent spin-off for the Museum and the academic public in the form of the learned catalogues that are associated with them. Some are successful in raising public awareness and pay for themselves – as did that on the Vikings, in 1980. But many are extremely expensive to mount and can be achieved only with the help of major sponsorship. Even in the Department of Prints and Drawings it is not always easy to cover costs, as loans from other museums – especially those abroad – are expensive to organize and fund. The host museum must pay for necessary conservation, photography, copyright fees, security, transport, packing, and the subsistence and travel expenses of the curatorial courier who accompanies the loan. For this reason the Museum has had to charge for entry to many of its special exhibitions, including in recent years those largely made up from its own collections (which had previously been free). Although there has been a fall-off in the number of paying visitors to special exhibitions in the period leading up to the opening of the Great Court, it is planned to increase the number to 300,000 in 2001–2.[85] This is a far cry from the 465,000 paying visitors who went to the Viking exhibition in 1980, but it is also an indicator of a more jaded public palate which demands more and greater spectacles in ever narrowing fields of interest, best provided at the Royal Academy. The number of temporary exhibitions mounted by the Museum, however, averages between twenty and thirty annually, some being comparatively small displays put on in one or two show-cases.

The traffic in loan exhibitions is two-way, for the Museum also lends willingly to similar exhibitions both in this country and abroad. This is conceived as a duty, in that the collections are held in trust and must be made as freely available as possible. It is an expensive process, as the time employed by Museum staff can never, save in the most exceptional circumstances, be recouped. Only when whole exhibitions are lent can reasonable returns be expected, and, although there is a tendency to avoid general 'treasure' exhibitions, they are sometimes necessary for propaganda or fund-raising purposes. Generally loans are more mundane, sometimes being simply of regional interest. In 1999–2000 114 separate loans of individual items or groups of objects, short-term and long-term, were made within the British Isles, of which about a quarter were renewals of previous long-term loans. A hundred foreign loans were made during the same period to museums and galleries in eighteen countries, of which only a handful was long-term. Often only two or three objects of high importance will be lent to a major foreign exhibition, but sometimes – as particularly with prints and drawings – a major group of images of one artist or school will be sent.[86]

In the last thirty years a programme of travelling exhibitions from the Museum's own collections has been developed, often, but not exclusively, in the United Kingdom, based on exhibitions first shown in the Museum. Other travelling exhibitions are specially developed to be shown abroad. Thus in 1999–2000 specially arranged exhibitions went to New York, Charleston, Shanghai, Singapore, Tokyo, Kobe and Fukuoka.[87] Such exhibitions can be useful in raising money, most recently making possible the refurbishment of two of the upper Egyptian galleries by means of the profits of touring exhibitions of Egyptian material in the United States. These exhibitions sometimes play a major diplomatic role, as with the exhibition of treasures of the British Museum which was sent to India, in co-operation with the British Council, as part of the celebration of fifty years of Indian independence. Opened by the Queen and the President of the Indian Republic, the show travelled from Delhi to Bombay.[88]

As the Museum holds in trust a large, diversified and, in some ways, invisible collection, the public both in Britain and abroad has a right to see this material. But there are associated problems. Occasionally an object is damaged; very occasionally something goes missing. But the problems tend to reside elsewhere; the strain on the curatorial staff has increased enormously. In 1985 the Museum lent to only forty-seven foreign venues in twelve countries, about half the number recorded fifteen years later. At that time I was lamenting the fact that the Museum had to cut its loans programme partly on the grounds of cost.[89] Robert Anderson managed to reverse this trend without significantly increased resources; but the expansion must have limits even if a dedicated registrar's department is set up to relieve the strain on departmental staff. One of the minor irritants of lending objects is that important pieces are often absent from display for quite long periods of time. This is a disappointment for visitors, who have a right to expect to see such material; it also detracts from the Museum's own displays, as the items cannot always be replaced and the visitor sees a lot of empty pins instead of fine objects – often without any information as to where they are. (There are instructions about this, but the staff are often too busy to prepare labels to explain where they have gone.) Something, ultimately, must give, and it is unlikely to be the government!

Who Visits the Museum?

The first survey of visitors to the Museum was carried out at the request of the government between October and December 1971.[90] It encompassed the British Museum and two other national museums, but its results were of minimal value as, like so many such surveys, it did not extend throughout the year and underestimated such matters as the impact of tourists. In 1982–3 the Museum itself initiated a survey and repeated it ten years later; in both cases the survey sampled visitors at various periods throughout the year.[91] Even so the surveys were perforce slanted in that they could not question schoolchildren, and also did not question the significant number of parties of Jehovah's Witnesses who visit the Museum on Saturdays throughout the year to look at material related to the Bible. These omissions might have skewed the results of the socio-economic status of visitors. Work continues to refine the type of surveys carried out in order better to understand the needs of the visitors.

The results of all these surveys are, however, fairly consistent. Approximately half the visitors in practically every survey came from the socio-economic class AB; 35 per cent came from C1, 8 per cent from C2 and 7 per cent from DE classes. More than half of the visitors had been to university, and nearly a quarter of the visitors were in their twenties. In the winter nearly half the visitors came from the United Kingdom (almost three-quarters from London and the south-east), while at the height of the summer up to 70 per cent were foreigners, mostly Europeans. American and Japanese were the next most numerous foreign visitors.[92] Such numbers are useful and might even be interesting, but only in marketing and lobbying terms. Partly as a consequence of such results the Museum has, for example, published souvenir guides in nine languages.

The Museum was early in the field of disabled access. One of its education officers was in 1984 seconded to the Carnegie Council for the Arts and Disabled People as administrator to promote the Attenborough Report on disabled access to the arts. On returning to the Museum she was able to help with many problems in this area. In 1997 Lloyds TSB funded a three-year post for an Access Officer to develop work for the disabled. On a practical level, lifts and slopes have been installed for wheelchair access throughout, and since 1978 sessions for disabled groups and 'handling exhibitions' for the visually impaired have been held, at which the help of volunteers is essential. Sign language was introduced into gallery talks on a regular basis and Braille information sheets are provided. All staff undertake disability training. The Education Department is conscious that it works for all, including the socially and culturally deprived, despite frequent accusations of elitism.[93]

Almost as a matter of course important official visitors to London visit the Museum. Heads of state, members of foreign governments and foreign delegations are dealt with on a daily basis. Not all are as grand as the President of China or the President of the United States, who have both made recent visits, but the contacts made during such tours are of diplomatic service to the country and often provide new and useful contacts for the Museum itself.

Charging

In the 1980s the Museum led the way, with the National Gallery and the Tate Gallery, in resisting admission charges. In 1997–8, despite great pressure and a reduction in government funding – to the great credit of Robert Anderson, who was fighting a tougher battle than his predecessor – the Museum held the line. Backed by an excellent specialist report,[94] the Trustees insisted that even the smallest charges would inhibit visits and refused to introduce them. That this was true is confirmed by visitor numbers, which at the Museum have continued to rise towards six million annually, whereas they shrank in those museums that charged for entry. Only the Natural History Museum, which played the popular dinosaur card with skill, bucked the trend. The Victoria and Albert Museum indeed was criticized by the National Audit Office for failing to reach its visitor number targets when the figure fell to 1.27 million in 1999–2000 (in 1985, the last year before charging, there were 2.097 million). The refusal to charge was not without pain for the British Museum, as it was unable (unlike charging museums) to reclaim Value Added Tax either on running costs or on its capital expenditure – a ruling which over the years has cost it £27 million. The Labour party, always against charging for entry, was at first unable to fund the tax cost. In the March budget in 2001 the Chancellor of the Exchequer, however, announced that all museums would be able to reclaim the tax, a decision met by a sigh of relief in the British Museum. It is possible now that visitors will be attracted away from the Museum by free entry elsewhere, but a major battle has been won for the general public and the Museum was in the van.

Research and Publication

Geoffrey Robinson (the Treasury Minister who later resigned from the Blair Government over the first Mandelson affair), apparently more in tune with modern art galleries than museums, made a judgement which is fairly typical of the uninformed but influential:

> It is probably fair to say that the British Museum has further to go than the others in making the change to an outward-looking entrepreneurial culture. The monastic roots of pure scholasticism run deep in Great Russell Street.[95]

Not only did he not understand the outward-looking nature of the Museum's culture – probably because he had never attempted to – but he used the term 'scholasticism' as one of opprobrium. Without scholarship and without research the Museum could not function as a popular and many-faceted institution of great popular appeal. This does not mean that the curators live in an ivory tower.

Research is as essential to the Museum as it is to any other national institution concerned with art and culture. Modern populism too often equates 'academic' with 'dry as dust' and consequently condemns it. But scholarship raises the excitement and the fascination of the Museum experience. The vitality of the British Museum is unashamedly based on its scholarship – and has been since its foundation. Sometimes this may appear arid, but without it the Museum would have been unable to reach out to the general public – both national and international – who have made it the most visited museum in the country and possibly in the world. Scholarship informs its public face. The Museum has made a firm statement about such concerns and it would be a sorry day if it were to be dismissed by populists as irrelevant:

> Research into all [these] cultures underlies every aspect of the Museum's work. No exhibition can be mounted without detailed research into the concepts or cultures it embodies, and indeed the objects and ideas which it includes. The collections themselves need research for their good order and development, while they rely on research in the field of conservation for their continuing existence in good shape. Hundreds of thousands of people every year contact the Museum for information, whether about the objects in their own or the Museum's collections, or about almost any aspect of the cultures covered by the Museum.... The books and articles which the Museum publishes are intended both to advance knowledge and, like the exhibitions in the main galleries, to bring the results of that new knowledge to as broad a public as possible, whether the academic community, schoolchildren and students, or the general public.
>
> ... In the late 18th and 19th centuries, the Museum was seen as the physical embodiment of an encyclopaedia, encompassing the sum of human knowledge, ...driven by a desire to establish a taxonomy of the Museum's contents, be they fossils, flints, coins or prints. The focus today is much more on the ways that these objects can be used to help us grasp the ideas or social groupings which produced them and of which they are an expression. A symbol of this change can perhaps be seen in the... way the Museum's galleries are presented; rooms arranged with classical antiquities arranged by shape or material have been replaced in recent years by displays illustrating such themes as the history of money or the cultural diversity of the Roman Empire.[96]

Lightly carried scholarship informs the many popular books produced by the staff – books which range from children's 'activity' books to guides and small highly illustrated descriptions of specific themes or groups of objects, which sell in large numbers. This scholarship is firmly grounded and is expressed in catalogues and papers in learned journals, which cover vast areas of the Museum's interests and holdings.[97] Thus Elizabeth Eames's small popular book on medieval tiles, which has been reprinted many times, is firmly based on the work for her massive two-volume catalogue of the same material, which is an essential tool of medieval archaeological scholarship.[98] Museums generally, and the British Museum in particular, now provide, as has been shown, the main expertise in that material culture which gives such immediacy to the understanding and enjoyment of the past. The Museum communicates that expertise through the objects it displays and through its publications, information panels and labelling.

The British Museum Company, established on a wing and a prayer in the mid-

1970s, has been an important catalyst in the dissemination of the Museum's scholarship. Founded initially to ease the publication of scholarly material, it is now one of the largest British publishers of books on archaeology, material culture and art. In 1999 the British Museum Press published fifty-five books, ranging from full catalogues to children's books. The company also produced postcards and replicas, recordings and craft material. Its commercial success is emphasized by its balance sheet which shows its turnover in 1999 at £8,794,000, in which year it gave £641,000 to the Museum.[99]

Pope-Hennessy had killed off *the British Museum quarterly* and substituted in its place a *Yearbook*, with themed articles; this was a financial disaster and, after four numbers, it had to be closed down. In 1979, however, I inaugurated our own publication series – *British Museum Occasional Papers* – independently of the company. Produced cheaply by offset lithography from camera-ready copy, these formed a quick and inexpensive medium for publications relevant to the Museum's work. The series, which now comprises some 130 titles, includes monographs, minor catalogues, conference papers, consultative documents, and even the results of visitor surveys. Sales more or less cover the costs and, because they are cheap, they are widely disseminated.

The Museum's academic output is monitored by the Trustees' Scholarship Committee and was in the mid-1990s subject to peer review by university assessors. Apart from the books published by the British Museum Press, members of the Museum's staff in 1999 (the last available figures) published six occasional papers, fourteen books with other publishers and 270 articles in learned journals. Further, they have as always helped by providing information, opinions and material to scholars, and have acted as a general service for the identification of antiquities. The education service is dependent on the general scholarship of the Museum, as is the whole public face of the institution. Displays could not be mounted without scholarship.

Such scholarship does not represent elitism; rather it provides a base for the total use of the collections by anyone who wishes to use the Museum. Of course the Museum from time to time indulges in gimmicks – a 'sleep-over' in the galleries for children, for example – but these are simply the extreme face of a policy of inclusion. Three random examples of the Museum working towards social inclusion will suffice. A grant to provide an education officer by SmithKline Beecham has developed programmes for families, play-groups and children. The loan to Leicester of a major exhibition featuring daily life in an Indian village enabled the Asian community of the Midlands to introduce their children to something approaching their own culture. During 1999 an assessment of the HSBC Money Gallery was carried out in relation to visitor reaction and the information in the gallery was modified in accordance with the findings. The idea that the Museum is 'elitist' stems from the educated class, which has probably never considered it as a whole, and condemns it without thinking. Even the Secretary of State, visiting the Great Court while it was under construction, accused the Museum of being elitist, and this at a time when one could hardly move in the galleries for the back-packers and parties of schoolchildren – the Museum had 5.6 million visitors in that rather constricted year! It is in any case patronizing to think that these visitors cannot be presented with difficult as well as simple concepts. The Museum cannot descend to the lowest populist denominator. This would be to diminish the objects and underestimate the intelligence of the general public. It would produce a museum of benefit to nobody.

View from the Boardroom Table

To be a Trustee is a great honour, and those chosen are pleased to give a great amount of time to the welfare of the Museum. By long tradition Trustees meet on Saturdays (in my day nine times a year, now six times) for about two and a half hours, to advise on all aspects of the Museum's governance. The number of Trustees' committees has been reduced in the late 1990s to five – Finance and Planning, Audit and Governance, Remuneration and Nomination, Scholarship, Public Policy – as well as two 'major projects' committees. To these might be added the Board of Directors of the British Museum Company.

There are twenty-five Trustees, a number often said by outsiders to be unmanageable. In practice, however, they are all needed and, with good chairmanship and good humour, the Board functions easily. In my fifteen years as Director I worked to three consummate chairmen: Lord Trevelyan (an ex-diplomat), Lord Trend (pl.28; former Secretary of the Cabinet) and Lord Windlesham (former Leader of the House of Lords). They managed the Board in different ways, but all used a light rein. The long board table was not terribly convenient, but with such chairmen business was despatched with great efficiency. The Board of my period (and I can write only of this) would form a splendid subject for sociological study. Territory, for example, was important. The Chairman sat in the middle of one side, flanked on his right by the Duke of Gloucester and on his left by the Director, supported by his deputy and the Secretary and Assistant Secretary. There was an unspoken *placement* among board members. A certain amount of gentlemanly manoeuvring was noticeable for the seats opposite the Chairman; as one senior Trustee left he would tend to be replaced by the next most senior member of the Board – Lord Annan replaced Lord Boyd, and was himself succeeded by Professor Hall. To the Chairman's right and on the other side of the table the professionals tended to congregate – academics, architects and lawyers (although Professor Treitel, the senior of the two lawyers, sat on the Assistant Secretary's left). Sir Denis Hamilton and some of the other businessmen sat on the same side of the table as the Chairman and to his right. The Royal Academy representative (Dame Elisabeth Frink and later Allen Jones) always sat at the left-hand end of the table. Some mavericks moved their seats from meeting to meeting and appeared quite unashamed.

Trustees arrived up to half an hour before the meeting to examine objects which had been acquired or which were before the meeting for approval. This material was laid out on a long sideboard and members of the staff lobbied the Trustees' interest. The meetings were structured to a strict model agenda, the papers colour-coded to distinguish active matters from various types of formal business. Reports of the various sub-committees would be discussed, as would matters of finance and public and international policy. Senior appointments would be formally confirmed. Internal matters, such as permission to lend objects, reports on special leave and on minor gifts, would be reported formally. At each meeting one of the keepers would appear to discuss his annual report, the chair being demitted for his or her appearance to the departmental Trustee. This could be tricky for the Director, who had to think on his feet about all sorts of problems raised by the keeper but not in his circulated report. For most Trustees the business that gave most pleasure was the discussion of purchases. The keepers' and the Director's devolved purchasing powers were kept deliberately low (this is no longer the case), so that the Director could see practically everything bought by the staff, but also so that members of the Board could take part in the discussion of acquisitions and thus fulfil their responsibilities to the Museum as a trust. Constrained only by the limits of available funds, discussion, informed by written departmental submission, was often animated. Trustees would use their own special knowledge to argue cases. Sir John Hale, for example, could charm the birds off the trees when discussing drawings; Sir David Attenborough would lucidly defend ethnographic purchases, while Professor Watson would argue (often against an unconvinced Lord Weinstock, who disliked Japanese art) with passion and effectiveness. The most difficult decisions were those taken on financial grounds, when one – often very different – piece had to be set off against another.

The Board was remarkably good-tempered, although discussion was often passionate. In my fifteen years I believe that only one vote was taken – and I have forgotten what that was about! It is, however, at Board meetings that the Director's mettle is tested; he cannot afford to lose too many fights. The Trustees' lunch following the meeting was a good opportunity for Trustees and staff to discuss decisions and policy informally.

Purpose and Politics

In 1989, in a mood of frustration and impatience, I wrote a small book entitled *The British Museum. Purpose and politics*.[100] Its main purpose was to go beyond uninformed comment in the media and Parliament and explain the ethos of the Museum. It came at a particularly difficult time in the institution's history, for it was short of money, had an unsympathetic government and was being threatened with deficit funding unless it charged for entry. The book was basically a plea for government support at a time when the public service generally was being eroded in both size and confidence. Describing the history and functions of the Museum, I dealt with such matters as the Greek government's request for the return of the Elgin Marbles, the issue of scholarship as a central function, the collecting policy and the integrity of the collections. I also discussed the international functions and relationships of the Museum and our outreach within England. I pointed to the fact that the government no longer funded increases of salary for which they, through the system of national awards, were responsible. I built a closely argued and on the whole convincing case against charging for entry on grounds of both earning capacity and visitor numbers, producing figures to back my arguments. The book was well received and had some effect on national policy concerning museums, particularly on the debate about charging for entry.

The Museum's problems, then as now, are based on chronically bad and inconsistent funding which extends a long way back – perhaps to the creation of the Ministry for the Arts and the separation of financial control from the Treasury. For a short time in the 1970s the Museum was well funded. Coming from the university world in 1977, I was, however, astounded that the Museum could not see that cuts were bound to come as a result of the slashing of funds caused by the country's International Monetary Fund crisis of 1976. What is more, it had no long-term plan to accommodate such a possibility. That the writing was on the wall was demonstrated by the fact that for the first time a director was appointed on a five-year contract. In some ways museums were more able to face stringent financial control than universities in that they had for many years been directly answerable to the august Public Accounts Committee of Parliament and were liable to defend their actions in public. Successive directors had appeared before it and always managed to stand up to it. Indeed, the Committee had tended to back them. This process protected museums in the first vicious period of attack on universities by the Thatcher government, but soon the Office of Arts and Libraries (and its successors) became more intrusive, more demanding. Trimmers within the profession who had their own political agenda backed them, but many remained staunch.

There was a perception (to a large extent unfounded) that museums were financially inefficient. The government wanted them to be run as businesses. Museums were told to raise money so that they could improve their public facilities – new buildings, refurbished galleries, bigger and better exhibitions, more education, more public relations. At the same time grants were cut, and no money was given to run these new facilities. The ring-fenced purchase grant was abolished. Although to his credit Richard Luce, as Minister for the Arts in the late 1980s, managed to provide some extra money for building maintenance, the core grant was gradually whittled away, which meant that museums could not keep up with inflation. As by far the greatest expenditure in the British Museum was on staff salaries, the level of which was controlled not by the Museum but by the government, first the fat – and there was some – was cut, then staff who left by resignation or retirement were not replaced. Then in 1999 even more draconian steps were taken when a number of staff redundancies were enforced. Among the jobs abolished were curatorial posts, the loss of which could not easily be borne. Managers and public relations staff were brought in on a substantial scale as a consequence of these savings, often at higher salary scales than those allowed under the old dispensation.

Performance indicators were introduced by civil servants with no knowledge of the museum profession. Some of these were ludicrous. How do you set targets for conservation? By counting the number of objects treated? You can conserve 200 iron nails in a week, but a decorated iron helmet may take months. Does a career-long catalogue of a school of Indian sculpture count for less than three educational books? Such judgements have had to be made at all times by the Museum, but the government began to decide priorities and force high-sounding performance indicators on museums, often for no other reason than because they held the purse-strings. There is an 'event' culture at large, which demands more of everything with no funds to back it, more exhibitions, more 'visitor experiences', more column inches in the newspapers. The government department also calls the tune in other ways.

Under the terms of the Nolan report on standards in public life there has been a revision in the way trustees of all national museums are appointed. Whether this was intended by Nolan is a matter for discussion; he was mainly concerned with quangos, the members of which are paid and often appointed politically. Trustee bodies are different. As their name implies these bodies hold museums in trust for the nation and have seldom been the subject of political gerrymandering in the 250 years of their existence. Trustees have protected museums from government interference because of their independence and because of their influence and experience. They have not been political bodies; rather they have comprised men and women working unpaid for the public good – certainly not for their own advancement. The method of selection of trustees was admittedly never open; now nearly all appointments are made only after the vacancy has been advertised. While this may seem to be nice and democratic, it means that many potentially valuable trustees cannot be bothered to go through a lengthy and uncertain process. In the past busy people had to be persuaded to become trustees; now they must fill in a form and go through a selection process. (The system is not as transparent as it seems. People are encouraged to apply for diverse reasons, including political ones; and among those encouraging such applications are civil servants and ministers.) The process is long and fraught, and appointments are often held up for months – even straightforward appointments, nominees of the learned societies for example, lie on civil servants' desks for months before being submitted to ministers. Further, no trustee (having been re-appointed after five years) may now serve for more than ten years. This is indefensible in that an institution may thus lose some of its most experienced and useful governors, whose judgement and experience have been honed over the years. Some of the best trustees in my experience of many such bodies were those who had served at least fifteen years – indeed, the British Museum Act allows such long service (they are not geriatrics – in my time nobody's term at the British Museum was renewed after the age of seventy).

Trustee bodies are now treated by government departments with something amounting to contempt. In an interview with a journalist about the public service element of trusteeship, Graham Greene, then Chairman of the Museum's Trustees, was reported as saying that his position took up three days a week:

> For most people, this kind of job provides another dimension to their lives. The service part is central, and it spreads your interest. I feel it's not valued as it used to be, especially by ministers. Even though you're not paid, ministers pressure you discourteously, [for example] change times of meeting at short notice. They forget you're giving your time for nothing....[101]

For ministers, read also civil servants. As public service – so long a proud (and almost unique) element of this country's governance – is devalued, so particularly is voluntary service. The government, always financially mean to the British Museum, seems to support it less and less. At the same time it wishes to exercise greater control, particularly by discouraging the Trustees' supervisory role. (On the appointment of Suzanna Taverne, who preached the governmental line, Trustee meetings were reduced to six a year; this clearly made continuity of decision difficult, and in 2001, just before her departure, monthly meetings were restored.) Civil servants now interfere far too much in bodies which they are meant to oversee lightly at arm's length, as witness a frighteningly *dirigiste* extract from an official statement of the Department of Culture, Media and Sport in 2001:

> We are convinced that the arm's length principle remains valid but the arm has different lengths, and is sometimes too long. It has become a substitute for a strategic leadership which only a Department of State can provide. That role means that we must develop a wider understanding of how the sectors work – to become an informed customer. It also means being able to take forward Government objectives for and with those sectors, and, when necessary, taking action ourselves. We need to be clear that public money is being spent to deliver public objectives and within a strategic framework in which our bodies can operate and continue properly to be responsible for detailed spending decisions.[102]

While indulging in control at the most minuscule level, the government has also abrogated its responsibility in financing capital development or the purchase of major objects or collections. Not a single penny of government money went into the Great Court scheme (compared with France where the equivalent scheme for the Louvre received 8,000 million francs – about £800,000,000 – directly from their government). Having formed the National Lottery, the British government expects one of its externally funded arms, the Heritage Lottery Fund, to pick up expenditure which in the past was the government's responsibility. This has worked so far; but, as many foresaw, the government is becoming more *dirigiste* towards the Lottery and is pre-empting the judgement of its trustees, giving directions as to the way it is to be administered and spent, so that one doubts whether major grants in eight figures will ever be made again. Further, because of the unwillingness of its sponsoring department to approach the Treasury directly for special purchase grants, the Museum has lost such prizes as the Bradley collection of icons (p.318).

On a rare emotional note in 1989, I wrote:

> There are some services which a proud and civilised nation should provide free: the British Museum, cherished in this tradition for nearly two and a half centuries, is surely one of these. Britain should be proud to hold such an institution in trust for all time in the spirit enunciated by its founding trustees and defended so vigorously through so many vicissitudes.[103]

This could be the coda to this history. Unfortunately the philistines are still at the gate and, as so often in the past, the Museum, still starved of public funds, has increasingly to kowtow to a government department which holds the purse-strings, has apparently little real understanding of its function, and whose civil servants have recently been criticized officially for their lack of trust in their clients. The Museum has vast popular support, both nationally and internationally, and deserves to be more sympathetically dealt with by the government. The exemption from Value Added Tax on museum development, announced in the March 2001 budget, demonstrates that some in government have not entirely forgotten the Museum.

The Museum – hounded by the government – may be financially in deficit, it may spend too much money on its image and it has had to put its plans for the study centre on hold; but through the presentation of the collections – fed by the scholarship lying at its core – it provides excitement to the people who in increasing numbers visit it, drawn by the sort of curiosity of which Sir Hans Sloane would have approved when he set the scene for the foundation of the Museum 250 years ago. No other museum is held in such respect internationally; no other national museum expends more time and effort in communicating its collections to the public. An exciting place in which to work, an exciting place to visit, it remains the greatest museum in the world.

NOTES

INTRODUCTION

1 Caygill (1981).
2 Miller (1973).
3 Harris (1998); Stearn (1981).

CHAPTER 1

1 Lewis *et al.* (1955–71),iv, 358–9.
2 See particularly de Beer (1953), Brooks (1954) and MacGregor (1994). A good older source is Faulkner (1829), 338–75.
3 His supposed (not very grand) birthplace, which was rebuilt in 1880, is pictured by Brooks (1954), pl. opp. p.48 and Sloan (1981), pl.1. See also Sloan (1981), 1–10 and de Beer (1953), 13. His mother was Sarah Hicks whose lineage is obscure, see Sloan (1981), 13; MacGregor (1994), 36n.
4 Archives de Vaucluse, quoted by de Beer (1953), 20.
5 He later took the lease of the house next door, no.4.
6 Some figures of his income are quoted by de Beer (1953), 53–5. See also von Uffenbach (1754), 247–51. For chocolate, see Mason (1993), 453.
7 Quoted by de Beer (1953), 58.
8 *The British Museum quarterly*, xxviii (1953), 6.
9 Voltaire (1734), 24ième lettre. 'Quiconque dit en Angleterre: "J'aime les arts" et veut être de la Société [Royale], en est dans l'instant. Mais en France, pour être membre et pensionnaire de l'Académie, ce n'est pas assez d'être amateur; il faut être savant …'.
10 Heyworth (1989), 147.
11 *The British Museum quarterly*, xxvvii (1953), 2. From Bodleian Library, Oxford, MS Eng. Misc. e. 260, fol. 101v.
12 MacGregor (1994), 41, n.134.
13 Franklin (1962), 50: 'I had brought over a few curiosities, among which the principal was a purse made of asbestos, which purifies by fire. Sir Hans Sloane heard of it, came to see me, and invited me to his house in Bloomsbury Square, where he show'd me all his curiosities, and persuaded me to add that to the number, for which he paid me handsomely.' See also letter BL, Sloane MS 4047, f.347, de Beer (1953), 123.
14 Von Uffenbach (1754), 247–51; Nickson (1994), 271.
15 Porter (2000), 239.
16 Berlin (2000), 39.
17 MacGregor (1994); much of what follows is dependent on this source.
18 A summary list of Sloane's catalogues, which have been subject to elaborate bibliographical scrutiny, is published by MacGregor (1994), 291–4. For full details see Jones (1988).
19 *Moral Essays*, Epistle IV, ll.6–10.
20 De Beer (1959), 936–7.
21 Edwards (1870), 248–73; Wood (1997). At some stages in his life Courten was known as Charleton, see *Dictionary of national biography, s.n.*
22 De Beer (1959), 856–7.
23 Gray (1953); Impey (1994). Brown (1994) gives a good account of Kaempfer.
24 Impey (1994), 226 and pl.23.
25 Quoted by Evans (1956), 71. The coins were separated from their labels when they were too loosely packed after Sloane's death; their provenances, therefore, are mostly unknown; see Archibald (1994), 150.
26 King has discussed the problem of calculating the actual numbers of ethnographia in the collection in MacGregor (1994), 232. He makes it clear that Braunholtz's suggestion (Braunholtz 1953; repeated Braunholtz 1970, 19–20) of some 350 specimens is an under-estimate.
27 King (1994), 233 and 241n.
28 King (1994), 233 and 241n.
29 King (1994), 233.
30 Petiver (1695–1703).
31 King (1994), 234 and 243n. For Sloane's North American collections see King (1985).
32 Jenkins (1994a), 167.
33 MacGregor (1994), 175.
34 For the history of this object before it entered Sloane's collection, see MacGregor (1994), 181.
35 Frere (1800), 205.
36 Cherry (1994).
37 Cherry (1994), 217 and figs 76–7; Emanuel (2000).
38 Rowlands (1994), 260. Rowlands discusses the collection of prints and drawings, pp. 245–62.
39 Van Gelder (1985), 201–2.
40 Rowlands (1994), 253.
41 For Sloane as a print collector see Griffiths, 21–42.
42 Evans (1956), 85n.
43 Griffiths (1996), 23, 28.
44 See below, p.78.
45 CE3/2, 536 (19 May 1759). It has been said that the picture had once belonged to Sloane, see Thackray (1992), 51–2. CE3/2, 536 (19 May 1759).
46 See below, p.29.
47 Cherry (1994), fig.67. Some pictures of the historical series not passed to other museums which probably belonged to Sloane are still in the Museum; they include portraits of the Grand Vizier (painted for Lord

Paget in 1702), of Henry III, of Princess Maria (1537) and of the Archduchess Isabella Clara Eugenia of Austria (1566–1633) (Thompson and Roe (1961a), 193). Other pictures closely connected to the collections and which almost certainly came from Sloane include a portrait of Sloane himself, perhaps by John Vanderbank (Thompson and Roe (1961), 116 and 117), and a portrait of William Courten, whose collection Sloane inherited (Thompson and Roe (1961a), 192 and 193).

48 Quoted by Cherry (1994), 216.
49 For his books see Nickson (1994).
50 Miller (1973), 40.
51 *The gentleman's magazine*, xviii (1748), 302. The account of this visit is reprinted by MacGregor (1994), 34–5.
52 The history of Sloane's will is complicated, see Caygill (1994), 45–68, for much of this section. *The will of Sir Hans Sloane Bart. deceased* was published in London in 1753. The British Library copy, which was purchased by Sir Henry Ellis in 'a Curiosity Shop in Sevenoaks Aug. 25. 1836', is shelved at C.61.b.13. It is much annotated. There is a copy in the Museum's Central Archive.
53 BL. Add. MSS 4241, f.14. For Birch see Gunther (1984).
54 *The will of Sir Hans Sloane...*, 16–29.
55 *Ibid.*, 22.
56 Notes of the meetings of the trustees of Sloane's will which follow are bound in with the British Library copy of *The will of Sir Hans Sloane...* (see n.52).
57 See *Daily Advertiser*, 7 February 1753.
58 *Journals of the House of Commons*, xxvi, 647 *et passim*. The accounts of the parliamentary proceedings are supplemented by the MS notes referred to n.56.
59 *The will of Sir Hans Sloane....*
60 Dolley (1954).
61 For these collections see most conveniently Miller (1973), 27–36 and 45–6.
62 The British Museum Act, 26 George II, c.22.
63 The question of the use of the term 'British' at this period has recently received some attention, e.g. Colley (1992), 85ff. There has never been a serious attempt to change the Museum's name.
64 The composition of the Board of Trustees, until the British Museum Act of 1963, was: the Archbishop of Canterbury, the Lord Chancellor, the Speaker of the House of Commons (the three Principal Trustees *ex officio*); the Lord President of the Council, the Lord Privy Seal, the Lord High Admiral or the First Commissioner of the Admiralty, the Lord Steward of the Household, the Lord Chamberlain, the Bishop of London, the Prime Minister and each of the Principal Secretaries of State, the Chancellor of the Exchequer, the Lord Chief Justice of the King's Bench, the Master of the Rolls, the Lord Chief Justice of Common Pleas, the Attorney General, the Solicitor General, the President of the Royal Society, the President of the College of Physicians (all *ex officio*); two members each nominated by the Sloane, Harley and Cotton families and fifteen other persons. These were supplemented or reduced from time to time – for example the post of Lord Chief Justice of Common Pleas was abolished in 1880, while the Presidents of the Royal Academy, the Royal Society and the British Academy, a Royal Trustee and a single Trustee nominated by the Townley, Payne-Knight and Elgin families were added. An Act of Parliament was necessary to add to this list; see, for example, 5 George IV, c.39, where the names of newly nominated societies are added.
65 CE1/1, 1–2 (11 Dec. 1753).
66 CE1/1, 63–4 (17 May 1755).
67 This committee, the membership of which varied according to the interest and availability of the members, is thoroughly minuted from 17 January

1754, initially in the General Meeting Minute Book.
68 CE1/1, 43–5 (1 June 1754). Three drafts were submitted (and five mottoes) – one was approved with the motto BONARUM ARTIUM CULTORIBUS (for those who care for the arts). (pl. 4) The drafts are preserved in BL Add. MS 4449, 152. See also Add. 36,269, f.159-61.
69 See for example Miller (1973), 47, for a summary of the lottery and its ramifications. See also Caygill (1994), 51–2 and Caygill (1992).
70 A copy of a letter to Charles Long written 10 April 1823 (CE115/3, 10) gives some idea of where the money went:

To the executors of Sir Hans Sloane	£20,000. 0. 0
To the Earl and Countess of Oxford the Harleian Manuscripts	£10,000. 0. 0
To the Earl of Halifax for Montague House	£10,250. 0. 0
To Repairs of Montague House	£12,873. 0. 0
For furniture peculiar to the Museum	£3,942.18. 21½
Items of minor expenditure	£718. 4. 6
To Mr Widmore for Cotton Liby till 1757	£160. 0. 0
Lost by the difference of Price between the times of buying and selling stock	£3,000. 0. 0
Set apart as a fund for the paymt. of Salaries, Taxes and other Expenses	£30,000. 0. 0
	£90,944. 2. 8½

The surplus went to the liquidation of numerous general expenses.

71 The document gifting the Royal Library and an annuity of £300 to the Museum, signed by the King, is at BL Add. MS 36,269, f.153-4. With the Royal Library came the privilege of receiving copyright deposit books.
72 The estimated shelf footage of the various libraries as reported to the Trustees has been summarized by Harris (1998), 3, 6: Sloane 4,600, Harley 1,700, Cotton 384, Edwards 576, the Royal Library 1,890.
73 MacGregor and Turner (1986).
74 The Society's museum at this period was described by Grew (1681).
75 For Arundel, see Howarth (1985).
76 Gundestrup (1991); Rasmussen (1979), 23–4, sets it in context.
77 Gutfleisch and Menzhausen (1989).
78 Olearius (1674); Spielmann and Drees (1997).
79. Worm (1655); Schlepern (1971).
80 Ruysch (1691); see *Dictionary of scientific biography, s.n.*
81 Major (1674); this was followed by Neickelius (1717), who mentions private London cabinets, among them Sloane's, 67n. Valentini (1704–14).
82 Crook (1973), 26–34, gives a succinct account of the continental private collections and their availability to the public. For a series of essays on European curiosity cabinets see Impey and MacGregor (1985).
83 Marchand (1933), 16–17.
84 There is a great deal of confusion concerning the spelling 'Montagu'. The confusion is caused by the spelling of the modern street behind the Museum – Montague Place. The family spells the name without the final e; but at various times the house itself appears in the literature with a final e.

85 There are many descriptions of Montagu House. The earliest published delineation and short description is in *Vitruvius Britannicus* (Campbell (1715), 4 and pls 34, 35 and 36). Two convenient summaries are Clinch (1890), 132–6, and Phillips (1964), 212–14. Campbell started the hare about Pouget, who, everybody agrees, cannot be the sculptor Pierre Puget, who was also an architect – vide Summerson (1993), 247 and 534n. – although his brother Gaspard has been suggested (Caygill and Date (1999), 10 – see Crook (1973), 56, for further discussion). Batten (1936–7), 95–6, suggested that Montagu House was not totally destroyed in the fire as the rather dramatic contemporary accounts say, but that its walls still stood and were used as the basis for the building after the fire – in which case M. P(o)uget might have been consulted. Recent excavations (in 1998 and 1999) have revealed no trace of the fire so Miss Batten's suggestion might well be accepted and the well-known exterior engravings may well reveal the original design of Hooke. Proof is, however, difficult as there is no known representation of Hooke's house apart from a possible depiction on Morgan's map of London (1682), which Caygill and Date (1999), 10, say is almost identical to the appearance of the building after the fire.

86 Vide Ackerman, *Microcosm of London*. Plans of all floors and of the wings, beautifully executed in ink and wash on vellum by Henry Flitcroft, dated 1725, are at CE48/1. Copies of these plans by W. Brasier, dated 1740, with pencilled and inked additions, were clearly used as working drawings by the Trustees, and were supplemented (probably by H. Keene, who signed one of them) to show the proposed layout for the Museum and the residences; they are at CE48/2.

87 CE48/1, plan 6.

88 This was perhaps rather fortunate as the title to the house was complicated by the fact that part of the building had been erected on leasehold property (the Crown lease of which ran out in 1771); perhaps that is why George III paid such a modest price for what was to become Buckingham Palace. See Colvin *et al.* (1976), 134.

89 CE1/1, 35 (3 April 1754). A further £250 was ultimately paid as interest on this sum, CE1/1, 54 (12 April 1755).

90 CE1/1, 36 (29 April 1754). 28 Geo II c.3. The deed of purchase (BM Central Archives) is dated 5 April 1755.

91 CE 1/1. Discussion on this matter will be found in the General Committee minutes of the April and May meetings of 1754.

92 The Trustees kept a careful account of their expenditure, but this can only be a rough estimate and is taken from Harris (1998), 2. It agrees roughly with that given by Ellis, n.70.

93 CE11, 91 (3 April 1756). This included the cost of the scaffolding.

94 BL Add. MS 4449, 178–9.

95 Messenger £20; porter £20. Two watchmen at 7s a week, £36 10s; Principal housemaid £10; three other maids at £7 each, £21. £101 13s 7s was allowed in board wages for the messenger, porter and housemaids, CE1/1, 78–9 (17 Jan. 1756).

96 The residences had an extremely complicated layout; the planning stage of their division is at CE48/2.

97 Summarized by Langford (1989), 447–52.

98 BL Add. MS 4449, f.108–9.

99 CE 1/1, 95–8 (3 June 1756).

100 The applications of the two men are in BL Add. MS 36,269, f.29, 31 and 93.

101 CE 1/1, 234 (2 Dec. 1758).

102 Nichols (1812–15), ix, 739n.

103 See Harris (1998), 12.

104 Gibbon (1887), 65. Maty was acquainted with Voltaire (see e.g. Besterman (1956), 83–4) and may well have given to the Museum the fine portrait by Théodore Gardelle which still hangs in the private apartments – Thompson and Roe (1961a), fig.3.

105 See, for example, Edwards (1870), 343.

106 According to *The gentleman's magazine*, lxi (1791), 189, his second wife had an income for life of more than £2,000 p.a.

107 His application to the Earl of Hardwick is at BL Add. 36,269, f.97.

108 BL Add. MS 36,269, f.99.

109 The appointments of these assistants are recorded in CE3/1. One of those appointed in the first batch was Henry Rimius (CE3/1), 99 (9 July 1756). He died within the year.

110 *Dictionary of national biography, s.n.*, and sources there cited.

111 Nichols (1817–58), vii, 377n., *The gentleman's magazine*, lxxiii (1803), 697, and Harris (1998), *passim*.

112 *Dictionary of national biography, s.n.*

113 CE1/2, 247–9 (22 Dec. 1758). His resignation is noted on 30 Jan. 1761 in the margins of the same minute.

114 *Dictionary of national biography, s.n.*

115 Gunther (1980), 9.

116 Quoted by Miller (1973), 67.

117 Caygill (1980).

118 CE1/1, 132 (8 Dec. 1756). Sloane's daughter, Sarah Stanley, solicited a place for him of the Lord Chancellor; Hardwicke Papers, BL Add. MS 36,269, f.99. For the assistant see CE1/2, 263 (21 June 1759). 'His wages and board cannot be less than £30 per Annum. He may be lodged over the Porters room, and may have the use of the Maids Kitchin in the day time'.

119 CEGeneral Payments, 21 (31 Dec. 1756).

120 CE3/2, 502 (20 Jan. 1759).

121 CE1/2, 268 (21 June 1759).

122 CE 1/1, 51 (1 April 1755); 60 (8 May 1755).

123 CE1/1, 71 (13 Dec. 1754). The figures and details in the following paragraph are taken from the minutes either of the General or the Standing Committee on the relevant dates.

124 On 3 June 1756 the Trustees agreed that Mr Phillips' company complete the order at £3 6s 6d per foot.

125 BL Add. MS 4449, f.123.

126 CE1/1, 212 (18 March 1758).

127 BL Add. MS 4449, f.101.

128 CE1/1, 210 (18 March 1758). The decision on coins had been taken earlier: CE1/1, 122 (31 July 1756).

129 CE1/1, 83–4 (20 Feb. 1756).

130 For the Lethieullier connection see James (1981), 5.

131 CE1/1, 133 (8 Dec. 1756).

132 CE1/1, 158–9 (19 March 1757).

133 CE1/1, 178 (17 June 1757).

134 E.g. a picture of the painter Rousseau who had been concerned with the decoration of Montagu House. CE1/1, 213 (18 March 1758).

135 CE30/1–106. A vellum copy was initiated as a permanent record, but was discontinued in 1820.

136 Harris (1998), 22–75.

137 CE1/1, 206 (19 Nov. 1757).

138 CE4/1, 49–50 (7 Jan. 1757).

139 Quoted by Caygill and Date (1999), 13.

140 CE1/1, 381 (21 Oct. 1757).

141 CE1/1, 117 (19 June 1756).

142 For example, CE1/1, 102 (3 June 1756), where gifts of plants were received from the Attorney General, the Duke of Argyll, Philip Carteret Webb, Mr Watson and Mr Alexander. Up to this date £205 16s 8d had been spent on the restoration and replanting of the garden.

143 An early nineteenth-century blank ticket survives in CE115/3, 85.

144 Quoted by Caygill and Date (1999), 15.

145 There has been much disagreement about this staff. It is almost certainly the object now known as the

mace which is placed on the board table at Trustees' meetings (pl. 2). Dated 1759, it fits the description in CE1/1, 239 (2 Dec. 1758) with some precision. It was bought of Thomas Gylpin, for six guineas. CE86/ General Payments, 42 (20 Jan. 1759). At a later date the warders in the Museum's galleries carried wands, seen for instance in a figure to the right in pl. 12 (of which one survived until the 1950s when it was seen by the present author).

CHAPTER 2

1 *The will of Sir Hans Sloane…*, op. cit., 28–9.
2 BL Add. MS 6179, f.18.
3 *Statutes and rules to be observed in the management and use of the British Museum*, London 1757 and 1758.
4 BL Add. MS 4302, f.12. See also BL Add. MS 4449 for various drafts.
5 BL Add. MS 6179, f.61–2.
6 For example in 1765 by a French visitor, Grosley (1772), ii, 25.
7 Miller (1973), 67–9; Harris (1998), 8–9.
8 BL Add. MS 45,867–45,875.
9 CE3/3, 609 (21 March 1760).
10 Mitford (1853), 183–4.
11 See Harris (1998), 9.
12 CE1/2, 256 (7 April 1759).
13 CE1/2, 266 (21 June 1759).
14 CE3/2, 521 (17 March 1759).
15 CE3/2, 522 (17 March 1759).
16 *Annual Register* 1759, 149–52.
17 CE1/2, 267 (21 June 1759).
18 CE1/2, 304 (5 April 1760).
19 CE1/2, 322 (23 May 1760).
20 Parliamentary Papers (Commons), 1808, vi, 48.
21 Quoted by Edwards (1870), 338.
22 CE3/5, 1368 (19 Feb. 1773).
23 Hutton (1785), 187–8.
24 Thompson (1767), 6. For the Egyptian objects see James (1981), 5–6.
25 Much of this description of the layout of Montagu House in the early 1760s is taken from Powlett (1762). International interest in the Museum is illustrated by the short translation of this guide into German – *Britisches Museum: nebst der Beschreibung des berumten Ritters H. Sloane*, Berlin 1764.
26 *Mozart in the British Museum*, 1968, 3 and pl.3.
27 BL Add. MS 27,276, f.11–12.
28 Thompson (1767), 28–9. The bust was given by Lord Exeter, who bought it at Dr Mead's sale in 1755 (ex-Arundel Collection). It is now identified more simply as the head of a poet (Walters 1899, no.847), although Michael Lort had some fun at Lord Exeter's expense in a letter to Horace Walpole (14 March 1762), 'Notwithstanding it bears so great a resemblance to the head in Hollar's print of Lord and Lady Arundel, there are some people pretend to say it is a modern piece, which Sir A. Fountayne procured and passed off as antique', Lewis and Wallace (1952), 153.
29 Matheson (1924), London 68–9.
30. CE1/2, 496–9 (25 Feb. 1764), see also Caygill (1988), 25. For the Duke of Brunswick's visit to London generally see Fitzmaurice (1901), 14–16.
31 Mr Bramble to Dr Lewis in Smollett's *Humphry Clinker* (1771).
32 Hutton (1785), 189–96.
33 Faujas Saint-Fond, B. (1799), 89.
34 CE1/2, 288–9 (8 March 1760).
35 CE1/2, 295–300 (22 March 1760); 309–14 (5 April 1760).
36 A good account of the financial plight of the Museum at this period is found in BL Add. MS 52,292, ff.121–3.

37 Hollis (1780), 112, 169–71.
38 CE1/4, 816 (3 June 1780).
39 *The gentleman's magazine*, xxiii (1803), 94.
40 Nichols (1812–15), vi, 359–79; *Dictionary of national biography*, s.n.
41 *Dictionary of national biography*, s.n., and Duyker and Tingbrand (1995).
42 See Duyker and Tingbrand (1995), *passim*, and particularly a letter from Banks to Johan Alströmer, President of the Royal Swedish Academy of Science (16 Nov. 1784), after Solander's death, *ibid.*, 411.
43 D'Arblay (1842), i, 297.
44 Solander was not, however, the only connection between the Cook explorations and the Museum, for Matthew Maty's daughter was married to Captain Charles Clerke who succeeded to Cook's command after his death.
45 CE1/4, 790 (26 Sept. 1778), 790. A letter on this subject, 11 Sept. 1778, is published by Duyker and Tingbrand (1995), 380.
46 Cf. Duyker and Tingbrand (1995), 2–5. The most recent commentator on Linnaeus, however, is not so positive and has pointed out that, after his return from the Cook voyage, he spurned his old teacher and his son; Koerner (1999), 155–6.
47 For Banks see Carter (1988) and Gascoigne (1994) and the sources there cited. His correspondence is calendared by Dawson (1958).
48 Cf., for example, Gascoigne (1994), 11, for the quarrel with Planta.
49 For details of this dispute see Carter (1988), 194–202. As a contemporary wrote of Maty, 'in this as in other instances in his life, his vivacity out-ran his judgement'; Nichols (1812–15), iii, 261.
50 Kaeppler (1979) and King (1981), 12–14.
51 Kaeppler (1979), 170. For New Zealand objects specifically see Starzecka (1998), 151.
52 CE1/3, 740–1 (28 Sept. 1775).
53 Fabricius (1784), quoted by Kaeppler (1979), 174.
54 King (1981), 14.
55 Carter (1988), frontispiece.
56 Even as late as the 1970s the Museum was able to acquire a small group of objects that had been in this collection; *Report of the Trustees*, 1969–72, 65.
57 The whole sorry tale is told by Kaeppler (1979), 175–7.
58 Hauser-Schäublin and Krüger (1998). Other material went to Göttingen by way of J.R. Forster, although some returned to Oxford and was transferred to the Pitt-Rivers Museum in the 1880s; Chapman (2000), 501.
59 CE1/4, 922 (13 Feb. 1796).
60 p.xxiv.
61 CE3/8, 2220I (9 April 1802).
62 Gascoigne (1994), 145.
63 *The gentleman's magazine*, lxxxiv (1814), 352. Sir Henry Ellis, who copied this reference into his scrapbook, CE115/3, 85v., commented, 'this bust was removed from its place at the top of the great staircase in 1830: it was the most hideous of Mrs Damer's prodns.'
64 Hollis (1780), 82.
65 Caygill (1985), 147–9.
66 CE4/1, 359 (Feb. 1779); Dawson (1999), 193–204.
67 Dawson (1999), *passim*.
68 King (1994a).
69 For the Roman collections of the eighteenth century see Haskell and Penny (1981), 62–73.
70 Winckelmann (1764), part of which was translated into English by G.H. Lodge in 1856 as *The history of ancient art*; for Winckelmann see Justi (1866–72).
71 For these representations see Jenkins and Sloan (1996), 42–3. The *Archaeologia* paper is Hamilton (1777).

72   See Jenkins and Sloan (1996). For a detailed discussion of some of his collections not covered in this volume see the volume of *Journal of the history of collections* (ix; 2, 1997) which is devoted to Hamilton. A drawing by Castiglione, once in the Hamilton collection, was purchased by the Museum with the aid of the Heritage Lottery Fund as late as 1997. P&D, 1997, 6–7, 10.

73   Quoted by Jenkins and Sloan (1996), 68, from BL Add. MS 34,048, f.15.

74   Quoted in Jenkins and Sloan (1996), 67, from *Philosophical transactions of the Royal Society*, lviii (1769), 11.

75   His gifts are listed by Jenkins and Sloan (1996), 305. See also *Journal of the history of collections* ix; 2.

76   The history of the vase is recounted in Williams (1989), 22–9.

77   CE1/3, 691–2 (11 April 1772). There was apparently no formal discussion of the application for this grant either in the Trustees' minutes nor in any surviving official correspondence; the first mention is in *Journals of the House of Commons*, xxxiii, 602 (20 March 1772).

78   CE4/1, 275 (9 April 1772).

79   CE4/1, 293v. (6 Oct. 1775).

80   For d'Hancarville see Haskell (1987), 30–45. There are many letters from d'Hancarville in the Townley archive, CETY 7/161–294.

81   The Museum Trustees, after a certain amount of trouble with d'Hancarville, made a grant from the residue of the Hamilton fund to help pay for the completion of the project, CE1/4, 782 (28 Feb. 1778).

82   Now in the Burrell Collection, Glasgow. Jenkins and Sloan (1996), 220–2.

83   Tischbein (1791–5). The Museum salvaged a large number of fragments of pottery from this collection during underwater explorations led by Roland Morris, helped by Anne Birchall, an assistant keeper, in the 1970s. Morris (1979).

84   Young (1995). Catherine was deeply interested in classical antiquity and purchased the great sculpture collection formed by the Englishman John Lyde Brown in 1785–7, which forms the core of the Hermitage's collection; Neverov (1984).

85   For Wedgwood pottery generally see Reilly (1989).

86   For this plaque see Scheidemantel (1969). I am grateful to Gaye Blake-Roberts and Lynn Miller of the Wedgwood Museum for this reference and to them and Helen Burton of Keele University library for much help with regard to the relationship between Wedgwood and the British Museum.

87   Weiss (1995).

88   Weiss (1995), 162–76.

89   The Portland Vase itself was loaned to the Museum in 1810.

90   For the Museum's collection see Dawson (1984). See also below, p.169.

91   CE3/5, 1206–7 (21 April 1769). See Griffiths and Williams (1987), 114.

92   Lewis, Smith and Lam (1955–71), viii, 304.

93   Cobbett (1814), xix, 189. CE115/3, 50–1. For Wilkes and his ideas for the British Museum see Thomas (1996), 210–1.

94   Moore (1996), summarized by Norman (1997), 36–7.

95   Bourgeois had briefly considered leaving his collection to the Museum, Beresford (1998), 16–17.

96   Confirmed CE1/4, 819 (24 June 1780).

97   23 July 1780; reprinted from Duyker and Tingbrand (1995), 389.

98   CE1/4, 832 (26 May 1781). For the riots and the Museum see CE1/4 and CE3/7 for 1780 *passim* and Caygill (1980). For the Gordon riots see de Castro (1926).

99   CE4/2, 851 (21 April 1807).

100   Thompson (1964).

101   CE1/4, 931; 932 (12 May; 16 June 1798).

102   Astle's letter (31 Aug. 1786) recommending himself as Trustee is at BL Add. MS 36,269, f.173.

103   'As there was not Money enough to defray the whole of the Expences of the last year; only part of the Tradesmens bills have been paid'; CE1/4, 814 (27 May 1780). At the same meeting (p.815) there is evidence (repeated elsewhere) of the hypothecation of money from the Treasury to repay money temporarily removed from Trust Funds.

104   A senior member of the Museum staff presented the accounts at the bar of the House of Commons.

105   CE1/4, 762 (15 Feb. 1777) is the first apparent record of a loss of books. The Trustees referred it to the Standing Committee for action.

106   CE3/7, 1830 (4 April 1783).

107   CE4/1, 618 (18 Sept. 1784).

108   CE4/1, 274 (11 March 1772).

109   CE4/1, 608 (not dated).

110   CE3/7, 1863 (12 March 1784); CE3/7, 1865 (26 March 1784).

111   CE86/1, 227 (5 June 1784); CE3/1, 1866 (7 May 1784). The other maids were Judith Stanley, Dorothy Staniland and Elizabeth Markland, who by 1790 was replaced by Katherine (sometimes Elizabeth) James. In 1800 Mary King became head maid.

112   CE3/8, 2223 (11 June 1802).

113   CE4/1, 601 (24 Aug. 1781).

114   CE1/4, 835 (29 Sept. 1781).

115   CE3/8, 2170 (9 Aug. 1799).

116   CE1/4, 903 (4 Feb. 1792); 907 (9 Feb. 1793).

117   CE1/4, 817 (3 June 1780).

118   CE1/4, 886 (1 Nov. 1788).

119   CE1/4, 782 (28 Feb. 1778). See also CE4/1, 319, 321 (26, 28 Feb. 1778).

120   CE1/4, 930 (10 Feb. 1798); CE1/4, 883 (3 Dec. 1787).

121   Van Rymsdyk (1778), iii. Cf. *Journals of the House of Commons*, xxxiv, 1774, 648, which seems to refer to this discussion in Committee. Harris, one of the MPs referred to by van Rymsdyk, wrote to Lord Monboddo concerning it at an early stage of the proceedings, implying that he believed in charging for entry – Knight (1900), 89.

122   CE1/4, 858–9 (31 Jan. 1784).

123   For the van Rymsdyks see Thornton (1982).

124   CE1/4, 858 (31 Jan. 1784).

125   CE4/2, 623 (23 Feb. 1784). The popularity of collecting casts of antique gems in the eighteenth century is discussed by Haskell and Penny (1981), 98. Tassie was a leading player in the field.

126   Particularly Strutt (1773) and (1796–9).

127   CE3/8, 2160 (8 March 1799).

128   The varied religious and national backgrounds of the staff make it unlikely that in the 1770s William Godwin was refused a post in the Museum because he was 'not a member of the Church of England and therefore could not hold this office of profit under the Crown', St Clair (1989), 36. In fact officers were employed by the Trustees, as they are today, and were never considered as civil servants, although they now have comparable status.

129   For Woide see *Dictionary of national biography, s.n.*

130   Planta (1776).

131   For the Orleans collection see Herrmann (1972), 133–45.

132   Cf. Bjurström (1992), 141.

133   Cantarel-Besson (1981).

134   For the Musée des Monuments Français see Haskell (1993), 237–52. A museum of antiquities was created at the Bibliothèque Nationale in 1795, Georgel (1994), 280.

CHAPTER 3

1 For his life see a brief entry in the *Dictionary of national biography*, s.n., and a bland chapter in Edwards (1870), 515–26.

2 Nicholls (1817–58), vii, 677.

3 It is usual to qualify her position at court by adding the word 'probably' to any statement concerning her, presuming that there is no direct evidence that they were siblings. Court memoirs of the period, however, tell a different story. Mrs Papendiek, whose daughter married Planta's son and who was at court as the same time (but in a more junior post) as Miss Planta, mentions Miss Planta's relationship to Joseph on a number of occasions and states that she had replaced Fanny Burney as the Queen's private treasurer about 1792; Broughton (1887), ii, 269. Lady Llanover, who edited Mrs Delany's diary and correspondence, describes Miss Planta in the index as a 'maid of honour' to Queen Charlotte, Delany (1862), 559; General Dyott in his diary describes her as 'a lady in waiting to good old Queen Charlotte', Jeffery (1907), ii, 207. These and other letters and diaries make it clear that she was a close companion and trusted servant of the Queen.

4 Planta's son also became a diplomat, and later an MP and Privy Councillor.

5 D'Arblay (1842), v, 39.

6 CE4/2, 745–8 (18 May 1801).

7 CE4/2, 749–50 (22 May 1801).

8 CE1/4, 955–6 (8 May 1802).

9 Printed regulations at CE4/2, 760 (14 Jan. 1803). The regulations were reported to Parliament, CE4/2, 774 (13 Feb. 1805).

10 As has been pointed out by Cash (1994), 64.

11 CE1/4, 949 (3 June 1801); 960 (11 Dec. 1802).

12 CE1/4, 949–50 (3 June 1801).The Principal Librarian now got £320 p.a., Under Librarians (Keepers) £200 and Assistant Librarians £120. Assistants' salaries were initially £60 but, as in the case of Ellis, this was increased to £80. In 1805 the Principal Librarian's salary was increased to £500, CE1/5, 1016 (28 Feb. 1805).

13 Esdaile (1946), 355.

14 A brilliant sketch of him will be found in the *Dictionary of national biography*. Just before he retired in 1812 he wrote out a number of reasons for resignation, which would strike a chord with every ambitious Assistant in the years to come: '1. The nature and constitution of the M[useum is] altogether objectionable; 2. The coldness, and even danger, in frequenting the great house in winter; 3. The vastness of the business remaining to be done & continually flowing in; 4. The total impossibility of my individual efforts, limited, restrained & controlled as they are, to do any real, or at least much, good; 5. An apparent, & I believe real, system of espionage throughout the place & certainly a want of respect towards & confidence in the officers; 6. The total absence of all aid in my department...;9. The want of society with the members, their habits wholly different & their manners far from fascinating & sometimes repulsive; 10. The want of power to do any good, & the difficulty of making the motley & often trifling committees sensible that they could do any good; 11. The general pride and affected consequence of these committees; 12. Their assumption of power, that I think not vested in them; 13. Their fiddle faddle requisition of incessant reports, the greatest part of which can inform them of nothing, or, when they do, of what they are generally incapable of understanding or fairly judging of.' Bodleian Library MSS Douce e 28.

15 Esdaile (1946), 74.

16 For details of Beloe's dismissal see p.62.

17 Professor of Drawing at the Royal Military Academy,

1802–8. A short article on his Chinese drawings is in Wood (1992); for his part in the Macartney Mission to China see Singer (1992), passim. He died in 1816 and a fulsome obituary appears in the The *gentleman's magazine*, lxxxvi (1816), 369–71; see also *Dictionary of national biography*, s.n., and Griffiths (1996), 11. The runner-up for his appointment was R. Duppa, who later became Professor of Painting at the Royal Academy, see Farrington (1978–98), ix, 3209. An engraved portrait of Alexander by Picart after Eldridge is at CE115/3, 209v.

18 He was the son of Dr Charles Combe, a considerable bibliophile and numismatist, whose collection of Bibles had been purchased by the Museum. See the *Dictionary of national biography*, s.n.

19 BL Add. MSS 36524, 34 (4 Feb. 1803).

20 Foreigners were still sometimes appointed. In 1807, for example, Charles König (who had been Banks's Librarian since 1801) was appointed Assistant Keeper of Minerals and in 1813 became Keeper of Natural History. He had been born in Brunswick and educated at Göttingen; *Dictionary of national biography*, s.n. For other foreigners who worked in the library departments see Harris (1998), 61.

21 CE3/8, 2236 (5 Aug. 1803).

22 Combe (1814) and Combe (1826).

23 Malcolm (1803), 499–531.

24 This may have been one of the original inscriptions recorded in the Trustees' minutes in 1758, 'Inscriptions have been put up in the several rooms of the Museum, distinguishing the contents thereof, and the person to whom they may formerly have belonged, or by whom they have been given'. CE1/1, 233 (2 Dec. 1758).

25 Given by the Earl of Exeter in 1775, CE4/3, 950 (10 March 1810). It appears to have been lost. Such cork models were much collected in the late eighteenth and early nineteenth centuries; an important collection may be seen in the Musée des Antiquités Nationales at Saint-Germain-en-Laye.

26 For Cracherode, see below, p.62.

27 Griffiths (1996), 43–51, provides a brilliant portrait of the man and his print collections. The reader is referred to this essay for further reference. See also the *Dictionary of national biography*. A copy of Cracherode's draft will is at CE115/3, 64.

28 BL Add. MS 47,611.

29 CE1/4, 936 (11 May 1799); CE3/8, 2169 (13 July 1799). Subsequently the books were kept separately in a Cracherode Room in the Department of Printed Books.

30 Griffiths (1996), 47–9; Griffiths and Williams (1987), 104.

31 The documents are printed by Griffiths (1996), 276–83.

32 CE3/8, 2270 (28 Feb. 1802).

33 Griffiths (1996), 91 and 99n. Mr Griffiths has pointed out to me that Maclennan (2000) has gone some way towards reconstructing some of Monro's collection.

34 Copies of the documents relating to this transaction between F. Fourier of the French Institute and Colonel Turner of the British Army, together with details of the vessels (HMS *Madras* and HMS *L'Egyptienne*) in which the objects were shipped are at CE115/3, 69. A list of antiquities from Egypt taken from the French was submitted to the Trustees on 10 July 1802, CE3/8, 2225; a month later a temporary covering was ordered for them, CE3/8, 2226 (6 Aug. 1802).

35 In *Vetusta monumenta*, iv, 1803, plsv–vii.

36 For an up-to-date account of the history and decipherment of the stone in a book to celebrate its recent cleaning and the special exhibition arranged around it, see Parkinson (1999).

37 *Description de l'Égypte, ou recueil des observations et des*

recherches qui ont été faites en Égypte, pendant l'expédition de l'Armée Français, Paris 1808–22.

38 CE3/8, 2228 (18 Dec. 1802).
39 CE1/4, 963; 995–6 (14 May 1803).The full report of this sub-committee is at CE4/2, 768–70 (14 May 1803).
40 Crook (1972), fig.21.
41 CE1/4, 965 (14 May 1803).
42 For contract with Saunders see CE/Misc papers A11 (Contracts), 3 Aug. 1804. It is agreed that Saunders's fee is equivalent to 5% of the contract price. The plans and elevations are at CE48/4/4–5.
43 CE3/8, 2261 (22 June 1805).
44 Charles Townley's Catholicism was significant; his family were Jacobite and were much affected by the penal laws. His father's uncle was executed in 1745 for high treason, having been deeply involved in the Jacobite rebellion, following in a family tradition of support for the Stuarts which went back to the 1715 rising, when his grandfather, although tried for treason, was acquitted for want of evidence. It was, therefore, probably wise for Townley – in view of the '45 rebellion – to have been sent abroad by his guardians after the death of his father to be educated at Douai.
45 This collection was published by Blundell himself between 1803 and 1810, but is now being republished in a series of volumes by the National Museum and Galleries on Merseyside, see Fejfer and Southworth (1991) and Fejfer (1997). Letters from Blundell to Townley are in CETY 7/1314–60.
46 For the history and content of the Townley Collection see Cook (1977) and (1985). In 1992 the Museum bought the Townley archive of some 5,500 letters for £200,000, a catalogue of which will shortly be published by S.J. Hill.
47 Smith (1892–1904), no.1874. Cook (1985), 15. Re-identified by Walker (1992).
48 Smith (1892–1904), no.2201. Cook (1985), 51 and fig. 47 (where the joins can clearly be seen). See also Vaughan (1992), 42.
49 Townley also collected a certain amount of Asian material, including some fine eighteenth-century wood-carving.
50 Cook (1977), 39–52 discusses the layout of the collection in Park Street.
51 For an identification of the objects in this famous painting see Cook (1977), 37–8 and Ian Jenkins in Wilton and Bignamini (1996), 260–1. Two water-colours by William Chambers of the display at 7 Park Street were acquired by the Museum in 1995, *ibid.*, 258–9.
52 Townley's sketch of the proposed new gallery is at CETY 7/2229–30.
53 The negotiations can be followed in the calendared correspondence of Banks, see Dawson (1958), *passim*.
54 CE1/4, 977 (3 June 1805).
55 An Act to vest the Townleian Collection of Ancient Sculpture in the Trustees of the British Museum...; 45, George III, c. cxxvii. CE86 General Accounts, 390 (20 Aug. 1805).
56 *Journals of the House of Commons*, lx, 460 (3 July 1805). A full account of all these negotiations and the various designs of the Townley Gallery is recorded in Cook (1977), which is much fuller than that of Crook (1973).
57 For a section through the building and a view of the exterior see Caygill and Date (1999), pl.3 and fig.4.
58 CE5/1, 116 (10 June 1808).
59 Combe (1810) and (1812–61). A two-volume detailed guide to the Townley Gallery was published anonymously in 1836 by the Society for the Diffusion of Useful Knowledge (Ellis, 1836).
60 While most of the sculpture displayed in the new gallery was from the Townley collection, acknowl-edgement was rarely made in early descriptions of sculpture displayed there from the Sloane, Hollis and Hamilton collections, as well as odd pieces donated by other collectors.
61 CE5/1, 103 (9 April 1808).
62 CE1/5, 1034–5 (14 May 1808); 1041–4 (21 May 1808).
63 CE5/1, 137 (12 Nov. 1808).
64 Combe *et al.* (1812–61).
65 CE4/3, 954–5 (4 April 1810). The memorandum of appointment was signed by the Archbishop of Canterbury, the Speaker and the Lord Chancellor as Principal Trustees. Their names were: Benjamin Bromley, John Church, John Keates, John Saunders, John James Brown, John Game, David Masters and William Turner.
66 CE1/5, 1074–6 (24 March 1810).
67 CE4/3, 1161 (undated 1814).
68 CE1/5, 1128–9 (26 Nov. 1814).
69 Smith (953), 313.
70 (1810), pt.2, 209.
71 Jenkins (1992), 31.
72 Bindman and Riemann (1993), 74.
73 Haskell and Penny (1981), 108–16. For the Borghese collection see Kalveram (1995).
74 Letter from Planta to Abbot, 30 Aug. 1811. Abbot (1861), 348–9.
75 Abbot (1861), 399 (28 July 1812). Abbot had not been present at the Trustees' meeting on 20 July when the matter was discussed, CE1/5, 1103–4; it was then agreed to approach the Treasury for purchase money.
76 Abbot (1861), 413. It is clear, from the lack of discussion in the Trustees' meetings, that the matter was confidential and was being dealt with orally, as must have been many similar decisions about major projects. Combe submitted a detailed memorandum of his adventures in Malta to the Trustees on 9 Jan. 1813 (CE5/3, 495). Combe kept a (now lost) diary of his trip; Henry Ellis records having tea with him later in the year and reading from it, BL Add. MS 36,653 (1) (17 Oct. 1813).
77 Abbot (1861), 450, 2 June 1813. The Speaker writes in his diary: 'Vansittart promised to speak to Lord Liverpool to-morrow, that the Ægina marbles might be bought for the same price (10,000 sequins) as the artists had agreed to take from the agent of the Prince Royal of Bavaria. And also for the Treasury to give Mr Combe a gratuity of 200l. or more for his trouble on the mission to Malta'. A good summary account of the story of the recovery of the Ægina and Bassae sculptures is in Stoneman (1987), 179–98.
78 Edwards (1870), 399, was the first to suggest that Combe was sent to Zakynthos to purchase the frieze; this is clearly a conflation of the Bassae and Ægina stories. Much of the correspondence concerning the purchase survives in the archives of the British Museum.
79 CE4/3, 1219 (1 May 1814). The scorpion is referred to in Ellis's scrapbook, CE115/3, 87r.
80 Combe (1812–61), 3n.
81 Smith (1829), 358.
82 Abbot (1861), 564.
83 Another recorded visit of Metternich was after his fall in 1848, when, faintly smiling, he met Guizot on the steps of the Museum. 'L'erreur ne s'est jamais approché de mon esprit', he said, Namier (1958), 24.
84 Ellis diary, BL Add. MSS 36,653 (1) (5 April, 8, 16 and 21 June 1814).
85 Hagen (1997), 52ff.
86 CE4/3, 990 (6 Dec. 1810); CE3/9, 2477 (12 Jan. 1811).
87 See letter offering the collection from Peregrine Townley, CE4/3, 1121–2 (12 May 1814). Parliamentary approval was granted on 24 June 1814, Ellis scrapbook in BM central archive, 84.

88 £300 approved CE3/9, 2525–6 (2 June 1812).
89 CE4/3,1014 (14 Dec. 1811).
90 54 Geo. III, c.156.
91 See Harris (1998), 34–7.
92 St Clair (1998); Smith (1916). See also *Report from the Select Committee of the House of Commons on the Earl of Elgin's collection of sculptured marbles*, London 1816.
93 Quoted by St Clair (1998), 263.
94 *English bards and scotch reviewers*, ll.1027–32.
95 For this sorry story see St Clair (1998), 68–79 and 238–44.
96 W.R. Hamilton (no relation of Sir William) later became an active Trustee of the Museum.
97 An Italian version of this document survives in the possession of Mr St Clair; St Clair (1998), 337–41.
98 The English version as reported to the Select Committee states 'that when they [Elgin's party] wish to take away any pieces of stone with old inscriptions or figures theron, that no opposition is made thereto', *Report*, p. xxv. In the Italian version the relevant and much quoted passage reads, '*e non si faccia opposizione al portar via qualche pezzi di pietra con inscrizioni, e figure...*', St Clair (1998), 337–41.
99 Legrand (1897).
100 Elgin's secretary, W.R. Hamilton (1810), published a sober and modest account of his ambitions in Athens, insisting, as he had consistently, that his collections should be used for the better education of artists.
101 *Childe Harold's Pilgrimage* II, xi.
102 Eisler (1999), 243, expresses the general puzzlement about the personal vendetta Byron carried on against Elgin and offers some explanation.
103 Brøndsted (1926), 134.
104 Farrington (1978–98), ix, 1945.
105 For Aberdeen and the Marbles see Chamberlain (1983), 67–71.
106 56 Geo. III, c.99 (1 July 1816).
107 Abbot (1861), 349.
108 CE4/3, 1187–8 (21 March 1815). There being no guarantee that they would be bought for the Museum, the request was turned down.
109 CE1/5, 1137 (8 April 1815).
110 CE3/9, 2627 (9 March 1816); CE1/5, 1143–4 (11 May 1816).
111 CE1/5, 1153–5 (12 Aug. 1816).
112 The Marbles were much drawn and copied. John Henning, for example, was encouraged by Charlotte, Princess of Wales, to make miniaturized plaster copies of the Parthenon frieze and of the Bassae frieze, which were widely copied; Clay *et al.* (1999), 42–3; the Museum has the slate moulds (Jenkins (2000), fig.2). A more public expression was a copy of the frieze carved in Bath stone by Henning and his son on two sides of the Athenæum – the gentlemen's club for scholars and scientists, in Pall Mall – Jenkins (2000). The committee of the club 'had no hesitation in selecting the Panathenaic procession which formed the frieze of the Parthenon as the most appropriate as well as the most beautiful specimen of sculpture which could be adopted. To an edifice which borrows its name from Athens, intended for a Society professedly connected with Literature and the Fine Arts, they flatter themselves that the celebrated production of Athenian taste, restored as it is here to a degree of perfection in which it had never been seen in modern times, would not be considered inappropriate'. Ward (1926), 37.
113 Jolliffe (1990), 49.
114 Peterson (1996), 3.
115 For a good account of the temporary Elgin and Phigalian rooms, with complete critical apparatus, see Jenkins (1992), 75–81.
116 The casts of the frieze are now displayed in the public restaurant in the south-west corner of the Museum.
117 CE5/5, 1116–7 (13 June 1818); CE3/10, 2700 (13 June 1818), *et seq.*
118 CE4/3, 1009 (13 July 1811).
119 For Salt see Halls (1834); for Belzoni see Mayes (1959).
120 The relevant Trustees' Minutes on the subject are published as Appendix 20 of the Select Committee (1835).
121 Belzoni offered the sarcophagus to the Museum on 10 September 1821 (CE4/4, 1681a). The decision to reject its purchase was effectively taken on 8 February 1823 at the meeting of the Trustees on which they accepted the gift of the Royal Library, CE1/5, 1202 (8 Feb. 1823). It may well be that the thought of such a purchase, at a time when the Trustees would have to go to Parliament to request money for a new building, seemed impolitic. As in so many cases before and after, special pleading must be looked at in a larger context. See also CE3/10, 2871 (10 April 1824).
122 For a summary of the Trustees' relations with Salt see James (1981), 10–14. See also Manley and Rée (2001), 197–211.
123 CE3/13, 3805–6 (10 May 1834).
124 See Clarke and Penny (1982).
125 *Ibid.*, 57.
126 Save the appointment of a royal nominee after 1832, in recognition of the gift of the Royal Library.
127 Briefly recorded by Carter (1988), 520. See also CE3/10, 2708 (14 Nov. 1818).
128 Griffiths and Williams (1987), 82–4.
129 Calendared by Dawson (1958).
130 The story is summarized in Stearn (1981), 22. The deal is itemized in Select Committee (1835), 30. Brown was to receive £200 p.a., with £75 p.a. for each additional day (in 1835 he was working four days a week). He was also allowed extra leave. His senior officer (König) was paid at the same rate and had less leave. The normal base rate for an assistant librarian was £150 for two days' attendance.
131 Stearn (1981), 22.
132 Select Committee (1835), 316; the figures are confirmed by the original salaries, wages and accounts held in the British Museum central archives. The salaries of the officers in the quoted year totalled £3,771 5s; that of the other staff was £1,626 14s 6d. These sums include extra allowances.
133 Leach, assistant librarian in Natural History, became mentally incapacitated in 1821 and by special dispensation was granted £100 p.a. as pension by the Treasury.
134 Summarized from Select Committee (1835), 398–400.
135 For Cary see *Dictionary of national biography, s.n.*, and Edwards (1870), 543–52.
136 Cary (1847), I, 156–7.
137 Edwards (1870), 548. *The Times*, 17 July 1837.
138 '...he felt disgraced in the eyes of the World by Mr Panizzi's being put over his head', Henry Ellis in his diary, BL. Add. MS 36,653 (5), f.11v (13 Oct. 1837). On 9 Nov. the Trustees discussed the matter with Ellis at their meeting, being clearly reluctant to let him go (*ibid.*, f.23r–25r).
139 E.g. CE1/5, 1175 (13 May 1820).
140 CE4/3, 1209 (16 June 1815).
141 See Crook (1973), 97–104. Crook's book gives a good account of Smirke's life and ideas.
142 See Crook (1976).
143 Smirke's sketch of the proposed new gallery is at CE4/3, 1266 (10 Feb. 1816). In presenting it to the Trustees (*ibid.*, 1267), Planta enthused, 'Thus in every Branch, at any time, and without enormous Expense, might the Museum be made to keep pace with the most extensive Establishments which Foreign

144 CE4/4, 1621 (8 Feb. 1821); CE1/5, 1180 (14 April 1821).

145 CE3/10, 2780 (10 March 1821).

146 CE1/5, 1198 (3 Feb. 1823).

147 CE1/5, 1213 (12 July 1823); 1215 (21 July 1823).

148 The brief to oppose the action is in the Central Archives of the Museum. *In Chancery. Suit between the Most Noble John, Duke of Bedford, and the Trustees of the British Museum...* [1822]. The action was dismissed in Chancery, 6 July 1822. A transcription of the case *In Chancery: the Duke of Bedford versus the British Museum* is also in the Central Archives of the Museum.

149 The committee originally consisted of Lord Liverpool, Lord Ripon, Lord Aberdeen, Sir Thomas Lawrence and Sir George Beaumont – the latter not a British Museum Trustee. Sir Robert Peel and Lord Dover were added in 1827. The first Keeper of the Gallery was William Seguier, a dealer and restorer, appointed by Treasury Minute, 30 March 1824. Understanding of the foundation of the National Gallery is complicated by the fact that there is no documented history of the institution. Holmes and Baker (1924) is really more of a pamphlet than a history – the authors describe it as 'the most hurried of summaries'. Herrmann (1999), 266–73, reprints some of the Angerstein correspondence first published by Whitley (1930). At first the National Gallery functioned effectively as part of the British Museum, to which the Trustees transferred their most important pictures (but not their portraits). Periodically the Museum Trustees inspected their pictures and minuted their visits, until they handed over control of them to the Gallery in 1868, after a recommendation of the 1853 Select Committee, first by means of a Treasury Minute of 27 March 1855, which was formalized in an Act of Parliament of 1856 establishing the Gallery as an independent body. See the sub-committee minutes on the Department of Pictures, Prints and Drawings for 14 June 1828, CE7/1, 15–19, the recommendations of which were adopted by the Trustees, CE1/5, 1309–11 (13 Dec. 1828). The recommendations included the statement that 'all future donations to the Trustees of Old Masters should be added to the National Gallery'. See also Select Committee (1835), 37–9; 92–3, etc. As late as the middle 1860s the Trustees printed a list of the pictures belonging to the British Museum in the National Gallery, at which time they enumerated 59.

150 For the full history of this gift and of the negotiations which led up to it see Miller (1973), 124–31, Harris (1998), 31–2 and Paintin (1989) and the references cited.

151 Hibbert (1998), 62.

152 The Library did not come to the Museum until the following year.

153 Cherry and Pevsner (1998), 294.

154 It is now planned to borrow well-bound books relevant to the Museum's interests from the House of Commons library to replace many of the King's Library books. Some of the bookcases will be used to display ceramics, and there will be a tactful exhibition in the original showcases. The Roubiliac Shakespeare will be placed in the centre of the gallery. Generous grants from the Wolfson and Sainsbury Foundations have initiated this project.

155 For these beams see Crook (1973), 141–2. A drawing of a beam is in Fox (1992), 57.

156 Schinkel, who visited the King's Library while it was being built, sketched the beams and plates in position before the ceiling had been hung. Bindman and Riemann (1993), fig.38.

157 Quoted by Crook (1972), 132.

158 CE3/10, 2885 (13 Nov. 1824). A Committee of the House of Commons approved the purchase of Rich's collection for £7,500 on 25 March 1825. For a summary of Rich's life in the context of Mesopotamian studies see Lloyd (1955), 18–91.

159 CE30/2, 8 March 1817; CE3/10, 2911 (21 April 1825); Mitchell (2000).

160 Bowdich (1819), McLeod (1977).

161 Griffiths (1996), 12.

162 CE3/10, 2985 (11 Nov. 1826). The Trustees, unusually, resolved to thank Combe's son not only for the manuscript but gave 'an Assurance of the strong feeling entertained by the Trustees of Mr. Combe's Services as an Officer and their sense of his Merits'.

163 The last volume written by him was Combe (1812–61), v. This volume dealt with the funerary monuments. In an introductory paragraph Edward Hawkins tells how he had seen it through the press and added to it.

164 Select Committee (1835), 294 and 346.

165 Select Committee (1835), 359.

166 Select Committee (1835), 569.

167 A Treasury minute specifically rejecting either a move or split is at CE4/6, 2165 (26 July 1826). It came at the end of a long battle and is the real signal for the continuation of Smirke's new building; CE1/5, 1261–5 (23 May 1826); CE4/6, 2158 (23 May).

168 Rather grudgingly acknowledged by Miller (1979), 3.

169 CE1/5, 1268–9 (10 Feb. 1827).

170 CE1/5, 1219 (14 Feb. 1824).

171 CE5/11, 2255 (8 March 1828).

172 Zwalf (1985), 150.

173 CE1/5, 1084 (12 May 1810).

174 CE4/3, 1244–5 (9 Nov. 1815); CE1/5, 1142 (10 Feb. 1816). The collection is now in the Devizes Museum. For Cunnington see Cunnington (1975); for a more critical assessment see Piggott (1989), 153–6.

175 CE4/6, 2143–6 (6 April 1826); CE3/10, 2957 (8 April 1826). This may have included two heads from the Parthenon frieze of which he presented casts to the Museum two years later – Jenkins (1992), 81. For Brøndsted's travels in Greece, see Haugsted (1996), 11–28. Brøndsted (who became keeper of the royal coin cabinet in Denmark) continued to offer parts of his collection to the Museum, cf., for example, CE3/12, 3338 (12 March 1831), when the Trustees turned down a bronze found near the River Siris and three other Greek bronzes for a total of £1,600. Two of this group (Walters (1899), nos 285–6) were later bought by the Trustees with the aid of money raised by two of their number, W.R. Hamilton and Alexander Baring, CE3/12, 3588 (20 April 1833); a copy of the original appeal document is at CE115/3, 138 (10 May 1833), by which time £435 had been raised towards the asking price of £1,000 or £1,100. The full list of subscribers (many of them members of the Society of Dilettanti) is at CE4/11 (March 1834), by which time the Museum had only £200 to pay. Again, CE3/12, 3448 (11 Feb. 1832), they once more turned down the Parthenon heads, Jenkins, *loc. cit.*; they are now in the National Museum, Copenhagen. All this despite the fact that he had given them a large paper copy of his book *Voyages et recherches dans la Grèce*, CE3/12, 3322 (12 Feb. 1831). The major part of Brøndsted's collection was put on display in Paris in 1833 and was apparently sold for a good price to the French government. Brøndsted was at this time very active in the market, as agent for the Crown Prince of Denmark (later Christian VIII) who was building up with expertise his great collection of classical antiquities which now forms part of the Danish National Museum (Rasmussen (1999), *passim*); he was later to act as an agent of the British Museum at the sale of the Durand collection, see below, p. 103. He was well known in the Museum and clearly became a friend of

Ellis, who records, for instance, taking him to the theatre, BL Add. MS 36,657 (7), 16 Dec. 1839.

176 CE4/6, 2093–101 (16 Jan. 1826). For the ultimate destination of part of this collection see Jahn (1854), xiv n. and Heydemann (1872), 1.

177 CE3/10, 3001 (13 Jan. 1827); CE4/6, 2198 (7 Feb. 1827).

178 CE3/10, 2650 (8 Feb. 1817).

179 CE1/5, 1268 (11 Dec. 1826).

180 CE1/6, 1370–1 (12 June 1830); CE4/8, 20 (19 June 1830). See also an anonymous engraved memorandum suggesting a public appeal for the purchase of the collection, CE115/3, 194 (12 April 1830). The collection was eventually bought in 1835 by the great dealer in works on paper, Samuel Woodburn, for £16,000, at which time its purchase was considered by the National Gallery, at that time to some extent governed by the Museum.

181 He was made a Knight of Hanover (the Guelphic Order) in 1832 and a Knight Bachelor in 1833. He records receiving his knighthood from the King in his diary, 'I had scarcely been at home two hours when a Letter came from the Lord Chamberlain's Office to tell me of the Fees, £108 2s 6d.' BL Add. MS 36,653 (4), f.111r (22 Feb. 1833).

182 After Combe's death Ellis also became Editor of the Society of Antiquaries and was paid £100 p.a. for this chore; Evans (1956), 242. In 1837 Ellis was being paid £150 p.a. as joint Secretary of the Society, CE5/21 (10 June 1837), and was allowed by the Trustees to keep the post.

183 Dictionary of national biography, s.n.

184 Miller (1973), passim.

185 Edwards (1870), 534–5.

186 Douglas (1951), 39–40, was influentially critical of his work, which was rooted in the eighteenth-century antiquarian tradition. In 1986 his work on Domesday was re-evaluated in a British Library exhibition for which Andrew Prescott published a four-page pamphlet.

187 Brand (1813). This was originally prepared for publication in 1795 (at which time it already needed wholesale revision); it would not have appeared without Ellis's editorial effort.

188 Ellis (1833) and (1836). The identity of the author of these volumes emerges in the Select Committee (1835), 22; a third book in the same series on Egyptian Antiquities was published in 1836.

189 The story is well told by Miller (1973), 131–2. The appointment was made quite quickly, for Ellis laid the King's sign manual before the Trustees' Committee only some six weeks after Planta's death, CE3/11, 3058 (12 Jan. 1828). Ellis, in reassuring Panizzi that he would support his selection as Principal Librarian in 1856, gives a version of the events which led to his own appointment. Add. MS 36,717, 297–8 (14 Feb. 1856). A copy of the Archbishop's letter to Clinton telling of Ellis's appointment is at Add. MS 36,717, 301 (20 Dec. 1827).

190 There are many biographies of Panizzi, and even a memoir from his own pen. For full references see Miller (1967).

191 Howley had previously been Bishop of London and thus an ex-officio Trustee.

192 Ackerman (1979).

193 His family on and off had a long connection with the Museum. His architect third son (Major Rhode Hawkins) went with Fellows to Xantos in 1841 and drew the Harpy Tomb and other monuments for the Museum publication. His grandson was Sir Frederic Kenyon, Principal Librarian of the Museum (see below), whose daughter Dame Kathleen Kenyon, an archaeologist, was a Trustee from 1965 to 1978.

194 CE1/5, 1246 (14 May 1825); CE3/10, 2999 (13 Jan. 1827).

195 This criticism is fully discussed by Cash (1995), 167–99.

196 Hansard, Parliamentary Debates, 3rd ser. xvi, 1003 (25 March 1833).

197 Edwards (1870), 541, and Harris (1998), 81 and 102, for details.

198 Madden Diary, 2 July 1835.

199 Miller (1973), 138.

200 Select Committee (1835).

201 Select Committee (1836).

202 Select Committee (1835), 154.

203 Madden Diary, 9 July 1836.

204 Select Committee (1835), 1. Patronage was so much in the hands of the Principal Trustees that in 1838 Ellis and the keepers first heard the names of appointed Assistants from Forshall after a Trustees' meeting. See Ellis diary, BL Add. MS 33,653 (6) (1 March 1838). It was clear that Ellis had no part in appointing assistants. Neither did the keepers.

205 19 April 1836, 296.

206 Elsewhere it is pointed out that they include 'one duke, three marquises, five earls, four barons, and three members of Parliament'. Select Committee (1835), 52.

207 Select Committee (1835), 9.

208 Select Committee (1835), 53.

209 Select Committee (1835), 27.

210 Select Committee (1836), 100.

211 The Times, 15 Oct. 1851.

212 Select Committee (1836), 407.

213 Select Committee (1836), 391.

214 Select Committee (1835), 249–54; Select Committee (1836), 469–77.

215 Appointed 13 Jan. 1827; CE5/10, 2112 (Feb. 1827).

216 Select Committee (1835), 255–9.

217 Select Committee (1836), 429–33.

218 Select Committee (1836), iii.

219 Select Committee (1836), iii–v).

220 CE3/15, 4330 (23 July 1836). The committee consisted of the Archbishop of Canterbury, the Bishop of London, the Chancellor of the Exchequer, the president of the Society of Antiquaries, Earl Cawdor, Lord Stanley, Lord Farnborough, Lord Ashburton and Sir Robert Inglis. A printed copy of the report is at CE115/3, 153 (2 Aug. 1836).

221 Select Committee (1837).

222 Appointed in the first instance as Extra Assistant Librarian, CE3/10, 2638 (16 Nov. 1816).

223 Appointed 21 March 1833; CE3/12, 3585 (20 April 1833). His two major publications are Ottley (1816 and 1823). His role in the history of print collecting is recounted by Griffiths (1996), 93; as a collector of drawings see Gere (1953).

224 Josi was appointed on the recommendation of the Archbishop of Canterbury after an intervention at a full board meeting, CE1/6, 1492 (13 Feb. 1836); this was confirmed at Standing Committee two weeks later, CE3/15, 4202 (1 Mar. 1836).

225 Appointed initially on a short-term contract, CE3/12, 3392 (14 Sept. 1831).

226 This was an open letter and was published in The gentleman's magazine, xcviii (1828), 61–4.

227 CE5/11, 2244–5 (8 Feb. 1828).

228 Faussett's collection, ultimately given by Joseph Meyer to the Liverpool Museum (now the National Museums and Galleries on Merseyside), was to be significant in the history of the establishment of a department for British antiquities at the British Museum (p.132). His excavations were not published until 1856; Faussett (1856).

229 CE3/11, 3068 (9 Feb. 1828).

230 The most prestigious British object purchased at this period was the Early Bronze Age gold cape from Mold in North Wales (1836, 9-1, 2). It was originally

offered for £100; the Trustees suggested £80, CE3/14, 4056 (8 Aug. 1835), an offer refused by the owner, CE3/14, 4064 (28 Aug. 1835). Eventually, with the help of Gage, Secretary of the Society of Antiquaries, it was bought for £95, CE3/15, 4189–90 (13 Feb. 1836). The acquisition of the Lewis chessmen for £80 in 1832 is discussed below (p.105). At random, a few other British acquisitions were an Anglo-Saxon brooch purchased for £4, CE3/12, 3551 (12 Jan 1833); 'several Celts and other ancient instruments in flint and stone', which cost £9 10s, CE3/12, 3605 (11 May 1833); two gold arm-rings from Ireland purchased for £15 5s, CE3/14, 3888 (8 Nov. 1834); a group of 'flint arrowheads, and spearheads, Stone hatchets, hammers, &c, Brass spearheads and other antiquities collected in Ireland' purchased for £30, CE3/13, 3852 (12 July 1834), CE5/16, 3686 (July 1834). More interesting were a group of models of cromlechs which were placed on tables in the galleries, CE5/16, 3690 (1 Aug. 1834).

231 Select Committee (1837), 13.
232 Stevenson (1981).
233 Levine (1986), 182–3, lists county and local societies founded before 1886.
234 Pyrah (1988), 14–30.
235 Hawkins (1841).
236 Babelon (1901), 210–326, Carson and Pagan (1986), 1.
237 Hawkins was instructed to withdraw from office in the Society in 1840, as was Samuel Birch as Secretary, by a strict interpretation by the Trustees of the plurality clause defined by the Select Committee (despite the fact that there were no emoluments). Carson and Pagan (1986), 9.
238 The society was granted a royal charter in 1904, becoming the Royal Numismatic Society, and was for many years the major conduit for the publication of numismatic papers by the staff of the Museum.
239 The origins and early history of the Danish National Museum are recounted in Jensen (1992), from which much of the following is taken. Nyerup's crucial publication was Nyerup (1806).
240 Thomsen (1836). The origin of the Three-Age system is best explained in English by Daniel (1943); Gräslund (1981) discusses the acceptance and formulation of the Three-Age system by Thomsen. An up-to-date assessment of Thomsen will be found in Danish, with English summaries, in the proceedings of a symposium published as Aarbøger for nordisk Oldkyndighed og Historie for 1988.
241 A useful, if sometimes rather slanted, discussion of national museums will be found in von Plessen (1992).
242 See above, p.57.
243 Gaehtgens (1992), Stonge (1998).
244 Galard (1993) provides an anthology of such visits – and many others.
245 Much has been written about the polymathic Denon – diplomat, politician, artist, writer, antiquarian, pornographer, specialist in gems – there is even a national committee 'pour le développement de la recherche et des études sur la vie et l'oeuvre de Vivant Denon'. See, for example, Lelièvre (1993), Claudon and Bailly (1997). For a major exhibition at the Louvre on Denon, see Chatelain (1999).

CHAPTER 4
1 John Dutt, Thomas Finch, John Garrett and George Spencer. It should be noted that at the same time the Prints and Drawings Department's staff consisted of a Keeper (Josi) and one attendant, George Reid; this was not to change for some time (Reid's son was appointed as a second attendant in 1842 – CE3/21, 6005 (30 Aug. 1842)).

2 Appointed 22 Jan. 1836; CE1/6, 1490 (3 Feb. 1836). For an outline of his career see Dictionary of national biography, s.n.
3 Appointed 10 Mar. 1840; CE3/18, 5391 (13 June 1840). See Cook (1997).
4 Appointed 13 April 1841, CE3/19, 5618 (1 May 1841). For an outline of his career see Dictionary of national biography, s.n. Vaux (1850).
5 CE3/23, 7594 (14 Oct. 1848).
6 The move of the printed books was completed by the end of 1840; it is chronicled by Harris (1991), 75–101.
7 The Builder (1863), xxi, 209. This building was demolished in 1885 to provide further space for classical antiquities, now the Payava and Caryatid rooms.
8 Quoted Griffiths (1996), 12.
9 CE1/6, 1723 (19 March 1842).
10 A ghostly photograph of the front of Montagu House records its passing, Caygill (1981), 17. Excavations in 1998 and 1999 have revealed traces of the debris created in pulling down the old house, as well as the foundations of some walls and even a few fragments of painted ceiling, Spence (1999).
11 Caygill and Date (1999), 28; see also Miller (1973), 197. Fragments of painted plaster were found during excavation in the forecourt in 1998, Spence (1999), 27.
12 The Builder, i (1843), 477, quoted by Caygill and Date (1999), 30. For a summary of the criticism see Crook (1973), 146–50.
13 For views of the Egyptian and Etruscan rooms on the upper floor at this period see Illustrated London News, 13 Feb. 1847, 108.
14 Illustrated London News, 24 Aug. 1847, 269, with an engraving. The scheme was triumphantly restored to its original gloomy appearance in 1999–2000 (Anderson (2000), 76), although with disastrously styled and pathetically hung pendant lights of late nineteenth-century design.
15 Jenkins (1992), fig.62, reprints an engraving of the Front Hall, c. 1850, with its original north wall temporarily occupied by Assyrian sculpture.
16 CE: The British Museum Conservation Plan, ii, 57–61.
17 The technical details of the structure of the building are ably summarized by Crook (1973), from which much of this paragraph derives.
18 The first mention of Smirke providing drawings of wall cases occurs in CE3/14, 3989 (27 May 1835) (the drawings – one initialled and dated by Smirke – survive in the BM Archives). Details of furnishing were regularly communicated to the Trustees, for example when Smirke submitted drawings of cases in the gallery of the south front intended for the ethnographical collections (these also survive in the BM Archives). In this instance Hawkins asked for more cases than were proposed; his plea was upheld by the Trustees; CE1/7, 1799–1800 (6 July 1844).
19 Wilson (1989), fig.11.
20 Original drawings by Smirke of cabinets with both legs and drawers (the drawers covered by doors) survive in the BM Archives (pl. 22). Date and Hamber (1990), fig. 8, reproduce a Fenton photograph of the Mineral Gallery in 1860 which shows the original form of both the legged table-cases and the wall-cases. The cases with drawers or cupboards continued in use until the late twentieth century (and some survive in storage) but were removed for reasons of security and because of the need for better conservation conditions. See also CE: The British Museum Conservation Plan, ii, 57.
21 The wall-cases in the King's Library were not glazed until 1853, CE3/26, 8538 (9 April 1853).
22 CE5/32, 9919 (April 1844).
23 CE5/39, 12450v (9 July 1847).
24 A poster advertising the sale of such materials is reproduced by Caygill and Date (1999), fig.15.

25 CE4/39 (7 April 1848).
26 A number of these drawings are reproduced in Caygill and Date (1999).
27 P&D 1900, 7–14, 63.
28 Caygill (1981), 32; Date and Hamber (1990), fig. 4. An Act of Parliament (2 Victoria, c.x) had in 1839 enabled the Trustees to purchase all the houses on the south side of the Museum site on Great Russell Street.
29 For a full description see Caygill and Date (1999), 39–40.
30 Twelve of the original lions were transferred in 1899 to the rails round Wellington's tomb in St Paul's Cathedral, which was also designed by Stevens. Another original lion is displayed in the Museum's nineteenth-century gallery. The railings are illustrated in Caygill and Date (1999), fig. 24.
31 CE3/23, 7509 (6 May 1848).
32 CE4/40 (24 and 26 June 1848).
33 This is Westmacott's own description quoted in *Synopsis of the contents of the British Museum*, 60th edition, 1853, ii–iii n.
34 *Pictorial half-hours of London topography*, Sept. 1851, 191, gives a contemporary description; the colour is analysed in Jenkins and Middleton (1992).
35 Caygill and Date (1999), 42–3 and fig. 26. For the drinking-fountain see Caygill (1981), 32.
36 Most of the figures quoted here are taken from the annual printed accounts of the Museum as presented to Parliament. For a discussion of the admission of the working class to the Museum in this period see Date (1996).
37 *Report of the Select Committee on national monuments and works of art in Westminster Abbey, in St Paul's Cathedral and other national edifices*, Parliamentary papers, House of Commons, 1841 (416), vi. 437, iii and question 3144.
38 *Ibid.*, questions 3007–8. Children under eight years of age were not admitted to the Museum and a number of cases of attempts to breach this rule were reported to the Trustees, who were adamant that such a regulation should be adhered to. Cf. the case of an eighteen-month-old child, CE5/63, 52–3 (15 Jan. 1859), where a legal opinion was sought.
39 The opening of the reading rooms is recorded, with a picture, in *The Illustrated London News*, 7 June 1851, 505–6 and 585. A few years later, the cases in the King's Library, the central Manuscript Saloon and the Grenville Library having been glazed, they were permanently opened to the public with a full cased display.
40 BL Add. MS 36,653 (7) (26 Dec. 1838).
41 *The Illustrated London News*, 29 March 1845, 202. More than 15,000 people visited the Museum on this day.
42 CE5/63, 52–3 (5 July 1859).
43 Date (1996), 35 et passim.
44 Hansard, 1856, 3 ser., cxli, col. 1358.
45 Gray had recommended that a smaller guide should be produced at 4d, 'but if it could reduced to 4d it would be better', *Report of the Select Committee on National Monuments and Works...*, 1841, paras. 3191–2.
46 The most ubiquitous was a series of cheap pamphlets of extreme bibliographical complexity of which Clarke (1843), published at 6d, is one of the earliest. Clarke's guides sold for at least eight years under various guises. Another, published in the same year, is Scott and Kesson (1843), sold at 3d, which went into a second edition in the same year. A slightly less well-produced version of Vaux (1851) was Masson (1848), which had a series of rather poor wood-engravings.
47 Select Committee (1860), xiii.
48 Jenkins (1992), 31–4, makes a valiant effort to explain the phenomenon.
49 BM: ANE Correspondence, vi, 1882 (15 April 1836).
50 CE3/14, 4057–8 (8 Aug. 1835). The Trustees were

51 informed that the Admiralty were willing to help in surveying and digging in Asia Minor on classical sites. Even the Treasury were not unimpressed.
51 Fellows (1839).
52 CE5/23, 6137 (8 Mar. 1839).
53 CE4/20 (dated 'Friday evg', i.e. 7 March 1839).
54 CE3/17, 5017 (9 March 1839).
55 Fellows (1843), 2n.
56 CE3/17, 5024–5 (20 March 1839); 5029–30 (6 April 1839).
57 CE3/18, 5464 (26 Sept. 1840); CE1/6, 1703–5 (5 June 1841).
58 CE3/19, 5696–7 (25 Sept. 1841). See Fellows (1843). Fellows had already sent detailed instructions (together with a sketch map) to Captain Graves (the naval officer in charge) on the stones which he thought should be removed, CE4/25 (28 Sept. 1841). The problems concerning permission are detailed in Jenkins (1992), 142.
59 CE3/19, 5727–8 (13 Nov. 1841); CE3/20, 6092–3 (24 Dec. 1842).
60 CE3/21, 6519–20 (9 Nov. 1844).
61 Scharf and Fellows (1847); Fellows (1852) also wrote a popular account.
62 CE3/21, 6697 (14 June 1845).
63 A view of the room was published in *The Illustrated London News*, 15 Jan. 1848, 15. For a fully documented account of the mounting of these sculptures see Jenkins (1992), 145–53.
64 CE3/18, 5278–9 (11 Jan. 1840).
65 CE5/18, 4396 (April 1836).
66 CE4/14 (17 April 1836).
67 The committee meetings of the middle months of 1836 were much exercised by this collection. The most important references are CE3/15, 4239–46 (16 April 1836); 4262–3 (23 April 1836); and letters from Hamilton and Brøndsted, CE4/14 (17 April 1836). Brøndsted received expenses and a fee of £210, CE86/Principal Librarian's Accounts 1833–37, 131. See Jenkins (1992a) for the collection and its importance.
68 CE5/18, 4477 (June 1836).
69 Rasmussen (1999), 36.
70 CE3/15, 4338 (32 July 1836). To be just, Brøndsted denied that he was responsible. He told Forshall that the parcel was packed by the French packer and was intended for the Duke of Hamilton (a Trustee), but 'this be confidentially between you and me' (29 June 1836). CE Miscellaneous papers, Box J.
71 CE3/18, 5254 (14 Dec. 1839); 5393 (13 June 1840).
72 CE3/24, 7936–7 (26 Jan. 1850); 7941 (9 Feb. 1850).
73 CE3/23, 7605 (14 Oct. 1848).
74 CE3/16, 4699 (27 Jan. 1838).
75 The problems of Treasure Trove rumbled on during the middle years of the nineteenth century. A rather one-sided, but useful, review of some of these discussions is in Ebbatson (1994), 47–9.
76 CE3/16, 4725–6 (31 March 1838). The Treasury reply, CE3/16, 4738–9 (14 April 1838), is typical of that institution: 'upon consulting their Solicitor the Lords Commissioners understood that it did not frequently occur that objects of interest as curiosities became the property of the Crown, but that their Lordships would order in such cases in future a report to be made to their Board in order that they might communicate with the Trustees on the subject'.
77 Hawkins himself published the hoard and the coins in it; three letters asking his advice concerning the distribution of objects from it which had been retained by the duchy office are preserved in BM: ANE Correspondence, ii, 128 (27 July 1842); iv, 1203 (13 Dec. 1842) and 1204 (24 Dec. 1842). For the Cuerdale hoard see Graham-Campbell (1992).
78 The Treasure Act 1996, Eliz. II, c.24.

79 Madden's diary for 17 Oct. 1831, quoted by Stratford (1997) in a fully documented description of the find and its circumstances. Madden did indeed write the find up in *Archaeologia* in a most remarkable and perspicacious paper, Madden (1832).

80 CE5/14, 2959 (Nov. 1831). Purchase reported CE3/12, 3434 (14 Jan. 1832).

81 CE3/15, 4347 (27 July 1836); CE3/17, 4935 (15 Dec. 1839).

82 CE1/7, 1799 (6 July 1844); for cost see CE4/34 (8 Jan. 1846).

83 BM: ANE Antiquities Correspondence, iv, 1160 (17 Nov. 1842).

84 Useful popular summary histories of Assyrian studies are Lloyd (1980) and Larsen (1994), which have full bibliographies. Budge (1925), if chauvinistic, is an invaluable study by a member of the Museum staff who knew many of the personalities involved.

85 Budge (1925), 26, gives a summary of the Assyrian finds in Rich's collection.

86 A fulsome biography is Rawlinson (1898).

87 For Hincks see Larsen (1996), *passim* and particularly pp. 178–88 and 333–7.

88 For Layard see Waterfield (1963).

89 Fontan (1994).

90 BM: ANE Correspondence, 1826–60, viii, 3198 (undated).

91 CE4/36 (16 Nov. 1846) in a private letter to Forshall, accompanying a more formal memorandum. The Trustees (presumably wishing to control the excavations properly) refused to accept his offer, CE3/22, 7131–5 (9 Jan. 1847). In a letter to Layard, CE27/28, 173–5 (22 Jan. 1847), Forshall hopes that Layard will agree to the fee. The matter seems to have remained unresolved.

92 Forshall explained this to Canning, CE27/28, 64 (15 Sept. 1846), in sending him draft instructions to Layard: 'There is', he writes, 'a little moralisation in the Memorandum, perhaps not altogether unsuited to the relative position of the T[rustee]s as a grave and dignified body, and Mr Layard as an enterprising young man'.

93 CE27/28, 45 (9 Sept. 1846).

94 CE4/36 (16 Nov. 1846).

95 Bruce (1903), ii, 177.

96 Rassam was British Vice-consul in Mosul and continued Layard's work when he left in 1851.

97 Entitled *A popular account of discoveries at Nineveh*, it was abridged from Layard (1849).

98 CE3/23, 7412 (8 Jan. 1848).

99 CE4/42 (20 March 1849); CE3/24, 7746–7 (24 March 1849).

100 Bruce (1903), ii, 188.

101 Layard communicated his decision at a meeting of a Trustees' sub-committee specifically set up to consider the Assyrian antiquities, CE7/2, 508–11 (2 Aug. 1851). The Trustees at the same meeting charged Rawlinson with the task of co-ordinating the Museum's efforts in Babylon.

102 Ellis to Layard, CE27/40, 93–4 (28 Nov. 1851). *The Illustrated London News* published articles on the Nimrud sculptures on 16 Dec. 1848, 2 March 1850, and 26 Oct. 1850; and on the Nineveh room, 26 March 1853.

103 The best-known is the engraving of the arrival of one of the Assyrian bulls at the Museum in *The Illustrated London News*, 28 Feb. 1852.

104 For a fully documented description of the construction and display of these galleries, see Jenkins (1992), 158–67.

105 Layard (1851).

106 Rawlinson (1861).

107 I rely in this section on the summary in Griffiths (1996), 11–13.

108 Griffiths (1996), 288–9.

109 Griffiths (1996), 65.

110 CE4/14 (15 and 24 March 1836).

111 CE4/14, undated (March 1836).

112 See p.103.

113 Josi applied to the Trustees for £500 to purchase prints from this sale, CE1/6, 1540 (28 April 1837); although they refused this sum, they ultimately relented and granted him £100 to add to the balance of the departmental grant, CE1/6, 1553 (27 May 1857).

114 CE3/21, 6580 (8 Feb. 1845).

115 CE3/23, 7448 (29 Jan. 1848).

116 Griffiths (1996), 13.

117 See *Dictionary of national biography, s.n.,* and Griffiths (1996), 13, 98–9.

118 Carpenter (1844).

119 Griffiths (1996), 100–1.

120 CE5/54, 15985 (9 Aug. 1854); CE3/26, 8747 (14 Oct. 1854); CE7/2, 886 (19 Jan. 1855).

121 CE3/24, 8024 (29 June 1850).

122 A fully documented account of this acquisition is in Thornton and Warren (1998).

123 Royal Commission (1850), 35.

124 Madden Diary, 7 Feb. 1845.

125 CE4/32 (9 Feb. 1845); on 12 Feb. they wrote again to the Duke asking his permission to restore the vase.

126 Caygill (1985a) tells the whole story.

127 CE27/25, 88.

128 CE27/26, 150; CE3/22, 6830 (13 Dec. 1845). Doubleday was the first specialist restorer to have worked in the Museum, he was followed by Robert Ready, who joined in 1858/9; his sons also worked there and the last one retired or died in 1930; Oddy (1993), 11.

129 The fascinating story of the latest reconstruction is told by Williams (1989), 8–21.

130 CE5/59, 491 (5 June 1857).

131 CE5/43, 13941 (4 April 1849).

132 CE1/7, 2075 (4 April 1849).

133 CE4/39 (April 1848).

134 Miller (1967), 167–72.

135 For Edwards's lively and individual comments on the riot see the summary in Munford (1963), 51–4.

136 Madden's Diary, 10 April 1848.

137 Cowtan (1872), 151. In all 341 people were catered for at this picnic, CE4/39 (10 April 1848).

138 *The Times*, 22 Jan. 1852.

139 Martin (1980), 365.

140 CE3/28, 9679–80 (12 Nov. 1859); 9709 (11 Feb. 1860); CE3/29, 9799–800 (14 July 1860).

141 CE4/114, 568–72 (9 June 1871). For Maskelyne see Morton (1987). A short typescript history and memorabilia of the Club are at CE Bay 6/G/2.

142 Figures quoted from Harris (1998), 132–3, 149n.

143 Harris (1998), 150.

144 Harris (1998), 158.

145 Ackerman (1979).

146 All figures from Harris (1998), chapters 4 and 5.

147 Figures abstracted from the annual *Accounts and income and expenditure of the British Museum* submitted to Parliament (the accounting methods changed during this period, thus the figures for 1836–47 are approximate).

148 Madden's diary, which he left to the Bodleian Library at Oxford, is now being transcribed for publication by a team of scholars. It is one of the great diaries of the nineteenth century, of enormous social and academic interest. It is also racy and as regards his colleagues – and particularly Panizzi – often vituperative. It has been much used – often to the detriment of Madden's own very considerable reputation – by historians of the Museum. While it is impossible to ignore it, I have attempted to use it only in relationship to events or facts, although it is practically impossible for anyone who has used it to refrain from occasional colourful

quotation. One wonders what Panizzi's diary would have been like – if he had kept one – and what it would have done to his reputation.

149 Miller (1973), 172, quotes *The Saturday Review*, 8 March 1856, 'If discord, envy, hatred, wrath, malice and all uncharitableness have a favourite house in England, it will be found between Bloomsbury Square and Tottenham Court Road.'

150 *Memorial to the First Lord of the Treasury on 10 March 1847 by members of the British Association for the Advancement of Science and of other Scientific Societies regarding the management of the British Museum*, Parliamentary Papers, House of Commons, 1847 (268), xxiv, 253.

151 Royal Commission (1850), 13.

152 Royal Commission (1850).

153 CE1/7, 2083–2104 (27 April, 4 May, 25 May, 1 June 1850). The committee's report was approved by the Trustees, CE1/7, 2103 (1 June 1850) and printed by order of the House of Commons: *Copies of all communications addressed to the Treasury by the Trustees of the British Museum, with reference to the report of the Commissioners appointed to inquire into the constitution and management of the British Museum*. Sessional papers, House of Commons, xxxiii (1850), 247–57.

154 For details see Harris (1998), 175–6.

155 CE1/7, 2103 (1 June 1850).

156 Royal Commission (1850), 42–4.

157 Royal Commission (1850), question 3230.

158 Royal Commission (1850), question 8066.

159 Royal Commission (1850), question 8145. One of the Trustees, W.R. Hamilton (hero of the classicists and one of the most active members of the board), admitted that he had not really thought about the matter.

160 Royal Commission (1850), question 8271.

161 Royal Commission (1850), 39.

162 Royal Commission (1850), 35.

163 Royal Commission (1850), questions 8171–7, 8186–8.

164 Royal Commission (1850), question 8120 et seq.

165 Royal Commission (1850), 35.

166 *Copies of all communications made by the Architect and Officers of the British Museum to the Trustees concerning the Enlargement of the Building of that Institution… 30 June 1852*, Sessional papers, House of Commons, xxviii, 226.

167 See Cowtan (1872), 214–5; Harris (1979), 11.

168 Quoted by Caygill and Date (1999), 44.

169 The original sketch is reproduced by Harris (1979), fig.5. Harris (1998), 187–8, discusses and documents some of the earlier plans to fill the space suggested by various people, including Hawkins and William Hosking, Professor of Architecture and Engineering at King's College London. See also Crook (1973), 168–81, who puts the idea of a round reading room in a wider context.

170 *Copies of all communications made by the Architect and Officers of the British Museum to the Trustees concerning the Enlargement of the Building of that Institution… 30 June 1852*, Sessional papers, House of Commons, xxviii. The drawing of this scheme is reproduced by Crook (1973), fig.76b. Rather alarmingly Sir Charles Barry now stepped in with a plan to roof the whole of the courtyard with glass and re-arrange some of the antiquities galleries to house books. This was firmly squashed by the Trustees who, for once, asked Ellis to consult the keepers (who were unanimously against the plan). Harris (1998), 183–4, recounts the full story.

171 Crook (1973), fig.76c.

172 CE4/50 (26 Jan. 1854). These sums were increased after the tenders were opened and as certain additions were made to the original design; see Harris (1998), 184–6, for details.

173 Wright (1997). Copies of the photographs are at CE114/148–9.

174 Boase (1954).

175 CE5/54, 15933 (10 Aug. 1854); CE3/26, 8731 (12 Aug. 1854).

176 Crook (1973), figs 84–5.

177 A famous BBC recording demonstrates that the noise caused by readers and staff was indeed muffled and not deadened.

178 Harris (1998), 187 and cited sources.

179 CE3/25, 8170 (8 March 1851). For the exiguous correspondence concerning his appointment see Caygill (1997), 105n.

180 Franks was an excessively private person, a bachelor whose private papers do not in the main survive. Until recently he has received little attention, but see Wilson (1984) and Caygill and Cherry (1997).

181 For the Cambridge Camden Society and its demise, see White (1962) and Pevsner (1972), 123–38.

182 Franks (1849). Franks's first gift of antiquities to the Museum was in March 1851 – an axe-head and a medieval brick – 1851, 4–28, 1–2.

183 CE5/46, 15375 (12 Dec. 1850).

184 Rickman (1817).

185 CE3/22, 6799 (28 Oct. 1845), 6806 (8 Nov. 1845), 6827 (13 Dec. 1845), CE1/7, 2111 (14 Dec. 1850).

186 Clark (1928), 226.

187 Wetherall (1998), 33.

188 For a contemporary description of this split, in which Ellis was involved, see the first volume of *The Journal of the British Archaeological Association*, 1845, i–xiv. See also Wetherall (1994), 16–20. Once things had settled down six members of the Museum staff had joined the committee of the Institute, and a further twelve were members of it.

189 Kemble (1849). Kemble, a member of the great theatrical family, was in the opinion of many 'the best of the English medievalists before Stubbs'. He was later a candidate for the post of Principal Librarian of the Museum, see below, p.129. For Kemble see Dickins (1939).

190 Kemble (1855). Republished in Kemble (1863), 221–51.

191 CE3/22, 6827 (13 Oct. 1845).

192 Lindenschmit (1848). This was reprinted in 1969 with an introduction on its importance by Kurt Böhner.

193 Wylie (1855).

194 For Cochet see *Centenaire de l'Abbé Cochet 1975. Actes du colloque international d'archéologie, Rouen 3-4-5 Juillet 1975*. fasc.i, Rouen 1978.

195 Again Wylie (1854) had drawn English attention to one of Cochet's excavations (at Envermeu).

196 For the process of collection at the Victoria and Albert Museum see Baker and Richardson (1997). For a history of the Museum itself see Burton (1999). For the history of the collections see also Cocks (1980).

197 See below p.135.

198 The principle was finally enunciated (if in rather delphic terms) in *Report of the select committee on the South Kensington Museum*, 1860. An early example of co-operation to this end occurred in 1867 when Franks was one of the three commissioners appointed to buy objects for the South Kensington Museum at the Exposition Universelle in Paris.

199 Guest and John (1989), 227; for the collection see Rackham (1915).

200 This act was superseded in 1850 by the Public Library and Museums Act, which narrowed the powers of local authorities with regard to museums. Emending statutes were added up to 1885.

201 The Academy was followed by the Royal Dublin Society, which two years later petitioned Parliament for the same purpose. See *Copy of a memorial transmitted by the Royal Dublin Society to the Lords Commissioners of the Treasury, in the month of January 1843, praying for a*

grant of money for the erection of a National Museum…, Parliamentary Papers, House of Commons, 1843 (372), 501.

202 Ash (1981), 104–5.

203 For the origins of the Royal Scottish Museum see Waterson (1997).

204 [Thomsen] (1836).

205 The system had a very mixed reception in Germany, where influentially Lindenschmit rejected it, Eggers (1959), 43–52. It was, however, well received in Switzerland and ultimately in France, Daniel (1950), 79, 85.

206 Worsaae (1843). This was translated into German in the following year and into English in 1849, Worsaae (1849).

207 Worsaae (1934),135–7; Worsaae (1938), 16–8. For a recent estimate of Worsaae's political and nationalistic stance in relation to his academic work see Ødegaard (1994).

208 Worsaae (1934). 304. See also the version of the story told by Thoms in Worsaae, (1849), x.

209 Quoted from Jensen (1992), 207.

210 Worsaae (1934), 304.

211 For Worsaae's more general archaeological influence in England see Wilkins (1961).

212 'The remains of the British islands, previous to the Roman invasion, embrace the Stone, Bronze and a portion of the Iron period of the Northern Antiquaries. They have, for convenience, been classed according to their materials, and in the order corresponding to that of the supposed introduction of such materials into this country'. With them were 'objects of similar date from other countries'. British Museum. A guide to the exhibition rooms of the Departments of natural History and Antiquities, London 1859, 98. The statement does not appear in the Synopsis for 1856. The first person to apply in any major manner the Three-Age system to British archaeology was the Scotsman Daniel Wilson – Wilson (1851).

213 The generalities of what follows are taken from Jenkins (1992) and Cook (1997), both of which provide full references.

214 See pp.147–9.

215 Lane-Poole (1894–5), 624. One of Newton's comments to Panizzi concerning Lane-Poole is at BL Add. MS 36,718, f.500 (14 Dec. 1858).

216 BL Add. MS 36,717, f.612–20 (9 Nov. 1856) and 36,718, f.500–1 (14 Dec. 1858), see below, p.149.

217 Much of the information concerning casts is taken from Jenkins (1990).

218 Haskell and Penny (1981), 79–91 et passim.

219 Haskell and Penny (1981), 123. The French in the Napoleonic period set up a cast section at the Louvre as an 'instrument de propagande artistique', Dominique-Vivant Denon, l'œil de Napoléon, Paris 1999, 188.

220 CE3/9, 2631 (11 May 1816); CE3/10, 2644 (11 Dec. 1816); CE1/5, 1151 (8 July 1816), 1152 (13 July 1816); CE4/4, 1327 (n.d., July 1816).

221 CE1/5, 1157 (8 Feb. 1817), 1158–9 (22 Feb. 1817). Jenkins (1990), 102, prints the reduced list. The original estimate is at CE4/4, 1356–7 (19 Nov. 1816), the reduced estimate is at CE4/4, 1370 (15 Feb. 1817).

222 CE3/10, 2731–2 (10 July 1819).

223 Gazi (1998).

224 Jenkins (1992), 35.

225 For the Egyptian casts see Tillett (1984). The Royal Academy donation is at CE3/12, 3396 (12 Nov. 1831). For a summary concerning the Academy's use of the collection see Jenkins (1992), 30–7; see also Hutchinson (1986), passim.

226 Simpson (2000).

227 Graham (1977), 141. Maudslay's mould-makers were later used at Persepolis by Weld; Simpson (2000), 29.

228 Quoted by Graham (1977), 153.

229 The Victoria and Albert Museum retained the casts of material in its own collections. From the middle of the nineteenth century casts of many objects from both the British Museum and the Victoria and Albert Museum were supplied under licence by the firm of D. Brucciani and Co. This firm was taken over by the Victoria and Albert Museum in 1922, the British Museum having taken back the moulds and casts of its own material in 1907. BM Registry file A68/108/01.

230 A full discussion of the early history of photography at the Museum is provided by Date and Hamber (1990), from which much of this section is derived.

231 British Library Map Department C26F7.

232 The British Museum. Friends of Prints and Drawings, Newsletter, i:8.

233 Panizzi revealed some of the Museum's thinking in evidence published in Report from the select committee on the South Kensington Museum, 1860, paras. 1624–6. Fenton also gave evidence, paras. 1546–1620.

234 CE3/41, 16327–8 (14 April 1883); 16812 (28 June 1884).

235 Pinney (1974–81), v, 477–8.

236 The Trustees had first applied to the Treasury for permission to pay pensions in 1836; Ellis was the first officer to receive a pension on official retirement (Leach in 1822 and Forshall in 1851 had received them on different grounds); CE3/25, 8940 (8 March 1856).

237 BL Add. MS 36,717 is replete with letters to Panizzi on the subject, not all totally favourable.

238 Miller (1967), 215.

239 BL Add. MS 36,717, f.298 (14 Feb. 1856).

240 Journal, ix, 104 (23 Feb. 1856) quoted by Pinney (1974–81), vi, 20n. Kemble, whose great work was the six-volume Codex diplomaticus aevi saxonici, had a wide experience of antiquities but expressed his opposition to the Three-Age system in Horæ Ferales, Kemble (1863), 71–2. Strangely, Franks, who was to edit the plates in this book after Kemble's death, managed to avoid agreeing with him in this matter.

241 BL Add. MS 36,717, f.327. The debate on the Museum's estimates in Parliament in 1856 revealed xenophobic criticism of Panizzi, Hansard 3, ser. cxli (1856), col. 1343–67. On different grounds Layard on the same occasion revealed that he had not wanted Panizzi, but not because of his original nationality.

242 BL Add. MS 36,717, f.343 and 349.

243 Madden Diary, 5 March 1856.

244 Madden Diary, 2 April 1856.

245 Harris (1998), 241.

246 CE3/27, 9011 (7 June 1856): For Owen see Rupke (1994) and Gruber and Thackray (1992).

247 Macaulay to Lord Lansdowne, 29 Feb. 1856, Pinney (1974–81) vi, 21–2.

248 Esdaile (1946), 123, quoting Percy Gardner.

249 British Museum. Statements and suggestions respecting the want of space in that institution (privately printed by and for the exclusive use of the Trustees), 8 Oct. 1857.

250 Copies of letter from Mr Wilson… 27 November 1857, of letter from Sir Benjamin Hall… 20 January 1858: and of letter from Mr Panizzi 27 January 1858, relative to the National Gallery and the British Museum. Parliamentary Papers. House of Commons, xxxiv, 1857–8.

251 Ibid., 3: A copy of report of the Keeper of Antiquities to the Trustees of the British Museum, respecting the want of accommodation for that Department, dated the 7th day of July 1858. Parliamentary Papers, House of Commons, xxxiv, 1857–8, 195.

252 Copy of memorial addressed to Her Majesty's Government by the promoters and cultivators of science on the subject of the proposed severance from the British Museum of its Natural History collections, Parliamentary Papers, House of Commons, 1857–8, xxxiii, 499.

253 Select Committee (1860).

254 Newton had long held this view. In a letter to Panizzi, dated Bodrum, 15 Feb. 1857, BL Add. MS 36,718, 24v– 26v, he writes: 'I certainly prefer the arrangement of the Louvre to any other I know. There ancient, mediæval and modern art of all kinds dwell under the same roof in suggestive juxtaposition... However I do not think it absolutely right that such a perfect centralization should be carried out in London. 'Circumstances have created a collection of Antiquities and Ancient Sculpture in the central position of Russell Square and a Picture Gallery and incipient collection of Mediæval & Renaissance Sculpture in the more fashionable locality of Trafalgar Square & Pall Mall.'
'I think that sufficient unity might be obtained by combining Pictures with Medieval and Renaissance Sculpture and Antiquities and limiting the British Museum to Classical Art. The natural limit of Classical Art is that period when paganism becomes extinct, say the 4th century of the Christian era.' Proposing that all Christian art should be moved to Marlborough House, he adds, 'It is monstrous to have two rival collections of Mediæval Antiquities as at present.'

255 41 and 42 Victoria, c.lv.

256 BM: ANE Antiquities, i 162 et seq. (29 July 1851). Bähr (1850).

257 British Museum. Guide to the exhibition rooms of the Departments of Natural History and Antiquities, London 1859, 50.

258 1851,4–28,1–2. See Potter (1997), 131 and pl.9.

259 1853,4–1,1–39 and 1853,4–23,1–17. Eames (1980), 763–4, has identified many of these.

260 Franks (1852). Franks's activities with this society did not always meet with the approval of the Trustees, who placed obstacles in his way with regard to his attendance at the annual meetings. Franks was firm in his rejection of these restrictions, writing to Birch, 'I do not however think that I myself I ought to accept that leave on the terms on which it has been granted which are the deduction of this time from my vacation next year... I am charged here specially with the formation and arrangement of the British Collection the progress of which I hope has given satisfaction to the Trustees...'. BM: ANE Correspondence, new ser. 5, F. 2225.

261 CE3/26, 8613 (8 Oct. 1853); details of bid at CE5/52, 15006 (7 Oct. 1853).

262 CE4/50 (7 Nov. 1853); CE3/26, 8622 (12 Nov. 1853); (CE4/50, 12 Jan. 1854) and CE3/26, 8643 (14 Jan. 1854). Vaux to Layard, BL Add. MS 38,984, f.374 (April 1856) (quoted by Miller (1973), 210).

263 Copies of all reports, memorials, or other communications to or from the Trustees of the British Museum, on the subject of the Faussett collection of Anglo-Saxon antiquities, Parliamentary Papers, House of Commons, xxxix, 297, 1854, 315–22.

264 White (1988) provides a full account of the story. There is a splendid picture of a public lecture in Liverpool in 1854, on the occasion of a lecture on the Faussett collection, MacGregor (1998), fig. 28.

265 White (1988), 122.

266 Faussett (1856).

267 Mayer Papers, Liverpool City Record Office (22 April 1856), quoted by White (1988), 121.

268 Interestingly, Layard (who might have been expected to take a Mediterranean view) expressed himself about the collection in forthright terms in Parliament, 'the trustees were men mostly connected with the classics, and could not appreciate a collection of "Saxon rubbish"', Hansard 1856, 3 ser., cxli, col.1357.

269 Smith (1854), Kidd (1977).

270 CE3/26, 8788 (1 Feb. 1855) et seq.

271 Quoted by Kidd (1977), 128–9. I have used this paper, on the acquisition of the Roach Smith collection, extensively here.

272 Stead (1985).

273 Evans (1956), 306–7.

274 CE3/28, 9325–6 (13 Jan. 1858); CE5/61, 89 (21 Jan. 1858); CE3/28, 9335–6 (13 Feb. 1858). This developed into an enormous row. Despite the fact that the hour of the Society's meeting was altered to 4 p.m. so as not to interfere with Franks's Museum work, the Trustees by a narrow vote again turned it down, CE5 /21, 271 (11 March 1858); CE3/28, 9350 (27 Feb. 1858). The matter was referred to a general meeting, where Lord John Russell proposed that he be allowed to accept the post and it was agreed, CE3/28 9363–4 (13 March 1858); see also Evans (1956), 294. The request had got tied up with the question of what sort of jobs could be taken on by staff (Ellis had been a paid officer of the Society since 1813); a survey having been conducted by the Trustees, the whole process was loosened up.

275 CE3/26, 8849–50 (9 June 1855); 8856 (23 June 1855); 8867 (7 July 1855). BM: ANE Correspondence, New ser. 5, F, 2194 (undated memo from Franks).

276 Gibson (1994), xviii–xx.

277 1856, 6–23, 1–170. CE7/2, 926–7 (1 May 1856); CE3/27, 8984 (26 April 1856); 9014 (7 June 1856).

278 Much of the detail about the negotiations leading to the national museums' purchases at this sale is documented in Wilson (1985), 73–80.

279 1855, 12–1, 1–231.

280 Catalogue of the celebrated collection of works of art, from the Byzantine period to that of Louis Seize, of that distinguished collector Ralph Bernal, Esq.... Christie and Manson, 1855. A catalogue annotated by Franks is in the Department of Medieval and later Antiquities of the British Museum.

281 Lasko (1994), 41–2.

282 Wilson (1985).

283 In giving them he wrote to Birch, 'Before I came to the Museum I commenced a collection of earthenwares of various kinds including Italian Majolica. My collection has never as you are aware interfered with purchases for the Museum as I have preferred seeing them in the Museum cases than in my own.' BM: ANE Antiquities correspondence, New ser. 5, F, 2221 (6 March 1855).

284 Haynes (1985), no. 64.

285 Hawkins (1852). The Trustees retained a few copies, one of which is in the Department of Coins and Medals. For this story see Syson (1997) and references there cited.

286 CE3/26, 8434 (19 June 1852). The presence of two historians – Macaulay and his friend Henry Hallam – at the meeting might explain the tough line taken by the Trustees. Hallam was perhaps the first historian to research the medieval period critically from the documents. He was a Whig historian before the term was invented and the criticism expressed in the minute sounds as though it might have been drafted by him. He would no doubt have been at one with Macaulay, who had little sympathy for Hawkins.

287 Hawkins (1885).

288 Pinney (1974–81), v, 477–8 (11 Dec. 1855).

289 CE5/63, 173 (24 Feb. 1859).

290 A catalogue of this collection is preserved in the Central Archive of the Museum.

291 CE5/71, 5601 (6 July 1863); CE3/30, 10398 (8 Aug. 1863).

292 1868, 8–8, 3207–13802; for the complicated bibliography of the published catalogues, see Griffiths and Williams (1987), 49–51.

293 BL Add. MS 36,720, f.498.

294 Miller (1973), 299.

295 Macaulay to Stanhope: 'We are likely, I rejoice to find, to get rid of Hawkins. Either Birch or Newton would be a good successor'; Pinney (1974–81), vi, 23 (3 March 1856).

296 Just as Hawkins's resignation was announced in October, Franks was involved in a major row with Panizzi about some small purchases he had made abroad – a row which might have proved fatal to his future in the Museum. Caygill (1997), 64–5.

297 Hawkins incidentally was the first keeper (although not the first member of staff) to retire with a pension – an extremely generous one of £530; see Treasury memorandum, CE4/68 (6 Dec. 1860).

298 Panizzi did not simply dabble in politics, he was very close to Gladstone (one of the elected Trustees), and with his full agreement – even to the extent of encouraging him to apply for money from the Secret Service Fund – went to Naples in 1855 on a pretext involving the museum, but in reality to try and rescue a group of prisoners; see Miller (1967), 242–67 and Shannon (1982), 315–16. For Gladstone and Panizzi see Foot (1979).

299 The accounts were presented in printed form to Parliament by one of the MP Trustees – Inglis and Walpole were prominent in this period. Its title varied slightly but typically is *An account of the income and expenditure of the British Museum for the financial year ended the 31st day of March 18XX; of the estimated charges and expenses for the year [following] and of the number of persons admitted to visit the Museum [for the previous five years]; together with a statement of the progress made in the arrangement of the collections, and an account of objects added to them in the year 18XX.* (Referred to here as *Accounts*.) The figures used here are derived from these documents, a bound-up set of which is deposited in the central library of the Museum.

300 *Journal*, iv, 280 (11 Oct. 1851), quoted by Pinney (1874–81), v, 201n.

301 Pinney (1974–81), v, 201–2 (11 Oct. 1851).

CHAPTER 5

1 CE7/2, 1159–60 (5 July 1860); CE3/29, 9791 (14 July 1860); 9803 (28 July 1960); 9813 (13 Oct. 1860); 9835 (27 Oct. 1860); 9842 (10 Nov. 1860); 985–2 (8 Dec. 1860); 9889 (26 Jan. 1861); 9896 (2 Feb. 1861).

2 CE5/67 (25 Jan. 1861).

3 CE3/29, 9896 (2 Feb. 1861).

4 One need not, however, be as paranoid as Madden in reading hidden meanings into the appointments, but his diary entry for 23 Jan. 1861 is worth quoting as a typical example of the jungle rumours of the kind that still sweep the Museum: 'Dr Gray informed me that the Dept. of Antiquities was to be divided and Messrs Birch, Newton and Vaux severally appointed heads. Newton's return is a great job, partly arranged by the interest of his future wife's mother, who was a natural daughter of Lord Eglington, with this additional little job, that the post of Consul, vacated by Newton at Rome, is to be filled by Mr Severn, father of the young lady Mr N. is going to marry!' Cook, B.F. (1997), 14, seems to confirm that there was some truth in the latter statement.

5 Even before Hawkins wrote his confidential letter about his intending retirement, Panizzi was clearly discussing the matter with Newton. Writing from Rome on 10 June 1860, Newton agreed that, 'Nothing would be more satisfactory to me than to form part of the new management of the Department of Antiquities as you propose'. BL Add. MS 36,720, f.485. A fortnight later he began discreetly to lobby Trustees.

6 For Oldfield's work see Jenkins (1992), 160–2, 202–3, with references there cited.

7 BL Add. MS 36,717, ff.590, 603.

8 Miller (1967), 271.

9 CE/Miscellaneous Papers, Box S.

10 Oldfield was probably fairly well off and could afford to resign; his father was prosperous and had lived near the Ruskins in Camden Hill, London. (Oldfield was a friend and contemporary of Ruskin and in 1844 had with him designed a window for St Giles, Camberwell; Cook and Wedderburn (1904), pl.22.) Oldfield sadly disappears from view, although he appears occasionally as an author in the archaeological journals of the late nineteenth century. He served as secretary to Layard, when the latter was First Commissioner of Works in 1868–9 (at which period he was involved in correspondence about the proposed new building for the natural history collections). In 1872 he married the Hon. Harriet Rivers, co-heir of the sixth Lord Rivers, who was related to two of the most influential people in British archaeology – General Pitt Rivers and Sir John Lubbock.

11 Burton (1999), 99–100.

12 BL Add. MS 38,988, f.145-50 (25 May 1862).

13 CE7/3, 1232–1263 (3 Dec. 1861) (note that this minute was printed and inserted in the cited volume on 21 Jan. 1862). A special committee was appointed to deal with the matter at an unusually well-attended meeting of the full board of Trustees, CE1/8, 2,270 (3 Dec. 1861). The decision to move to South Kensington was never formally reported to the Trustees, who in a series of minutes accepted it as a *fait accompli*. Waterhouse, the architect ultimately appointed by the Trustees, had in 1869 even favoured a 'magnificent' building on the Embankment between Waterloo Bridge and Charing Cross. For some personal correspondence with Layard about the new building see BL Add. MS 38,996, vol. lxvi, f.13 and *passim*.

14 See Caygill (1997), 68–70 for details and references. Franks told Birch only on 10 March, and, unusually, Birch wrote a memorandum about the conversation; BM: ENA Correspondence, new ser.5, 2379 (10 March 1866).

15 CE5/77, 9 March 1866.

16 CE3/31, 10,944–6 (10 March 1866), 10,968 (14 April 1866).

17 For Reid see *Dictionary of national biography, s.n.*

18 CE3/31, 11,038–9 (14 July 1866); 11,056–7 (4 Aug. 1866).

19 CE3/31, 10,821–2 (24 June 1865); 10,833 (8 July 1865). He was granted a huge pension of £1,400 (his salary had been £1,200, together with a rent-free residence). Much of the detail of Panizzi's resignation and the appointment of his successor is recorded with references in Miller (1967), 278–84.

20 BL Add. MS 36,723, f.485. Cole thought that Panizzi would have liked him to direct both the British Museum and the South Kensington Museum; Burton (1999), 99.

21 CE3/31, 11,040 (14 July 1866). Jones's appointment as Principal Librarian, signed by the Queen, is in the BM Central Archives. He paid stamp duty of £75.

22 Cf., for example, Richard Garnett in *Dictionary of national biography, s.n.*

23 Garnett (1899), 319.

24 The complete documentation of this story, unless otherwise indicated, is bound together in the BM Central Archives as *Negotiations with reference to the South Kensington and Bethnal Green Museums to the Trustees of the British Museum*. Many of the original drafts are at CE/Miscellaneous Papers, Bay 6/E/4.

25 The South Kensington side of the story is colourfully told in Burton (1999), 95–9.

26 These were: in the Department of Oriental, British and Mediaeval Antiquities and Ethnography, Hawkins, Franks and W.H. Coxe; in Greek and Roman, Newton and J.G. Grenfell; in Coins and Medals, Vaux, R.S. Poole, J.G. Pfister and Fred. W.

27   Madden (the son of Sir Frederic); while in the Department of Prints and Drawings, the staff consisted of the keeper, carpenter, and a 'transcriber', George William Reid.

27   Harris (1998), 271. The figures in this paragraph are extracted from this section of Harris's book.

28   CE3/15, 4205–7 (12 March 1836); 4231–2 (16 April 1836).

29   CE5/25, 6692–3 (11 Jan. 1840). See also CE4/21 (19 Dec. 1839); CE3/18, 5313 (15 Feb. 1840).

30   As late as the 1950s the 'heavy gang' often worked at Covent Garden in the evening and regaled the rest of the staff with stories of the ballerinas.

31   Its original printed rules are preserved at CE115/3, 327. A later version of the rules and a broken run of the annual reports of the Society between 1845 and 1870 are in the Madden scrapbook: British Library, Dept. of Printed Books, C.55.i.1 ('General History'), ff.84v et passim.

32   CE3/29, 10,058 (14 Dec. 1861).

33   A detailed account of the negotiations concerning pay and pensions, with references, is in Harris (1998), 291–5. See also CE/Bay 6/C/12.

34   CE3/37, 14111 (12 Jan. 1878). Keepers after 1878 received salaries on the scale £650–£750; assistant keepers, £500–£600. Assistants were now placed in two classes: the first class were paid £250–£450; those of the second class, £120–£240. These scales were below the equivalent grades in the civil service, but above those paid in the South Kensington Museum, which did not achieve parity with the British Museum until the twentieth century, Burton (1999), 170.

35   For Gladstone's (almost over-enthusiastic) commitment to the reforms see Shannon (1982), 278–83, and *passim*.

36   *Copies of the correspondence subsequent to 1st October 1864, between the Civil Service Commissioners and the Principal Librarian of the British Museum, respecting the examination of candidates for situations in that department* (493; 512), Parliamentary Papers, House of Commons, 1866, xxxix, 241.

37   He was paid £100 p.a. and does not appear on the staff lists as the cuneiform inscription publications were funded separately, CE3/32, 11,161 (9 Feb. 1867). He was established as a senior assistant, in the lower section, on 21 March 1870, CE3/33, 11,833 (26 March 1870).

38   Such rights are revealed only in the annual budgets set by the Finance Committee and from the discussion of individual cases in the General Committee minutes. CE7/3, 1349 (14 Dec. 1864), provides the first mention of provision of a retirement allowance for an attendant.

39   CE3/34, 12,268 (11 Nov. 1871).

40   BL Add. MS 36,717, ff.612–20 (9 Nov. 1856).

41   Newton (1862–3).

42   Newton (1865) and Newton (1880).

43   Cf. Cook, B.F. (1997), 17.

44   Most importantly in a printed memorandum concerning the display of the Parthenon sculptures, dated 1 March 1861. A copy is in CE/Correspondence on the display of the Parthenon sculptures, 1928–38.

45   Smith and Porcher (1864). Smith and Porcher were paid £200 each by a grateful board of Trustees, CE3/29, 10,061 (14 Dec. 1861).

46   Wood (1877).

47   CE3/29, 9982 (8 June 1861); CE3/33, 11824 (12 March 1872).

48   CE30/8, 213 (12 Feb. 1863).

49   Shelton (1981).

50   Ward (1997), 282. These objects had been catalogued by Reinaud (1828).

51   Walters (1926), no. 3577.

52   CE97/Newton to George Grote (the historian), 5 Dec. 1866.

53   CE5/78, 59 (Oct. 1866); CE3/31, 11,087 (13 Oct. 1866); 11,115 (8 Dec. 1866). A copy of the contract note is at CE5/78 (6 Dec. 1866).

54   CE3/30, 10,628–9 (9 Jan. 1864).

55   Haseloff (1990), 20 and pl.18.

56   CE5/76 (6 July 1865).

57   Michaelis (1908), 101–2, tells the story.

58   For details see Cook, B.F. (1997), 16.

59   Jones (1990), no.1.

60   Shannon (1982), 350–1. A more charitable view will be found in Jones (1982), 110–25.

61   Gladstone was present at a lecture Schliemann gave to the Society of Antiquaries on 25 June 1875 and made a long speech afterwards. Max Müller of Oxford was scandalized by Gladstone's twisting of the evidence to support his own theories, 'So great a man, so imperfect a scholar'; quoted Shannon (1999), 158. A member of the Museum staff, Sidney Colvin, later said of Gladstone, 'no Homeric critic has ever shown, along with so minute and systematically tabulated a knowledge of the text, such ingenious perversity as he in comment and interpretation', Colvin (1921), 193.

62   Quoted by Vaio (1990), 416.

63   For the Newton/Schliemann correspondence see Fitton (1991). For Schliemann and Gladstone see Vaio (1990).

64   British Library, Gladstone Papers, 44440, 176 (9 Oct. 1873); Burton (1999), 124.

65   It is interesting, for example, that Alain Schnapp, a leading specialist in Greek archaeology, should end his fascinating history of archaeology, *The discovery of the past*, in the middle years of the nineteenth century with an admiring bow towards the European prehistorians of that period with the words, 'From then on the great archaeological debate was no longer the opposition of a philological model [that of the classical archaeologist] to one of natural history, but a consideration of the application, extension and consequences of the natural history model...', implying the end of the heroic days of classical archaeology. Schnapp (1996), 324.

66   Newton in his early years was interested in the generality of European archaeology. In a lecture to the Archaeological Institute in 1850 (reprinted Newton (1880), 1–38), he not only refers his audience to the museum in Copenhagen and to Worsaae's work, but ranges wide in his discussion of what evidence can be drawn from archaeology in such fields as technology, the marriage of medieval literature with medieval art, and (referring to the upcoming 1851 Exhibition) he writes, 'the object which Archæology would achieve is not less than the Exhibition of the Industry of all nations for all time'.

67   Kenyon (1993).

68   Quoted from Daniel (1976), 9, who in this, his inaugural lecture to the Disney chair, gives an outline of its history.

69   Babington (1865), 10.

70   It is interesting that the Disney chair (and incidentally the Slade chair) seem so unimportant in the history of Cambridge that they are not mentioned in the volume of the latest standard history of the university which deals with the period, Searby (1997).

71   Rupke (1994), 220–58.

72   Evans (1943), 102. Evans's lecture was published in *Archaeologia*, Evans (1860).

73   But see Cook, J. (1997), 119.

74   BM: ANE Correspondence, new ser. 2, BO-BY, 433 (11 Oct. 1860) – 436 (1 Aug. 1861).

75   Chadwick (1970), 77.

76   An excellent summary of the early history of biblical archaeology is Moorey (1991), 1–24. The most important objects in the Museum's collection illustrating this subject are published in Mitchell (1992).

77 Birch (1872), 12.
78 Quoted Moorey (1991), 4.
79 Smith (1873).
80 This was first commented upon approvingly by de Mortillet (1867), 328.
81 For Pitt Rivers see Thompson (1977) and Bowden (1991).
82 Evans (1943), 122; Barth and Hodson (1976).
83 The others were Vogt of Germany, Sven Nilsson of Sweden and the American diplomat/newspaper proprietor/archaeologist Ephraim George Squier. Squier was one of the two or three pioneers of early American archaeology, having himself excavated in the Mississippi valley and in Nicaragua. Franks never visited America, but this contact with Squier was probably important. Franks had a copy of Squier's book on central America (it is now in the Society of Antiquaries of London), Squier (1855), and presumably had quite a bit to do with him in relation to the Congress.
84 Some of Franks's travels have been documented by Caygill (1997), 80–9.
85 Fabricius (1854).
86 Briggs (1988), 141–4. For an example of Green's interest in artefacts see Burrow (1981), 202.
87 The applied arts were catalogued by Waring (1858). Modern appraisals of the exhibition are in Finke (1985) and (for the Old Masters) Haskell (2000), 82–97.
88 Burton (1999), 34–6.
89 The Burlington Fine Art Club was finally wound up in 1951. For these clubs see Coppel (1996), 162–4, and the references there cited.
90 King (1997), 136.
91 Barley (1999), 11–12.
92 Snow (1858). A notebook including drawings by Franks and another hand of this material is at BM Ethno. Franks notebooks, ss.26.
93 CE4/84 (7 Nov. 1865).
94 Franks's visit is referred to, without sources, in a booklet accompanying a British Museum exhibition, Henry Christy, a pioneer of anthropology in 1965. The excavations were written up at the request of the trustees of Christy's estate by the geologist T.R. Jones and published in 1875 – Lartet and Christy (1875). The collection of palaeolithic art has recently been catalogued by Sieveking (1987).
95 For this collection see Jensen (1992), 350–4; Gilberg (1999); Nyt fra Nationalmuseet, Dec.–Feb. 1999/2000. The Rijksmuseum voor Volkenkunde in Leiden sometimes claims that it is an earlier foundation than its Copenhagen equivalent. Based on the royal collection of Chinese rarities founded by William I in 1821, it became public as the Ethnografisch Museum in 1838.
96 Steinhauer (1862).
97 'In the spring of 1856, I met with Mr Christy accidentally in an omnibus in Havana. He had been in Cuba leading an adventurous life, visiting sugar-plantations, copper-mines, and coffee-estates, descending into caves, and botanizing in tropical jungles, cruising for a fortnight in an open boat among the coral reefs, hunting turtles and manatis, and visiting all sorts of people from whom information was to be had, from foreign consuls and Lazarist missionaries down to retired slave-dealers and assassins', Tylor (1861), 1. The Museum's masks of Xipe Totec, sometimes considered to be fakes, are now on balance accepted as genuine Aztec antiquities, Jones (1990), 298–9. The mask illustrated is 1956. Am.x.6.
98 CE4/84 (7 Nov. 1865), document C, p. 4. Caygill (1985), 30–5.
99 Grey, 1854,12–29,1–142; for details of Grey's acquisition of the material see Starzecka (1998), 152; Fiji, 1857,3–18,1–24; Haslar, 1853,2–20,1–293.

100 CE7/3, 1400–1 (18 Nov. 1865).
101 CE4/85 (10 Jan. 1866).
102 King (1997), 140.
103 King (1997), 141–2. This was the precursor of the Notes and queries booklets issued to travellers and others by the Anthropological Institute until well on in the twentieth century.
104 BM: MME Out letters, 3 (26 April 1890), 396; Franks to Sir C. Euan Smith. A few days earlier Read had written to C.R. Bishop in Honolulu offering to exchange a feather cloak and other objects 'among our private duplicates' for objects of a type not in the Museum's collection, as he was trying to negotiate the purchase of a collection formed by a member of Cook's party. Ibid. (21 March 1890).
105 Frobenius (1898), ix, quoted by Plankensteiner (1998), 61.
106 It went into seven editions, the last one appearing in 1913, and was, significantly, published in Danish in 1874. Much of what follows in the next two paragraphs depends on more detailed discussion by Mack (1997), 41–8.
107 Spencer (1851).
108 CE4/84 (7 Nov. 1865), Document C.
109 Childe (1951), ch.1, gives a good, if Marxist, survey of this problem.
110 It is interesting in this context that a department of prehistory was erected under A. Voss in the Berlin ethnographical museum in 1874.
111 Copies of letter from General Pitt Rivers in which he offers to present his collection to the nation, of the report of the committee appointed by the government declining to accept the collection. Sessional papers, House of Commons, lxxiii, 1881. For the Pitt Rivers Museum see Petch (1998) and Chapman (2000).
112 CE29/1 (20 July 1880); (4 Sept. 1880); (9 Oct. 1880).
113 New dictionary of national biography, s.n.
114 Trigger (1989) in his standard History of archaeological thought does not even mention him. But he only mentions the British Museum once – and then critically.
115 The standard history of archaeology, Daniel (1950), for example, refers to him only four times; the only major mention implies that Franks was reluctant to accept the Three-Age system (p.82) – wrongly (see p.125). Casson (1940), writing from the viewpoint of an Oxford classical archaeologist trained in anthropology concerning the origins of the twin studies of archaeology and anthropology, does not mention him once.
116 Caygill and Cherry (1997).
117 Wilson (1997).
118 Caygill and Cherry (1997), 334–46.
119 Nilsson (1866).
120 Evans (1872). Cook, J. (1997), 124, points out that Evans apparently used some of Franks's drawings in this book as in his Ancient bronze implements – Evans (1881).
121 De Navarro (1936), 306.
122 Daniel (1950), 116.
123 Franks (1868).
124 He was the only Englishman, for example, to sit on a large committee set up by the International Congress of Archaeology and Anthropology in 1872 to investigate the controversy about the Abbé Bourgeois's chipped flints from Thenay, Loir-et-Cher. Like the majority of the committee he was wrong! Daniel (1950), 98–9.
125 For example, Franks was only the fourth Englishman (and first English archaeologist) out of the first sixty-two foreign members to be elected to the Swedish Academy of Letters (founded in 1753). He was elected in 1876, Evans in 1883. Hildebrand et al. (1992), 113.
126 MacEnery's work and ideas were being independently

reflected elsewhere in Europe in the 1820s and 30s, see de Laet (1981), 116–17.

127 Cook, J. (1997), 117–18.
128 Evans gives a lively account of a visit in March 1864 to de Lastic, 'rather a wideawake bird', and his English wife; Evans (1943), 120–1.
129 Cook, J. (1997), 119, records the circumstances of the acquisition. See also Owen (1869).
130 Cook, J. (1997), 119–20, 123–4.
131 A further tranche of material was purchased for the Museum in 1909 by the American collector J. Pierpont Morgan. Kinnes and Longworth (1985).
132 Longworth (1991).
133 CE3/32, 11,582–3 (9 Jan. 1869); CE3/33, 11,714–5 (24 July 1869). For the Klemm collection see Orlińska (2002).
134 Keller (1866).
135 E.g. 1880, 8–2, 115–30.
136 Material from the earliest excavations at Hallstatt was given in 1863 by J.G. Ramsauer, who had excavated there for the Vienna Museum from 1846 (1863,9–22,1–4 and 1863,9–30,1–4). Objects from the 1866 excavations drifted in over the years, given by Franks, Colonel Schwab and others, culminating in the material excavated by Lubbock and Evans between 1867 and 1916. A small collection from La Tène was built up by gifts from Franks in the 1880s and Professor E. Desor and Colonel Schwab in 1867 (1867,7–1, 1; 1867,7–2,1–2 and 1880,12–14,2–10).
137 The Iron Age content of the Morel collection has been catalogued by Stead and Rigby (1999) – the Somme-Bionne grave is at pp.160–2. In 1904 certain items were transferred to the Department of Greek and Roman Antiquities.
138 Particularly the fourth-century mosaic pavements excavated at Woodchester and Withington, Glos., by Samuel Lysons – 1808,2–27,1 and 1812,6–13,1, and the splendid second-century bronze head of Hadrian from the River Thames – 1848,11–3,1.
139 CE3/22, 6807 (8 Nov. 1845). The Colchester collection was added to by the acquisition in 1870 of the Polle-fexen collection, 1870,4–2,1–821. The collection was purchased from a number of sources: CE3/33, 11,767 (11 Dec. 1869); 11,826–7 (12 March 1870). 1870,4–2,1–821.
140 One of the most important pieces which probably comes from the Roman wall is the gilded copper figure of Hercules, said to be from near Birdoswald, given by Franks, 1895,4–8,1. The Hod Hill material was acquired in two tranches – 1892,3–1–1797 and 1893,6–1,1–472 – Brailsford (1962). CE4/191 (10 Feb. 1892), (11 May 1892), (6 July 1892); CE3/46, 19,012 (9 July 1892).
141 CE3/31, 11,148 (12 Jan. 1867); Webster and Backhouse (1991), no 70.
142 Collingwood (1927), 126 and fig.137.
143 Wilson (1964), 179–91.
144 The story is told by Wilson (1964), 118–19.
145 From Rooves More Fort, Aglish, Co. Cork (1866,5–11,1–3); Macalister (1945), nos. 124–6.
146 Allen and Anderson (1903), ii, fig. 127. Another major piece of Pictish sculpture, the Hilton of Cadboll slab, came to the Museum in 1921, but after protest was returned to Scotland and is now in the National Museums of Scotland, Close-Brooks and Stevenson (1982), 32.
147 Stevenson (1981), 180–1.
148 Evans (1943), 124–8, provides an amusing and illuminating account of her father's activities there.
149 Mac Dermott (1955); Henry (1970), pl.18.
150 CE7/3, 1402 (18 Nov. 1865). Witt, a medical doctor, had trained at Leiden. He practised in Bedford before going to Sydney, where he made his fortune, returning to London in 1849; Gaimster (2000).
151 In the accounts presented to Parliament, 1 May 1867,

26, they are described as illustrating 'the superstitions connected with the evil eye and nature worship' – equivocation on a grand scale!
152 CE3/31, 10,918 (13 Jan. 1866). Permission was, for example, given to display objects from the collection 'illustrative of the Roman bath', CE3/32, 11,176 (23 Feb. 1867).
153 For the Printed Book collection see Cross (1991).
154 BM: MME Out letters 3, 439 (24 Aug. 1893).
155 The best account of Slade is Griffiths (1996), 113–22, who has discussed his collecting in depth. I have used this work extensively here. For glass collecting see Tait (n.d.) and for Franks's English glass see Dawson (1999). See also New dictionary of national biography.
156 Franks (1871), 167–83, lists all the items Slade gave or bequeathed to the Museum (as well as two portraits presented to the National Portrait Gallery). The Tiberius sword is G&R 1866,8–6,1; Walters (1899), no.867.
157 CE4/94 (22 April 1868).
158 CE5/81 (22 April 1868; 20 May 1868). Papers about the administration of the codicil in relation to the printed books, manuscripts, prints and drawings are at CE4/95 (23 July 1868); CE4/98, 379–82 (6 April 1869).
159 Franks (1869); a second edition with notes and appendices has references.
160 BM: MME Out letters, 12 Nov. 1886, 421. Franks wished it to be labelled 'the Nesbitt Collection'.
161 CE4/95 (23 July 1868).
162 An exhibition of some of the prints was mounted almost immediately; Reid (1869).
163 Waagen (1857), 217–19.
164 Franks (1849) and (1858), see also the section 'Vitreous art' in Waring (1858).
165 CE5/81 (11 March 1868); Slade's letter is dated 10 March.
166 Tait (n.d.), 76; Dawson (1999).
167 Dawson (1997), 201, has pointed to the paucity of the pre-Slade collection.
168 Tait (n.d.), 77.
169 BM: MME 1852,6–30,1.
170 The Demmin reference is quoted by Dawson (1997), 203. In discussing the acquisition of European ceramics I am deeply indebted to Dawson (1997), from which most of the information in this section is culled. For the Godman collection see Godman (1901) and Ward (1997), 278–9. Godman, whose family money was derived from South African gold mining, later became a Trustee of the Museum and was a specialist in tropical birds. There is a portrait memorial plaque dedicated to him in the Natural History Museum, Thackray (1995), pl.34.
171 Gaimster (1997).
172 Evans (1943), 103; Demmin (1867), 924. For the documented continental porcelain see Dawson (1985) and for the French porcelain see Dawson (1994). Just before his death Franks wrote a catalogue of his continental collection and put them on display at the Bethnal Green branch of the South Kensington Museum; Franks (1896). There is a curious note concerning his collection in Franks's manuscript apologia: 'I should have been glad to place it to the British Museum, but I do not think there is room for it there. I offered it on loan to the South Kensington Museum, but it was not accepted. I should be sorry to see it broken up, and I might present it to the South Kensington Museum. I doubt whether that institution would very much care for it as I have heard there disparaging remarks on the similar collection of English porcelain, presented to the South Kensington Museum by Lady Charlotte Schreiber by my advice.' Caygill and Cherry (1997), 323.
173 Hobson (1905), I.1 and I.2. Found during sewer work.
174 Dawson (1984).
175 It is unclear when Franks passed his English collec-

176 Hobson (1903) and (1905).

177 Guest and John (1989), 227.

178 Ward (1997), 274–9. Interestingly, Franks had obtained a piece of Turkish pottery which had been displayed at the Great Exhibition of 1851, perhaps directly in view of his contacts with Cole; Franks (1896), no. 512.

179 Ward (1997), 276.

180 BM: OA 1878 12–30,1–970.

181 Rogers (1984).

182 Harrison-Hall (1997) has written on this subject and the information in this section relies heavily on her work.

183 CE3/32, 11,177 (23 Feb. 1867).

184 Franks (1876); 655 pieces were shown.

185 CE4/172 (4 Oct. 1878). Harrison-Hall (1997) gives further documentary references.

186 Harrison-Hall (1997), 221. In offering his collection to the Museum – CE4/172 (4 Oct. 1878), he adds 'that from the very comprehensive nature of the collection, I do not anticipate that it will at any time be necessary to make any considerable outlay to complete the series'.

187 Caygill and Cherry (1897), 323.

188 For Franks's Japanese interest see Smith (1997), on which I rely heavily.

189 CE3/40, 15,665–6 (25 June 1881); 15,782 (12 Nov. 1881); 15,807 (10 Dec. 1881). The Trustees had approached the Treasury for a grant, but this was refused. Payment was consequently made in three annual instalments from the Museum's grant-in-aid. (The collection also included some Chinese classical paintings.)

190 Franks (1869a).

191 CE30/7, 330 (18 July 1857).

192 Smith (1997), 267–8.

193 The Henderson collection is registered at 1878,12–30,1–970. The Meyrick collection, which is the residue of a collection withdrawn from display at the South Kensington Museum and sold by Pratt of Bond Street about 1876, included a considerable amount of medieval material and much else besides. Some of the material came from the Douce collection, about which Meyrick wrote a series of articles in *The gentleman's magazine*, n.s. v–vi, 1836, 245 *et passim*. See departmental register, 1878,11–1,381–580, and Franks's memorandum to the Trustees, CE4/172 (9 Oct. 1878).

194 Portal (2000), 15–16.

195 Quoted by Jenkins (1992), 211, from CE3/15 (14 July 1836). In 1817 the Trustees had turned down the offer of a collection of Indian sculpture and inscriptions formed by Colonel Franklin, CE1/5, 1161 (22 May 1817).

196 Willis (1997) has charted the growth of the Indian collection until the death of Franks. Much of what follows is based on his chapter, and the references quoted there.

197 For the India Museum see Desmond (1982).

198 OA 1872,7–1,1–106. The catalogue of the abortive sale was published by Norton, Trist, Watney and Co, 20 June 1872, and consisted of 104 lots. A manuscript note by H.J. Braunholtz in the Museum's copy of the sale catalogue (written in the 1920s) quotes a doubtful statement that Franks 'was the only bidder at this sale. Auctioneer objected to sell, but Franks insisted. Eventually the daughters of J. Bridge gave them to the Museum. *sic* Longworth James.' A Trustee's minute CE3/34, 12,502–3 (13 July 1872) explicitly thanks Bridge's three daughters and orders that the sculpture be labelled as from the 'Bridge Collection'. For this confusing episode see Willis (1997), 253–5.

199 Franks records that at one stage of the discussions the India Museum was offered as a whole to the British Museum; Caygill and Cherry (1997), 322.

200 The South Kensington Museum received most of the decorative arts, textiles, metal and woodwork, which now form the bulk of their Indian collections.

201 Knox (1992).

202 Zwalf (1996).

203 It is not impossible that Rassam had suggested the Museum's participation in the expedition, although he makes no mention of it in the book he wrote about his mission.

204 CE3/32, 11, 318–20 (16 Oct. 1867).

205 CE3/32, 11,336–7 (9 Nov. 1867); 11,342 (23 Nov. 1867); 11,361 (7 Dec. 1867); 11,369–70 (14 Dec. 1867).

206 CE3/32, 11,526 (25 July 1868); 11,550 (14 Nov. 1868). In 1870 Holmes became Librarian at Windsor Castle and was knighted in 1905. See *Dictionary of national biography*, *s.n.*

207 They were registered in the ethnographic register, 1868,10–1,1–28, and included a number of strictly ethnographic items.

208 CE4/94 (16 April 1868), (28 April 1868). He was, however, allowed to retain a gold-covered shield, for which he paid £25.

209 CE5/82 (1 July 1868); CE3/32, 11,502 (4 July 1868).

210 *Copy of all correspondence... between the British Museum, the Treasury, the War Office and Colonel Millward R.A.... relative to the Purchase of the Abyssinian Abanas Crown and a Gold Chalice captured at Magdala.* Sessional papers, House of Commons, xxxix (1871).

211 Pollen (1878), 372–4.

212 CE3/34, 12,564–5 (14 Dec. 1872). George V in 1924 returned to the Emperor Haile Selassie a crown said to have belonged to Téwodros, which had been deposited by the Treasury in the Victoria and Albert Museum. Queen Elizabeth II returned Téwodros's cap and silver seal to Haile Selassie during her State Visit in 1962. The British Museum manuscripts were catalogued by Wright (1877) and were also discussed in detail by Sylvia Pankhurst (Pankhurst, 1955) in her cultural history of the country. Her son continues to lead a moderately toned campaign to return some of the objects to Ethiopia; see, for example, Pankhurst (1986).

213 For the full story see *The art newspaper*, no. 80, April 1998.

214. Willis (1997), 259.

215 Curtis (1997) is the most recent account of the treasure. See also Dalton (1905) and Zeimal (1979), the latter being a book written for the exhibition of the treasure in the State Hermitage Museum in Leningrad.

216 Curtis discusses the complicated problems of the find-place in some detail, and provides a map; Curtis (1997), 230 and 235–8.

217 The treasure, which Franks considered as part of his collection of drinking vessels, was loaned for display to the Museum in 1893; CE3/46, 19,240 (10 June 1893).

218 BM: MME Gold Cup [MSS] Documents. For the cup see Dalton (1924); bibliography in Stratford (1993), 319–25.

219 For Franks's purchase and his subsequent negotiations see Cherry (1997), 196–7.

220 CE4/191 (6 April 1892); CE3/46, 18,973 (14 May 1892). The cup was registered at 1892,5–1,1. The principal donors at £500 were the Duke of Northumberland, Lord Crawford, Lord Iveagh (who originally gave the sum anonymously), Lord Savile, C. Drury Fortnum, Franks, The Goldsmiths' Company and the Wertheimer heirs. Lord Derby, J.E. Taylor, Charles E. Keyser, Sir Henry Peek, William Minet, Capt. John Peel and a number of City Companies gave smaller sums.

221 Van Tilburg (1992).
222 Anderson (1997), 293.
223 A rather unreliable catalogue of the European portion of the collection is Ward (1981).
224 Burton (1999), 120.
225 Anderson (1997), 291.
226 Tait (1968), 24–6 and pls 13–17.
227 Tait (1983), 35–7 and pls 40–4.
228 For a summary account of his work see Reade (1993).
229 CE4/172 (8 Oct. 1878): Birch reports the purchase of Assyrian material by Rassam, which included the plates from the Balawat gates and more than 1,000 fragments of tablets from Kuyunjik.
230 Leichty (1986), xxv.
231 For a reasonably objective summary of Budge's activities at this time, see Lloyd (1980), 165–72. See also Budge's own account, Budge (1920), i, 123ff. The purchase of small objects (antikas) was a major activity by travellers in all parts of the Turkish empire until the Great War. David Hogarth, later Keeper of the Ashmolean Museum, gives a revealing account of typical deals; Hogarth (1896), 21–6. There was money to be made by the knowledgeable purchaser, but many treated it like T.E. Lawrence, 'to buy antikas is a sport, not commerce'; quoted Wilson (1989), 101 (Lawrence, in fact, was collecting seriously for the Ashmolean as well as the British Museum).
232 For a lively account of Chester's dealings in Egypt and elsewhere, see Budge (1920), i, 84–5n.
233 Moran (1992).
234 CE3/38, 14,454–5 (12 Oct. 1878). For Bond see Dictionary of national biography, s.n.
235 Newton had been appointed CB in 1875 and KCB in 1877. Newton's refusal appears not to be documented. Franks's refusal is recorded by Read in his entry on Franks in the Dictionary of national biography and in a passing reference in a letter to a friend, see Caygill (1997), 98.
236 Prescott (1997), 196.
237 Prescott (197), 206–7.
238 For the National Portrait Gallery see CE3/38, 14,413–4 (12 Oct. 1878). The Museum retained the foreign portraits and those of people connected with the Museum and its collections. Strangely, the Museum acquired a remarkable Gilbert Stuart portrait of a native American – Thayondaneagea, a Mohawk – between 1879 and 1936, Thompson (1969), but otherwise has only collected paintings to do with the history of the Museum, as for example John Wood's portrait of Sir Charles Fellows purchased in 1988. For the National Gallery proposal, see CE3/41, 16,507 (13 Oct. 1883). The Museum also collects, rather haphazardly, portrait sculpture, see Dawson (1999a).
239 CE3/42, 16,958 (14 Feb. 1885).
240 Bond was knighted shortly before his death in 1898.
241 Quoted by Prescott (1997), 210.
242 CE3/44, 17,987–8 (14 July 1888). In 1898 the title of his office was changed to Director and Principal Librarian.
243 Miller (1973), 259–60, recounts two of the more bizarre stories concerning his ruthless behaviour towards members of staff. For Thompson see Dictionary of national biography and Kenyon (1929), which – although he was cold – does show a human side of the man. Esdaile (1951), 90, who joined the Museum in 1903, gave a typical judgement, 'a terrifying person, with his stature, eagle face, white beard and piercing blue eyes, [he] had something of the schoolboy in him and could unbend'.
244 Prescott (1997), 196–7.
245 Thompson (1912).
246 Vaux later became Secretary of the Royal Society of Literature and of the Royal Asiatic Society, the latter presumably because of his interest in Assyriology

about which he wrote a number of books; New dictionary of national biography, s.n.
247 Edwards (1837); Hawkins (1852).
248 Carson (1974), 39–41.
249 Walker (1953).
250 Hill (1988), 39.
251 Drower (1982), 14.
252 New dictionary of national biography, s.n. Two of his nephews also worked in the Museum; Reginald Lane Poole, being briefly employed in the Department of Manuscripts in 1880–1, became a major and influential Oxford historian. Stanley Edward Lane Poole, like his uncle, was a numismatist and an Egyptologist, being an assistant in the Department of Coins and Medals between 1877 and 1892; he resigned to write and to excavate in Egypt. In 1896 he was appointed Professor of Arabic at Trinity College Dublin. Poole was clearly not on good terms with Newton – EES archive: letter Poole to Amelia Edwards (12 Feb. 1885).
253 Dictionary of national biography, s.n.
254 Budge (1920), i, 20–1.
255 Pinches left in 1900 to become a lecturer in Assyrian at University College London.
256 For Renouf see The dictionary of national biography, s.n. It is to be remembered that Gladstone was Budge's patron (he had paid for him to go to Cambridge – Budge was an orphan) and was a powerful Trustee at the time, see Shannon (1999), 226. Budge was backed in his application not only by Gladstone but by a considerable body of scholars – Peile, Lowe, Sayce, Vaux and W. Wright, and by two other Trustees, Rawlinson and W.H. Smith, in one of whose shops Budge was then working as a full-time assistant. BM Central Archives; staff applications and testimonials.
257 James (1981), 23.
258 Budge (1920), ii, 300–18. A letter of apology, written before the case by Budge to Layard (who was the whistle-blower) is in the Layard papers, BL Add. MS 52,292, f.130. The action was funded by the Trustees; the Museum's side of the story, together with press clippings and depositions, is bound up at CE/43 Rassam v. Budge 1893.
259 Dictionary of national biography, s.n.
260 Walters (1926), xi–xii.
261 Tatton-Brown (1987).
262 CE3/38, 14,845 (11 Oct. 1879). A portion of the collection had been on view at the South Kensington Museum in 1879; Burton (1999), 124.
263 CE3/35, 13,246–7 (24 April 1875); CE3/35, 13,257–8 (8 May 1875); 13,277 (12 June 1875).
264 CE3/36, 13,797–8 (24 Feb. 1877); CE3/37, 13,835–6 (24 March 1877); 14,076 (24 Nov. 1877).
265 Dictionary of national biography, s.n. Colvin was a close friend of R.L.B. Stevenson, whose letters he edited, and of Joseph Conrad. He and his second wife kept a literary salon in London and this was so important in their lives that the Museum is hardly named in the book about their circle written by E.V. Lucas (1928). In his own memoirs he devoted only a single chapter to the Museum, Colvin (1921).
266 Fagan (1880).
267 Dodgson was appointed in April 1893, Binyon in September 1893 (initially in the library) and Hind in October 1903 – all three became keepers.
268 CE3/47, 19,576–7 (14 July 1895).
269 The Trustees were keen to acquire the collection; CE3/47, 19,721–2 (15 June 1895). Coppel (1996) and Royalton-Kisch et al. (1996). Colvin wrote a catalogue for an exhibition of this collection with comparative pieces from the Museum's collection, as part of his strategy to publicize its importance in applying for the grant. It went into two editions; Colvin (1894). The Treasury approved the purchase; CE3/47, 19,741 (12 July 1895).

270 For Mitchell (and Malcolm's print collection) see Coppel (1996).

271 *Annual Return*, 1896, 41.

272 CE3/47, 19,745–6 (12 July 1895). O'Donoghue (1901).

273 Budge (1920), i, 21–2.

274 The antiquities departments had hitherto occupied 8,457 square metres.

275 CE3/41, 16,002 (10 June 1882). The best account of White and his bequest is by Bond in Franks (1888), 1–4. See also Caygill (1982).

276 So near was the building to the residence that Bond was forced to install stained glass in the bow-window of his drawing-room which was immediately over-looked by office windows in the new wing; Caygill and Date (1999), 54. Kenyon was the first Director to live in the present Director's Residence in the middle of the west wing.

277 CE3/42, 16,959 (14 Feb. 1885).

278 CE3/42, 16,936–8 (17 Jan. 1885). The Treasury threat-ened to reduce the purchase grant to make good the overspend.

279 *Annual Return* 1915, 83.

280 For an outline description of the reorganization of the classical sculpture see Jenkins (1992), 212–21, and Caygill and Date (1999), 53–5.

281 The negotiations with the various firms and govern-ment departments have been carefully sorted out by Harris (1998), 313–15. See also Caygill and Date (1999), 56. The Museum continued to generate its own electricity until 1931.

282 See Harris (1998), 316, for references.

283 Harris (1998), 381.

284 Esdaile (1951a).

285 Quoted by Miller (1973), 256.

286 Caygill (1997), 77.

287 Opening hours were: 10 a.m. – 4 p.m. from November to February; 10 a.m. – 5 p.m. March and April and September and October; 10 a.m. – 7 p.m. mid-August and September; 10 a.m. – 8 p.m. Mondays and Saturdays from 1 May to mid-July.

288 *Accounts* 1898, 14.

289 *Forty-fourth report of the Department of Science and Art,* 1896.

290 *Annual Return* 1898, 48. The painting of labels and of registration numbers on objects was until well into the 1960s in the hands of the Steele family, who worked on piece rates.

291 The *Synopsis* had ceased publication in 1856 and was gradually replaced by a series of guides to individual galleries, priced between 2d and 6d. The general *Guide to the exhibition galleries of the British Museum, Bloomsbury* was first published in 1880 at 6d and went into a number of editions. The first special exhibition guide apparently concerned the Wycliffe exhibition in the King's Library, which was published in 1884 at 4d.

292 *Annual Return* 1902, 16–17.

293 A printed copy of the 1881 proposals and the keepers' replies was submitted to the Trustees, BM Central archives, Miscellaneous Papers K; CE3/40, 15,579–80 (30 April 1881). This was not the first time that there had been suggestions about formal lectures in the Museum. As early as 1841 J.S. Buckingham, encour-aged by Lord Abinger, wrote to Sir Robert Peel with proposals for a series of popular lectures, but this had come to nothing (BL Add. MS 40485, vol. cccv, ff.240–5), although many of the staff lectured outside the Museum informally to working men's clubs and mechanics' institutes.

294 CE3/45, 18,678 (9 May 1891). See below, p.208.

295 Peacock (1988), 59; Stewart (1959), 10; Beard (2000), 54–5.

296 CE3/42, 16,863 (11 Nov. 1884).

297 Silver (1962), 234–5.

298 CE3/47, 19,712 (17 June 1895).

299 Johnson (1988).

300 Harris (1998), 383–4.

301 CE3/42, 16,968 (14 Feb. 1885).

302 Salisbury to Professor Herbert MacLeod, 1885, quoted by Roberts (1999), 281.

303 Colvin (1921), 195. He made a similar remark to Budge, Budge (1920), i, 67.

304 CE3/49, 620–8 (11 June 1898).

305 CE3/48, 195–6 (13 Feb. 1897).

306 Quoted from Wilson (2001).

307 Ellis (1981).

308 Gunther (1967), 8.

309 Johnson (1989), 16.

310 Johnson (1989) and Johnson (1993).

311 Johnson (1993), 38.

312 Personal information from the late Dame Kathleen Kenyon, daughter of Sir Frederick Kenyon.

313 Johnson (1989), 208.

314 Hilton (1985), 49.

315 Colvin (1921), 209–23.

316 Askwith (1969), 55.

317 Worsaae (1938), 210 (8 May 1880). See also Caygill (1997), 94.

318 Wilson (1984), 7.

319 See Harris (1998), 376, and below, p.203.

320 When Lubbock first brought forward a bill for the protection of ancient monuments in 1876, he proposed that the British Museum should be respon-sible for executing the task. See Evans (1943), 156.

321 For Dilke as art historian see Askwith (1969), 196–203.

322 Wiell (1997), 219.

323 Lundbeck-Culot (1997).

324 Dalton (1898), 7.

325 The Charleston Museum, founded in 1773, claims to be America's first museum, see Borowsky (1963).

326 Caygill and Cherry (1997), 318–24.

327 Much of this material is published in catalogues either dedicated to, or including, his bequest: Franks (1896), Marshall (1911), Dalton (1905) and (1912), Read and Tonnochy (1928).

328 Howe (1903–4).

329 The Montague Guest collection was given on condi-tion that it be catalogued, see Tonnochy *et al.* (1930). For Lady Charlotte Schreiber see Guest and John (1989).

330 The collection was originally catalogued by Read (1902) and is now the subject of a major re-evaluation in a catalogue by Tait (1986–).

CHAPTER 6

1 This was Dr Lionel Barnett, a major figure in Indian scholarship. Basham (1950).

2 Vincent (1984), 486.

3 Quoted Lockhart (1949), 384.

4 CE1/10, 3249 (11 Jan. 1924). Esher had for some time been campaigning against Prime Ministerial nomina-tions. As early as 29 Nov. 1921 he was writing to Kenyon in a similar vein; CE/Sir F. Kenyon: unregis-tered correspondence concerning official Museum business, approx. 1910–28. Kenyon returned to the fray in his evidence before the Royal Commission on National Museums and Galleries a few years later, but got nowhere; *Royal Commission* [1928–30], *oral evidence, memoranda and appendices to the interim report,* 192, 52.

5 After 1932 candidates for curatorial posts no longer had to take a written examination (see below, p.215). The letters and papers of the Principal Trustees (CE15 and 18) survive to illustrate the incredible bureaucracy required to save their face.

6 CE3/48, 462 (8 Jan. 1898).

7 *Dictionary of national biography, s.n.* Bell (1952).

367

8 A letter to J. Pierpont Morgan, in the Pierpont Morgan Library, New York, archives expresses some of his disappointment.

9 Miller (1973), 292.

10 He was one of the historians of this curious institution, of which Maunde Thompson was a member; as, later, were two other Directors, Kendrick and the present author.

11 Vincent (1984), 498. On Hill's first meeting as Director, Crawford managed to persuade the Trustees that they could retain their minutes, subject to the proviso that they be returned to the Museum on their resignation or death. CE3/63, 4727 (10 Jan. 1931).

12 The Clerical Grade was retained only in the Director's Office; the rest of the grade were re-designated as Technical or Library Assistants, in two classes. Attendants were retained but were eligible for promotion to the Technical or Library Assistantships. Junior technical grades were labelled the 'Manipulative Class'. A little earlier the curatorial grades had been re-named – Assistant Keepers became Deputy Keepers and the old Assistants were classed by age as Assistant Keeper First Class and Assistant Keeper Second Class (D27368B–650JH – copy in CE/Director's Papers, Sir Frederic Kenyon).

13 Some of the detail in this section is taken from BM Central Archives, Staff Applications and Testimonials, which is ordered alphabetically. CE33 (1833–1933).

14 Smith (1965), 16.

15 Dictionary of national biography, s.n. For his career in the Victoria and Albert Museum see Burton (1999), 166–74.

16 Kenyon (1941).

17 Smith (1892–1904); (1910).

18 Smith (1916).

19 CE18/9 (25 March 1896).

20 Griffith was an extremely distinguished Egyptologist. His bequest of his magnificent library and his estate to the University of Oxford led to the foundation of the Griffith Institute of Egyptology.

21 The examination at this time was competitive and consisted of: writing from dictation, orthography, elementary mathematics, English composition, précis, geography, English history from the Norman Conquest to the eighteenth century, and at least three languages. Other subjects could also be examined. CE8/9 (18 Nov. 1895). In 1899 a more focused series of examinations was agreed to by Order in Council, the more elementary papers were abolished and new papers were introduced. For example, examinations were to be set in a branch of numismatics for the Department of Coins and Medals and 'History of Renaissance and Modern art', with questions on the schools and methods of Engraving and with practical tests' for the Department of Prints and Drawings. CE8/9, 29 July 1898 et seq. The competitive examination was abolished in 1921 and replaced by qualifying written examination, followed by a selection board organized by the Civil Service Commission.

22 CE18/9, 2062 (22 May 1895).

23 Hill (1945).

24 Read and Dalton (1899).

25 Hobson (1903) and Hobson (1905). Typically Hobson had a first-class degree in classics from Jesus College, Cambridge, and had filled in the four years before his appointment as a schoolmaster.

26 The full and rather terrible story of Hawkes and Smith is told in Webster (1991), 205–12.

27 See, for example, the estimate by Roe (1981), 215.

28 A charitable view of Smith is in Kendrick (1971).

29 The antiquaries journal, xx (1940), 293.

30 King had been to Rugby and was an exhibitioner of King's College, Cambridge, where he had received a first-class degree in 1891 in theology and had then started to study Syriac.

31 Budge (1925), 178.

32 Driver (1944).

33 Mallowan (1977), 304.

34 Thompson (1930), 481.

35 Dictionary of national biography, s.n.; Thompson (1930); Dawson and Uphill (1995), s.n.

36 Wiseman (1980).

37 An excellent account of Dodgson is provided by Carey (1998). See also Popham (1950) and Carey (1996).

38 His chauffeur was the father of Len Deighton, the novelist. Dodgson was not the only member of staff who had a chauffeur; William King of the Department of British and Mediaeval Antiquities had not only a chauffeur, but a Rolls Royce to go with him; King (1976), 167.

39 Dictionary of national biography, s.n.

40 Hill (1988), 39.

41 Barnett (1937).

42 One of his fellow candidates at this competition was (Sir) Charles Peers, later Chief Inspector of Ancient Monuments, President of the Society of Antiquaries and a Trustee of the Museum. His career and that of his intimate friend Hill were always closely intertwined.

43 Dictionary of national biography, s.n. Robinson (1950), Hill (1988).

44 Hill (1915) and Hill (1936).

45 A Bill to authorize the Trustees of the British Museum to deposit copies of local newspapers with local authorities, and to dispose of valueless printed matter (PP, House of Lords, iv, (1899), 89). Ironically, almost a century later, the British Library has been disposing of non-British newspapers because of space problems, but now in the light of the ability to record newspapers in microform, cf. The Times, 7 and 12 Aug. 2000.

46 The Times, 5 June 1900.

47 2 Edward VII, c.12. The need to keep all the collections under one roof had been breached with the passing of the British Museum Act 1878, 41 and 42 Victoria, c.55, which allowed the transfer of collections from Bloomsbury. Nowadays permission to store objects off-site is given by Order in Council, e.g. the British Museum (Authorized Repositories Order) 1984 (Statutory instruments, no. 1181).

48 The site (following the precedent of the Natural History Museum) was vested not in the Trustees, but in the Office of Works. For the complicated manoeuvrings which led to the out-housing of the newspapers at Colindale see the detailed documentation in Harris (1998), 376–8.

49 Purchased by Act of Parliament, 57 and 58 Victoria, c.34. 1 Montague Place, which did not belong to the Bedford Estate, was the rectory of St George's, Bloomsbury. It was purchased in 1905 for £5,000, CE3/52, 2118 (14 Oct. 1905).

50 Caygill and Date (1999), fig.36; Crook (1972), figs 92–5.

51 The Act states that 'The said property shall be managed in such a manner as the Treasury direct, and the net rents and profits accruing therefrom shall be paid into the Exchequer'. Miller (1973), 261, has a point when he states that 'Successive Chancellors of the Exchequer were more interested in the rentals to be obtained from these houses, than in giving the Museum more space.'

52 Kenyon (1914), 8.

53 For documentation CE47. Unless otherwise stated, all the information used here is taken from this source and is not referred to in detail.

54 Cherry and Pevsner (1998), 296.

55 Peace (1994), no.220.

56 Previously the Map and Music Rooms.

57 Quoted by Caygill and Date (1999), 59.
58 Kenyon (1914) was written to celebrate the opening.
59 Caygill and Date (1999), fig.39.
60 The railings – poor replicas of those at the front of the Museum – were removed for scrap during the Second World War. They were replaced in 2000.
61 This was never intended as an entrance; the main entrance in Burnet's original scheme was to have been on Bedford Square.
62 CE/BY6/A/5. The intrusive staircase, fortunately, was never built.
63 *Annual return* 1896, 70.
64 The Steele family fulfilled this function in a freelance capacity for more than eighty years. Before they were employed, the painting of labels had been in the hands of various junior members of staff, most recently the Museum plumber, James Frid. Mrs M. Steele was first employed in the 1880s; two of her sons and her grandson, Donald, continued to work until Donald retired in the 1960s. They also painted the registration numbers on the objects. They were employed on similar projects as far away as Hadrian's Wall. They charged by letter. In the 1930s Donald, for example, was charging 9d a dozen for gold letters under ½ inch in height and 1s 6d per dozen for letters over one inch in height (information from M. Hall).
65 *Annual return* 1902, 68. As late as 1961 Edward Croft Murray, then Deputy Keeper of Prints and Drawings, produced all the labels for an exhibition on fakes in his elegant renaissance hand.
66 E.g. *Annual return* 1890, 62.
67 Plate 23 shows a striking picture of the empty gallery, which demonstrates the airy effect he was trying to achieve. Almost immediately panels were introduced which divided most of the cases laterally and prevented long vistas through cases.
68 Similar, rather smaller, cases are known to have been used in the upper galleries in the 1890s.
69 E.g. *Annual return* 1910, 72.
70 Prices varied; in the first years of the twentieth century there seems to have been a standard price of a shilling or 1s 6d. By the 1920s they had risen to 2s or 2s 6d. They were still being produced in the 1950s, when they sold for about 6s. The sales counter can be seen in a photograph of *c*.1906; Dawson (1999a), fig.9.
71 Burton (1999), 125–6.
72 Waterhouse retired, after an extension, in 1956.
73 He sold his equipment to the Museum for £10. It is believed to survive at Colindale.
74 Kenyon (1914).
75 CE3/49, 678 (9 July 1898).
76 CE Director's papers, Sir Frederic Kenyon – Guide-lecturers' salaries (28 Feb. 1925).
77 Department of Egyptian and Assyrian Antiquities. Students' Room [Regulations], 11 May 1907.
78 Victoria and Albert Museum *Review*... 1926, 108. British Museum *Annual report* 1928, 3.
79 Much of the information in this section comes from a lecture given by Kenyon – Kenyon (1934). An undated and unpublished paper by Kenyon, 'Military and other war service of the staff', on which this is apparently based, is at CE/BAY6/A/7.
80 CE3/57, 3275–80 (22 Sept. 1914).
81 CE3/57, 3280 (22 Sept. 1914).
82 CE3/58, 3380 (12 June 1915).
83 CE3/58, 3390 (10 July 1915); 3481 (8 July 1916).
84 CE3/58, 3553 (13 Oct. 1917). The others were J.V. Scholderer (seconded to War Office) and J. Leveen (in the Army Service Corps).
85 CE3/58, 3560 (10 Feb. 1917); 3577 (9 March 1918); 3607 (12 Oct. 1918).
86 CE3/58, 3558 (10 Nov. 1917).
87 Sandys (1919). There is a volume of press cuttings concerning this episode in the Museum Archives.

88 Beaverbrook (1956), 332–3. See also Gilmour (1994), 491.
89 This was quite a complicated exhibition and included many patriotic documents and books. It was pointed out, for example, that the battle of Malplaquet was fought on part of the same ground as the retreat from Mons; *A short guide to the temporary war-time exhibition in the British Museum*, London 1918.
90 The propaganda medals were a far-sighted purchase as many of them were produced by major German Expressionist artists, such as Goetz and Zadikow; Jones (1978). 217 were bought in 1917 for £48 from HM Procurator General; CE3/58, 3521 (13 Jan. 1917). Others were given by M. Frankenhuis and M. van den Bergh. The purchase of books is recorded by Harris (1998), 462–3.
91 CE3/58, 3555 (13 Oct. 1917).
92 Literature on the history of scientific conservation in the Museum is sparse, but see Oddy (1997) and Plenderleith (1998).
93 Kenyon (1934), 31–3, 36–7.
94 CE3/59, 3674 (11 Oct. 1919); 3683 (8 Nov. 1919); 3733 (8 May 1920); 3/60, 3934 (10 June 1922).
95 Royal Commission [1928–30], *Final report*, ii, 1930, 20–1, 84.
96 Plenderleith (1998), 130–1.
97 Rathgen (1905).
98 Plenderleith (1956).
99 Documents at CE/BY6/H/6.
100 Much of the detail of this restructuring will be found in Harris (1999), 538–40.
101 The last keeper to live on site was Basil Gray, Keeper of Oriental Antiquities, who retired in 1969. The Director now pays rent at 10 per cent of his gross salary. For a pleasant account of being duty officer in residence see King (1991), 293–8, and as an example of a rather more harrowing side of the job see Burnett and Reeve (2001), 87.
102 CE3/61, 4285 (12 June 1926).
103 CE4/250, 4979 (Dec. 1933).
104 CE3/58, 3542 (9 June 1917).
105 CE 3/60, 4201 (13 June 1925).
106 CE18/15 (27 March 1934). A single mother, Senior was allowed to retain her post after the birth of her daughter. She was killed by a bomb in the Second World War and, bizarrely, her name does not appear on the war memorial.
107 Figures from *Estimates*.
108 *Twenty-five years of the National Art Collections Fund*, 1903–1928, Glasgow 1928.
109 CE30/50, 14 June 1911.
110 See *Royal Commission* (1928–30).
111 A minute of the meeting with Baldwin is at CE4/231, 924 (7 March 1927).
112 Kenyon was also an unashamed propagandist, giving the Romanes Lecture at Oxford on 'Museums and National Life' – a lecture which pulled few punches.
113 British Museum Act, 1930. 20–21 George V, c.45.
114 The subsequent Act of Parliament, 14 & 15 George V, c.23, allowed the loan of material in Great Britain only.
115 For Lawrence's role in the excavations at Carchemish, see Wilson (1989), 73–148.
116 E.g. Winstone (1990), 35–7. Woolley was never one to play down a good story, see, for example, Woolley (1962), *passim*.
117 The correspondence in CE32/Carchemish blends glorious end-of-Empire sentiment with cool academic judgement.
118 The pre-war excavation documentation is bound as a separate volume, CE32/Carchemish. For Morrison see *Dictionary of national biography, s.n.*
119 Many fragments, however, survive and are now in the Ankara Museum (one piece was later bought by the

British Museum and some objects reached the Louvre).

120 Woolley and Lawrence (1914), in reprint of 1969, viii.

121 The third and final volume of the excavation report was not published until 1952; Woolley and Barnett (1952).

122 The Germans, digging at Warka, were also at the same time adding greatly to the knowledge of Sumerian civilization. Their meticulous, publicly funded excavation produced, however, no synthetic account and the site is known only to specialists.

123 Woolley (1927–76).

124 Sidney Smith was seconded as Director of Antiquities in Iraq from 1928–31. CE3/62, 4483 (28 July 1928); CE3/63, 4741 (14 Feb. 1931).

125 Curtis (1982) celebrates the first fifty years of the School's history.

126 Budge (1920), i, 241.

127 James (1982).

128 For Petrie see Drower (1985).

129 Petrie (1904) expresses many of these ideas.

130 One such piece was the wooden statue of Meryre-hashtef from Petrie's excavations at Sedment, given by the National Art Collections Fund in 1923. See Drower (1985), pl. 74.

131 Gardiner (1955).

132 For the Petrie Museum at University College London see Janssen (1992).

133 He offered the Lahun Treasure to the British Museum for £8,000; this was turned down by Kenyon as too expensive, without consulting Budge. The material went to New York. Kenyon's action was attacked vociferously by Read in his Presidential Address to the Society of Antiquaries in 1920, see Evans (1956), 393. Drower (1985), 333, implies that it was Budge who turned the offer down. For the finding of the treasure see Drower (1985), 328–9.

134 For Brunton and Caton-Thompson see Dawson and Uphill (1995), s.n.

135 E.g. CE3/64, 5375 (12 June 1937) – I.E.S. Edwards was allowed twenty weeks' special leave, the Society paying his expenses.

136 Curtis (1990).

137 Quoted by James (1997), 274.

138 James (1997) and Edwards (2000).

139 Another Egyptologist in the Department, Arthur Shorter, was unpopular with Smith, who froze him out.

140 A summary history of the Department of Ethnography is provided by Braunholtz (1970).

141 Willey and Sabloff (1974), 82. Almost immediately after the publication of Joyce's book on Mexico in 1914, H.J. Spinden introduced his 'Archaic hypothesis', which was to revolutionize the study of the cultural history of prehistoric America; see Willey (1981).

142 The importance of Haddon's work here is summarized by Mack (n.d.), 21–3.

143 Coombes (1994), 60, in an admirable if controversial book, does not appreciate the power structure of the Museum in describing the position of ethnography at the turn of the century as fragile. Read within a few years had two ethnographic assistants and he, a powerful figure in the Museum's hierarchy and himself an ethnographer, continued to collect aggressively with full documentation in this area.

144 Dalton (1898). See Mack (n.d.), 27–9. Dalton's report was published by the Trustees and widely circulated. CE3/49, 681 (9 July 1898); 731 (22 Oct. 1898).

145 For Torday see Mack (n.d.).

146 Bassani and McLeod, M. (n.d.). Maternity is illustrated in many places, but see, for example, Gardiner (1992), pl.3.

147 Silber (1996), 130–1, pls. ix, 119–22. See also the wooden figure ibid., pls 134–5 (Cat.94), which is also attributed to Gaudier.

148 Mack (1998), 76.

149 Moore (1981).

150 Braunholtz (1953a), 112–14.

151 Braunholtz (1970), 44–5. Museum legend has it that, because of a private tiff over a minor matter, Smith was not on speaking terms with Joyce. He apparently communicated with him through a departmental messenger, 'Mr Smith presents his compliments to Mr Joyce...'.

152 Boletín Bibliográfico de Antropologica Americana, xiii: 2, 252–8, quoted Braunholtz (1970), 47.

153 Braunholtz (1952).

154 Report of Trustees, 1966, 49.

155 For his obituary see the Sunday Telegraph, 17 Feb. 1991. Museum gossip tells that he was eased out for being disgracefully drunk in one of the galleries. Viva King (1976), 139, tells another story: 'His attendance was very erratic and when, after several weeks' absence, he turned up only to change his clothes (he kept many clothes in a cupboard there) and announced that he was off to the Derby, Hobson decided that he had had enough...'.

156 For a portrait of King, see his wife's autobiography, King (1976). See also King (1991), 271–2.

157 CE3/60, 4003 (10 March 1923).

158 Hobson (1923).

159 CE3/63, 4976 (10 June 1933).

160 Harris (1998), 492.

161 CE/ Miscellaneous papers, BY 6/A/5 (25 April 1936).

162 CE3/65, 5877 (13 Oct. 1945).

163 Pinder Wilson (2000), Dictionary of national biography, s.n.

164 A pressure group, 'the executive committee for a museum of Asiatic art in London', was set up in 1931. It conducted a campaign by letter in The Times and published a privately printed pamphlet which includes a verbatim account of a meeting at India House at which the Museum was fully represented – The project of a museum of Asiatic art in London, London [1931]. See files at CE/Central Museum of Oriental Art and Antiquities.

165 The project of a museum of Asiatic art in London, London [1931], 24–5.

166 CE3/51, 1749 (8 Nov. 1902).

167 Stein collection documents at CE32/23, 1–121 and CE32/24, 1–70. Wang (1999) is a useful source for his collections and documentation in the United Kingdom.

168 Most conveniently summarized by Whitfield and Farrar (1990).

169 For his life and work, see Oldham (1943). A useful biography is Walker (1995).

170 Binyon was given leave to prepare for an official visit to China and Japan before the war, CE3/57, 3266 (11 July 1914). The visit was overtaken by events and he eventually went in 1928, although the Treasury refused to grant him any money towards the journey. He was financed by a committee based in the Imperial University of Tokyo and also visited Korea, China, Siam and Cambodia; Hatcher (1995), 243–58. I have been unable to trace any earlier official visit to the Far East by a member of staff.

171 McCausland (2001).

172 Binyon (1916).

173 Annual report 1926.

174 Annual report 1924.

175 Jenyns (1954).

176 The Museum ultimately received nearly 700 objects: Report of the Trustees, 45, Watson et al. (1952); Gadd (1952a).

177 Long (1991).

178 CE3/64, 5108 (13 Oct. 1934); 5139 (12 Jan. 1935).

179 The British Museum quarterly, ix (1935–6), 86–8.

180 For Salting see Coppel (1996a).

181 At his death probate was granted at a gross value of £1,332,000 (net personality £1,287,906).

182 Colvin (1910).

183 These were surveyed by Alan Donnithorne of the Department of Conservation in 1982, but the survey is unpublished. Christopher Date, the Museum Archivist, undertook a further survey in 1991.

184 See Carey (1996) and (1998).

185 Carey (1996), 211.

186 Carey (1996a), 242.

187 *Annual report* 1925 and 1926.

188 An exhibition was mounted in 1933 to display the major acquisitions of Dodgson's keepership; Popham (1933).

189 King (1991), 271.

190 Hind (1938–48).

191 Hind (1952).

192 For Binyon see Hatcher (1995).

193 Binyon was appointed Companion of Honour on his retirement, the only member of staff to receive this high distinction. Long after his retirement, Arthur Waley was awarded it as a poet in 1956 (he had also been awarded the Queen's Medal for Poetry).

194 Waley (1931).

195 Carson (1986), 20–24.

196 Robinson (1966).

197 Sutherland (1977).

198 Sutherland (1977), 435.

199 Robinson (1952).

200 *New dictionary of national biography, s.n.,* Bruce-Mitford (1990).

201 Kendrick (1925).

202 Kendrick (1971), 3.

203 Kidd (1994).

204 Smith (1931).

205 Dalton describes his own pathological shyness in a book written under a pen-name, Leith (1908). For Hawkes, see Webster (1991) and Harding (1993).

206 Armstrong later went to the College of Heralds.

207 Kendrick and Hawkes (1932), a much used textbook for many years.

208 Kitzinger (1940). Kitzinger later became A. Kingsley Porter Professor of Art at Harvard and Director of Studies at Dumbarton Oaks Center for Byzantine Studies.

209 Bruce-Mitford (1975–83). Bruce-Mitford was greatly indulged by the Trustees in producing this monograph; he assembled a large team of helpers, particularly worthy of mention being Angela Care Evans, who carried much of the burden of collaborating with a difficult and obsessive colleague.

210 Phillips (1987), 70–9, has left a personal account of his involvement. Two of the chief excavators – Stuart Piggott and W.F. Grimes – later became senior and distinguished figures in British archaeology. Associated with them was Grimes's chief, O.G.S. Crawford, Archaeology Officer of the Ordnance Survey, who was to provide a forum in the journal *Antiquity*, which he owned and edited, for a preliminary account of the find only a year after its discovery.

211 Webster (1991), 172–3.

212 CE3/65, 5943 (12 Oct. 1946). Treasure Trove was claimed on behalf of the Crown and the finder (not the landowner) was customarily awarded the full market value of the find, which was paid by the institution to which it was offered.

213 Painter (1977).

214 Kenyon was to have a long, active and productive retirement, including spells as Secretary of the British Academy and President of the Society of Antiquaries. It is typical of the man that he attended a conference in Berlin in late August 1939, on the last day of which he made a forthright speech against German attitudes. He nearly got caught there by the outbreak of war, and had to leave hurriedly and return to England by way of Sweden. Crawford (1955), 205.

215 Vincent (1984), 532.

216 In 1925 A.H. Smith had been succeeded by H.B. Walters as Keeper of Greek and Roman Antiquities.

217 Hill (1988).

218 In 1930, as a result of a recommendation of the Royal Commission of 1928–30, the Director at Bloomsbury ceased to have responsibility for the Natural History Museum, although the Trustees still controlled it; 20 & 21 George V, c.46.

219 The Prime Minister did not approve of the appeal, CE3/64, 5059 (14 April 1934). The figure ultimately provided by the government is rather obscure; I have taken the round sum from a note in *Estimates* for 1950–1, 11.

220 CE3/64, 5131–2 (8 Dec. 1934); 5139 (12 Jan. 1935). Oscar Raphael guaranteed the interest up to £80 p.a.

221 *New dictionary of national biography, s.n.*

222 Jenkins (1992), 213–14, gives a fully documented summary of the history of the cast room. Some of the casts were retained by the Museum and the cast of the Laocoon went to the Ashmolean Museum, Oxford. For the collection of classical casts at the Victoria and Albert Museum see Burton (1999), 122 and fig.8.6.

223 CE3/64, 5032 (13 Jan. 1934).

224 The account of the re-housing of the Parthenon sculptures rests heavily on Jenkins (1992), 225–30, who has quoted the primary sources.

225 Smith (1892–1904), (1910).

226 Quoted by Jenkins (1994), 203–5.

227 Smith (1930).

228 Gardiner (1992), 216–17. Quoted from *The Times*, 2 May 1921. Reprinted Epstein (1942), 181, as an introduction to Epstein's long-running and immoderate feud with the Museum.

229 The consultation documents are at CE/103 (MD25/1A, 1B, 2–6).

230 Jenkins (1992), 226.

231 17 June 1930, Vincent (1984), 534. For further difficulties with Duveen, who insisted on Pope as architect for the gallery he was giving to the Tate Gallery, see Spalding (1998), 62.

232 Vincent (1984), 536–7.

233 CE103 (MD25/5) (22 Jan. 1937).

234 CE3/64, 5339 (13 Feb. 1937).

235 Behrman (1986), 165, 207–8.

236 Secrest (1984), 98–100.

237 Vincent (1984), 537.

238 The 23rd British Museum Classical Colloquium, held in Nov. 1999, entitled 'Cleaning the Parthenon Sculptures', was accompanied by copies of most of the relevant papers concerning the 1930s cleaning, now on file in the Museum's Central Archives. This account is drawn largely from these papers.

239 After the war he joined the British Council, in which he stayed until his death in 1963.

240 *The Times*, 18 May 1939.

241 Goldsmith (1984), 52.

242 See his autobiography, Ashmole (1994), and Robertson (1989).

243 *British Museum magazine*, no. 21, 1995, 28–9.

244 Ashmole (1994), 71.

245 Dodgson (1903–11).

246 Hind (1910).

247 The exhibitions are listed by Griffiths and Williams (1987), 17–19.

248 For the Cambridge school of archaeology see Clark (1989).

249 Anthropology was formally recognized at Cambridge as long ago as 1890 – in the Department of Anatomy under pressure from the professor, Alexander Macalister. His interest was primarily in physical

anthropology and to this end he appointed W.H.L. Duckworth to a post in the subject. At about the same time a social anthropologist, A.C. Haddon (p.224), was appointed, supported by J.G. Frazer, Fellow of Trinity and author of *The golden bough*, and William Ridgeway, the Disney Professor of Archaeology. A Board of Studies was set up in 1904.

250 Webster (1991), 232.

251 Murray (2000), *passim*.

252 For classical archaeology at Oxford see Boardman (1985).

253 The first professor, William Ramsay, was appointed in 1885, but left in the following year to take up a post in Aberdeen, for reasons which Arthur Evans recorded in doggerel: 'Oxford to glorify her Lapidarium/Made a Professor, minus honararium;/The new Professor finding stones and bread/Were not convertible, discreetly fled.' Boardman (1985), 45. For Gardner see *Dictionary of national biography*, *s.n.*

254 An interesting sidelight on the classical archaeologist's overweening perception of his own subject is provided by D.G. Hogarth, Keeper of the Ashmolean Museum, in 1899: '... wherever archaeology is pursued as a serious study, classical archaeology is regarded as supplying a basis and a training in method, much as classical languages are recognized as offering the indispensable foundation for the literary and linguistic education of our schools and universities'. Hogarth (1899), 295.

255 Green (1981), 56–7, gives an account of the foundation of this chair.

256 For Childe: Trigger (1980); Green (1981).

257 The Trustees 'desired particularly to promise such co-operation as was possible to the Institute of Archaeology, and instructed the Director to write to the University to that effect'. CE3/63, 4948 (11 March 1933).

258 Harrison (1994), 222.

259 Elegantly discussed by Burton (1999), 178–81.

260 The problem of collecting by members of staff has never been satisfactorily resolved. In 1928 Kenyon had attempted to control the practice, quoting a Trustees' regulation of 8 Aug. 1863, 'Let the Officers of the Museum be informed that it is expected by the Trustees that every person in their service will refrain from making a collection of the same kind as those which are preserved in the Museum for public use, and from dealing in such articles in the way of sale or exchange.' Kenyon, conscious presumably of Campbell Dodgson's collecting activities, almost half-heartedly re-affirmed this regulation in a memorandum to staff, 'Collecting is objectionable in an Officer (and especially a Keeper) unless he intends his collection ultimately to come to the Museum. This is normally the case where the collection is of any importance, and was so in that of Franks, who was a known collector and an Assistant at the date of that order. Probably it is best that the regulation should stand in case of need...'. CE/Director's Papers: Sir Frederic Kenyon (15 June 1928). It is clear that this memorandum was triggered by the five-day sale (which realized more than £20,000) at Sotheby's in November 1928 of Sir Hercules Read's collection, which must have seemed as scandalous then as it does now; Herrmann (1980), 237n. It is clear that the curators of the 1920s and 1930s hardly honoured this admonition. As late as 1971, one of their contemporaries, Kenneth (Lord) Clark, formerly Director of the National Gallery and then a Trustee of the Museum, approved the practice, believing that it improved a curator's 'eye' and ability to do his job – CE22/3, 1198 (11 Dec. 1971); 1212 (22 Jan. 1972). Although Clark's view was endorsed by the Trustees, it is now accepted that collecting by staff is only allowed if objects are

offered to the Museum through the Director before or after purchase; CE22/4, 1864 (17 May 1975).

261 Dr Lionel Barnett, who is mentioned in the first paragraph of this chapter, was a world expert in Indian languages, but never went to the sub-continent. It is alleged that he once started out to receive a prestigious award in India, but turned back at Cairo because he found the heat unbearable.

262 The machinations concerning German representation on the Permanent Council of the International Congress of Pre- and Protohistoric Sciences in 1936 are recounted by Krämer (2002), 52–7.

263 Harris (1998), 468–9.

264 Harris (1998), 469–71.

265 These works are carefully described and documented by Harris (1998), 472–4.

266 In 1924 there had been a proposal to house ethnography in one of the buildings constructed for the British Empire exhibition at Wembley. Later there were proposals to move it to South Kensington. Caygill and Date (1999), 67.

267 Forsdyke (1952); Caygill (1989), (1990), (1992a).

268 CE/Minutes of National Museum Directors' Conference, 15 Nov. 1933.

269 BM Ethno., Digby MS, 11.

270 Adrian Digby has written up his experiences of the wartime repositories, see BM Ethno., Digby MS.

271 Vol. xv (1952).

272 Harris (1998), 555 and fig.91.

273 In addition to the description of the damage to the south-west quadrant recorded in Forsdyke (1952), see a rather more detailed account in King (1991), 261–6.

274 A plan showing the extent of the war damage is published in Report of Trustees, 1966, figs 1 and 2.

275 Quoted Caygill (1992a), 40.

CHAPTER 7

1 Two curatorial members of the staff of antiquities departments, Derek Allen (Coins and Medals) and H.G.M. Bass (Egyptian and Assyrian Antiquities), stayed on as civil servants. Allen, who was to retire as an Under Secretary in the Board of Trade, continued to write on numismatic subjects. In 1969 he became Secretary of the British Academy and was from 1972 until his death in 1975 a Trustee of the Museum – see Turner (1976). Bass went into the Foreign and Colonial Office, where he specialized in Africa and was ultimately High Commissioner in Lesotho before retiring to become Chapter Clerk of St George's Chapel, Windsor.

2 CE3/65, 5832 (14 Oct. 1944).

3 The Tate Gallery had also suffered serious damage, but not on the scale of the British Museum. It was able to re-open all its galleries in February 1949; Rothenstein (1966), 81–9, 183; Spalding (1998), 82–8, 101. The Victoria and Albert Museum came through the war virtually unscathed, which enabled its brilliant director, Leigh Ashton, to mount innovative permanent exhibitions setting new standards for Britain.

4 King (1991), 265.

5 CE3/65, 5918 (11 May 1946).

6 CE3/65, 5943 (12 Oct. 1946).

7 CE3/65, 6000 (11 Oct. 1947).

8 Quoted Ashmole (1994), 125 (caption to figure which shows the result). The Trustees, CE7/7 (12 July 1950), noted that this room, together with the Egyptian and Assyrian sculpture galleries, had re-opened.

9 CE7/7 (14 June 1951).

10 CE3/65, 5867 (14 July 1945); 5877 (13 Oct. 1945).

11 CE3/65, 5870 (14 July 1945). Cohn had been in Britain since 1934.

12 The title of this sub-department caused a great deal of

discussion – and did until in 2000 it was renamed the Department of Prehistory and Early Europe (a still unsatisfactory title); CE3/65, 5867 (14 July 1945); 5877 (13 Oct. 1945).

13 CE3/65, 5906 (13 April 1946).
14 Scrutton became Director of the National Galleries of Scotland 1971–7. French joined the Royal Commission for Historic Monuments (England) and became a major expert on medieval stained glass (obituary: *The Times*, 10 March 2001).
15 CE3/65, 5993 (12 July 1947).
16 CE3/65, 5937 (12 Oct. 1946). After a two-year probationary period, a minimum of five and a maximum of seven years was to be served in the cadet grade, although exceptions were made for returning servicemen. CE3/65, 5962 (8 Feb. 1947).
17 CE3/65, 5963 (8 Feb. 1947).
18 CE3/65, 5990 (12 July 1947).
19 The substantive decision is recorded in CE7/7 (8 Dec. 1948).
20 CE3/65, 5836 (14 Oct. 1944).
21 CE3/65, 5849 (10 Feb. 1945). Braunholtz left for Africa in February 1946 and returned in July having visited Nigeria, the Gambia, Sierra Leone and the Gold Coast; CE3/65, 5897 (9 Feb. 1946); 5927 (13 July 1946).
22 Winstone (1990), 217–42.
23 CE3/65, 5857 (14 April 1945). The Trustees later granted £3,000 from the Carchemish Trust Fund for this project, another £1,000 being raised from other sources; CE3/65, 5900 (9 Feb. 1946). A further £1,000 was granted as a final payment for work on the site in February 1947; CE3/65, 5967 (28 Feb. 1947).
24 Douglas Barrett, now in Oriental Antiquities, for example, after fighting with the Combined Operations Bombardment Unit in North Africa, Italy and France, had been involved in the reorganization of local government in Germany. William Watson, in British and Medieval Antiquities (who in 1949 transferred to Oriental Antiquities), had been in Far Eastern Intelligence, based in India; while Donald Wiseman, of Egyptian and Assyrian Antiquities, had been a Group Captain in Mediterranean Intelligence and had been awarded an OBE and the American Bronze Star. One or two, like R.A. Higgins of the Department of Greek and Roman Antiquities, had been prisoners of war.
25 CE7/7 (31 May 1949).
26 CE3/65, 2923 (13 July 1946).
27 CE3/65, 5900 (9 Feb. 1946).
28 CE3/65, 6189 (12 Nov. 1949). Sheridan Bowman has pointed out to me that this minute predates Libby's first publication on radiocarbon dating by at least a month.
29 A picture of the first laboratory is in *The Times science review*, no.14 (Winter 1954). The first results were published in Barker and Mackey (1959).
30 *British Museum quarterly news supplement*, May 1962, 3.
31 CE3/65, 6144 (9 July 1949).
32 CE3/65, 6149 (9 July 1949).
33 Allan pointed out to the Trustees in 1945 that the medieval post had been withdrawn forty years earlier; CE3/65, 5866 (14 July 1945).
34 He became deeply and romantically attached to Ireland and left the Museum in 1963 for Queen's University, Belfast. After a short and unhappy time at Armidale in Australia, he died prematurely in 1981, Lyon (1982).
35 In 1973 he became Master of University College, Durham, and was later Director of the Polytechnic of North London.
36 A. Griffiths, personal communication. For Popham see Shaw (1971).
37 Croft Murray is remembered with little affection in the Department, but a warmer view of his social side

is to be found in King (1991), 271. See also obituary, *The Times*, 24 Sept. 1980.
38 Spalding (1998), 106.
39 White (1995).
40 Coldstream (1994).
41 CE3/66, 6248 (22 July 1950).
42 CE3/65, 6102 (11 Dec. 1948).
43 One of the grounds for Edwards's promotion was that he might move to the chair at University College London; he was the only Egyptologist in the department, and another appointment was clearly needed, but the promotion could have waited until Gadd's retirement. CE3/65, 6195 (10 Dec. 1949).
44 *Dictionary of national biography, s.n.*
45 Personal experience.
46 Harris (1998), 669.
47 For documented details of the Secretary's office at this period see Harris (1998), 669–70.
48 CE3/67, 6837 (14 July 1956).
49 Members of the library departments also joined this brain-drain; some of them went to university libraries and some to chairs, as did T.J. Brown of the Department of Manuscripts, who became Professor of Palaeography at King's College London in 1960. For others see Harris (1998), 670, and above, pp.259–60.
50 Television cameras were first allowed in the galleries in 1950. The curatorial staff demonstrated the objects; CE3/66, 6200 (28 Jan. 1950).
51 Tait (1959).
52 CE3/67, 6846 (14 July 1956).
53 Tait and Cherry (1978), Cherry and Tait (1980).
54 The Museum was a pioneer in the use of Perspex as a material for mounts.
55 Hansard, 9 July 1952, 1318.
56 15 and 16 George 6 & 1 Eliz.2.
57 Heath (1998), 241–2.
58 See, for example, a story told by Dame Joan Evans, the Museum's first woman Trustee, Pope-Hennessy (1991), 203.
59 Information from P. Harris, then Assistant Secretary.
60 E.g. CE3/68, 7524 (11 May 1961).
61 Sir Richard Thompson, who was appointed by the Prime Minister when the 1963 Act came into force, survived as a Trustee until 1984.
62 BM Central Registry, MG105/3. I can trace no evidence for the assertion made by Edward Heath (1998, 242) that it was a discussion between him and Henry Brooke, one of the Treasury Ministers, in 1961 that led to the reform of the Trustees.
63 British Museum Act 1963, Elizabeth II, Chapter 24. The Committee to consider the new bill consisted initially of Lord De L'Isle, Lord Cambridge, Lord Radcliffe, Sir Victor Goodman and Mr Chuter Ede.
64 CE3/67, 7403 (8 Oct. 1960).
65 CE3/68, 7869 (13 July 1963).
66 CE22/1, 171–2 (12 Dec. 1964).
67 Ashmole (1994), 126.
68 *British Museum Society Bulletin*, no.2 (1969), 5.
69 Cherry and Pevsner (1998), 294.
70 Barnett (1970), 3.
71 I am grateful to Margaret Hall for providing me with the skeleton of this section.
72 *Report of Trustees*, 1966.
73 *Report of Trustees*, 1966, 9.
74 Only by the Trustee Investments Act of 1961 were trustees of any institution given power to invest in equities. Brooke Sewell had insisted that his monies should not be subject to this ruling.
75 To the chagrin of the staff they did not mention staff facilities, including the truly horrific staff canteen housed in the temporary sheds on the west side of the Museum which had originally been built for the display of the cast collection.
76 *Report of Trustees*, 1966, frontispiece. The history of the

negotiations to this point is conveniently chronicled and documented by Harris (1998), 673–5.

77 Some of the invective engendered by the decision will be found in Crook (1973) 222–3.

78 Radcliffe (1968), 7.

79 Heward (1994), 201.

80 Cancellation costs were £2m.

81 CE22/2, 624 (9 Dec. 1967). Harris (1998), 621ff., details the negotiations about the transfer of the Patent Office.

82 The other members of the committee were Sir Roy Allen, Professor of Statistics in London University, Sir John Brown, Publisher of the Oxford University Press, and Sir Bernard Miller, Chairman of the John Lewis Partnership. Roy Allen resigned halfway through the proceedings on health grounds and was replaced by H.J. Habbakuk, the newly appointed Principal of Jesus College, Oxford.

83 *Dainton report*, 1.

84 *Principal Documentary Evidence submitted to the National Libraries Committee*, i, A7–A91. The views of the keepers of the antiquities departments are printed at A90–1.

85 BL DH2/134, III, 41 (30 July 1969).

86 *The British Library* (Cmnd. 4572).

87 The British Library Act (1972), Elizabeth II, c.54.

88 For a detailed account of the mechanics which prepared the way for total separation, see Harris (1998), 682–6.

89 A note on the accounts published in *Report of Trustees*, 1999–2000, 38, states, 'Agreement is currently being sought from the Charity Commissioners to share this fund equally with the British Library ...'.

90 Wolfenden (1976), 163.

91 CE/Booze-Allen and Hamilton reports, 1972.

92 CE22/3, 1242–4 (8 April 1972), 1409–11 (14 April 1973), 1638–40 (6 April 1974).

93 Morris had been Assistant Secretary from 1965 to 1968, before returning to the Slavonic section of the Library.

94 Wolfenden (1976), 174.

95 Haynes, Keeper of Greek and Roman Antiquities, was, for example, asked by the Trustees to re-write one of his sections when Kathleen Kenyon 'emphasised the importance of acquiring commonplace objects provided they came from well-documented excavations', CE22/3, 1178 (11 Dec. 1971).

96 CE22/3, 1070 (23 Jan. 1971).

97 Initially the Director was also a director of the company, but this ceased at the time of Pope-Hennessy's departure in order to reserve his position in relation to the Parliamentary Committee on Public Accounts. The Director still, however, attended board meetings of the company.

98 CE/MO 203/7/5.

99 House of Commons, *Fourth report from the Committee of Public Accounts*, Session 1974–5, 319–20.

100 Central Registry file, 33/10/29 (11 June 1973).

101 House of Commons, *Fourth report from the Committee of Public Accounts*, Session 1974–5, xxii.

102 E.g. Caygill and Date (1999), 67.

103 pp. 39–40.

104 Derived from the French – Musée de l'Homme. There may have been some resistance from the keeper about this title, CE22/3, 1155 (18 Sept. 1971). The title, which may have been Kenneth Clark's suggestion, was approved by the Board, who delayed its christening until June 1972; CE22/3, 1169 (30 Oct. 1971).

105 CE22/3, 1146 (24 July 1971).

106 Edwards (2000), 247–98, gives his own view of the exhibition. Edwards (1972) for the catalogue.

107 His attitude was, however, often counter-productive. At a visitation to the Department in 1975 the Trustees – unusually outspoken – said that 'they had been

dissatisfied at the conduct of the Visitation by Mr Gere and at the scant effort which seem to have been made to show either the problems or the achievements of the Department.' CE22/4, 1925 (20 Sept. 1975).

108 Mack (1982).

109 Bateman *et al.* (1966).

110 *Report of Trustees*, 1972–5, 58.

111 Cranstone (1966).

112 CE3/67, 6841 (14 July 1956).

113 Hammond (1972).

114 *Report of Trustees*, 1966, 47–8.

115 Allison (1965).

116 *Report of Trustees*, 1966, 49.

117 Gadd (1952).

118 Higgins (1961).

119 542 items in all, *Report of Trustees*, 1966, 46.

120 *Report of Trustees*, 1966, 46.

121 Tait (1962).

122 Stead (1996).

123 The story of this cross is told in glorious technicolor, which must be taken with a grain of salt, in Hoving (1981).

124 Carson (1966–7).

125 Exemption from Estate Duty of unalienable heirlooms had been allowed since the Finance Act of 1896. This exemption was extended in 1910 to objects of artistic interest, whether they were settled heirlooms or not. The 1930 Finance Act, section 40, provided a wider definition of exempted objects of national importance; further, if exempted objects were sold to certain public institutions Estate Duty was not payable. By 1957 duty on estates valued at over £1m had increased to 80 per cent (in 1930 it was 30 per cent), and the possibilities of exemption had thus become more attractive to owners. CE/Central Registry files PG25, I *et seq.* A record of those items purchased under this 'in lieu' procedure may be found in the annual reports of the Reviewing Committee on the Export of Works of Art.

126 Robertson (1975), pl.62b.

127 CE22/4 1787–8 (1 March 1975); 1804 (12 April 1975). Camber and Cherry (1977).

128 H.M.Treasury. *Report of the committee on the export of works of art, etc.*, London 1952.

129 CE3/67, 6971–2 (13 July 1957); 6994–5 (12 Oct. 1957); 7026 (14 Dec. 1957); 7028 (25 Jan. 1958); 7043 (8 Feb. 1958); 7126 (11 Oct. 1958); 7183 (14 Feb. 1959). Tait (1968), 11–14. Catalogues of the collection are now beginning to appear: Tait and Coole (1987); Randall and Good (1990).

130 Popham (1952), 40.

131 Popham (1935).

132 Hulton (1977).

133 Popham (1952), 47. Christmas cards are the province of the Victoria and Albert Museum; this collection was accepted for its social and royal interest.

134 Carey (1996a), 242.

135 See, for example, *Report of Trustees*, 1969–72, 39–40.

136 Bruce-Mitford (1956), 255.

137 Evison (1987).

138 *Report of Trustees*, 1969–72, 51.

139 Brailsford (1962), Richmond (1968).

140 Ashton (1992).

141 Alexander (1954).

142 Painter (1967).

143 *Report of Trustees*, 1966, 29.

144 E.g. CE3/68, 7529 (13 May 1961).

145 Mallowan (1978).

146 Simpson (2000a).

147 *Report of Trustees*, 1972–5, 52.

148 Addis (1979).

149 Pope-Hennessy (1991), 206.

CHAPTER 8

1   Pope-Hennessy (1991), 201.
2   CE22/4, 2183–4.
3   *British Museum magazine*, no.13, 26–7.
4   The union representing the senior grades made repre-
    sentations to the Trustees about this matter, who
    'remained unshaken in [their] conviction that
    Keepers should be appointed by open competition'.
    CE22/4, 1944–5 (25 Oct. 1975).
5   Pope-Hennessy (1991), 230.
6   The Accounting Officer is responsible to Parliament
    for 'the propriety and regularity of the public finances
    for which she is answerable and for the keeping of
    proper records.' *Report of Trustees* 1998–9, 18.
7   Funding for the post of Eccles Librarian was provided
    by Lady Eccles in memory of her husband.
8   The committees were set up in June 1974; CE22/3,
    1673–4 (15 June 1974).
9   CE22/3, 1660 (11 May 1974).
10 CE22/3, 1764–5 (7 Dec. 1974); CE22/4, 1780 (18 Jan.
    1975).
11 *Report of Trustees* 1978–81, 13.
12 *Report of Trustees* 1975–8, 41; 1981–5, 68.
13 Hanna and Lee (1988), 94–5.
14 The Museum's experience of this stone was not
    unique; examples in Indian museums and on the site
    itself suffered similar deterioration.
15 Oddy (1997).
16 For some figures on such internships see *Report of
    Trustees* 1984–7, 39.
17 Damon, *et al.* (1989).
18 For a convenient summary of these two techniques in
    relation to the Museum see Bowman (1991), 117–38.
19 Craddock *et al.* (1990).
20 Jones (1990), 280.
21 *Report of Trustees* 1999–2000, 82.
22 Burton (1999), 224.
23 Following the successful transfer of the Turner water-
    colours to the Tate Gallery in 1986, it became clear
    that further such logical transfers should be made.
    In the 1990s, under the chairmanship of Robert
    Anderson, a committee of national museum directors
    made recommendations for similar deposits. One
    of the major transfers was of the photographic and
    poster collections of the Department of Prints and
    Drawings which went to the Victoria and Albert
    Museum; the Museum received works on paper and
    mummy portraits from the National Gallery.
24 Khan, Knox and Thomas (1991).
25 Hewitt and Keyworth (1987).
26 Carey and Griffiths (1980); Carey and Griffiths (1984);
    Carey (1997); Carey and Griffiths (1990).
27 In the Department of Prints and Drawings the most
    frequently requested loans at present are works by
    Otto Dix and Picasso.
28 Goldscheider (1986).
29 Rudoe (1991).
30 Carey (1991).
31 Smith (1983) and (1985).
32 McLeod (1993).
33 *Report of Trustees* 1993–6, 20.
34 *The Friends of Prints and Drawings. Newsletter*, i: 8, Feb.
    2001. Lecture by Antony Griffiths, 28 March 2001.
35 For the netsuke see Harris (1987).
36 For the Martinware collection see Rudoe (1991), 71–7.
37 Munn (1986) gives a personal view of this eccentric
    lady.
38 Tait (1984). The other major beneficiary of her
    generosity was the Fitzwilliam Museum, Cambridge.
39 His autobiography – Wharton-Tigar (1987) – recounts
    something of his extraordinary life. See also Griffiths
    (1997).
40 The report was published by the Department for
    Culture, Media and Sport. The Culture, Media and

Sport Committee of the House of Commons also
    looked at this and similar problems and published a
    report with recommendations in July 2000 (*Cultural
    property: return and illicit trade*, Seventh report). The
    Museum gave evidence.
41 The statement is printed in *Report of Trustees*
    1999–2000, 67. In 2001 Britain decided to sign the
    UNESCO Convention on Cultural Property, which is
    intended to stamp out the illicit trade in works of art
    and antiquities, but has not yet signed the much more
    draconian 1995 UNIDROIT convention.
42 The Museum's reaction to this process was praised by
    the Culture, Media and Sport Committee of the House
    of Commons in 2000 (Seventh report, vol. i, liii).
43 BM Central Registry file, A48/51/130.
44 'The British Museum and the Chatsworth drawings:
    Trustees for the Museum or the Nation?', *Burlington
    Magazine*, cxxvi, no. 978 (Sept. 1984), 539. *Export of
    works of art 1984–85. Thirty-first report of the reviewing
    committee...*, 1.
45 Jaffé (1993).
46 Caygill (1999), 159; Buckton (1994), 205.
47 BM Central Registry file, A45/51/142.
48 BM Central Registry file, A44/51/045.
49 This was not the first time the Museum had ventured
    into the acquisition of property in Wiltshire. In 1913
    it attempted, with the anonymous aid of John Jacob
    Astor, to buy Stonehenge. This fortunately fell
    through. See documents in BM Central archive.
50 CE22/5, 2629 (16 Dec. 1978); 2656–7 (27 Jan. 1979);
    2674–7 (3 March 1979); 2707–8 (7 April 1979);
    2720–4 (12 May 1979); 2762–3 (23 June 1979); 2813
    (6 Oct. 1979).
51 CE22/3, 1528–9 (27 Oct. 1973).
52 CE22/3, 1723–6 (26 Oct. 1974).
53 The Keeper of Western Asiatic Antiquities disagreed
    with this assessment.
54 CE22/4, 1930 (25 Oct. 1975).
55 Jackson and Potter (1996).
56 Curtis (1989).
57 Curtis and Green (1997).
58 *Report of Trustees* 1998–9, 66.
59 Wilson (1989), 92.
60 Wilson (1989), 113.
61 *Report of Trustees* 1981–4, 11. For a more discursive
    statement see Wilson (1989), 112–17.
62 Painter (1977a).
63 Johns (1993).
64 Johns and Potter (1983).
65 Stead (1998).
66 Wilson (1989), 33–4.
67 Treasure Act 1996, Elizabeth II, c.24.
68 A useful summary of the results of the Portable Anti-
    quities Scheme is Hull (2001).
69 *Report of Trustees* 1981–4, 14–16.
70 This Fund was made up of grants from the Wolfson
    Family Charitable Trust, the Wolfson Foundation and
    the Department of National Heritage.
71 A succinct, illustrated account of this project is
    Anderson (2000). See also Foster (2001).
72 Central Registry file A/23/82/16.
73 It has been noted that the library of the Royal Anthro-
    pological Institute had been deposited in the
    Museum. This was formally transferred to it in
    1976–9, members of the Institute retaining borrow-
    ing rights. Together with the pre-existing departmen-
    tal library, this in effect created the most important
    anthropological/ethnographical library in Britain,
    comprising some 110,000 books. The Museum's
    original collection was based on Christy's books and
    a further 2,000 splendid items given by Franks.
    Gregson (1992).
74 *A celebration of two and a half centuries. A plan for the British
    Museum.*

75 'The Great Court' was allegedly christened by
    Marjorie Caygill, Fran Dunkels and Erica Bolton
    (personal communication).

76 The brief was short, *The British Museum. Guidelines for
    the future use of the inner courtyard*.

77 Informed gossip has it that the grant might have been
    higher if certain members of the Commission had not
    – strangely – considered the Museum to be 'elitist'.

78 The donors are listed in Anderson (2000), 109.

79 From the beginning it had been agreed that the
    remaining cast-iron quadrant of Panizzi's library
    would be conserved. It was unbolted, dismantled and
    sold at auction.

80 Caygill (2000), 34–41.

81 A virulent, nit-picking and nasty attack by 'Piloti' in
    Private eye, no.1021, 9 (9–22 Feb. 2001), was well
    answered by Ben Goodger in *Private eye*, no. 1022, 14
    (23 Feb.–8 March 2001).

82 The report was immediately posted on the Museum's
    website.

83 www.thebritishmuseum.ac.uk

84 Townsend (1985), 115.

85 The British Museum Plan 1999/2000 to 2001/2002, 22.

86 *Report of Trustees 1999–2000*, 87–94.

87 *Report of Trustees 1999–2000*, 86.

88 Blurton (1997).

89 Wilson (1989), 108–9.

90 Digby (1974).

91 Caygill and House (1986); Caygill and Leese (1994).

92 63 per cent of visitors to the Louvre are foreigners; 19
    per cent come from the Île de France; *The Art Newspa-
    per*, no 115 (2001), 13.

93 *British Museum review*, 2000, 19.

94 *British Museum: the impact of charging on visitor profile*,
    AEA Management Consultants, 1997.

95 Robinson (2000), 162.

96 *British Museum. Research register*, 1994–6, 1–2.

97 From 1991 to 1996 the research product of the
    Museum was published in British Museum. *Research
    register*. Latterly it has appeared in the *Report of Trustees*.

98 Eames (1968) and Eames (1980).

99 *Report of Trustees 1999–2000*, 35. This year's figure is
    quoted, as 1999–2000 was not a typical trading year in
    that the Museum shops were reduced to a temporary
    building in the forecourt and a small temporary
    children's shop in one of the galleries.

100 Wilson (1989).

101 *The Guardian*, 20 March 2001.

102 *2001 Comprehensive Spending Review for Heritage, Libraries
    and Museums*, as published on the website of the
    Department for Culture, Media and Sport.

103 Wilson (1989), 104.

SELECTIVE PLANS

The public display areas in the British Museum are known sometimes as galleries, sometimes as rooms (a terminology that changes from time to time without any discernible logic). Occasionally they are labelled eccentrically, and some preserve long-vanished features or names. They have been numbered and re-numbered many times – never permanently. On these plans (which are only roughly accurate) only the rooms and galleries mentioned in the text are shown; they are numbered arbitrarily for ease of reference. The names listed are the original names; inset below them are subsequent names.

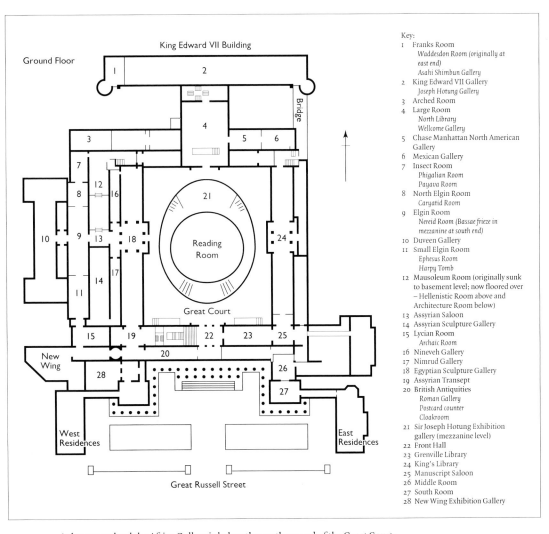

Key:
1 Franks Room
     Waddesdon Room (originally at east end)
     Asahi Shimbun Gallery
2 King Edward VII Gallery
     Joseph Hotung Gallery
3 Arched Room
4 Large Room
     North Library
     Wellcome Gallery
5 Chase Manhattan North American Gallery
6 Mexican Gallery
7 Insect Room
     Phigalian Room
     Payava Room
8 North Elgin Room
     Caryatid Room
9 Elgin Room
     Nereid Room (Bassae frieze in mezzanine at south end)
10 Duveen Gallery
11 Small Elgin Room
     Ephesus Room
     Harpy Tomb
12 Mausoleum Room (originally sunk to basement level; now floored over – *Hellenistic Room above* and *Architecture Room below*)
13 Assyrian Saloon
14 Assyrian Sculpture Gallery
15 Lycian Room
     Archaic Room
16 Nineveh Gallery
17 Nimrud Gallery
18 Egyptian Sculpture Gallery
19 Assyrian Transept
20 British Antiquities
     Roman Gallery
     Postcard counter
     Cloakroom
21 Sir Joseph Hotung Exhibition gallery (mezzanine level)
22 Front Hall
23 Grenville Library
24 King's Library
25 Manuscript Saloon
26 Middle Room
27 South Room
28 New Wing Exhibition Gallery

At basement level the Africa Gallery is below the northern end of the Great Court; the lecture theatres are below the Court's southern end. The Assyrian Basement is below Gallery 13. The Townley sculptures are below the south end of the Duveen Gallery. The Islamic Gallery is at sub-basement level off the west of the North Entrance Hall in the middle of the north side of the King Edward VII Building.

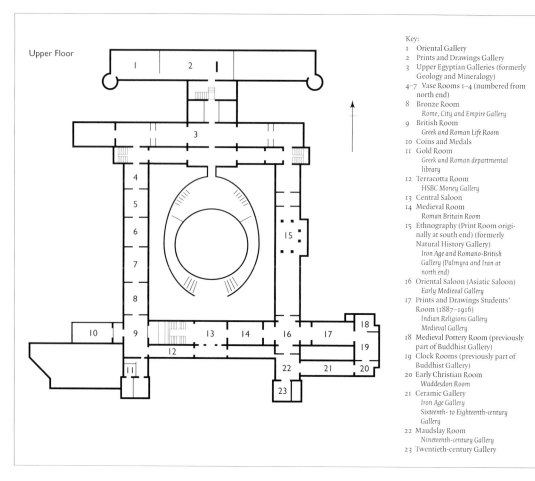

Upper Floor

Key:
1 Oriental Gallery
2 Prints and Drawings Gallery
3 Upper Egyptian Galleries (formerly
   Geology and Mineralogy)
4–7 Vase Rooms 1–4 (numbered from
   north end)
8 Bronze Room
       Rome, City and Empire Gallery
9 British Room
       Greek and Roman Life Room
10 Coins and Medals
11 Gold Room
       *Greek and Roman departmental
       library*
12 Terracotta Room
       HSBC Money Gallery
13 Central Saloon
14 Medieval Room
       Roman Britain Room
15 Ethnography (Print Room originally at south end) (formerly
   Natural History Gallery)
       *Iron Age and Romano-British
       Gallery (Palmyra and Iran at
       north end)*
16 Oriental Saloon (Asiatic Saloon)
       Early Medieval Gallery
17 Prints and Drawings Students'
   Room (1887–1916)
       Indian Religions Gallery
       Medieval Gallery
18 Medieval Pottery Room (previously
   part of Buddhist Gallery)
19 Clock Rooms (previously part of
   Buddhist Gallery)
20 Early Christian Room
       Waddesdon Room
21 Ceramic Gallery
       Iron Age Gallery
       *Sixteenth- to Eighteenth-century
       Gallery*
22 Maudslay Room
       Nineteenth-century Gallery
23 Twentieth-century Gallery

The Korean Gallery is on a mezzanine below the Oriental Gallery. The
Japanese Galleries are above the Oriental and Prints and Drawings Galleries.

DEPARTMENTAL STRUCTURE

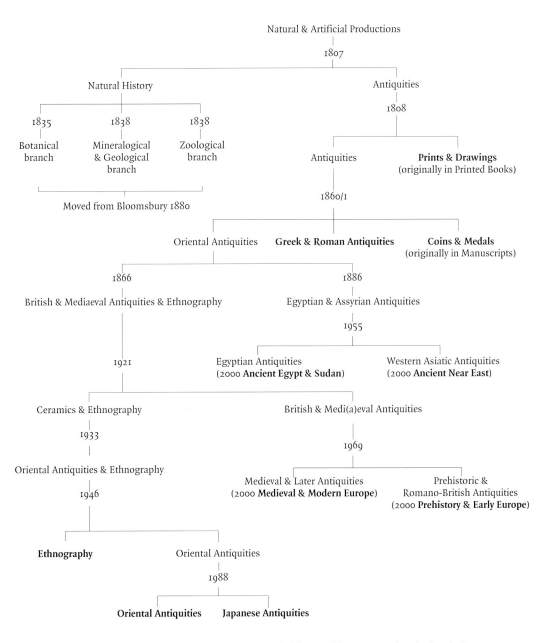

Above is shown the descent of the present departments (in bold type) of the Museum since its foundation (adapted from Bowman (1991), 174). The modern scientific departments are not shown. In 1931 the Museum took over the administration of a laboratory established within it in 1920 (funded by the government's Department of Scientific and Industrial Research) and labelled it the Research Laboratory. In 1975 this was divided into (1) Research Laboratory and (2) Department of Conservation and Technical Services. Briefly re-united in 1982 under one keeper, the departments divided again in 1985 as (1) Department of Scientific Research and (2) Department of Conservation.

Appendix 3

CURATORIAL STAFF
1756–May 2002

by Marjorie Caygill

It has unfortunately not been possible to list all the staff of the Museum since the first appointments were made in 1756: that would have taken up more space than is available here. The aim therefore is merely to trace curatorial responsibility for the antiquities collections with the addition of a few scientific, conservation and administrative staff. The Appendix therefore provides only a partial record of those who have made the Museum what it is today. Amongst the omissions are administrators, designers, educationalists, illustrators, information technologists, museum assistants, photographers, security and works staff, whose titles testify to the wide range of skills found in today's Museum and all of whom have made valued contributions.

Listed below therefore are the curatorial staff of the antiquities departments and all the curatorial staff of the Museum before the establishment of the Department of Antiquities in 1807 equivalent to the present Grade 5 and above. Also listed are the heads of the Museum, their deputies, the Museum Secretaries, the senior grades in the Conservation Department and the Research Laboratory (Scientific Research) and some others appointed to curatorial grades. Members of staff are listed according to their original and current or final departmental appointments – the changing names and structures of the departments are recorded in Appendix 2.

Over the years titles of posts have changed. From the appointment of the first officers in 1756 the head of the institution was known as *Principal Librarian* (PL); between 1898 and 1973 his title was *Director and Principal Librarian*; in 1973 on the splitting off of the British Library the post was re-named *Director*. The post of *Managing Director* was held from 1999 to 2001. From 1968 to 1971 there was an *Assistant Director* whose title was changed between 1971 and 1997 to *Deputy Director*.

Heads of departments were at first known as *Under Librarians* (UL) (although the term 'keeper' was in use at least as early as 1814). In the 1830s the title of *Keeper* became the official designation – now graded as Band 1. Heads of department were originally assisted by an *Assistant Librarian* (the equivalent *Assistant Keeper* label was used from c. 1820). In 1921 this grade was re-named *Deputy Keeper* (DK) – now Band 2.

The original *Assistants* were introduced in the 1820s as a grade intermediate between Assistant Librarian and Attendant. Supernumerary Assistants were employed in 1838. In 1851 they were divided into two grades – 1st class (previously the permanent Assistants) and 2nd Class (previously Supernumeraries). In 1861 Assistants 1st Class were divided into an Upper and a Lower section. In 1867 Assistants 1st Class of the Upper Section were renamed Senior Assistants Upper Section. Assistants 1st Class Lower Section were amalgamated with Assistants 2nd Class into a new grade called Senior Assistant Lower Section. In 1921 this confusing grade structure was changed so that Assistants of the 1st and 2nd class became *Assistant Keepers* (AK). In 1929 Assistant Keepers and Assistants were renamed *Assistant Keeper Class I* (AKI), with the post *Assistant Keeper Class II* (AKII) being in effect a cadet grade.

A new grade of *Research Assistant* (RA) was introduced in 1960. This included *Research Assistants I* (RA) and *Research Assistants II*. In 1963 *Senior Research Assistants* (SRA) were appointed.

In 1980, as part of Civil Service restructuring, curatorial grades were replaced by new designations A–G. In 1996 a 12-grade banding system was introduced for the Museum. Curatorial grades now include (previous designations in brackets): 1 (Keeper, 5, A); 2 (DK, 6, B); 3 (AKI/II, 7, C); 4 (SRA, D); 5 (RAI, E), 6 (RAII, F).

The heads of the scientific departments are also known as *Keepers*. Previously they and their staff held grades equivalent to those in the scientific civil service, and were known as *Scientific Officers* (SO) and *Chief Conservation Officers* (CCO). The professional staff are now designated as *Scientists* or *Conservators*. Only senior members of these departments are listed.

The following departmental abbreviations are used:

AES	Ancient Egypt and Sudan		Nat Hist	Natural History
ANE	Ancient Near East		NHMA	Natural History and Miscellaneous
Ants	Antiquities			Antiquities
BMA	British and Mediaeval Antiquities		NRLSI	National Reference Library of Science
BME	British and Medi(a)eval Antiquities			and Invention
	and Ethnography		OA	Oriental Antiquities
C&E	Ceramics and Ethnography		OAE	Oriental Antiquities and Ethnography
C&M	Coins and Medals		OOA	(Old – i.e. 1860–86) Oriental Antiquities
Cons	Conservation		OPB	Oriental Printed Books and Manu-
C&TS	Conservation and Technical Services			scripts
Dir	Director's Office		PB	Printed Books
EA	Egyptian Antiquities		P&D	Prints and Drawings
EAA	Egyptian and Assyrian Antiquities		P&EE	Prehistory and Early Europe
Educ	Education		PRB	Prehistoric and Romano-British
GRA	Greek and Roman Antiquities			Antiquities
JA	Japanese Antiquities		PS	Public Services
L&A	Library and Archives		RL	Research Laboratory
MLA	Medieval and Later Antiquities		Sec	Secretariat
MME	Medieval and Modern Europe		SR	Scientific Research
MSS	Manuscripts		SRC	Scientific Research and Conservation
NAP	Natural and Artificial Productions		WAA	Western Asiatic Antiquities

NAME	DEPT OF FIRST APPOINTMENT	DATES	BM DATES *	FINAL OR CURRENT POST
Abdy, Richard Anthony	GRA	1970–	1993–	Curator 6 (C&M)
Abe, Mitsuhiro	Cons	1937–	(1998–2001)	Conservator 3
Ackermann, Dr Silke Maren	MLA	1961–	1995–	Curator 5
Ager, Barry Melvin	MLA	1948–	(1979) 1985–	Curator 5
Akehurst, David	Dir	1931–	1948–82	CCO (GRA)
Alexander, William	P&D	1767–1816	1808–16	Under Librarian (1808)
Allan, John	C&M	1884–1955	1907–49	Keeper (1931)
Allden, Alison Jean	MLA	1954–	1985–9	Curator E
Allen, Derek Fortrose	C&M	1910–75	1935–47	AKI
Anderson, Dr Robert Geoffrey William	Dir	1944–	1992–2002	Director (1992)
Andrews, Carol Ann Ray	EA	1945–	1971–2000	Curator 4

* ( ) = UNESTABLISHED, TEMPORARY OR FIXED-TERM APPOINTMENT

NAME	DEPT OF FIRST APPOINTMENT	DATES	BM DATES	FINAL OR CURRENT POST
Archibald, Marion MacCallum	C&M	1935–	1963–97	Curator 3
Arrowsmith, Jean Cherry	Ethno	1947–	1976–89	RAI
Ashmole, Bernard	GRA	1894–1988	(1939) 1948–56	Keeper (1939)
Ashton, Nicholas Mark	PRB	1961–	(1983) 1987–	Curator 4
Attwood, Philip	GRA	1954–	(1978) 1979–	Curator 4 (C&M)
Ayscough, Rev. Samuel	Nat Hist	1745–1804	1787–1804	Asst Librarian, PB (1791)
Bailey, Dr Donald Michael	GRA	1931–	(1955) 1957–96	Curator D
Baker, Stanley	EA	1919–	(1935) 1938–79	CCO (C&TS)
Barker, Harold	RL	1919–	1947–79	Keeper Cons (1975)
Barley, Dr Nigel Frederick	Ethno	1947–	1980–	Curator 3
Barnett, Dr Richard David	EAA	1909–86	1932–74	Keeper WAA (1955)
Barnwell, Charles Frederick	Ants	1781–1849	1827–43	AK
Barrett, Douglas Eric	OA	1917–92	1947–77	Keeper (1969)
Bartrum, Giulia	P&D	1954–	1979–	Curator 4
Bass, Harry Godfrey Mitchell	EAA	1914–2002	1939–47	AKII
Baty, Jeremy Robin	MLA	1955–	(1979–84)	Curator E
Bayliss, Gordon	Sec	1944–	1979–90	Curator E (Central Librarian)
Baynes-Cope, Arthur David	RL	1928–	1960–84	Principal SO
Bedford, Horace Walpole	PB	d.1808	1805–8	Asst Librarian (Ants)
Beloe, Rev. William	PB	1756–1817	1803–6	UL (PB)
Bennet-Clark (Carey), Margret Aithna	Ethno	1929–	1953–61	AKI
Besly, Edward Michael	C&M	1951–	(1974) 1977–86	Curator E
Bierbrier, Dr Morris Leonard	EA	1947–	1975–2000	Curator 3
Binyon, Robert Laurence	P&D	1869–1943	1893–1933	Keeper (1932)
Birch, Dr Samuel	Ants	1813–85	1836–85	Keeper OOA (1861)
Birchall, Dr Ann	GRA	1936–	1962–78	AKI
Blake-Hill, Philip Victor	Dir	1917–	1937–71	SRA BMA (1969), MSS (1971)
Bland, Dr Roger Farrant	C&M	1955–	1979–	Curator 2
Blurton, Thomas Richard	OA	1952–	(1986) 1990–	Curator 3
Boalch, Donald Howard	OAE	1914–	1947–8	AKII
Boff, Dr Ruth Minna	C&TS	1952	1980–82	Principal SO (SRC)
Bolton, Dr Lissant	Ethno	1954–	1999–	Curator 3
Bond, Sir Edward Augustus	MSS	1815–98	1838–88	Keeper MSS (1866), PL (1878)
Bonsall, John Clive	PRB	1948–	1974–8	RAI
Boscawen, William St Chad	OOA	1855–1913	1875–7	Senior Asst, Lower Section
Boston, David Merrick	Ethno	1931–	1962–5	AKI
Bowman, Dr Sheridan Gail Esther	RL	1950–	1976–	Keeper SR (1989)
Bowring, Joanna	Sec	1958–	(1991) 1996–	Central Librarian 5
Bradley, Susan Margaret	RL	1948–	1972–	Scientist 3 (Cons)
Brailsford, John William	BMA	1918–88	(1946) 1947–73	Keeper PRB (1969)

NAME	DEPT OF FIRST APPOINTMENT	DATES	BM DATES	FINAL OR CURRENT POST
Brankston, Archibald Dooley	OAE	d.1941	1938–41	AKII
Braunholtz, Hermann Justus	BME	1888–1963	1913–53	Keeper OAE (1938), Ethno (1946)
Bray, Edward	Sec	d.1814	1806–14	Secretary (1806)
Bresc, Cécile	C&M	1974–	2001–	Curator 6 (C&M)
Bridgewater, Bentley Powell Conyers	PB	1911–96	1937–73	Secretary (1948), Keeper (1961)
Brooke, George Cyril	C&M	d.1934	1908–34	DK (1932)
Bruce-Mitford, Marilyn Roberta	BMA	1945–	1967–90	AKI (Management Services Unit)
Bruce-Mitford, Dr Rupert Leo Scott	BME	1914–94	1938–76	Keeper BMA (1954), MLA (1969)
Buckton, David	MLA	1935–	1978–2000	Curator 3
Budge, Sir (Ernest Alfred Thompson) Wallis	OOA	1857–1934	1883–1924	Keeper EAA (1894)
Burgon, Thomas	Ants	1787–1858	1844–58	Supernumerary Asst
Burn, Dr Lucilla Mary	GRA	1954–	(1982) 1985–2001	Curator 4
Burnett, Dr Andrew Michael	C&M	1952–	1974–	Keeper (1992)
Burt, Dr Ben W.	Ethno	1948–	1974–	Curator 5
Callaghan, Peter John	GRA	1947–	(1983–4)	Curator E
Camber, Dr Richard Monash	MLA	1944–	1970–78	AKI
Canby, Dr Sheila Randolph	OA	1949–	1991–	Curator 3
Carey (Bindman), Frances Anne	P&D	1948–	1975–	DK (1994)
Carmichael, Elizabeth Margaret	Ethno	1937–	(1961–2) 1964–97	AKI
Carpenter, William Hookham	P&D	1792–1866	1845–66	Keeper (1845)
Carradice, Dr Ian Arthur	C&M	1953–	1977–91	Curator D
Carson, Dr Robert Andrew Glendinning	C&M	1918–	1947–83	Keeper (1978)
Caygill, Marjorie Lancaster	Sec	1940–	1973–	Asst to Director 3
Cayzer, Elizabeth	P&D	1946–	(1979–80)	RAI
Chapman, Hugo Downes	P&D	1963–	1995–	Curator 3
Cherry, John	BMA	1942–	1964–2002	Keeper MLA (1998)
Christensen, Birthe K.	Cons	1960–	2001–	Conservator 3
Clark, Timothy Thorburn	JA	1959–	1987–	Curator 3
Clifford, Sir Timothy (Peter Flint)	P&D	1946–	1976–8	AKI
Cohn, Dr William	OA		(1945–6)	Temp AKI
Coldstream, John Nicolas	GRA	1927–	(1956–7)	Temp AKII
Cole, Dennis Neligan	P&D	1921–	(1971–5)	Temp RAI
Collins, Dr Michael Denis	MLA	1950–	1979–86	AKI
Collon, Dr Dominique Petronella Margaret	WAA	1940–	(1964–8) (1977–88) 1988–	Curator 3
Colvin, Sir Sidney	P&D	1845–1927	1883–1912	Keeper (1883)
Combe, Taylor	NAP	1774–1826	1803–26	Keeper Ants (1807)
Cook, Dr Barrie John	C&M	1959–	1985–	Curator 4

NAME	DEPT OF FIRST APPOINTMENT	DATES	BM DATES	FINAL OR CURRENT POST
Cook, Dr Brian Francis	GRA	1933–	1969–93	Keeper (1976)
Cook, Jill May	PRB	1954–	1986–	Curator 3
Cooper, Sidney Pool	PB	1919–	1963–76	Head of PS (1973)
Coppel, Stephen Leonardo	P&D	1955–	1992–	Curator 4
Corbett, Peter Edgar	GRA	1920–92	(1949) 1950–61	AKI
Corkran, Sutton Fraser	BME	d.1871	1863–71	Senior Asst, Lower Section
Cowell, Michael Robin	RL	1947–	1970–	Scientist 3
Coxe, William Henry	OOA	d.1869	1861–9	Senior Asst, Lower Section
Craddock, Dr Paul Terence	RL	1945–	1966–	Scientist 3
Cran, Robert Andrew Duncan	OA	1949–	1974–9	RAI
Cranstone, Dr Bryan Allan Lefevre	Ethno	1918–89	1947–76	DK (1969)
Cribb, Joseph Edmond	C&M	1947–	1970–	DK (2001)
Croft-Murray, Edward Frederick	P&D	1907–80	1933–73	Keeper (1954)
Crossman, Yvonne	MSS	1928–	1961–8	RAI (BMA)
Cruickshank, Philippa	C&TS	1957–	1977–	Conservator 4 (Cons)
Cureton, James Edwin	C&M	1848–81	1869–70	Senior Asst, Lower Section
Curtis, Dr John Edward	WAA	1946–	1971–2002	Keeper (1989)
Curtis, Dr Vesta	C&M	1951–	(1995–)	Curator 5
Cust, Sir Lionel H.	P&D	1859–1929	1884–95	2nd Class Asst
Dalton, Ormond Maddock	BME	1866–1945	1895–1927	Keeper (1921)
Daniels, Dr Vincent D.	Cons	1948–	1974–	Scientist 3
Date, Christopher N.	PS	1950–	(1975) 1978–	Archivist L&A 4
Davies, Roy William	GRA	d.1977	1977	RAI
Davies, William Vivian	EA	1947–	1974–	Keeper (1988)
Davis, Allan John Henry	Ethno	1925–	(1952) 1957–85	RAI
Dawson, Mary Aileen Mackenzie	MLA	1949–	1976–	Curator 3
Digby, Adrian	BME	1909–2001	1932–69	Keeper Ethno (1953)
Dodgson, Campbell	P&D	1867–1948	1893–1932	Keeper (1919)
Dolley, Reginald Hugh Michael	C&M	1925–83	1951–63	AKI
Donnithorne, Alan	C&TS	1951–	1976–94	CCO (Cons)
Donoghue (O'Donoghue), Freeman Marius	P&D	b.1848	1867–1909; 1916–17	AK
Doubleday, Ian Anthony	Sec	1959–	1999–	Secretary 3
Durrans, Dr Brian	Ethno	1946–	1976–	Keeper (2000)
East, Katherine	MLA	1926–	1973–86	RAI
Edwards, Dr Iorwerth Eiddon Stephen	EAA	1909–96	1934–74	Keeper EA (1955)
Elgood, Dr Heather Mary	OA/Educ	1950–	(2001–)	Curator 3
Ellis, Sir Henry	PB	1777–1869	(1800) 1805–56	Keeper PB (1806), MSS (1812), PL (1827)
Empson, James	Sloane & PB	d.1765	1756–65	UL (NHMA)

NAME	DEPT OF FIRST APPOINTMENT	DATES	BM DATES	FINAL OR CURRENT POST
Entwistle, Christopher John Speight	MLA	1953–	(1980) 1985–	Curator 5
Errington, Dr Elizabeth Ann	C&M	1947–	(1995–)	Curator 5
Esdaile, Arundell James Kennedy	PB	1880–1956	1903–40	Secretary (1926)
Evans, Angela Care	BMA	1940–	1967–	Curator 4
Evans, Jeremy Lancelotte	MLA	1951–	1971–	Curator 5
Evetts, Basil Thomas Alfred	EAA	b.1858/9	1885–91	2nd Class Asst
Fagan, Louis Alexander	P&D	1845–1903	1869–92	1st Class Asst
Fagg, William Buller	OAE	1914–92	1938–74	Keeper, Ethno (1969)
Farrer, Dr Anne Selina Lucy	OA	1953–	1984–2000	Curator 4
Fearon, Roger Douglas John	Dir	1941–75	1964–75	RAI (Ethno)
Fenton, Terry Leonard	WAA	1936–	1963–6	AKII
Filer, Joyce	EA	1952	(1992–2002)	Research Curator
Finkel, Dr Irving Leonard	WAA	1951–	1979–	Curator 3
Fisher, Penelope Anne Gilmour	C&TS	1957–	1977–94	Conservator D (Cons)
Fitton, Josephine Lesley	GRA	1953–	(1980) 1984–	Curator 4
Fitzgerald, James Edward	Ants	d.1896	1844–9	Assistant Secretary
Fleming, Lore Erwine	OPB	1930–	1972–95	Conservator D (Cons)
Forsdyke, Sir (Edgar) John	GRA	1883–1979	1907–50	Keeper GRA (1932), Director & PL (1936)
Forshall, Rev. Josiah	MSS	1795–1863	1824–50	UL (1828–37), Secretary (1828–50)
Foster, Geoffrey Bromley	C&TS	1934–	1978–94	Conservator D (Cons)
Francis, Sir Frank (Chalton)	PB	1901–88	1926–68	Secretary (1946), Keeper PB (1948), Director & PL (1959)
Frankel, David	WAA	1946–	1975–8	RAI
Franks, Sir (Augustus) Wollaston	Ants	1826–97	1851–97	Keeper BME (1866)
Freestone, Dr Ian Charles	RL	1951–	1979–	Scientist 2
French, Thomas Worden	GRA	1917–2001	(1946–7)	Temp AKII
Friedman (Davies), Dr Renée	EA	1957–	(1998–)	Research Curator
Gadd, Cyril John	EAA	1893–1969	1919–55	Keeper (1948)
Gaimster, David Richard Michael	MLA	1962–	1986–	Curator 4
Gardner, Percy	C&M	1846–1937	1871–87	1st Class Asst
Gere, John Arthur Giles	P&D	1921–95	(1946) 1947–81	Keeper (1972)
Gifford, Rev. Dr Andrew	MSS	1700–84	1756–84	Asst Librarian
Gillman, Derek Anthony	OA	1952–	1981–5	Curator E
Glanville, Stephen Ranulf Kingdon	EAA	1900–56	1924–33	AKI
Goldman, Paul Henry Joseph	P&D	1950–	1974–97	Curator E
Good, Richard	MLA	1926–	1976–93	Curator E
Gowers, Harold James	Dir	1920–89	1939–80	CCO (Cons)
Gray, Basil	C&E	1904–89	1928–69	Keeper OA (1946), Acting Director & PL (1968)

NAME	DEPT OF FIRST APPOINTMENT	DATES	BM DATES	FINAL OR CURRENT POST
Gray, Dr Edward Whitaker	NAP	1748–1806	?1774–1806	UL (1787)
Gregson, Audrey Grace	Ethno	1938–	1970–96	Curator D (Librarian)
Grenfell, John Granville	GRA	1839–	1861–6	2nd Class Asst
Griffith, Francis Llewellyn	BME	1862–1934	1888–96	2nd Class Asst
Griffiths, Antony Vaughan	P&D	1951–	1976–	Keeper (1991)
Grueber, Herbert Appolld	C&M	1846–1927	1866–1912	Keeper (1906)
Haith, Catherine Elizabeth	MLA	1954–	(1976) 1984–2001	Curator 5
Hake, Sir Henry (Mendelssohn)	P&D	1892–1951	1914–28	AK
Hall, Harry Reginald Holland	EAA	1873–1930	1896–1930	Keeper (1924)
Hall, Margaret	Design	1936–	1964–2001	DK (Head of Design)
Handcock, Percy Stewart Peache	EAA		1908–12	2nd Class Asst
Hanna, James (Seamus) Bernard	C&TS	1953–	1979–88	CCO (Cons)
Harding, Eric George	P&D	1929–	1966–89	CCO (Cons)
Harper, Rev. Samuel	NAP	c.1733–1803	1756–1803	UL PB (1765)
Harris, Terence Victor	OA	1942–	1978–	Keeper JA (1997)
Harrison-Hall, Jessica Lucy	OA	1965–	(1991) 1992–	Curator 4
Hawkes, Professor Charles Francis Christopher	BME	1905–92	1928–46	AKI
Hawkins, Edward	Ants	1780–1867	1825–60	Keeper (1826)
Haynes, Dr Denys Eyre Lankester	GRA	1913–94	1939–76	Keeper (1956)
Head, Barclay Vincent	C&M	1844–1914	1864–1906	Keeper (1893)
Hewitt, Virginia Helen	C&M	1955–	1979–	Curator 4
Higgins, Dr Reynold Alleyne	GRA	1916–93	1947–77	DK (1965)
Higgs, Dr Peter John	GRA	1966–	(1993) 1995–	Curator 5
Hill, Sir George Francis	C&M	1867–1948	1893–1936	Keeper (1912), Director & PL (1931)
Hill, Dr Jeremy David	PRB	1963–	1999–	Curator 4
Hind, Arthur Mayger	P&D	1880–1957	1903–45	Keeper (1933)
Hinks, Roger Packman	GRA	1903–63	1926–39	AKI
Hobbs, Dr Richard	C&M	1969–	(1991) 1992–3; 2002–	Curator 5 (P&EE)
Hobson, Robert Lockhart	BME	1872–1941	1897–1938	Keeper C&E (1921), OAE (1934)
Hopley, Ann	Sec	1948–	1973–9	RAI (Archivist)
House, Geoffrey Alan Leslie	Educ	1948–	1976–	DK Head PS (1987), Head Design & Exhibitions (2000)
Hudson, Julie	Ethno	1964–	(1986) 1988–	Curator 6
Hudson, William	NAP	c.1730–93	1757–8	Asst Librarian (Nat Hist)
Hughes, Dr Michael J.	RL	1944–	1967–2000	Scientist 3
Hulton, Paul Hope	P&D	1918–90	1951–81	DK (1973)
Hunt, Charles Garth	Ethno	1943–	(1965)	Temp AKII

NAME	DEPT OF FIRST APPOINTMENT	DATES	BM DATES	FINAL OR CURRENT POST
Hutchinson, Beresford	BMA	1936–	1964–79	RAI
Hyslop, Miranda Mary	BMA		(1964)	Temp AKII
Jackson, Ralph Peter John	PRB	1950–	1977–	Curator 3
James, Thomas Garnet Henry	EAA	1923–	1951–88	Keeper EA (1974)
Jenkins, Dr Gilbert Kenneth	C&M	1918–	1947–78	Keeper (1965)
Jenkins, Dr Ian D.	GRA	1953–	1978–	Senior Curator 2
Jenyns, Roger Soame	C&E	1904–76	1931–68	DK OA (1950)
Johns, Dr Catherine M.	PRB	1941–	(1967) 1968–	Curator 3
Jones, John Winter	PB	1805–81	1837–78	Keeper (1856), PL (1866)
Josi, Henry	P&D	1802–45	1836–45	Keeper (1836)
Joyce, Thomas Athol	BME	1878–1942	1902–38	DK C&E (1921)
Justamond, Dr John Obadiah	NAP		(1773)–8	Asst
Keary, Charles Francis	C&M	1848–1917	1872–87	1st Class Asst
Kendrick, Sir Thomas Downing	BME	1895–1979	1922–59	Keeper (1938), Director & PL (1950)
Kent, Dr John (Philip Cozens)	C&M	1928–2000	1953–90	Keeper (1983)
Kenyon, Sir Frederic (George)	MSS	1863–1952	1889–1930	AK MSS (1898), Director & PL (1909)
Kerry, John Edward	Educ	1924–	1972–5	DK (Head of Education)
Kidd, Dafydd Simon Whitney	MLA	1948–	1974–99	Curator 3
King, Jonathan Colin Harmsworth	Ethno	1952–	1975–	Curator 3
King, Leonard William	EAA	1869–1919	1892–1919	AK
King, William Augustus Henry	C&E	1894–	1926–54	DK BMA (1952)
Kinnes, Dr Ian Alexander	PRB	1944–	1974–98	AKI
Knight, Dr Gowin	PL	1713–72	1756–72	Principal Librarian (1756)
Knox, John Robert	OA	1946–	1978–	Keeper (1994)
Lane, Hannah Patricia	RL	1940–	(1961) 1963–95	Conservator C (Cons)
Langton, Leslie Reginald	Dir	1916–84	1935–76	CCO (C&TS)
Lasko, Professor Peter Erik	BMA	1924–	1950–65	AKI
Lee, David John	Dir	1938–	(1957) 1962–98	Conservator 4 (Cons)
Leeper, Alexander Wigram Allen	EAA	1887–1935	1912–19	2nd Class Asst
Leopold, Dr Jan Hendrik	MLA	1935–	1988–95	AKI
Lidchi, Dr Henrietta J.	Ethno	1966–	(1994) 2000	DK (2000)
Lightfoot, Christopher Sherwin	GRA	1955–	(1982–6)	Curator E
Lodge, Alice Lallie	GRA		(1945–6)	Temp AKII
Logan-Smith, Alexandrina Jean	EA	1950–	1976–80	RAI
Longworth, Dr Ian Heaps	BMA	1935–	(1963) 1963–95	Keeper P&RB (1973)
Lowick, Dr Nicholas Manning	C&M	1940–86	1962–86	DK (1979)
Lyttelton, Dr Margaret Bessie	GRA	1936–93	1974–9	DK (Educ) (1975); AKI (GRA) (1978)
McCall, Henrietta	ANE	1948–	(2001–)	Curator 5

NAME	DEPT OF FIRST APPOINTMENT	DATES	BM DATES	FINAL OR CURRENT POST
McCord, Margaret Elisabeth Anne	C&TS	1944–	1976–89	CCO (Cons)
MacDowall, Dr David William	C&M	1930–	1956–60	AKI
McEwan, Dr Colin	Ethno	1951–	1993–	Curator 3
MacGregor, Robert Neil	Dir	1946–	2002–	Director (2002)
Mack, Professor Brian John	Ethno	1949–	1976–	Keeper (1991); Senior Keeper (2000)
Mackay, Sheila Thorne	Ethno	1926–	1976–91	RAI
Mackie, Sheila	Ethno	1950–	1989–	Librarian 5
McLeod, Professor Malcolm D.	Ethno	1941–	1974–90	Keeper (1974)
Macnamara, Dr Ellen Floyd	GRA	1924–	(1983–7)	Curator E
Madden, Frederic William	Ants	1839–1904	1858–68	Senior Asst, Upper Section, C&M (1867)
Maher, Pauline Ann O'Regan	BMA	1933–	(1955–7)	Temp AKII
Main, Dr Peter Livingstone	RL	1952–	1978–	Scientist 3
Males, Dr Valerie Jean	OA	1950–	1979–81	RAI
Malone (Stoddart), Dr Caroline Ann Tuke	P&EE	1957–	2000–	Keeper (2000)
Manning, William H.	BMA	1936–	1963–4	RAII
Marée, Marcel	AES	1969–	(2000–)	Curator 5
Marks, Professor Richard Charles	MLA	1945–	1973–9	AKI
Marshall, Frederick Henry	GRA	1878–1955	1901–12	1st Class Asst
Martin, Joan Steel	C&M	1919–83	1953–76	RAI
Mattingley, Harold	C&M	1884–1964	1910–47	AKI
Maty, Dr Matthew	PB	1718–76	1756–76	UL PB (1756), NAP (1765), PL (1772)
Maty, Rev. Paul Henry	NAP	1745–87	1776–87	UL (1782)
Maurice, Rev. Thomas	MSS	1754–1824	1799–1824	Asst Librarian
Meadows, Andrew Robert	C&M	1965–	1995–	Curator 4
Mealy, Henry Aubury	Ants	b.1832–3	1857–98	2nd Class Asst
Michaelson, Carol Jeanne Day	OA	1946–	(1991) 1995–	Curator 4
Middleton, Dr Andrew Philip	RL	1949–	1983–	Scientist 3
Millard, Alan Ralph	WAA	1937–	(1961–3)	Temp AKII
Mitchell, Dr Terence Croft	WAA	1929–	(1959) 1966–89	Keeper (1985)
Morris, George Bernard	PB	1932–	1960–94	Secretary (DK) (1973)
Morris, Justin Collard	PRB	1973–	(1995) 2001–	Curator 6 (OA)
Morton, Dr Charles	MSS	1719–99	1756–99	UL (1756), PL (1776)
Moss, Dr Alfred Allinson	RL	1912–90	1939–53	PSO
Murray, Alexander Stuart	GRA	1841–1904	1867–1904	Keeper (1886)
Nares, Rev. Robert	MSS	1753–1829	1795–1807	UL (1799)
Needham, Dr Stuart Paul	PRB	1953–	1977–	Curator 3
Nenk, Beverley	MLA	1957–	1989–	Curator 5
Neverson, Yvonne Vanessa	Ethno	1952–	1977–82	RAI
Newell, Jennifer	Ethno	1971–	2001–	Curator 5

NAME	DEPT OF FIRST APPOINTMENT	DATES	BM DATES	FINAL OR CURRENT POST
Newey, Hazel Mary	MLA	1949–	1972–93	CCO (Cons)
Newton, Sir Charles (Thomas)	Ants	1816–94	1840–52; 1861–86	Keeper GRA (1861)
Nimmo, Baron Arthur Francis	Dir	1913–89	(1929) 1931–75	CCO (C&TS)
Norville-Day, Heather Elizabeth	Cons	1959–	1998–	Conservator 4
O'Connell, Sheila Mary	P&D	1947–	(1979) 1991	Curator 4
Oddy, Dr William Andrew	RL	1942–	(1966) 1967–2002	Keeper Cons (1986), Head of Cons (1991)
O'Hanlon, Dr Michael David Peter	Ethno	1950–	1983–98	AKI
Oldfield, Edmund	Ants	1816–1902	1848–61	1st Class Asst
Omar, Sherif Ali Tawfik	C&TS	1945–	1981–6	CCO (Cons)
Opper, Thorsten	GRA	1969–	2001–	Curator 5
Organ, Robert Muller	RL	1917–	1951–65	Chief Experimental Officer
Orna-Ornstein, John	C&M	1972–	(1994–2001) 2001–	Curator 5
Ottley, William Young	Ants	1771–1836	1833–6	Keeper, P&D (1833)
Ozanne, James William	P&D	d.1931	1866–9	Senior Asst, Lower Section
Painter, Dr Kenneth Scott	BMA	1935–	1960–88	DK PRB (1974), GRA (1977)
Paintin, Elaine Margaret	PRB	1947–	1975–6	RAI
Panizzi, Sir Anthony (Antonio Genesio Maria)	PB	1797–1879	1831–66	Keeper (1837), PL (1856)
Parker, Claire Nihoul	Sec	1946–	1994–8	Secretary (DK) (1994)
Parker, Sir Karl Theodore	P&D	1895–1992	1928–33	AKII
Parkinson, Dr Richard Bruce	EA	1963–	1992–	Curator 4
Pascoe, Dr Michael William	C&TS	1930–	1976–81	Keeper C&TS (SPSO) (1979)
Penneck, Rev. Richard	PB	c. 1728–1803	1761–1803 (1761)	Keeper of Reading Room
Penny, Joyce Mary Freeman	OA	1912–	(1948–9)	Temp AKII
Persaud, Harry	PB	1946–	(1968) 1970–	Curator 5 (Ethno)
Pfister, Johann Georg	Ants		(1850) 1857–76 C&M (1871)	Senior Asst, Upper Section,
Picton, Dr John Wyndham	Ethno	1938–	(1961) 1970–79	DK (1974)
Pilbeam, Janet Mavis	JA	1946–	1992–	Curator 6
Pimpaneau, Sara	Ethno	1968–	1999–	Curator 5
Pinches, Theophilus Goldridge	OOA	1856–1934	1878–1900	1st Class Asst
Pinder-Wilson, Ralph Hutchinson	OA	1919–	1949–76	DK (1969)
Planta, Rev. Andrew	PB	1717–73	1758–73	Asst, PB (1765)
Planta, Joseph	PB	1744–1827	1773–1827	Keeper MSS (1776), PL (1799)
Plenderleith, Dr Harold James	RL	1898–1997	(1924) 1931–59	Keeper (1949)
Poole, Reginald Stuart	Ants	1832–95	1852–93	Keeper C&M (1870)
Pope-Hennessy, Sir John (Wyndham)	Dir	1913–94	1974–6	Director (1974)

NAME	DEPT OF FIRST APPOINTMENT	DATES	BM DATES	FINAL OR CURRENT POST
Popham, Arthur Ewart	P&D	1889–1970	1912–54	Keeper (1945)
Portal, Jane Virginia	OA	1955–	(1987) 1990–	Curator 3
Porter, Alexandra	ANE	1972–	(2001–)	Curator 6
Porter, Dr Venetia Ann	C&M/OA	1955–	(1987) 1989–	Curator 4
Posey, Sarah	Ethno	1962–	(1987) 1987–	Curator 5
Potter, Dr Timothy William	PRB	1944–2000	1978–2000	Keeper (1995)
Pouncey, Philip Michael Rivers	P&D	1910–90	1945–66	DK (1954)
Powell-Jones, Mark Ellis	C&M	1951–	1974–92	Keeper (1990)
Prescott, Arthur George	GRA	1911–84	(1934) 1936–75	CCO
Price, Dr Martin Jessop	C&M	1939–95	1966–94	DK (1978)
Pryce, Frederick Norman	GRA	1888–1953	1911–39	Keeper (1936)
Quirke, Stephen Gerald John	EA	1962–	(1987) 1989–99	Curator 3
Rae, Allyson	Cons	1955–	1978–	Conservator 4
Rankine (Hall), Jean Morag	PB	1941–	1967–97	Head PS (1978), Deputy Director (1983)
Rapson, Edward James	C&M	1861–1937	1887–1906	1st Class Asst
Rawson, Dame Jessica (Mary)	OA	1943–	1967–94	Keeper (1989)
Read, Sir Charles Hercules	BME	1857–1929	1880–1921	Keeper (1896)
Reade, Dr Julian Edgeworth	WAA	1938–	1975–2000	Curator 3
Reeve, John Frederick	Educ	1951–	1980–	Head of Education (DK) (1998)
Reeves, Carl Nicholas	EA	1956–	(1984–91)	Curator E
Reid, George William	P&D	1819–87	1842–83	Keeper (1866)
Renouf, Sir Peter le Page	EAA	1822–97	1886–91	Keeper (1886)
Rigby, Valery	PRB	1938–	1978–99	Curator 4
Rimius, Henry	PB	d.1756	1756	Asst Librarian
Roberts, Alison Jane	PRB	1959–	1987–96	Curator E
Roberts, Dr Paul C.	GRA	1961–	(1994) 1994–	Curator 5
Robertson, Charles Martin	GRA	1911–	1936–48	AKI
Robinson, Sir Edward Stanley Gotch	C&M	1887–1976	1912–52	Keeper (1949)
Robinson, James Patrick	MLA	1962–	1991–	Curator 5
Rogers, Professor John Michael	OA	1935–	1977–91	DK (1982)
Rosenfeld, Dr Andrée Jeanne Berthe	BMA	1934–	1964–72	SRA (PRB)
Ross, (Sir) Edward Denison	P&D	1871–1940	1914–16	1st Class Asst
Rowlands, John Kendall	P&D	1931–	1965–91	Keeper (1981)
Roy, Gillian S.	P&D	1939–	(1968–73) 1995–2001	Conservator 3 (Cons)
Royalton-Kisch, Martin Bruce	P&D	1952–	1975–8; 1982–	Senior Curator 2
Rudoe, Judith Ann	MLA	1951–	1974–	Curator 3
Russell, John Francis O'Neill	MLA	1923–85	1970–85	RAI
Samson, Dr Otto W.	OAE	1900–	(1944–7)	Temporary AKII
Schofield, Louise Eva Marian	GRA	1958–	(1987–2000)	Curator 5

NAME	DEPT OF FIRST APPOINTMENT	DATES	BM DATES	FINAL OR CURRENT POST
Scott, Dr Alexander	RL	1853–1947	(1920) 1931–8	Director of RL (1931)
Scott-Moncrieff, Philip David	EAA	1879–1911	1903–11	2nd Class Asst
Scrutton, Thomas Hugh	P&D	1917–	(1946–7)	Temp AKII
Senior, Elizabeth	P&D	d.1941	1934–41	AKII
Shaw, Dr George	NAP	1751–1813	1791–1813	Keeper NAP (1807)
Shelton, Anthony Alan	Ethno	1955–	1985–91	Curator E
Shore, Arthur Frank	EAA	1924–94	1957–74	AKI
Shorter, Alan Wynn	EAA	1905–38	1929–38	AKII
Sieveking, Dr Gale de Giberne	BMA	1925–	1956–85	DK PRB (1974)
Simpson, Dr St John	WAA	1962–	1993–	Curator 4
Sloan, Dr Kim M.T.	P&D	1953–	1992–	Curator 3
Smith, Arthur Hamilton	GRA	1860–1941	1886–1925	Keeper (1909)
Smith, (Sir) Cecil Harcourt	GRA	1859–1944	1879–1908	Keeper (1904)
Smith, George	OOA	1840–76	(1867) 1870–76	Senior Asst, Lower Section
Smith, John Thomas	P&D	1766–1833	1816–33	Asst [Keeper of P&D] (1816)
Smith, Lawrence Roger Hines	MSS	1941–	1962–97	Keeper OA (1977); JA (1987)
Smith, Pamela Manton	L&A	1946–	1998–	Fleming Librarian 5
Smith, Reginald Allender	BME	1873–1940	1898–1938	Keeper BMA (1927)
Smith, Sandra Melanie	Cons	1962–	1985–	Conservator (3) Acting Keeper (2002)
Smith, Sidney	EAA	1889–1979	1914–48	Keeper (1931)
Snelgrove, Dudley Francis	P&D	1906–92	(1920) 1941–64	SRA
Solander, Dr Daniel Charles	NAP	1736–82	1763–82	UL (1773)
Sollberger, Dr Edmond	WAA	1920–89	(1961) 1967–83	Keeper (1974)
Southern, Dinah Margaret Bonnell Baird	P&D	1947–	1970–75	RAI
Southgate, Rev. Richard	MSS	1749–95	1784–95	Asst
Spence, Anthony John Macduff	PRB	1961–	1984–	Curator 5
Spencer, Dr Alan Jeffrey	EA	1949–	1975–	Curator 3
Spencer, Neal Andrew	EA	1974–	(2000–)	Curator 5
Spratling, Dr Mansel Gilwern	PRB	1944–	1975–7	RAI
Spring, Christopher James	Ethno	1951–	1976–	Curator 5
Sproston, Alison	L&A	1941–	2000–	Eccles Librarian 3
Stainton (Campbell), Lindsay Raymonde Clifford	P&D	1947–	1978–91	AKI
Starzecka, Dorota	Ethno	1939–	1968–99	AKI
Stead, Dr Ian Mathieson	PRB	1936–	1974–96	DK (1977)
Stead, Miriam Joan	EA	1953–	1981–7	Curator E
Stratford, Neil Martin	MLA	1938–	1975–98	Keeper (1975)
Strong, Dr Donald Emrys	GRA	1927–73	1956–68	AKI
Strudwick, Dr Nigel C.	EA		(1999–)	Curator 6
Swaddling, Dr Judith	GRA		1976–	Curator 4
Syson, Luke	C&M	1965–	1991–	Curator 4

NAME	DEPT OF FIRST APPOINTMENT	DATES	BM DATES	FINAL OR CURRENT POST
Tait, Gerald Hugh	BMA	1927–	1954–92	DK (1969)
Tatton-Brown, Dr Veronica Ann	GRA	1944–	1974–	Curator 3
Taverne, Suzanna	Dir	1960–	1999–2001	Managing Director (1999)
Tayler, Donald Bertram	Ethno	1931–	(1963)	Temp AKI
Taylor, Dr John Hilton	EA	1958–	(1988) 1990–	Curator 4
Taylor, Michael Reding	MLA	1934–	(1965) 1966–70	AKI
Templeman, Dr Peter	PB	1711–69	1759–60	Keeper Reading Room
Thompson, David Robert	MLA	1950–	(1979) 1981–	Curator 3
Thompson, Sir (Edward) Maunde	MSS	1840–1929	1861–1909	Keeper (1878), PL (1888)
Thompson, Philip Andrew	Cons	1953–	1981–	Conservator 4
Thompson, Reginald Campbell	EAA	1876–1941	1899–1905	2nd Class Asst
Thornton (Warren), Dr Dora Frieda	MLA	1961–	1990–	Curator 4
Tite, Dr Michael Stanley	RL	1938–	1975–89	Keeper (1981)
Tonnochy, Alec Bain	BME	1889–1963	1914–54	Keeper BMA (1950)
Tubb, Jonathan Nicholas	WAA	1951–	1979–	Curator 4
Turner, Nicholas James Lindsay	P&D	1947–	1974–94	DK (1991)
Uprichard, Robert Kenneth	WAA	1948–	(1976) 1979–	Conservator 4 (Cons)
Usherwood, Nicholas John	PS	1943–	1977–8	DK
Vainker, Shelagh Jane	OA	1960–	1986–91	Curator E
Varndell, Gillian Louise	PRB	1951–	1973–6; (1981) 1982–	Curator 5
Vaux, William Sandys Wright	C&M	1818–85	1841–70	Keeper (1861)
Villing, Dr Alexandra C.	GRA	1968–	2001–	Curator 5
Waley, Arthur David (b. Schloss)	P&D	1889–1966	1913–30	AKI
Walker, Christopher Bromhead Fleming	WAA	1942–	(1967) 1970–	DK (1995)
Walker, John	C&M	1900–64	1931–64	Keeper (1952)
Walker, Dr Susan Elizabeth Constance	GRA	1948–	1977–	DK (1995)
Wallace, Kathleen Janet	Sec	1941–	1979–2001	Curator 4 (Archivist)
Walters, Henry Beauchamp	GRA	1867–1944	1890–1932	Keeper (1925)
Wang, Helen K.	C&M	1965–	(1991) 1993–	Curator 4
Ward, Rachel Mary	OA	1955–	1983–2000	Curator 4
Wartenberg, Dr Ute	C&M	1963–	1991–93	Curator E
Waterhouse, David Boyer	OA	1936–	1961–4	AKII
Watkins, Sarah Ceinwen	Cons	1956–	1994–	Conservator 4
Watson, Professor William	BMA	1917–	(1946) 1947–66	AKI, BMA (1947); OA (1949)
Webb, Maysie Florence	NRLSI	1923–	1966–83	Keeper, Asst Director (1963), Deputy Director (1971)
Webb, William			[1756]	Asst Librarian (did not take up post)
Weber, Catherine	PRB	1944–	(1970–2)	RAII

NAME	DEPT OF FIRST APPOINTMENT	DATES	BM DATES	FINAL OR CURRENT POST
Webster, Leslie Elizabeth	BMA	1943–	1964–	DK (1985); Acting Keeper (MME) (2002)
Weir, Shelagh G.	Ethno	1942–	1965–97	AKI
Welsby, Dr Derek Anthony	EA	1956–	(1991) 1992–	Curator 4
Werner, Dr Alfred Emil Anthony	RL	1911–	1954–75	Keeper (SPSO) (1959)
White, Sir Christopher (John)	P&D	1930–	1954–64	AKI
Whitfield, Professor Roderick	BMA	1937–	1968–84	AKI (OA)
Wiggins, Colin Peter	P&D	1953–	(1973–81)	RAII
Wilcox, Timothy	P&D	1955–	(2001–)	Curator 5
Wilkinson, Alexandra	EA	1932–	(1956) 1958–69	RAI
Williams, Dr Daniel Gareth Edmund	C&M	1969–	1996–	Curator 5
Williams, Dr Dyfri John Roderick	GRA	1952–	1979–	Keeper (1993)
Williams, Dr Jonathan Hugh Creer	C&M	1967–	(1993) 1994	Curator 4
Williams, Dr Nigel Ruben Rook	BMA	1944–92	(1961) 1964–92	CCO (D) (Cons)
Williams, Reginald	P&D	1922–	1953–86	SRA
Willis, Dr Michael D.	OA		1994–	Curator 3
Wills, Paul	C&TS	1945–	1980–6	CCO (D) (Cons)
Wilson, Sir David (MacKenzie)	BMA	1931–	1955–63; 1977–92	Director (1977)
Wilson, Gillian Mary	PRB	1950–	1977–80	RAI
Wilson, Dr Timothy H.	MLA	1950–	1979–90	AKI
Wilton, J. Andrew R.	P&D	1942–	(1959) 1967–84	AKI
Winkworth, William Wilberforce	C&E	1897–1991	1922–6	Asst
Wiseman, Professor Donald John	EAA	1918–	(1948) 1949–61	AKI (WAA)
Witney, John Humphrey	PB	1879–1964	1896–1946	Secretary (1940)
Woide, Rev. Charles Godfrey (Karl Gottfried)	PB	1725–90	1782–90	Asst Librarian
Wolfenden, Sir John (Frederick) (later Lord Wolfenden)	Dir	1906–85	(1969–73)	Director and PL (1969)
Wood, Norma Rosalind	P&D	1924–	(1976–80)	RAI
Wroth, Warwick William	C&M	1858–1911	1878–1911	AK
Yeames, Arthur Henry Savage	GRA	b.1881	1905–7	2nd Class Asst (GRA); (C&M) (1906)
Youngs, Susan Mabury	MLA	1947–	1973–	Curator 4
Zwalf, Wladimir	OPB & MSS	1932–	1962–93	AKI (OA)

LIST OF SOURCES

Manuscripts

BRITISH MUSEUM CENTRAL ARCHIVES (CE)
CE1. Minutes of General Meeting of the Trustees, 1753–1963.
CE3. Minutes of Standing Committee of the Trustees, 1754–63.
CE4. Original papers, 1743–1946.
CE5. Officers' reports to General Meetings and Standing Committee, 1805–69.
CE6. Minutes to officers, 1888–1963.
CE7. Minutes of sub-committees of the Trustees, 1828–1963.
CE9. Indexes of minutes of General Meetings, Standing Committee and sub-committees of Trustees, 1754–1939.
CE15. Letter books of Principal Trustees relating to staff, 1847–57.
CE18. Papers of Principal Trustees relating to staff matters and routine, 1860–1944.
CE22. Minutes of Board of Trustees, 1963–.
CE25. Board papers, 1963–.
CE30. Book of Presents, 1756–1960.
CE32. Papers relating to excavations overseas.
CE33. Staff applications and testimonials.
CE43. Miscellaneous litigation.
CE48. Buildings; plans and drawings.
CE53. Reports of sub-committees of the Trustees, 1805–9.
CE54. Minutes of special committees of the Trustees.
CE 86. Accounts.
CE98–113. Registered files.
CE114. Photographs.
CE115. Scrapbooks and illustrations of the Museum.
CE Bay6/G/2. History of the British Museum Rifle Club.
CE Acc No 147. Braunholtz papers.
CE Booze-Allen and Hamilton reports, 1972.
CE The British Museum conservation plan, 2000.
CE Catalogue of the Hawkins collection of medals, April 1860.
CE Confidential correspondence on the display of the Parthenon Sculpture, 1928–38.
CE Directors' papers.
CE In Chancery. Between the Most Noble John, Duke of Bedford, Plt., and the Trustees of the British Museum, Defts. Brief for Defendants (1822).
CE In Chancery. The Duke of Bedford versus the British Museum... Application for an injunction, 6 July 1822.
CE John Winter Jones's appointment as Principal Librarian signed by Victoria.

CE Minutes of National Museum Directors' Conference.
CE The British Museum Plan, 1999/2000 to 2001/2002.
CE TY The Townley archive.

BRITISH MUSEUM (BM) CENTRAL REGISTRY FILES
BM DEPARTMENTAL FILES
BM: ANE (Department of the Ancient Near East) Antiquities correspondence.
BM: Ethno. (Department of Ethnography) Digby MS (Adrian Digby, 'Evacuated ethnography at Drayton and the quarry, 1939–45').
BM: MME (Department of Medieval and Modern Europe) Gold Cup Documents.
BM: MME (Department of Medieval and Modern Europe) Out letters.

BODLEIAN LIBRARY, OXFORD
Douce e 28.
Madden's Diary MSS.Eng.hist c.140–82.

BRITISH LIBRARY (BL)
BL Add. 4241. Birch, T. Memoirs relating to the Life of Sr. Hans Sloane Bart.
BL Add. 4302. Letters to Dr Birch.
BL Add. 4449. Birch Collection. Papers relating to the British Museum.
BL Add. 6179. Ward, J. Papers relating to the British Museum.
BL Add. 27,276. Weedon, Rev. W. Pleasing recollection of a walk through the British Museum.
BL Add. 36,269. Hardwicke papers.
BL Add. 38,996. Layard papers.
BL Add. 40,485. Peel papers.
BL Add. 52,292. Thompson, E. Maunde. History of the British Museum.
BL DH2 Correspondence, Trustees' Minutes and Reports of the Keepers of Printed Books.
BL Sloane MS 4047.

UNIVERSITY LIBRARY, CAMBRIDGE (ULC)
ULC Add.9389 Letters to Joseph Bonomi.

FIONA WRIGHT
Franks, A.W. The apology for my life (MS).

Printed sources

Abbot, C. (1861) The diary and correspondence of Charles Abbot, Lord Colchester, speaker of the House of Commons, 1802–1817, ii, London.

Accounts. Accounts and income and expenditure of the British Museum submitted to Parliament.

A celebration of two and a half centuries. A plan for the British Museum, London (1990).

Ackerman, R.W., and G.P. (1979) Sir Frederic Madden, a biographical sketch and bibliography, New York and London.

Addis, J.M. (1979) Chinese porcelain from the Addis collection..., London.

Alexander, E.M.M. (1954) 'Finds from the Mesolithic habitation-site at Star Carr, Seamer, near Scarborough, Yorkshire', The British Museum quarterly, xix, 52–4.

Allen, J.R., and Anderson, J. (1903) The early Christian monuments of Scotland, Edinburgh.

Allison, P.A. (1965) 'African ethnography from Kew', The British Museum quarterly, xxix, 103–9.

Anderson, R. (1997) 'Early scientific instruments and horology', in Caygill and Cherry (1997), 286–95.

Anderson, R. (2000) The Great Court and the British Museum, London.

Annual report. Annual report of the general progress of the Museum and of the British Museum (Natural History).

Annual return. Return... of the account of the income and expenditure of the British Museum... (to the House of Commons).

Archibald, M.M. (1994) 'Coins and medals', in MacGregor (1994), 150–60.

Ash, M. (1981) '"A fine, genial and hearty band": David Laing, Daniel Wilson and Scottish archaeology', in Bell (1981), 31–85.

Ashmole, B. (1994) Bernard Ashmole 1894–1988. An autobiography (ed. D. Kurtz), Oxford.

A short guide to the temporary war-time exhibition in the British Museum, London 1918.

Ashton, N.M. (ed.) High Lodge. Excavations by G. de G. Sieveking, 1962–8, and J. Cook, 1988, London.

Askwith, B. (1969) Lady Dilke, a biography, London.

Babelon, E.C.F. (1901) Traité des monnaies grecques et romaines, I, Paris.

Babington, C. (1865) An introductory lecture on archaeology, Cambridge.

Bähr, J.C. (1850) Die Gräber der Liven. Ein Beitrag zur nordischen Alterthumskunde und Geschichte, Dresden.

Baker, M., and Richardson, B. (eds.) (1997) A grand design. The art of the Victoria and Albert Museum, London.

Barker, H., and Mackey, C.J. (1959) 'British Museum natural radiocarbon measurements, i', American journal of science radiocarbon supplement, i, 81–6.

Barley, N. (ed.) (1999) The golden sword. Stamford Raffles and the East, London.

Barnett, L.D. (1937) 'Edward James Rapson, 1861–1937', Proceedings of the British Academy, xxiii, 526–37.

Barnett, R.D. (1970) 'Re-building of the Assyrian galleries', British Museum Society, Bulletin, no.3, 2–3.

Barth, F.E., and Hodson, F.R. (1976) 'The Hallstatt cemetery and its documentation: some new evidence', The Antiquaries journal, lvi, 161–76.

Basham, A.L. (1960) 'Lionel David Barnett, 1871–1960', Proceedings of the British Academy, lxvi, 333–40.

Bassani, E., and McLeod, M. (n.d.) Jacob Epstein collector, Milan.

Bateman, C.A., et al. (1966) Presentation and production of clay tablets and the conservation of wall paintings, London.

Batten, M.I. (1936–7) 'The architecture of Dr Robert Hooke F.R.S.', The Walpole Society, xxv, 83–113.

Battiscombe, C.F. (ed.) (1956) The relics of St Cuthbert, Durham.

Beard, M. (2000) The invention of Jane Harrison, Cambridge (Mass.) and London.

Beaverbrook, M. (1956) Men and power, 1917–1918. London.

Behrman, S.N. (1986) Duveen, new ed., London.

Bell, A.S. (ed.) (1981) The Scottish antiquarian tradition. Essays to mark the bicentenary of the Society of Antiquaries of Scotland and its museum, 1780–1980, Edinburgh.

Bell, H.I. (1952) 'Sir Frederic George Kenyon, 1863–1952', Proceedings of the British Academy, xxxviii, 269–94.

Beresford, R. (1998) Dulwich Picture Gallery, complete illustrated catalogue, London.

Berlin, I. (2000) The power of ideas, London.

Besterman, T. (1956) Voltaire's correspondence, xviii, Geneva.

Bimson, M., and Freestone, I.C. (1983) 'An analytical study of the relationship between the Portland Vase and other Roman cameo glasses', Journal of glass studies, xxx.

Bindman, D., and Riemann, G. (eds.) (1993) Carl Friedrich Schinkel, 'The English Journey'. Journal of a visit to France and Britain in 1826, New Haven and London.

Binyon, L. (1916) A catalogue of Japanese and Chinese woodcuts preserved in the Sub-department of Oriental Prints and Drawings in the British Museum, London.

Birch, S. (1872) 'The progress of biblical archæology', Transactions of the Society for Biblical Archæology, i, 1–12.

Bjurström, P. (1992) 'Die Entstehung der Nationalgalerien im 18 Jahrhundert. Aspecte der Grundungsgeschichte des Schwedischen Nationalmuseums' in von Plessen (1992), 142–7.

Blurton, T.R. (1997) The enduring image: treasures from the British Museum, London.

Boardman, J. (1985) '100 years of classical archaeology at Oxford' in Kurtz (1985).

Boase, T.S.R. (1954) 'The decoration of the new Palace of Westminster 1841–63', Journal of the Warburg and Courtauld Institutes, xvii, 319–58.

Borowsky, C.M. (1963) 'The Charleston Museum', Museum news, xli; 6, 11–21.

Borrie, M. (1979) 'Panizzi and Madden', The British Library journal, v, 18–37.

Bowden, M. (1991) Pitt Rivers, the life and archaeological work of Lieutenant-General Augustus Henry Lane Fox Pitt Rivers, Cambridge.

Bowdich, T.E. (1819) Mission from Cape Coast Castle to Ashantee..., London.

Bowman, S. (1990) Radiocarbon dating, London.

Bowman, S. (ed.) (1991) Science and the past, London.

Brailsford, J.W. (1962) Hod Hill, i, Antiquities from Hod Hill in the Durden collection, London.

Brand, D. (1998) The study of the past in the Victorian Age, Oxford. Oxbow Monograph, 73.

Brand, J. (1813) Observations on the popular antiquities: chiefly illustrating the origin of our vulgar and provincial customs, ceremonies and superstitions. London.

Braunholtz, H.J. (1952) 'The Beasley collection', The British Museum quarterly, xv, 103–5.

Braunholtz, H.J. (1953) 'The Sloane Collection: ethnography', The British Museum quarterly, xviii: 1, 23–6.

Braunholtz, H.J. (1953a) 'History of ethnography in the Museum 1753–1938 (Pt.II)', The British Museum quarterly, xviii, 109–20.

Braunholtz, H.J. (1970) Sir Hans Sloane and ethnography, London.

Briggs, A. (1988) Victorian things, London.

British Museum. A guide to the exhibition rooms of the Departments of Natural History and Antiquities, London 1859 et seq.

British Museum quarterly news supplement.

British Museum. Research register, 1994–6.

British Museum Review, 1996–8.

Brock, M.G., and Corthoys, M.C. (eds.) (2000) The history of Oxford University. Nineteenth-century Oxford, part 2, Oxford. The History of the University of Oxford.

Brøndsted, P.O. (1926) Breve fra P.O. Brøndsted 1801–33. Copenhagen.

Brooks, E. St. J. (1954) Sir Hans Sloane, the great collector and his circle, London.

Broughton, A.M.C. (1887) Court and private life in the time of Queen Charlotte; being the private journals of Mrs Papendiek, Assistant Keeper of the Wardrobe to Her Majesty, London.

Brown, Y.-Y. (1994) 'Japanese books and manuscripts.

Sloane's Japanese library and the making of the *History of Japan*', in MacGregor (1994), 278–90.

Bruce, W.N. (1903) *Sir A. Henry Layard G.C.B., D.C.L. Autobiography and letters from his childhood to his appointment as ambassador at Madrid*, ii, London.

Bruce-Mitford, R.L.S. (1956) 'National museums and local material', *The museums journal*, lv: 10, 251–8.

Bruce-Mitford, R.L.S. (1971), 'Envoi', *The British Museum quarterly*, xxxv, 8–15.

Bruce-Mitford, R.L.S. (1975–83) *The Sutton Hoo ship-burial*, London.

Bruce-Mitford, R.L.S. (1990) 'Thomas Downing Kendrick, 1895–1979', *Proceedings of the British Academy*, lxxvi, 445–71.

Buckton, D. (ed.) *Byzantium. Treasures of art and culture*, London.

Budge, E.A.W. (1920) *By Nile and Tigris. A narrative of journeys in Egypt and Mesopotamia on behalf of the British Museum between the years 1886 and 1913*. London.

Budge, E.A.W. (1925) *The rise and progress of Assyriology*, London.

Burnett, A., and Reeve, J. (2001) *Behind the scenes at the British Museum*, London.

Burrow, J.W. (1981) *A liberal descent*, London.

Burton, A. (1999) *Vision and Accident. The story of the Victoria and Albert Museum*, London.

Calder, W.M., and Cobet, J. (eds.) (1990) *Heinrich Schliemann nach hundert Jahren*, Frankfurt/Main.

Camber, R., and Cherry, J. (1977) 'The Savernake horn', *The British Museum yearbook*, ii, 201–11.

Campbell, C. (1715) *Vitruvius Britannicus*, i, London.

Cantarel-Besson, Y. (1981) *La naissance du musée du Louvre*, Paris.

Carpenter, W.H. (1844) *Pictorial notices, consisting of a memoir of Sir A. van Dyck, with a descriptive catalogue of the etchings executed by him...*, London.

Carey, F. (1977) 'Henry Moore drawings in the British Museum', *The British Museum yearbook*, ii, 245–52.

Carey, F. (1991) *Collecting the 20th century*, London.

Carey, F. (1996) 'Campbell Dodgson (1867–1948)', in Griffiths (1996), 211–35.

Carey, F. (1996a) 'Curatorial collecting in the twentieth century', in Griffiths (1996), 236–55.

Carey, F. (1997) *Modern Scandinavian prints*, London.

Carey, F. (1998) *Campbell Dodgson, scholar and collector, 1867–1948*, London.

Carey, F., and Griffiths, A. (1980) *American prints 1879–1979*, London.

Carey, F., and Griffiths, A. (1984) *The print in Germany 1880–1933*, London.

Carey, F., and Griffiths, A. (1990) *Avant-garde British print-making, 1940–60*, London.

Carson, R.A.G. (1966–7) 'The Sir George Allen bequest', *The British Museum quarterly*, xxxi, 32–4.

Carson, R.A.G. (1974) 'The Department of Coins and Medals. British Museum', *Compte rendu, Commission Internationale de Numismatique*, xxi, 35–45.

Carson, R.A.G., and Pagan, H. (1986) *A history of the Royal Numismatic Society 1836–1986*, London.

Carter, H.B. (1988) *Sir Joseph Banks 1743–1820*, London.

Cary, H. (1847) *Memoir of the Rev. Francis Cary...*, London.

Cash, D. (1994) *Access to museum culture: the British Museum from 1753 to 1836*, Unpublished thesis, University of Cambridge.

Casson (1940) *The discovery of man. The story of the inquiry into human origins*, London.

Caygill, M.L. (1980) 'The Gordon riots', *The British Museum Society bulletin*, no.34, 26–9.

Caygill, M.L. (1981) *The story of the British Museum*, London.

Caygill, M.L. (1982) 'William Who's Wing' *The British Museum Society bulletin*, no.40, 13–17.

Caygill, M.L. (1985) *Treasures of the British Museum*, London.

Caygill, M.L. (1985a) 'Whodunit', *British Museum Society bulletin*, no.48, 28–31.

Caygill, M.L. (1988) 'After the bowing is over', *The British Museum Society bulletin*, no.57, 25–9.

Caygill, M.L. (1989) '1939: Evacuating the BM's treasures', *The British Museum Society bulletin*, no.62, 17–21.

Caygill, M.L. (1990) 'The British Museum at war', *British Museum magazine*, no.6, 35–9.

Caygill, M.L. (1992) 'The British Museum lottery', *British Museum magazine*, no.10, 7–10.

Caygill, M.L. (1992a) 'The protection of national treasures at the British Museum during the Second World War' in Vandiver (1992), 29–40.

Caygill, M.L. (1994) 'Sloane's will and the establishment of the British Museum', in MacGregor (1994), 45–68.

Caygill, M.L. (1997) 'Franks and the British Museum – the cuckoo in the nest', in Caygill and Cherry (1997), 51–114.

Caygill, M.L. (1999) *The British Museum. A-Z companion*, London.

Caygill, M.L. (2000) *The British Museum Reading Room*, London.

Caygill, M.L., and Cherry, J. (1997) *A.W. Franks. Nineteenth-century collecting and the British Museum*, London.

Caygill, M.L., and Date, C. (1999) *Building the British Museum*, London.

Caygill, M., and House, G. (eds) (1986) *A survey of visitors to the British Museum (1982–1983) by Peter H. Mann*, London. British Museum occasional paper, no.64.

Caygill, M., and Leese, M.N. (1994) *A survey of visitors to the British Museum (1992–3)*, London. British Museum occasional paper, no.101.

Centenaire de l'Abbé Cochet 1975. Actes du colloque international d'archéologie, Rouen 3-4-5 Juillet 1975. fasc. i, Rouen 1978.

Chadwick, O. (1970) *The Victorian church*, ii, London.

Chamberlain, M.E. (1983) *Lord Aberdeen. A political biography*, London.

Chatelain, J.(1999) *Dominique Vivant Denon et le Louvre de Napoléon*, London.

Chapman, W.R. (2000) 'The Pitt Rivers collection', in Brock and Curthoys (2000), 499–503.

Cherry, B., and Pevsner, N. (1998) *London, 4, North*, London (The Buildings of England).

Cherry, J. (1994) 'Medieval and later antiquities', in MacGregor (1994), 198–221.

Cherry, J. (1997) 'Franks and the medieval collections', in Caygill and Cherry (1997), 184–99.

Cherry, J., and Tait, G.H. (1989) 'Excavations at the Longton Hall porcelain factory. Part II', *Post-medieval archaeology*, xiv, 1–22.

Childe, V.G. (1951) *Social Evolution*, London.

Christian Jürgensen Thomsen 29 December 1788 –1988, Copenhagen 1988 (*Aarbøger for nordisk Oldkyndighed og Historie*).

Clark, G. (1989) *Prehistory at Cambridge and beyond*, Cambridge.

Clark, K. (1928) *The gothic revival, an essay in the history of taste*, London.

Clarke, H.J. (1843) *The British Museum; a hand-book guide for visiters [sic]*, London.

Clark, J.A. (1980) 'Sir Hans Sloane and Abbé Jean Paul Bignon: notes on collection building in the eighteenth century', *Library quarterly*, l, 475–82.

Clarke, M., and Penny, N. (ed.) (1982) *The arrogant connoisseur: Richard Payne Knight 1751–1824*, Manchester.

Claudon, F., and Bailly, B. (ed.) (1997) *Vivant Denon, colloque de Chalon sur Saône*, Chalon sur Saône.

Clay, A., et al. (1999) *British sculpture in the Lady Lever Art Gallery*, Liverpool.

Clinch, G. (1890) *Bloomsbury and St Giles: past and present*, London.

Close-Brooks, J., and Stevenson, R.B.K. (1982) *Dark age sculpture. A selection from the collections of the National Museum of Antiquities of Scotland*, Edinburgh.

Cobbett, W. (1814) *The parliamentary history of England*, London.

Cocks, A. Somers (1980) *The Victoria and Albert Museum. The making of the collection*, Leicester.

Coldstream, J.N. (1994) 'Reginald Alleyne Higgins 1916–93', *Proceedings of the British Academy*, lxxxvii, 309–26.

Colley, L. (1992) *Britons, forging the nation 1707–1837*, New Haven and London.

Collingwood, W.G. (1927) *Northumbrian crosses of the pre-Norman age*, London.

Colvin, H.M., *et al.* (1976) *The history of the king's works*, v.

Colvin, S. (1895) *Guide to an exhibition of drawings and engravings by the old masters, principally from the Malcolm collection...*, 2nd edn, London.

(Colvin, S.) (1910) *Exhibition of drawings bequeathed to the British Museum by the late Mr George Salting*, London.

Colvin, S. (1921) *Memories and notes of persons and places 1852–1912*, London.

Combe, T. (1810) *A description of the collection of ancient terracottas in the British Museum*, London.

Combe, T., *et al.* (1812–61) *A description of the collection of ancient marbles in the British Museum*, London.

Combe, T. (1814) *Veterum populorum et regum numi qui in Museo Britannico adservantur*, London.

Combe, T. (1826) *Description of the Anglo-Gallic coins in the British Museum*, London.

Cook, B.F. (1977) 'The Townley Marbles in Westminster and Bloomsbury', *The British Museum yearbook*, ii, 34–78.

Cook, B.F. (1985) *The Townley marbles*, London.

Cook, B.F. (1997) 'Sir Charles Newton, KCB (1816–1894)', in Jenkins and Waywell (1997), 9–23.

Cook, E.T., and Wedderburn, A. (1904) *The works of John Ruskin*, xii, London.

Cook, J. (1997) 'A curator's curator: Franks and the Stone Age collections', in Caygill and Cherry (1997), 115–29.

Coombes, A.E. (1994) *Reinventing Africa, museums, material culture and popular imagination in late Victorian and Edwardian England*, New Haven and London.

Coppel, S. (1996) 'William Mitchell (1820–1908) and John Malcolm of Poltalloch (1805–93)', in Griffiths (1996), 159–88.

Coppel, S. (1996a) 'George Salting (1835–1909)', in Griffiths (1996), 189–210.

Cowtan, R. (1872) *Memories of the British Museum*, London.

Craddock, P.T. (1990) 'Zinc in India', in Craddock, P.T. *et al.* (ed.) *2000 years of zinc and brass*, London, 29–72. British Museum Occasional Paper, l.

Crane, S.A. (1999) 'Story, history and the passionate collector', in Myrone and Peltz (1999), 187–204.

Cranstone, B. (1966) *New Guinea: the Sepik head-waters, 1963–64*, London.

Crawford, O.G.S. (1955) *Said and done, the autobiography of an archaeologist*, London.

Crook, J.M. (1973) *The British Museum; a case study in architectural politics* (Pelican Books edition), Harmondsworth.

Crook, J.M. (1976) 'Sidney Smirke: the architecture of compromise', in J. Fawcett, *Seven Victorian architects*, London, 50–65.

Cross, P.J. (1991) 'The Private Case: a history', in Harris (1991), 201–40.

Cunnington, R.H. (1975) *From antiquary to archaeologist. A biography of William Cunnington 1754–1810*, Aylesbury.

Curtis, J.E. (1982) *Fifty years of Mesopotamian discovery. The work of the British School of Archaeology in Iraq, 1932–1982*, London.

Curtis, J.E. (1989) *Excavations at Qasrij Cliff and Khirbet Qasrij*, London.

Curtis, J.E. (1990) 'Richard David Barnett 1909–1986', *Proceedings of the British Academy*, lxxvi, 321–45.

Curtis, J.E. (1997) 'Franks and the Oxus Treasure', in Caygill and Cherry (1997), 228–49.

Dainton report. *Report of the national libraries committee* (Cmnd. 4028), London 1969.

Curtis, J.E., and Green, A.R. (1997) *Excavations at Khirbet Katuniyeh*, London.

Dalton, O.M. (1898) *Ethnographic museums in Germany*, London.

Dalton, O.M. (1905) *The Treasure of the Oxus*, London.

Dalton, O.M. (1912) *Catalogue of the finger rings, Early Christian, Byzantine, Teutonic, mediaeval and later... in the British Museum*, London.

Damon, P.E., *et al.* (1989) 'Radiocarbon dating of the Shroud of Turin', *Nature*, cccxxxvii, 611–15.

Daniel, G.E. (1943) *The Three Ages, an essay on archaeological method*, Cambridge.

Daniel, G.E. (1950) *A hundred years of archaeology*, London.

Daniel, G.E. (1976) *Cambridge and the back-looking curiosity*, Cambridge.

Daniel, G.E. (1981) *Towards a history of archaeology*, London.

Daniels, V. (ed.) (1988) *Early advances in conservation*, London. British Museum occasional papers, 65.

D'Arblay, F. (1842) *Diary and letters of Madame d'Arblay*, London.

Darley, G. (1999) *John Soane, an accidental romantic*, New Haven and London.

Date, C. (1996) 'For the instruction and moral improvement of the People', The British Museum and the working man in mid-Victorian London, London (University of London, unpublished MA thesis).

Date, C., and Hamber, A. (1990) 'The origins of photography at the British Museum, 1839–1860', *History of Photography*, xiv: 4, 309–25.

Davies, F. (1999) 'John Charles Robinson's work at the South Kensington Museum, part II', *Journal of the history of collections*, xi; 1, 95–115.

Dawson, A. (1984) *Masterpieces of Wedgwood in the British Museum*, London.

Dawson, A. (1985) *Documentary continental ceramics from the British Museum*, London.

Dawson, A. (1994) *A catalogue of the French porcelain in the British Museum*, London.

Dawson, A (1997) 'Franks and European ceramics, glass and enamels', in Caygill and Cherry (1997), 200–19.

Dawson, A. (1999) 'English glass in the British Museum, the legacy of Augustus Wollaston Franks', *Glass collectors and their collections in museums in Great Britain*, London, 1–7.

Dawson, A. (1999a) *Portrait sculpture: a catalogue of the British Museum collection c. 1675–1975*, London.

Dawson, W.D. (1958) *The Banks letters, a calendar of the letters of Sir Joseph Banks*, London.

Dawson, W.R., and Uphill, E.P. (1995) *Who was who in Egyptology*, 3rd edn, revised by M.L. Bierbrier, London.

de Beer, E.S. (1959) *The diary of John Evelyn*, London.

de Beer, G.R. (1953) *Sir Hans Sloane and the British Museum*, London.

de Castro, J.P. (1926) *The Gordon riots*, London.

de Laet, S. (1981) 'Philip-Charles Schmerling (1791–1836)', in Daniel (1981), 112–19.

Delany, M. (1862) *Autobiography and correspondence of Mary Granville, Mrs Delany: with interesting reminiscences of King George III and Queen Charlotte*, iii. London (ed. Lady Llanover).

Demmin, A. (1867) *Guide de l'amateur des faïences et porcelaines*, London.

de Mortillet, G. (1867) *Promenades préhistoriques à l'Exposition Universelle*, Paris.

de Navarro, J.M. (1936) 'A survey of research on an early phase of Celtic culture', *Proceedings of the British Academy*, xxii, 297–341.

Description de l'Égypte, ou recueil des observations et des recherches qui ont été faites en Égypte, pendant l'expedition de l'Armée Français, Paris 1808–22.

Desmond, R. (1982) *The India Museum 1801–1879*, London.

Dickins, B. (1939) 'John Mitchell Kemble and Old English scholarship', *Proceedings of the British Academy*, 51–84.

Digby, P.W. (1974) *Visitors to three London museums, a survey carried out on behalf of the Department of Education and Science*, London.

Dodgson, C. (1903–11) *Catalogue of early German woodcuts in the British Museum*, London.

Dolley, R.H.M. (1954) 'The Cotton collection of Anglo-Saxon coins', *The British Museum quarterly*, xix, 75–81.

Douglas, D. (1951) *English Scholars 1660–1730*, 2nd edn, London.

Driver, G.R. (1944) 'Reginald Campbell Thompson 1876–1941', *Proceedings of the British Academy*, xxx, 447–85.

Drower, M.S. (1982) 'The early years', in James (1982), 9–36.

Drower, M.S. (1985) *Flinders Petrie, a life in archaeology*, London.

Duyker, E., and Tingbrand, P. (1995) *Daniel Solander, collected correspondence 1735–1782*, Melbourne.

Eames, E.S. (1968) *Medieval tiles, a handbook*, London.

Eames, E.S. (1980) *Catalogue of medieval lead-glazed earthenware tiles in the Department of Medieval and Later Antiquities in the British Museum*, London.

Ebbatson, L. (1994) 'Context and discourse: Royal Archaeological Institute membership 1845–1942', in Vyner (1994), 22–74.

Edwards, E. (1837) *A brief descriptive catalogue of the medals struck in France, and its dependencies, between 1759 and 1830*, London.

Edwards, E. (1870) *Lives of the founders of the British Museum with notices of its chief augmentors and other benefactors*, London (reprinted New York 1969).

(Edwards, I.E.S.) (1972) *Treasures of Tutankhamun*, London.

Edwards, I.E.S. (2000) *From the pyramids to Tutankhamun*, Oxford.

Eggers, H.J. (1959) *Einführung in die Vorgeschichte*, Munich.

Eisler, B. (1999) *Byron, child of passion, fool of fame*, London.

Ellis, E.F. (1981) *The British Museum in fiction. A check-list*, Buffalo (NY).

(Ellis, H.) (1833) *The British Museum. Elgin and Phigaleian marbles*, London.

(Ellis, H.) (1836) *The British Museum. The Townley Gallery*, London.

Emanuel, R.R. (2000) 'The Society of Antiquaries' Sabbath lamp', *The Antiquaries journal*, lxxx, 308–15.

Epstein, J. (1942) *Let there be sculpture*, London.

Esdaile, A. (1946) *The British Museum library, a short history and survey*, London.

Esdaile, A. (1951) 'Bookmen of the British Museum', *Library review*, no.98, 90–6.

Esdaile, A. (1951a) 'The British Museum in my time', *Library review*, no.100, 228–32.

Esdaile, A. (1952) 'The British Museum in my time: more memories', *Library review*, no.101, 301–5.

Estimates. Estimates for civil services (presented annually to Parliament).

Evans, J. (1860) 'On the occurrence of flint implements in undisturbed beds of gravel, sand and clay', *Archaeologia*, xxxviii, 280–307.

Evans, J. (1872) *The ancient stone implements, weapons, and ornaments of Great Britain and Ireland*, London.

Evans, J. (1881) *The ancient bronze implements, weapons, and ornaments of Great Britain and Ireland*, London.

Evans, J. (1943) *Time and chance, the story of Arthur Evans and his forebears*, London.

Evans, J. (1956) *A history of the Society of Antiquaries*, London.

Evans, J.D., et al. (ed.) (1981) *Antiquity and man, essays in honour of Glyn Daniel*, London.

Evison, V.I. (1987) *Dover: the Buckland Anglo-Saxon cemetery*, London. Historic Buildings and Monuments Commission for England. Archaeological reports, no.3.

Fabricius, A. (1854) *Illustreret Danmarkshistorie for folket*, Copenhagen.

Fabricius, J. (1784) *Briefe aus London vermischten Inhalts*, Dessau and Leipzig.

Fagan, L. (1880) *The life of Sir Anthony Panizzi, K.C.B., etc.*, London.

Farrington, J. (1978–98) *The diary of Joseph Farrington* (various editors), London.

Faujas Saint-Fond, B. (1799) *Travels in England, Scotland and the Hebrides*, London.

Faulkner, T. (1829) *An historical and topographical description of Chelsea and its environs*, i, Chelsea.

Faussett, B. (1856) *Inventorium sepulchrale: an account of some antiquities dug up... in the county of Kent, from A.D.1757 to A.D.1773*, London.

Fejfer, J. (1997) *The Ince Blundell collection of classical sculpture*, i, 2, Liverpool (Corpus signorum imperii romani, Great Britain iii, 9).

Fejfer, J., and Southworth, E. (1991) *The Ince Blundell collection of classical sculpture*, i, 1, London (Corpus signorum imperii romani, Great Britain iii, 2).

Fellows, C. (1839) *A journal written during an excursion to Asia Minor*, London.

Fellows, C. (1843) *The Xanthian marbles; their acquisition, and transmission to England*, London.

Fellows, C. (1852) *Travels and researches in Asia Minor, more particularly in the province of Lycia*, London.

Finke, U. (1985) 'The Art-Treasures exhibition', in Archer, J.H.G. (ed.), *Art and architecture in Victorian Manchester*, Manchester, 102–26.

Fitton, L. (1991) *Heinrich Schliemann and the British Museum*, London (British Museum. occasional papers, 83).

Fitton, L. (1995) 'Charles Newton and the discovery of the Greek Bronze Age', in Morris (1995), 73–8.

Fitzmaurice, E. (1901) *Charles William Ferdinand, Duke of Brunswick. An historical study, 1735–1806*, London.

Fontan, E. (1994) *De Khorsabad à Paris. La découverte des Assyriens*, Paris.

Foot, M.R.D. (1979) 'Gladstone and Panizzi', *The British Library journal*, v, 48–56.

Forsdyke, J. (1952) 'The Museum in war-time', *The British Museum quarterly*, xv, 1–9.

Foster, N., et al. (2001) *Norman Foster and the British Museum*, London.

Fothergill, B. (1969) *Sir William Hamilton, envoy extraordinary*, London.

Fourth report from the Committee of Public Accounts, Session 1974–5 (House of Commons).

Fox, C. (ed.) (1992) *London – world city*, New Haven and London.

Franklin, B. (1962) *The autobiography of Benjamin Franklin* (ed. Leary), New York.

Franks, A.W. (1849) *A book of ornamental glazing quarries, collected and arranged from ancient examples*, London/Oxford.

Franks, A.W. (1852) 'The collection of British antiquities in the British Museum', *The archaeological journal*, ix, 7–15.

Franks, A.W. (1858) *Examples of oriental art in glass and enamels*, London.

Franks, A.W. (1868) *Guide to the Christy Collection of prehistoric antiquities and ethnography*, London.

(Franks, A.W. (ed.)) (1869) *Catalogue of the collection of glass formed by Felix Slade, Esq., F.S.A.*, London.

Franks, A.W. (1869a) 'Notes on the discovery of some stone implements in Japan', *International Congress on Prehistoric Archaeology, Transactions...*, 258–66.

Franks, A.W. (1876) *The catalogue of a collection of oriental porcelain lent for exhibition by A.W. Franks, Esq., F.R.S., F.S.A.*, London.

(Franks, A.W.) (1888) *Guide to the English ceramic ante-room and the glass & ceramic gallery*, London.

Franks, A.W. (1896) *Catalogue of a collection of continental porcelain...*, London.

Frere, J. (1800) 'Account of some ancient weapons discovered at Hoxne in Suffolk', *Archaeologia*, xiii, 204–5.

Frobenius, L. (1898) *Der Ursprung der afrikanischen Kulturen*, Berlin.

Gadd, C.J. (1952) 'The Southesk collection of cylinder-seals', *The British Museum quarterly*, xv, 60–1.

Gadd, C.J. (1952a) 'The Raphael bequest. I. Egyptian and West Asiatic antiquities', *The British Museum quarterly*, xv, 57–60.

Gaehtgens, T.W. (1992) *Die Berliner Museumsinsel in Deutschen Kaiserreich*, Munich.

Gaimster, D. (1997) *German stoneware 1200–1900, archaeology and cultural history...*, London.

Gaimster, D. (2000) 'Sex and sensibility at the British Museum', *History today*, l: 9, 10–15.

Galard, J. (1993) *Visiteurs du Louvre. Un florilège*, Paris.

Gardiner, A. (1955) *The Ramasseum papyri*, Oxford.

Gardiner, S. (1992) *Epstein, artist against the establishment*, London.

Garnett, R. (1899) *Essays in librarianship and bibliography*, London.

Gascoigne, J. (1994) *Joseph Banks and the English Enlightenment. Useful knowledge and polite culture*, Cambridge.

Gazi, A. (1998) 'The Museum of Casts in Athens (1846–1874)', *Journal of the history of collections*, x; 1, 87–92.

Georgel, C. (1990) *La jeunesse des Museés. Les musées de France au xixe siècle*, Paris.

Gere, J.A. (1953) 'William Young Ottley as a collector of drawings', *The British Museum quarterly*, xviii, 44–53.

Gibbon, E. (1887) 'Memoirs of my life and writings', in W. Smith (ed.), *The history of the decline and fall of the Roman Empire*, i, London 1887.

Gibson, M. (1994) *The Liverpool ivories. Late antique and medieval ivory and bone carving in Liverpool Museum and Walker Art Gallery*, London.

Gibson, M., and White, S.M. (1988) *Joseph Mayer of Liverpool 1803–1886*, London.

Gilberg, R. (1999) 'Etnografisk samlings historie...', *Jordens folk*, xxxiv: 3, 29–57.

Gilmour, D. (1994) *Curzon*, London.

Godman, F.D. (1901) *The Godman collection of oriental and Spanish pottery and glass 1865–1900*, London.

Goldscheider, I. (1986) *Czechoslovak prints from 1900 to 1970*, London.

Goldsmith, J. (ed.) (1984) *The gymnasium of the mind. The journals of Roger Hinks 1933–63*, Salisbury.

Graham, I. (1977) 'Alfred Maudslay and the discovery of the Maya', *The British Museum yearbook*, ii, 137–55.

Graham-Campbell, J. (ed.) (1992) *Viking treasure from the North-West. The Cuerdale hoard in its context*, Liverpool. National Museums and Galleries on Merseyside; occasional papers, 5.

Gräslund, B. (1981) 'The background of C.J. Thomsen's Three-Age system', in Daniel (1981), 45–50.

Gray, B. (1953) 'Sloane and the Kaempfer collection', *The British Museum quarterly*, xviii: 1, 20–3.

Gray, B. (1951) 'The Oppenheim bequest', *The British Museum quarterly*, xvi, 21–2.

Green, S. (1981) *Prehistorian. A biography of V. Gordon Childe*, Bradford-on-Avon.

Gregson, A.G. (1992) 'The Ethnography Library', *British Museum magazine*, no.10, 22–3.

Grew, N. (1681) *Museum regalis societatis...*, London.

Griffiths, A. (ed.) (1996) *Landmarks in print collecting. Connoisseurs and donors at the British Museum since 1753*, London.

Griffiths, A. (1997) 'Wharton-Tigar collection of trade cards', *British Museum magazine*, no.28, 27–8.

Griffiths, A., and Williams, R. (1987) *The Department of Prints and Drawings in the British Museum, user's guide*, London.

Grosley, P.J. (1772) *A tour of London or new observations on England and its inhabitants*, London.

Gruber, J.W., and Thackray, J.C. (1992) *Richard Owen commemoration*, London.

Guest, R., and John, A.V. (1989) *Lady Charlotte. A biography of the nineteenth century*, London.

Gundestrup, B. (1991) *Det kongelige danske Kunstkammer 1737*, Copenhagen.

Gunther, A.E. (1967) *Robert T. Gunther. A pioneer in the history of science 1869–1940*, Oxford (Early Science in Oxford, xv.)

Gunther, A.E. (1980) *The founders of science at the British Museum 1753–1900...*, London.

Gunther, A.E. (1984) *An introduction to the life of the Rev. Thomas Birch D.D. F.R.S.*, Halesworth.

Gutfleisch, B., and Menzhausen, J. (1989) 'How a Kunstkammer should be formed', *Journal of the history of collections*, i, 3–32.

Hagen, A. (1997) *Gåten om kong Raknes grav. Hovedtrekk i norsk arkeologi*, Oslo.

Halls, J.J. (1834) *The life and correspondence of Henry Salt, esq., F.R.S., &c*, London.

Hamilton, W. (1777) 'Account of the discoveries at Pompeii...', *Archaeologia*, iv, 160–75.

(Hamilton, W.R.) (1810) *Memorandum on the subject of the Earl of Elgin's pursuits in Greece*, Edinburgh.

Hammond, N. (1972) *Lubaantún 1926–70; the British Museum in British Honduras*, London.

Hanna, S.B., and Lee, N.J. (1988) 'The consequences of previous adhesives and consolidants used for stone conservation at the British Museum,' in Daniels (1988), 89–102.

Harding, D.W. (1993) 'Charles Francis Christopher Hawkes, 1905–1992', *Proceedings of the British Academy*, lxxxiv, 323–44.

Harris, P.R. (1979) *The Reading Room*, London.

Harris, P.R. (ed.) (1991) *The library of the British Museum. Retrospective essays on the Department of Printed Books*, London.

Harris, P.R. (1998) *A history of the British Museum library 1753–1973*, London.

Harris, V. (1987) *Netsuke, the Hull Grundy collection in the British Museum*, London.

Harrison, B. (1994) *The history of the University of Oxford, viii, The twentieth century*, Oxford.

Harrison-Hall, J. (1997) 'Oriental pottery and porcelain', in Caygill and Cherry (1997), 220–9.

Haseloff, G. (1990) *Email im Frühen Mittelalter. Frühchristliche Kunst von der Spätantike bis zu den Karolingern*, Marburg (Marburger Studien zur Vor- und Frühgeschichte, Sonderband, i).

Haskell, F. (1987) *Past and present in art and taste*, New Haven and London.

Haskell, F. (1993) *History and its images. Art and the interpretation of the past 1500–1900*, New Haven and London.

Haskell, F. (2000) *The ephemeral museum. Old Master paintings and the rise of the art exhibition*, New Haven and London.

Haskell, F., and Penny, N. (1981) *Taste and the Antique. The lure of classical sculpture*, New Haven and London.

Hatcher, J. (1995) *Laurence Binyon. Poet, scholar of East and West*, London.

Haugsted, I. (1996) *Dream and reality. Danish architects and artists in Greece*, London.

Hauser-Schäublin, B., and Krüger, G. (ed.) (1998) *Gifts and treasures from the South Seas. The Cook/Forster collection*, Göttingen, Munich and New York.

Hawkins, E. (1841) *The silver coins of England...*, London.

Hawkins, E. (1852) *Numismata britannica. A description of medals illustrative of the history of Great Britain from the Conquest to the demise of William III*, London.

Hawkins, E. (1885) *Medallic illustrations of the history of Great Britain and Ireland to the death of George II* (ed. A.W. Franks et al.), London.

Haynes, S. (1985) Etruscan bronzes, London.

Heath, E. (1998) The course of my life, London.

Henry Christy, a pioneer of anthropology, London 1965.

Henry, F. (1970) Irish art in the Romanesque period (1020–1170 A.D.), London.

Herrmann, F. (1972) The English collectors, a documentary chrestomathy, London.

Herrmann, F. (1980) Sotheby's, portrait of an auction house, London.

Herrmann, F. (1999) The English as collectors. A documentary sourcebook, London.

Heward, E. (1994) The great and the good. A life of Lord Radcliffe, Chichester.

Hewitt, V.H., and Keyworth, J.M. (1987) As good as gold, 300 years of British bank note design, London.

Heyworth, P.L. (1989) Letters of Humfrey Wanley, palaeographer, Anglo-Saxonist and librarian, 1672–1726, Oxford.

Heydemann, H. (1872) Die Vasensammlungen des Museo Nazionale zu Neapel, Berlin.

Hibbert, C. (1998), George III, a personal history, London.

Higgins, R.A. (1961) 'The Elgin jewellery', The British Museum quarterly, xxiii, 101–7.

Hildebrand, B., et al. (1992) Matrikel över ledamöter av Kungl. Vitterhetsakademien och Kungl. Vitterhets Historie och Antikvitets Akademien, Stockholm.

Hill, G.F. (1915) The development of Arabic numerals in Europe…, Oxford.

Hill, G.F. (1936) Treasure Trove in law and practice from the earliest time to the present day, Oxford.

Hill, G.F. (1944) 'Ormond Maddock Dalton, 1866–1945', Proceedings of the British Academy, xxxi, 357–74.

Hill, G.F. (1988) 'An autobiographical fragment', The Medal, no.12, 37–48.

Hilton, T. (1985) John Ruskin, the early years, New Haven and London.

Hind, A.M. (1910) Catalogue of early Italian engravings in the British Museum, London.

Hind, A.M. (1938–48) Early Italian engraving, A critical catalogue, London.

Hind, A.M. (1952) 'The Schwerdt collection of sporting prints and drawings', The British Museum quarterly, xiv: 1, 12–16.

H.M. Treasury. Report of the committee on the export of works of art, etc., London 1952.

Hobhouse, J.C. (1813) A journey through Albania and other provinces of Turkey in Europe and Asia, to Constantinople, during the years 1809 and 1810, London.

Hobson, R.L. (1903) Catalogue of English pottery in the Department of British and Mediaeval Antiquities and Ethnography in the British Museum, London.

Hobson, R.L. (1905) Catalogue of English porcelain in the Department of British and Mediaeval Antiquities and Ethnography in the British Museum, London.

Hobson, R.L. (1923) Catalogue of the Frank Lloyd collection of Worcester porcelain of the Wall period in the… British Museum, London.

Hogarth, D.G. (1896) A wandering scholar in the Levant, London.

Hogarth, D.G. (ed.) (1899) Authority and archaeology, sacred and profane, London.

Hollis, T. (1780) Memoirs of Thomas Hollis esq., F.R. and A.SS., London.

Holmes, C., and Baker, C.H.C. (1924) The making of the National Gallery, 1824–1924, London.

Hoving, T. (1981) King of the confessors, London.

Howard, S. (1992) 'Fakes, intention, proofs and impulsion to know: the case for Cavaceppi and clones', in Jones (1992), 51–62.

Howarth, D. (1985) Lord Arundel and his circle, New Haven and London.

Howe, E.R.J.G. (1903–4) Franks bequest. Catalogue of British and American book plates bequeathed to the Trustees of the British Museum by Sir Augustus Wollaston Franks, KCB, FRS, PSA, Litt.D., London.

Hull, L. (2001) 'Hand in trove', Museums journal, March 2001, 27–8.

Hulton, P. (1977) The work of Jacques le Moyne de Morgues…, London.

Hutchinson, S.C. (1986) The history of the Royal Academy, 1768–1986, 2nd edn, London.

Hutton, W. (1785) A journey from Birmingham to London, Birmingham.

Impey, O. (1994) 'Oriental antiquities', in MacGregor (1994), 222–7.

Impey, O., and MacGregor, A. (1985) The origins of museums. The cabinet of curiosities in sixteenth- and seventeenth-century Europe, Oxford.

Jackson, R.P.J., and Potter, T.W. (1996) Excavations at Sonea, Cambridgeshire, 1980–85, London.

Jaffé, M. (1993) Old Master drawings from Chatsworth, London.

Jahn, O. (1854) Beschreibung der Vasensammlung König Ludwigs in der Pinakothek zu München, Munich.

James, T.G.H. (1981) The British Museum and ancient Egypt, London.

James, T.G.H. (1982) Excavating in Egypt. The Egypt Exploration Society 1882–1982, London.

James, T.G.H. (1997) 'Iorwerth Eiddon Stephen Edwards 1909–1996', Proceedings of the British Academy, xcvii, 273–90.

Janssen, R.M. (1992) The first hundred years, Egyptology at University College London, 1892–1992, London.

Jeffery, R.W. (ed.) (1907) Dyott's diary, 1781–45, London.

Jenkins, I. (1990) 'Acquisition and supply of casts of the Parthenon sculptures by the British Museum 1835–1939', Annual of the British School at Athens, xlviii, 89–114.

Jenkins, I. (1992) Archaeologists and aesthetes in the sculpture galleries of the British Museum 1800–1939, London.

Jenkins, I. (1992a) 'La vente des vases Durand (Paris 1836) et leur réception en Grande Bretagne', in Laurens and Pomian (1992), 269–78.

Jenkins, I. (1994) 'Bernard Ashmole and the British Museum' in Ashmole (1994), 203–9.

Jenkins, I. (1994a) 'Classical antiquities', in MacGregor (1994), 167–73.

Jenkins, I. (2000) 'John Henning's frieze for the Athenaeum', in Tait and Walker (2000), 149–156.

Jenkins, I., and Middleton, A. (1992) 'Painted pediment', British Museum magazine, no.11, 9.

Jenkins, I., and Sloan, K. (1996) Vases and volcanoes, Sir William Hamilton and his collections, London.

Jenkins, I., and Waywell, G.B. (eds) (1997) Sculptors and Sculpture of Caria and the Dodecanese, London

Jensen, J. (1992) Thomsens museum. Historien om Nationalmuseet, Copenhagen.

Jenyns, S. (1954) 'The A.D. Brankston collection of Chinese porcelain', The British Museum quarterly, xix, 54–7.

Johns, C. (1993) The Hoxne treasure, London.

Johns, C., and Potter, T. (1983) The Thetford treasure: Roman jewellery and silver, London.

Johnson, B.C. (1988) Rorke's Drift and the British Museum. The life of Henry Hook, V.C., London.

Johnson, B.C. (ed.) (1989) Tea and anarchy! The Bloomsbury diary of Olive Garnett 1890–1893, London.

Johnson, B.C. (ed.) (1993) Olive and Stepniak. The Bloomsbury diary of Olive Garnett 1893–1895, London.

Jolliffe, J. (1990) Neglected genius. The diaries of Benjamin Robert Haydon 1808–1846, London.

Jones, M. (1978) The Dance of Death: medallic art of the First World War, London.

Jones, M. (ed.) (1990) Fake? The art of deception, London.

Jones, M. (ed.) (1992) Why fakes matter. Essays on problems of authenticity, London.

Jones, P.M. (1988) 'A preliminary check-list of Sir Hans

Sloane's catalogues', *The British Library Journal*, xiv: 1, 38–51.

Journals of the House of Commons.

Justi, C. (1866–72) *Winckelmann. Sein Leben, seine Werke und seine Zeitgenossen*, Leipzig.

Kaeppler, A.E. (1979) 'Tracing the history of the Hawaiian Cook voyage artefacts in the British Museum', *Captain Cook and the South Pacific*, London, 167–98 (The British Museum yearbook, 3).

Kahn, F., Knox, J.R., and Thomas, K.D. (1991) *Exploration and excavations in Bannu District, North-West Frontier Province, Pakistan*, London (British Museum occasional papers, 80).

Kalveram, K. (1996) *Die Antikensammlung des Kardinals Scipione Borghese*, Worms am Rhein (Römische Studien der Bibliotheca Herziana, 11).

Keller, F. (1866), *The lake dwellings of Switzerland and other parts of Europe*, London.

Kemble, J.M. (1849) *The Saxons in England*, London.

Kemble, J.M. (1855) 'On mortuary urns found at Stade-on-the-Elbe...', *Archaeologia*, xxxvi, 270–83.

Kemble, J.M. (1863) *Horæ ferales; or studies in the archaeology of the northern nations*, London.

Kendrick, T.D. (1925) *The Axe Age*, London.

Kendrick, T.D. (1971) 'In the 1920s', *The British Museum quarterly*, xxxv, 2–8.

Kendrick, T.D., and Hawkes, C.F.C. (1932), *Archaeology in England and Wales, 1914–1931*, London.

(Kenyon, G.F.) (1914) *The buildings of the British Museum, illustrated from prints and drawings*, London.

Kenyon, F.G. (1929) 'Sir Edward Maunde Thompson, 1840–1929', *Proceedings of the British Academy*, xv, 477–90.

Kenyon, F.G. (1934) *The British Museum in War Time*, Glasgow.

Kenyon, F.G. (1941) 'Arthur Hamilton Smith 1860–1941', *Proceedings of the British Academy*, 393–404.

Kenyon, J. (1993) *The history men. The historical profession in England since the Renaissance*, 2nd edn, London.

Kidd, D. (1977) 'Charles Roach Smith and his Museum of London Antiquities', *The British Museum yearbook*, ii, 105–36.

Kidd, D. (1994) 'The Gotlandic collection of James Curle of Melrose (1862–1944)', *Journal of the history of collections*, vi: 1, 87–101.

Kinnes, I.A., and Longworth, I.H. (1985) *Catalogue of the excavated prehistoric and Romano-British material in the Greenwell collection*, London.

King, A.H. (1991) 'Quodlibet: some memoirs of the British Museum and its Music Room 1934–76', in Harris (1991), 242–98.

King, J.C.H. (1981) *Artificial curiosities from the northwest coast of America. Native American artefacts in the British Museum collected on the third voyage of Captain James Cook and acquired through Sir Joseph Banks*, London.

King, J.C.H. (1985) 'North American ethnography in the collections of Sir Hans Sloane' in Impey and MacGregor, 232–6.

King, J.C.H. (1994) 'Ethnographic collections', in MacGregor (1994), 228–44.

King, J.C.H. (1994a) 'Vancouver's ethnography', *Journal of the history of collections*, vi: 1, 35–58.

King, J.C.H. (1997) 'Franks and ethnography', in Caygill and Cherry (1997), 136–59.

King, V. (1976) *The weeping and the laughter*, London.

Kitzinger, E. (1940) *Early medieval art*, London.

Knight, W. (1900) *Lord Monboddo and some of his contemporaries*, London.

Knox, R. (1992) *Amaravati. Buddhist sculpture from the Great Stupa*, London.

Krämer, W. (2002) *Gerhard Bersu, ein deutscher Prähistoriker, 1889–1964*, Mainz (Vorabsonderdruck Bericht der Römisch-Germanischen Kommission, lxxxii).

Kurtz, D. (1985) *Beazley and Oxford*, Oxford. Oxford University Committee for Archaeology, Monograph, no.10.

Lane-Poole, S. (1894–5) 'Sir Charles Newton K.C.B., D.C.L., Litt.D.', *The national review*, xxiv, 616–27.

Langford, P. (1989) *A polite and commercial people. England 1727–1783*, Oxford.

Larsen, M.T. (1995) *The conquest of Assyria: excavations in an antique land 1840–1860*, London.

Lartet, E., and Christy, H. (1875) *Reliquiae Aquitanicae, being contributions to the archaeology and palaeontology of Périgord and the adjoining provinces of southern France*, London.

Lasko, P.E. (1994) *Ars sacra, 800–1200*, 2nd edn, New Haven and London.

Laurens, A.-F., and Pomain, K. (ed.) (1992) *L'anticomanie. La collection d'antiquités aux 18e et 19e siècles*, Paris.

Layard, A.H. (1849) *Nineveh and its remains: with an account of a visit to the Chaldean Christians of Kurdistan, and the Yezidis, or devil-worshippers; and an enquiry into the manners and arts of the ancient Assyrians*, London.

Layard, A.H. (1851) *Inscriptions in the cuneiform character from Assyrian monuments*, London.

Leichty, E. (1986) *Catalogue of the Babylonian tablets in the British Museum, vi, Tablets from Sippar, I*, London.

Leith, W. (1908) *Apologia diffidentis*, London.

Lelièvre, P. (1993) *Vivant Denon, homme des lumières, "ministre des arts de Napoléon"*, Paris.

Legrand, P.E. (1897) 'Biographie de Louis-François-Sébastien Fauvel', *Revue archéologique*, 3 ser. xxx, 41–66 and xxxi, 185–201.

Levine, P. (1986) *The amateur and the professional. Antiquarians, historians and archaeologists in Victorian England, 1838–1886*, Cambridge.

Lewis, W.S, Smith, W.H., and Lam, G.L. (ed.) (1955–71) *Horace Walpole's correspondence with Sir Horace Mann, i–xi*, London. The Yale edition of Horace Walpole's correspondence, xvii–xxvii.

Lewis, W.S., and Wallace, A.D. (1952) *Horace Walpole's correspondence with Thomas Chatterton, Michael Lort...*, London. The Yale edition of Horace Walpole's correspondence, xvi.

Lindenschmit, W. and L. (1848) *Das germanische Totenlager bei Selzen in der provinz Rheinhessen*, Mainz.

Lloyd, S. (1980) *Foundations in the dust; a story of Mesopotamian exploration*, revised edn, London.

Lloyd-Jones, H. (1982) *Blood for the ghosts. Classical influences in the nineteenth and twentieth century*, London.

Lockhart, J.G. (1949) *Cosmo Gordon Lang*, London.

Long, H. (1991) 'The unobtrusive collector', *Antique Collector*, Sept. 1991.

Longworth, I.H., et al. (1991) *Excavations at Grimes Graves, Norfolk, 1972–1976, fasc.3*, London.

Lubbock, J. (1865) *Pre-historic times as illustrated by ancient remains, and the manners and customs of modern savages*, London.

Lucas, E.V. (1928) *The Colvins and their friends*, London.

Lundbeck-Culot, K. (1997) 'Frédéric VII, roi du Danemark, Napoléon III et l'archéologie. Les deux premiers donateurs du Musée des Antiquités Nationales de Saint-Germain-en-Laye', *Antiquités nationales*, xxix, 99–118.

Lyon, S. (1982) 'Dr Michael Dolley MRIA, FSA', *The British Numismatic Journal*, lii, 265–71.

Macalister, R.A.S. (1945) *Corpus inscriptionum insularum celticarum, i*, Dublin.

McCausland, S. (2001) 'A new date for the Admonitions scroll', *British Museum magazine*, no.41, 10.

Mac Dermott, M. (1955) 'The Kells Crozier', *Archaeologia*, xcvi, 59–113.

MacGregor, A. (1994) *Sir Hans Sloane. Collector, scientist, antiquary, founding father of the British Museum*, London.

MacGregor, A. (1998) 'Antiquities inventoried: museums and "national antiquities" in the mid nineteenth century', in Brand (1998), 125–37.

MacGregor, A., and Turner, A.J. (1986) 'The Ashmolean Museum', in Sutherland, L.S., and Mitchell, L.G., 639–58.

Mack, J. (1982) 'Material culture and ethnic identity in Southeastern Sudan', in Mack, J., and Robertshaw, P. (eds) (1982) Culture history in the southern Sudan. Archaeology, linguistics and ethnohistory, Nairobi, 111–30. Memoir no.8 of the British School in Eastern Africa.

Mack, J. (1997) 'Antiquities and the public: the expanding Museum, 1851–96', in Caygill and Cherry (1997), 34–50.

Mack, J. (n.d.) Emil Torday and the art of the Congo, 1900–1909, London.

Mack, J. (1998) 'Kuba art and the birth of ethnography', in Schildkrout, E., and Keim, C.A. (1998), The scramble for art in Central Africa, Cambridge, 63–78.

Maclennan, H. (2000) Antiquarianism, master prints and aesthetics in the collecting culture of the nineteenth century, London (unpublished University of London Ph.D thesis).

McLeod, M. (1977) 'T.E. Bowdich: an early collector in West Africa', The British Museum yearbook, ii, 79–104.

McLeod, M.D. (1993) Collecting for the British Museum, Milan.

Madden, F. (1832) 'Historical remarks on the introduction of the game of chess into Europe, and on the ancient chessman discovered on the Isle of Lewis', Archaeologia, xxiv, 203–91.

Major, J.D. (1674) Unvorgreiffliches Bedenken von Kunst- und Naturalien-Kammern, Kiel.

Malcolm, J.P. (1803) Londinium redivivum or an ancient history and modern description of London..., ii, London.

Mallowan, M.E.L. (1960) 'Memories of Ur', Iraq, 1–19.

Mallowan, M.E.L. (1970) 'Cyril John Gadd, 1893–1969', Proceedings of the British Academy, lvi, 363–402.

Mallowan, M.E.L. (1977) Mallowan's Memoirs, London.

Mallowan, M.E.L. (1978) The Nimrud ivories, London.

Manley, D., and Rée, P. (2001) Henry Salt, artist, traveller, diplomat, Egyptologist, London.

Marchand, J. (ed.) (1933) A Frenchman in England, 1784. Being the 'Mélanges sur l'Angleterre' of François de la Rochefoucauld, Cambridge.

Marshall, F.H. (1911) Catalogue of the jewellery, Greek, Etruscan, and Roman, in the Departments of Antiquities in the British Museum, London.

Martin, B.R. (1980) Tennyson, the unquiet heart, Oxford.

Mason, A.S. (1993) 'Hans Sloane and his friends', Journal of the Royal College of Physicians of London, xxvii, 4, 450–5.

(Masson, D.) (1848) The British Museum; historical and descriptive, London. Chambers Instructive and Entertaining Library.

Matheson, P.E. (ed.) (1924) Travels of Carl Philipp Moritz in England in 1782, London.

Mayes, S. (1959) The great Belzoni, London.

Michaelis, A. (1908) A century of archaeological discoveries, London.

Miller, E. (1967) Prince of Librarians. The life and times of Antonio Panizzi of the British Museum, London.

Miller, E. (1973) That noble cabinet. A history of the British Museum, London.

Miller, E. (1979) 'Antonio Panizzi and the British Museum', The British Library journal, v, 1–17.

Mitchell, T. (1992) The Bible in the British Museum, interpreting the evidence, London.

Mitchell, T. (2000) 'The Persepolis sculptures in the British Museum', Iran, xxxviii, 49–56.

Mitford, J. (ed.) (1853) The correspondence of Thomas Gray and William Mason..., London.

Moore, A. (1996) Houghton Hall, the Prime Minister, the Empress and the Hermitage, Norwich and London.

Moore, H. (1981) Henry Moore at the British Museum, London.

Moorey, R. (1991) A century of biblical archaeology, Cambridge.

Morris, C. (ed.) (1995) Klados. Essays in honour of J.N. Coldstream, London.

Morris, R. (1979) HMS Colossus, the story of the salvage of the Hamilton treasure, London.

Morton, V. (1987) Oxford rebels, the life and friends of Nevil Story Maskelyne 1823–1911..., Gloucester.

Mozart in the British Museum, London 1968.

Munford, W.A. (1963) Edward Edwards, 1812–1886, portrait of a librarian, London.

Munn, G. (1986) 'Mrs Anne Hull Grundy', Antique collector, Feb. 1986, 42–7.

Myrone, M., and Peltz, L. (1999) Producing the past. Aspects of antiquarian culture and practice, 1700–1850, Aldershot.

Murray, O. (2000) 'Ancient history, 1872–1914', in Brock and Curthoys (2000), 333–60.

Namier, L.B. (1958) Vanished supremacies, London.

Neickelius, C.F. (1717) Museographia, oder Anleitung zum rechten und ütlicher Anlegung der Museorum oder Räriteten-Kammer, Leipzig and Breslau.

Neverov, O. (1984) 'The Lyde Brown collection and the history of ancient sculpture in the Hermitage Museum', American Journal of Archaeology, lxxxviii, 33–42.

Newton, C.T. (1862–3) A history of the discoveries at Halicarnassus, Cnidus and Branchidæ..., London.

Newton, C.T. (1865) Travels and discoveries in the Levant, London.

Newton, C.T. (1880) Essays in art and archæology, London.

Nichols, J. (1812–15) Literary anecdotes of the eighteenth century, London.

Nichols, J. (1817–58) Illustrations of the literary history of the eighteenth century, London.

Nickson, M.A.E. (1994) 'Books and manuscripts', in MacGregor (1994), 263–77.

Nilsson, S. (1866) The primitive inhabitants of Scandinavia, London.

Norman, G. (1997) The Hermitage; the biography of a great museum, London.

Nyerup, R. (1806) Oversigt over fædrelandets mindesmærker fra oltiden, saaledes som samme kan tænkes opstillede i et tilkommende National Museum, Copenhagen.

Oddy, A. (1993) 'The history and prospects for the conservation of metals in Europe', Current problems in the conservation of metal antiquities, 1–37, Tokyo (The thirteenth international symposium on the conservation and restoration of cultural property).

Oddy, A. (1997) The British Museum Department of Conservation; history, organisation, role and activities, London.

Ødegaard, V. (1992) 'Mellem sagnhistorie, videnskab og nationalpolitik', Fortid og nutid, pt. 1, 3–23.

O'Donohogue, F.M. (1901) The catalogue of the playing cards... bequeathed... by the late Lady Charlotte Schreiber, London.

Oldham, C.E.A.W. (1943) 'Sir Aurel Stein, 1862–1943', Proceedings of the British Academy, xxix, 329–48.

Olearius, A. (1674) Gottorffische Kunst-Cammer, Schleswig.

Orlińska, G. (2002) Catalogue of the 'Germanic' antiquities from the Klemm collection in the British Museum, London.

Ottley, W.Y. (1816) An inquiry into the origin of the early history of engraving, London.

Ottley, W.Y. (1823) The Italian school of design: being a series of fac-similes of original drawings, London.

Owen, R. (1869) 'Description of the cavern of Bruniquel and its organic contents', Philosophical Transactions of the Royal Society, clix, 517–33 and 535–7.

Painter, K.S. (1967) 'The Roman site at Hinton St Mary, Dorset', The British Museum quarterly, xxiii, 15–31.

Painter, K.S. (1977) The Mildenhall treasure, London.

Painter, K.S. (1977a) The Water Newton Early Christian silver, London.

Paintin, E. (1989) The King's Library, London.

Pankhurst, R. (1986) 'The case for Ethiopia', Museum, no.149, 58–60.

Pankhurst, S. (1955) Ethiopia, a cultural history, London.

Parkinson, R. (1999) Cracking codes. The Rosetta stone and decipherment, London.

Peace, D. (1994) Eric Gill; a descriptive catalogue, London.

Peacock, S.J. (1988) Jane Ellen Harrison, the mask and the self, New Haven and London.

Petch, A. (1998) 'Man as he was and as he is': General Pitt Rivers's collections', Journal of the history of collections, x: 1, 75–86.

Peterson, C. (1996) 'Innovative use of wrought and cast iron', Association for preservation technology bulletin, xxvii: 3.

Petiver, J. (1695–1703) Musei petiveriani... rariora naturae continens, London.

Petrie, W.F. (1904) Methods and aims in archaeology, London.

Pevsner, N. (1953) 'British Museum. Some unresolved problems of its architectural history', The architectural review, pt.1, 179–83.

Pevsner, N. (1972) Some architectural writers of the nineteenth century, Oxford.

Phillips, C.W. (1987) My life in archaeology, Gloucester.

Phillips, H. (1964) Mid-Georgian London, London.

Piggott, S. (1989) Ancient Britons and the antiquarian imagination. Ideas from the renaissance to the regency, London.

Pinder-Wilson, R. (2000) 'Basil Gray, 1904–1989', Proceedings of the British Academy, cv, 439–57.

Pinney, T. (1974–81) The letters of Thomas Babington Macaulay, Cambridge.

Plankensteiner, B. (1998) Austausch. Kunst aus südlichen Afrika um 1900, Vienna.

Planta, J. (1776) An account of the romansh language... read at the Royal Society, Nov. 10. 1775, London.

Plenderleith, H.J. (1956) 'The methods used in the preservation of the relics' in Battiscombe (1956), 531–44.

Plenderleith, H.J. (1998) 'A history of conservation', Studies in conservation, xliii, 129–43.

Pollen, J.H. (1878) Ancient and modern gold and silver smiths' work in the South Kensington Museum, London.

Pope-Hennessy, J. (1991) Learning to look, London.

Popham, A.E. (1933) Guide to an exhibition of the more important prints and drawings acquired during the keepership of Mr Campbell Dodgson 1912–1932, London.

Popham, A.E. (1935) Catalogue of the drawings in the collection formed by Sir Thomas Phillips, Bart. F.R.S., now in the possession of his grandson, T. Fitzroy Phillips Fenwick..., privately printed.

Popham, A.E. (1939) A handbook of the drawings and watercolours in the... British Museum, London.

Popham, A.E. (1950) 'Campbell Dodgson, 1867–1948', Proceedings of the British Academy, xxxvi, 291–7.

Popham, A.E. (1952) 'Department of Prints and Drawings', The British Museum quarterly, xv, 40–7.

Portal, J. (2000) Korea. Art and archaeology, London.

Potter, T.W. (1997) 'Later prehistory and Roman Britain: the formation of the national collections', in Caygill and Cherry (1997), 130–5.

Principal Documentary Evidence submitted to the National Libraries Committee, i, 1969.

(Powlett, E.) (1761) The general contents of the British Museum: with remarks. Serving as a directory for viewing that noble cabinet, London.

Prescott, A. (1997) 'The Panizzi touch: Panizzi's successors as Principal Librarian', The British Library Journal, xxiii: 2, 194–236.

Pyrah, B.J. (1988) The history of the Yorkshire Museum and its geological collections, York.

Rackham, B. (1915) Catalogue of English porcelain earthenware enamels etc. collected by Charles Schreiber, Esq., M.P., and the Lady Charlotte Schreiber, London.

Radcliffe, C. (1968) Government by contempt, London.

Randall, A.G., and Good, R. (1990) Pocket chronometers, marine chronometers and other portable precision timekeepers, London. Catalogue of the watches in the British Museum, vi.

Rasmussen, B.B., et al. (1999) Christian VIII og Nationalmuseet, Copenhagen.

Rasmussen, H. (1979) Dansk museums historie, de kulturhistoriske museer, Hjørring.

Rathgen, F. (1905) The preservation of antiquities, a handbook for curators, Cambridge.

Rawlinson, G. (1898) A memoir of Major-general Sir Henry Creswicke Rawlinson, London.

Rawlinson, H.C. (1861) A selection from the historical inscriptions of Chaldæa, Assyria and Babylon, London.

Read, C.H. (1902) The Waddesdon Bequest, London.

Read, C.H., and Dalton, O.M. (1899) Antiquities from the city of Benin and from other parts of West Africa in the British Museum, London.

Read, C.H., and Tonnochy, A.B. (1928) Catalogue of the silver plate, mediaeval and later, bequeathed to the British Museum by Sir Augustus Wollaston Franks, K.C.B..., London.

Reade, J.E. (1993) 'Hormuzd Rassam and his discoveries', Iraq, lv, 3962.

Reilly, R. (1989) Wedgwood, London and New York.

(Reid, G.W.) A guide to that portion of the collection of prints bequeathed... by the late F. Slade ..., London.

Reinaud, M. (1828) Monumens arabes, persans, et turcs du cabinet de M. le Duc de Blacas..., Paris.

Report of the national libraries committee, see Dainton report.

Report of the Select Committee on national monuments and works of art in Westminster Abbey, in St Paul's Cathedral and other national edifices, Parliamentary papers, House of Commons, 1841.

Report from the Select Committee of the House of Commons on the Earl of Elgin's collection of sculptured marbles, London 1816.

Report of Trustees: The British Museum. Report of the Trustees. (Also: The British Museum. Annual Report of the Trustees)

Richmond, I. (1968) Hod Hill, ii, Excavations carried out between 1951 and 1958 for the Trustees of the British Museum, London.

Rickman, T. (1817) An attempt to discriminate the styles of English architecture from the Conquest to the Reformation, London.

Roberts, A. (1999) Salisbury, Victorian titan, London.

Robertson, M. (1975) A history of Greek art, Cambridge.

Robertson, M. (1989) 'Bernard Ashmole, 1894–1998', Proceedings of the British Academy, lxxv, 313–28.

Robinson, E.S.G. (1950) 'George Francis Hill, 1867–1948', Proceedings of the British Academy, xxxvi, 241–50.

Robinson, E.S.G. (1952) 'The Lloyd collection of coins of Western Greece', The British Museum quarterly, xvi: 1, 14–15.

Robinson, E.S.G. (1966) 'John Walker, 1900–1964', Proceedings of the British Academy, lii, 287–92.

Robinson, G. (2000) The unconventional minister. My life inside New Labour, London.

Robinson, J.C. (1854) An introductory lecture on the museum of ornamental art of the Department [of Science and Art], London.

Roe, D. (1981) 'Amateurs and archaeologists: some early contributions to British Palaeolithic studies', in Evans et al. (1981), 214–20.

Rogers, J.M. (1984) 'The Godman bequest of Islamic pottery', Apollo, cxx (July), 24–31.

Rothenstein, J. (1966) Brave day, hideous night. Autobiography 1939–1965, London.

Rowlands, J. (1994) 'Prints and drawings', in MacGregor (1994), 245–62.

Royalton-Kisch, M., (1999) 'Diana and Aurora at home', British Museum magazine, no.33, 11–14.

Royalton-Kisch, M. et al. (1996) Old master drawings from the Malcolm collection, London.

Royal Commission (1850) Report of the commissioners appointed to inquire into the constitution and government of the British Museum with minutes of evidence, London.

Royal Commission (1928–30) Royal commission on national museums and galleries, I, Interim report 1928; Final report, part 1, 1929; Final Report, part 2, 1930; Oral evidence, memoranda and appendices to the interim report, 1928, London.

Rudoe, J. Decorative arts, 1850–1950. A catalogue of the British Museum collection, London.

Rupke, N.A. (1994) Richard Owen, Victorian naturalist, New Haven and London.

Russell, R.D., and Goodden, R.Y. (1969) 'The new Greek and Roman galleries', British Museum Society bulletin, no.2, 4–6.

Ruysch, F. (1691) Observationum anatomico-chirurgicarum centuria. Accedit catalogus... in Museo Ruyschiano asserevantur..., Amsterdam.

St. Clair, W. (1989) The Godwins and the Shelleys. The biography of a family, London.

St. Clair, W. (1998) Lord Elgin and the marbles, (3rd edn), Oxford.

St. Clair, W. (1999) 'The Elgin Marbles: questions of stewardship and accountability', International journal of cultural property, viii, 391–521.

Sandys, J. (ed.) (1919) A selection from... letters... published... between January 1 and 9, protesting against the proposal for taking over the British Museum as offices for the Air Board, rev. edn, Cambridge.

Scharf, G., and Fellows, C. (1847) Lycia, Caria, Lydia..., London.

(Scott, R.T., and Kesson, J.) (1843) A complete guide to the British Museum forming a correct catalogue..., London.

Scheidemantel, V.J. (1969) '"The Apotheosis of Homer": a Wedgwood and Bentley plaque', The Wedgwoodian, June 1969, 68–76.

Schlepern, H.D. (1971) Museum Womianum. Dets forudsætninger og tilblevelse, Aarhus.

Schnapp, A. (1992) 'La pratique de la collection par le chevalier d'Hancarville', in Laurens and Pomian (1992), 209–18.

Schnapp, A. (1996) The discovery of the past. The origins of archaeology, London.

Searby, P. (1997) A history of the university of Cambridge, iii, Cambridge.

Select Committee (1835) Report from the Select Committee on the condition, management and affairs of the British Museum; together with minutes of evidence, London.

Select Committee (1836) Report from the Select Committee on the British Museum..., London.

Select Committee (1837) Report from the Select Committee on the British Museum..., London.

Select Committee (1838) Report from the Select Committee on the British Museum..., London.

Select Committee (1860) Report from the Select Committee on the British Museum..., London.

Secrest, M. (1984), Kenneth Clark, a biography, London.

Shannon, R. (1982) Gladstone, 1809–1865, i, London.

Shannon, R. (1999) Gladstone, heroic minister, 1865–98, London.

Shaw, J. Byam (1971) 'Arthur Ewart Popham, 1889–1970', Proceedings of the British Academy, lvii, 487–96.

Shelton, K.J. (1981) The Esquiline Treasure, London.

Sieveking, A. (1987) A catalogue of palaeolithic art in the British Museum, London.

Silber, E. (1996) Gaudier-Brzeska. Life and art, with a catalogue raisonné of the sculpture, London.

Silver, A. (ed.) The family letters of Samuel Butler 1841–1886, London.

Singer, A. (1992) The lion and the dragon. The story of the British embassy to the court of the Emperor Qianlong in Peking, 1792–94, London.

Simpson, St. J. (2000) 'Rediscovering past splendours from Iran. 19th-century casts of sculptures from Persepolis', British Museum Magazine, 28–9.

Simpson, St. J. (2000a) 'Parthian and Bronze Age grave groups from Bahrain', British Museum Magazine, no.36, 34.

Sloan, W.R. (1981) Sir Hans Sloane, founder of the British Museum; legend and lineage, Helen's Bay.

Smith, A.H. (1892–1904) A catalogue of sculpture in the Department of Greek and Roman Antiquities of the British Museum, 3 vols, London.

Smith, A.H. (1910) The sculptures of the Parthenon, London.

Smith, A.H. (1916) 'Lord Elgin and his collection', The journal of Hellenic studies, xxxvi, 163–372.

Smith, A.H. (1930) Memorandum on the proposed new Elgin room, n.p.

Smith, C.R. (1854) Catalogue of London antiquities. Collected by, and the property of, Charles Roach Smith, London.

Smith, G. (1873) 'The Chaldean account of the Deluge', Transactions of the Society of Biblical Archaeology, ii, 213–34.

Smith, J.T. (1829) Nollekens and his times..., London.

Smith, L. (1983) The Japanese print since 1900: old dreams and new visions, London.

Smith, L. (1985) Contemporary Japanese prints. Symbols of a society in transition, London.

Smith, L. (1997) 'The art and antiquities of Japan', in Caygill and Cherry (1997), 261–72.

Smith, N.C. (1953) Letters of Sidney Smith, Oxford.

Smith, R.A. (1931) The Sturge collection..., London.

Smith, R.M., and Porcher, E.A. (1864) History of recent discoveries at Cyrene..., London.

Smith, W.C. (1965) A Handelian's notebook, London.

Smollett, T. (1771) The expedition of Humphry Clinker, London.

Snow, W.P. (1858) A catalogue of the arctic collections in the British Museum..., London.

Southworth, E. (1991) 'The Ince Blundell collection. Collecting behaviour in the eighteenth century', Journal of the history of collecting, iii, 219–34.

Spalding, F. (1998) The Tate. A history, London.

Spence, T. (1999) 'Excavations at the British Museum', Minerva, x: 5, 26–7.

Spencer, H. (1851) Social statics: or, the conditions essential to human happiness and the first of them developed, London.

Spielmann, H., and Drees, J. (1997) Gottorf im Glanz der Barock, i, Schleswig.

Squier, E.G. (1855) Notes on Central America; particularly the states of Honduras and San Salvador..., New York.

Starzecka, D.C. (1998) 'The Maori collections in the British Museum', in Starzecka, D.C. (ed.) Maori art and culture, London, 147–58.

Stead, I.M. (1985) The Battersea shield, London.

Stead, I.M. (1996) Celtic art in Britain before the Roman conquest, 2nd edn, London.

Stead, I.M. (1998) The Salisbury hoard, Stroud.

Stead, I.M., and Rigby, V. (1999) The Morel collection, Iron Age antiquities from the British Museum, London.

Stearn, W.T. (1981) The Natural History Museum... A history of the British Museum (Natural History), 1753–1980, London.

Steinhauer, C.L. (1862) Catalogue of a collection of ancient and modern stone implements, and of other weapons, weapons, tools and utensils of the aborigines of various countries, in the possession of Henry Christy, FGS, FLS, London.

Stevenson, R.B.K. (1981) 'The museum, its beginnings and its development' in Bell (1981), 31–85 and 142–211.

Stewart, A. (1990) Greek sculpture, London.

Stewart, J. (1959) Jane Ellen Harrison, a portrait from letters, London.

Stoneman, R. (1987) Land of lost gods. The search for classical Greece, London.

Stonge, C. (1998) 'Making private collections public: Gustav Friedrich Waagen and the Royal Museum in Berlin', Journal of the history of collections, x: 1, 61–74.

Stratford, J. (1993) The Bedford inventories, the worldly goods of John, Duke of Bedford..., London.

Stratford, N. (1997) The Lewis chessmen and the enigma of the hoard, London.

Strutt, J. (1773) The regal and ecclesiastical antiquities of England, London.

Strutt, J. (1796–9) *A compleat view of the manners, dress and habits of the people of England...*, London.

Summerson, J. (1993) *Architecture in Britain, 1530–1830*, 9th edn, New Haven.

Sutherland, L.S., and Mitchell, L.G. (eds) (1986) *The history of the University of Oxford, v. The eighteenth century*, Oxford.

Sutherland, C.H.V. (1977) 'Edward Stanley Gotch Robinson, 1887–1976', *Proceedings of the British Academy*, lxiii, 423–40.

Synopsis of the contents of the British Museum, London 1808–56.

Syson, L. (1997) 'The legacy of Edward Hawkins: Franks as numismatist', in Caygill and Cherry (1997), 296–307.

Tait, G.H. (1959) *Bow porcelain 1744–1776. A special exhibition to commemorate the bi-centenary of... Thomas Frye...*, London.

Tait, G.H. (1962) 'The Passmore gift', *The British Museum quarterly*, xxv, 41–4.

Tait, G.H. (1968) *Clocks in the British Museum*, London.

Tait, G.H. (1983) *Clocks and watches*, London.

Tait, G.H. (ed.) (1984) *The art of the jeweller. A catalogue of the Hull Grundy gift to the British Museum: jewellery, engraved gems and goldsmiths' work*, London.

Tait, G.H. (1986–) *Catalogue of the Waddesdon bequest in the British Museum*, London.

Tait, G.H. (n.d.) 'Felix Slade (1790–1868)', *Glass Circle journal*, viii, 70–87.

Tait, G.H., and Cherry, J. (1987) 'Excavations at Longton Hall porcelain factory', Part I, *Post-medieval archaeology*, xii, 1–29.

Tait, G.H., and Coole, P.G. (1987) *The stackfreed*, London. Catalogue of watches in the British Museum, i.

Tait, G.H., and Walker, R. (2000) *The Athenæum collection*, London.

Tatton-Brown, V. (1987) *Ancient Cyprus*, London.

Thackray, J.C. (1992) *A catalogue of the portraits, paintings, drawings and sculpture at the Natural History Museum*, London.

The British Library (Cmnd. 4572). (Parliamentary White Paper).

The British Museum quarterly, news supplement, 1962–6.

The British Museum Review, 1996–

The project of a museum of Asiatic art in London, London (1931).

The will of Sir Hans Sloane Bart, deceased, London 1753.

Thomas, P.D.G. (1996) *John Wilkes, a friend to liberty*, Oxford.

(Thompson, A.) (1767) *Letters on the British Museum*, London.

Thompson, J.R.F. (1964) 'The Guards at the British Museum', *Household Brigade Magazine*, Autumn 1964, 172–5.

Thompson, J.R.F. (1969) 'Thayendanegea the Mohawk and his several portraits', *The connoisseur*, clxx, 49–53.

Thompson, J.R.F., and Roe, F.G. (1961) 'Some oil portraits in the British Museum', *The Connoisseur*, cxlvii, 114–18.

Thompson, J.R.F., and Roe, F.G. (1961a) 'More paintings at the British Museum', *The Connoisseur*, cxlvii, 189–95.

Thompson, M.W. (1977) *General Pitt Rivers. Evolution and archaeology in the nineteenth century*, Bradford-on-Avon.

Thompson, R.C. (1930) 'Harry Reginald Holland Hall, 1873–1930', *Proceedings of the British Academy*, xvi, 475–85.

(Thomsen, C.J.) (1836) *Ledetraad til nordisk Oldkyndighed*, Copenhagen (English edition 1848).

Thorkelin, G.J. (1815) *... Poëma danicum dialecto anglosaxonica... Ex bibliotheca Cottoniae...*, Hafniae.

Thornton, D., and Warren, J. (1998) 'The British Museum's Michelangelo acquisitions and the Casa Buonarroti', *Journal of the history of collections*, x: 1, 9–30.

Thornton, J.L. (1982) *Jan van Rymsdyk, medical artist of the eighteenth century*, Cambridge.

Tillett, S. (1984) *Egypt itself*, London.

Tischbein, W. (1791–5) *Collection of engravings from ancient vases discovered... in the kingdom of the Two Sicilies between 1789–90*, Naples.

(Tonnochy, A.B., et al.) (1930) *Catalogue of the Montague Guest collection of badges, tokens and passes...*, London.

Townsend, S. (1985) *The Adrian Mole diaries*, London.

Trigger, B.G. (1980) *Gordon Childe. Revolutions in archaeology*, London.

Trigger, B.G. (1989) *A history of archaeological thought*, Cambridge.

Turner, E.G. (1976) 'Derek Fortrose Allen. 1910–1975', *Proceedings of the British Academy*, lxii, 435–57.

Twenty-five years of the National Art Collections Fund, 1903–1928, Glasgow 1928.

Tylor, E.B. (1861) *Anahuac: or Mexico and the Mexicans, ancient and modern*, London.

Vaio, J. (1990) 'Gladstone and the early reception of Schliemann in England', in Calder and Cobet (1990), 415–30.

Valentini, M.B. (1704–14) *Museum Museorum*, Frankfurt/Main.

Vandiver, P.B., et al. (ed.) (1992) *Materials issues in art and archaeology III*, Pittsburgh. Materials Research Society symposium proceedings, cclxvii.

van Gelder, J.G. (1985) *Jan de Bisschop and his Icones and Paradigmata*, Doornspijk.

van Rymsdyk, J. and A. (1778) *Museum Britannicum being an exhibition of a great variety of antiquities and natural curiosities of that noble and magnificent cabinet the British Museum...*, London.

van Rymsdyk, J. and A. (1791) *Museum Britannicum or a display in thirty two plates of the antiquities and natural curiosities of that noble and magnificent cabinet the British Museum ...*, 2nd edn, London.

van Tilburg, J.A. (1992) *HMS Topaze on Easter Island*, London. British Museum occasional papers, 73.

Vaughan, G. (1992) 'The restoration of classical sculpture in the eighteenth century and the problem of authenticity', in Jones (1992), 41–50.

Vaux, W.S.W. (1850) *Nineveh and Persepolis; an historical account of ancient Assyria and Persia, with an account of the recent researches in those countries*, London.

Vaux, W.S.W. (1851) *Handbook to the antiquities of the British Museum: being a description of the remains of Greek, Assyrian, and Etruscan art preserved there*, London.

Victoria and Albert Museum Review: Review of the principal acquisitions during the year...

Vincent, J. (1984) *The Crawford papers. The journals of David Lindsay, twenty-seventh Earl Crawford and tenth Earl of Balcarres, 1871–1940, during the years 1892 to 1940*, Manchester.

Voltaire, F.-M. (1734) *Lettres philosophiques*, Paris.

von Plessen, M.-L. (1992) *Die Nationen und ihre Museum*, Frankfurt.

von Uffenbach, Z. (1754), *Merkwürdige Reisen durch Niedersachsen, Holland und Engelland*, ii, Ulm and Memmingen.

Vyner, B. (ed.) (1994) *Building on the past. Papers celebrating 150 years of the Royal Archaeological Institute*, London.

Waagen, G.F. (1857) *Galleries and cabinets of art in Great Britain*, London.

Waley, A. (1931) *A catalogue of the paintings recovered from Tun-Huang by Sir Aurel Stein... in the sub-Department of Oriental Prints and Drawings in the British Museum, and in the Museum of Central Asian Antiquities, Delhi*, London.

Walker, A. (1995) *Aurel Stein, pioneer of the silk road*, London.

Walker, J. (1953) 'The early history of the Department of Coins and Medals', *The British Museum quarterly*, xvii, 76–80.

Walker, S. (1992) 'Clytie – a false woman', in Jones (1992), 32–40.

Walters, H.B. (1899) *Catalogue of the bronzes, Greek, Roman and Etruscan in the... British Museum*, 2nd edn, London.

Walters, H.B. (1926) *Catalogue of the engraved gems and cameos, Greek, Etruscan and Roman in the British Museum*, London.

Wang, H. (ed.) (1999) *Handbook to the Stein collections in the UK*, London. British Museum occasional papers, 129.

Ward, F.A.B. (1981) A catalogue of European scientific instruments in the Department of Medieval and Later Antiquities of the British Museum, London.

Ward, H. (1926) History of the Athenæum, 1824–1925, London.

Ward, R. (1997) 'Islamism, not an easy matter', in Caygill and Cherry (1997), 272–85.

Waring, J.B. (ed.) (1858) Art treasures of the United Kingdom from the art treasures exhibition, Manchester, London.

Waterfield, G. (1963) Layard of Nineveh, London.

Waterston, C.D. (1997) Collections in context. The museum of the Royal Society of Edinburgh and the inception of a national museum for Scotland, Edinburgh.

Watson, W., et al. (1952) 'The Raphael bequest, II, Oriental Antiquities', The British Museum quarterly, xv, 82–95.

Webster, D.B. (1991) Hawkeseye, the early years of Christopher Hawkes, Stroud.

Webster, L., and Backhouse, J. (eds) (1991) The making of England, Anglo-Saxon art and culture, London.

Weiss, T. (ed.) (1995) Wedgwood, englische Keramik in Wörlitz, Leipzig.

Wetherall, D. (1994) 'From Canterbury to Winchester: the foundation of the Institute', in Vyner (1994), 8–21.

Wetherall, D. (1998) 'The growth of archaeological societies', in Brand (1998), 21–34.

Wharton-Tigar, E. (1987) Burning bright. The autobiography of Edward Wharton-Tigar, n.p.

White, C. (1995) 'John Arthur Giles Gere, 1921–1995', Proceedings of the British Academy, xc, 367–90.

White, J.F. (1962) The Cambridge movement. The ecclesiologists and the gothic revival, Cambridge.

White, R.H. (1988) 'Mayer and British archaeology', in Gibson and Wright (1988), 118–22.

Whitfield, R., and Farrer, A. (1990) Caves of the Thousand Buddhas, Chinese art of the silk route, London.

Whitley, W.T. (1930) Art in England 1821–1837, London.

Wiell, S. (1997) Flensborgsamlingen 1824–1864 og dens skæbne, Flensborg.

Wilkins, J. (1961) 'Worsaae and British antiquities', Antiquity, xxxv, 214–20.

Willey, G.R. (1981) 'Spinden's Archaic Hypothesis', in Evans et al. (1981), 35–41.

Willey, G.R., and Sabloff, V.A. (1974) A history of American archaeology, London.

Williams, N. (1989) The breaking and remaking of the Portland Vase, London.

Willis, M.D. (1997) 'Sculpture from India', in Caygill and Cherry (1997), 250–61.

Will of Sir Hans Sloane: The will of Sir Hans Sloane Bart. deceased, London 1753.

Wilson, D. (1851) The archaeology and prehistoric annals of Scotland, Edinburgh.

Wilson, D.M. (1964) Anglo-Saxon ornamental metalwork 700–1100 in the British Museum, London.

Wilson, D.M. (1984) The forgotten collector. Augustus Wollaston Franks of the British Museum, London.

Wilson, D.M. (1989) The British Museum. Purpose and politics, London.

Wilson, D.M. (1997) 'Augustus Wollaston Franks – towards a portrait', in Cherry and Caygill (1997), 1–5.

Wilson, D.M. (2001) 'The British Museum and the Athenæum', in F.F. Armesto (ed.) Armchair Athenians. Essays from the Athenæum, London, 221–8.

Wilson, J. (1989) Lawrence of Arabia, the authorised biography of T.E. Lawrence, London.

Wilson, T. (1985) 'The origins of the maiolica collections of the British Museum and the Victoria & Albert Museum', Faenza, lxxi, 68–81.

Wilton, A., and Bignamini, I. (1996) Grand Tour. The lure of Italy in the eighteenth century, London.

Winckelmann, J.J. (1764) Geschichte der Kunst des Alterthums, Dresden.

Winstone, H.V.F. (1990) Woolley of Ur, the life of Sir Leonard Woolley, London.

Wiseman, D.J. (1980) 'Sidney Smith', Proceedings of the British Academy, lxvi, 463–71.

Wolfenden, J. (1976) Turning points. The memoirs of Lord Wolfenden, London.

Wood, C.G. (1979) 'Classification and value in a seventeenth-century museum. William Courten's collection', Journal of the history of collections, ix; 1, 61–77.

Wood, F. (1992) 'Britain's first view of China', British Museum Magazine, no.11, 20–21.

Wood, J.T. (1877) Discoveries at Ephesus, including the site and remains of the great temple of Diana, London.

Woolley, C.L. (1927–76) Excavations at Ur, London and Philadelphia.

Woolley, C.L. (1962) As I seem to remember, Shaftesbury.

Woolley, C.L., and Barnett, R.D. (1952) Carchemish..., iii, London.

Woolley, C.L., and Lawrence, T.E. (1914) Carchemish. Report on the excavations at Djerabis on behalf of the British Museum, London.

Worm, O. (1655) Musei Wormiani historia..., Leiden.

Worsaae, J.J.A. (1843) Danmarks oldtid oplyst ved oldsager og gravhøie, Copenhagen.

Worsaae, J.J.A. (1849) The primeval antiquities of Denmark, London.

Worsaae, J.J.A. (1934) En oldgrandskers erindringer, 1821–1847, Copenhagen.

Worsaae, J.J.A. (1938) Af en oldgrandskers breve, 1848–1885, Copenhagen.

Wright, C.J. (1997) 'Consort and cupola: Prince Albert, Panizzi and the Reading Room of the British Museum', The British Library journal, xxii; 2, 176–93.

Wright, W. (1877) Catalogue of the Ethiopic manuscripts in the British Museum acquired since the year 1847, London.

Wylie, W.W. (1854) 'Some account of the Merovingian cemetery at Envermeu...', Archaeologia, xxxv, 223–31.

Wylie, W.W. (1855) 'The graves of the Alemanni at Oberflacht in Suabia', Archaeologia, xxxvi, 129–60.

Young, H. (1995) The genius of Wedgwood, London.

Zeimal, E.V. (1979) Amudarinskii Klad, Leningrad.

Zwalf, W. (1985) Buddhism. Art and faith, London.

Zwalf, W. (1996) Catalogue of the Gandhara sculpture in the British Museum, London.

INDEX